W9-APH-268

MAPS

Circled letters in text correspond to letters on the photographs. For more information on the sights pictured, turn to
the indicated page number Ⓐⵒ on each photograph.

Fodor's 2nd Edition

Brazil

Fodor's Travel Publications • New York, Toronto, London, Sydney, Auckland
www.fodors.com

CONTENTS

DESTINATION
BRAZIL

Brazil is vast, captivating, and as full of surprises as it is of samba. It lures you this way with glorious shores and pulls you that way with primeval rain forest and then tempts you elsewhere with snow-capped peaks, arid plateaus, and enormous plains. Rio entices with its happy heart and its bossa-nova beats. São Paulo invigorates with its ethnic diversity and its energy. Salvador intrigues with its African traditions. And Brasília astonishes with its modern shapes. From the baroque statuary of a colonial church to the statuesque figures of Copacabana, the country's sights will captivate your senses and capture your imagination. And just when you think you've seen it all, there's yet another surprise waiting down the road, around the bend, or beyond the next palm tree.

RIO DE JANEIRO

Ⓐ⟩ 38

Cariocas, as Rio's citizens are called, refer to their home as "the marvelous city." To see why, you need only take in the views from atop Ⓒ**Corcovado** or Pão de Açúcar (Sugarloaf). Rio cascades down and between mountains carpeted with green. It ribbons out to beaches awash with blue waters of ocean and bay. It dangles like a sun-washed jewel from the south-central edge of a state of the same name. Although this urban gem will dazzle you any time, it glows with exceptional brilliance during the pre-Lenten festivities of ⑧**Carnaval** (Carnival), the world's largest and most colorful party. And deep within the city burn the hues of Portugal, whose legacy is most evident in the Ⓐ**Beco do Comércio** as well as in and around the tiled plazas of ⒸCentro (downtown). For a more intimate glimpse of this European heritage, visit the 1641 Mosteiro de São Bento, a Benedictine church full of gold-painted wood carvings, or the hilltop Igreja de Nossa Senhora da Glória do Outeiro, a baroque church dating from 1739 that once looked directly over Guanabara Bay. You can also see Rio's many Brazilian facets over a meal in ⒹColombo, a Belle Epoque café; on a tour of the Palácio do Catete, home to 18 of the nation's presidents; on a stroll through the Jardim Botânico, gardens fit for an exiled king; or on a drive through the Floresta da Tujuca, a forest in the middle of town.

Ⓓ56

Ⓔ37

RIO DE JANEIRO

(F) 72

Is Rio a city bordered by a series of beaches? Or is Rio a series of beaches across the street from a city? Contemplate these and other contemporary questions while digging your toes into the sands of long, broad Ⓖ**Copacabana.** Later, revise your opinions over a beer at one of the countless sidewalk cafés alongside. Alternatively, sip some ice-cold coconut water while sunning yourself on the neighboring beach of ③**Ipanema.** Slightly farther afield, at São Conrado, you can watch, or even join, the hang gliders who float down onto the shore. Or perhaps you need a *tanga* (Brazilian bikini) or some other teeny memento. You can shop like a true *senhor* or *senhora* at the chic little São Conrado Fashion

(G) 48

Mall, or lose yourself amid all the merchandise in Barra da Tijuca's Barra Shopping, one of South America's largest retail centers. For a serious souvenir, take a seat in one of the many branches of Ⓕ**H. Stern** and select a stone or finished piece of jewelry. To see the "beautiful game" and hear Rio roar, catch a *futebol* match at Ⓗ**Maracanã,** the world's largest open-air soccer stadium. To escape all the frenzy, do as the cariocas do. Head for the sophisticated resort of Ⓘ**Búzios,** the sailing mecca of Angra dos Reis, the imperial city of Petrópolis, or the colonial town of Parati. Don't be surprised, however, if your heart flutters at the thought of returning to Rio. It is, after all, the *cidade maravilhosa.*

SÃO PAULO

The rivalry between Rio de Janeiro and São Paulo goes back many years. *Paulistanos* don't know how to relax, say cariocas. Cariocas know more about relaxing than anything else, say paulistanos. You'll see the truth very quickly for yourself, of course, because this city, like Rio, has found a balance between getting things done and not doing much of anything. In São Paulo, no place is busier than the trading floor of ⒷBOVESPA, the country's major stock exchange. You'll also sense that important affairs are being conducted as you stride along ⒶAvenida Paulista. Once a country road, it's now lined with so many skyscrapers that you can almost hear the urgent buzz of business deals. This urban energy is contagious. Work off some of yours while shopping at antiques fairs and handicrafts markets or at malls like Shopping Center Iguatemi or D&D Decoração & Design Center. Alternatively,

Ⓑ 92

Ⓒ 102

visit a singular sight such as the Ⓒ**Instituto Butantã,** on the Universidade de São Paulo campus, where venom is extracted from snakes, spiders, and other poisonous creatures to make antidotes that are used all over Latin America. Theaters and museums are everywhere. Corporate portals often swing open to reveal art. Orchestras and opera and dance companies from all over the world stop in São Paulo while on tour. Film and other festivals take place the whole year round. State-of-the-art discos and an array of other clubs provide every kind of beat your feet might desire. You can also give your feet a rest while you report home from one of the many stylish cybercafés. On Sunday, tune in to the music at the frequent (and often free) shows held in Ⓓ**Parque Ibirapuera.** You can also jog through this park's 395 acres, visit its cultural pavilions or its planetarium, and—in October and November of even-numbered years—attend the renowned Bienal art show. Paulistanos, it seems, know how to play as hard as they work.

Ⓓ 100

SÃO PAULO

Such a great and sophisticated metropolis as São Paulo attracts people from throughout Brazil and beyond. It's also both a gathering place for artists and a repository for their work. In Parque Ibirapuera the Ⓕ**Museu de Arte Moderna** houses supurb permanent collections of Brazilian modernist paintings, drawings, and sculptures. On a wooded estate in the residential neighborhood of Morumbi, you can view everything from tapestries and sacred art to objects once owned by Brazil's royal family at the Ⓔ**Fundação Maria Luisa e Oscar Americano.** Many other museums are crammed with Brazilian masks and jewelry, the works of Europe's great masters, and even samurai artifacts. An international city, São Paulo will also feed you well.

Ⓔ 101

Settlers from Germany, Portugal, Spain, Russia, and the Middle East have added flavors from around the world to the cultural stew. The Bixiga neighborhood, the city's Little Italy, is filled with such restaurants as ①**Lellis Trattoria,** and a meal in the Liberdade district will make you feel as if you're dining in Japan. After so much activity, you may want to escape inland or along the coast of São Paulo State. Within 100 miles or so of town, you can slow your pace in the mountain retreat of ⑥**Campos de Jordão,** soothed by its pleasant cafés, alpine breezes, icy waterfalls, and rugged trails. You can hike, too, on the island of ⑭**Ilhabela.** The ocean here may also beckon you to ride its waves, explore its offshore wrecks, or simply collapse on its beachy shore. After all, when it comes to mastering the art of urban living, relaxing is just as important as seeing and doing.

⑭⟩ 135

① ⟩ 108

THE SOUTH

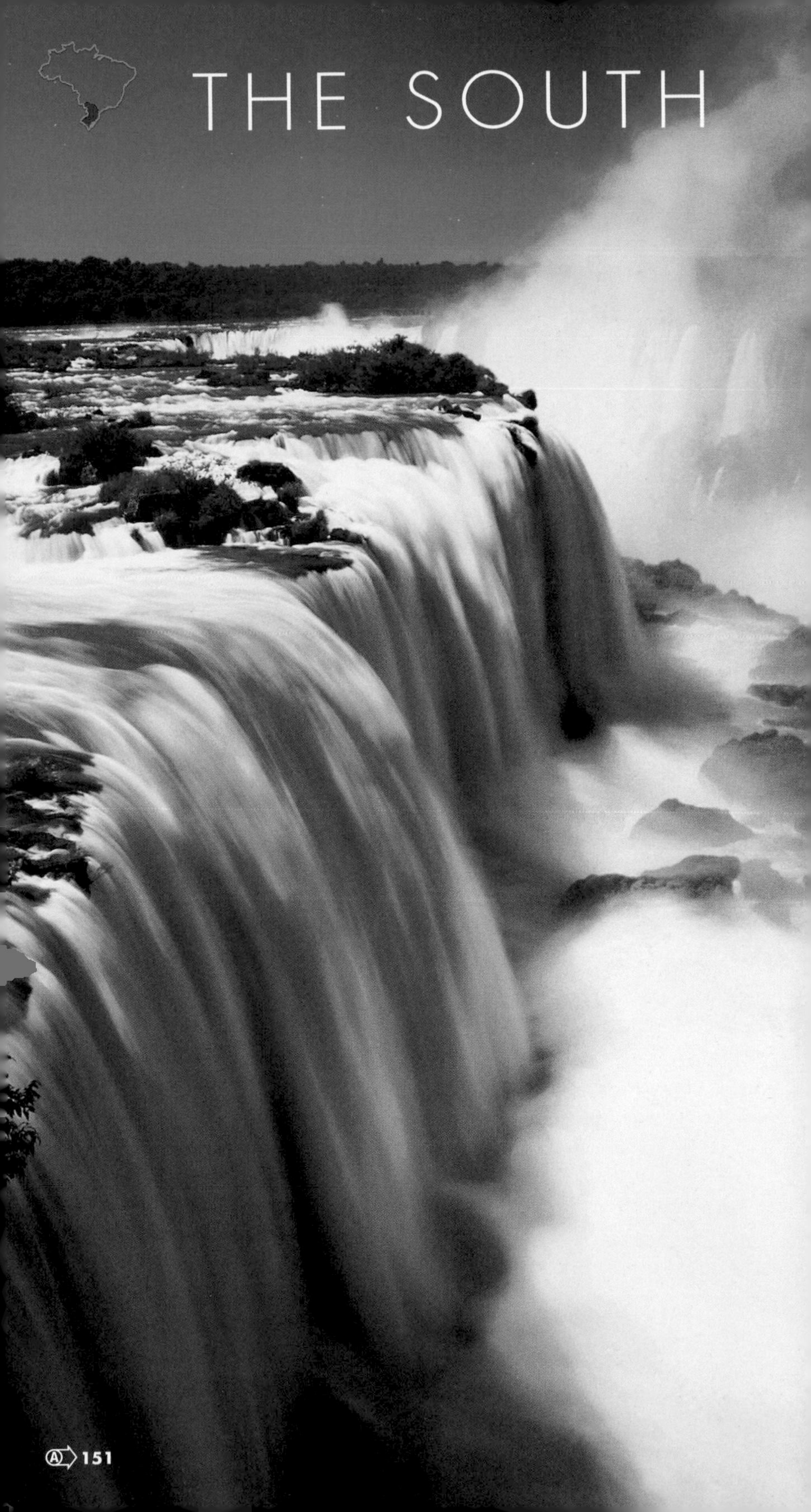

Ⓐ 151

Summer isn't the only season in the land of the German shopkeeper, the Italian vintner, and the Latin American *gaúcho* (cowboy). The south's climate and landscapes are as varied as its settlers. Its three states—Paraná, Santa Catarina, and Rio Grande do Sul—run along the coast and inland to the border of Uruguay, Argentina, and Paraguay. Here you'll find sunny shores, forest-covered mountains, flat farmlands, and dense jungle. In

Ⓑ 162

Ⓒ 145

western Paraná, nearly 300 waterfalls make up the Ⓐ**Foz do Iguaçu.** Curitiba, the state capital, displays its 300 years of history amid such modern amenities as the Ⓒ**Rua 24 Horas,** a glass-covered alley lined with cafés open 24 hours a day. In communities around multicultural Ⓑ**Porto Alegre,** Rio Grande do Sul's capital, you might hear farmers speaking German. Some of Santa Catarina's mountain towns evoke Bavaria. In contrast, the Atlantic beaches at Ⓓ**Ilha de Santa Catarina,** near the state capital at Florianópolis, might just make you forget Rio.

Ⓓ 154

The state that ultimately fulfilled Portugal's dreams of treasure chests brimming with gold and diamonds has the deceptively cold name of "General Mines." The title of its capital city, Belo Horizonte (Beautiful Horizon), is more indicative of its vistas: rugged hills and mountains, fertile valleys, and Brazilian baroque villages that were paid for by gems. This wealth not only gave

MINAS GERAIS

Ⓐ▷194

rise to colonial towns but also attracted great craftsmen. In the town of Ⓑ**Ouro Preto** you can reflect amid an air of devotion in the 18th-century Ⓒ**Igreja de São Francisco de Assis.** This masterpiece of design and sculpture is the work of the beloved Brazilian artist Aleijadinho. His carved cherubs, tropical fruits, and allegorical figures are all the more amazing when you consider that a mysterious illness left him without the use of his hands. The quiet yet passionate resolve expressed in his work exemplifies the nature of the *mineiros*, as locals are called. Although proud of their

Ⓑ▷190

accomplishments and earnest about their politics, they're a reserved, stalwart bunch. It's no wonder that Brazil's first attempt at independence started here. You can learn something of this 1789 rebellion in the Ⓐ**Museu da Inconfidência,** also in Ouro Preto. The art and artifacts here and in other museums still seem warm from the hands that made and used them, perhaps because craftsmanship is still a way of life. You're sure to find a handmade treasure of your own in one of the many shops that line the streets of Ouro Preto, Tiradentes, Diamantina, and other gold-rush communities.

BRASÍLIA AND THE WEST

Ⓐ216

Brazil has a history of bold ideas, but surely Brasília was the boldest. For more than 100 years, there were discussions about moving the capital inland. And then, in 1960, only four years after the site and Lúcio Costa's master plan were selected, the new city made its debut in the country's geographic center amid a vast, flat *cerrado* (savanna). Its sight lines and modernist structures are as grand as its story. The great Brazilian architect Oscar Niemeyer designed many buildings, including the Ⓐ**Palácio do Itamaraty,** fronted by a huge reflecting pool created by Brazilian land-

Ⓑ217

scape artist Roberto Burle Marx. The circular cathedral, ©**Catedral Metropolitana de Nossa Senhora da Aparecida,** also by Niemeyer, welcomes you with its broad interior and abundant natural light. The bronze sculpture ®*Os Candangos* is a tribute to the laborers—many of them northeastern migrants—who built the capital in such a short time. Indeed, many of Brasília's

⑩▷ 225

residents hail from elsewhere. And where do these "locals" go to escape city life? They head west to places like Pirenópolis, an 18th-century gold-rush town. Farther south and west, beyond the city of Goiâna, is a region of ranches that feel light years from Brasília, among them the ⑩**Pousada do Rio Quente/Hotel Tourismo,** two lovely hotels and a beautifully landscaped water park. Yet farther from civilization is the massive Ⓔ**Pantanal,** an untamable mosaic of swamp and forest teeming with wildlife, including vultures in all hues of the rainbow.

Ⓔ▷ 233

Nowhere does Brazil's African heritage seem more alive than in the northeastern coastal city of Salvador, capital of Bahia State. You'll hear Africa in the rhythms of the music. You'll taste its flavors in the palm oil, coconut, and spices that enliven the food. And you'll witness Brazilian adaptations of its traditions

SALVADOR

Ⓐ 256

on street corners and squares. The white-clad followers of Ⓑ **Candomblé,** the dominant Afro-Brazilian religion, worship their gods and goddesses in spiritual centers and on beaches. The half-clad practitioners of *capoeira,* a blend of African dance and the martial arts, perfect their skills in just about any open space. There's music every night in the Ⓒ **Largo do Pelourinho,** a plaza named for the pillory where slaves were once punished. Many of the colonial buildings that surround this square have been completely restored. Here, as in many another old Brazilian city,

Ⓑ 258

you'll see the influence of the Portuguese, who made fortunes, first from the *pau-brasil* (brazilwood) trees and later from vast tracts of sugar-cane. With the colonizers came the priests and their churches. In the 18th-century Ⓐ**Igreja de São Francisco,** elaborate cedar and rose-wood carvings appear to shimmer both with gold leaf and with life. The baroque Igreja de Nossa Senhora do Rosário dos Pretos, built by and for slaves, embodies the local spirit. And on a street not far from such old, well-pre-served churches and squares is the former home of Jorge Amado, whose novels cele-brate the traditions—both African and Brazilian—that you can still experience daily in Salvador.

RECIFE AND FORTALEZA

North of Salvador, on Brazil's most curvaceous bit of coast, are two colonial cities where old and new are stitched together almost seamlessly. As history would have it, the influences here are often Dutch as well as Portuguese and African. In Recife, capital of Pernambuco State, you can stroll along beaches, cross bridges spanning three rivers, and wander amid new high-rises and old churches. The 16th-century suburb of ⒷOlinda was once the state capital. Today it's a UNESCO World Cultural Site with an enchanting Carnaval, fine ocean views, and hilly streets. In Fortaleza, capital of Ceará State, you can revel in miles of urban beaches with warm ocean waters and cooling breezes or watch the city's fabric unfold on tours of its neoclassical concert hall, its

1846 lighthouse, and its modern Gothic cathedral. Or spend a day in the Mercado Central, where fine lace and other handicrafts fill some 500 shops. About 48 kilometers (30 miles) east is Ⓐ**Iguape,** whose dunes are so high and smooth that you can ski down their slopes. Another 113 kilometers (70 miles) east lies Ⓒ**Canoa Quebrada,** where red cliffs collide with white, palm-dotted sands. It's easy to forget about clocks and calendars on such timeless swaths of shore.

THE AMAZON

Through the centuries, many have tried to conquer Brazil's vast northwestern region. From conquistadors and captains of industry to adventurers and anthropologists, no one has solved all the mysteries that envelop this mystical land. Laced with hundreds of streams, it's dominated by just one, the gargantuan Ⓐ**Amazon River,** an inland sea of waterway that runs for more than 6,000 kilometers (4,000 miles) and is so wide in places that you can't see the shore from a riverboat's deck. As you move beneath the bordering rain-forest canopy on guided trips into the wilds, narrow rays of sunlight slice through steam and mist, flocks of green and yellow parrots fly amid branches, monkeys chatter from hidden posts, butter-

flies of all colors fill the air, and caimans splash at water's edge. Everything about this floodplain is as dramatic as it is oversized, including the Ⓑ Ⓕ **Ilha do Marajó.** The world's largest river island sits at a split in the Amazon, which flows around and sometimes through it. While basking on one of its many beaches you

24

can contemplate such Amazonian mysteries as how this island came to have more water buffalo than it has Aruã Indians or why the indigenous *capybara*, the world's largest rodent, is considered sweet.

THE AMAZON

©⟩ 314

The Amazon throbs with life, its pulse alternating between wild and calm. About 113 kilometers (70 miles) inland from the Atlantic is Belém, a city that's undergoing a rebirth while

Ⓓ⟩ 330

trying to preserve its historic boomtown heritage. At the Ⓖ**Museu Emílio Goeldi** you can take long, safe looks at wildlife or learn about Marajó Indian culture. Hawkers in the ©**Ver-o-Peso** market sell everything from local pottery and produce to magical charms and potions. A thousand miles from the sea, in South America's center, you can marvel at the wealth of the rubber barons who built the city of Ⓔ**Manaus.** This free-trade zone is filled with electronics markets as well as handsome municipal buildings and opulent residences created by European artisans in the

Ⓔ⟩ 327

19th century. To get an idea of the era's riches, visit the Ⓓ**Teatro Amazonas,** an 1896 opera house filled with Italian marble, English wrought-ironwork, and French tiles and crystal. The rain forest, however, is never far away. Just outside town, you can stay in jungle lodges and arrange heart-racing trips to bayous covered with giant water lilies or heart-stopping voyages on tributaries filled with piranha. Along the way you may see fishermen in canoes or pass settlements where trees hang heavy with fruit, jute hangs out to dry, and life's pulse is as slow today as it was yesterday.

FODOR'S
CHOICE

Even with so many special places in Brazil, Fodor's writers and editors have their favorites. Here are a few that stand out.

BEACHES

Barra do Sahy. São Paulo families in search of relief from the city favor this beach on a North Shore bay. ☞ p. 102

Barra da Tijuca. Rio's citizens adore this stretch of sand for its refreshing waters, its cool breezes, and its nearby amenities. ☞ p. 47

Boa Viagem. The aquamarine waters along this urban strand form pools near the *arrecifes* (reefs) that give Recife its name. ☞ p. 276

Ⓕ **Búzios.** Just two hours from Rio, this resort and its gorgeous sands attract the chic and the savvy. ☞ p. 82

Canoa Quebrada. Dunes, red cliffs, and palm groves are among the bounties of this strand near Fortaleza. ☞ p. 287

Ilha do Mel. You must hike to the unspoiled beaches of this southern island, where cars aren't allowed and the number of visitors is limited. ☞ p. 150

Ilha de Santa Catarina. It's hard to resist the charms of the 42 beaches on this, the "Magic Island." ☞ p. 154

Prainha and Grumari. These two crescents are so isolated that it's hard to believe they're part of Rio. ☞ p. 49

Stella Maris. Sun worshipers and surfers prize this Salvador beach's sands and shores; its food kiosks also entice. ☞ p. 260

DINING

Yemanjá, Salvador. Murals with ocean motifs and bubbly aquariums set the scene for generous portions of seafood prepared using regional ingredients. $$$–$$$$ ☞ p. 261

La Bohème, Fortaleza. Only one room in this mansion serves as a restaurant. The rest are galleries hung with art. $$–$$$$ ☞ p. 288

Boulevard, Curitiba. This place feels more like France than Brazil. $$–$$$$ ☞ p. 147

Famiglia Mancini, São Paulo. The atmosphere is jovial, the decor unique, and the food Italian. $$–$$$$ ☞ p. 108

La Via Vecchia, Brasília. Politicians and other notables come for a feast that's eclectic yet elegant. $$–$$$$ ☞ p. 221

La Chaumière, Brasília. This has been the capital's finest French restaurant for years. $$–$$$ ☞ p. 221

Claude Troisgros, Rio. Sensitive use of Brazilian ingredients and chefs whose creativity knows no end yield out-of-this-world meals. $$–$$$ ☞ p. 57

Le Coq d'Or, Ouro Preto. The Cordon Bleu–trained executive chef here brings French inspiration to Brazilian cuisine. $$–$$$ ☞ p. 194

Porcão, Rio. This restaurant epitomizes the *churrascaria* experience: waiters zip among tables, slicing sizzling chunks of grilled beef, pork, and chicken onto your plate. $$ ☞ p. 53

Il Gattopardo Ristorante, Porto Alegre. The beautiful people choose this restaurant for its fine Italian cuisine and its sophisticated ambience. $–$$$$ ☞ p. 164

Ⓔ **Chalezinho, Belo Horizonte.** This chalet-style, hilltop restaurant attracts couples in search of magical evenings of fondue and music. $–$$$ ☞ p. 184

Marina Ponta da Areia, Ilha de Santa Catarina. Locals are fond of this seafood spot for its superb location overlooking the Lagoa da Conceição. $–$$$ ☞ p. 157

Antigamente Lago Sul, Brasília. A lakefront setting and delicious Brazilian fare make for memorable meals here. $–$$$ ☞ p. 220

Canto da Peixada, Manaus. This restaurant owes its popularity to masterful preparation of river fish. $–$$ ☞ p. 332

Caso do Ouvidor, Ouro Preto. This is the place to sample typical *mineira* food. $–$$ ☞ p. 194

Galpão, São Paulo. The modern setting reflects the tastes of the architect-owner, and the pizzas are inventive and delicious. $–$$ ☞ p. 109

Quatro Sete Meia, Rio. The seafood in this restaurant, in a fishing village just outside the city, is served both indoors and outside in a garden. $–$$ ☞ p. 59

Lá em Casa, Belém. Outstanding interpretations of Amazon dishes have given this restaurant international renown. ¢–$$$ ☞ p. 317

LODGING

Ⓒ **Copacabana Palace, Rio.** Old World elegance joins contemporary amenities and white-glove service. $$$$ ☞ p. 60

Fazenda Carmo, Ilha do Marajó. A stay at this Amazon buffalo farm makes for a memorable experience. $$$$ ☞ p. 322

Gran Meliá São Paulo. The location is as big a draw as the creature comforts, some of them high-tech. $$$–$$$$ ☞ p. 111

Lago Salvador, Manaus. One of several famed jungle lodges offers seclusion and a sense of unity with the forest as well as simple comforts. $$$ ☞ p. 334

Caesar Park Hotel, Fortaleza. The interior is sleek and modern, and the sea views are classic. $$–$$$ ☞ p. 290

Ouro Minas Palace Hotel, Belo Horizonte. This fine hotel offers elegant surroundings, excellent service, and many amenities. $$–$$$ ☞ p. 185

Bonaparte Hotel Residence, Brasília. Stylish decor, spacious rooms, and great business services are among the draws. $$ ☞ p. 221

Ⓚ **Caiman Ecological Refuge, Pantanal.** This deluxe ranch, which promotes ecological awareness, is one of the region's top lodges. $$ ☞ p. 239

FODOR'S
CHOICE

Naoum Plaza Hotel, Brasília. Politicians and royalty often check into the Naoum. $$ ☞ p. 221

Academia de Tênis Resort, Brasília. This former tennis club is now a resort with chalets, pools, and, of course, tennis courts. $–$$ ☞ p. 222

Costão do Santinho Resort, Florianópolis. This comfortable resort has a beach and a solid roster of amenities. $–$$ ☞ p. 158

Maison Joly, São Paulo. Amenities such as a heliport stand out at this Ilhabela establishment. $–$$ ☞ p. 135

Ⓓ Hotel das Cataratas, Foz do Iguaçu. The ambience here is almost as unique as the location. $ ☞ p. 154

Ⓑ Pousada dos Pireneus, Pirenópolis. Well-heeled families flee stark Brasília for this landscaped resort. $ ☞ p. 230

Solar Nossa Senhora do Rosário, Ouro Preto. Impeccable service and elegant rooms are the hallmarks here. $ ☞ p. 195

Ⓐ Solar da Ponte, Tiradentes. This colonial inn charms you with its immaculate garden and its afternoon teas. $ ☞ p. 199

Blue Tree Caesar Towers, Porto Alegre. The city's finest hotel is in a quiet neighborhood with views of the Rio Guaíba. ¢–$$ ☞ p. 165

Manacá, Belém. This comfortable, well-situated hotel costs astonishingly little. ¢ ☞ p. 319

Pousada do Príncipe, Parati. As its name implies, this is the inn of a prince—literally. ¢ ☞ p. 85

MONUMENTAL STRUCTURES

Basilica de Nazaré, Belém. Built of marble, this church holds its own next to Europe's finest. ☞ p. 316

Catedral Metropolitana, Brasília. Oscar Niemeyer's masterpiece, a structure resembling a crown of thorns, honors Brazil's patron saint. ☞ p. 213

Corcovado and Christo Redentor, Rio. The city's icon gazes out benevolently from Corcovado Mountain. ☞ p. 51

Edifício Itália, São Paulo. The top of this building offers a 360-degree view and the chance to see how big this city really is. ☞ p. 93

Hidrelétrica de Itaipú. The world's largest dam tames the mighty Rio Paraná. ☞ p. 153

Igreja Bom Jesus do Matosinho, Congonhas do Campo. The 12 Old Testament prophets standing before this church are among Brazil's most cherished artworks. ☞ p. 198

Igreja de São Francisco, Salvador. The ornate carvings and profusion of gold leaf are breathtaking. ☞ p. 256

Igreja São Francisco de Assis, Ouro Preto. This baroque church's lavish altars and soapstone sculptures are masterpieces. ☞ p. 193

Ⓖ Memorial JK, Brasília. Immerse yourself in a pyramid containing displays on city history. It's also the tomb of Juscelino Kubitschek, the man who made it all happen. ☞ p. 213

Palácio do Catete, Rio. The former presidential palace's details are as incredible as its history. ☞ p. 46

Palácio do Itamaraty, Brasília. This modernist structure houses Brazil's foreign ministry, an impressive art collection, and an interior tropical garden. A memorable waterscape is outside. ☞ p. 216

Teatro Amazonas, Manaus. No building better represents the opulence of the rubber boom. ☞ p. 330

MUSEUMS

Centro de Preservação da Arte, Cultura, e Ciências Indigena, Santarém. The collection here helps preserve the art, culture, and science of Latin America's indigenous peoples. ☞ p. 325

Ⓘ Museu de Arte Naif do Brasil, Rio. The canvases that grace the walls bring to art what Brazilians bring to life: verve, color, and joy. ☞ p. 52

Museu de Arte de São Paulo. MASP is the pride of São Paulo, and its image is linked to the city in the same way that the Eiffel Tower is linked to Paris. ☞ p. 98

Museu Emílio Goeldi, Belém. In a small chunk of rain forest you'll find interesting flora and fauna as well as a great museum with Indian artifacts. ☞ p. 316

Museu da Inconfidência, Ouro Preto. This museum commemorates Brazil's first attempt at independence. ☞ p. 194

Museu da Mineralogia e das Pedras, Ouro Preto. The large collections illustrate Minas's gold and the wealth and variety of its gems. ☞ p. 194

PARKS AND PRESERVES

Ⓗ Pantanal Wetlands. This vast floodplain is the best place to see wildlife outside of sub-Saharan Africa. Its savannas, forests, and swamps are home to more than 600 bird species as well as anacondas, jaguars, monkeys, and other creatures. ☞ p. 233

Parque da Pedreira, Curitiba. Impressive landscaping and unique structures have given an abandoned quarry new life. ☞ p. 146

Ⓙ Parque Nacional do Iguaçu. This amazing preserve has one of the world's most fantastic waterfalls. ☞ p. 152

Parque Nacional dos Aparados da Serra. The pine-fringed canyons here are often hidden by fog, evoking an otherworldly atmosphere. ☞ p. 169

Sítio Roberto Burle Marx, Rio. Inland amid mangrove swamps and jungle, this museum honors Brazil's finest landscape designer. ☞ p. 50

1   RIO DE JANEIRO

The spectacular beauty of Rio is compelling. This glamorous metropolis is kissed by the sun, scalloped by gorgeous wide beaches, and dotted with dramatic mountains. Yet its history marked it not as a playground but as an important port—for the shipment of gold, gemstones, and coffee—and as a seat of colonial power.

Updated by
Ana Lúcia
do Vale

RIO WAS NAMED—OR MISNAMED—BY the crew of a Portuguese ship that arrived in what is now the city on January 1, 1502. Thinking they had found the mouth of a river, instead of the bay that became known as the Baía de Guanabara (Guanabara Bay), they dubbed the spot Rio de Janeiro (January River). Sixty-five years later, on the feast of St. Sebastian, the city was founded with the official name of São Sebastião do Rio de Janeiro.

In 1736, Brazil's colonial capital was moved to Rio from Salvador and, in 1889 when the country became independent, Rio was declared the capital of the Republic of Brazil. It held this title until 1960 when the federal government was moved to Brasília.

Today, this pulsating city is synonymous with the girl from Ipanema, the dramatic Pão de Açúcar Mountain, and the wild and outrageous Carnaval (Carnival) celebrations. But Rio is also a city of stunning architecture, good museums, and marvelous food; it's a teeming metropolis where the very rich and the very poor live in uneasy proximity and where enthusiasm is boundless—and contagious.

As you leave the airport and head to your hotel, you'll be tossed onto a massive, chaotic, not-so-scenic urban roadway. But, by the time you reach breezy, sunny Avenida Atlântica—flanked on one side by white beach and azure sea and on the other by the pleasure-palace hotels that testify to the city's eternal lure—your heart will leap with expectation. Now you're truly in Rio, where the 10 million wicked angels and shimmering devils known as *cariocas* dwell.

The term "carioca" comes from the country's early history, when it meant "white man's house" and was used to describe a Portuguese trading station. Today the word defines more than birthplace, race, or residence: it represents an ethos of pride, a sensuality, and a passion for life. Much of the carioca verve comes from the sheer physical splendor of a city blessed with seemingly endless beaches and sculpted promontories.

Prepare to have your senses engaged and your inhibitions untied. You'll be seduced by a host of images: the joyous bustle of vendors at Sunday's Feira Hippie (Hippie Fair); the tipsy babble at sidewalk cafés as patrons sip their last glass of icy beer under the stars; the blanket of lights beneath Pão de Açúcar; the bikers, joggers, strollers, and power walkers who parade along the beach each morning. Borrow the carioca spirit for your stay; you may find yourself reluctant to give it back.

Pleasures and Pastimes

Beaches

Rio's beaches define its culture: vibrant, joyful, beautiful. From infants to women in barely-there string bikinis—known as *tangas*—and thong-wearing men to senior citizens, the beach culture seduces all. The strands of tawny sand are exercise centers, gathering places, lovers' lanes—in effect, the city's pulse points. And every beach has its own flavor: from grande dame Copacabana with its volleyball nets and outdoor cafés to the seductive Ipanema; from São Conrado with its hang gliders to the hip, expansive Barra da Tijuca. A day at the beach doesn't necessarily mean swimming. Although cariocas wander into the water to surf or cool off, most spend their time crammed on the sand, sunning and socializing. (Note: beach vendors aren't supposed to charge more than R$5.50 for a bottle of beer or other alcoholic beverage, R$3 for a coconut water.)

Carnaval

Of the great carnivals of the world—Venice in Europe, Trinidad and Tobago in the Caribbean, and Mardi Gras in New Orleans—the most amazing may be Brazil's. And although Carnaval celebrations unfold all over this South American country, there's none with more glitter, glitz, or downright decadence than Rio's. During the four official days of the celebration, which ends the day before Lent begins, *escolas de samba* (samba schools, which are actually neighborhood groups, not schools at all) compete in two nights of opulent parades, weaving through the aptly named Sambódromo from sunset to dawn. Costumed revelers writhe at street parties and gala balls to the seductive samba beat. "Costume" is a relative term: some are wildly elaborate; others are barely there.

These competitions draw some of Rio's best percussionists, dozens of lavish floats, and thousands of marchers—including statesmen, beauty queens, veteran samba musicians, soccer personalities, and would-be celebrities (even a few seconds of TV exposure marching with a samba school is enough to launch a modeling or acting career). The joyous free-for-all infects even the most staid.

Dining

With more than 900 restaurants, Rio's dining choices are broad, from savory Middle Eastern, where sandwiches and fresh juices are the mainstays, to elegant eateries with posh decor, award-winning kitchens, and first-class service. Be sure to sample some local fare such as that found at the *churrascarias* (restaurants specializing in grilled meats). *Feijoada* (a hearty stew of black beans and pork) is the national dish. Wash it down with a *chopp* (the local draft beer; pronounced "shop," as in "born to") or a *caipirinha* (made with crushed lime, crushed ice, and a potent sugarcane liquor called *cachaça*).

Lodging

From luxury high-rise hotels gazing out over the beaches and ocean to small inland inns, you'll find a range of lodging options here. You may also find prices high, but that surprise will be softened by the top-rate service that's synonymous with carioca hospitality. Many hotels have computers and business services, and some include generous breakfast buffets in their rates; the concierges are more than willing to help you nab samba show tickets, tables at the best eateries, or a reliable, English-speaking tour guide. If you plan to spend time at the beach, your best bet is a hotel along Copacabana, Ipanema, or Barra da Tijuca (Copacabana has the advantage of being on the *metrô*, or subway, line).

Side Trips

As tantalizing as the city is, you'll have a far richer taste of Brazil—of both its imperial past and its jet-setting present—if you wander outside town. Just across Guanabara Bay is Niterói, where ancient forts provide a window on history and a great view of Rio. A scenic road leads northeast to Petrópolis and the opulent imperial palace that was the summer home of Brazil's emperor. Swiss-settled Nova Friburgo peeks from a lush valley speckled with waterfalls farther north. Sailboat-jammed Cabo Frio is a popular eastern coastal resort, and although Brigitte Bardot in a bikini may have put nearby Búzios on the map, the 23 beaches, temperate weather, and sophisticated ambience have kept it there.

West of Rio, on Brazil's Costa Verde (Green Coast), Angra dos Reis is the jumping-off point for 365 islands that pepper a picturesque bay. One of the loveliest, Ilha Grande, is lapped by emerald waters and retains an unspoiled flavor despite its popularity. The most amazing gem, however, is the southwestern coastal town of Parati with its 18th-century architecture; the lovely cays sprinkled along its bay have attracted the likes of British rocker Mick Jagger and Brazilian actress Sonia Braga.

EXPLORING RIO DE JANEIRO

Cariocas divide their city into three sections: Zona Norte (North Zone), Zona Sul (South Zone), and Centro, the downtown area that separates them. Except for some museums, churches, and historic sights, most of the tourist activity is in beach- and hotel-laden Zona Sul. To sense the carioca spirit, spend a day on Copacabana and walk from the Avenida Atlântica to Ipanema. The western extension of Ipanema, Leblon, is an affluent, intimate community flush with good, small restaurants and bars (sadly, the water is polluted). The more distant southern beaches, beginning with São Conrado and extending past Barra da Tijuca to Grumari, become richer in natural beauty and increasingly isolated.

Although Rio's settlement dates back nearly 500 years, it's in every respect a modern city. Most of the historic structures have fallen victim to the wrecking ball, though a few churches and villas are still tucked in and around Centro. As these colonial vestiges are far-flung, consider seeing them on an organized walking or bus tour. You can use the metrô (and comfortable walking shoes) to explore, or the bus is another option. Just be sure you know where you're going, and memorize some key phrases in Portuguese as bus drivers don't speak English. Police have put a dent in crime, but as in any large city, be cautious and aware.

Great Itineraries

IF YOU HAVE 3 DAYS

If you only have three days, you must visit Rio's two most famous peaks: try Pão de Açúcar your first morning and Corcovado—and the nearby Museu de Arte Naif do Brasil—that afternoon. Weekdays, swing by the little Museu Carmen Miranda to see the Brazilian bombshell's costumes, jewelry, and wild headdresses. In the evening, join the fun at a samba show. Set your second day aside for exploring historic Rio—perhaps having lunch in Centro at the opulent do Teatro—and for shopping. By your third day, the sun and sand will be irresistible. Explore Copacabana and Ipanema, or settle in under a beach umbrella on breezy Barra da Tijuca. In the evening, try the national dish at Ipanema's Casa da Feijoada.

IF YOU HAVE 5 DAYS

On your first day, explore Centro, take the cable car to Pão de Açúcar, and head to a samba show at Plataforma. The next day, jump on the cogwheel train to Corcovado and set aside time for the captivating Museu de Arte Naif do Brasil near its base before indulging in a Brazilian barbecue at Mariu's or Porção. Bike or walk off lunch at Lagoa Rodrigo de Freitas, then slide into a shopping center. On your third day, stroll from Copacabana to Ipanema, stopping en route to order a tropical pizza at Bar Garota de Ipanema or grab an icy drink on Barra da Tijuca.

Take an organized *favela* (shantytown) tour in the afternoon and, in the evening, dine on feijoada or churrasco. On the fourth day, head for Petrópolis to see the imperial palace, or make the 40-minute drive to Sítio Roberto Burle Marx to see the country house and gardens of Brazil's most famous landscaper. Have your concierge check the evening schedule at the Banco do Brasil Cultural Center. On your last day, take the Santa Teresa trolley to the Museu Chácara do Céu before you hop the metrô to the opulent Palácio do Catete. Weekdays, wind up the day at the kitschy Museu Carmen Miranda.

IF YOU HAVE 7–10 DAYS

Begin in the Flamengo and Botafogo neighborhoods and Pão de Açúcar; work in visits to the Museu Carmen Miranda and the Museu de Arte Moderna. On the second day, wander through Centro and head for the Palácio do Catete. Then take the trolley to Santa Teresa and the Museu Chácara do Céu. On the third day, beach-hop by bus early in the day and then do some shopping. On your fourth day, slide out of town to Petrópolis or down the coast to Angra dos Reis or Parati for a day or two. When you return to Rio, visit Corcovado and the nearby Museu de Arte Naïf do Brasil; spend the afternoon roaming through the Jardim Botânico or biking around Lagoa Rodrigo de Freitas. Your final days could include an escape to Prainha and Grumari beaches and the Sítio Roberto Burle Marx, or you could do a favela tour. In the evenings catch a samba revue or a bossa nova or jazz show or head out dancing. If you're in the city on Sunday, wander through Ipanema's Feira Hippie.

When to Tour

Carnaval is the best time to soak in the city's energy. Arrive a few days before the celebrations begin, or stay a few days after they end, to enjoy the museums and other sights that close for the four days of revelry. Be sure to book your hotel and flight at least one year in advance. To tour the city at a quieter time with gentler temperatures (it usually stays in the 90s during Carnaval) and lower prices, the off-season runs from May to October (Brazil's winter).

Centro and Environs

What locals generally refer to as Centro is a sprawling collection of several districts that contain the city's oldest neighborhoods, churches, and most enchanting cafés. Rio's beaches, broad boulevards, and modern architecture may be impressive; but its colonial structures, old narrow streets, and alleyways in leafy inland neighborhoods are no less so.

Numbers in the text correspond to numbers in the margin and on the Rio Centro and Environs map.

A Good Tour (or Two)

Start at the **Mosteiro de São Bento** ① for your first taste of Brazilian baroque architecture. From here, move south into the heart of Centro. At the beginning of Avenida Presidente Vargas you'll find the solid **Igreja de Nossa Senhora da Candelária** ②. From this church there are several options: soccer fans can take a cab or the metrô to **Maracanã** soccer stadium, where *o jogo bonito* (the beautiful game) is played; those who prefer a more bucolic setting can head (by cab or metrô) to **Quinta da Boa Vista;** and history buffs can walk south along Avenida 1° de Março, crossing it and heading west to a network of narrow lanes and alleys highlighted by the **Beco do Comércio** ③, a pedestrian street. After wandering this area, return to Avenida 1° de Março and walk southeast to the Praça 15 de Novembro, a square that's dominated by the **Paço Imperial** ④. A few blocks away is the large **Museu Histórico Nacional** ⑤.

From the Museu Histórico Nacional, follow Rua Santa Luzia southeast to Avenida Rio Branco, Centro's main thoroughfare. North one block is the Victorian **Biblioteca Nacional** ⑥, and one block up from it is the French neoclassical **Museu Nacional de Belas Artes** ⑦. In the middle of the next block up, and across Rio Branco, you'll find the **Teatro Municipal** ⑧ and its elegant café. Continue north on Rio Branco and turn left on Avenida Almirante Barroso. A short walk northwest brings you to the Largo da Carioca, a large square near the Carioca metrô stop. Atop a low hill overlooking it are the **Igreja de São Francisco da Penitência** ⑨ and the **Convento do Santo Antônio** ⑩. The architecturally striking (or absurd, depending on your viewpoint) **Catedral de São Sebastião do Rio de Janeiro** ⑪ is just south, off Avenida República do Chile, as is the station where you can take a *bonde* (trolley) over the **Aqueduto da Carioca** ⑫ and along charming Rua Joaquim Murtinho into Santa Teresa. This eccentric neighborhood is famed for its cobblestone streets and its popular **Museu Chácara do Céu** ⑬, whose works are displayed in a magnificent former home with beautiful city views.

TIMING AND PRECAUTIONS

Although you can follow this tour in a day if you set out early, you might want to break it up into two days or be selective about which museums you fully explore. You can also mix some of the southernmost sights in with those (the Aterro do Flamengo, Museu de Arte Moderna, or Monumento aos Pracinhas) in the Flamengo, Botafogo, and Pão de Açúcar tours. However you organize your day, you'll need plenty of energy to get everything in. Leave your camera at your hotel if you're planning to use public transportation. Wear no jewelry, and keep your cash in a money belt or safe pocket.

Sights to See

⑫ **Aqueduto da Carioca.** The imposing Carioca Aqueduct, with its 42 massive stone arches, was built between 1744 and 1750 to carry water from the Rio Carioca in the hillside neighborhood of Santa Teresa to Centro. In 1896 the city transportation company converted the then-abandoned aqueduct to a viaduct, laying trolley tracks along it. Since then, Rio's distinctive trolley cars (called "bondes" because they were financed by foreign bonds) have carried people between Santa Teresa and Centro. (Guard your belongings particularly closely when you ride the open-sided bondes; the fare is about R$1.) *Metrô: Carioca or Cinelândia.*

③ **Beco do Comércio.** A network of narrow streets and alleys centers on this pedestrian thoroughfare. The area is flanked by restored 18th-century homes, now converted to offices. The best known is the Edifício Telles de Menezes. A famous arch, the Arco dos Telles, links this area with Praça 15 de Novembro. ⊠ *Praça 15 de Novembro 34, Centro. Metrô: Uruguaiana.*

⑥ **Biblioteca Nacional.** Corinthian columns adorn the neoclassical National Library (built between 1905 and 1908), the first such establishment in Latin America. Its original archives were brought to Brazil by King João VI in 1808. Today it contains roughly 13 million books, including two 15th-century printed Bibles, and manuscript New Testaments from the 11th and 12th centuries; first-edition Mozart scores as well as scores by Carlos Gomes (who adapted the José de Alencar novel about Brazil's Indians, *O Guarani,* into an opera of the same name); books that belonged to Empress Teresa Christina; and many other manuscripts, prints, and drawings. Tours aren't available in English, but the devoted staff of docents will try to work something out to accommodate English-speaking book lovers. ⊠ *Av. Rio Branco 219,* ☏ *021/2262–8255.* ☐ *Tours R$2.* ☺ *Weekdays 9–8, Sat. 9–3; tours: weekdays at 11, 1, 3, and 5. Metrô: Cinelândia.*

⑪ **Catedral de São Sebastião do Rio de Janeiro.** The exterior of this metropolitan cathedral (circa 1960), which looks like a concrete beehive, can be off-putting (as the daring modern design stands in sharp contrast to the baroque style of other churches). But don't judge until you've stepped inside. Outstanding stained-glass windows transform the interior—which is 80 m (263 ft) high and 96 m (315 ft) in diam-

Rio Centro and Environs

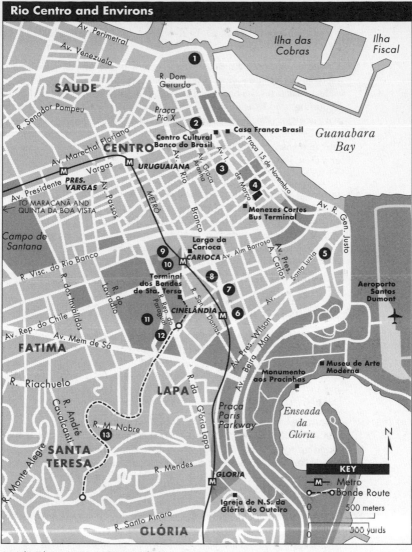

Ilha das Cobras

Ilha Fiscal

SAUDE

R. Dom Gerardo

Av. Perimetral

Av. Venezuela

R. Senador Pompeu

Praça Pío X

Guanabara Bay

Centro Cultural Banco do Brasil

Casa França-Brasil

CENTRO

Av. Marechal Floriano

Av. Presidente Vargas

PRES. VARGAS

URUGUAIANA

TO MARACANÃ AND QUINTA DA BOA VISTA

Praça 15 de Novembro

Menezes Cortes Bus Terminal

Largo da Carioca

CARIOCA

Terminal dos Bondes de Sta. Tersa

CINELÂNDIA

R. Visc. do Rio Banco

Av. Rep. do Chile

Av. Mem de Sá

FATIMA

R. Riachuelo

LAPA

Praça Paris Parkway

Monumento aos Pracinhas

Museu de Arte Moderna

Aeroporto Santos Dumont

Enseada da Glória

N

R. André Cavalcanti

R. M. Nobre

SANTA TERESA

R. Mendes

GLORIA

R. Santo Amaro

GLÓRIA

Igreja de N.S. da Glória do Outeiro

KEY
Ⓜ — Metro
Bonde Route

0   500 meters

0   500 yards

eter—into a warm yet serious place of worship that accommodates up to 20,000 people. An 8½-ton granite rock lends considerable weight to the concept of an altar. ⊠ *Av. República do Chile 245,* ☎ *021/2240–2869.* ☞ *Free.* ☉ *Daily 7–5:30. Metrô: Carioca or Cinelândia.*

⑩ **Convento do Santo Antônio.** The Convent of St. Anthony was completed in 1780, but some parts date from 1615, making it one of Rio's oldest structures. Its baroque interior contains priceless colonial art—including wood carvings and wall paintings. The sacristy is covered with *azulejos* (Portuguese tiles). Note that the church has no bell tower: its bells hang from a double arch on the monastery ceiling. An exterior mausoleum contains the tombs of the offspring of Dom Pedro I and Dom Pedro II. ⊠ *Largo da Carioca 5,* ☎ *021/2262–0129.* ☞ *Free.* ☉ *Weekdays 2–5. Metrô: Carioca.*

❷ **Igreja de Nossa Senhora da Candelária.** The classic symmetry of Candelária's white dome and bell towers casts an unexpected air of sanity over the chaos of downtown traffic. The church was built on the site of a chapel founded in 1610 by Antônio de Palma after he survived a shipwreck; paintings in the present dome tell his tale. Construction on the present church began in 1775, and although it was formally dedicated by the emperor in 1811, work on the dome wasn't completed until 1877. The sculpted bronze doors were exhibited at the 1889 world's fair in Paris. ⊠ *Praça Pio X,* ☎ *021/2233–2324.* ☞ *Free.* ☉ *Weekdays 7:30–noon and 1–4:30, weekends 8–1. Metrô: Uruguaiana.*

❾ **Igreja de São Francisco da Penitência.** The church was completed in 1737, nearly four decades after it was started. Today it's famed for its wooden sculptures and rich gold-leaf interior. The nave contains a painting of St. Francis, the patron of the church—reportedly the first painting in Brazil done in perspective. ⊠ *Largo da Carioca 5,* ☎ *021/2262–0197.* ☉ *By appointment. Metrô: Carioca.*

OFF THE
BEATEN PATH

MARACANÃ – From the Igreja de Nossa Senhora da Candelária, you can walk 3½ blocks to the Uruguaiana station and take the metrô to the world's largest soccer stadium. Officially called Estádio Mario Filho after a famous journalist, it's best known as Maracanã, for the neighborhood in which it's situated and for a nearby river. The 178,000-seat stadium (with standing room for another 42,000) went up in record time to host the 1950 World Cup. Brazil lost its chance at the cup by losing a match 2–1 to Uruguay—a game that's still analyzed a half century later. Here soccer star Pelé made his 1,000th goal in 1969. The smaller, 17,000-seat arena in the same complex has hosted events featuring such notables as Madonna, Paul McCartney, and Pope John Paul II. Stadium tours are offered daily (except on match days) from 9 to 5. ⊠ *Rua Prof. Eurico Rabelo, Gate 16,* ☎ *021/2568–9962.* ☞ *R$3. Metrô: Maracanã.*

❶ **Mosteiro de São Bento.** Just a glimpse of this church's main altar will fill you with awe. Layer upon layer of curvaceous wood carvings—coated in gold—create a sense of movement. Spiral columns whirl upward to capitals topped by cherubs so chubby and angels so purposeful they seem almost animated. Although the Benedictines arrived in 1586, they didn't begin work on this church and monastery until 1617. It was completed in 1641, but such artisans as Mestre Valentim (who designed the silver chandeliers) continued to add details almost through to the 19th century. On some Sundays, mass is accompanied by Gregorian chants. ⊠ *Rua Dom Gerardo 32,* ☎ *021/2291–7122.* ☞ *Free.* ☉ *Weekdays 8–11 and 2:30–5:30.*

★ ⑬ **Museu Chácara do Céu.** With its cobblestone streets and bohemian atmosphere, Santa Teresa is a delightfully eccentric neighborhood. Gabled Victorian mansions sit beside alpine-style chalets as well as more prosaic dwellings—many hanging at unbelievable angles from the flower-encrusted hills. Set here, too, is the quaintly named Museum of the Small Farm of the Sky. The outstanding collection of mostly modern works was left—along with the hilltop house that contains it—by one of Rio's greatest arts patrons, Raymundo de Castro Maya. Included are originals by such 20th-century masters as Pablo Picasso, Georges Braque, Salvador Dalí, Edgar Degas, Henri Matisse, Amedeo Modigliani, and Claude Monet. The Brazilian holdings include priceless 17th- and 18th-century maps and works by leading modernists. The grounds afford fine views of the aqueduct, Centro, and the bay. ⊠ *Rua Murtinho Nobre 93,* ☎ *021/2507–1932.* 🎟 *Free.* ☉ *Wed.–Mon. noon–5.*

NEED A | Santa Teresa attracts artists, musicians, and intellectuals to its eclectic
BREAK? | slopes. Their hangout is **Bar do Arnaudo** (⊠ Rua Almirante Alexandrino 316-B, ☎ 021/2252–7246), which is always full.

❺ **Museu Histórico Nacional.** The building that houses the National History Museum dates from 1762, though some sections—such as the battlements—were erected as early as 1603. It seems appropriate that this colonial structure should exhibit relics that document Brazil's history. Among its treasures are rare papers, Latin American coins, carriages, cannons, and religious art. ⊠ *Praça Marechal Ancora,* ☎ *021/2550–9266.* 🎟 *Free.* ☉ *Tues.–Fri. 10–5:30, weekends 2–6. Metrô: Carioca or Cinelândia.*

❼ **Museu Nacional de Belas Artes.** Works by Brazil's leading 19th- and 20th-century artists fill the space at the National Museum of Fine Arts. Although the most notable canvases are those by the country's best-known modernist, Cândido Portinari, be on the lookout for such gems as Leandro Joaquim's heartwarming 18th-century painting of Rio (at once primitive and classical, the small oval canvas seems a window on a time when fishermen still cast nets in the waters below the landmark Igreja de Nossa Senhora da Glória do Outeiro). After wandering the picture galleries, consider touring the extensive collections of folk and African art. ⊠ *Av. Rio Branco 199,* ☎ *021/2240–0068.* 🎟 *R$8, free Sun.* ☉ *Tues.–Fri. 10–6, weekends 2–6. Metrô: Carioca or Cinelândia.*

❹ **Paço Imperial.** This two-story colonial building is notable for its thick stone walls and ornate entrance. It was built in 1743, and for the next 60 years was the headquarters for Brazil's captains (viceroys), appointed by the Portuguese court in Lisbon. When King João VI arrived, he made it his royal palace. After Brazil's declaration of independence, emperors Dom Pedro I and II called the palace home. When the monarchy was overthrown, the building became Rio's central post office. Restoration work in the 1980s transformed it into a cultural center and concert hall. The third floor has a restaurant, and a ground-floor shop sells stationery and CDs. The square on which the palace is set, Praça 15 de Novembro, has witnessed some of Brazil's most significant historic moments. Known in colonial days as Largo do Paço, here two emperors were crowned, slavery was abolished, and Emperor Pedro II was deposed. Its modern name is a reference to the date of the declaration of the Republic of Brazil: November 15, 1889. ⊠ *Praça 15 de Novembro 48, Centro,* ☎ *021/2533–4407.* 🎟 *Free.* ☉ *Tues.–Sun. noon–6:30.*

OFF THE | **QUINTA DA BOA VISTA –** West of downtown, set in the entrancing land-
BEATEN PATH | scaped grounds of a former royal estate, you'll find pools and marble statues as well as the Museu Nacional and the Jardim Zoológico.

Housed in what was once the imperial palace (circa 1803), the museum has exhibits on Brazil's past and on its flora, fauna, and minerals—including the biggest meteorite (5 tons) found in the southern hemisphere. At the zoo, you can see animals from Brazil's wilds in re-creations of their natural habitats. A highlight is the Nocturnal House, where you can spot such night creatures as bats and sloths. *Entrance at corner of Av. Paulo e Silva and Av. Bartolomeu de Gusmão, ☎ 021/ 2568–8262 for museum, 021/2569–2024 for zoo. ☑ R$3 for museum; R$4 for zoo. ☉ Tues.–Sun. 9–4:30. Metrô: San Cristóvão.*

⑧ Teatro Municipal. Carrara marble, stunning mosaics, glittering chandeliers, bronze and onyx statues, gilded mirrors, German stained-glass windows, brazilwood inlay floors, and murals by Brazilian artists Eliseu Visconti and Rodolfo Amoedo make the Municipal Theater opulent, indeed. Opened in 1909, it's a scaled-down version of the Paris Opera House. The main entrance and first two galleries are particularly ornate. As you climb to the upper floors, the decor becomes more ascetic, a reflection of a time when different classes entered through different doors and sat in separate sections. The theater seats 2,357—with outstanding sight lines—for its dance performances and classical music concerts. Tours are available by appointment. ⊠ *Praça Floriano 210, ☎ 021/2297–4411. Metrô: Cinelândia or Carioca.*

NEED A
BREAK?

Elegance joins good food at the charming **Café do Teatro** (⊠ Praça Floriano 210, ☎ 021/2297–4411), in the lower level of the Teatro Municipal. Have a light lunch (weekdays 11–3) or coffee and a pastry (served at lunch or during evening performances) as you drink in the atmosphere. The decor is classical, replete with columns and wall mosaics that look like something out of a Cecil B. DeMille epic. The bar resembles a sarcophagus, and two sphinxes flank the sunken dining area. Note that this is one of the few cafés where you may be turned away if you're dressed too shabbily.

Flamengo, Botafogo, and Pão de Açúcar

These neighborhoods and their most famous peak—Pão de Açúcar—are like a bridge between the southern beach districts and Centro. Several highways intersect here, making it a hub for drives to Corcovado, Copacabana, Barra, or Centro. The metrô also travels through the area. Although the districts are largely residential, you'll find Rio Sul, one of the city's most popular shopping centers, as well as good museums and fabulous public spaces.

The eponymous beach at Flamengo no longer draws swimmers (its gentle waters look appealing but are polluted; the people you see are sunning, not swimming). A marina sits on a bay at one end of the beach, which is connected via a busy boulevard to the smaller beach (also polluted), at Botafogo. This neighborhood is home to the city's yacht club, and when Rio was Brazil's capital, it was also the site of the city's glittering embassy row. The embassies were long ago transferred to Brasília, but the mansions that housed them remain. Among Botafogo's more interesting mansion- and tree-lined streets are Mariana, Sorocaba, Matriz, and Visconde e Silva.

Botafogo faces tiny sheltered Urca, which is separated by Pão de Açúcar from a small patch of yellow sand called Vermelha. This beach is, in turn, blocked by the Urubu and Leme mountains from the 1-km (½-mi) Leme Beach at the start of the Zona Sul.

Numbers in the text correspond to numbers in the margin and on the Rio de Janeiro City map.

A Good Tour

Start at the northern end of the lovely, landscaped **Aterro do Flamengo** and the **Museu de Arte Moderna (MAM)** ⑭. Nearby is the **Monumento aos Pracinhas** ⑮, which honors the dead of World War II. Wander south along the Aterro before hopping into a cab and heading inland to the hilltop **Igreja de Nossa Senhora da Glória do Outeiro** ⑯. Get on the metrô at the Glória station and take it one stop to the Catete terminal, or walk south along Rua da Glória da Lapa to Rua da Catete, and you'll find the **Palácio do Catete** ⑰. From here you can either return to the Aterro by cab and walk south to the **Museu Carmen Miranda** ⑱, or you can take the metrô to the Botafogo stop and the nearby **Casa Rui Barbosa** ⑲. Finish the tour by riding the cable car up the **Pão de Açúcar** ⑳ for panoramic views of the bay and the neighborhoods you've just explored.

TIMING AND PRECAUTIONS

This tour takes a full day and involves a lot of walking and time outdoors. You can shorten the itinerary by taking a cab to sights off the Aterro do Flamengo and/or from one end of the Aterro to the other. As always, keep your money and other valuables out of sight while strolling.

Sights to See

Aterro do Flamengo. This waterfront park flanks Baía de Guanabara from the Glória neighborhood to Flamengo. It gets its name from its location atop an *aterro* (landfill), and was designed by landscape architect Roberto Burle Marx. Paths used for jogging, walking, and biking wind through it. There are also playgrounds and public tennis and basketball courts. On weekends the freeway beside the park is closed to traffic; the entire area becomes one enormous public space.

⑲ **Casa Rui Barbosa.** Slightly inland from the Aterro is a museum in what was once the house of 19th-century Brazilian statesmen and scholar Rui Barbosa (a liberal from Bahia State who drafted one of Brazil's early constitutions). The pink mansion dates from 1849 and contains memorabilia of Barbosa's life, including his 1913 car and an extensive library that's often consulted by scholars from around the world. During the ongoing reconstruction, admission is free. ⊠ *Rua São Clemente 134, Botafogo,* ☎ *021/2537–0036.* ☞ *Free.* ☉ *Tues.–Fri. 9–4, weekends 2–5. Metrô: Botafogo.*

⑯ **Igreja de Nossa Senhora da Glória do Outeiro.** Set atop a hill, this baroque church is visible from many spots in the city, making it a landmark that's truly cherished by the cariocas. Its location was a strategic point in the city's early days. Estácio da Sá took this hill from the French in the 1560s and then went on to expand the first settlement and found a city for the Portuguese. The church, which wasn't built until 1739, is notable for its octagonal floor plan, large dome, ornamental stonework, and vivid tilework. ⊠ *Praça Nossa Senhora da Glória 135, Glória,* ☎ *021/2557–4600.* ☞ *Free.* ☉ *Tues.–Fri. 9–noon and 1–5, weekends 9–noon. Tours first Sun. of month by appt. only. Metrô: Glória.*

⑮ **Monumento aos Pracinhas.** The Monument to the Brazilian Dead of World War II (the nation sided with the Allies during the conflict) is actually a museum and monument combined. It houses military uniforms, medals, stamps, and documents belonging to soldiers. Two soaring columns flank the tomb of an unknown soldier. The first Sunday of each month, Brazil's armed forces perform a colorful changing of the guard. ⊠ *Parque Brigadeiro Eduardo Gomes, Flamengo,* ☎ *021/ 2240–1283.* ☞ *Free.* ☉ *Tues.–Sun. 10–4. Metrô: Cinelândia.*

44

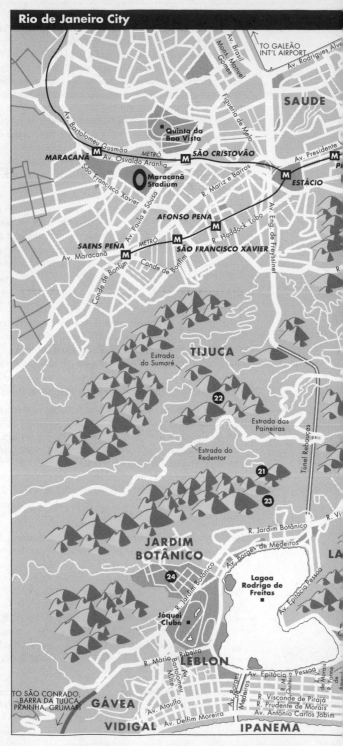

Ilha das Cobras

Av. Perimetral

Baía de Guanabara

R. Senador Pompeu

METRÔ

M CENTRAL

CENTRAL

PRES. VARGAS

URUGUAIANA

Menezes Cortes Bus Terminal

M

CENTRO

CARIOCA

M

See Rio Centro and Environs Map

① – ⑬

PRAÇA 11

Av. Mem de Sá

CINELÂNDIA

Aeroporto Santos Dumont

FÁTIMA

LAPA

⑮ ⑭

SANTA TERESA

GLÓRIA

⑯

Túnel Santa Bárbara

GLÓRIA

CATETE

CATETE

M

⑰

LARGO DO MACHADO

M

FLAMENGO

Praia do Flamengo

R. Pinheiro Machado

R. Paissandu

R. Osvaldo Cruz

FLAMENGO

M

R. das Laranjeiras

R. Rui Barbosa

⑱

Infante / Aterro Dom Henrique

URCA

Av. João Luis Alves

Av. São Sebastião

⑳

BOTAFOGO

⑲

BOTAFOGO

M

Praia de Botafogo

Av. das Nações Unidas

Av. Pasteur

Av. Portugal

São Clemente

R. Voluntários da Pátria

Mena Barreto

R. General

A. Quintela

VERMELHA

Visconde de Silva

R. Real Grandeza

R. Alvaro Ramos Monteiro

CARDEAL AREOVERDE

CARDEAL AREOVERDE

M

Av. Princesa Isabel

R. Gustavo Sampaio

LEME

GOA

R. Toneleiro

R. Barata Ribeiro

R. Figueiredo Magalhães

Av. Atlântica

Av. Copacabana

ATLANTIC OCEAN

Parque da Catacumba

R. Santa Clara

Av. Henrique Dodsworth

R. Raul Pompéia

R. Nossa Senhora de

COPACABANA

R. F. Otaviano

N

KEY

•••• Cable Car

M Metrô

0 ——— 1 mile

0 ——— 1 km

⑭ **Museu de Arte Moderna (MAM).** Set in a striking concrete-and-glass building, the Modern Art Museum has a collection of some 1,700 works by artists from Brazil and elsewhere. It also hosts significant special exhibitions, and has a movie theater that plays art films. ⊠ *Av. Infante Dom Henrique 85, Flamengo,* ☎ *021/2210–2188.* ☞ *Free.* ☉ *Tues.– Sun. noon–6. Metrô: Cinelândia.*

⑱ **Museu Carmen Miranda.** This tribute to the Brazilian bombshell is in a circular building that resembles a concrete spaceship (its door even opens up rather than out). On display are some of the elaborate costumes and incredibly high platform shoes worn by the actress, who was viewed as a national icon by some and as a traitor to true Brazilian culture by others. Hollywood photos of Miranda, who was only 46 when she died of a heart attack in 1955, show her in her trademark turban and jewelry. You'll also find her records, movie posters, and such memorabilia as the silver hand-held mirror she was clutching when she died. ⊠ *Av. Rui Barbosa 560, Flamengo,* ☎ *021/2551–2597.* ☞ *Free.* ☉ *Weekdays 11–5. Metrô: Flamengo.*

NEED A BREAK?   Flamengo contains some of Rio's better small restaurants. For authentic Brazilian fare, the bohemian community heads to **Lamas** (⊠ Rua Marques de Abrantes 18, ☎ 021/2556–0799).

★ ⑰ **Palácio do Catete.** Once the villa of a German baron, the elegant, 19th-century, granite-and-marble palace became the presidential residence after the 1889 coup overthrew the monarchy and established the Republic of Brazil. Eighteen presidents lived here.

You can gaze at the palace's gleaming parquet floors and intricate bas-relief ceilings as you wander through its **Museu da República** (Museum of the Republic). The permanent—and frank—exhibits include a shroud-draped view of the bedroom where President Getúlio Vargas committed suicide in 1954 after the military threatened to overthrow his government. Presidential memorabilia, furniture, and paintings that date from the proclamation of the republic to the end of Brazil's military regime in 1985 are also displayed. A small contemporary art gallery and a theater operate within the museum. ⊠ *Rua do Catete 153, Catete,* ☎ *021/2558–6350.* ☞ *R$5, free Wed.* ☉ *Tues.–Sun. noon–5, weekends 2–6. Metrô: Catete.*

★ ⑳ **Pão de Açúcar.** This soaring 1,300-m (390-ft) granite block at the mouth of Baía de Guanabara was originally called *pau-nh-acugua* (high, pointed peak) by the indigenous Tupi Indians. To the Portuguese the phrase seemed similar to *pão de açúcar,* or "sugarloaf"; the rock's shape reminded them of the conical loaves in which refined sugar was sold. Italian-made bubble cars holding 75 passengers each move up the mountain in two stages. The first stop is at Morro da Urca, a smaller, 212-m (705-ft) mountain; the second is at the summit of Pão de Açúcar itself. The trip to each level takes three minutes. In high season, long lines form for the cable car; the rest of the year, the wait is seldom more than 30 minutes. ⊠ *Av. Pasteur 520, Praia Vermelha, Urca,* ☎ *021/2546–8400.* ☞ *R$18.* ☉ *Daily 8 AM–10 PM.*

Zona Sul

Rio is home to 23 *praias* (beaches), an almost continuous 73-km (45-mi) ribbon of sand. All are public and are served by buses and taxis. At intervals along the beaches at Copacabana and Ipanema are small *postos* (bathhouses) with washrooms, showers, and dressing rooms that can be used for about R$2. Kiosks manned by police also pepper the avenues running parallel to the beach, and crime has dropped dramatically as a result.

A Good Beach Strategy

Although the circuit starts to the northeast at the beaches of Flamengo, Botafogo, Urca, and Vermelha, the waters off their shores are often polluted. The best sands are farther south. Leme, which is popular with senior citizens, runs into the city's grande dame, **Copacabana.** Its 3-km (2-mi) stretch is lined by a sidewalk whose swirling pattern was designed by Roberto Burle Marx. You'll also find outdoor cafés, high-rise hotels, and juice kiosks. At the end, cut around on the small Arpoador Beach (favored by surfers), or take Avenida Francisco Otaviano to **Ipanema.** Note that the final leg of this beach, called Leblon, is polluted; swimming isn't recommended.

Beyond Ipanema and Leblon, mountains again form a natural wall separating you from the next beach, little Vidigal. Still more mountains block it from **São Conrado,** a beach where hang gliders land after leaping from a nearby peak. A highway through a mountain tunnel forms the link between São Conrado and the long, spectacular **Barra da Tijuca.** Its waters are clean and cool, and its far end, known as Recreio dos Bandeirantes, was home to a small fishing village until the late 1960s. Beyond are **Prainha,** whose rough seas make it popular with surfers, and the lovely **Grumari,** whose copper sands are often packed. Just before Prainha, you can take a slight detour to visit the **Museu Casa do Pontal,** Brazil's largest folk-art museum. It's worth continuing down the hill beyond Grumari to the **Sítio Roberto Burle Marx** for an in-depth look at one of Brazil's greatest artists.

City buses and small green minivans pick you up and drop you off wherever you request along the shore. If you're brave enough to drive, the city has established small, affordable parking lots (look for attendants in green-and-yellow vests) along waterfront avenues. There are several organized tours that take in the beaches, and agents at Turismo Clássico can arrange for drivers and guides.

TIMING AND PRECAUTIONS

Although you can tour the shoreline in several hours, consider spending a full day just wandering from Copacabana to Ipanema or sunbathing on Barra da Tijuca. Remember that Rio's beaches aren't just about sunning and swimming; they're also about volleyball games, strolling, biking, and people-watching.

Don't shun the beaches because of reports of crime, but *do* take precautions. Leave jewelry, passports, and large sums of cash at your hotel; avoid wandering alone and at night; and be alert when groups of friendly youths engage you in conversation. (Sometimes they're trying to distract you while one of their cohorts snatches your belongings.) The biggest danger is the sun. From 10 to 3 the rays are merciless, making it essential to have heavy-duty sunscreen, hats, cover-ups, and plenty of liquids (you can also rent a beach umbrella from a vendor or your hotel). Hawkers stroll the beaches with beverages—take advantage of their services. Lifeguard stations are found once every kilometer.

Sights to See

★ **Barra da Tijuca.** Cariocas consider the beach to be Rio's best, and the 18-km-long (11-mi-long) sweep of sand and jostling waves certainly is dramatic. Pollution isn't a problem, and in many places neither are crowds. Barra's water is also cooler and its breezes more refreshing than those at other beaches. The waves can be strong in spots; this attracts surfers, windsurfers, and jet skiers, but you should swim with caution. The beach is set slightly below a sidewalk, where cafés and restaurants beckon. Condos have also sprung up here, and the city's largest shopping centers and supermarkets have made inland Barra their home.

RITES ON THE BEACH

ALTHOUGH RIO'S ANNUAL CARNAVAL is an amazing spectacle, there is perhaps no stranger sight than that which takes place on the beaches each New Year's Eve. Under the warm tropical sky and with the backdrop of the modern city, thousands faithful to the Macumba religion honor Iemanjá, the goddess of the sea.

The advent of the new year is a time for renewal and to ask for blessings. The faithful—of all ages, colors, and classes—determined to start the year right, pour onto the beaches at around 10 PM. Some draw mystic signs in the sand. Others lay out white tablecloths with gifts befitting a proud, beautiful goddess: combs, mirrors, lipsticks, hair ribbons, perfumes, wines. Still others bring flowers with notes asking for favors tucked amid the blossoms. Worshipers chant and sing over their offerings and set candles around them.

By 11:30 PM, the beaches are a mass of white-clad believers with flickering candles—the shore looks as if it has been invaded by millions of fireflies. At midnight, the singing, shrieking, and sobbing is accompanied by fireworks, sirens, and bells. The faithful rush to the water for the moment of truth: if the goddess is satisfied with an offering, it's carried out to sea, and the gift giver's wish will come true. If, however, Iemanjá is displeased with an offering, the ocean will throw it back; the gift giver must try again another year.

At the far end of Barra's beachfront avenue, Sernambetiba, is Recreio dos Bandeirantes, a 1-km (½-mi) stretch of sand anchored by a huge rock, which creates a small protected cove. Its quiet seclusion makes it popular with families. The calm, pollution-free water, with no waves or currents, is good for bathing, but don't try to swim around the rock—it's bigger than it looks.

Copacabana. Maddening traffic, noise, packed apartment blocks, and a world-famous beach—this is Copacabana, Manhattan with bikinis. A walk along the neighborhood's classic crescent is a must. You'll see the essence of beach culture, a cradle-to-grave lifestyle that begins with toddlers accompanying their parents to the water and ends with graying seniors walking hand in hand along the sidewalk. It's here that athletic men play volleyball using only their feet and heads, not their hands. As you can tell by all the goal nets, soccer is also popular (Copacabana hosts the world beach soccer championships every January and February). You can swim here, although pollution levels and a strong undertow can sometimes be discouraging.

Copacabana's privileged live on beachfront Avenida Atlântica, famed for its wide mosaic sidewalks, hotels, and cafés. On weekends, two of the avenue's lanes are closed to traffic and are taken over by joggers, rollerbladers, cyclists, and pedestrians. Two blocks inland from and parallel to the beach is Avenida Nossa Senhora de Copacabana, the main commercial street, with shops, restaurants, and sidewalks crowded with the colorful characters that give Copacabana its flavor.

At the Pão de Açúcar end is Leme, a natural extension of Copacabana. A rock formation juts into the water here, forming a quiet cove that's less crowded than the rest of the beach. Along a sidewalk, at the side of the mountain overlooking Leme, anglers stand elbow to elbow with their lines dangling into the sea.

NEED A BREAK?

Stop in for a drink at one of Avenida Atlântica's few air-conditioned cafes. The windows of **Manoel & Juaquin** (⊠ Av. Atlântica 1936, Copacabana, ☎ 021/2236–6768) face the sands so you can settle in with a cold draft beer or a light meal (the garlic potatoes are unbeatable) while watching carioca life unfold. Bring cash; this eatery takes no credit cards.

Ipanema. As you stroll along this beach, you'll catch a cross section of the city's residents, each favoring a particular stretch. There's an area dominated by families; a spot near Copacabana, known as Arpoador, that tantalizes surfers; and even a strand favored by the gay community. Ipanema, nearby Leblon (off whose shores the waters are too polluted for swimming), and the blocks surrounding Lagoa Rodrigo de Freitas are part of Rio's money belt. For a close-up look at the posh apartment buildings, stroll down beachfront Avenida Vieira Souto and its extension, Avenida Delfim Moreira, or drive around the lagoon on Avenida Epitácio Pessoa. The tree-lined streets between Ipanema Beach and the lagoon are as peaceful as they are attractive. The boutiques along Rua Garcia D'Ávila make window-shopping a sophisticated endeavor. Other chic areas near the beach include Praça Nossa Senhora da Paz, which is lined with wonderful restaurants and bars; Rua Vinicius de Moraes; and Rua Farme de Amoedo.

NEED A BREAK?

Have you ever wondered if there really *was* a girl from Ipanema? The song was inspired by schoolgirl Heloisa Pinheiro, who caught the fancy of songwriter Antônio Carlos (a.k.a. Tom) Jobim and his pal lyricist Vinicius de Moraes as she walked past the two bohemians sitting in their favorite bar. They then penned one of last century's classics. That was in 1962, and today the bar has been renamed **Bar Garota de Ipanema** (⊠ Rua Vinicius de Moraes 49-A, Ipanema, ☎ 021/2267–8787).

OFF THE BEATEN PATH

MUSEU CASA DO PONTAL – If you're heading toward Prainha or beyond to Grumari, consider taking a detour to Brazil's largest folk-art museum. One room houses a wonderful mechanical sculpture that represents all of the escolas de samba that march in the Carnaval parades. Another mechanical "scene" depicts a circus in action. This private collection is owned by a French expatriate, Jacques Van de Beuque, who has been collecting Brazilian treasures—including religious pieces—since he arrived in the country in 1946. ⊠ Estrada do Pontal 3295, Grumari, ☎ 021/2490–3278 or 021/2539–4914. ☑ R$5. ⊙ Tues.–Sun. 9–5.

★ **Prainha and Grumari.** The length of two football fields, Prainha is a vest-pocket beach favored by surfers, who take charge of it on weekends. Set about 35 minutes west of Ipanema on a road that hugs the coast, it's accessible only by car from Avenida Sernambetiba. The swimming is good, but watch out for surfboards. About five minutes farther, off Estrada de Guaratiba, is Grumari, a beach that seems an incarnation of paradise. What it lacks in amenities (you'll find only a couple of groupings of thatch-roof huts selling drinks and snacks) it makes up for in natural beauty: the glorious red sands of its quiet cove are backed by low, lush hills. On weekdays, especially in the off-season, these beaches are almost empty; on weekends, particularly in peak season, the road to and from them is so crowded it almost becomes a parking lot.

NEED A BREAK?

From Grumari, Estrada de Guaratiba climbs up through dense forest, emerging atop a hill above the vast Guaratiba flatlands. Here you'll find the **Restaurante Pont de Grumari** (✉ Estrada do Grumari 710, Grumari, ☎ 021/2410–1434), an eatery famed for grilling fish to perfection. With its shady setting, glorious vistas, and live music performances (samba, bossa nova, jazz), it's the perfect spot for lunch (open daily 11:30–7) after a morning on the beach and before an afternoon at the Sítio Roberto Burle Marx or the Museu Casa do Pontal.

São Conrado. In Leblon, at the end of Ipanema blocked by the imposing Dois Irmãos Mountain, Avenida Niemeyer snakes along rugged cliffs that offer spectacular sea views on the left. The road returns to sea level again in São Conrado, a natural amphitheater surrounded by forested mountains and the ocean. Development of what is now a mostly residential area began in the late '60s with an eye on Rio's high society. A short stretch along its beach includes the condominiums of a former president, the ex-wife of another former president, an ex-governor of Rio de Janeiro State, and a one-time Central Bank president. In the middle of the small valley is the exclusive Gávea Golf and Country Club. The far end of São Conrado is marked by the towering Pedra da Gávea, a huge flat-top granite block. Next to it is Pedra Bonita, the mountain from which gliders depart. (Although this beach was the city's most popular a few years ago, contaminated water has discouraged swimmers.)

Ironically, the neighborhood is surrounded by shantytowns. Much of the high ground has been taken over by Rio's largest favela, Rocinha, where an estimated 200,000 people live. This precarious city within a city seems poised to slide down the hill. It, and others like it, are the result of Rio's chronic housing problem coupled with the refusal by many of the city's poor to live in distant working-class neighborhoods. Though the favelas are dangerous for the uninitiated, they have their own internal order, and their tremendous expansion has even upper-class cariocas referring to them not as slums but as neighborhoods. Notice that the favelas enjoy prime vistas, and most of them are constructed of brick.

OFF THE
BEATEN PATH

SÍTIO ROBERTO BURLE MARX – Beyond Grumari the road winds through mangrove swamps and tropical forest. It's an apt setting for the plantation-turned-museum where Brazil's famous landscape designer, Roberto Burle Marx, is memorialized. Marx, the mind behind Rio's mosaic beachfront walkways and the Aterro do Flamengo, was said to have "painted with plants" and was the first designer to use Brazilian flora in his projects. More than 3,500 species—including some discovered by and named for Marx as well as many on the endangered list—flourish at this 100-acre estate. He grouped his plants not only according to their soil and light needs but also according to their shape and texture. Marx also liked to mix modern things with old ones—a recurring theme throughout the property. The results are both whimsical and elegant. In 1985 he bequeathed the farm to the Brazilian government, though he remained until his death in 1994. His house is now a cultural center full of his belongings, including collections of folk art. The grounds also contain his large, ultramodern studio (he was a painter, too) and a small, restored colonial chapel dedicated to St. Anthony. *Estrada de Guaratiba 2019, Guaratiba, ☎ 021/2410–1412 or 021/2410–1171. ✉ R$4. ☺ By appointment only.*

The Lush Inland

Beyond the sand and sea in the Zona Sul are lush parks and gardens as well as marvelous museums, seductive architecture, and tantalizing restaurants. You can't say you've seen Rio until you've taken in the view from Corcovado and then strolled through its forested areas or beside its inland lagoon—hanging out just like a true carioca.

Numbers in the text correspond to numbers in the margin and on the Rio de Janeiro City map.

A Good Tour

Head first to the imposing **Corcovado** ㉑ and its hallmark Cristo Redentor statue. As you slide up the side of the steep mountain in the train, you'll pass through the lush forested area known as **Floresta da Tijuca** ㉒. (If you want to explore the forest more, you'll need to hire a cab or join a tour that offers both Corcovado and Floresta da Tijuca.) Back down the hill and at the train station again, stroll downhill a short distance to the **Museu de Arte Naïf do Brasil** ㉓, which houses a renowned collection of primitive art from around the world. The same street leads uphill to the delightful colonial square called Largo do Boticário—a good place to rest your feet. From here, grab a taxi and journey west to the inviting **Jardim Botânico** ㉔, across from which is the Jóquei Clube. The botanical gardens are within walking distance from the Lagoa Rodrigo de Freitas, the giant saltwater lagoon that serves as one of the city's playgrounds—for children and adults alike.

TIMING AND PRECAUTIONS

You can see these sights in a day if you start early. Try to visit Corcovado on a clear day, clouds often obscure the Christ statue on its summit. You can join an organized tour or hire a cabbie to take you out for the day (public transportation doesn't conveniently reach these sights). The security is good at Corcovado and Floresta da Tijuca, so you can usually carry your camera without worry. At the Jardim Botânico and the Lagoa Rodrigo de Freitas, however, be alert. Throughout this tour, keep valuables in a money belt or somewhere else out of sight.

Sights to See

★ ㉑ **Corcovado.** There's an eternal argument about which view is better, from Pão de Açúcar or from here. Corcovado has two advantages: at 690 m (2,300 ft), it's nearly twice as high and offers an excellent view of Pão de Açúcar itself. The sheer 300-m (1,000-ft) granite face of Corcovado (the name means "hunchback" and refers to the mountain's shape) has always been a difficult undertaking for climbers.

It wasn't until 1921, the centennial of Brazil's independence from Portugal, that someone had the idea of placing a statue atop Corcovado. A team of French artisans headed by sculptor Paul Landowski was assigned the task of erecting a statue of Christ with his arms apart as if embracing the city. (Nowadays, mischievous cariocas say Christ is getting ready to clap for his favorite escola de samba.) It took 10 years, but on October 12, 1931, the *Cristo Redentor* (Christ the Redeemer) was inaugurated. The sleek, modern figure rises more than 30 m (100 ft) from a 6-m (20-ft) pedestal and weighs 700 tons. In the evening a powerful lighting system transforms it into a dramatic icon.

There are two ways to reach the top: by cogwheel train (originally built in 1885) or by winding road through the Floresta da Tijuca. The train provides delightful views of Ipanema and Leblon (from an absurd angle of ascent) as well as a close look at the thick vegetation and the butterflies and birds it attracts. (You may wonder what those oblong medicine balls hanging from the trees are, the ones that look like spiked watermelons tied to ropes—they're *jaca,* or jackfruit.) Trains leave the **Cosme Velho station** every 30 minutes, daily 8:30–6:30, for the steep 5-km (3-mi), 17-minute ascent. Late-afternoon trains are the most popular; on weekends be prepared for a long wait. ⊠ *Rua Cosme Velho 513, Cosme Velho,* ☎ *021/2558–1329.* 🚇 *R$18.*

Driving up through the forest is free, but if you want to visit the statue by car, you have to pay R$5 for each person plus R$5 for parking.

Whether you arrive by train, tour bus, or car, a climb up a series of steep, zigzagging staircases and landings is necessary before you get to the summit, the statue, and the viewing points. There are no elevators or ramps for wheelchairs. You'll pass little cafés and shops selling film and souvenirs along the way. Once at the top, all of Rio stretches out before you.

㉒ **Floresta da Tijuca.** Surrounding Corcovado is the dense, tropical Tijuca Forest. Once part of a Brazilian nobleman's estate, it's studded with exotic trees and thick jungle vines and has a delightful waterfall, the Cascatinha de Taunay. About 180 m (200 yards) beyond the waterfall is the small pink-and-purple Capela Mayrink (Mayrink Chapel), with painted panels by the 20th-century Brazilian artist Cândido Portinari.

From several points along this national park's 96 km (60 mi) of narrow, winding roads the views are breathtaking. Some of the most spectacular are from Dona Marta, on the way up Corcovado; the Emperor's Table, supposedly where Brazil's last emperor, Pedro II, took his court for picnics; and, farther down the road, the Chinese View, the area where Portuguese king João VI allegedly settled the first Chinese immigrants who came to Brazil in the early 19th century to develop tea plantations. A great way to see the forest is by Jeep; you can arrange tours through a number of agencies. *Entrance at Praça Afonso Viseu 561, Tijuca,* ☎ *021/2492–2253.* ☒ *Free.* ☉ *Daily 7–7.*

㉔ **Jardim Botânico.** The 340-acre Botanical Garden contains more than 5,000 species of tropical and subtropical plants and trees, including 900 varieties of palms (some more than a century old) and more than 140 species of birds. The temperature is usually a good 12°C (22°F) cooler in the shady garden that was created in 1808 by Portuguese King João VI during his exile in Brazil. In 1842 the garden gained its most impressive adornment, the Avenue of the Royal Palms, 720-m-long (800-yard-long) double row of 134 soaring royal palms. Elsewhere in the gardens, the Casa dos Pilões, an old gunpowder factory, has been restored and displays objects that pertained to both the nobility and to their slaves. Also on the grounds are a library, a small café, and a gift shop that sells souvenirs with ecological themes (the shop is a product of the Earth Summit that was held in 1992). ☒ *Rua Jardim Botânico 1008,* ☎ *021/2294–6012.* ☒ *R$4.* ☉ *Daily 8–5.*

NEED A BREAK?
Cool off with some homemade ice cream featuring a tropical twist. The flavors at **Mil Frutas Sorvetes** (☒ Rua J. J. Seabra, Jardim Botânico, ☎ 021/2511–2550) are concocted using such local fruits as *acerola* and jaca.

★ ㉓ **Museu de Arte Naif do Brasil.** More than 8,000 art naïf works by Brazil's best (as well as works by other self-taught painters from around the world) grace the walls of this lovely colonial mansion that was once the studio of painter Eliseu Visconti. The pieces in what is reputedly the world's largest and most complete collection of primitive paintings date from the 15th century through contemporary times. Don't miss the colorful, colossal (7 × 4-m/223 × 13-ft) canvas that depicts the city of Rio; it reportedly took five years to complete. This museum sprang from a collection started decades ago by a jewelry designer who later created a foundation to oversee the art. A small gift shop sells postcards, T-shirts, and other items. ☒ *Rua Cosme Velho 561, Tijuca,* ☎ *021/2205–8612 or 021/2205–8547.* ☒ *R$5.* ☉ *Tues.–Fri. 10–6, weekends noon–6.*

DINING

Meat lovers will be mesmerized by the succulent offerings in Rio's churrascarias, especially those that serve *rodízio* style (grilled meat on skewers is continuously brought to your table—until you can eat no more). Hotel restaurants often offer feijoada on Saturday (sometimes Friday, too). Vegetarians will appreciate the abundance of salad bars, where you pay for your greens by the kilo. And seafood restaurants are in abundance. (Note that it's perfectly safe to eat fresh produce in clean, upscale places; avoid shellfish in all but the best restaurants.)

Cariocas have scaled back on *almoço* (lunch), which used to be a full meal, and have turned more to *lanche* (a sandwich). Dinner is a late affair; if you arrive at 7, you may be the only one in the restaurant. Popular places seat customers until well after midnight on weekends, when the normal closing hour is 2 AM. Cariocas love to linger in *choperias*, plain but pleasant bars that may also serve food, and such establishments abound. Most serve dishes in the $–$$ range, and portions are large enough for two people to share.

Many restaurants offer a special fixed-price menu as well as à la carte fare. Many also include what is referred to as cover charge for the bread and other appetizers placed on the table. Leaving a 10% tip is enough, but check your bill: the service charge may already have been added. Some restaurants don't accept credit cards, many are closed on Monday, and dress is almost always casual.

For price categories, *see* the chart *under* Dining *in* Smart Travel Tips A to Z.

Brazilian

$$$ ✕ **Mariu's.** This highly regarded churrascaria serves more than a dozen types of sizzling meats, rodízio style (R$32 per person). Its popularity sparked the opening of a second restaurant in Leme. Reservations are a good idea. ⊠ *Rua Francisco Otaviano 96, Ipanema,* ☎ *021/2521–0500. DC, MC, V.* ⊠ *Av. Atlântica 290A, Leme,* ☎ *021/2542–2393. DC, MC, V.*

$$$ ✕ **Porção.** Waiters at these quintessential rodízio-style churrascarias
★ fly up and down between rows of linen-draped tables wielding giant skewers laden with sizzling barbecued beef, pork, and chicken. All the branches resonate with the good humor that seems to accompany this slightly primitive form of eating. Save room if you can: the papaya creme pudding topped by a bit of cassis shouldn't be missed. ⊠ *Rua Barão da Torre 218, Ipanema,* ☎ *021/2522–0999. Reservations not accepted. AE, DC, MC, V.* ⊠ *Av. Armando Lombardi 591, Barra da Tijuca,* ☎ *021/2492–2001. Reservations not accepted. AE, DC, MC, V.* ⊠ *Av. Infante Dom Henrique, Parque do Flamengo,* ☎ *021/2554–8862. Reservations not accepted. AE, DC, MC, V.*

$$$ ✕ **Siri Mole.** If you want to eat typical food from the northeast of Brazil,
★ this is the place. It's a small but absolutely comfortable restaurant that makes exotic dishes, such as *acarajé,* a mix of fried smashed white beans and shrimp. Don't miss the *moqueca de siri,* a hot stew made of crabs, *dendê* oil (a kind of spicy olive oil), and coconut milk. ⊠ *Rua Francisco Otaviano 50, Copacabana,* ☎ *021/2267–0894. AE, DC, MC, V.*

$$–$$$$ ✕ **Esplanada Grill.** This churrascaria serves high-quality meat like T-bone steak (R$29) or picanha, a tasty Brazilian cut of beef marbled with some fat (R$23 half portion). All the grilled dishes come with fried palm hearts, baked potatoes, and rice. Brazilian TV stars like to hang out at this upscale eatery. ⊠ *Rua Barão da Torre 600, Ipanema,* ☎ *021/2512–2970. DC, MC, V.*

54

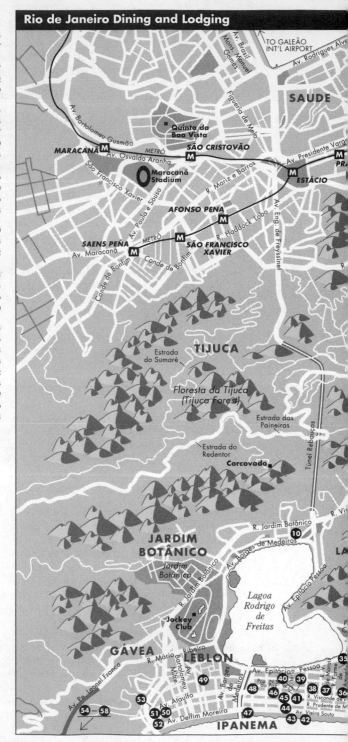

Rio de Janeiro Dining and Lodging

Lodging

$$–$$$ ✕ **Barra Grill.** Informal and popular, this steak house serves some of the best meat in town and is a favorite stop after a long day at the beach. Prices for the rodízio-style meals are slightly more expensive on weekends than during the week. ✉ *Av. Ministro Ivan Lins 314, Barra da Tijuca,* ☏ *021/2493–6060. Reservations not accepted. AE, DC, MC, V.*

$$–$$$ ✕ **Yorubá.** The menu reflects owner Neide Santos's origins. A *baiana* ★ (woman from the northeastern Brazilian state of Bahia) by birth, she offers African-Brazilian dishes typical of that region. African sculptures, blue windows, and green leaves spread all over the place, make up the decor. The *piripiri* (a spicy rice with ginger, coconut milk, and shrimp) is worth it at R$65 for two. ✉ *Rua Arnaldo Quintela 94, Botafogo,* ☏ *021/2541–9387. No credit cards.*

$$ ✕ **Casa da Feijoada.** Brazil's savory national dish is the specialty here, ★ where huge pots of the stew simmer every day (R$25 per person). The restaurant does a superb job with desserts as well, whipping up a lovely selection of traditional sweets with flavors like banana or pumpkin. To drink, try the caipirinha made with cachaça and not only lime but also other fruits like tangerine, passion fruit, pineapple, strawberry, or kiwi. Be careful though, caipirinha is strong, and the sweet taste can be deceptive. ✉ *Rua Prudente de Morais 10, Ipanema,* ☏ *021/2523–4994 or 021/2247–2776. AE, DC, MC, V.*

$–$$ ✕ **Terra Brasilis.** Large windows overlooking a tree-lined street, cool white-ceramic tile, and stucco walls painted buttercup yellow and celery green give this "weigh-and-pay" restaurant a cheery atmosphere. For lunch, simply help yourself to the Brazilian buffet (including a good selection of salads) and head to a counter, where your plate is weighed. It works out to about R$16 a kilo on weekdays, R$18 on weekends, but it's really hard to eat that much. And, yes, they do take the plate's weight into account. For dinner, the system changes to rodízio-style service of several Brazilian dishes: fried, dried meat, and red and black beans. ✉ *Rua Humberto de Campos 699, Leblon,* ☏ *021/2274–4702,* WEB *www.cozinhatipica,com.br. AE, DC, MC, V.*

$–$$ ✕ **Yemanjá.** Featuring typical food from Bahia, this restaurant serves portions big enough for two. Try the *bobó de camarão,* made of shrimp and mashed *aipim* (a root vegetable similar to potato). For dessert, opt for the white or black *cocada,* a sugar and coconut confection cooked either a short time (white), or a longer time (black). ✉ *Rua Visconde de Pirajá 128, Ipanema,* ☏ *021/2247–7004. AE, DC, MC, V.*

Cafés

¢–$$ ✕ **Garcia & Rodrigues.** It's a combination café, delicatessen, liquor shop, ★ and trendy restaurant. High-society cariocas breakfast at this expensive but cozy place. At lunchtime, choose from a selection of sandwiches, made with ingredients such as salmon. ✉ *Av. Ataulfo de Paiva 1251, Leblon,* ☏ *021/2512–8188. AE, DC, MC, V.*

¢–$ ✕ **Colombo.** At the turn of the century, this belle epoque structure was ★ Rio's preeminent café, the site of afternoon teas for high-society *senhoras* and a center of political intrigue and gossip. Jacaranda-framed mirrors from Belgium and stained glass from France add to the art nouveau decor. Portions are generous, but you can also just stop by for a pastry and coffee while you absorb the opulence. ✉ *Rua Gonçalves Dias 32, Centro,* ☏ *021/2232–2300. Reservations not accepted. No credit cards. Closed Sun. No dinner. Metrô: Carioca.*

Eclectic

$$$–$$$$ ✕ **Spices.** A Caribbean flair presides over the creative menu here. An extensive array of mixed drinks includes the Nêga Sings the Blues (a variation of the caipirinha made with cachaça, lime, ginger, and honey). The entrées have similarly offbeat names, and many of the seafood, fowl, and meat dishes employ fruits and nuts in their preparation. Try the ginger tuna with mango or the grilled beef with Gorgonzola and pumpkin purée. Spices has some of the best-looking salads in town as well. ⊠ *Av. Epitácio Pessoa 864, Lagoa,* ☎ *021/2259–1041. AE.*

$–$$$$ ✕ **Alho & Óleo.** On Ipanema's Praça Nossa Senhora da Paz, this restau-
★ rant features an eclectic menu with a hint of Italy. Interesting fowl dishes include partridge with dates and grilled duck with apricots; the arugula salad with eggplant, mushrooms, and sea bass is also recommended. Homemade pasta dishes include a farfalle with seafood and artichokes. ⊠ *Rua Barão da Torre 348, Ipanema,* ☎ *021/2247–6711 or 021/2247–6712. AE.* ⊠ *Rua Buarque de Macedo 13, Flamengo,* ☎ *021/2225–3418, AE.*

$ ✕ **Garfo Livre.** The by-the-kilo buffets at this eatery two blocks from the beach give economical eating a new twist. As you enter, you're given a card on which the items you select are marked. Grab a plate, help yourself to the buffet—which has many Middle Eastern dishes—get your plate weighed, and then pay on your way out. The salad bar has a large selection that includes beans, hummus, and steamed and raw veggies. Commuters come on weeknights beginning at 7 trading rush hour for happy hour. ⊠ *Av. Nossa Senhora de Copacabana 1003, Copacabana,* ☎ *021/3813–5571. AE, DC, MC, V.*

French

$$$$ ✕ **Carême.** The R$70 prix-fixe menu here includes a choice of some
★ of the best French desserts in town. *Delícia de limão* (lemon delight) is a must-try. It's made of several thin layers of a hazelnut biscuit lightly soaked with lemon juice and stacked with honey mousse and lemon cream; atop it all are merengue, small pieces of white chocolate, and a strawberry. ⊠ *Rua Visconde de Caravelas 113, Botafogo,* ☎ *021/2537–5431. Reservations essential. No lunch. DC, MC.*

$$$$ ✕ **Le Pré-Catalan.** In the hotel Sofitel Rio Palace is a carioca version of the charming Parisian restaurant of the same name in the Bois du Boulogne. Reopened in 1998 with chef Roland Villard, this has become one of the best French restaurants in Rio. Every two weeks it has a new prix-fixe menu—R$65 with three choices for appetizers, main dish, and a dessert. ⊠ *Av. Atlântica 4240, Level E, Copacabana,* ☎ *021/2525–1160. Reservations essential. AE, DC, MC, V. No lunch.*

$$$$ ✕ **Le Saint Honoré.** Le Saint Honoré offers diners French cuisine and an extraordinary view of Copacabana Beach from atop Le Meridien hotel. Brazilian fruits and herbs tucked into dishes produce such gems as *les pièces du boucher marquées sauces gamay et béarnaise,* a fillet with both béarnaise and red-wine sauces. A jacket and tie are advised. ⊠ *Av. Atlântica 1020, 37th floor, Copacabana,* ☎ *021/3873–8880. Reservations essential. AE, DC, MC, V.*

$$$–$$$$ ✕ **Claude Troisgros.** Many consider this Rio's finest restaurant, though
★ Claude Troisgros himself has left and Chef Antônio Costa is now at the helm. The menu is famed for nouvelle cuisine relying entirely on Brazilian ingredients. Every dish—from the crab or lobster flan to chicken, fish, and duck prepared with exotic herbs and sauces—is pure pleasure and always exceptionally light. The dessert menu is headed by a to-die-for passion-fruit mousse. ⊠ *Rua Custódio Serrão 62, Jardim Botânico,* ☎ *021/2537–8582. Reservations essential. AE, DC.*

$$–$$$$ ✕ **Monseigneur.** Modern and traditional French cuisine meet here, where the grand decor matches the meals—two striking lighted columns of translucent crystal dominate the center of the restaurant. The disadvantage is that to get to the Inter-Continental Rio hotel you'll need a

cab. ⊠ *Av. Prefeito Mendes de Morais 222, São Conrado,* ☏ *021/3323–2200. Reservations essential. AE, DC, MC, V. No lunch.*

Italian

$$$–$$$$ ✕ **Cipriani.** The Copacabana Palace hotel's restaurant offers a superb dining experience. Start with a Cipriani—champagne with fresh peach juice (really a Bellini). The snook carpaccio with apple and fennel is a marvelous appetizer; so is the salad of endive marinated in red wine. The pastas must be imported from heaven, and the meat and fish entrées are, appropriate to their lavish surroundings, fit for kings. None of this, of course, comes cheaply. ⊠ *Av. Atlântica 1702, Copacabana,* ☏ *021/2545–8747. Reservations essential. AE, DC, MC, V.*

$$–$$$$ ✕ **Margutta.** A good wine list complements the cuisine here. The pasta,
  ★   fish, and risottos are all top drawer—and always fresh. ⊠ *Av. Henrique Dumont 62, Ipanema,* ☏ *021/2511–0878. AE, DC, V. No lunch weekdays.*

$$–$$$ ✕ **Alfredo.** The mainstay is the pasta, especially the fettuccine Alfredo. Start your meal with a selection from the ample cold buffet of antipasti, which may include traditional pastas served with a variety of sauces. The restaurant is in the Inter-Continental hotel and has a view of the pool area. ⊠ *Av. Prefeito Mendes de Morais 222, São Conrado,* ☏ *021/3323–2200. AE, DC, MC, V. No lunch.*

$–$$$$ ✕ **D'Amici.** This restaurant is a pleasant surprise formed from the collaboration of two maître d's, Antonio Salustiano and Candido Alves, and a sommelier, Walmir Pereira. None of the three is Italian; in fact, they all come from the northeast of Brazil. But the lamb with rice and herbs is divine, and the boar meat with red wine sauce is irresistible. Many dishes aren't listed on the fixed menu—ask for suggestions. ⊠ *Rua Antônio Vieira 18, Leme,* ☏ *021/2541–4477. AE, DC, MC, V.*

Mexican

$–$$ ✕ **Guapo Loco.** The bustling crowds feast on tamales, enchiladas, and other Mexican favorites until closing time at 3 AM. Tequila has garnered quite a following among the young; the margaritas are good. ⊠ *Rua Rainha Guilhermina 48, Leblon,* ☏ *021/2294–2915. AE, DC, MC, V. No lunch weekdays.*

Portuguese

$$–$$$$ ✕ **Adega Aragon.** Simple, but original, this restaurant has more than
  ★   20 kinds of *bacalhau* (cod) on the menu. There's also the *sinfonia marítima,* R$38 for two, a grilled seafood medley of shrimp, squid, and fresh fish served with rice. ⊠ *Rua Siqueira Campos 18B, Copacabana,* ☏ *021/2257–1427. AE, D, DC, MC, V.*

$$–$$$$ ✕ **Antiquarius.** This much-loved establishment is as famous for its flaw-
  ★   less—and award-winning—rendering of Portuguese classics as for its high prices. Wander through the antiques shop at the restaurant before settling in at a table. A recommended dish is the *cozido,* a stew with a multitude of ingredients, including bananas. The *cataplana,* a seafood stew with rice, is also marvelous, and the *perna de cordeiro* (leg of lamb) is the most requested dish on the menu. The wine list impresses even Portuguese gourmets. ⊠ *Rua Aristides Espínola 19, Leblon,* ☏ *021/2294–1049. Reservations essential. DC.*

Seafood

$$$$ ✕ **Galani.** Although it overlooks action-packed Ipanema, the mood at this Caesar Park hotel restaurant is quiet. The buffet (R$43 weekdays, R$59 weekends) has everything from salads and seafood to pasta and carpaccio. ⊠ *Av. Antônio Carlos Jobim 460, Ipanema,* ☎ *021/2525–2525. AE, DC, MC, V.*

$$$–$$$$ ✕ **Satyricon.** This eclectic Italian seafood restaurant, which also has
★ a branch in Búzios, is rumored to have been Madonna's favorite eatery
when she was in town. The *pargo* (fish baked in a thick layer of rock
salt) is a specialty, and the sushi and sashimi are well loved. It's ex-
pensive, but it has some of the best seafood in town. ⊠ *Rua Barão da
Torre 192, Ipanema,* ☎ *021/2521–0627. DC, MC, V.*

$–$$$$ ✕ **Shirley.** Homemade Spanish seafood casseroles and soups are the
★ draw at this traditional Copacabana restaurant tucked onto a shady
street. Try the *zarzuela,* a seafood soup, or *cazuela,* a fish fillet with
white-wine sauce. Don't be turned off by the simple decor (a few
paintings hung on wood-paneled walls): the food is terrific. ⊠ *Rua Gus-
tavo Sampaio 610, Leme,* ☎ *021/2275–1398. Reservations not accepted.
No credit cards.*

$–$$$ ✕ **Don Camillo.** There's always something new on the menu at this Co-
★ pacabana beachfront restaurant. Try the fried seafood platter (R$22)
with shrimp, sardines, and fresh fish of the day. The Italian atmosphere
is completed by a musical group that sings traditional songs. ⊠ *Av.
Atlântica 3056, Copacabana,* ☎ *021/2549–9958,* WEB *www.tempero.
com.br. AE, D, DC, MC, V.*

$–$$$ ✕ **Quatro Sete Meia.** Internationally renowned, this restaurant is one
★ hour by car west of Copacabana, at the end of a highway that offers
stunning coastal views. Simplicity is the soul of the restaurant—whose
name is its street number—and the village in which it's set. There are
only 11 tables: five indoors and six in a garden at water's edge. The
menu carries seven delicious options, including *moquecas* (seafood stews),
grilled seafood, and curries. ⊠ *Rua Barros de Alarcão 476, Pedra da
Guaratiba,* ☎ *021/2417–1716. Reservations essential. No credit cards.
Closed Mon.–Tues. No dinner Wed.–Thurs.*

Vegetarian

$$$ ✕ **Celeiro.** What may be Rio's sole organic restaurant is always full
for lunch. The buffet offers approximately 40 salads as well as a wide
selection of pastas for R$33 per kilo. ⊠ *Rua Dias Ferreira 199, Leblon,*
☎ *021/2274–7843. D, MC, V. No dinner.*

¢–$ ✕ **Bistrô do Paço.** A good option for a light lunch, the daily buffet of
salads (R$9 per person) includes carrot salad with oranges, potatoes,
and apples. For R$10 you can try also an onion, cheese, or spinach
quiche. ⊠ *Praça Quinze 48, Centro,* ☎ *021/2262–3613. MC, V. No
dinner.*

¢–$ ✕ **Doce Delícia.** Make your own salad by choosing 5 to 15 of the 42
items offered daily. Dressings run the gamut from light and yogurt
based to innovative, with mustard and lemon. A large portion is R$11,
a small R$9. ⊠ *Rua Aníbal de Mendonça 55, Ipanema,* ☎ *021/2259–
0239. V.*

LODGING

Most hotels are in Copacabana and Ipanema. Copacabana hotels are
close to the action (and the metrô), but the neighborhood is noisier
than Ipanema (which is itself noisier than São Conrado and Barra da
Tijuca). Note that Rio's "motels" aren't aimed at tourists. They attract
couples looking for privacy, and usually rent by the hour.

In the days just prior to and during Carnaval, already peak-season rates
can double, even triple. Expect to pay a premium for a room with a
view. Many hotels include breakfast in the rate, but the quality varies
from a full buffet to a hard roll with butter. Remember that if you're

traveling during peak periods, make reservations as far in advance as possible. Air-conditioning is standard in most hotels, as are room safes. Room service is available in all $$$–$$$$ establishments; in $$–$$$$ hotels, you'll find concierges or, at the very least, reception personnel who perform concierge duties.

For price categories, *see* the chart *under* Lodging *in* Smart Travel Tips A to Z.

$$$$ 🏨 **Caesar Park.** This beachfront hotel has established itself as a favorite
★ of business travelers, celebrities, and heads of state, who appreciate its impeccable service. To assist business guests, the hotel provides secretarial services, as well as fax machines and laptops for in-room use. ⊠ *Av. Vieira Souto 460, Ipanema 22120,* ☎ *021/2525–2525, 800/2223–6800 in the U.S,* WEB *www.caesarpark-rio.com. 186 rooms, 32 suites. Restaurant, bar, pool, beauty salon, massage, sauna, exercise room, baby-sitting, laundry service, business services, meeting room. AE, DC, MC, V.*

$$$$ 🏨 **Copacabana Palace.** Built in 1923 for the visiting king of Belgium,
★ this was the first luxury hotel in South America. To this day, it retains more soul and elegance than any other hotel. Igor Stravinsky, Marlene Dietrich, Orson Welles, Eva Peron (who reportedly showed up with 100 suitcases in tow), Robert De Niro, and Princess Di are just a few of the luminaries who have stayed here. It also served as the set for much of the 1933 Fred Astaire and Ginger Rogers film *Flying Down to Rio.* A face-lift restored its facade and left the individually decorated guest rooms with such luxurious touches as inlaid agate and mahogany; and computer, fax, and modem facilities. The Copa also has a rooftop tennis court and Rio's largest hotel pool. The Saturday feijoada is a social event extraordinaire, rivaling the gala Carnaval ball held here each year. ⊠ *Av. Atlântica 1702, Copacabana 22021,* ☎ *021/2548–7070, 800/237–1236 in the U.S.,* FAX *021/2235–7330,* WEB *www.copacabanapalace.orient-express.com. 122 rooms, 102 suites. 2 restaurants, 2 bars, in-room data ports, pool, sauna, tennis court, health club, theater, business services, meeting room. AE, DC, MC, V. Metrô: Cardeal Arcoverde.*

$$$$ 🏨 **Inter-Continental Rio.** One of the city's only resorts is in São Conrado, on its own slice of beachfront next to the Gávea Golf and Country Club. Attractions include a cocktail lounge, a discotheque, a French restaurant (the Monseigneur), an Italian restaurant (the Alfredo), business facilities, and golf privileges. Every room has an original tapestry done by a Brazilian artist and a balcony overlooking the ocean. The nearby mall is much less crowded than those with more central locations. ⊠ *Av. Prefeito Mendes de Morais 222, São Conrado 22600,* ☎ *021/3323–2200 or 800/327–0200 in the U.S.,* FAX *021/3323–5500,* WEB *www.interconti.com. 391 rooms, 20 cabanas, 53 suites. 5 restaurants, 2 bars, piano bar, 3 pools, beauty salon, sauna, golf privileges, 3 tennis courts, health club, shops, dance club, nightclub, business services, convention center, travel services, car rental. AE, DC, MC, V.*

$$$$ 🏨 **Sheraton Rio Hotel & Towers.** Built so that it dominates Vidigal, between Leblon and São Conrado, this is the only hotel in Rio with its own private beach (it's set on a bluff above the water and has a stairway down to the sand). Guest rooms are decorated in pastels, and all have beach views. Four floors in a section called the Towers are reserved for business travelers, who receive separate check-in service and have access to a private lounge, a business center, a buffet breakfast, and around-the-clock butler service. The landscaping out by the pools is fabulous, and though the hotel isn't long on intimacy, the vistas are sublime. Be prepared for numerous taxi rides from this prime, though isolated, location. ⊠ *Av. Niemeyer 121, Vidigal 22450,* ☎ *021/2274–*

1122 or 800/325–3589 in the U.S., FAX 021/2239–5643, WEB www.
sheraton-rio.com. 561 rooms, 22 suites. 4 restaurants, 2 bars, 3 pools,
sauna, 3 tennis courts, exercise room, shops, nightclub, business services, meeting room, travel services, car rental. AE, DC, MC, V. BP.

$$$$ ⊞ **Sofitel Rio Palace.** Anchoring one end of Copacabana Beach, this
hotel has been given a top-to-bottom face-lift and is, once again, one
of the best on the strip. The building's H shape givess all rooms views
from the balconies of the sea, the mountains, or both. One pool gets
the morning sun; the other, afternoon rays. The rooftop bar areas are
always lively. ⊠ Av. Atlântica 4240, Copacabana 22070, ☎ 021/
2525–1232, 800/7763–4835 in the U.S. 388 rooms, 12 suites. 2 restaurants, 2 bars, tea shop, 2 pools, sauna, health club, shops, nightclub,
business services, convention center. AE, DC, MC, V.

$$$–$$$$ ⊞ **Excelsior.** This hotel, part of the Windsor chain, may have been built
in the 1950s, but its look is sleek and contemporary—from the sparkling
marble lobby to the guest-room closets paneled in gleaming jacarandá
(Brazilian redwood). Service is top rate. The expansive breakfast buf-
fet—free for guests—is served in the hotel's window-banked restau-
rant facing the avenue and beach. The equally elaborate lunch and dinner
buffets cost roughly R$25. The rooftop bar–pool area offers an escape
from the hustle and bustle. Ask for a room with a water view. ⊠ Av.
Atlântica 1800, Copacabana 22000, ☎ 021/2257–1950 or 800/444–
UTELL in the U.S., FAX 021/2257–1850, WEB www.windsonrhoteis.
com.br. 230 rooms. Restaurant, 2 bars, pool, health club, meeting room.
AE, DC, MC, V. BP. Metrô: Cardeal Arcoverde.

$$$–$$$$ ⊞ **Le Meridien.** Of the leading Copacabana hotels, the 37-story French-
owned Meridien is the closest to Centro, making it a favorite of busi-
ness travelers. Rooms are done in pastel tones with dark wood furniture.
If you have work to do, the hotel has a complete executive center. Af-
terward, relax over a meal in Le Saint Honoré restaurant and then head
for the jazz bar, which books some of the best acts in town. ⊠ Av. Atlân-
tica 1020, Copacabana 22012, ☎ 021/3873–8888, FAX 021/3873–8777,
WEB www.meridien-br.com/rio. 443 rooms, 53 suites. 3 restaurants, bar,
pool, beauty salon, sauna, business services. AE, DC, MC, V.

$$$ ⊞ **Rio Othon Palace.** The flagship of the Brazilian Othon chain, this 30-
story hotel is not new, but it does offer a prime view of Copacabana's
distinctive black-and-white sidewalk mosaic from the rooftop pool, bar,
and sundeck. The hotel has an executive floor, with secretarial support,
fax machines, and computer hookups. ⊠ Av. Atlântica 3264, Copacabana
22070, ☎ 021/522–1522, FAX 021/522–1697, WEB www.hoteis-othon.
com.br. 554 rooms, 30 suites. 2 restaurants, 2 bars, pool, sauna, health
club, nightclub, business services. AE, DC, MC, V.

$$–$$$ ⊞ **Everest Rio.** With standard service but one of Rio's finest rooftop views
(a postcard shot of Corcovado and the lagoon), this hotel is in the heart
of Ipanema's shopping and dining district, a block from the beach. Back
rooms offer sea views. ⊠ Rua Prudente de Morais 1117, Ipanema
22420, ☎ 021/2525–2200, FAX 021/2521–3198, WEB www.everest.
com.br. 156 rooms, 11 suites. Restaurant, bar, pool, sauna, business services. AE, DC, MC, V.

$$–$$$ ⊞ **Miramar Palace.** The beachfront Miramar is a strange mix of old
and new. Rooms are among the largest in Rio, and public areas are dominated by classic touches, from the Carrara marble floor of the lobby
to the spectacular glass chandeliers that light the two restaurants. The
hotel's 16th-floor bar is notable for its unobstructed view of the entire
sweep of Copacabana; after 6 PM live Brazilian music adds a touch of
romance. ⊠ Av. Atlântica 3668, Copacabana 22010, ☎ 021/2521–1122,
FAX 021/2521–3294, WEB www.hotelmiramar.com.br. 133 rooms, 11
suites. 2 restaurants, 2 bars, coffee shop, tearoom. AE, DC, MC, V. BP.

$$–$$$ ⊞ **Praia Ipanema.** This hotel isn't deluxe, but it has a great location, and you can see the sea from all its rooms. Take in the dramatic beach view from the pool area on the roof of the 15-story building. You can also catch a breeze from your private balcony (every room has one). ✉ *Av. Vieira Souto 706, Ipanema 22420,* ☎ *021/2540–4949,* 𝔽𝔸𝕏 *021/ 2239–6889,* 𝕎𝔼𝔹 *www.praiaipanema.com. 105 rooms. Bar, pool, beach. AE, DC, MC, V. BP.*

$$–$$$ ⊞ **Rio Atlântica.** Though it's not luxurious, the Atlântica is well appointed and well maintained, offering rooftop sunbathing and swimming, a health club, and a bar with a view of Copacabana Beach. Although breakfast isn't included in the rates, standard rooms are (relatively) reasonably priced, and the service is superb. Business travelers will appreciate the meeting rooms and the secretarial support, which includes such services as simultaneous translation. ✉ *Av. Atlântica 2964, Copacabana 22070,* ☎ *021/2548–6332,* 𝔽𝔸𝕏 *021/2255–6410. 108 rooms, 120 suites. Restaurant, 2 bars, pool, health club, business services, meeting room. AE, DC, MC, V.*

$$–$$$ ⊞ **Rio Internacional.** The red frame of this beachfront hotel has become a Copacabana landmark. Swiss owned and aimed at business travelers, the hotel offers a rarity for Avenida Atlântica: all rooms have balconies with sea views. All guests are welcomed with a glass of champagne. ✉ *Av. Atlântica 1500, Copacabana 22010,* ☎ *021/2543–1555,* 𝔽𝔸𝕏 *021/ 2542–5443,* 𝕎𝔼𝔹 *www.riointernacional.com.br. 117 rooms, 12 suites. Restaurant, 2 bars, pool, sauna, business services. AE, DC, MC, V.*

$$ ⊞ **Leme Othon Palace.** Large rooms and a quiet beachfront location have made this a hotel of choice with repeat visitors. Built in 1964, it has a subdued, conservative air, lacking a few of the most modern amenities. ✉ *Av. Atlântica 656, Leme 22010,* ☎ *021/2543–8080 or 021/ 2546–1010,* 𝕎𝔼𝔹 *www.hoteis-othon.com.br. 168 rooms, 26 suites. Restaurant, bar. AE, DC, MC, V.*

$$ ⊞ **Sol Ipanema.** Another of Rio's crop of tall, slender hotels, this one has a great location, anchoring the eastern end of Ipanema Beach. All rooms have motel-style beige carpets and drapes and light-color furniture; deluxe front rooms have panoramic beach views, while back rooms from the eighth floor up, which are the same size, have views of the lagoon and Corcovado. ✉ *Av. Vieira Souto 320, Ipanema 22420,* ☎ *021/2525–2028,* 𝔽𝔸𝕏 *021/2247–8484,* 𝕎𝔼𝔹 *www.solipanema.com.br. 66 rooms, 12 suites. Restaurant, bar, pool. AE, DC, MC, V. BP.*

$–$$ ⊞ **Grandville Ouro Verde.** For three decades, folks have favored this hotel for its efficient, personalized service. The tasteful Brazilian colonial decor and dark-wood furniture are in step with the emphasis on quality and graciousness. All front rooms face the beach; those in the back on the 6th to 12th floors have a view of Corcovado. ✉ *Av. Atlântica 1456, Copacabana 22041,* ☎ *021/2543–4123,* 𝔽𝔸𝕏 *021/ 2542–4597,* 𝕎𝔼𝔹 *www.grandville.com.br. 61 rooms, 5 suites. Restaurant, bar, library. AE, DC, MC, V.*

$–$$ ⊞ **Guanabara Palace Hotel.** Another member of the Windsor chain, the recently renovated Guanabara is one of the only solid hotel choices right in Centro. Rooms are reasonably sized and tastefully done in brown and beige. Like the one in its sister hotel, the Excelsior, the restaurant serves elaborate buffet meals, and breakfast is included in the rate. The contemporary rooftop pool area, with its stunning views of Guanabara Bay, absolutely gleams thanks to its pristine white tiles, white trellises, and white patio furnishings. ✉ *Av. Presidente Vargas 392, Centro 22071,* ☎ *021/2518–0333,* 𝔽𝔸𝕏 *021/2516–1582,* 𝕎𝔼𝔹 *www.windsorhoteis.com.br. 326 rooms. Restaurant, bar, minibars, room service, pool, sauna, health club, business services, meeting room, parking (R$11). AE, DC, MC, V. BP. Metrô: Uruguaiana.*

$ ⊡ **Arpoador Inn.** This pocket-size hotel occupies the stretch of sand known as Arpoador. Surfers ride the waves, and pedestrians rule the roadway—a traffic-free street allows direct beach access. The hotel is simple but comfortable. At sunset the view from the rocks that mark the end of the beach is considered one of Rio's most beautiful. The spectacle is visible from the hotel's back rooms; avoid the front rooms, which are on the noisy side. ⊠ *Rua Francisco Otaviano 177, Ipanema 22080,* ☎ *021/ 2523–6092,* FAX *021/2511–5094,* WEB *www.ipanema.com/hotel/arpoador.inn. htm. 46 rooms, 2 suites. Restaurant, bar. AE, DC, MC, V. BP.*

$ ⊡ **Atlântico Copacabana.** The large lobby may look modern to some, pretentious to others. Guest rooms are slightly larger than average. Although the Atlântico is in a noisy residential area, it's only four blocks from the beach. ⊠ *Rua Sigueira Campos 90, Copacabana 20000,* ☎ *021/2548–0011,* FAX *021/2235–7941,* WEB *www.atlanticocopacabana. com.br. 97 rooms, 18 suites. Restaurant, 3 bars, pool, beauty salon, sauna. AE, DC, MC, V. BP. Metrô: Cardeal Arcoverde.*

$ ⊡ **Debret.** This former apartment building scores points for keeping its prices moderate despite a beachfront location. The decor honors Brazil's past: the lobby has baroque statues and prints depicting colonial scenes, and the rooms are furnished in dark, heavy wood. The hotel has a loyal following among diplomats and businesspeople who are more interested in functionality and low prices than elegance. ⊠ *Av. Atlântica 3564, Copacabana 22041,* ☎ *021/2522–0132,* FAX *021/ 2521–0899,* WEB *www.debret.com. 90 rooms, 10 suites. Restaurant, bar. AE, DC, MC, V. BP.*

$ ⊡ **Glória.** A grande dame of Rio's hotels, this classic was built in 1922 and is full of French antiques. What makes it a draw for business travelers (it's a five-minute cab ride from Centro) may discourage sun worshipers (it's a slightly longer cab ride from the beaches). ⊠ *Rua do Russel 632, Glória 22210,* ☎ *021/2205–7272,* FAX *021/2555–7282,* WEB *www. hotelgloriario.com.br. 596 rooms, 20 suites. 4 restaurants, 3 bars, 2 pools, sauna, exercise room, meeting room. AE, DC, MC, V. BP. Metrô: Glória*

$ ⊡ **Ipanema Inn.** This small, no-frills hotel was built for those who want to stay in Ipanema but have no interest in paying the high prices of beachfront accommodations. Just a half block from the beach, it's convenient not only for sun worshipers but also for those seeking to explore Ipanema's varied nightlife. ⊠ *Rua Maria Quitéria 27, Ipanema 22410,* ☎ *021/2523–6092 or 021/2274–6995. 56 rooms. Bar, dining room. AE, DC, MC, V. BP.*

$ ⊡ **Royalty Copacabana.** Set three blocks from the beach, this hotel is convenient for beachgoers yet removed enough to satisfy those looking for peace and quiet. Moderate prices are a plus. The back rooms from the third floor up are the quietest and have mountain views; front rooms face the sea. ⊠ *Rua Tonelero 154, Copacabana 22030,* ☎ *021/ 2548–5699,* FAX *021/2255–1999. 130 rooms, 13 suites. Restaurant, bar, pool, sauna, exercise room. AE, DC, MC, V. BP. Metrô: Cardeal Arcoverde.*

$ ⊡ **Toledo.** Although it has few amenities, the Toledo goes the extra mile to make the best of what it does have. The staff is friendly, the service is efficient, and the location—on a quiet back street of Copacabana, a block from the beach—isn't bad either. Back rooms from the 9th to the 14th floors have sea views and sliding floor-to-ceiling windows. ⊠ *Rua Domingos Ferreira 71, Copacabana 22050,* ☎ *021/2257– 1990,* FAX *021/2287–7640. 87 rooms, 8 suites. Bar, coffee shop. DC, MC, V. BP.*

$ ⊡ **Vermont.** This hotel is clean, reliable, and just two blocks from the beach—a good choice for budget travelers. Its only drawback is its location on the main street of Ipanema, which means incessant noise during the day (it tends to quiet down after the shops close). ⊠ *Rua Visconde de Pirajá 254, Ipanema 22410,* ☎ *021/2522–0057,* FAX *021/2267–7046. 54 rooms. Bar, dining room. AE, DC, MC, V. BP.*

¢–$ ⊡ **Novo Mundo.** A short walk from the Catete metrô station, this traditional hotel sits astride Guanabara Bay in Flamengo, near Glória. Convention rooms are popular with the business crowd, and there is a parking garage with daily or hourly rates. All rooms have air-conditioning, closet with safe, TV with cable channels in English, a small refrigerator, and a writing desk. Deluxe rooms have a view of the bay. ⊠ *Praia do Flamengo 20, Flamengo 22210–030,* ☎ *021/2557–6226 or 0800/225–3355. 217 rooms, 10 suites. Restaurant, bar, hair salon. AE, D, MC, V. BP. Metrô: Catete.*

NIGHTLIFE AND THE ARTS

Rio's nightlife is as hard to resist as its beaches. Options range from samba shows shamelessly aimed at visitors to sultry dance halls that play *forró*, a music style that originated in Brazil's northeast during World War II. (American GIs stationed at refueling stops opened up their clubs "for all," which, when pronounced with a Brazilian accent, became "forró.") You'll find spots that feature the sounds of big band, rock, and everything in between. One of the happiest mediums is *música popular brasileira* (MPB), the generic term for popular Brazilian music, which ranges from pop to jazz. Note that establishments in this carefree city often have carefree hours; call ahead to confirm opening times.

There are also many performing arts options, including opera, theater, music, dance, and film. For current listings, pick up the bilingual *Rio Guia*, published by Riotur, the city's tourist board; *Este Mês no Rio/This Month in Rio* and similar publications are available at most hotels, and your hotel concierge is also a good source of information. The Portuguese-language newspapers *Jornal do Brasil* and *O Globo* both publish schedules of events in the entertainment sections of their Friday editions.

Nightlife

Bars, Choperias, and Lounges

Bars and lounges often ask for a nominal cover in the form of either a drink minimum or a music charge. Choperias attract an unattached crowd looking for an ice-cold Brazilian draft beer.

Bar Bofetada. Downstairs the tables flow out onto the street; upstairs large windows open to the sky and afford a good view of the action below. The young, energetic crowd downs chopp and caipirinhas and delicious seafood (the owners are Portuguese) or meat platters large enough to share. ⊠ *Rua Farme de Amoedo 87–87A, Ipanema,* ☎ *021/2522–9526 or 021/2523–3992.*

Bar Garota de Ipanema. The choperia where regulars Tom Jobim and Vinicius de Moraes, authors of *The Girl from Ipanema*, sat and longingly watched the song's heroine head for the beach. (See if you can guess where they usually sat. Hint: it's a table for two near a door.) ⊠ *Rua Vinicius de Moraes 39, Ipanema,* ☎ *021/2267–5757.*

Barril 1800. An unpretentious beachfront choperia, this Ipanema landmark is usually jammed with people grabbing an icy beer or cocktail and a snack. ⊠ *Av. Antônio Carlos Jobim 110, Ipanema,* ☎ *021/2287–0085.*

Bracarense. Don't expect to find fancy people in this small, informal place where cariocas linger with their beer on the sidewalk in front of the bar. It's perfect for after a soccer game in Maracanã; many just go

HOW TO USE THIS GUIDE

Great trips begin with great planning, and this guide makes planning easy. It's packed with everything you need—insider advice on hotels and restaurants, cool tools, practical tips, essential maps, and much more.

COOL TOOLS

Fodor's Choice Top picks are marked throughout with a star.

Great Itineraries These tours, planned by Fodor's experts, give you the skinny on what you can see and do in the time you have.

Smart Travel Tips A to Z This special section is packed with important contacts and advice on everything from how to get around to what to pack.

Good Walks You won't miss a thing if you follow the numbered bullets on our maps.

Need a Break? Looking for a quick bite to eat or a spot to rest? These sure bets are along the way.

Off the Beaten Path Some lesser-known sights are worth a detour. We've marked those you should make time for.

POST-IT® FLAGS

Dog-ear no more!

"Post-it" is a registered trademark of 3M.

ICONS AND SYMBOLS

Watch for these symbols throughout:

★	Our special recommendations
✕	Restaurant
🏠	Lodging establishment
✕🏠	Lodging establishment whose restaurant warrants a special trip
☺	Good for kids
☞	Sends you to another section of the guide for more information
✉	Address
☎	Telephone number
FAX	Fax number
WEB	Web site
🎫	Admission price
☉	Opening hours
$-$$$$	Lodging and dining price categories, keyed to strategically sited price charts. Check the index for locations.
①❶	Numbers in white and black circles on the maps, in the margins, and within tours correspond to one another.

ON THE WEB

Continue your planning with these useful tools found at **www.fodors.com**, the Web's best source for travel information.

"Rich with resources." —*New York Times*

"Navigation is a cinch." —*Forbes* "Best of the Web" list

"Put together by people bursting with know-how."
—*Sunday Times* (London)

Create a Miniguide Pinpoint hotels, restaurants, and attractions that have what you want at the price you want to pay.

Rants and Raves Find out what readers say about Fodor's picks—or write your own reviews of hotels and restaurants you've just visited.

Travel Talk Post your questions and get answers from fellow travelers, or share your own experiences.

On-Line Booking Find the best prices on airline tickets, rental cars, cruises, or vacations, and book them on the spot.

About our Books Learn about other Fodor's guides to your destination and many others.

Expert Advice and Trip Ideas From what to tip to how to take great photos, from the national parks to Nepal, Fodors.com has suggestions that'll make your trip a breeze. Log on and get informed and inspired.

Smart Resources Check the weather in your destination or convert your currency. Learn the local language or link to the latest event listings. Or consult hundreds of detailed maps—all in one place.

there to talk about sports. ⊠ *Rua José Linhares 85B, Leblon,* ☎ *021/ 2294–3549.*

Cervantes. The chopp here goes well with the meat-and-pineapple combo dishes for which Cervantes is famous. ⊠ *Av. Prado Júnior 335, Copacabana,* ☎ *021/2275–6174.*

Chico's Bar. Owned by nightspot entrepreneur Chico Recarey, both the bar and the adjoining restaurant, Castelo da Lagoa, are big with affluent carioca singles and couples. ⊠ *Av. Epitácio Pessoa 1560, Lagoa,* ☎ *021/2523–3514.*

Hipódromo. Good chopp, honest food, and many young, happy people are the norm at this bar near the Jóquei Clube. ⊠ *Praça Santos Dumont, Gávea,* ☎ *021/2294–0095.*

Jazzmania. If you arrive before nightfall, you get a superb view of Ipanema Beach at sunset from one of the better jazz clubs in town. ⊠ *Av. Rainha Elizabeth 769, Ipanema,* ☎ *021/2227–2447.*

Mistura Fina. Fine jazz combines with excellent food at Mistura Fina, which is open from midnight to 3 AM. ⊠ *Av. Borges de Medeiros 3207, Lagoa Rodrigo de Freitas, Lagoa,* ☎ *021/2537–2844.*

Cybercafés

Cyber Place. Plenty of terminals, snacks, and a zippy connection make this the best place to get your E-mail. You'll pay about R$8 per hour, and access is available Monday to Saturday from noon until 2 AM, Sunday from noon to midnight. Cyber Place is in an entertainment complex at the very top of the Rio Sul shopping center. ⊠ *Av. Lauro Müller 116, Loja D91, Botafogo,* ☎ *021/2541–1006.*

Internet House. A peaceful place, one block from Copacabana Beach, Internet House has 12 computers, laser and deskjet color printers, and fax and scanner services available. You'll pay about R$10 per hour; access is available Monday–Saturday from 9 AM until 10 PM. ⊠ *Av. Nossa Senhora de Copacabana 195, Shop 106, Copacabana,* ☎ *021/ 2542–3348.*

Tudo é Fácil Estação Internet. Access is available Monday–Saturday from 10–10 and Sunday from 3–9; you'll pay about R$3 per 15 minutes. ⊠ *Rua Xavier da Silveira, 19B, Copacabana,* ☎ *021/2522–3970;* ⊠ *Rua Prado Júnior 78, Copacabana,* ☎ *021/2543–7229.*

Dance Clubs

Rio's *danceterias* (discos) offer flashing lights and loud music. At a number of places, including samba clubs, you can dance to live Brazilian music. *Gafieiras* are old-fashioned ballroom dance halls, usually patronized by an equally old-fashioned clientele. Upon entry to some clubs you're given a card to carry—each successive drink is marked on it. You pay on departure for what you've consumed.

Asa Branca. The decor combines modern geometric designs with old-fashioned fixtures at Chico Recarey's large nightclub. Big bands and popular Brazilian musicians keep the crowd moving until dawn. ⊠ *Av. Mem de Sá 17, Lapa,* ☎ *021/2252–4428.*

Ballroom. Wear your most comfortable clothes—Bermudas and sandals or sundresses—to dance forró here on Thursday. It also hosts concerts, so check which band which is playing. ⊠ *Rua Humaitá 110, Humaitá,* ☎ *021/2537–7600.*

B.A.S.E. Be prepared for loud music and modern people. The expensive but fashionable B.A.S.E. club is conveniently located near Copacabana Beach. ⊠ *Rua Francisco Otaviano 20A, Copacabana,* ☎ *021/ 2522–0544.*

Biblo's Bar. This is *the* place for live music and dancing, particularly if you're single and more than 45 years old. ⊠ *Av. Epitácio Pessoa 1484, Lagoa,* ☎ *021/2521–2645.*

DabliüBar. As it's always crowded, you should arrive early, around 10 PM, or after 2 AM. Fancy youngsters fill the place (capacity 550) in between those hours. ⊠ *Rua Visconde de Pirajá 22, Ipanema,* ☎ *021/2523–0302.*

El Turf. A hot spot with a cool location in the Jóquei Clube, the large dance space often fills up with the young and the beautiful. ⊠ *Praça Santos Dumont 31, Gávea,* ☎ *021/2274–1444.*

Estudantina. Opened as a dance hall in 1932, this has become an eternally popular nightclub. On weekends, it packs in as many as 1,500 people. ⊠ *Praça Tiradentes 79, Centro,* ☎ *021/2232–1149.*

Hard Rock Cafe. Even in Rio you can find this megachain outlet in the Shopping Center América. As at other branches, such as in New York or Cannes, you can find huge burgers and beautiful people. ⊠ *Av. das Américas, 700, 3rd floor, Barra da Tijuca,* ☎ *021/2232–1149.*

Méli Mélo. A place where fashionable 18- to 25-year-olds go, Méli Mélo is a huge nightclub with two dance floors (one DJ plays '70s music; the other, hip hop and techno). There's also a Japanese restaurant and a cybercafé on-site. ⊠ *Av. Borges de Medeiros 1426, Lagoa,* ☎ *021/2219–3132.*

Studio 54. In the New York City Center shopping mall is a copy of the disco that was really hot in 1970s Manhattan. The original is gone, but here you can dance all night in one of the most modern, newest, and coolest places in Rio. Be prepared: the DJs play the electronic music really loud. ⊠ *Av. das Américas 5000, Stores 114–115, Barra da Tijuca,* ☎ *021/3325–1874.*

Sôbre as Ondas. Dance to live music, usually MPB or samba, overlooking Copacabana Beach. The crowd is mostly over 35. You can also dine at the Terraço Atlântico restaurant, downstairs. ⊠ *Av. Atlântica 3432, Copacabana,* ☎ *021/2521–1296.*

Gay and Lesbian Clubs

Rio is a relatively gay-friendly city; the community even has its own gala during Carnaval. Style Travel Agency offers tours targeted to gay and lesbian travelers, an has information on local happenings.

The hippest cariocas—both gay and straight—hang out in Ipanema and Leblon.

Bar do Hotel (⊠ Av. Delfim Moreira 630, Leblon, ☎ 021/2540–4990) is inside the hotel Marina Palace. It serves lunch and dinner, but gets really crowded for drinks on Friday and Saturday nights. The **Galeria Café** (⊠ Rua Teixeira de Mello, 31 E–F, Ipanema, ☎ 021/2523–8250) is a bar with house/techno music for sophisticated gays. From Thursday to Saturday it's not only crowded inside, patrons overflow out onto the sidewalk. Drink minimum is R$10. **Le Boy** (⊠ Rua Paul Pompéia 94, Copacabana, ☎ 021/2521–0367) is a gay disco that draws an upscale crowd. If you prefer to be where the trends are set, **00** (⊠ Av. Padre Leonel Franca, 240, Gávea, ☎ 021/2540–8041) is a new restaurant–café–sushi bar with a dance floor. It's open from 7 PM until 1 PM, but the coffee shop operates 24 hours.

Nightclubs

Although nightclubs often serve food, their main attraction is live music; it's best to eat elsewhere earlier.

If you're interested in entertainment of a steamier variety, stroll along Avenida Princesa Isabel at the end of Copacabana—near Le Meridien hotel—to one of the numerous burlesque, striptease, and sex shows. Be warned, some of the female patrons may be prostitutes.

Canecão. Seating up to 5,000 people at tiny tables in a cavernous space, this is the city's largest nightclub, the logical place for some of the biggest names on the international music scene to hold concerts. Reserve a table up front. ⊠ *Av. Venceslau Brás 215, Botafogo,* ☎ *021/ 2543-1241.*

Plataforma. The most spectacular of Rio's samba shows has elaborate costumes and a variety of musical numbers including samba and rumba. A two-hour show costs about $38.50, drinks not included. Downstairs is a hangout for many local luminaries and entertainers. Upstairs you can eat at Plataforma's famed barbecue restaurant. ⊠ *Rua Adalberto Ferreira 32, Leblon,* ☎ *021/2274-4022.*

Vinicius. You may rightly associate sultry bossa nova with Brazil, but it's increasingly hard to find venues that offer it. This club is one. Along with nightly live samba, jazz, popular music, or bossa nova music, this club has a good kitchen. ⊠ *Rua Vinicius de Moraes 39, Ipanema,* ☎ *021/2287-1497.*

The Arts

Although MPB may have overshadowed *música erudita* (classical music), Rio has a number of orchestras. The Orquestra Sinfônica Brasileira and the Orquestra do Teatro Municipal are the most prominent. Tickets to performing arts events are inexpensive by international standards and may be purchased at the theater or concert hall box offices. Dress is generally smart casual, although the conservative upper crust still likes to dress elegantly for the Teatro Municipal. Just don't wear valuable jewelry or carry lots of cash.

Rio has an avid film-going public and a well-regarded film industry (you may catch a flick that later hits the international movie circuit). Films are screened in small *cineclubes,* or state-of-the-art movie theaters (many in shopping malls). Foreign movies are shown in their original language with Portuguese subtitles (only children's films are dubbed). After dark, exercise caution in Cinelândia, where there's a large concentration of theaters.

In addition to its many museums, there are several privately funded cultural centers. These host changing, often exceptional art and photography exhibits as well as film series, lectures, and children's programs. All the big newspapers have daily cultural sections that tell what's going on in the city—in Portuguese.

Venues

ATL Hall (⊠ Av. Ayrton Senna 3000, Barra da Tijuca, ☎ 021/3385-0516 for tickets, 021/2285-3773 for schedules) is a posh, 4,500-seat performance center in the Via Parque shopping complex. It hosts theater and dance performances, as well as shows by top-name performers.

Centro Cultural Banco do Brasil (⊠ Rua 1° de Março 66, Centro, ☎ 021/2216-0237, 021/2216-0626) was constructed in 1888 and was once the headquarters of the Bank of Brazil. In the late 1980s, this six-story domed building with marble floors was transformed into a cultural center for art exhibitions and music recitals. The complex features a library, two theaters, four video rooms, an auditorium, and a permanent display of Brazilian currency. Its gift shop is full of stunning coffee-table tomes on art and history—some in English. It's open Tuesday–Sunday 10–8.

Fundação Casa França–Brasil (⊠ Rua Visconde de Itaboraí 78, Centro, ☎ 021/2253-5366) links France and Brazil in a cultural and artistic exchange. The interior of what was once a customs house has been completely restored, leaving an elegant, neoclassical space of gracious columns and arcades. Exhibits have included everything from photography and painting to displays on Carnaval and Brazil's environment. Musical shows (Gilberto Gil was a recent performer), poetry readings, and lectures round out the events. The center's hours are Tuesday–Sunday 10–8.

Sala Cecília Meireles (⊠ Largo da Lapa 47, Centro, ☎ 021/2232–4779) is a center for classical music.

Teatro Dulcina (⊠ Rua Alcindo Guanabara 17, Centro, ☎ 021/2240–4879), a 600-seat theater, features opera and classical concerts.

Teatro João Caetano (⊠ Praça Tiradentes, Centro, ☎ 021/2221–0305) offers nightly variety shows—comedy, music, and dance—in a large theater setting.

Teatro Municipal (Praça Floriano, Centro, ☎ 021/2297–4411) is the city's main performing arts venue, hosting dance, opera (often with international divas as guest artists), symphony concerts, and theater events year-round—although the season officially runs from April to December. The theater also has its own ballet company, and is the site of an international ballet festival during April and May.

Teatro Paço Imperial (⊠ Praça 15 de Novembro 48, Centro, ☎ 021/2533–4407), like the Teatro Municipal, features a varied schedule of theater, music, and dance performances.

OUTDOOR ACTIVITIES AND SPORTS

Participant Sports

Bicycling and Running

Bikers and runners share the boulevards along the beach and, for cooler and quieter outings, the path around Lagoa Rodrigo de Freitas. On weekends many cariocas also bike or run along the stretch of Floresta da Tijuca Road that becomes pedestrians only. Although hotels can arrange bike rentals, it's just as easy to rent from stands along beachfront avenues or the road ringing the lagoon. Rates are about R$10 per hour. You're usually asked to show identification and give your hotel name and room number, but deposits are seldom required. (Note that helmets aren't usually available.)

Boating and Sailing

Captain's Yacht Charters (⊠ Rua Conde de Lages 44, Glória, ☎ 021/2224–0313) charters all types of crewed vessels for any length of time. You can arrange an afternoon of water-skiing with a speedboat or a weekend aboard a yacht.

Golf

If you're staying at the Sheraton, Inter-Continental, Copacabana Palace, or Rio Atlântica, you get a R$50 discount on the R$150 greens fee at the 18-hole **Gávea Golf Club** (⊠ Estrada da Gávea 800, São Conrado, ☎ 021/3322–4141). Golf lessons run R$30 per half hour. You can rent equipment for the par 3, six-hole greens of the **Golden Green Golf Club** (⊠ Av. Canal de Marapendi 2901, Barra da Tijuca, ☎ 021/2433–3950). But you have to be invited by a club member to have lessons or play at the nine-hole course.

Hang Gliding

At **Just Fly** (☎ 021/2268-0565) a 30-minute hang glider flight—jumping from Pedra Bonita in the Parque Nacional da Tijuca, and landing at Praia do Pepino in São Conrado—costs approximately R$170 including transportation to and from your hotel. For a little more, you can have 12 pictures taken as well. **Superfly** (⊠ Estrada das Canoas 1476, Casa 2, São Conrado, ☎ 021/3332–2286) offers hang-gliding classes and tandem flights with instructors. A package including pickup at your hotel and 12 photos taken in-flight costs about R$220.

THE BEAUTIFUL GAME

BRAZILIANS ARE MAD about *futebol* (soccer), their "jogo bonito," and players here are fast and skillful. The best possess *jinga*, a quality that translates roughly as feline, almost swaggering grace. Some of their ball-handling moves are so fluid they seem more akin to ballet—or at least to the samba—than to sport.

Futebol is believed to have been introduced in the late 19th century by employees of British-owned firms. By the early 20th century, upper-class Brazilians had formed their own leagues, as had the nation's European immigrants, who were already familiar with the game. Because it requires little equipment, the sport also found a following in Brazil's poor communities.

You can see young *brasileiros* everywhere practicing—any of these boys could be a future futebol hero. Brazil has turned out many international stars: the most famous, Pelé, retired more than 20 years ago and is still revered as a national hero. The country's team is consistently included in World Cup competitions and is a repeat title holder.

Fans come to games with musical instruments, flags, banners, streamers, talcum powder, and firecrackers. There's no better spot for the brave to witness the spectacle than at the world's largest soccer stadium, Rio's Estádio Maracanã. Here, you and 219,999 other people can make merry. Even if you don't have a great view of the field, you'll certainly be a part of the event.

Hiking

Centro Excursionista Brasileiro (✉ Av. Almirante Barroso 2–8, Centro, ☎ 021/2252-9844) provides guides, maps, and gear for hiking expeditions throughout the metropolitan area.

Tennis

There are nine courts for rent at **Fazenda Clube Marapendi** (✉ Av. das Américas 3979, Barra da Tijuca, ☎ 021/3325-2440). The large, well-equipped health club **Rio Sport Center** (✉ Av. Ayrton Senna 2541, Barra da Tijuca, ☎ 021/3325-6644) has six tennis courts (three covered). Court time runs from R$16–R$69 per hour depending on whether you want to play in the morning or at night on the covered courts. You can also rent equipment and arrange lessons.

Spectator Sports

Auto Racing

Brazilian race-car drivers rank among the world's best and frequently compete in international events. You'll get a taste of the speed if you watch the checkered flag drop on competitions in the Formula I Grand Prix circuit named after one of the country's most famous racers, Emerson Fittipaldi. The racetrack is the **Autódromo Internacional Nelson Piquet** (✉ Av. Embaixador Abelardo Bueno, Jacarepagua, ☎ 021/2441-2158).

Futebol

You can watch a match at the **Estádio Maracanã** (✉ Rua Prof. Eurico Rabelo, Maracanã, ☎ 021/2264-9962). The fans are half the spectacle. During the season the top game is played each Sunday at around

5 PM. The three most popular teams are Flamengo, Fluminense, and Vasco da Gama. Play between any of them is soccer at its finest.

Horse Racing

Races are held year-round in the **Jóquei Clube** (✉ Praça Santos Dumont 31, Gávea, ☎ 021/2512–9988) beginning Monday and Thursday at 7 PM and weekends at noon. The big event of the year, the Brazilian Derby, is held the first Sunday of August.

SHOPPING

From sophisticated jewelry and Euro-style clothes to teeny tangas and funky tie-dyed dresses, the selection is broad. You can stroll down streets lined with fashionable boutiques, barter with vendors at street fairs, or wander through one of more than two dozen air-conditioned malls. Good bets include leather, suede, jewelry, and cool summer clothing in natural fibers—appropriate for the climate. Also look for coffee, samba and bossa nova CDs, and art. (Note that larger shoe sizes, once difficult to find in Rio, are now common.)

Ipanema is Rio's most fashionable shopping district. Its many exclusive boutiques are in arcades, with the majority along Rua Visconde de Pirajá. In Copacabana you'll find souvenir shops, bookstores, and branches of some of Rio's better shops along Avenida Nossa Senhora de Copacabana and the streets just off it. If upscale jewelry catches your fancy, head for Avenida Atlântica.

Brazil is one of the world's largest producers of gold and the largest supplier of colored gemstones, with important deposits of aquamarines, amethysts, diamonds, emeralds, rubellites, topazes, and tourmalines. To get an idea of what's available, figure out what stones interest you and compare their quality and price at various shops. If you're planning to go to Minas Gerais, save your jewelry shopping for there; otherwise, stick with shops that offer certificates of authenticity and quality.

Centers and Malls

Barra Shopping (✉ Av. das Américas 4666, Barra da Tijuca, ☎ 021/2431–9922) is one of South America's largest complexes. Although it's slightly out of the way, shoppers from all over town head for this mall, which features a medical center, eight movie theaters, and a bowling alley as well as shops.

New York City Center (✉ Av. das Américas 5000, Barra da Tijuca, ☎ 021/2432–4980), just beside Barra Shopping, is one of the newest in town, easily recognizable by the enormous replica of the Statue of Liberty that hangs out front. There are 18 movie theaters, the nightclub Studio 54, upscale restaurants, and Gameworks—where you can play with flying simulators. The best way to reach Barra da Tijuca is by car or by taxi (R$50 roundtrip). But there's also the CityRio bus.

Rio Off Price Shopping (✉ Rua General Severiano 97, Botafogo, ☎ 021/2542–5693), just down the street from the Rio Sul shopping center, is a mall with prices 20% lower than usual. The complex has snack bars and two movie theaters.

Rio Sul (✉ Av. Lauro Müller 116, Botafogo, ☎ 021/2295–1332) is one of the city's most popular retail complexes, with more than 400 shops. The shopping is sophisticated, and the food court is endless.

São Conrado Fashion Mall (✉ Estrada da Gávea 899, São Conrado, ☎ 021/3322–0300) sells a wide array of international and domestic fashions and is Rio's most appealing mall, as it's the least crowded and has an abundance of natural light.

Shopping Center Cassino Atlântico (✉ Av. Nossa Senhora de Copacabana, Copacabana, ☎ 021/2247–8709), adjoining the Rio Palace hotel, is dominated by antiques shops, jewelry stores, art galleries, and souvenir outlets.

Shopping Center da Gávea (✉ Rua Marquês de São Vicente 52, Gávea, ☎ 021/2274–9896) has a small but select mix of fashionable clothing and leather goods stores. It also has several top art galleries, of which the best are Ana Maria Niemeyer, Beco da Arte, Borghese, Bronze, Paulo Klabin, Saramenha, and Toulouse.

Via Parque (✉ Av. Ayrton Senna 3000, Barra da Tijuca, ☎ 021/3385–0100) is a 230-store complex popular for its outlets and ample parking (nearly 2,000 spaces). In addition to movie theaters and fast-food restaurants, the mall is home to the ATL Hall Theater.

Markets

The **Feira Hippie** is a colorful handicrafts street fair held every Sunday 9–6 in Ipanema's Praça General Osório. Offerings run the gamut from jewelry and hand-painted dresses and T-shirts to paintings and wood carvings, leather bags and sandals, rag dolls, knickknacks, and even furniture. A handful of booths sell samba percussion instruments.

In the evenings and on weekends along the median of **Avenida Atlântica,** artisans spread out their wares. You'll find paintings, carvings, handicrafts, sequined dresses, and hammocks from the northeast. Saturday (during daylight hours) an open-air fair near the **Praça 15 de Novembro** has such goods as china and silver sets, watches, Asian rugs, and chandeliers. Vendors at **Rio Antique Fair,** on Rua do Lavradio in Centro, sell antiques, rare books, records, and all types of objets d'art on Saturday afternoon. The antiques sellers move to the **Casa Shopping Center,** in Barra da Tijuca, on Sunday.

The crowded, lively **Feira Nordestina** (Northeastern Fair), held every Sunday 6–1 at the Campo de São Cristóvão, is a social event for northeasterners living in Rio. They gather to hear their own distinctive music, eat regional foods, and buy tools and cheap clothing.

Babilônia Feira Hype (☎ 021/2253–9800 or 021/2263–7667, WEB www.babiloniahype.com.br) opens weekends from 3–11 every fortnight inside the Jóquei Club Brasileiro, at Rua Jardim Botânico. This fair brings together fashion, design, art, and gastronomy. It's not only good for shopping, but for watching the beautiful people go by. Admission is R$3, but it's free for children under eight.

Specialty Shops

Art

Bonino (✉ Rua Barata Ribeiro 578, Copacabana, ☎ 021/2294–7810) has been around for some 30 years, and is the most traditional, best known, and most visited of Rio's art galleries.

Cohn Edelstein (✉ Rua Jangadeira 14B, Ipanema, ☎ 021/2523–0549; Rua Barão da Torre 185A, Ipanema, ☎ 021/2287–9933) is an internationally respected contemporary art gallery showing Brazilian works.

Contorno (✉ Shopping Center da Gávea, Rua Marquês de São Vicente 52, Gávea, ☎ 021/2274–3832) hosts an eclectic gallery, but the art it displays is certainly Brazilian.

Rio Design Center (✉ Av. Ataulfo de Paiva 270, Leblon, ☎ 021/2274–7893) contains several galleries, including Borghese, Beco da Arte, Montesanti, Museum, and Way.

Beachwear

Blueman (✉ Rio Sul, Av. Lauro Müller 116, Botafogo, ☎ 021/2220–4898), a bikini shop with many mall locations in addition to the Rio

Sul branch, carries the bathing suits–tangas—that virtually define Brazil in much of North America's imagination. Tangas are said to have been invented in Ipanema—and they don't take up much room in your luggage.

Bum Bum (⊠ Rua Vinicius de Moraes 130, Ipanema, ☎ 021/2521–1229) is the market leader in beachwear, with locations in Rio Sul and Barra Shopping in addition to its Ipanema branch.

Salinas (⊠ Forum de Ipanema, Visconde de Pirajá 351, Ipanema), a *très* chic bikini designer, is the label de rigueur with the fashionable in Búzios and other resort areas.

CDs

Toca do Vinicius (⊠ Rua Vinicius de Moraes 129, Ipanema, ☎ 021/2247–5227) bills itself as a "cultural space and bossa nova salon." The shop, though tiny, does indeed seem like a gathering place for bossa-nova aficionados from around the world (if you're one of them, there's a good chance you'll leave the shop with an e-mail address for at least one new pal). Amid the atmosphere of bonhomie, you'll find books (a few in English), sheet music, and T-shirts as well as CDs.

Clothing

Alice Tapajós (⊠ Fórum de Ipanema, Visconde de Pirajá 351, Ipanema, ☎ 021/2247–2594) carries DKNY and other well-known sportswear in its Ipanema, São Conrado Fashion Mall, and Barra Shopping locations.

Ar Livre (⊠ Av. Nossa Senhora de Copacabana 900, Copacabana, ☎ 021/2549–8994) has an exceptional selection of good quality T-shirts and beachwear at appealing prices.

Krishna (⊠ Rio Sul, Av. Lauro Müller 116, Botafogo, ☎ 021/2542–2443; ⊠ São Conrado Fashion Mall, Estrada da Gávea 899, São Conrado, ☎ 021/3322–0437) specializes in classic feminine dresses and separates—many in fine linens, cottons, and silks.

Lojas Americanas (⊠ Rua do Passeio 42–56, Centro, ☎ 021/2524–0138), Rio's largest chain department store, focuses on mostly casual fashions for men, women, and children. But it also has a wide selection of toys, records, cosmetics, and sporting goods.

Handicrafts

Casa do Pequeno Empresário (⊠ Rua Real Grandeza 293, Botafogo, ☎ 021/2286–9464) is an exposition center for handcrafted items made of everything from porcelain to wood and papier-mâché to clay.

Folclore (⊠ Rua Visconde de Pirajá 490, Ipanema, ☎ 021/2259–7442). This handicrafts shop bursts with primitive paintings, costume jewelry, leather and ceramic crafts, and birds and flowers carved from stone. Quality is high, but take note: some items have been imported from other South American nations.

Jewelry

Amsterdam Sauer (⊠ Rua Visconde de Pirajá 484, Ipanema, ☎ 021/2512–9878) is one of Rio's top names in jewelry, with top prices, to boot. Jules Roger Sauer, the founder of these stores (with branches in Brazil, the United States, and the Caribbean), is particularly known for his fascination with emeralds. The on-site gemstone museum (☎ 021/2239–8045) is open weekdays 10–5 and Saturday 9:30–1 (tour reservations are a good idea).

Antônio Bernardo (⊠ Gávea, Forum Ipanema, and Fashion Mall shopping malls) has been making gorgeous jewelry with contemporary designs for nearly 30 years.

H. Stern (⊠ Rua Visconde de Pirajá 490, Ipanema, ☎ 021/2259–7442) is owned by the eponymous Hans Stern, who started his empire in 1945 with an initial investment of about $200. Today his interests include mining and production operations as well as 170 stores in Europe, the Americas, and the Middle East. His award-winning designers create truly distinctive contemporary pieces (the inventory runs to about 300,000 items). At H. Stern world headquarters you can see exhibits of rare stones and watch craftspeople transform rough stones into sparkling jewels. There's also a museum you can tour (by appointment only). If you feel the prices are too high in the upstairs salons, there are shops downstairs that sell more affordable pieces as well as folkloric items.

Leather Goods

Bottega Veneta (⊠ Shopping Center da Gávea, Rua Marquês de São Vicente 52, Gávea, ☎ 021/2274–8248) has fine women's shoes and bags.

Formosinho (⊠ Av. Nossa Senhora de Copacabana 582, Copacabana, ☎ 021/2287–8998) sells men's and women's shoes at low, wholesale prices. In addition to its Copacabana location, it has three other stores along Ipanema's Rua Visconde de Pirajá.

Frankie Amaury (⊠ Shopping Center da Gávea, Rua Marquês de São Vicente 52, Gávea, ☎ 021/2294–8895) is *the* name in leather clothing.

Mariazinha (⊠ Forum de Ipanema, Praça Nossa Senhora da Paztel, Ipanema, ☎ 021/2541–6695) carries fashionable footwear.

Nazaré (⊠ Shopping Center da Gávea, Rua Marquês de São Vicente 52, Gávea, ☎ 021/2294–9849) has bags and fine women's shoes.

Victor Hugo (⊠ Rio Sul, Av. Lauro Müller 116, Botafogo, ☎ 021/2275–3388) carries women's handbags.

RIO DE JANEIRO A TO Z

To research prices, get advice from other travelers, and book travel arrangements, visit www.fodors.com.

AIR TRAVEL

CARRIERS
Nearly three dozen airlines regularly serve Rio. Several of the international carriers also offer Rio–São Paulo flights. International carriers include: Aerolíneas Argentinas, American Airlines, British Airways, Canadian Airlines, Delta, and United. Several domestic carriers serve international and Brazilian destinations: Transbrasil, Varig, and VASP. Nordeste/RioSul covers domestic routes.

➤ AIRLINES AND CONTACTS: **Aerolíneas Argentinas** (☎ 021/3398–3520 or 021/2292–4131). **American Airlines** (☎ 021/3398–4053 or 021/2210–3126). **British Airways** (☎ 021/3398–3888 or 021/2221–0922). **Canadian Airlines** (☎ 021/3398–3604 or 021/2220–5343). **Delta** (☎ 021/3398–3492, 021/2507–7262, or 0800/222–1121). **Nordeste/RioSul** (☎ 021/2507–4488, 021/2524–9387, or 0800/99–2004). **Transbrasil** (☎ 021/3398–5485 or 021/2297–4477). **United** (☎ 021/3804–1200, 021/3398–4050, 021/2532–1212, or 0800/224–5532). **VASP** (☎ 021/3814–8079, 021/2292–2112, 021/2462–3363, or 0800/99–8277). **Varig** (☎ 021/3398–2122, 021/2534–0333, 021/2217–4591, or 0800/99–7000).

AIRPORTS AND TRANSFERS
All international flights and most domestic flights arrive and depart from the Aeroporto Internacional Antônio Carlos Jobim, also known as Galeão. The airport is about 45 minutes northwest of the beach area and most of Rio's hotels. Aeroporto Santos Dumont, 20 minutes from the beaches and within walking distance of Centro, serves the Rio–São Paulo air shuttle and a few air-taxi firms.

➤ AIRPORT INFORMATION: **Aeroporto Internacional Antônio Carlos Jobim** (☎ 021/3398–4526 or 0800/99–9099). **Aeroporto Santos Dumont** (☎ 021/2524–7070 or 0800/224–4646).

AIRPORT TRANSFERS
Special airport taxis have booths in the arrival areas of both airports. Fares to all parts of Rio are posted at the booths, and you pay in advance (about R$35–R$50). Also trustworthy are the white radio taxis parked in the same areas; these charge an average of 20% less. Three reliable special-taxi firms are Transcoopass, Cootramo, and Coopertramo.

Air-conditioned *frescão* buses run by Empresa Real park curbside outside customs at Galeão and outside the main door at Santos Dumont; for less than R$7 they make the hour-long trip from the former into the city, following the beachfront drives and stopping at all hotels along the way. If your hotel is inland, the driver will let you off at the nearest corner. Buses leave from the airport every half hour from 5:20 AM to 11 PM.

➤ TAXIS AND SHUTTLES: **Cootramo** (☎ 021/2560–5442). **Coopertramo** (☎ 021/2560–2022). **Empresa Real** (☎ 021/2290–5665 or 021/2270–7041). **Transcoopass** (☎ 021/2560–4888).

BUS TRAVEL TO AND FROM RIO
Regular service is available to and from Rio. Long-distance buses leave from the Rodoviária Novo Rio station, near the port. Any local bus marked RODOVIÁRIA will take you to the station. You can buy tickets at the depot or, for some destinations, from travel agents. Buses also leave from the more conveniently located Menezes Cortes Terminal, near Praça 15 de Novembro.

➤ BUS INFORMATION: **Rodoviária Novo Rio station** (✉ Av. Francisco Bicalho 1, São Cristóvão, ☎ 021/2291–5151). **Menezes Cortes Terminal** (✉ Rua São José 35, Centro, ☎ 021/2533–7577).

BUS TRAVEL WITHIN RIO
Much has been made of the threat of being robbed on Rio's buses. However, crime has dropped significantly in the last few years; if you're discreet, you shouldn't have any problems. Just don't wear expensive watches or jewelry, carry a camera or a map in hand, or talk boisterously in English. It's also wise to avoid buses during rush hour.

CityRio, run by Riotur, takes you to 270 sightseeing points—including the beaches—in air-conditioned comfort. Tickets are R$16, R$30, or R$40 for 24-, 36-, or 48-hour passes. Buses operates from 8 to 6, at half-hour intervals. A map with the schedule and description of each route in English and three other languages is available.

Local buses are inexpensive and can take you anywhere you want to go. (Route maps aren't available, but the tourist office has lists of routes to the most popular sights.) You enter buses at the rear, where you pay an attendant and pass through a turnstile, then exit at the front. Have your fare in hand when you board to avoid flashing bills or wallets. Be aware that bus drivers speak no English, and they drive like maniacs.

The upscale, privately-run, and air-conditioned frescão buses run between the beaches, downtown, and Rio's two airports. These vehicles, which look like highway buses, stop at regular bus stops but also may be flagged down wherever you see them. Also recommended are the *jardineira* buses, open-sided vehicles (they look like old-fashioned streetcars) that follow the beach drive from Copacabana to São Conrado as well as beyond to Barra da Tijuca. White posts along the street mark jardineira stops. They offer excellent views of the scenery and drive slowly along the beach avenue, a welcome relief to anyone who has ridden the regular city buses. Green minivans also run back and forth along beachfront avenues, stopping to pick up and drop off people wherever they're flagged. (Fares start at about R$5.)

➤ BUS INFORMATION: **CityRio** (☎ 0800/225–8060).

CAR RENTAL

Car rentals can be arranged through hotels or agencies and cost about R$80–R$226 a day for standard models. Agencies include Hertz and Unidas. Both also have desks at the international and domestic airports.

➤ MAJOR AGENCY: **Hertz** (✉ Av. Princesa Isabel 334, Copacabana, ☎ 021/2275–7440; ✉ Aeroporto Internacional Antônio Carlos Jobim, ☎ 021/3398–4338; ✉ Aeroporto Santos Dumont, ☎ 021/2262–0612).

➤ LOCAL AGENCIES: **Localiza Rent a Car** (✉ Av. Princesa Isabel 214, Copacabana, ☎ 021/2275–3340; ✉ Aeroporto Internacional Antônio Carlos Jobim, ☎ 021/3398–5445; ✉ Aeroporto Santos Dumont, ☎ 021/2533–2677). **Unidas** (✉ Av. Princesa Isabel 350, Copacabana, ☎ 021/2275–8299).

CAR TRAVEL

The carioca style of driving is passionate to the point of abandon: traffic jams are common, the streets aren't well marked, and red lights are often more decorative than functional. Despite new parking areas along the beachfront boulevards, finding a spot can still be a problem. If you do choose to drive, exercise extreme caution, wear seat belts at all times, and keep the doors locked. When frustrations get the best of you, the book *How to Be a Carioca* offers some advice: even when you are angry, smile.

Arriving from São Paulo (429 km/266 mi on BR 116) and Brasília (1,150 km/714 mi on BR 040), you enter Rio via Avenida Brasil, which runs into Centro's beachside drive, the Avenida Infante Dom Henrique. This runs along Rio's Baía de Guanabara and passes through the Copacabana Tunnel to Copacabana Beach. The beachside Avenida Atlântica continues into Ipanema and Leblon along Avenidas Antônio Carlos Jobim (Ipanema) and Delfim Moreira (Leblon). From Galeão, take the Airport Expressway (known as the Linha Vermelha, or Red Line) to the beach area. This expressway takes you through two tunnels and into Lagoa. Exit on Avenida Epitácio Pessoa, the winding street encircling the lagoon. To reach Copacabana, exit at Avenida Henrique Dodsworth (known as the Corte do Cantagalo). For Ipanema and Leblon, there are several exits, beginning with Rua Maria Quitéria.

Turismo Clássico Travel, one of the country's most reliable travel and transport agencies, can arrange for a driver, with or without an English-speaking guide (four hours with a driver only is R$200). Classico's owners, Liliana and Vera, speak English, and each has 20 years of experience in organizing transportation—often working with film crews. They also offer sightseeing tours.

➤ CONTACTS: **Turismo Clássico Travel** (✉ Av. Nossa Senhora de Copacabana 1059, Sala 805, Copacabana, ☎ 021/2523–3390).

GASOLINE

There's a gas station on every main street in Rio: for example, on Avenida Atlântica in Copacabana; around the Lagoa Rodrigo de Freitas and at Avenida Vieira Souto in Ipanema. International companies, such as Shell and Esso, are represented. The gas stations run by Brazilian oil company Petrobras are called BR. Ipiranga is another local option. Half of the gas stations are open from 6 AM until 10 PM and the other half are open 24 hours with convenience stores. As gas stations don't have emergency service, it's better to ask if car-rental insurance includes it.

➤ GAS STATIONS: **BR** (✉ Posto de Gasolina Cardeal: Av. Atlântica s/n, Leme, ☎ 021/2275–5696; ✉ Posto Santa Clara: Av. Atlântica s/n, Copacabana, ☎ 021/2547–1467). **Ipiranga** (✉ Ponei Posto de Gasolina: Av. Borges de Medeiros 3151, Lagoa, ☎ 021/2539–1283).

CONSULATES
➤ CONTACTS: **Australia** (✉ Av. Rio Branco 1, Room 810, Centro, ☎ 021/2518–3351). **Canada** (✉ Rua Lauro Müller 116, Room 1104, Botafogo, ☎ 021/2542–7593). **United Kingdom** (✉ Praia do Flamengo 284, 2nd floor, Flamengo, ☎ 021/2553–6850). **United States** (✉ Av. Presidente Wilson 147, Centro, ☎ 021/2292–7117).

EMERGENCIES
➤ EMERGENCY SERVICES: **Ambulance and Fire** (☎ 193). **Police** (☎ 190). **Tourism Police** (✉ Av. Afrânio de Melo Franco, Leblon, ☎ 021/3399–7170).
➤ PRIVATE MEDICAL CLINICS: **Cardio Plus** (✉ Rua Visconde de Pirajá 330, Ipanema, ☎ 021/2521–4899). **Galdino Campos Cardio Copa Medical Clinic** (✉ Av. Nossa Senhora de Copacabana 492, Copacabana, ☎ 021/2548–9966). **Medtur** (✉ Av. Nossa Senhora de Copacabana 647, Copacabana, ☎ 021/2235–3339). **Policlínica Barata Ribeiro** (✉ Rua Barata Ribeiro 51, Copacabana, ☎ 021/2275–4697).
➤ 24-HOUR PHARMACIES: **Drogaria Pacheco** (✉ Av. Nossa Senhora de Copacabana 534, Copacabana, ☎ 021/2548–1525). **Farmácia do Leme** (✉ Av. Prado Junior 237, Leme, ☎ 021/2275–3847).

ENGLISH-LANGUAGE MEDIA
Bookstores that carry some English-language publications include Letras & Expressões, Livraria Argumento, Livraria Kosmos, and Sodiler. In Ipanema, newstands Banca Nossa Senhora da Paz and Banca General Osório sell international newspapers 24 hours a day.
➤ BOOKSTORES: **Letras & Expressões** (✉ Rua Visconde de Pirajá 276, Ipanema, ☎ 021/2521–6110. **Livraria Argumento** (✉ Rua Dias Ferreira 417, Leblon, ☎ 021/2239–5294). **Livraria Kosmos** (✉ Rua do Rosário 155, Centro, ☎ 021/2224–8616). **Sodiler** (✉ Aeroporto Internacional Antônio Carlos Johim, ☎ 021/3393–9511; ✉ Aeroporto Santos Dumont, ☎ 021/3393–4377).
➤ NEWSSTANDS: **Banca General Osório** (✉ corner of Praça General Osório and Rua Jangadeiros, Ipanema, ☎ 021/2287–9248). **Banca Nossa Senhora da Paz** (✉ Rua Visconde de Pirajá 365, Ipanema, ☎ 021/2522–0880).

GAY AND LESBIAN TRAVELERS
Style Travel, an offshoot of the established Brasil Plus travel agency, is a great source of information on gay and lesbian lodging, tour, and nightlife options in the area. They can also supply knowledgeable, English-speaking gay and lesbian guides and arrange trips to outlying areas. Style Travel is a member of the International Gay and Lesbian Travel Association (IGLTA).

G Magazine is Rio's gay and lesbian glossy magazine. It's available at most newsstands and lists local arts, music, and style events—in Portuguese. Visit Rio's on-line "Gay Guide" at www.ipanema.com/rio/gay. The site is a wealth of information—from the practical to the downright sexy. Rio's gay beach scene is at Bolsa, on Copacabana Beach in front of the Copacabana Palace, and at Ipanema by Posts 8 and 9, east of Rua Farme de Amoedo, a.k.a. Farme Gay. Locals on these sandy stretches are usually open to questions about what's happening in the gay and lesbian community.

➤ CONTACTS: **Grupo Arco-Íris de Conscientização Homossexual** (☎ 021/2552–5995, 021/9295–7229). **Style Travel** (Rua Visconde de Pirajá 433, 6th floor, Ipanema, ☎ 021/2247–8915 or 021/2522–0709).

HEALTH

You should avoid tap water (note that ice in restaurants and bars is safe as it's usually made from bottled water), and take care not to soak up too much sun. Despite Rio's reputation, crime is no more likely than in any large city. Most crimes involving visitors occur in crowded public areas: beaches, busy sidewalks, intersections, and city buses. Pickpockets, usually children, work in groups. One will distract you while another grabs a wallet, bag, or camera. Be particularly wary of children who thrust themselves in front of you and ask for money or offer to shine your shoes. Another member of the gang may strike from behind, grabbing your valuables and disappearing into the crowd.

Another tactic is for criminals to approach your car at intersections. Always keep doors locked and windows partially closed. Leave valuables in your hotel safe, don't wear expensive jewelry or watches, and keep cameras out of sight. Walking alone at night on the beach isn't a good idea; neither is getting involved with drugs—penalties for possession are severe, and dealers are the worst of the worst.

MAIL, INTERNET, AND SHIPPING

Brazilians are joining the Internet community in increasing numbers, and the staff at many hotels can arrange Internet access for guests. In addition, you can head to several cybercafés around town for coffee while you check your e-mail.

The main post office is in Centro, but there are branches all over the city, including one at Galeão, several on Avenida Nossa Senhora de Copacabana in Copacabana, and one on Rua Visconde de Pirajá in Ipanema. Most are open weekdays 8–5 and Saturday 8–noon.

Federal Express and DHL have offices here that are open weekdays, but shipping usually takes longer than just overnight. You can call a day ahead to schedule pick-up.
➤ COURIER SERVICES: **DHL** (✉ Rua Teófilo Otoni 15 A, Centro, ☎ 021/2263–5454). **Federal Express** (✉ Av. Calógeras 23, Centro, ☎ 021/2262–8565).
➤ POST OFFICE: **Main Branch** (✉ Av. Presidente Vargas 3077, ☎ 021/2503–8222).

MONEY MATTERS

Generally, exchange rates are better in the city than at the airport and cash gets better rates than traveler's checks. Most Brazilian banks don't exchange money. One that does is Banco do Brasil. The branch at Galeão offers good exchange rates, but it won't provide credit-card advances.

Casas do câmbio (exchange houses) are found all over the city, especially along the beaches and on Avenida Nossa Senhora de Copacabana and Rua Visconde de Pirajá in Ipanema. Many change money without charging a service fee. Sometimes, depending on the amount of money you wish to exchange, exchange houses have a better rate than the banks. American Express is another option.

Some hotels, such as the Caesar Park and the Copacabana Palace, offer competitive rates but will charge a commission if you're not a guest there. On weekends, hotels may be your best bet because few other places are open. Or try the automatic-teller machines (ATMs) throughout town that dispense reais.

➤ BANKS: **Banco do Brasil** (✉ Rua Bartolomeu Mitre 438 A, Leblon, ☎ 021/2512–2999; ✉ Av. Nossa Senhora de Copacabana 594, ☎ 021/2548–8992; ✉ Aeroporto Internacional Antônio Carlos Jobim, third floor, ☎ 021/3398–3652). **Banco 24 Horas ATM** (✉ Av. Nossa Senhora de Copacabana 202; ✉ Av. Nossa Senhora de Copacabana 599; ✉ Av. Nossa Senhora de Copacabana 1366; ✉ Visconde de Pirajá 174, Ipanema.

➤ EXCHANGE SERVICES: **American Express** (✉ Av. Atlântica 1702 B, Copacabana, ☎ 021/2548–2148 or 0800/778–5050. **Casa Universal** (✉ Av. Nossa Senhora de Copacabana 371 E, Copacabana, ☎ 021/2548–6696).

METRÔ TRAVEL

Rio's subway system, the metrô, is clean, relatively safe, and efficient—a delight to use—but it's not comprehensive. Reaching sights distant from metrô stations can be a challenge, especially in summer when the infamous carioca traffic fans what is already 90-degree exasperation. Plan your tours accordingly; tourism offices and some metrô stations have maps.

Trains run daily from 6 AM to 11 PM along two lines: Linha 1 runs north from the Cardeal Arcoverde stop in Copacabana, parallel to the coast and into downtown, then west to its terminus at Saens Pena station; Linha 2 starts four stops before Saens Pena at Estácio and heads northwest to Rio's edge at the Pavuna station. A single metrô ticket costs R$1, a 10-pack is R$10 (but there are discounts for riding the subway during the nonrush hours, between noon and 4). Combination metrô-bus tickets allow you to take special buses to and from the Botafogo station: the M-21 runs to Leblon via Jardim Botânico and Jóquei; the M-22 goes to Leblon by way of Túnel Velho, Copacabana, and Ipanema.

➤ METRÔ INFORMATION: **Information Line** (☎ 021/2292–6116 or 021/2255–5552).

TAXIS

Yellow taxis are just like those in New York, except that even fewer drivers speak English. They have meters that start at a set price and have two rates: "1" for before and "2" for after 8 PM. The "2" rate also applies to Sunday, holidays, the month of December, the neighborhoods of São Conrado and Barra da Tijuca, and when climbing steep hills. Drivers are required to post a chart noting the current fares on the inside of the left rear window. Carioca cabbies are wonderful people by and large, but there are exceptions. Remain alert and trust your instincts; a few drivers have taken nonnatives for a ride.

Radio taxis and several companies that routinely serve hotels (and whose drivers often speak English) are also options. They charge 30% more than other taxis but are reliable and, usually, air-conditioned. Other cabs working with the hotels will also charge more, normally a fixed fee that you should agree on before you leave. Reliable radio cab companies include Centro de Taxis, Coopacarioca, and Coopatur.

➤ TAXI COMPANIES: **Centro de Taxis** (☎ 021/2593–2598). **Coopacarioca** (☎ 021/2253–3847). **Coopatur** (☎ 021/2290–1009).

TELEPHONES

Rio's area code is 021. There are public phones on corners throughout the city. They work with cards that you can buy in a variety of denominations at newsstands, banks, and some shops (some phones also work with credit cards). For long-distance calls, there are phone offices at the main bus terminal, Galeão, downtown at Praça Tiradentes 41, and in Copacabana at Avenida Nossa Senhora de Copacabana 540.

To make international calls through the operator, dial 000111. For operator-assisted long-distance within Brazil, dial 101; information is 102.

TOURS

You can ride around the Floresta da Tijuca and Corcovado, Angra dos Reis, or Teresópolis in renovated World War II Jeeps (1942 Dodge Commanders, Willys F-75s, and others) with the well-organized Atlantic Forest Jeep Tours. Guides speak English, French, German, and Spanish. The company also offers a range of ecological tours, including some on horseback. The superb guides at Gray Line speak your language. In addition to a variety of city tours, the company also offers trips outside town, whether you'd like to go white-water rafting on the Rio Paraíbuna, tour a coffee plantation, or spend time in Petrópolis. Helicopter tours are also an option.

Carlos Roquette is a history teacher who runs Cultural Rio, an agency that hosts trips to 8,000 destinations. Most are historic sites. A guided visit costs around R$100 per hour, depending on the size of the group. Ecology and Culture Tours offers hiking and jeep tours of Tijuca, Sugar Loaf, Santa Teresa, and various beaches. Guides speak English: morning and afternoon excursions are available. Favela Tour offers a fascinating half-day tour of two favelas. For anyone with an interest in Brazil beyond the beaches, such tours are highly recommended. The company's English-speaking guides can also be contracted for other outings.

Qualitours will take you and yours in a jeep around old Rio, the favelas, Corcovado, Floresta da Tijuca, Prainha, and Grumari. They can explain everything in English, Hungarian, French, or German. Hang glide or paraglide over Pedra da Gávea and Pedra Bonita under the supervision of São Conrado Eco-Aventura.
➤ CONTACTS: **Atlantic Forest Jeep Tours** (☎ FAX 021/2495–9827, ☎ 021/2494–4761). **Cultural Rio** (☎ 021/9911–3829 or 021/3322–4872, WEB www.culturalrio.com). **Ecology and Culture Tours** (☎ 021/2522–1620). **Favela Tour** (☎ 021/3322–2727). **Gray Line** (☎ 021/2512–9919). **Qualitours** (☎ 021/2232–9710). **São Conrado Eco-Aventura** (☎ 021/2522–5586).

TRAIN TRAVEL

Intercity trains leave from *the* central station that starred in the Oscar-nominated movie by the same name, Estação Dom Pedro II Central do Brasil. Trains, including a daily overnight train to São Paulo, also leave from the Estação Leopoldina Barao de Maria, near Praça 15 de Novembro.
➤ TRAIN INFORMATION: **Estação Dom Pedro II Central do Brasil** (✉ Praça Cristiano Otoni on Av. President Vargas, Centro, ☎ 021/2233–8818). **Estação Leopoldina Barao de Maria** (✉ Av. Francisco Bicalho, São Cristóvão, ☎ 021/2273–1122 or 021/2575–3399).

VISITOR INFORMATION

The Rio de Janeiro city tourism department, Riotur, has an information booth, which is open 8–5 daily. There are also city tourism desks at the airports and the Novo Rio bus terminal. The Rio de Janeiro state tourism board, Turisrio, is open weekdays 9–6. You can also try contacting Brazil's national tourism board, Embratur.
➤ TOURIST INFORMATION: **Embratur** (✉ Rua Uruguaiana 174, Centro, ☎ 021/2509–6017). **Riotur** (✉ Rua da Assembléia 10, near Praça 15 de Novembro, Centro, ☎ 021/2217–7575). **Riotur information booth** (✉ Av. Princesa Isabel 183 Copacabana, ☎ 021/2541–7522). **Turisrio** (✉ Rua da Assembléia 10, 7th and 8th floors, Centro, ☎ 021/2531–1922).

SIDE TRIPS FROM RIO

Rio the state has just as much allure as Rio the city. Across Guanabara Bay, Niterói is a mix of new and old: the ultramodern Museu de Arte Contemporânea is set not too far from historic forts. A scenic northeast road into the mountains leads to Petrópolis, a city that bears testimony to the country's royal legacy. Beyond, tucked into a lush valley, is charming Nova Friburgo with its Swiss ambience. Due east of the city, dangling off the yacht-frequented coast, are the sophisticated resort towns of Cabo Frio and Búzios, where Rio's chic escape for weekends. And to the southwest along the Costa Verde sit the stunning Angra dos Reis—facing the offshore island of Ilha Grande—and the colonial city of Parati, with its 18th century Portuguese architecture and plethora of offshore islets.

Niterói

14 km (9 mi) east of Rio.

Ranked as having the highest quality of life in Rio de Janeiro state, Niterói, literally, "hidden waters," was founded in 1573. Old and new come together in this city of 453,000, where both a modern naval industry and traditional fishing help support the economy. Ocean beaches and the Fortaleza de Santa Cruz—an ancient fortress built in 1555 to protect the bay—draw visitors, but so does the ultramodern Museu de Arte Contemporânea. Ferries from Riio's Praça 15 de Novembro cross the bay, arriving at Praça Araribóia in a pleasant 20 minutes.

The must-see **Museu de Arte Contemporânea** was constructed by the well-known architect Oscar Niemeyer (he designed most of Brazil's capital—Brasília). Opened in September 1996, the building looks a bit like a spaceship. The modern art museum shelters the collection donated by João Sattamini. Just five minutes from Praça Araribóia (in downtown Niterói where the ferries stop), enjoy a nice walk along the coastline. Upon leaving, try the fresh coconut water sold outside. ⊠ *Estrada de Boa Viagem, Boa Viagem,* ☎ *021/2620–2400.* 🎫 *R$2.* ☉ *Tues.– Fri. 11–7, Sat. 1–9, Sun 11–7.*

The **Fortaleza de Santa Cruz** was the first fort built on Guanabara Bay, in 1555. Distributed on two floors are cannons, a sun clock, and the Santa Barbara Chapel—dating from the 17th century. It's best to visit in the cool morning hours. Fifteen minutes from downtown, it's an easy taxi ride (R$15), or there's a bus that goes straight to Jurujuba (No. 33) from the ferry dock. ⊠ *Estrada General Eurico Gaspar Dutra, Jurujuba,* ☎ *021/2711–0462.* 🎫 *R$3.* ☉ *Daily 9–5.*

Built as an lookout point, **Forte Barão do Rio Branco** was armed and turned into a battery in 1567. Inside is the Forte do Imbuí, another fortress, which is a wonderful place to walk, with a great view of Guanabara Bay and Rio. ⊠ *Av. Marechal Pessoa Leal 265, Jurujuba,* ☎ *021/2711–0366 or 021/2711–0566.* 🎫 *R$3.* ☉ *Weekends, holidays 9–5.*

Petrópolis

65 km (42 mi) northeast of Rio.

The hilly highway northeast of the city rumbles past forests and waterfalls en route to a mountain town so refreshing and picturesque that Dom Pedro II, Brazil's second emperor, spent his summers in it. (From 1889 to 1899, it was also the country's year-round seat of government.)

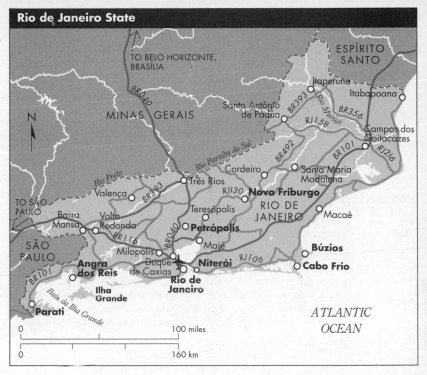

Rio de Janeiro State

Horse-drawn carriages shuttle between the sights, passing flowering gardens, shady parks, and imposing pink mansions.

The **Museu Imperial** is a museum housed in the magnificent 44-room palace that was Dom Pedro's summer home, the colossal structure is filled with polished wooden floors, 19th-century artwork, and grand chandeliers. You can also see the diamond-encrusted gold crown and scepter of Brazil's last emperor, as well as other royal jewels. ⊠ *Rua da Imperatriz 220,* ☎ *024/2237–8000.* ▣ *R$4.* ☉ *Tues.–Sun. noon–5:30.*

From the Museu Imperial, you can walk three long blocks or take a horse-drawn carriage to **São Pedro de Alcantara,** the Gothic cathedral containing the tombs of Dom Pedro II; his wife, Dona Teresa Cristina; and their daughter, Princesa Isabel. ⊠ *Av. Tiradentes,* ☎ *no phone.* ▣ *Free.* ☉ *Weekdays 8–noon, Sun. 8–6.*

The **Palácio de Cristal** (Crystal Palace), a stained-glass and iron building made in France and assembled in Brazil, was a wedding present to Princesa Isabel. During the imperial years it was used as a ballroom: it was here the princess held a celebration dance after she abolished slavery in Brazil in 1888. ⊠ *Praça da Confluencia, Rua Alfredo Pacha,* ☎ *no phone.* ▣ *Free.* ☉ *Tues.–Sun. 9–5.*

Dining and Lodging

$–$$ ✕ **Bauernstube.** German food is the backbone of this log cabin–style eatery. The bratwurst and sauerkraut are properly seasoned, and the strudel is an excellent choice for polishing off a meal. ⊠ *Dr. Nelson de Sá Earp 297,* ☎ *024/2442–1097. AE, DC, MC, V. Closed Mon.*

$–$$$ ✕▣ **Pousada de Alcobaça.** Just north of Petrópolis, this is considered by many to be the loveliest inn in the area. The grounds have beautiful gardens and a swimming pool. The kitchen turns out exceptional breakfasts, lunches, and high teas with an emphasis on fresh ingredients. Meals, which include savory pastas, are served in the garden. ✉ *Agostinho Goulao 298, Correa,* ☎ *024/2221–1240,* FAX *024/2222–3390. 10 rooms. Restaurant, pool, sauna, tennis court. AE, DC, MC, V. BP.*

$–$$$ ✕▥ **Pousada Monte Imperial.** A few minutes from downtown, this Euro-style inn has 14 double rooms with private baths, a pool, a lobby with a fireplace, and a restaurant-bar. Drinks and meals can also be taken in the lovely garden. ✉ *Rua Joséde Alencar 27,* ☎ *024/2237–1664. 14 rooms. Restaurant, bar, pool. AE, DC, MC, V. BP.*

¢ ▥ **Hotel Margaridas.** Three chalets and 12 apartments make up this comfortable complex just five minutes from the heart of downtown. You'll find well-tended gardens and a swimming pool. ✉ *Rua Bispo Pereira Alves 235,* ☎ *024/2442–4686. 12 apartments, 3 chalets. Pool. AE, DC, MC, V. BP.*

Nova Friburgo

131 km (79 mi) northeast of Petrópolis; 196 km (121 mi) northeast of Rio.

This summer resort town was settled by Swiss immigrants in the early 1800s, when Brazil was actively encouraging European immigration and when the economic situation in Switzerland was bad. Woods, rivers, and waterfalls dot the terrain encircling the city. Homemade liquors, jams, and cheeses pack the shelves of the town's small markets. Cariocas come here to unwind in the cool mountain climate.

A cable car rises more than 600 m (2,000 ft) to **Morro da Cruz,** which offers a spectacular view of the mountain. ✉ *Praça Teleférica,* ☎ *no phone.* ▱ *Admission R$10.* ☉ *Weekends 9–6.*

Lodging

$ ▥ **Hotel Bucsky.** Long walks through the several thousand kilometers of forests that surrounds the hotel are among the draws at this country-house inn. Meals are included, and if the restaurant is not luxurious, it does serve honest food, self-service style. ✉ *Estrada Rio-Friburgo, Km 76.5, Ponte Saudade 28615-160,* ☎ *024/2522–5052 or 024/2522–5500.* FAX *024/2522–9769. 60 rooms, 10 suites. Pool, sauna, miniature golf, tennis court. AE, DC, MC, V. FAP.*

Cabo Frio

168 km (101 mi) east of Rio.

Set up as a defensive port from which to ship wood to Portugal nearly four centuries ago, Cabo Frio has evolved into a resort town renowned for its fresh seafood. It's also a prime jumping-off point for the endless number of white-sand beaches that crisscross the area around town and the offshore islands. A favorite sailing destination, its turquoise waters are crowded with sailboats and yachts on holidays and weekends. The town itself has attractive baroque architecture.

Praia do Forte is popular thanks to its calm, clear waters and long stretch of sand. On weekends it's jammed with colorful beach umbrellas, swimmers, and sun lovers. Some distance away, Praia Brava and Praia do Foguete lure surfers to their crashing waves.

Búzios

★ *25 km (15 mi) northeast of Cabo Frio; 193 km (126 mi) northeast of Rio.*

Búzios, a little more than two hours from Rio, is a string of gorgeous beaches that draws resort fans year-round from Europe and South America. This is the perfect place to do absolutely nothing. It was little more than a fishing village until the 1960s, when Brigitte Bardot was photographed here in a bikini. Since then, Búzios's rustic charm has given way to *pousadas,* or inns (some of them luxurious, few inexpensive); restaurants; and bars run by people who came on vacation and never left. The balance between the cosmopolitan and the primitive is seductive.

March through June is low season, when temperatures range from about 27°C (80°F) to 32°C (90°F), and prices often drop 30%–40%. The water is still warm, yet the crowds aren't as great; the area seems much more intimate than in the summer months of October through December. Though not a great deal of English is spoken here, a little Spanish or French will get you a long way.

Each of the beaches offers something different: the lovely, intimate Azeda and Azedinha are local favorites (and the spots where you may find topless bathing); Ferradura is known for the gastronomic excellence of its kiosks and its jet skiing; Lagoinha is referred to by all as a magic beach and has a natural amphitheater where world-class musicians hold concerts; Brava is the surfers' beach; and Manguinhos is popular with windsurfers.

Dining and Lodging

$$$–$$$$ ✕ **Satyricon.** The Italian fish restaurant famous in Rio has opened up
★ shop here as well. The menu's highlight is the expensive but great seafood, including the restaurant's famous rock salt–baked whole fish, which music star Madonna has tried and approved. ⊠ *Av. José Bento Ribeiro Dantas 412,* ☎ *024/2223–1595. AE, DC, MC, V.*

$$–$$$$ ✕ **Cigalon.** The restaurant has a veranda overlooking the beach. It's
★ the only place that serves lamb steak for R$27. The cooked lobster with rice and almonds for R$42 is a must-eat. If you're having trouble making up your mind among the tempting options, the tasting menu for R$33 might be your best bet. ⊠ *Rua das Pedras 151,* ☎ *024/2223–6284. AE, DC, MC, V.*

$ ✕ **Chez Michou.** This *crêperie* on the main drag in the center of town is the best place to eat if you want something quick, light, and inexpensive. You can choose from about 500 different crepe fillings and then eat your meal outdoors. At night locals and visitors alike congregate to drink and people-watch. ⊠ *Rua José Bento Ribeiro Dantas 90,* ☎ *024/2223–6137. No credit cards.*

$$–$$$ 🏨 **Barracuda.** This hotel is included in Brazil's esteemed Roteiros de
★ Charme club, a highly exclusive association of the nation's best places to stay. The view of the sea from the deck is breathtaking. ⊠ *Ponta da Sapata,* ☎ *021/2287–3122, ext. 601 for reservations from Rio,* ☎ FAX *024/2223–1314. 23 rooms. Restaurant, pool, sauna, 2 tennis courts. AE, DC, MC, V. BP.*

Angra dos Reis

151 km (91 mi) west of Rio.

Angra dos Reis, the Bay of Kings, anchors the rugged Costa Verde in an area of beautiful beaches, colonial architecture, and clear emerald waters. Schooners, yachts, sailboats, and fishing skiffs thread among the 365 offshore islands, one for every day of the year. Indeed, Angra dos Reis's popularity lies in its strategic location—ideal for exploring those islands, many of which are deserted patches of sand and green that offer wonderful swimming and snorkeling opportunities. Organized boat tours from shore can take you to favored island haunts.

One of the most popular islands is the lush, mountainous **Ilha Grande.** Just 2 km (1 mi), a 90-minute ferry ride off the shore from Angra dos

Reis, it has more than 100 idyllic beaches—sandy ribbons that stretch on and on with a backdrop of tropical foliage. The boats arrive at Vila do Abraão. From there you can roam paths that lead from one slip of sand to the next or negotiate with local boatmen for jaunts to the beaches or more remote islets.

A 10-minute walk takes you to the hot waters off the beaches Praia da Júlia and Comprida. After a 25-minute walk is the transparent sea at Abraãozinho Beach. If you choose to go by boat, don't miss the big waves of Lopes Mendes Beach or the astonishing blue, Mediterraneanlike water of Lagoa Azul. Scuba diving fans should head to Gruta do Acaiá to see turtles and other colorful South American fish.

Dining and Lodging

$$$–$$$$ ✕🏨 **Hotel do Frade & Golf Resort.** Guest-room balconies overlook the sea and a private beach at this modern resort hotel. For those who love sports, the property offers many options: an 18-hole golf course, seven tennis courts, a soccer field, and, of course, jet skis and other boat rentals. The hotel can also arrange excursions on the Ilha Grande Bay or scuba diving. It's no surprise that seafood is good at the buffet restaurant Scuna. In the summer, other resort restaurants offer a variety of international cuisines. ⊠ *BR 101, Km 123, Praia do Frade,* ☎ *024/3369–9500,* 𝔽𝔸𝕏 *024/3369–2254. 160 rooms. 3 restaurants, bar, swimming pool, tennis courts, 18-hole golf, soccer, jet skiing, boating, cinema, baby-sitting. AE, D, DC, MC, V. FAP.*

$$–$$$$ 🏨 **Paraíso dos Reis.** Opened in 2000, this comfortable hotel has a private beach. Electric cars shuttle guests from the door of their chalets to the sand. Water activities abound, including jet ski and boat rental. ⊠ *Estrada do Contorno 3700, Retiro,* ☎ *024/3367–2654,* 𝔽𝔸𝕏 *024/3367–2654. 30 rooms. Bar, pool, massage, sauna, jet skiing, boating. AE, D, DC, MC, V.*

$–$$ 🏨 **Portogalo Suíte.** Perched on the top of a hill with a wonderful view of the bay, the exposed-brick buildings have a rustic appeal. The rooms are cozy and comfy and a cable car is available to take guests down the hillside to the beach and the marina. ⊠ *BR 101, Km 71, Praia de Itapinhoacanga,* ☎ *024/3361–4343,* 𝔽𝔸𝕏 *024/3361–4361. 70 rooms. Bar, pool, sauna, 2 tennis courts, jet skiing. AE, D, DC, MC, V.*

Parati

100 km (60 mi) southwest of Angra dos Reis.

This stunning colonial city is one of South America's gems. Giant iron chains hang from posts at the beginning of the mazelike grid of cobblestone streets, closing them to all but pedestrians, horses, and bicycles. Until the 18th century, this was an important transit point for gold plucked from the Minas Gerais—a safe harbor protected from pirates by a fort. (The cobblestones are the rock ballast brought from Lisbon, then unloaded to make room in the ships for their golden cargoes.) In 1720, however, the colonial powers cut a new trail from the gold mines straight to Rio de Janeiro, bypassing the town and leaving it isolated. It remained that way until contemporary times, when artists, writers, and others "discovered" the community and UNESCO placed it on its World Heritage Site list. Brazilian actress Sonia Braga comes here to relax, and Rolling Stone Mick Jagger used it as the backdrop for a music video.

Parati isn't a city peppered with lavish mansions and opulent palaces; rather it has a simple beauty. By the time the sun breaks over the bay each morning—illuminating the whitewashed, colorfully trimmed buildings—the fishermen will have begun spreading out their catch at the outdoor market. The best way to explore is simply to begin walking winding streets banked with centuries-old buildings that hide quaint inns, tony restaurants, shops, and art galleries. Once you've finished your in-town exploration, you can begin investigating what makes this a weekend escape for cariocas: the lush, tropical offshore islands and not-so-distant strands of coastal beach.

Parati is jammed with churches, but the most intriguing are the trio whose congregations were segregated by race during the colonial era. **Igreja de Nossa Senhora do Rosário** (⊠ Rua do Comércio) was built by the town's slaves so they could have their own place of worship. Simple and clean-lined **Igreja de Santa Rita** (⊠ Rua Santa Rita), meanwhile, was built in 1722 and earmarked for free mulattoes; today it houses a small religious art museum. On the far extreme of the social spectrum, **Igreja de Nossa Senhora das Dores** (⊠ Rua Dr. Pereira) was the church of the community's small but elite white population. The fortress, **Forte Defensor Perpétuo** (⊠ Morro da Vila Velha), was built in the early 1700s (and rebuilt in 1822) as a defense against pirates and is now home to a folk-arts center. It sits north of town.

Dining and Lodging

$–$$ ✕ **Amigo do Rei.** You can find typical food from the Brazilian countryside, as well as seafood at this cozy, quiet spot. It's one of the best eateries in town—both because of the kitchen and because of the prices. ⊠ *Rua Dona Geralda 174, Centro Histórico de Parati,* ☎ *024/3371–1049. No credit cards. No lunch.*

$ 🏨 **Porto Pousada Parati.** Rooms in this historic structure in the old-
★ est part of town ring a series of courtyards and a swimming pool. Rates include breakfast. ⊠ *Rua do Comércio,* ☎ *024/3371–1205,* FAX *024/ 3371–2111. 51 rooms. Restaurant, bar, pool, sauna. AE, DC, MC, V.*

¢–$ 🏨 **Pousada do Ouro.** Inside an 18th-century building with a garden courtyard, this is the inn most likely to host celebrities who come to the area for sun and atmosphere. ⊠ *Rua da Praia 145,* ☎ *024/3371– 1378,* FAX *024/3371–1311. 18 rooms, 8 suites Restaurant, bar, pool. AE, DC, MC, V. BP.*

¢ 🏨 **Pousada do Príncipe.** A prince (the great grandson of Emperor
★ Pedro II) owns this aptly named inn at the edge of the colonial city. The hotel is painted in the yellow and green of the imperial flag, and its quiet, colorful public areas are graced by photos of the royal family. Rooms are small but comfortable (and air-conditioned). The swimming pool in the plant-filled patio beckons. The kitchen is impressive, too; its chef turns out an exceptional feijoada. ⊠ *Av. Roberto Silveira 289,* ☎ *024/3371–2266,* FAX *024/3371–2120. 34 rooms. Restaurant, pool, sauna, 2 tennis courts. AE, DC, MC, V.*

Side Trips from Rio A to Z

BOAT AND FERRY TRAVEL

To get to Niterói, there are ferries available at Praça 15 de Novembro in Rio. In 20 minutes you'll arrive at Praça Araribóia, in downtown Niterói. There is no car service available. Barcas boats are bigger and slower than the newer Catamaran Jumbo Cat fleet.

To get to Ilha Grande, Vila do Abraão, you have two options run by Barcas. A ferry leaves Angra dos Reis, from Cais da Lapa at Avenida dos Reis Magos, daily at 3:15 PM. The return ferry departs weekdays at 10 AM and weekends at 11 AM. Or depart from Mangaratiba, at Avenida Mangaratiba, weekdays at 8 AM and weekends at 9 AM. The ferry back from Vila do Abraão to Mangaratiba leaves daily at 5:30 PM. Either trip takes an hour and a half.

➤ BOAT AND FERRY INFORMATION: **Barcas S/A** (✉ Praça Araribóia 6–
8, Niterói, ☎ 021/2719–1892 or 021/2620–6766; ☎ Ilha Grande information: 021/2533–6661). **Catamaran Jumbo Cat** (✉ Praça Araribóia
s/n, Niterói, ☎ 021/2620–8589 or 021/2620–8670).

BUS TRAVEL
Several bus companies, including 1001, depart for Niterói from the
Menezes Cortes Terminal (downtown Rio); from Avenida Princesa Is-
abel in Copacabana; and from Botafogo at the beach.

Leaving hourly from Rio's Rodoviária Novo Rio, Costa Verde buses
travel to Petrópolis, Única buses to Angra dos Reis, and 12 buses a
day head for Parati. Regional bus services connect Petrópolis with Nova
Friburgo and Parati with Angra dos Reis.

Buses, a shuttle service, and airplanes regularly travel to and from popular Búzios and Rio. The best option is the shuttle service, which will
pick you up in Rio in the morning and drop you at your pousada before noon. Contact Turismo Clássico Travel in Rio for reservations.
Municipal buses connect Cabo Frio and Búzios.
➤ BUS INFORMATION: **Costa Verde** (☎ 021/2573–1484). **1001** (☎ 021/
2613–1001 or 021/3849–5001). **Única** (☎ 021/2263–8792).

CAR TRAVEL
To reach Niterói by car, take the 14-km-long (9-mi-long) Presidente
Costa e Silva Bridge, also known as Rio-Niterói. BR 101 connects the
city to the Costa Verde and Parati. You'll need to head north and along
BR 040 to reach the mountain towns of Petrópolis and Novo Friburgo.
Coastal communities Cabo Frio and Búzios are east of Rio along or
off RJ 106.

MONEY MATTERS
There are banks and ATMs in each community, but it's best to get reais
before leaving Rio. Check in advance with your hotel to make sure credit
cards are accepted.

TRANSPORTATION AROUND OUTLYING AREAS OF RIO
You can rent cars, dune buggies, motorcycles, and bicycles at most of
these destinations—or you can simply take taxis around each area. Ask
the staff at your hotel or at the tourist offices for recommendations.

VISITOR INFORMATION
Tourist offices are generally open weekdays from 8 or 8:30 to 6 and
Saturday from 8 or 9 to 4; some have limited Sunday hours, too. The
Niterói Tourism Office is open daily 9 to 6.
➤ TOURIST INFORMATION: **Angra dos Reis Tourism Office** (✉ Across
from bus station on Rua Largo da Lapa, ☎ 024/3365–1175, ext.
2186). **Búzios Tourism Office** (✉ Praça Santos Dumont 111, ☎ 024/
2623–2099). **Cabo Frio Tourism Office** (✉ Av. de Contorno, Praia do
Forte, ☎ 024/2647–1689). **Niterói Tourism Office** (✉ Estrada Leopoldo
Fróes 773, São Francisco, ☎ 021/2710–2727). **Nova Friburgo Tourism
Office** (✉ Praça Dr. Demervel B. Moreira, ☎ 024/2523–8000). **Parati
Tourism Office** (✉ Av. Roberto Silveira, ☎ 024/3371–1266, ext. 217).
Petrópolis Tourism Office (✉ Praça da Confluencia 3, ☎ 024/2243–
3561).

2 SÃO PAULO

Recognized as the economic capital of Latin America, São Paulo is a place of fancy restaurants and hotels, grand avenues, skyscrapers, and busy folk. It's also a cultural crossroads that has attracted people from all over Brazil and from abroad. Elegant cuisine, lively nightlife, abundant arts attractions, and opportunities for a better life are among its magnets. When the hustle-bustle becomes too much, savvy city dwellers escape to the mountains, spa towns, and beaches in surrounding São Paulo State.

Updated by
Karla Brunet

C ROWDED BUSES GRIND DOWN streets spouting black smoke, endless stands of skyscrapers block the horizon, and the din of traffic deafens the ear. But native *paulistanos* (inhabitants of São Paulo city; inhabitants of São Paulo State are called *paulistas*) love this megalopolis of 17 million. São Paulo now sprawls across 7,951 square km (3,070 square mi), 1,502 square km (580 square mi) of which make up the city proper. The largest city in South America makes New York City look small.

In 1554 Jesuit priests, including José de Anchieta and Manoel da Nóbrega, founded the village of São Paulo de Piratininga and began converting Indians to Catholicism. Wisely set on a plateau, the mission town was protected from attack and was served by many rivers. It remained unimportant to the Portuguese Crown until it became the departure point for the *bandeira* (literally, "flag") expeditions, whose members set out to look for gemstones and gold, to enslave Indians, and, later, to capture escaped African slaves. In the process, these adventurers established roads into vast portions of previously unexplored territory. São Paulo also saw Emperor Dom Pedro I declare independence from Portugal by the Rio Ipiranga (Ipiranga River), near the city.

In the late 19th century, São Paulo became a major coffee producer, attracting both workers and investors from many countries. Italians, Portuguese, Spanish, Germans, and Japanese put their talents and energies to work. By 1895, 70,000 of the 130,000 residents were immigrants. Their efforts transformed the place from a sleepy mission post into a dynamic financial and cultural hub. Avenida Paulista was once the site of many a coffee baron's mansion. Money flowed from these private domains into civic and cultural institutions. The arts began to flourish, and by the 1920s São Paulo was attracting such great artists as Mário and Oswald de Andrade, who introduced modern elements into Brazilian art.

In the 1950s, the auto industry began to develop and contributed greatly to São Paulo's contemporary cityscape. In the last 30 years, people from throughout Brazil have come seeking jobs, many in the Cubatão Industrial Park—the largest in the developing world—just outside the city limits. Today, like many major European or American hubs, São Paulo struggles to meet its citizens' transportation and housing needs, and goods and services are expensive. Yet, even as the smog reddens your eyes, you'll see that there's much to explore. As a city committed to making dreams come true, São Paulo offers top-rate nightlife and dining and thriving cultural and arts scenes.

The city faces the Atlantic shore in the southeast region of the state that shares its name. From town it's easy to travel by car or bus to the state's many small, beautiful beaches and beyond to the states of Paraná, Rio de Janeiro, and Minas Gerais. Although most sandy stretches are a couple of hours from the city, good side trips can be as close as the 30-minute drive to Embu.

Pleasures and Pastimes

Dining

With more than 12,000 restaurants and a melting pot of cultures, there's a cuisine for every craving. Japanese and Italian restaurants abound. Indeed, paulistanos are very proud of their pizza, especially pies topped with mozzarella, arugula, and sun-dried tomatoes. Establishments that serve Portuguese, German, French, and Spanish dishes are also popular. Be sure to try the *beirute*, a popular Lebanese contribution that's like a Middle Eastern submarine sandwich, served hot in toasted Syrian bread and sprinkled with oregano.

Of course many restaurants offer traditional Brazilian specialties such as *feijoada* (the national dish of black beans and a variety of meats), *churrasco* (barbecued meats), and *moqueca* (fish stew made with coconut milk and *dendê*, or palm oil). Some places specialize in regional food from Bahia (whose spicy dishes are often toned down), Minas Gerais, and elsewhere. *Virado à paulista* (beans, eggs, and collard greens) is a typical São Paulo dish. Nothing goes better with Brazilian food than a *caipirinha* (a drink with the rumlike *cachaça*, lemon, and sugar).

Lodging

You'll find many world-class hotels here; most are in big buildings on or around Avenida Paulista. Regardless of the price category, most hotels have good restaurants and buffet breakfasts.

Nightlife

From romantic garden terraces where you can grab a quiet drink to clubs where you can dance to throbbing techno music till dawn, the nightlife reflects the city's eclectic heritage. The chic and wealthy head for establishments, many of which serve food, in the Vila Olímpia and Itaim neighborhoods. The Pinheiros neighborhood, near Vila Madalena, has a large concentration of Brazilian clubs and alternative bars. The neighborhood of Jardins has some of the city's best dance clubs as well as a selection of gay and lesbian bars.

São Paulo's music clubs often feature jazz and blues artists. On weekends you'll find samba and *pagode* (musicians sitting around a table playing for a small crowd) in clubs throughout the city. At *forró* couples dance close to the fast beat and romantic lyrics of music that originated in the country's northeast. Forró has become quite popular in the past few years.

Parks and Gardens

In Latin America's biggest urban park, Parque Ibirapuera, you can ramble for an entire day without seeing all the grounds, museums, and cultural attractions. On Sunday, you may well be accompanied by thousands of paulistanos seeking refuge from all the surrounding concrete. The Fundação Oscar e Maria Luisa Americano has a small forest and a museum. The Parque do Estado (also called the Parque do Ipiranga) surrounds the Museu do Ipiranga and has a beautiful garden.

Side Trips

São Paulo State is full of natural attractions and towns with artistic and historical treasures. Embu is famous for its furniture stores, and artisans from throughout Brazil sell their wares at its enormous weekend street fair. The healing waters beckon from the spas of Águas de São Pedro. You can go white-water rafting or hike past more than 17 waterfalls around Brotas. In Campos do Jordão you can imagine yourself at a European mountain retreat. On the island called Ilhabela, you can bask on a beautiful beach and swim, snorkel, or dive.

EXPLORING SÃO PAULO

Each neighborhood seems a testament to a different period of the city's history. The largely pedestrians-only hilltop and valley areas, particularly Vale do Anhangabaú, are where São Paulo's first inhabitants lived—Jesuit missionaries and treasure-hunting pioneers. Later these areas became Centro (downtown district), a financial and cultural center that's still home to the stock exchange and many banks. It's now the focus of revitalization efforts.

The Bela Vista and Bixiga (the city's little Italy) neighborhoods, near Centro, are home to many theaters and bars. In the 19th century, many families who made fortunes from coffee built whimsical mansions in the ridge-top Avenida Paulista neighborhood. Beginning with the post–World War II industrial boom, these homes gave way to skyscrapers. Many of the best hotels are also on or near this avenue.

During the economic growth of the 1970s, many businesses moved west, downhill to a former swamp. You'll find the tall buildings of Avenida Brigadeiro Faria Lima, the stylish homes of the Jardins neighborhood, and the Shopping Center Iguatemi (Brazil's first mall) just off the banks of the Rio Pinheiros. Large-scale construction of corporate headquarters continues south, between the Marginal Pinheiros Beltway and the Avenida Engenheiro Luís Carlos Berrini, not far from the luxurious Shopping Center Morumbi.

Great Itineraries

IF YOU HAVE 3 DAYS

On the first day, plan a walk along Avenida Paulista, with its many cultural attractions. Head to Centro on the second day to see such landmarks as the Edifício Itália and Teatro Municipal. Don't miss the Latin crafts exhibit at the Memorial da América Latina. On the third day, head for the Parque do Ibirapuera to visit one of its museums or just relax under the trees.

IF YOU HAVE 5 DAYS

In addition to the attractions outlined in the three-day itinerary, you can take a day to visit the snake museum at Instituto Butantã and/or the Fundação Maria Luisa e Oscar Americano. On your last day tour the Museu do Ipiranga and its environs, where Brazil's independence was declared.

IF YOU HAVE 7–10 DAYS

With so many days, you can explore the city as detailed above and take a side trip. If shopping is your passion, work in a weekend junket to Embu's street fair. If the outdoors beckons, head to Brotas, with its waterfalls, trails, and river rafting.

When to Tour

Most cultural events—film and music festivals and art exhibits—happen between July and December. During the South American summer (January through March) the weather is very rainy, and floods can disrupt traffic. In summer, make reservations for beach resorts as far in advance as possible, particularly for weekend stays. In winter (May through July), follow the same rule for visits to Campos do Jordão.

Centro

Even though the downtown district has its share of petty crime, it's one of the few places with a historical flavor. You can explore the areas where the city began and see examples of architecture, some of it beautifully restored, from the 19th century.

Numbers in the text correspond to numbers in the margin and on the São Paulo Centro map.

A Good Tour

The **Edifício Copan** ①, designed by Brazilian architect Oscar Niemeyer, seems an appropriate place to begin a tour. Farther up Avenida Ipiranga is the city's tallest building, the **Edifício Itália** ② (you might want to re-

São Paulo Centro

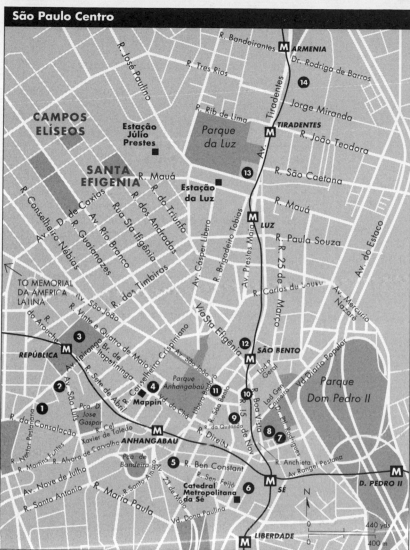

turn at the end of the day for a terrific view of the city from the bar or the restaurant on the 41st floor). Continue north along the avenue to the **Praça da República** ③. Cross Ipiranga and walk down the pedestrians-only Rua Barão de Itapetininga, with its many shops and street vendors. Follow it to the neobaroque **Teatro Municipal** ④, in the Praça Ramos de Azevedo. Head east across the square to the Viaduto do Chá, a monumental overpass above the Vale do Anhangabaú—the heart of São Paulo. At the end of this viaduct, turn right onto Rua Líbero Badaró and follow it to the baroque **Igreja de São Francisco de Assis** ⑤. A short walk along Rua Benjamin Constant will bring you to the **Praça da Sé** ⑥, the city's true center and the site of the Catedral Metropolitana da Sé.

You can take the *metrô* (subway) from the station at the cathedral west to the Barra Funda station and the **Memorial da América Latina.** Or you can head north out of Praça da Sé and follow Rua Roberto Simonsen to the **Solar da Marquesa de Santos** ⑦, the city's only surviving late-18th-century residence. Nearby is the **Pátio do Colégio** ⑧. Walk north along Rua Boa Vista; turn left onto Rua Anchieta and then left onto Rua 15 de Novembro. Number 275, on the left, houses **BOVESPA** ⑨, the São Paulo Stock Exchange. Near the end of Rua 15 de Novembro, at Rua João Brícola 24, stands the 36-floor **Edifício BANESPA** ⑩. To the northwest is the **Edifício Martinelli** ⑪. Walk two blocks up on Rua São Bento to the **Basílica de São Bento** ⑫, a church constructed at the beginning of the 20th century. Near it is Café Girondino, a good spot for a break. From the basilica, you can take a train north from the São Bento station to the Luz stop and the **Pinacoteca do Estado** ⑬, the state gallery. On Avenida Tiradentes walk north to see the religious art at **Museu de Arte Sacra** ⑭.

TIMING AND PRECAUTIONS

This route requires at least five hours on foot and use of the metrô, which is safe and clean. An early start will allow you to be more leisurely should one sight pique your interest more than another. If you're planning to take taxis or hire a driver, bear in mind that traffic jams are common.

Being a tourist in Centro is a bit hazardous. If you keep a low profile, and speak at least some Spanish (if not Portuguese), you'll most likely avoid being the target of thieves. Otherwise you might feel more comfortable touring with a guide. Whatever you do, leave your Rolex back at the hotel.

Sights to See

⑫ **Basílica de São Bento.** This church, constructed between 1910 and 1922, was designed by German architect Richard Berndl. Its enormous organ has some 6,000 pipes. ⊠ *Largo de São Bento,* ☎ *011/228–3633.* 🖬 *Free.* ⊙ *Mon., Wed., and Fri. 5–1 and 2–7:45, Thurs. 2–7:45, Sat. 6–1 and 3–7:30, Sun. 5–1 and 3–6. Metrô: São Bento.*

⑨ **BOVESPA.** If you leave an ID with the guard at the front desk, you can go up to the mezzanine and watch the hurly-burly of the busy São Paulo Stock Exchange—a hub for the foreign investment Brazil has attracted in its efforts to privatize state-owned companies. Computer terminals in the observation gallery carry the latest stock quotes as well as general information in various languages. BOVESPA offers tours in English, but only to representatives of foreign investment institutions. (If you fit this description, you can make arrangements in advance by faxing the Superintendência Executiva de Desenvolvimento at FAX 011/239–4981.) ⊠ *Rua 15 de Novembro 275,* ☎ *011/233–2000, ext. 2456.* 🖬 *Free.* ⊙ *Weekdays 9–noon and 2–6. Metrô: São Bento.*

Café Girondino is frequented by BOVESPA traders from happy hour until midnight. The bar serves good draft beer and sandwiches. Pictures on the wall depict Centro in its early days. ⊠ *Rua Boa Vista 365,* ☎ *011/ 229–4574. Metrô: São Bento.*

⑩ Edifício BANESPA. This structure offers a no-frills chance for a panoramic look at the city if you can't fit tea or drinks at the top of the Edifício Itália into your Centro tour. The 36-floor BANESPA Building was constructed in 1947 and modeled after New York's Empire State Building. A radio traffic reporter squints through the smog every morning from here. ⊠ *Praça Antônio Prado,* ☎ *no phone.* ☒ *Free.* ☉ *Weekdays 9–6. Metrô: São Bento.*

❶ Edifício Copan. The architect of this serpentine apartment and office block, Oscar Niemeyer, went on to design much of Brasília, the nation's capital. The building has the clean, white, undulating curves characteristic of his work. Although many Brazilians prefer colonial architecture, all take pride in Niemeyer's international reputation. The Copan was constructed in 1950, and its 1,850 apartments house about 4,500 people. If you want to shop in the first-floor stores, be sure to do so before dark, when the area is overrun by prostitutes and transvestites. ⊠ *Av. Ipiranga at Av. Consolação,* ☎ *no phone. Metrô: Anhangabaú.*

★ ❷ Edifício Itália. To see the astounding view from atop the Itália Building, you'll have to patronize the bar or dining room of the Terraço Itália restaurant, on the 41st floor. As the restaurant is expensive (and isn't one of the city's best), afternoon tea or a drink is the quickest, least expensive option. Tea is served 3–5:30, and the bar opens at 6. ⊠ *Av. Ipiranga 336,* ☎ *011/257–6566 (restaurant). Metrô: Anhangabaú.*

⑪ Edifício Martinelli. Note the whimsical penthouse atop the Martinelli Building, the city's first skyscraper, which was built in 1929 by Italian immigrant-turned-count Giuseppe Martinelli. The rooftop is open weekdays 10:30–4. To get there, you need to get permission from the building manager on the ground floor and leave a photo ID at the front desk. Then take the elevator to the 34th floor and walk up two more flights. ⊠ *Av. São João 35,* ☎ *no phone.* ☒ *Free. Metrô: São Bento.*

❺ Igreja de São Francisco de Assis. The baroque St. Francis of Assisi Church is actually two churches with a common name, one run by Catholic clergy and the other by lay brothers. One of the city's best-preserved Portuguese colonial buildings, it was built from 1647 to 1790. ⊠ *Largo São Francisco 133,* ☎ *011/606–0081.* ☒ *Free.* ☉ *Daily 7 AM– 8 PM; lay brothers' church weekdays 7–11:30 and 1–8, weekends 7 AM– 10 AM. Metrô: Sé or Anhangabaú.*

MEMORIAL DA AMÉRICA LATINA – A group of buildings designed by Oscar Niemeyer, the Latin American Memorial includes the Pavilhão da Criatividade Popular (Popular Creativity Pavilion), which has a permanent exhibition of Latin American handicrafts, and a model showing all the countries in Latin America. The Salão de Atos Building shows the panel *Tiradentes,* about an independence hero from Minas Gerais, painted by Cândido Portinari in 1949 and installed in 1989. ⊠ *Av. Auro Soares de Moura Andrade 664,* ☎ *011/3823–9611,* WEB *www.memorial.org.br.* ☒ *Free.* ☉ *Tues.–Sun. 9–6. Metrô: Barra Funda.*

⑭ Museu de Arte Sacra. If you can't get to Bahia during your stay in Brazil, the Museum of Sacred Art is a must-see. It houses an extremely interesting collection of wooden and terra-cotta masks, jewelry, and liturgical objects that date from the 17th century to the present. Don't miss the on-site convent, founded in 1774. ⊠ *Av. Tiradentes 676,* ☎ *011/ 3326–1373.* ▦ *R$4.* ⊙ *Tues.–Fri. 11–6, Sat.–Sun. 10–7. Metrô: Luz.*

❽ **Pátio do Colégio.** São Paulo was founded by the Jesuits José de Anchieta and Manoel da Nóbrega in the College Courtyard in 1554. The church was constructed in 1896 in the same style as the chapel built by the Jesuits. ⊠ *Pátio do Colégio 84,* ☎ *011/3105–6899.* ⊙ *Church: Mon.–Sat. 8:15 AM–midnight, Sun. mass at 10 AM. Metrô: Sé.*

❻ **Pinacoteca do Estado.** The building that houses the State Art Gallery was constructed in 1905 and renovated in 1998. In the permanent collection you can see the work of such famous Brazilian artists as Tarsila do Amaral (whose work consists of colorful, somewhat abstract portraits), Anita Malfatti (a painter influenced by fauvism and German expressionism), Cândido Portinari (whose oil paintings have social and historical themes), Emiliano Di Cavalcanti (a multimedia artist whose illustrations, oil paintings, and engravings are influenced by cubism and contain Afro-Brazilian and urban themes), and Lasar Segall (an expressionist painter). ⊠ *Praça da Luz 2,* ☎ *011/229–9844,* ▥ *www. uol.com.br/pinasp.* ▦ *R$5.* ⊙ *Tues.–Sun. 10–6. Metrô: Luz.*

❸ **Praça da República.** Republic Square is the site of a huge Sunday street fair with arts and crafts, semiprecious stones, food, and often live music. Some artisans display their work all week long, so it's worth a peek anytime. *Metrô: República.*

❻ **Praça da Sé.** Two major metrô lines cross under the large, busy Cathedral Square. Migrants from Brazil's poor northeast often gather to enjoy their music and to sell and buy such regional items as medicinal herbs. It's also the central hangout for street children, and the focus of periodic (and controversial) police sweeps to get them off the street. The square, and most of the historic area and financial district to its north, have been set aside for pedestrians, official vehicles, and public transportation only.

❼ **Solar da Marquesa de Santos.** This 18th-century manor house was bought by Marquesa de Santos in 1843. It now contains a museum that hosts temporary exhibitions. ⊠ *Rua Roberto Simonsen 136,* ☎ *011/3106–2218.* ▦ *Free.* ⊙ *Tues.–Sun. 9–5. Metrô: Sé.*

❹ **Teatro Municipal.** Inspired by the Paris Opéra, the Municipal Theater was built between 1903 and 1911 with art nouveau elements. *Hamlet* was the first play presented, and the house went on to host such luminaries as Isadora Duncan in 1916 and Anna Pavlova in 1919. Unfortunately, the fully restored auditorium, resplendent with gold leaf, moss-green velvet, marble, and mirrors, is open only to those attending cultural events, but sometimes you can walk in for a quick look at the vestibule. ⊠ *Praça Ramos de Azevedo,* ☎ *011/223–3022. Metrô: Anhangabaú.*

Liberdade

At the beginning of the 20th century, a group of Japanese arrived to work as contract farm laborers in São Paulo State. During the next five decades, roughly a quarter of a million of their countrymen followed, forming what is now the largest Japanese colony outside Japan. Distinguished today by a large number of college graduates and successful businesspeople, professionals, and politicians, the colony has made important contributions to Brazilian agriculture and the seafood industry. The Liberdade neighborhood, which is south of Praça da Sé behind the cathedral and whose entrance is marked by a series of red porticoes, is home to many first-, second-, and third-generation Nippo-

Brazilians. Clustered around Avenida Liberdade, you'll find shops with everything from imported bubble gum to miniature robots to Kabuki face paint. The Sunday street fair holds many surprises.

Numbers in the text correspond to numbers in the margin and on the São Paulo City map.

A Good Tour

From the **Praça Liberdade** ⑮, by the Liberdade metrô station, walk south along Rua Galvão Bueno. About six blocks from the square is the intriguing **Museu da Imigração Japonesa** ⑯.

TIMING AND PRECAUTIONS

The best time to visit Liberdade is on Sunday during the street fair, when you'll find tents that sell Asian food, crafts, and souvenirs. This tour takes about two hours—a little longer if you linger in the museum. Don't take this tour at night.

Sights to See

⑯ **Museu da Imigração Japonesa.** The Museum of Japanese Immigration has two floors of exhibits about Nippo-Brazilian culture and farm life and Japanese contributions to Brazilian horticulture. (They're credited with introducing the persimmon, the azalea, the tangerine, and the kiwi to Brazil, among other things.) Call ahead to arrange for an English-language tour. ⊠ *Rua São Joaquim 381,* ☎ *011/279-5465.* ✉ *R$3.* ☺ *Tues.–Sun. 1:30–5:30. Metrô: São Joaquim.*

⑮ **Praça Liberdade.** On Sunday morning Liberdade hosts a sprawling Asian food and crafts fair, where the free and easy Brazilian ethnic mix is in plain view; you may see, for example, Afro-Brazilians dressed in colorful kimonos hawking grilled shrimp on a stick. Liberdade also hosts several ethnic celebrations, such as April's Hanamatsuri, commemorating the birth of the Buddha. *Metrô: Liberdade.*

Avenida Paulista and Bixiga

Money once poured into and out of the coffee barons' mansions that lined Avenida Paulista, making it, in a sense, the financial hub. And so it is today, though instead of mansions you'll find many major banks. Like the barons before them, many of these financial institutions generously support the arts. Numerous places have changing exhibitions—often free—in the Paulista neighborhood. Nearby Bixiga, São Paulo's Little Italy, is full of restaurants.

A Good Tour

Begin your tour at the **Museu de Arte de São Paulo (MASP)** ⑰, which has Brazil's best collection of fine art. Across the street is **Parque Trianon** ⑱, where many businesspeople eat lunch. Leaving the park, veer right onto Avenida Paulista and head for the **Centro Cultural FIESP** ⑲, which frequently has art and theatrical presentations. Farther down Paulista is the **Espaço Cultural Citibank** ⑳, a gallery with temporary exhibitions. Continue a few more blocks along Paulista to the **Instituto Cultural Itaú** ㉑, a great place to see contemporary Brazilian art. In the next block is the **Casa das Rosas** ㉒, with yet another noteworthy gallery. From here you can hop a bus or a taxi to the **Museu Memória do Bixiga** ㉓, with its displays on Italian immigration.

TIMING AND PRECAUTIONS

This tour takes about five hours, including a visit to MASP and the Museu do Bixiga. Busy, well-lighted Avenida Paulista may well be the safest place in city. Even so, stay alert and hold onto your bags, particularly in Parque Trianon.

São Paulo City

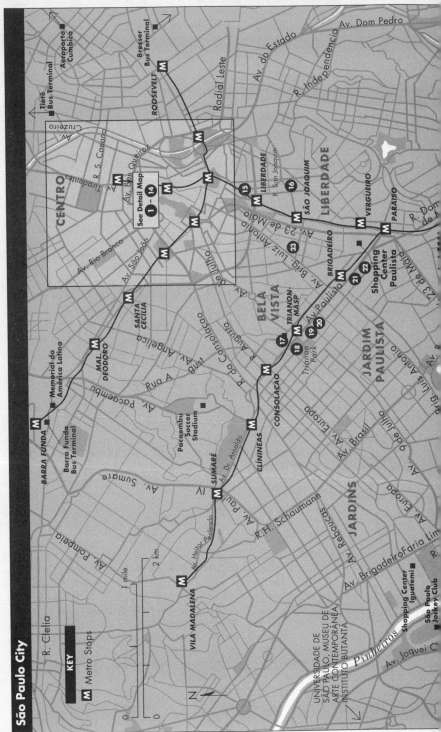

KEY

M Metro Stops

See Detail Map 1 – 14

CENTRO

BELA VISTA

LIBERDADE

JARDIM PAULISTA

JARDINS

VILA MADALENA

BARRA FUNDA

MAL. DEODORO

SANTA CECILIA

SUMARÉ

CLINICAS

CONSOLAÇÃO

TRIANON-MASP

BRIGADEIRO

SÃO JOAQUIM

VERGUEIRO

PARAÍSO

Tietê Bus Terminal

Aeroporto Cumbica

Bresser Bus Terminal

Barra Funda Bus Terminal

Memorial da América Latina

Pacaembu Soccer Stadium

Trianon Park

Shopping Center Paulista

Shopping Center Iguatemi

São Paulo Jockey Club

UNIVERSIDADE DE SÃO PAULO, MUSEU DE ARTE CONTEMPORÂNEA, INSTITUTO BUTANTÃ

Av. Dom Pedro

Av. do Estado

R. Independência

Radial Leste

ROOSEVELT

Av. Cruzeiro

R. S. Caetano

Av. Seb. Queiroz

Av. Tiradentes

Av. Rio Branco

Av. São João

Av. 9 de Julho

Av. 23 de Maio

Av. Brig. Luiz Antonio

R. San Joaquim

R. Dom de M

Av. Paulista

Av. Angélica

R. da Consolação

R. Augusta

Rua A

Av. Pacaembu

Av. Sumaré

Av. Dr. Arnaldo

Av. Heitor Penteado

Av. Pompéia

R.H. Schaumann

Av. Rebouças

Av. Brasil

Av. Europa

Av. Brigadeiro Faria Lim

Av. 9 de Julho

Av. Joaquei C

Pinheiros

R. Clelia

1 mile

2 km

N

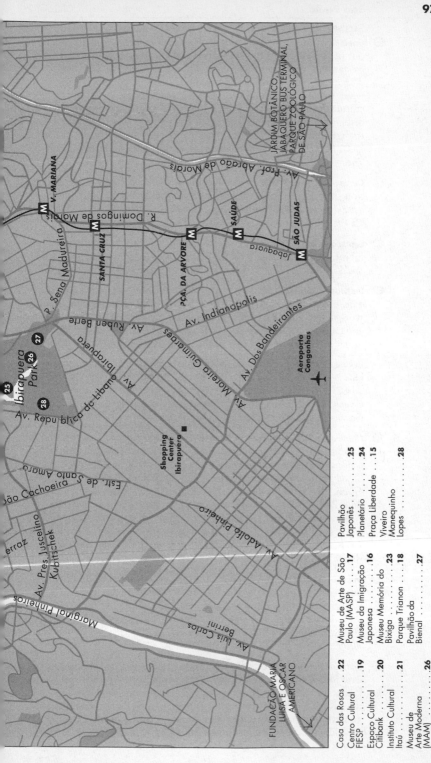

Casa das Rosas . . . **22**
Centro Cultural
FIESP **19**
Espaço Cultural
Citibank **20**
Instituto Cultural
Itaú **21**
Museu de
Arte Moderna
(MAM) **26**

Museu de Arte de São
Paulo (MASP) **17**
Museu da Imigração
Japonesa **16**
Museu Memória do
Bixiga **23**
Parque Trianon . . . **18**
Pavilhão da
Bienal **27**

Pavilhão
Japonês **25**
Planetário **24**
Praça Liberdade . . .**15**
Viveiro
Manequinho
Lopes **28**

Sights to See

㉒ Casa das Rosas. The House of the Roses, a French-style mansion, seems out of place next to the skyscrapers of Paulista. It was built in 1935 by famous paulistano architect Ramos de Azevedo for one of his daughters. The building was home to the same family until 1986, when it was made an official municipal landmark. It was opened as a cultural center—with changing fine-arts exhibitions and multimedia displays by up-and-coming artists—in 1991, and it's one of the avenue's few remaining early 20th-century buildings. ⊠ *Av. Paulista 37, Paraíso,* ☎ *011/251–5271,* ⟨WEB⟩ *www.dialdata.com.br/casadasrosas.* ▣ *Free.* ⊙ *Tues.–Sun. 2–8. Metrô: Brigadeiro.*

⑲ Centro Cultural FIESP. The cultural center of São Paulo State's Federation of Industry has a theater, a library of art books, and temporary art exhibits. ⊠ *Av. Paulista 1313, Jardim Paulista,* ☎ *011/253–5877.* ▣ *Free.* ⊙ *Tues.–Sun. 9–7. Metrô: Trianon.*

⑳ Espaço Cultural Citibank. Citibank's cultural space hosts temporary exhibitions of Brazilian art. ⊠ *Av. Paulista 1111, Jardim Paulista,* ☎ *011/5576–2744.* ▣ *Free.* ⊙ *Weekdays 9–7, weekends 10–5. Metrô: Trianon.*

㉑ Instituto Cultural Itaú. Maintained by Itaú, one of Brazil's largest private banks, this cultural institute has art shows as well as lectures, workshops, and films. Its library specializes in works on Brazilian art and culture. ⊠ *Av. Paulista 149, Paraíso,* ☎ *011/238–1700,* ⟨WEB⟩ *www.itaucultural.org.br.* ▣ *Free.* ⊙ *Tues.–Sun. 10–7. Metrô: Brigadeiro.*

NEED A
BREAK?   Before heading to the Museu Memória do Bixiga, try a *baurú* at **Ponto Chic** (⊠ Praça Osvaldo Cruz 26, Bixiga, ☎ 011/289–1480)—a block east of Instituto Cultural Itaú, across Avenida Paulista. The restaurant claims to have invented this sandwich, which is made with roast beef, tomato, cucumber, and steam-heated mozzarella.

★ ⑰ Museu de Arte de São Paulo (MASP). A striking low-rise elevated on two massive concrete pillars 77 m (256 ft) apart, the São Paulo Museum of Art contains the city's premier collection of fine arts. Highlights include dazzling works by Hieronymous Bosch, Vincent van Gogh, Pierre-Auguste Renoir, and Edgar Degas. Lasar Segall and Cândido Portinari are two of the many Brazilian artists represented in the collection. The huge open area beneath the museum is often used for cultural events and is the site of a Sunday antiques fair. ⊠ *Av. Paulista 1578, Bela Vista,* ☎ *011/251–5644,* ⟨WEB⟩ *www2.uol.com.br/masp/.* ▣ *R$10.* ⊙ *Tues.–Sun. 11–6. Metrô: Trianon.*

㉓ Museu Memória do Bixiga. This museum, established in 1980, contains objects that belonged to Italian immigrants who lived in the Bixiga neighborhood. On weekends you can extend your tour to include the **Feira do Bixiga,** at Praça Dom Orione, where handicrafts, antiques, and furniture are sold. ⊠ *Rua dos Ingleses 118, Bixiga,* ☎ *011/285–5009.* ▣ *Free.* ⊙ *Wed.–Sun. 2–5.*

⑱ Parque Trianon. The park was originally created in 1892 as a showcase for local vegetation. In 1968, Roberto Burle Marx (the Brazilian landscaper famed for Rio's mosaic-tile beachfront sidewalks) renovated it and incorporated new trees. You can escape the noise of the street and admire the flora while seated on one of the benches sculpted to look like chairs. ⊠ *Rua Peixoto Gomide 949, Jardim Paulista,* ☎ *011/289–2160.* ▣ *Free.* ⊙ *Daily 6–6. Metrô: Trianon.*

BRAZIL'S MELTING POT

SÃO PAULO IS A MICROCOSM of Brazil's melting pot. To be Brazilian means to share a heritage that's Native American, Portuguese, and African. The mix is further seasoned with offspring of settlers from other parts of Europe, from Asia, or from the Middle East.

Most of the indigenous peoples encountered by the first Portuguese were members of the Tupi-Guarani language group (2 of an estimated 180 languages spoken by roughly 200 tribes) and were nomadic hunter-gatherers who lived along the coast. Many Brazilian words and place names, such as Copacabana, are are words from those languages. Indeed, the country's name comes from *paubrasil*, the indigenous term for the brazilwood tree (it was used to make a coveted red dye and was the nation's first major export).

The Africans brought to Brazil as slaves were primarily Yoruban (from what are today Liberia, Nigeria, Benin, and parts of Sudan) and Bantu (from Angola, Mozambique, and Zaire). These groups blended their spiritualistic and animist beliefs with the Roman Catholic traditions of their Portuguese masters. Cults arose that likened African gods and goddesses to Catholic saints, creating a completely new pantheon of *orixás* (deities); some groups adopted beliefs of the indigenous peoples as well. Although 70% of Brazilians are Roman Catholic, many are also members of such thriving cults as Candomblé (from Salvador), Macumba (from Rio de Janeiro), and Xangô (from Recife),

to name a few. Those who aren't members are at least respectful of the cults and their traditions (politicians have even been known to court cult leaders). The nation's food and music were also strongly influenced by the Afro-Brazilians. And "samba" is an African word as well as an African rhythm.

When Napoléon invaded Portugal, King João VI and the royal family fled to Brazil. The marriage of his son, Dom Pedro, to the Austrian archduchess Leopoldina saw the advent of immigration by German-speaking colonists. Many put down roots in the south, where the climate was similar to that of their homelands. Today, there are southern communities filled with Bavarian-style architecture. After the American Civil War, some U.S. Southerners moved to Brazil; like the Germans, many settled in Brazil's south, though others chose the Amazon.

When Brazil abolished slavery in 1888, the nation actively recruited European agricultural laborers—Germans, Italians, Spaniards, and Portuguese came to work the fields. They were followed by groups from Eastern Europe, Russia, and the Middle East. In 1908, 640 Japanese immigrants arrived in Brazil; by 1969, more than 200,000 of their countrymen had followed. Most settled in São Paulo and its environs, and most worked in agriculture. Today the city has the largest Japanese community outside Japan. It also has many more varieties of fruits and vegetables than it would have had if the Japanese had not been so successful.

Parque Ibirapuera

Only 15 minutes by taxi from downtown, Ibirapuera is São Paulo's answer to New York's Central Park, although it's slightly less than half the size and gets infinitely more crowded on sunny weekends. In the 1950s the land, which originally contained the municipal nurseries, was chosen as the site of a public park to commemorate the city's 400th anniversary. Oscar Niemeyer was called in to head the team of architects assigned to the project. The park was inaugurated in 1954, and some pavilions used for the opening festivities still sit amid its 395 acres. You'll also find jogging and biking paths, a lake, and rolling lawns.

A Good Walk

Enter at Gate 9 and walk around the lake to the starry sights at the **Planetário** ㉔. As you exit the planetarium, veer left to the **Pavilhão Japonês** ㉕. Then turn left and follow the path to the Marquise do Ibirapuera, a structure that connects several buildings, including the **Museu de Arte Moderna (MAM)** ㉖ and the **Pavilhão da Bienal** ㉗, which houses the park branch of the Museu de Arte Contemporânea. When you exit the compound, walk toward Gate 7 and the **Viveiro Manequinho Lopes** ㉘, with its many species of Brazilian trees.

TIMING AND PRECAUTIONS

The park deserves a whole day, though you can probably do this tour in one afternoon. Avoid the park on Sunday, when it gets really crowded, and after sundown.

Sights to See

㉖ **Museu de Arte Moderna (MAM).** The permanent collection of the Museum of Modern Art includes more than 2,600 paintings, sculptures (some in a sculpture garden out front), and drawings from the Brazilian modernist movement, which began in the 1920s, when artists were developing a new form of expression influenced by the city's rapid industrial growth. The museum also hosts temporary exhibits that feature works by new local artists and has a library with more than 20,000 books, photographs, videotapes, and CD-ROMs. In a 1982 renovation, Brazilian architect Lina Bo Bardi gave the building a wall of glass, creating a giant window that beckons you to peek at what's inside. ⊠ *Gate 10,* ☎ *011/5549–9688.* ⊠ *R$5 (free on Tues.).* ◷ *Tues., Wed., Fri. noon–6, Thurs. noon–10, weekends and holidays 10–6.*

NEED A BREAK?   The **Bar do MAM,** inside the Museu de Arte Moderna, has sandwiches, pies, soda, coffee, and tea. The comfortable chairs enable you to thoroughly rest.

㉗ **Pavilhão da Bienal.** From October through November in every even-numbered year, this pavilion hosts the Bienal (Biennial) art exhibition, which draws more than 250 artists from more than 60 countries. The first such event was held in 1951 in Parque Trianon and drew artists from 21 countries. It was moved to this Oscar Niemeyer–designed building—with its large open spaces and floors connected by circular slopes—after Ibirapuera Park's 1954 inauguration. The pavilion also houses a branch of the **Museu de Arte Contemporânea** (MAC; Museum of Contemporary Art), whose main branch is at the Universidade de São Paulo. Exhibits are created from the museum's collection of works by such European artists as Pablo Picasso, Amedeo Modigliani, Wassily Kandinsky, Joan Miró, and Henri Matisse. Look also for the works of Brazilian artists such as Anita Malfatti, Tarsila do Amaral, Cândido Portinari, and Emiliano Di Cavalcanti. ⊠ *Gate 10,* ☎ *011/5573–9932,* WEB *www.mac.usp.br.* ⊠ *Free.* ◷ *Museum: Tues.–Sun. 12–6.*

㉕ **Pavilhão Japonês.** An exact replica of the Katsura Imperial Palace in Kyoto, Japan, the Japanese Pavilion is also one of the structures built for the park's inauguration. It was designed by University of Tokyo professor Sutemi Horiguti and built in Japan. It took four months to reassemble beside the man-made lake in the midst of the Japanese-style garden. In the main building you'll find displays of samurai clothes, 11th-century sculptures, and pottery and sculpture from several dynasties. Rooms used for traditional tea ceremonies are upstairs. ⊠ *Gate 10,* ☎ *011/5573–6453.* 🎟 *R$2.* ⊙ *Weekends and holidays 10–5.*

㉔ **Planetário.** Paulistanos love the planetarium and frequently fill the 350 seats under its 48-ft-high dome. You can see a projection of the 8,900 stars and five planets (Mercury, Venus, Mars, Jupiter, and Saturn) clearly visible in the southern hemisphere. Shows last 50 minutes and always depict the night sky just as it is on the evening of your visit. Be sure to buy tickets at least 15 minutes before the session. ⊠ *Gate 10, Av. Pedro Álvares Cabral,* ☎ *011/5575–5206.* 🎟 *R$5.* ⊙ *Weekends and holidays, projections at 3:30 and 5:30.*

㉘ **Viveiro Manequinho Lopes.** The Manequinho Lopes Nursery is where most plants and trees used by the city are grown. The original was built in the 1920s; the current version was designed by Roberto Burle Marx. You'll find specimens of such Brazilian trees as *ipê, pau-jacaré,* and *pau-brasil,* the tree after which the country was named (the red dye it produced was greatly valued by the Europeans). The Bosque da Leitura (Reading Forest) has a stand that provides books and magazines (all in Portuguese) as well as chairs so people can read among the trees. ⊠ *Enter park from Av. República do Líbano,* ☎ *no phone.* ⊙ *Daily 5–5.*

Elsewhere in São Paulo

Several far-flung sights are worth a taxi ride to see. West of Centro is the **Universidade de São Paulo (USP),** which has two very interesting museums: a branch of the Museu de Arte Contemporânea and the Instituto Butantã, with its collection of creatures that slither and crawl. Head southwest of Centro to the **Fundação Maria Luisa e Oscar Americano,** a museum with a forest and garden in the residential neighborhood of Morumbi. In the Parque do Estado, southeast of Centro, are the **Jardim Botânico** and the **Parque Zoológico de São Paulo.**

Sights to See

Fundação Maria Luisa e Oscar Americano. A private wooded estate is the setting for the Maria Luisa and Oscar Americano Foundation. Exhibits feature objects from the Portuguese colonial and imperial periods as well as modern pieces. You'll find paintings, furniture, sacred art, silver, porcelain, engravings, personal possessions of the Brazilian royal family, tapestries, and sculpture. ⊠ *Av. Morumbi 3700, Morumbi,* ☎ *011/3742–0077,* 🕸 *www.fundacaooscaramericano.org.br.* 🎟 *R$5.* ⊙ *Tues.–Fri. 11–5, weekends 10–5.*

Jardim Botânico. The Botanical Gardens contain about 3,000 plants belonging to more than 340 native species. You'll also find a greenhouse with Atlantic rain-forest species, an orchid house, and a collection of aquatic plants. ⊠ *Av. Miguel Stéfano 3031, Parque do Estado,* ☎ *011/5584–6300.* 🎟 *R$2.* ⊙ *Wed.–Sun. 9–5.*

★ 🐾 **Parque Zoológico de São Paulo.** The 200-acre São Paulo Zoo has more than 3,000 animals, and many of its 410 species—such as the *mico-leão-dourado* (golden lion tamarin monkey)—are endangered. Its attractions include a lake with small islands, where monkeys live in houses on stilts, and the Casa do Sangue Frio (House of Cold Blood) with reptilian and amphibian creatures. ⊠ *Av. Miguel Stéfano 4241,*

Parque do Estado, ☎ *011/276–0811,* 🌐 *www.zoologico.com.br.* 📧
R$7. ☉ *Tues.–Sun. 9–5.*

Universidade de São Paulo. Consider taking a stroll around the grounds
of the country's largest university (founded in 1934) just to soak in
the atmosphere of a Brazilian campus. Art lovers can also visit the university branch of the **Museu de Arte Contemporânea,** which consists
of a main building and an annex, to see works by world-renowned contemporary European and Brazilian artists. ✉ *Main bldg.: Rua da Re-
itoria 109, Cidade Universitária,* ☎ *011/3818–3538,* 🌐 *www.usp.br.*
📧 *Free.* ☉ *Tues.–Wed. and Fri. 10–7, Thurs. 11–8, weekends 10–4.*

In 1888 a Brazilian scientist, with the aid of the state government, turned
a farmhouse into a center for the production of snake serum. Today
the **Instituto Butantã** has more than 70,000 snakes, spiders, scorpions,
and lizards. It still extracts venom and processes it into serum that's
made available to victims of poisonous bites throughout Latin America. Unfortunately, the institute has suffered from underfunding; it's
somewhat run-down, and its exhibits aren't as accessible to children
as they could be. ✉ *Av. Vital Brasil 1500, Cidade Universitária,* ☎ *011/
3813–7222.* 📧 *R$1.5.* ☉ *Tues.–Sun. 9–4:30.*

Beaches

São Paulo rests on a plateau 72 km (46 mi) inland. If you can avoid
traffic, getaways are fairly quick on the parallel Imigrantes (BR 160)
or Anchieta (BR 150) highways, each of which becomes one-way on
weekends and holidays. Although the port of Santos (near the Cubatão
Industrial Park) has *praias* (beaches) in and around it, the cleanest and
best beaches are along what is known as the North Shore. Mountains
and bits of Atlantic rain forest hug numerous small, sandy coves. On
weekdays when school is in session, the beaches are gloriously deserted.

Buses run along the coast from São Paulo's Jabaquara terminal, near
the Congonhas Airport, and there are once-daily trains from the Estação da Luz to Santos and the sands along the North Shore. Beaches
often don't have bathrooms or phones right on the sands, nor do they
have beach umbrellas or chairs for rent. They generally do have restaurants nearby, however, or at least vendors selling sandwiches, soft
drinks, and beer.

Barra do Sahy. Families with young children favor this small, quiet beach
165 km (102 mi) north of the city on the Rio–Santos Highway. Its narrow strip of sand (with a bay and a river on one side and rocks on the
other) is steep but smooth, and the water is clean and very calm.
Kayakers paddle about and divers are drawn to the nearby Ilha das
Couves. Area restaurants serve only basic fish dishes with rice and salad.
Note that Barra do Sahy's entrance is atop a slope and appears suddenly—be on the lookout.

Camburi. The young and the restless flock here to sunbathe, surf, and
party. At the center of the beach is a cluster of cafés, ice-cream shops,
bars, and the Tiê restaurant. The service may be slow, but Tiê's menu
is extensive, and the open-air setup is divine. Another good bet is Bom
Dia Vietnã, with its delicious pizzas, sandwiches, sushi, salads, and banana pie. Camburi is just north of Barra do Sahy. If you're coming from
the south, use the second entrance; although it's unpaved, it's in better shape than the first entrance.

Maresias. Some of the North Shore's most beautiful houses line the
Rio–Santos road (SP 055) on the approach to Maresias. The beach itself is also nice, with its 4-km (2-mi) stretch of white sand and its clean,

green waters that are good swimming and surfing. Maresias is popular with a young crowd.

Ubatuba. Many of the more than 30 beaches around Ubatuba are truly beautiful enough to merit the 229-km (148-mi) drive north along the Carvalho Pinto and Oswaldo Cruz highways. For isolation and peace, try Prumirim Beach, which can only be reached by boat; for a little more action try the centrally located Praia Grande, with its many kiosks. Ubatuba itself has a very active nightlife. In nearby Itaguá you'll find several gift shops, a branch of the Projeto Tartarugas Marinhas (Marine Turtles Project), and a large aquarium.

DINING

São Paulo's social life centers on dining out, and there are a great many establishments from which to choose (new ones seem to open as often as the sun rises), particularly in the Jardins district. You'll find German, Japanese, Spanish, Italian, and Portuguese restaurants as well as top-quality French and Indian spots. There are innumerable *churrascarias* (places that serve a seemingly endless stream of barbecued meat), which are beloved by paulistanos. As in other Brazilian cities, many restaurants serve feijoada on Wednesday and Saturday; top restaurants do it up in fancy buffets.

São Paulo restaurants frequently change their credit-card policies, sometimes adding a surcharge for their use or not accepting them at all. Though most places don't generally require jacket and tie, people tend to dress up; establishments in the $$ to $$$$ categories expect you to look neat and elegant. You might feel uncomfortable in jeans.

For price categories, *see* the chart *under* Dining *in* Smart Travel Tips A to Z.

Brazilian

$$$ $$$$ ✕ **Bargaço.** The original Bargaço has long been considered the best Bahian restaurant in Salvador. If you can't make it to the northeast, be sure to have a meal in the São Paulo branch. Seafood is the calling card. ⊠ *Rua Oscar Freire 1189, Cerqueira César,* ☎ *011/3085–5058. AE, DC, MC, V. Metrô: Consolação.*

$$$ ✕ **Baby Beef Rubaiyat.** Galician Belarmino Iglesias was once an employee at this restaurant; today he owns it, and he and his son run it. The meat they serve is from their ranch in Mato Grosso do Sul State. The buffet features charcoal-grilled fare—from baby boar (on request at least two hours in advance) and steak to chicken and salmon—and a salad bar with all sorts of options. Wednesday and Saturday see a feijoada; on Friday the emphasis is on seafood. ⊠ *Alameda Santos 86, Paraíso,* ☎ *011/289–6366. V. No dinner Sun. Metrô: Paraíso.*

$$$ ✕ **Dona Lucinha.** Mineiro dishes—from the Minas Gerais State—are the specialties at this modest eatery with plain wooden tables. The classic cuisine is served as a buffet only: more than 50 stone pots hold dishes like *feijão tropeiro* (beans with manioc flour). Save room for a dessert of ambrosia. ⊠ *Av. Chibaras 399, Moema,* ☎ *011/5549–2050. AE, DC, MC, V.* ⊠ *Rua Bela Cintra 2325, Jardins,* ☎ *011/3062–1973. AE, DC, MC, V.*

$$–$$$$ ✕ **Esplanada Grill.** The beautiful people hang out in the bar of this highly
★ regarded churrascaria. The thinly sliced *picanha* steak (similar to rump steak) is excellent; it goes well with a house salad (hearts of palm and shredded, fried potatoes), onion rings, and creamed spinach. The restaurant's rendition of the traditional *pão de queijo* (cheese bread) is just right. ⊠ *Rua Haddock Lobo 1682, Jardins,* ☎ *011/3081–3199. V.*

$$–$$$ ✕ **Consulado Mineiro.** During and after the Saturday crafts and antiques fair in Praça Benedito Calixto, it may take an hour to get a table at this homey restaurant set in a house. Among the traditional mineiro dishes are the *mandioca com carne de sol* (cassava with salted meat) appetizer and the *tutu* (pork loin with beans, pasta, cabbage, and rice) entrée. ⊠ *Rua Praça Benedito Calixto 74, Pinheiros,* ☎ *011/3064–3882. AE, DC, MC, V. Closed Mon.*

$–$$ ✕ **Sujinho–Bisteca d'Ouro.** The modest Sujinho serves churrasco without any frills. It's the perfect place for those who simply want to eat an honest, gorgeous piece of meat. ⊠ *Rua da Consolação 2078, Cerqueira César,* ☎ *011/231–5207. No credit cards. Metrô: Consolação.*

¢–$ ✕ **Frevo.** Paulistanos of all ilks and ages flock to this Jardins luncheonette for its beirute sandwiches, draft beer, and fruit juices in flavors such as *acerola* (Antilles cherry), passion fruit, and papaya. ⊠ *Rua Oscar Freire 603, Jardins,* ☎ *011/3082–3434. No credit cards.*

Continental

$$–$$$$ ✕ **Paddock.** Both locations of this restaurant are considered ideal spots for relaxed business lunches; neither is open on weekends. Men and women of affairs eat and chat in comfortable armchairs. The Continental cuisine is prepared with finesse; try the lamb with mint sauce or the poached haddock. ⊠ *Av. São Luís 258, Centro,* ☎ *011/ 257–4768. AE, DC, MC, V. Closed weekends. Metrô: Anhangabaú or República.* ⊠ *Av. Brigadeiro Faria Lima 1912, Loja 110, Jardim Paulistano,* ☎ *011/3814–3582. AE, DC, MC, V. Closed weekends.*

$–$$$$ ✕ **Cantaloup.** That paulistanos take food seriously has not been lost on the folks at Cantaloup. The two dining areas are in a converted warehouse. Oversize photos decorate the walls of the slightly formal room, and a fountain and plants make the second area feel more casual. Try the filet mignon with risotto or the St. Peter's fillet with almonds and spinach. Save room for the papaya ice cream with mango soup or the mango ice cream with papaya soup. ⊠ *Rua Manoel Guedes 474, Itaim Bibi,* ☎ *011/3846–6445. AE, DC, MC, V.*

Eclectic

$$$–$$$$ ✕ **La Tambouille.** This Italo-French restaurant with a partially enclosed garden isn't just a place to be seen; many believe it also has the best food in town. Among chef André Fernandes's recommended dishes are the linguini with fresh mussels and prawn sauce and the filet mignon *rosini* (served with foie gras and risotto with saffron). ⊠ *Av. Nove de Julho 5925, Jardim Europa,* ☎ *011/3079–6276. AE, DC, MC, V.*

$$–$$$ ✕ **Bar des Arts.** A great place for lunch or drinks (it's a favorite with businesspeople), the Bar des Arts is set in a charming arcade near a flower shop, a wine shop, and a fountain. You'll find both a buffet and à la carte options at lunch. ⊠ *Rua Pedro Humberto 9, at Rua Horacio Lafer, Itaim Bibi,* ☎ *011/3849–7828. AE, DC, MC, V. Closed Mon.*

$–$$$ ✕ **Mestiço.** Tribal masks peer down at you from the walls of the large,
★   modern dining room. Consider the Thai *huan-hin* (chicken with shiitake mushrooms in ginger sauce and rice) followed by a dessert of lemon ice cream with *baba de moça* (a syrup made with egg whites and sugar). ⊠ *Rua Fernando de Albuquerque 277, Consolação,* ☎ *011/ 256–3165. AE, DC, MC, V. Metrô: Consolação.*

¢–$$ ✕ **Spot.** This place, the closest thing to a chic diner that you'll find, is just one door up from MASP. The salads and the pasta dishes are good bets; come early, though, as it gets crowded after 10 PM. ⊠ *Alameda Rocha Azevedo 72, Cerqueira César,* ☎ *011/283–0946. AE, DC, MC, V. Metrô: Consolação.*

¢–$ ✕ **Milk & Mellow.** Before or after a night of clubbing, stop for the great sandwiches, hamburgers, and milk shakes in a relaxed atmosphere. It's open weekdays until 4 AM and weekends until 6 AM. ⊠ *Av. Cidade Jardim 1085, Itaim Bibi,* ☎ *011/3849–8916. MC, V.*

French

$$$$ ✕ **Le Coq Hardy.** This upscale restaurant has two chefs: one is a veteran of the top French kitchens in Brazil, and the other spent many years cooking in France. The grilled foie gras and mango, the escargots with mushrooms in an anise-and-wine sauce, and the roast duck are all highly recommended. ⊠ *Rua Jerônimo da Veiga 461, Itaim Bibi,* ☎ *011/3079–3344. AE, DC, MC, V. Closed Sun.*

$$–$$$$ ✕ **Bistrô Jaú.** The name of this place has recently changed (formerly Laurent) but not much else has. Chef Laurent Suadeau, famous for his use of Brazilian ingredients to create French nouvelle cuisine, runs the kitchen. Businesspeople from Avenida Paulista appreciate the fine decor and and the superb yet inexpensive (compared with dinner) lunch menu. ⊠ *Alameda Jaú 1606, Jardins,* ☎ *011/3085–5573. AE, DC, MC, V.*

$$–$$$$ ✕ **La Casserole.** Facing a little Centro flower market, this charming bistro has been around for generations. Surrounded by wood-paneled walls decorated with eclectic posters, you can dine on such delights as *gigot d'agneau aux soissons* (roast leg of lamb in its own juices, served with white beans) and cherry strudel. ⊠ *Largo do Arouche 346, Centro,* ☎ *011/220–6283. AE, DC, MC, V. Closed Mon. No lunch Sat.*

$$–$$$$ ✕ **Freddy.** You'll leave behind the grunge and noise of the streets when you walk through the doors of this long-lived eatery with the feel of an upscale Parisian bistro. Try the duck with Madeira sauce and apple purée, the pheasant with herb sauce, or the hearty cassoulet (white beans, lamb, duck, and garlic sausage). ⊠ *Praça Dom Gastão Liberal Pinto 111, Itaim Bibi,* ☎ *011/3849–0977. AE, DC, MC, V. No dinner Sun., no lunch Sat.*

$
★ ✕ **La Tartine.** This small restaurant has movie posters on its walls and simple but comfortable furniture. The menu changes daily; a favorite is the classic coq au vin. ⊠ *Rua Fernando de Albuquerque 267, Consolação,* ☎ *011/259–2090. V. Closed Sun.–Mon. Metrô: Consolação.*

Indian

$$–$$$$ ✕ **Ganesh.** Many consider this the best Indian eatery in town. The traditional menu includes curries and *tandoori* dishes. The decor is all Indian artwork and tapestries. ⊠ *Morumbi Shopping Center, Av. Roque Petroni Jr. 1089, Morumbi,* ☎ *011/5181–4748. AE, DC, MC, V.*

Italian

$$$–$$$$ ✕ **Fasano.** A family-owned northern Italian classic, this restaurant is as famous for its superior cuisine as for its exorbitant prices. The new chef, Salvatore Loi, has added to the menu dishes like seafood ravioli with a white wine sauce. Despite the cost, the luxe decor—marble, mahogany, and mirrors—has seen better days. ⊠ *Rua Haddock Lobo 1644, Jardins,* ☎ *011/3062–4000. AE, DC, MC, V. Closed Sun. No lunch.*

$$–$$$$ ✕ **Ca' D'Oro.** This is a longtime northern Italian favorite among Brazilian bigwigs, many of whom have their own tables in the Old World–style dining room. Quail, osso buco, and veal and raisin ravioli are winners, but the specialty is the Piedmontese *gran bollito misto,* steamed meats and vegetables accompanied by three sauces and served from a cart. ⊠ *Grande Hotel Ca' D'Oro, Rua Augusta 129, Bela Vista,* ☎ *011/236–4300. AE, DC, MC, V. Metrô: Anhangabaú.*

Dining

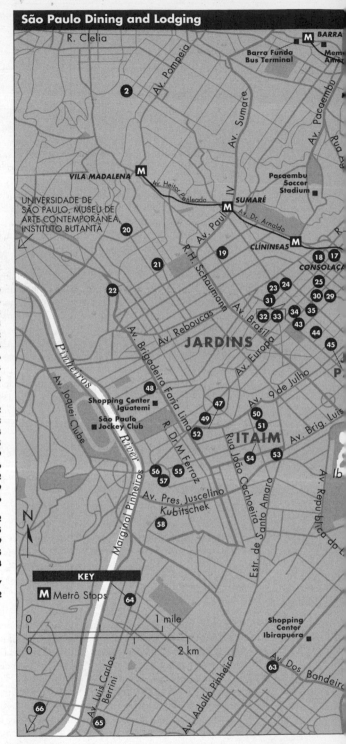

São Paulo Dining and Lodging

$$-$$$$ ✗ **Famiglia Mancini.** A huge provolone cheese is the first thing you see
★   at this warm, cheerful restaurant. An incredible buffet with cheeses,
       olives, sausages, and much more is the perfect place to find a tasty ap-
       petizer. The menu has many terrific pasta options, such as the cannel-
       loni with palm hearts and a four-cheese sauce. ⊠ *Rua Avanhandava
       81, Centro,* ☎ *011/256–4320. AE, DC, MC, V. Metrô: Anhangabaú.*

$$-$$$$ ✗ **Lellis Trattoria.** Photos of famous patrons (mostly Brazilian actors)
       hang on the walls, and the doors and bar are made of metal, giving
       this typical Italian cantina a sophisticated twist. Salmon fillet *marinatta*
       (in white sauce with potatoes, raisins, and rice) is the best choice on
       the menu. ⊠ *Rua Bela Cintra 1849, Jardim Paulista,* ☎ *011/3064–
       2727. AE, DC, MC, V.*

$$-$$$$ ✗ **La Vecchia Cucina.** Chef Sergio Arno changed the face of the city's
       Italian restaurants with his *nuova cucina,* exemplified by such dishes
       as frogs'-legs risotto and duck ravioli with watercress sauce. Well-to-
       do patrons feast either in the ocher-color dining room decorated with
       Italian engravings and fresh flowers or in the glassed-in garden gazebo.
       ⊠ *Rua Pedroso Alvarenga 1088, Itaim Bibi,* ☎ *011/3167–2822. AE,
       DC, MC, V. No dinner Sun., no lunch Sat.*

$-$$$$ ✗ **Gigetto.** The walls are adorned with theater posters, a tribute to the
       actors who dine here after performing. The modest decor is offset by
       the elaborate menu's more than 200 delicious options. Try the cappelletti
       à romanesca (with chopped ham, peas, mushrooms, and white cream
       sauce). ⊠ *Rua Avanhandava 63, Centro,* ☎ *011/256–9804. AE, DC,
       MC, V. Metrô: Anhangabaú.*

$-$$$ ✗ **Roperto.** Plastic flowers adorn the walls at this typical Bixiga cantina.
       You won't be alone if you order the traditional and ever-popular fusilli
       ao sugo (with tomato sauce). ⊠ *Rua 13 de Maio 634, Bixiga,* ☎ *011/
       288–2573. DC, MC, V.*

$-$$$ ✗ **Santo Colomba.** This Italian restaurant near the Paulista hotels isn't
       inexpensive, but some say that for the money you won't find better
       food in the city. It was originally built in Rio de Janeiro's Jóque Clube
       (Jockey Club) before being brought lock, stock, and barrel (or rather
       wooden walls, French tiles, and carved wooden bar) to its current lo-
       cation. You can feast on pasta with shrimp, squid, tomato, and garlic
       while listening to live piano music. ⊠ *Alameda Lorena 1165, Jardins,*
       ☎ *011/3061–3588. AE, DC, MC.*

$-$$ ✗ **Jardim di Napoli.** Just about everywhere you look in this restaurant
       you'll see the white, green, and red of the Italian flag. People come for
       the unmatchable *polpettone alla parmigiana,* a huge meatball with moz-
       zarella and tomato sauce. There are also many other meat dishes,
       pasta selections, and pizza. ⊠ *Rua Doutor Martinico Prado 463,
       Higienópolis,* ☎ *011/3666–3022. No credit cards.*

$ ✗ **Ritz.** An animated crowd chatters as contemporary pop music plays
       in the background. Although each day sees a different special, one of
       the most popular dishes is the *bife à milanesa* (a breaded beef cutlet)
       with creamed spinach and french fries. ⊠ *Alameda Franca 1088,
       Cerqueira César,* ☎ *011/3088–6808. AE, V. Metrô: Consolação.*

$ ✗ **Mamma Mia.** This buffet eatery is known for its grilled chicken, but
       you can also have salad and pasta here for R$15. ⊠ *Av. Moema 41,
       Moema,* ☎ *011/5051–5100. AE, DC, MC, V.*

Japanese

$$$-$$$$ ✗ **Nagayama.** Low-key, trustworthy, and well loved, both Nagayama
       locations consistently serve excellent sushi and sashimi. The chefs like
       to experiment: the California *uramaki* Philadelphia has rice, cream cheese,
       grilled salmon, roe, cucumber, and spring onions rolled together. ⊠
       Rua Bandeira Paulista 369, Itaim Bibi, ☎ *011/3079–7553. AE, DC,*

MC. ⊠ *Rua da Consolação 3397, Cerqueira César,* ☎ *011/3064–0110.
AE, DC, MC.*

$$ ✕ **Komazushi.** Real sushi connoisseurs will appreciate Komazushi.
Although master chef Takatomo Hachinohe died in 1998, Jun Sakamoto,
the sushiman in charge, maintains the high standards set by his pre-
decessor. The seats at the bar are reserved for customers known to order
expensive options. ⊠ *Rua São Carlos do Pinhal 241, Bela Vista,* ☎
011/287–1820. No credit cards. Closed Mon. Metrô: Trianon.

$–$$$$ ✕ **Nakombi.** A *Kombi* (Volkswagen van) in the middle of the dining
room acts as a balcony where chefs prepare sushi. In this eclectic en-
vironment, tables are surrounded by a small artificial river crowded
with fish. The menu includes a good variety of dishes. Try the salmon
fillet with *shimeji* mushrooms. ⊠ *Rua Pequetita 170, Vila Olímpia,*
☎ *011/3845–9911. AE, DC, MC, V.*

Lebanese

$$–$$$$ ✕ **Arábia.** For more than 10 years, Arábia has been serving traditional
Lebanese cuisine in a beautiful, high-ceiling location. Simple dishes such
as hummus and stuffed grape leaves are executed with aplomb. The
lamb melts in your mouth with astonishing speed. The "executive" lunch
includes one cold dish, one meat dish, a drink, and dessert—all at a
(relatively) reasonable price. Don't miss the rose syrup for dessert; it
comes over a pistachio delight that may leave you in tears. ⊠ *Rua Haddock Lobo 1397, Jardins,* ☎ *011/3061–2203,* WEB *www.arabia.com.br.
AE, DC, MC.*

$ ✕ **Almanara.** Part of a chain of Lebanese semi-fast-food outlets, Al-
★ manara is perfect for a quick lunch of hummus, tabbouleh, grilled
chicken, and rice. There's also a full-blown restaurant on the premises
that serves Lebanese specialties *rodízio* style (you get a taste of everything until you can ingest no more). ⊠ *Rua Oscar Freire 523, Jardins,*
☎ *011/3085–6916. AE, DC, MC, V.*

Pan-Asian

$$–$$$ ✕ **Sutra.** A coconut tree grows in the middle of this cozy bar–restau-
rant, a huge map of Thailand covers one wall, and sofas with pillows
provide a comfy place to relax. The chic, creative mix of Asian cuisines
includes Vietnamese, Thai, and Japanese. A recommended dish is
kaeng kung (prawns with broccoli and other vegetables in a curry-and-
coconut-milk sauce). To spice up your love life, you can choose from
aphrodisiac drinks with names inspired by the Kama Sutra (tabletop
cards even have illustrations). The "bamboo splitting," for example,
is made of Absolut, tequila, Cointreau, lemon juice, and Coca Cola.
⊠ *Rua Salvador Cardoso 20, Itaim Bibi,* ☎ *011/3849–4758. DC, MC,
V. Closed Sun.–Mon. No lunch.*

$–$$$ ✕ **Oriental Café.** High ceilings and tile floors convey a sense of space,
while candles flickering on tables keep things intimate. With such so-
phisticated dishes as shark-fin soup, this is considered the best restau-
rant of its kind. You'll also find less exotic dishes such as marinated
chicken thighs. ⊠ *Rua José Maria Lisboa 1000, Jardim Paulista,* ☎
011/3060–9495. AE, DC, MC, V. Closed Mon. No lunch Tues.– Sat.

Pizza

$–$$ ✕ **Galpão.** Owned by an architect, this pizzeria has such interesting
★ decor details as lights that shine from behind bottle bottoms embed-
ded in exposed brick walls. Fast service is also a hallmark. The best
menu choice is the arugula, sun-dried tomatoes, and mozzarella pizza.

✉ *Rua Doutor Augusto de Miranda 1156, Pompéia,* ☎ *011/3672–4767. DC, MC, V. Closed Mon.*

$–$$ ✗ **Oficina de Pizzas.** Both branches of this restaurant look like something designed by the Spanish artist Gaudí, but the pizzas couldn't be more Italian and straightforward. Try a pie with mozzarella and toasted garlic. ✉ *Rua Purpurina 517, Vila Madalena,* ☎ *011/3816–3749. DC, MC, V.* ✉ *Rua Inácio Pereira da Rocha 15, Vila Madalena,* ☎ *011/3813–8389. DC, MC, V.*

$–$$ ✗ **Piola.** Part of a chain started in Italy, this restaurant serves good pasta dishes as well as pizza. It's frequented by young people who seem to match the trendy decoration perfectly. ✉ *Rua Oscar Freire 512, Jardins,* ☎ *011/3064–6570,* WEB *www.piola.com.br. AE, DC, MC, V.*

$–$$ ✗ **Pizzaria Camelo.** Though it's neither fancy nor beautiful, its wide variety of thin-crust pies served has kept paulistanos enthralled for ages. The *chopp* (draft beer) is great, too. Avoid Sunday night, unless you want to wait an hour for a table. ✉ *Rua Pamplona 1873, Cerqueira César,* ☎ *011/3887–8764. DC, MC, V.*

$–$$ ✗ **Speranza.** One of the most traditional pizzerias, this restaurant is famous for its margherita pie. The crunchy *pão de linguiça* (sausage bread) appetizers have a fine reputation as well. ✉ *Rua 13 de Maio 1004, Bela Vista,* ☎ *011/288–8502. DC, MC, V.*

$–$$ ✗ **I Vitelloni.** The pizza with arugula, mozzarella, sun-dried tomatoes, and roasted garlic invented here has been copied by pizzerias all over town. The place is small, but the service is great. ✉ *Rua Conde Sílvio Álvares Penteado 31, Pinheiros,* ☎ *011/3819–0735. No credit cards.*

Seafood

$$–$$$$ ✗ **Amadeus.** The quality and preparation of the fish is famous among the business lunch crowd. Appetizers such as fresh oysters and salmon and endive with mustard, and entrées like shrimp in a cognac sauce, make it a challenge to find better fruits of the sea elsewhere in town. ✉ *Rua Haddock Lobo 807, Jardins,* ☎ *011/3061–2859. AE, DC. No dinner weekends. Metrô: Consolação.*

$$–$$$$ ✗ **Truta Rosa.** Fresh trout, prepared in endless ways, makes this small restaurant with a huge fish-shape window a hit. You'll cross a metal bridge over a small lagoon to reach the dining room, where sashimi and quenelles reel in the customers. ✉ *Av. Vereador José Diniz 318, Santo Amaro,* ☎ *011/5523–7021. AE, DC, MC, V. Closed Mon. No dinner Sun.*

LODGING

São Paulo's hotels are almost exclusively geared to business travelers, both homegrown and foreign. For this reason, most hotels are near Avenida Paulista, with a few in the Marginal Pinheiros and charming Jardins neighborhoods. Many hotels offer discounts of 20%–40% for cash payment or weekend stays. Few include breakfast in the room rate. São Paulo hosts many international conventions, so it's wise to make reservations well ahead of your arrival.

For information about youth hostels, contact the **Associação Paulista de Albergues da Juventude** (✉ Rua 7 de Abril 386, República, 01320-040, ☎ 011/258–0388). The association sells a book ($2.50) that lists hostels throughout Brazil.

For price categories, *see* the chart *under* Lodging *in* Smart Travel Tips A to Z.

$$$$ 🏨 **Gran Meliá São Paulo.** The Meliá is in the same building as São Paulo's
★ world trade center and the D&D Decoração & Design Center. Off the
large marble lobby is a bar whose comfortable leather chairs are perfect for unwinding after a day of meetings or shopping. Guest rooms
have king-size beds, two phone lines, living rooms with sofas, and small
tables that are the perfect places to set up your laptop. The apartment
floors have such special amenities as pass-key access and bathroom
faucets that can be programmed to maintain whatever water temperature you prefer. ⊠ *Av. das Nações Unidas 12559, Brooklin 04578-
905,* ☎ *011/3043–8000 or 0800/15–5555,* FAX *011/3043–8001,* WEB
*www.solmelia.es. 300 suites. Restaurant, bar, in-room data ports, in-
room safes, room service, indoor pool, beauty salon, massage, sauna,
tennis court, exercise room, paddle tennis, business services, meeting
room. AE, DC, MC, V.*

$$$$ 🏨 **L'Hotel.** Close to the major business hubs, this European-style hotel
has rooms and suites decorated in somewhat sterile floral patterns. The
place was modeled after the famous L'Hotel in Paris, and the small number of rooms allows it to focus on providing superior service. Though
at its inception L'Hotel wanted to retain an air of exclusivity, reports
have been mixed as to its success. ⊠ *Alameda Campinas 266, Jardins
01404-000,* ☎ FAX *011/283–0500,* WEB *www.lhotel.com.br. 82 rooms,
5 suites. 2 restaurants, pub, room service, pool, sauna, health club, business services, meeting room. AE, DC, MC, V. Metrô: Trianon.*

$$$$ 🏨 **Hotel Sofitel São Paulo.** Near the Congonhas Airport and Ibirapuera
Park, this modern, luxury hotel is noted for its French style. The
restaurant even serves French cuisine. ⊠ *Rua Sena Madureira 1355,
Bloco 1, Ibirapuera 04021-051,* ☎ *011/5574–1100 or 0800/11–1790,*
FAX *011/5575–4544,* WEB *www.accorbrasil.com.br. 219 rooms. Restaurant, bar, room service, pool, sauna, tennis court, exercise room, laundry, business services, meeting rooms. AE, DC, MC, V.*

$$$$ 🏨 **Inter-Continental São Paulo.** This exquisite hotel is by far the most
★ attractive of the city's top-tier establishments. Service is attentive, and
both the private and public areas are well appointed. Creams, pastels,
and marble come together with seamless sophistication and elegance.
⊠ *Av. Santos 1123, Jardins 01419-001,* ☎ *011/3179–2600,* FAX *011/
3179–2666,* WEB *www.interconti.com. 160 rooms, 33 suites. Restaurant, bar, room service, pool, massage, sauna, health club, business services, helipad. AE, DC, MC, V. Metrô: Trianon.*

$$$$ 🏨 **Renaissance São Paulo.** A stay at this Jardins hotel, a block from
Avenida Paulista, puts you close to both shops and businesses. From
the street, it has the appeal of a roll of tinfoil, but its interior is graceful and elegant. There are six Renaissance Club floors with 57 suites
that include a buffet breakfast, evening hors d'oeuvres, butler service,
express check-in and check-out, and fax machines. If you want to arrive in style, the hotel's helipad is key. ⊠ *Alameda Santos 2247, Jardins
01419-002,* ☎ *011/3069–2233; 800/468–3571 in the U.S.,* FAX *011/
3064–3344,* WEB *www.renaissancehotels.com. 452 rooms, 100 suites.
3 restaurants, 3 bars, room service, pool, massage, health club, squash,
shops, business services, travel services, helipad, parking (fee). AE, DC,
MC, V. Metrô: Consolação.*

$$$$ 🏨 **Sheraton Mofarrej Hotel & Towers.** Just behind Avenida Paulista and
★ next to Parque Trianon, the Mofarrej is part of Sheraton's A-class Luxury Collection hotels. Rooms are done in light hues, and the four
floors that have butler service offer other amenities that will make you
feel all the more pampered. Rooms on the west side overlook the park.
⊠ *Alameda Santos 1437, Jardins 01419-905,* ☎ *011/253–5544 or 0800/
11–6000,* FAX *011/283–0160,* WEB *www.sheraton-sp.com. 2 restaurants,
2 bars, room service, indoor pool, massage, sauna, exercise room,
business services, convention center. AE, DC, MC, V. Metrô: Trianon.*

$$$$ 📷 **Transamérica.** Directly across the Rio Pinheiros from the Centro Empresarial office complex, the home of many U.S. companies, this hotel is a comfortable and convenient choice for those working outside Centro. The skylighted lobby has granite, marble, Persian carpets, palm trees, leather sofas, and oversize modern paintings; the spacious rooms have no special charm, but their pastel colors, wood furnishings, and beige carpeting create a relaxing atmosphere. ✉ *Av. das Nações Unidas 18591, Santo Amaro 04795-901,* ☎ *011/5693–4511 or 0800/12–6060,* FAX *011/5693–4990,* WEB *www.transamerica.com.br. 396 rooms, 66 suites. Restaurant, bar, room service, pool, sauna, 9-hole golf course, 2 tennis courts, exercise room, jogging, business services. AE, DC, MC, V.*

$$–$$$ 📷 **Maksoud Plaza.** Ronald Reagan *almost* stayed here on a 1982 presidential visit, but the Secret Service thought the soaring atrium lobby—with its panoramic elevators, fountains, greenery, and shops—posed a security risk. The staff provides professional service, the hotel's restaurants aren't bad, and the in-house theater and the Maksoud 150 nightclub offer entertainment. ✉ *Alameda Campinas 1250, Jardins 01404-900,* ☎ *011/3145–8000,* FAX *011/3145–8001,* WEB *www.maksoud.com.br. 416 rooms, 99 suites. 6 restaurants, 3 bars, room service, indoor pool, health club, nightclub, theater, business services. AE, DC, MC, V. Metrô: Trianon.*

$$ 📷 **Eldorado Higienópolis.** Set in one of the city's oldest and most attractive
★   residential neighborhoods, only a five-minute taxi ride from Centro, this hotel has a large pool and a lobby dressed in travertine marble with a pink-granite floor. The on-site café is lovely, and the rooms are all pleasant; the noise level is lowest in those at the front above the fifth floor or those in back. ✉ *Rua Marquês de Itu 836, Higienópolis 01223-000,* ☎ *011/3361–6888,* FAX *011/222–7194,* WEB *www.hoteiseldorado.com.br. 152 rooms. Restaurant, bar, room service, pool. AE, DC, MC, V.*

$$ 📷 **Grande Hotel Ca' D'Oro.** Owned and run by a northern Italian family for more than 40 years, this Old World–style hotel near Centro has bar-side fireplaces, lots of wood and Persian carpeting, a great variety of room decor (all along classic European lines), ultrapersonalized service, and the beloved Ca' D'Oro restaurant. All these amenities attract many repeat customers, including quite a few Brazilian bigwigs. ✉ *Rua Augusta 129, Cerqueira César 01303-001,* ☎ *011/236–4300,* FAX *011/236–4311,* WEB *www.cadoro.com.br. 240 rooms, 50 suites. Restaurant, 2 bars, room service, indoor pool, sauna, exercise room. AE, DC, MC, V. Metrô: Consolação.*

$–$$ 📷 **Bourbon.** Both guests and furnishings are well cared for in this small hotel near the Largo do Arouche, a charming downtown district. A brass-accented basement bar features live piano music. The lobby has upholstered print sofas, an abstract handcrafted black-and-white wall hanging, and granite flooring. Rooms are done in beige and blue and have marvelously large, sunlit bathrooms. ✉ *Av. Vieira de Carvalho 99, Centro 01210-010,* ☎ *011/3337–2000,* FAX *011/220–8187. 123 rooms. Restaurant, bar, sauna. AE, DC, MC, V. Metrô: República.*

$ 📷 **Carillon Plaza.** Walk out of the heated hustle and bustle of the Jardins neighborhood and into this hotel's cool lobby full of mirrors and marble. You can retreat still farther by heading to the rooftop pool for an afternoon of sunbathing or by sinking into a leather chair for a meal in the restaurant. The multilingual staff is very helpful. ✉ *Rua Bela Cintra 652, Jardins 01415-000,* ☎ *011/257–9233,* FAX *011/255–3346,* WEB *www.redepandehoteis.com.br/carillon/carillon.htm. 39 rooms, 10 suites. Restaurant, bar, in-room safes, room service, pool. AE, DC, MC, V. Metrô: Consolação.*

$ ⊞ **Novotel São Paulo Ibirapuera.** Well located near Ibirapuera Park, with easy access to the city's main streets, Novotel São Paulo Ibirapuera offers solid service. In need of redecoration, it's still a decent choice, just not as great as it once was. ✉ *Rua Sena Madureira 1355, Ibirapuera 04021-051,* ☎ *011/5574–9099,* ℻ *011/5572–3499. 80 rooms. Restaurant, bar, room service, pool, sauna, tennis court, exercise room, laundry, business services, meeting rooms. AE, DC, MC, V.*

$ ⊞ **Parthenon Golden Tower.** A full-service establishment with apartmentlike amenities, this hotel is popular with business travelers and families alike. The rooms are nicely decorated, and each has a private balcony. ✉ *Av. Cidade Jardim 411, Pinheiros 01453-000,* ☎ *011/3081–6333,* ℻ *011/3088–3531,* 🖦 *www.accorbrasil.com.br. 73 suites. Restaurant, bar, room service, pool, sauna, meeting room, exercise room, laundry. AE, DC, MC, V.*

¢–$ ⊞ **La Guardia.** If you don't need to be surrounded by luxury, consider this simple, affordable (compared to many establishments) hotel. Rooms are small but comfortable and have thick carpets and marbletop tables. The environment is friendly, and the service is good. ✉ *Rua Peixoto Gomide 154, Cerqueira César 01409-000,* ☎ *011/255–0600,* ℻ *011/258–7398. 28 rooms, 14 suites. Restaurant, free parking. AE, DC, MC, V. Metrô: Consolação.*

¢–$ ⊞ **Ville Hotel.** In the lively Higienópolis neighborhood of apartment buildings, bars, and bookstores abutting Mackenzie University, this hotel costs about R$90 a night. The small lobby features a black-and-pink-granite floor, recessed lighting, and leather sofas; rooms are done in pastels with brown carpeting. ✉ *Rua Dona Veridiana 643, Higienópolis 01238-010,* ☎ *011/257–5288,* ☎ ℻ *011/239–1871. 54 rooms. Restaurant, meeting room. AE, DC, MC, V.*

¢ ⊞ **Ibis São Paulo Expo.** This large hotel has clean, budget rooms. The decoration is contemporary and functional. ✉ *Rua Eduardo Viana 163, Barra Funda 01133-040,* ☎ *011/3824–7373,* ℻ *011/3824–7374. 280 rooms. Restaurant, room service, laundry, meeting rooms. AE, DC, MC, V.*

NIGHTLIFE AND THE ARTS

Nightlife

São Paulo is a city beset by trends, so clubs and bars come and go at a dizzying pace. Though these were all thriving spots at press time, it's best to check with hotel concierges and paulistanos you meet to confirm that a place is still open before heading out on the town.

Bars

From the sophisticated to the casual, there is a bar for every taste. The most expensive places are in the Itaim neighborhood. Vila Madalena is full of trendy places.

Balcão. The word for "balcony" in Portuguese is *balcão*, and true to its name, this place has a sprawling one. If you'd like a little food to accompany your drinks and conversation, try the sun-dried tomato and mozzarella sandwich. ✉ *Rua Doutor Melo Alves 150, Jardim Paulista,* ☎ *011/3088–4630. Metrô: Consolação.*

Barnaldo Lucrécia. Live *música popular brasileira* (MPB; popular Brazilian music) is often a draw. The crowd is intense though jovial. ✉ *Rua Abílio Soares 207, Paraíso,* ☎ *011/3885–3425. Metrô: Paraíso.*

Elias. This place is a hangout for fans of the Palmeiras soccer team, whose stadium is just a few blocks away. If you want something to eat, the carpaccio is undoubtedly the best choice on the menu. ✉ *Rua Cayowaá 70, Perdizes,* ☎ *011/3864–4722.*

Empanadas. Most patrons stop for a beer en route to another Vila Madalena bar. It's a good place to "warm up" for an evening out with a quick drink and a bite to eat. The empanadas are particularly appealing. ✉ *Rua Wisard 489, Vila Madalena,* ☎ *011/3032-2116.*

Frangó. Because it's set in the Freguesia do Ó neighborhood, a stop makes you feel as if you've been transported to a small town. In addition to a pleasant location, Frangó also offers 90 varieties of beer, including the Brazilian export beer Xingu. Its rich, molasseslike flavor nicely complements the bar's unforgettable *bolinhos de frango com queijo* (chicken balls with cheese). ✉ *Largo da Matriz de Nossa Senhora do Ó 168, Freguesia do Ó,* ☎ *011/3932-4818 or 011/3931-4281.*

Grazie a Dio. The patrons may be different ages, but they're usually fashionable and always like good music. The best time to go is at happy hour for daily live performances. On Saturday it's jazz, and on Friday, bossa nova. The natural decorations, including trees and constellations, complement the Mediterranean food served in the back. ✉ *Rua Girassol 67, Vila Madalena,* ☎ *011/3031-6568.*

Original. This place was one of the first of many bars modeled on 1940s-era Rio clubs. It has good draft beer and snacks. ✉ *Rua Graúna 137, Moema,* ☎ *011/530-9486.*

Pirajá. The pictures of Rio de Janeiro on the walls will make you think fondly of Ipanema. The action starts at happy hour after 6 PM. ✉ *Av. Brigadeiro Faria Lima 64, Pinheiros,* ☎ *011/3815-6881.*

Bar Brahma. First opened in 1949, this used to be the meeting place of artists, intellectuals and politicians. It was closed down in 1997, but reopened in 2001 and is again a popular place to meet. ✉ *Av. São João 677, Centro,* ☎ *011/3333-0855.*

Brazilian Clubs
MPB clubs book quiet, largely acoustic instrumental and vocal music in the style of Milton Nascimento, Chico Buarque, and Gilberto Gil. The emphasis tends to be on samba and bossa nova.

Piratininga. The tiny round tables at this small bar-restaurant are perfect for a quiet rendezvous. The live MPB and jazz music add to the romance. ✉ *Rua Wisard 149, Vila Madalena,* ☎ *011/3032-9775.*

Sem Eira Nem Beira. The decor was inspired by Brazilian bars circa 1940. Previously called Vou Vivendo, the club is famous for its live MPB performances on Friday and Saturday. ✉ *Rua Fiandeiras 966, Itaim Bibi,* ☎ *011/3845-3444.*

Cybercafés
Espaço Ideal. You can keep up with your stocks on the six computers, which have Internet access and are connected to a printer. It costs R$4 for a half hour and R$7 for an hour. There's also a good selection of healthy sandwiches, juices, and coffee to satisfy your body as well as your mind. ✉ *Rua Artur de Azevedo 1339, Pinheiros,* ☎ *011/3081-9670.*

Frans Café at Fnac. Inside a well-known French store you'll find six computers connected Monday–Sunday 10–10. Access costs about R$4 for a half hour and R$7 per hour. ✉ *Av. Pedroso de Morais 858, Pinheiros,* ☎ *011/3814-2404.*

B.A.S.E./diesel. The space-age decor puts you in the mood for a little cyber-exploration. For R$6 per half hour, you can log onto one of eight computers Tuesday–Friday after 10 PM and Saturday after 11 PM, when this dance club is in full swing. ✉ *Av. Brigadeiro Luiz Antônio 1137, Bela Vista,* ☎ *011/3606-3244.*

Coffee & Book at Saraiva Megastore. This store sells CDs and books and has a café as well as five computers. You can log on Monday–Saturday 10–10 and Sunday 2–8; the cost is R$5 for the first half hour and R$4 for each additional 30 minutes. ⊠ *Shopping Eldorado, Av. Rebouças 3970, Pinheiros,* ☎ *011/3819–1770.*

Dance Clubs

People tend to go dancing very late. Still, you should arrive early to avoid the lines. Don't worry if the dance floor appears empty at 11 PM; things will start to sizzle an hour or so later.

Avenida Club. Some nights are dedicated to Caribbean rhythms, others to MPB. Regardless, the large wooden dance floor—one of the finest in town—attracts a crowd of thirtysomethings. ⊠ *Av. Pedroso de Morais 1036, Pinheiros,* ☎ *011/3814–7383.*

B.A.S.E./Diesel. In the '60s this was a bathhouse, but now it hosts hot dance parties from 9 PM until the wee hours. Three bars and an enormous dance floor reverberate to a mix of everything from Jimi Hendrix to cutting-edge dance hits. ⊠ *Av. Brigadeiro Luíz Antônio 1137, Bela Vista,* ☎ *011/3106–3191.*

Blen Blen Brasil. You can dance to live music—from reggae to salsa to Brazilian rock. ⊠ *Rua Inácio Pereira da Rocha 520, Pinheiros,* ☎ *011/ 3812–2890.*

Brancaleone. Even if you've always been told that you move to the beat of a different drum, you'll find a suitable rhythm here. Each night brings a new beat, including disco, rock, funk, soul, Brazilian pop, and forró. You can take a break on the patio; refreshments include food as well as drink. ⊠ *Rua Luis Murat 298, Jardim América,* ☎ *011/3819– 8873.*

Canto da Ema. Considered the best place to dance forró in town, here you'll find people of different ages and styles coming together on the dance floor. *Xiboquinha* is the official forró drink, made with *cachaça* (a Brazilian sugarcane-based alcohol), lemon, honey, cinnamon, and ginger. ⊠ *Av. Brigadeiro Faria Lima 364, Pinheiros,* ☎ *011/3813–4708.*

Carioca Club. *Carioca* is the name for a person from Rio de Janeiro, and this place has the decor of old-style Rio clubs. Its large dance floor attracts an eclectic mix of college students, couples, and professional dancers who move to samba, *axé* (a type of music from Bahia), and pagode. ⊠ *Rua Cardeal Arcoverde 2899, Pinheiros,* ☎ *011/3812–3782.*

Dolores Bar. DJs spin funk, soul, and hip-hop tunes for a crowd in its twenties and thirties. Wednesday and Friday nights are the most popular, and people really do fill up the floor only after the witching hour. ⊠ *Rua Fradique Coutinho 1007, Vila Madalena,* ☎ *011/3031–3604.*

KVA. Live or recorded forró is played every night. There are three stages, two dance floors, and one coffee shop. ⊠ *Rua Cardeal Arcoverde 2958, Pinheiros,* ☎ *011/3819–2153.*

A Lanterna. Because this venue is a mixture of restaurant, bar, and nightclub, you can go early for dinner and stay late for dancing. Actors, dancers, and musicians give performances that add to the entertainment. The walls are decorated with local artists' works. ⊠ *Rua Fidalga 531, Vila Madalena,* ☎ *011/3816–0904.*

Lov.e Club & Lounge. The interior design makes you feel like you're in a set from an *Austin Powers* movie. Before 2 AM the music isn't too loud, and you can sit and talk on the '50s-style sofas. Then the techno effects keep people on the small dance floor until sunrise. ⊠ *Rua Pequetita 189, Vila Olímpia,* ☎ *011/3044–1613.*

Nias. This is one of the few places left where you can still dance to true rock and roll. DJs play tunes from the '80s and '90s and also current international pop-rock tunes. ⊠ *Rua dos Pinheiros 688, Pinheiros,* ☎ *011/3062–3877.*

The Pool. Ever wish you could fully cool off during a hot night of dancing? Well, this place has a 8-m-long (26-ft-long) pool where you can do just that. The club will provide you with a swimsuit, but you can't wear it back on the dance floor. DJs play house music. ⊠ *Rua Teodoro Sampaio 1109, Pinheiros,* ☎ *011/3068–8307.*

Gay and Lesbian Clubs

A Lôca. You'll find a large dance floor, a video room, and two bars here. A mixed gay and lesbian crowd often dances until dawn and then has breakfast in the club. ⊠ *Rua Frei Caneca 916, Cerqueira César,* ☎ *011/ 3120–2055. Metrô: Consolação.*

Massivo. This fabulous underground disco and club welcomes gay, lesbian, and straight patrons. ⊠ *Rua Alameda Itu 1548, Jardins,* ☎ *011/ 3083–7505. Metrô: Consolação.*

Muzik. This place is frequented mostly by men between the ages of 18 and 35, and there's room for 1,200 of them. Bodybuilders in swim trunks dance on stages while DJ Mauro Borges and others play '70s and house music until the last patron leaves. ⊠ *Rua da Consolação 3032, Jardim Paulista,* ☎ *011/3081–5496.*

Stereo. The fashionable and exotic crowd is primarily gay, but straight patrons meet to dance as well. Decorations have a retro-futuristic look. Be prepared for a mob on Wednesday, which is '80s night. ⊠ *Alameda Olga 168, Barra Funda,* ☎ *011/3664–7925. Metrô: Barra Funda.*

Jazz Clubs

All of Jazz. People come to this small place to actually *listen* to very good jazz and bossa nova. Local musicians jam here weekly. Call ahead to book a table on weekends. ⊠ *Rua João Cachoeira 1366, Vila Olímpia,* ☎ *011/3849–1345.*

Bourbon Street. With a name right out of New Orleans, one of the world's coolest jazz towns, it's no wonder this is where the best jazz and blues bands play. ⊠ *Rua Dos Chanés 127, Moema,* ☎ *011/5561–1643.*

Café Piu Piu. Although this establishment is best known for jazz, it also hosts groups that play rock, bossa nova, and even tango. Decorations include statues, an antique balcony, and marble tables. ⊠ *Rua 13 de Maio 134, Bixiga,* ☎ *011/258–8066.*

Mr. Blues Jazz Bar. At this traditional jazz, blues, and soul venue, the audience drinks beer and whiskey and eats french fries with Parmesan cheese. ⊠ *Av. São Gabriel 558, Jardim Paulista,* ☎ *011/3884–9356.*

Sanja Jazz Bar. A few tables (arrive early to get a seat) in an old town house are the setting for live jazz, rock, and blues performances. ⊠ *Rua Frei Caneca 304, Consolação,* ☎ *011/255–2942.*

The Arts

The world's top orchestras, opera and dance companies, and other troupes always include São Paulo in their South American tours. Listings of events appear in the "Veja São Paulo" insert of the newsweekly *Veja.* The arts sections of the dailies *Folha de São Paulo* and *O Estado de São Paulo* also have listings and reviews. In addition, *Folha* publishes a weekly guide on Friday called "Guia da Folha."

Tickets for many events are available at booths throughout the city as well as at theater box offices Many of these venues offer ticket delivery for a surcharge. **Fun by Phone** (☎ 011/3097–8687) sells ticket to music concerts, theater, and theme parks. **Lucas Shows** (☎ 011/3858–5783) delivers tickets to your hotel door for a fee. At **Show Ticket at Shopping Center Iguatemi** (⊠ Av. Brigadeiro Faria Lima 1191, 3rd floor, ☎ 011/3814–9807) you can buy tickets to the main concerts and performances in town Monday–Saturday 10–10 and Sunday 2–8.

Classical Music, Dance, and Theater

The city is home to both a state and a municipal orchestra, though both suffer from a chronic lack of funds. The theater district, in the bohemian Bela Vista neighborhood, has dozens of theaters dedicated mostly to plays in Portuguese. The contemporary music ensemble **Grupo Novo Horizonte** (☎ 011/256–9766), a group of eight professional musicians, gives performances in town but does not have a permanent home.

PERFORMANCE VENUES

Sala São Luiz. This venue hosts chamber music performances. ⊠ *Av. Juscelino Kubitschek 1830, Itaim Bibi,* ☎ *011/3847–4111.*

Teatro Alfa. Opera, ballet, music, and symphony performances are held here. It's one of the newest theaters in the country, with all the latest sound and lighting technology—and the biggest foreign stars grace the stage. Tickets can be bought by phone and picked up a half hour before the performance. ⊠ *Rua Bento Branco de Andrade Filho 722, Santo Amaro,* ☎ *011/5693–4000 or 0800/55–8191,* WEB *www.teatroalfa. com.br.*

Teatro Cultura Artística. Its fine acoustics make this theater perfect for classical music performances. It also hosts dance recitals and plays. ⊠ *Rua Nestor Pestana 196, Cerqueira César,* ☎ *011/258–3616,* WEB *www.culturaartistica.com.br.*

Teatro Faculdade Armando Álvares Penteado (FAAP). The FAAP Theater presents concerts and Brazilian plays. ⊠ *Rua Alagoas 903, Pacaembú,* ☎ *011/3662–1992.*

Teatro João Caetano. This theater hosts state-sponsored festivals as well as Brazilian plays. ⊠ *Rua Borges Lagoa 650, Vila Mariana,* ☎ *011/ 5573–3774. Metrô: Santa Cruz.*

Teatro Municipal. Most serious music, ballet, and opera is performed in the intimate gilt and moss-green-velvet surroundings of this classic theater. There are lyrical performances on Monday at 8:30 and concerts on Wednesday at 12:30. A local cultural organization, the Mozarteum Brasileira Associação Cultural, holds classical music concerts, which include performances by visiting artists, April–October. ⊠ *Praça Ramos de Azevedo, Centro,* ☎ *011/222–8698. Metrô: Anhangabaú.*

TUCA. The Catholic University theater puts on alternative concerts as well as plays. ⊠ *Rua Monte Alegre 1024, Sumaré,* ☎ *011/3670–8453.*

Via Funchal. Capable of seating more than 3,000 people, this is the site of many large international shows. ⊠ *Rua Funchal 65, Vila Olímpia,* ☎ *011/3846–2300 or 011/3842–6855,* WEB *www.viafunchal.com.br.*

Escola de Samba

From December to February, many *escolas de samba* (samba "schools"—groups that perform during Carnaval) open their rehearsals to the public. Drummers get in sync with the singers, and everyone learns the lyrics to each year's songs. **Rosas de Ouro** (⊠ Av. Cel. Euclides Machado 1066, Freguesia do Ó, ☎ 011/3966–0608 or 011/3857–4555) has one of the most popular escola de samba rehearsals.

Film

Only foreign children's movies are dubbed; the rest have subtitles with the original dialogue intact. Arrive at blockbuster releases at least 40 minutes early, particularly on Sunday night. The region near Avenida Paulista, Avenida Consolação, and Rua Augusta has more than 10 movie theaters as well as many cafés and bars where you can hang out before or after the show. Movie theaters in shopping centers are also good options. Call ahead for confirmation because theaters often change their programming without notice.

The **Belas Artes** complex (✉ Rua da Consolação 2423, Consolação, ☎ 011/258–4092 or 011/259–6341) offers Hollywood films. **Centro Cultural São Paulo** (✉ Rua Vergueiro 1000, Paraíso, ☎ 011/3277–3611, ext. 279) usually features a series of theme films for free or nearly free. It also presents plays, concerts, and art exhibits. **Cinearte** (✉ Av. Paulista 2073, Jardim Paulista, ☎ 011/285–3696) hosts most of the premieres in town. Brazilian, European, and other non-American films are shown at the **Espaço Unibanco** (✉ Rua Augusta 1470/1475, Consolação, ☎ 011/288–6780).

Free Shows

Most free concerts—with performances by either Brazilian or international artists—are presented on Sunday in Parque Ibirapuera. City-sponsored events are held in Centro's Vale do Anhangabaú area. State-sponsored concerts take place at the Memorial da América Latina, northwest of Centro. **Serviço Social do Comércio** (SESC, Commerce Social Service; ☎ 011/3179–3400) is very active in cultural programming, and many of its events are free. The organization has units in several neighborhoods.

OUTDOOR ACTIVITIES AND SPORTS

Participant Sports

Bicycling

Night Biker's Club (✉ Rua Pacheco de Miranda 141, Jardim Paulista, ☎ 011/3887–4773) offers bike tours of the city at night. **Parque Ibirapuera** has places that rent bicycles for about R$8 an hour and a special bike path. There are also bike lanes on Avenida Sumaré and Avenida Pedroso de Morais. **Sampa Bikers** (✉ Rua São Sebastião 454, Chácara Santo Antônio, ☎ 011/9990–0083 or 011/5183–9477) offers tours in the city and excursions outside town. A day tour costs about R$60, including transport and lunch.

Climbing

Inspired, perhaps, by the skyscrapers on Avenida Paulista, climbers have recently crowded the gyms and rock-climbing schools that have sprung up around town. Most places offer training and rent equipment. At **Casa de Pedra** (✉ Rua da Paz 1823, Chácara Santo Antônio, ☎ 011/5181–7873) the daily fee for using the rock-climbing facilities is R$20, and an hour of instruction is R$30. **Jump** (✉ Av. Pompéia 568, Pompéia, ☎ 011/3675–2300) offers a three-day climbing course on its open walls. **90 Graus** (✉ Rua João Pedro Cardoso 107, Aeroporto, ☎ 011/5034–8775) opened in 1993 and offers climbing courses and individual training.

Golf

The greens fee at the 18-hole **Clube de Campo** (✉ Praça Rockford 28, Vila Represa, ☎ 011/5929–3111) is R$50. It's open Monday–Tuesday and Thursday–Friday 7–7. **Golf School** (✉ Av. Guido Caloi 2160, Santo Amaro, ☎ 011/5515–3372) is a driving range that offers 30-minute classes for R$20; R$10 gets you 100 balls.

Scuba Diving

Most dive schools take you to Ilhabela and other places outside town on weekends and offer NAUI and PADI certification courses. **Claumar** (✉ Av. Brigadeiro Faria Lima 4440, Itaim Bibi, ☎ 011/3846–3034) has a 15-m (49-ft) diving tower used during classes in São Paulo. **Deep Sea** (✉ Rua Manoel da Nóbrega 781, Paraíso, ☎ 011/3889–7721) has small group dive trips to Lage de Santos in a fast boat. **Diving Col-**

lege (⊠ Rua Doutor Mello Alves 700, Cerqueira César, ☎ 011/3061–1453) is one of the oldest diving schools in Brazil and offers all the PADI courses.

Tennis

Court fees at **Play Tênis** (⊠ Leopoldo Couto de Magalhães Jr. 1097, Itaim Bibi, ☎ 011/3845–7446) are R$35 an hour, but they don't rent rackets. **Tênis Coach** (⊠ Rua Dr. Francisco Tomás de Carvalho 940, Morumbi) rents courts and and has classes for people of all ages.

Spectator Sports

Auto Racing

São Paulo hosts a Formula I race every March, bringing this city of 4.5 million cars to heights of spontaneous combustion, especially when a Brazilian driver wins. The race is held at **Autódromo de Interlagos** (⊠ Av. Senador Teotônio Vilela 315, Interlagos, ☎ 011/5521–9911), which also hosts other kinds of races on weekends. For ticket information on the Formula I race contact the **Confederação Brasileira de Automobilismo** (⊠ Rua da Glória 290, 8th floor, Rio de Janeiro, RJ 20241-180, ☎ 021/2221–4895).

Futebol

Futebol (soccer) has always been a Brazilian passion. The nation's love affair with the sport became even stronger after Brazil won the 1994 World Cup and has reached the finals in subsequent years. São Paulo has several well-funded teams with some of the country's best players. The five main teams—São Paulo, Palmeiras, Portuguesa, Corinthians, and Juventus—even attract fans from other states. The two biggest stadiums are Morumbi and the municipally run Pacaembu. Note that covered seats offer the best protection, not only from the elements but also from rowdy spectators.

Morumbi (⊠ Praça Roberto Gomes Pedrosa, Morumbi, ☎ 011/3749–8000), the home stadium of São Paulo Futebol Clube, has a capacity of 85,000. The first games of the 1950 World Cup were played at the **Pacaembu** (⊠ Praça Charles Miller, Pacaembu, ☎ 011/3661–9111) stadium.

Horse Racing

Thoroughbreds race at the **São Paulo Jockey Club** (⊠ Rua Lineu de Paula Machado 1263, Cidade Jardim, ☎ 011/3816–4011), which is open Monday and Wednesday–Thursday 7:30 PM–11:30 PM and weekends 2–9. Card-carrying Jockey Club members get the best seats and have access to the elegant restaurant.

SHOPPING

People come from all over South America to shop in São Paulo, and shopping is considered an attraction in its own right by many paulistanos. In the Jardins neighborhood, stores that carry well-known brands from around the world alternate with the best Brazilian shops. Prices are high for most items, especially in Jardins and the major shopping centers.

Stores are open weekdays 9–6:30 and Saturday 9–1. A few are open on Sunday (for a list of these shops and their Sunday hours, call ☎ 011/210–4000 or 011/813–3311). Mall hours are generally weekdays 10–10 and Saturday 9 AM–10 PM; during gift-giving holiday seasons malls open on Sunday.

Areas

In **Centro,** Rua do Arouche is noted for leather goods. In **Itaim,** the area around Rua João Cachoeira has evolved from a neighborhood of small clothing factories into a wholesale- and retail-clothing sales district. Several shops on Rua Tabapuã sell small antiques. Also, Rua Dr. Mário Ferraz is stuffed with elegant clothing, gift, and home-decoration stores. **Jardins,** centering on Rua Augusta (which crosses Avenida Paulista) and Rua Oscar Freire, is the chicest area. Double-parked Mercedes-Benzes and BMWs point the way to the city's fanciest stores, which sell leather items, jewelry, gifts, antiques, and art. You'll also find many restaurants and beauty salons. Shops that specialize in high-price European antiques are on or around Rua da Consolação. A slew of lower-price antiques stores line Rua Cardeal Arcoverde in **Pinheiros.**

Centers and Malls

D&D Decoração & Design Center. This complex shares a building with the world trade center and the Gran Meliá hotel. It's loaded with fancy decoration stores, full-scale restaurants, and fast-food spots. ⊠ *Av. das Nações Unidas 12555, Brooklin Novo,* ☎ *011/3043–9000.*
Shopping Center Ibirapuera. For a long time the largest shopping mall in Brazil, Ibirapuera features more than 500 stores in addition to three movie theaters. ⊠ *Av. Ibirapuera 3103, Moema,* ☎ *011/5095–2300.*
Shopping Center Iguatemi. The city's oldest and most sophisticated mall offers the latest in fashion and fast food. Four movie theaters often show American films in English with Portuguese subtitles. The Gero Café, built in the middle of the main hall, has a fine menu. ⊠ *Av. Brigadeiro Faria Lima 2232, Jardim Paulista,* ☎ *011/3816–6116.*
Shopping Center Morumbi. Set in the city's fastest-growing area, Morumbi is giving Iguatemi a run for its money. That said, it houses about the same boutiques, record stores, bookstores, and restaurants as Iguatemi, though it has more movie theaters (a total of six). ⊠ *Av. Roque Petroni Jr. 1089, Morumbi,* ☎ *0800/17–7600.*

Markets

Almost every neighborhood has a weekly outdoor food market (days are listed in local newspapers), complete with loudmouthed hawkers, exotic scents, and piles of colorful produce.

On Sunday, there are **antiques fairs** near the Museu de Arte de São Paulo and (in the afternoon) at the Shopping Center Iguatemi's parking lot. Many stall owners have shops and hand out business cards so you can browse throughout the week at your leisure. An **arts and crafts fair**— selling jewelry, embroidery, leather goods, toys, clothing, paintings, and musical instruments—takes place Sunday morning in Centro's Praça da República. Many booths move over to the nearby Praça da Liberdade in the afternoon, joining vendors there selling Japanese-style ceramics, wooden sandals, cooking utensils, food, and bonsai trees. **Flea markets**—with second-hand furniture, clothes, and CDs—take place on Saturday at Praça Benedito Calixto in Pinheiros and on Sunday at the Praça Dom Orione in Bela Vista.

Specialty Shops

Antiques

Antiquário Paulo Vasconcelos. Folk art and 18th- and 19th-century Brazilian furniture are among the finds here. ⊠ *Alameda Gabriel Monteiro da Silva 1881, Jardins,* ☎ *011/3062–2444.*

Edwin Leonard. This collective of three dealers sells Latin American and European antiques. ✉ *Rua Oscar Freire 146, Jardins,* ☎ *011/3088–1394.*

Patrimônio. Come for Brazilian antiques at reasonable prices. It also sells some Indian artifacts as well as modern furnishings crafted from iron. ✉ *Alameda Ministro Rocha Azevedo 1068, Jardins,* ☎ *011/3064–1750.*

Renato Magalhães Gouvêa Escritório de Arte. This shop offers a potpourri of European and Brazilian antiques, modern furnishings, and art. ✉ *Av. Europa 68, Jardins,* ☎ *011/3081–2166.*

Art

Arte Aplicada. For Brazilian paintings, sculptures, and prints, this is the place. ✉ *Rua Haddock Lobo 1406, Jardins,* ☎ *011/3062–5128.*

Camargo Vilaça. The staff has an eye for the works of up-and-coming Brazilian artists. ✉ *Rua Fradique Coutinho 1500, Vila Madalena,* ☎ *011/3032–7066.*

Espaço Cultural Ena Beçak. You can shop for Brazilian prints, sculptures, and paintings and then stop in the café. ✉ *Rua Oscar Freire 440, Jardins,* ☎ *011/3088–7322.*

Galeria Jacques Ardies. If art naïf is your thing, this place is a must. ✉ *Rua do Livramento 221, Vila Mariana,* ☎ *011/3884–2916. Metrô: Paraíso.*

Galeria Renot. Here you'll find oil paintings by such Brazilian artists as Vicente Rego Monteiro, Di Cavalcanti, Cícero Dias, and Anita Malfatti. ✉ *Alameda Ministro Rocha Azevedo 1327, Jardins,* ☎ *011/3083–5933.*

Galeria São Paulo. This gallery is a leader in contemporary, mainstream art. ✉ *Rua Estados Unidos 1456, Jardins,* ☎ *011/3062–8855.*

Mônica Filgueiras Galeria. Many a trend has been set at this gallery. ✉ *Alameda Ministro Rocha Azevedo 927, Jardins,* ☎ *011/3082–5292.*

Clothing

Alexandre Herchovitch. Senhor Herchovitch is a famous Brazilian designer. His store has prêt-à-porter and tailor-made clothes. ✉ *Alameda Franca 631, Jardins,* ☎ *011/288–8005.*

Anacapri. This shop sells women's underwear, swimsuits, and clothes in large sizes. ✉ *Rua Juquis 276, Moema,* ☎ *011/5531–8913.*

Cori. Everyday outfits with classic lines are the specialty. ✉ *Rua Haddock Lobo 1584, Jardins,* ☎ *011/3081–5223.*

Daslu. You can mingle with elite ladies who enjoy personalized attention in this "closed" (no storefront) designer-label boutique. ✉ *Rua Domingos Leme 284, Vila Nova Conceição,* ☎ *011/3842–3785.*

Elite. Owned by the modeling agency of the same name, this store is a favorite among girls from 13 years old and up for dresses and sportswear. ✉ *Rua Oscar Freire 735, Jardins,* ☎ *011/3082–9449.*

Ellus. This is a good place to buy men's and women's jeans, sportswear, and street wear. ✉ *Shopping Eldorado, 3rd floor, Cerqueira César,* ☎ *011/3815–4554,* WEB *www.ellus.com.br.*

Fórum. Although it has a lot of evening attire for young men and women, this shop also sells sportswear and shoes. ✉ *Rua Bela Cintra 2102, Jardins,* ☎ *011/3085–6269.*

Le Lis Blanc. This shop is Brazil's exclusive purveyor of the French brand Vertigo. Look for party dresses in velvet and sheer fabrics. ✉ *Rua Oscar Freire 809, Jardins,* ☎ *011/3083–2549.*

Maria Bonita/Maria Bonita Extra. If you have a little money in your pocket, shop at Maria Bonita, which has elegant women's clothes with terrific lines. At Maria Bonita Extra, the prices are a little lower. ✉ *Rua Oscar Freire 702, Jardins,* ☎ *011/3062–6433.*

Petistil. Younger family members aren't forgotten at this store, which sells clothes for infants and children up to 11 years old. ⊠ *Rua Teodoro Sampaio 2271, Pinheiros,* ☎ *011/3816–2865.*

Reinaldo Lourenço. The women's clothes here are high quality and sophisticated. ⊠ *Rua Bela Cintra 2167, Jardins,* ☎ *011/3085–8150.*

Richard's. This store carries one of Brazil's best lines of sportswear. Its collection includes outfits suitable for the beach or the mountains. ⊠ *Rua Oscar Freire 1129, Jardins,* ☎ *011/3082–5399. Metrô: Consolação.*

Uma. Young women are intrigued by the unique designs of the swimsuits, dresses, shorts, shirts, and pants sold here. ⊠ *Rua Girassol 273, Vila Madalena,* ☎ *011/3813–5559,* WEB *www.uma.com.br.*

Vila Romana Factory Store. You can't beat the prices for suits, jackets, jeans, and some women's wear (silk blouses, for example) at this store, a 40-minute drive from Centro. The in-town branch is more convenient, but its prices are higher. ⊠ *Via Anhanguera, Km 17.5,* ☎ *011/ 3601–2211.* ⊠ *Rua Oscar Freire 697, Jardins,* ☎ *011/3081–2919,* WEB *www.vilaromana.com.br.*

Viva Vida. Long evening dresses—many done in shiny, sexy, exotic fabrics—steal the show. ⊠ *Rua Oscar Freire 969, Jardins,* ☎ *011/3088–0421,* WEB *www.vivavida.com.br.*

Zoomp. This shop is famous for its jeans and high-quality street wear. Customers from 13 to 35 mix and match the clothes, creating some unusual combinations. ⊠ *Rua Oscar Freire 995, Jardins,* ☎ *011/ 3064–1556,* WEB *www.zoomp.com.br.*

Handicrafts

Alfândega. The owners travel the world collecting things to sell in their shop. Just about every continent is represented, with such items as Indonesian dolls, painted Spanish bottles, Brazilian pottery, and candles. ⊠ *Pátio Higienópolis, Av. Higienópolis 618, Loja 450, Higienópolis,* ☎ *011/3662–4651.*

Art Índia. This government-run shop sells Indian arts and crafts made by tribes throughout Brazil. ⊠ *Rua Augusta 1371, Loja 119, Cerqueira César,* ☎ *011/283–2102. Metrô: Consolação.*

Casa do Amazonas. As its name suggests, you'll find a wide selection of products from the Amazon in this store. ⊠ *Galeria Metropôle, Av. São Luís 187, Loja 14, Centro,* ☎ *011/5051–3098. Metrô: São Luís.*

Galeria de Arte Brasileira. This shop specializes in Brazilian handicrafts. Look for objects made of pau-brasil wood, hammocks, jewelry, T-shirts, *marajoara* pottery (from the Amazon), and lace. ⊠ *Alameda Lorena 2163, Jardins,* ☎ *011/3062–9452.*

Jewelry

Antônio Bernardo. One of Brazil's top designers owns this store; his work includes both modern and classic pieces that use only precious stones. ⊠ *Rua Bela Cintra 2063, Jardins,* ☎ *011/3083–5622.*

Atelier Cecília Rodrigues. This designer crafts unique pieces of gold and precious stones. ⊠ *Rua Horácio Lafer 767, Itaim Bibi,* ☎ *011/3849–9393.*

Castro Bernardes. In addition to selling jewelry and precious stones, this store restores old pieces. ⊠ *Rua Jerônimo da Veiga 164, 19th floor, Itaim Bibi,* ☎ *011/3167–1001.*

SÃO PAULO A TO Z

To research prices, get advice from other travelers, and book travel arrangements, visit www.fodors.com.

AIR TRAVEL
CARRIERS
Aerolíneas Argentinas has daily flights from Buenos Aires and Madrid and twice-a-week service from Auckland, New Zealand, and Sydney, Australia. Air France has a daily flight from Paris. American Airlines offers three flights a day from Miami and one a day from both New York and Dallas. British Airways flies from London every day but Tuesday and Wednesday. Canadian Airlines flies from Toronto every day but Monday. Continental Airlines flies from New York daily; United Airlines flies daily from Miami, New York, and Chicago.

Rio-Sul and Nordeste connect São Paulo with most major Brazilian cities daily. TAM flies daily to Miami, Paris, and most major Brazilian cities. It serves Mercosur capitals as well. Transbrasil has daily flights to major Brazilian cities. Varig has daily service to many U.S. and Brazilian cities; it also offers regular service to more than 18 countries in Latin America, Europe, Asia, and Australia. VASP serves all major Brazilian cities daily. GOL, the youngest Brazilian airline, offers budget tickets to major national capitals.

➤ AIRLINES AND CONTACTS: **Aerolíneas Argentinas** (☎ 011/6445–3806). **Air France** (☎ 011/3049–0909). **American Airlines** (☎ 011/214–4000 or 011/258–1244). **British Airways** (☎ 011/3145—9700). **Canadian Airlines** (☎ 011/259–9066). **Continental Airlines** (☎ 0800/55–4777). **GOL** (☎ 0800/70–12131). **Rio-Sul and Nordeste** (☎ 0800/99–2004 or 011/5561–2161). **TAM** (☎ 0800/56–7890). **Transbrasil** (☎ 0800/15–1151). **United Airlines** (☎ 0800/16–2323 or 011/3145–6444). **Varig** (☎ 0800/99–7000 or 011/5091–7000). **VASP** (☎ 0800/99–8277).

AIRPORTS AND TRANSFERS
São Paulo's international airport, Aeroporto Cumbica, is in the suburb of Guarulhos, 30 km (19 mi) and a 45-minute drive (longer during rush hour or on rainy days) northeast of Centro. Aeroporto Congonhas, 14 km (9 mi) south of Centro (a 15- to 30-minute drive, depending on traffic), serves regional airlines, including the Rio–São Paulo shuttle. From June to September, both airports are sometimes fogged in during the early morning, and flights are rerouted to the Aeroporto Viracopos in Campinas; passengers are transported by bus (an hour's ride) to São Paulo.
➤ AIRPORT INFORMATION: **Aeroporto Congonhas** (☎ 011/5090–9000). **Aeroporto Cumbica** (☎ 011/6445–2945). **Aeroporto Viracopos** (☎ 019/725–5000).

AIRPORT TRANSFERS
EMTU *executivo* buses—fancy, green-stripe "executive" vehicles—shuttle between Cumbica and Congonhas (6 AM–10 PM, every 30 mins) as well as between Cumbica and the Tietê bus terminal (5:40 AM–10 PM, every 45 mins); the downtown Praça da República (5:30 AM–11 PM, every 30 mins); and the Hotel Maksoud Plaza (6:45 AM–11 PM every 35 mins), stopping at most major hotels on Avenida Paulista. The cost is R$12. Municipal buses, with CMTC painted on the side, stop at the airport and go downtown by various routes, such as via Avenida Paulista, to the Praça da Sé and the Tietê bus station.

The sleek, blue-and-white, air-conditioned Guarucoop radio taxis will take you from Cumbica to downtown for around $45; the fare to town from Congonhas is about R$20. *Comum* (regular) taxis also charge R$40 from Cumbica and around R$18 from Congonhas. Fleet Car Shuttle (counter at Cumbica Airport's arrivals Terminal 1) is open daily 6 AM–midnight, and serves groups of up to 10 people in a van, stopping at one destination of choice. The fee (for the vanload) is about R$70.

➤ TAXIS AND SHUTTLES: **EMTU** *executivo* buses (☎ 0800/19–0088).
Fleet Car Shuttle (☎ 011/945–3030). **Guarucoop radio taxis** (☎ 011/
208–1881).

BUS TRAVEL TO AND FROM SÃO PAULO

Combined, the four bus stations serve 1,105 destinations. The huge
main station—serving all major Brazilian cities (with trips to Rio every
hour on the half hour) as well as Argentina, Uruguay, Chile, and
Paraguay—is the Terminal Tietê in the north, on the Marginal Tietê
Beltway. Terminal Bresser, in the eastern district of Brás, serves southern Minas Gerais State and Belo Horizonte. Terminal Jabaquara, near
Congonhas Airport, serves coastal towns. Terminal Barra Funda, in
the west, near the Memorial da América Latina, has buses to and from
western Brazil. All stations have or are close to metrô stops. You can
buy tickets at the stations; although those for Rio de Janeiro can be
bought a few minutes before departure, it's best to buy tickets in advance for other destinations and during holiday seasons.
➤ BUS INFORMATION: **Bus stations** (☎ 011/235–0322 for information
on all stations). **Terminal Barra Funda** (✉ Rua Mário de Andrade 664,
Barra Funda). **Terminal Bresser** (✉ Rua do Hipódromo, Brás). **Terminal Jabaquara** (✉ Rua Jequitibas, Jabaquara). **Terminal Tietê** (✉
Av. Cruzeiro do Sul, Santana).

BUS TRAVEL WITHIN SÃO PAULO

There's ample municipal bus service, but regular buses (white with a
red horizontal stripe) are overcrowded at rush hour and when it rains.
Stops are clearly marked, but routes are spelled out only on the buses
themselves. To get a bus to stop, put out your arm horizontally. The
fare is R$1.15. You enter at the front, pay the *cobrador* (fare collec-
tor) in the middle, and exit at the back. The cobrador gives out *vale
transporte* slips, or fare vouchers (with no expiration time), and often
has no change.

The green-and-gray SPTrans executivo buses, whose numerical desig-
nations all end with the letter *E,* are more spacious and cost around
R$2 (you pay the driver upon entry). Many *clandestino* buses (unli-
censed, privately run) traverse the city. Although not very pleasing to
the eye—most are battered white vehicles that have no signs—it's perfectly fine to take them; they charge the same as SPTrans buses.

For bus numbers and names, routes, and schedules for SPTrans buses,
purchase the *Guia São Paulo Ruas,* published by Quatro Rodas and
sold at newsstands and bookstores for about R$30.
➤ BUS INFORMATION: **Municipal bus service** (☎ 0800/12–3133 transit
information). **SPTrans executivo** (☎ 158).

CAR RENTAL

Car-rental rates range from R$60 to R$100 a day. Major rental companies include Avis, Hertz, and Localiza.
➤ MAJOR AGENCIES: **Avis** (✉ Rua da Consolação 335, Centro, ☎
0800/55–0066). **Hertz** (✉ Rua da Consolação 439, Centro, ☎ 011/
258–8422).
➤ LOCAL AGENCY: **Localiza** (✉ Rua da Consolação 419, Centro, ☎
0800/99–2000).

CAR TRAVEL

The main São Paulo–Rio de Janeiro highway is the Via Dutra (BR 116
North), which has been repaved and enlarged in places. The speed limit
is 120 kph (74 mph) along most of it, and although it has many tolls,
you'll find many call boxes you can use if your car breaks down. The
modern Rodovia Ayrton Senna (SP 70) charges reasonable tolls, runs

parallel to the Dutra for about a quarter of the way, and is an excellent alternative route. The 429-km (279-mi) trip takes five hours. If you have time, consider the longer, spectacular coastal Rio–Santos Highway (SP 55 and BR 101). It's an easy two-day drive, and you can stop midway at the colonial city of Parati, in Rio de Janeiro State.

Other main highways are the Castelo Branco (SP 280), which links the southwestern part of the state to the city; the Via Anhanguera (SP 330), which originates in the state's rich northern agricultural region, passing through the university town of Campinas; SP 310, which also runs from the farming heartland; BR 116 south, which comes up from Curitiba (a 408 km/265 mi trip); plus the Via Anchieta (SP 150) and the Rodovia Imigrantes (SP 160), parallel roads that run to the coast, each operating one-way on weekends and holidays.

Driving isn't recommended because of the heavy traffic (nothing moves at rush hour, especially when it rains), daredevil drivers, and inadequate parking. If, however, you do opt to drive, there are a few things to keep in mind. Most of São Paulo is between the Rio Tietê and the Rio Pinheiros, which converge in the western part of town. The high-speed routes along these rivers are Marginal Tietê and Marginal Pinheiros. There are also *marginais* (beltways) around the city. Avenida 23 de Maio runs south from Centro and beneath the Parque do Ibirapuera via the Ayrton Senna Tunnel. You can take Avenida Paulista, Avenida Brasil, and Avenida Faria Lima southwest to the Morumbi, Brooklin, Itaim, and Santo Amaro neighborhoods. The Elevado Costa e Silva, also called Minhocão, is an elevated road that connects Centro with Avenida Francisco Matarazzo in the west.

In most commercial neighborhoods you must buy hourly tickets (called Cartão Zona Azul) to park on the street during business hours. Only buy them at newsstands, not from people on the street. Booklets of 20 tickets cost R$16. Fill out each ticket—you'll need one for every hour you plan to park—with the car's license plate and the time you initially parked. Leave the tickets in the car's window so they're visible to officials from outside. After business hours or at any time near major sights, people may offer to watch your car. Although paying these "caretakers" about R$3 is enough to keep your car's paint job intact, to truly ensure its safety opt for a parking lot. Rates are R$5–R$7 for the first hour and R$1–R$2 each hour thereafter.

CONSULATES
➤ CONTACTS: **Australia** (⊠ Av. Tenente Negrão 140/121, 12th floor, Itaim Bibi, ☎ 011/3849–6281). **Canada** (⊠ Av. Paulista 1106, 1st floor, Cerqueira César, ☎ 011/5509–4321). **New Zealand** (⊠ Rua Pais de Araújo 29, 12th floor, Jardim Europa, ☎ 011/3845–5532). **United Kingdom** (⊠ Av. Paulista 1938, 17th floor, Cerqueira César, ☎ 011/287–7722). **United States** (⊠ Rua Padre João Manoel 933, Jardins, ☎ 011/3081–6511).

EMERGENCIES
The three main pharmacies have more than 20 stores, each open 24 hours—Droga Raia, Drogaria São Paulo, and Drogasil. The police department in charge of tourist affairs, Delegacia de Turismo, is open weekdays 8–8.
➤ EMERGENCY SERVICES: **Ambulance** (☎ 192). **Delegacia de Turismo** (⊠ Av. São Luís 91, Centro, ☎ 011/3107–8712). **Fire** (☎ 193). **Police (military)** (☎ 190).
➤ HOSPITALS: **Albert Einstein** (⊠ Av. Albert Einstein 627, Morumbi, ☎ 011/3745–1233). **Beneficência Portuguesa** (⊠ Rua Maestro Cardim

769, Paraíso, ☎ 011/253–5022). **Sírio Libanês** (✉ Rua. D. Adma
Jafet 91, Bela Vista, ☎ 011/3155–0200).
➤ 24-HOUR PHARMACIES: **Droga Raia** (✉ Rua José Maria Lisboa 645,
Jardim Paulistano, ☎ 011/3884–8235). **Drogaria São Paulo** (✉ Av.
Angélica 1465, Higienópolis, ☎ 011/3667–6291). **Drogasil** (✉ Av.
Brigadeiro Faria Lima 2726, Cidade Jardim, ☎ 011/3812–6276).

ENGLISH-LANGUAGE MEDIA

Most Avenida Paulista newsstands sell major U.S. and European papers as well as magazines and paperbacks in English. Livraria Cultura
has a large selection of English books of all types in its store at Conjunto Nacional. Fnac sells many international books and periodicals.
Laselva usually receives magazines from abroad earlier than other
bookstores. Saraiva's megastore also has English-language titles.
➤ BOOKSTORES: **Fnac** (✉ Av. Pedroso de Morais 858, Pinheiros, ☎ 011/
3819–2119). **Laselva** (✉ Shopping Ibirapuera, Av. Ibirapuera 3103,
☎ 011/5561–9561). **Livraria Cultura** (✉ Av. Paulista 2073/153,
Cerqueira César, ☎ 011/285–4033). **Saraiva's** (✉ Shopping Eldorado,
Av. Rebouças 3970, Pinheiros, ☎ 011/3819–5999).

HEALTH

Don't drink tap water. Ask for juice and ice made with bottled water
in restaurants and bars. Don't eat barbecued meats sold by street vendors; even those served in some bars are suspect. The air pollution might
irritate your eyes, especially in July and August (dirty air is held in the
city by thermal inversions), so pack eye drops.

MAIL, INTERNET, AND SHIPPING

Internet access is available at many cybercafés around town. There's
a branch of the *correio* (post office) in Centro. International couriers
include DHL and FedEx.
➤ POST OFFICE: **Correio** (✉ Praça do Correio, ☎ 011/3831–5522).
➤ OVERNIGHT SERVICES: **DHL** (✉ Rua da Consolação 2721, Jardins,
☎ 0800/10–6023). **FedEx** (✉ Av. São Luís 187, Loja 43, Centro, ☎
011/5641–7788).

METRÔ TRAVEL

The metrô is safe, quick, comfortable, and clean, but unfortunately it
doesn't serve many of the city's southern districts. The blue line runs
north–south, the orange line runs east–west, and the green line runs
under Avenida Paulista from Vila Mariana to the new stations at
Sumaré and Vila Madalena, near Avenida Pompéia. The metrô operates daily 5 AM–midnight. Tickets are sold in stations and cost R$1.40
one-way. (You can get discounts on round-trip fares and when you buy
10 tickets at once; note that ticket sellers aren't required to change large
bills.) You insert the ticket into the turnstile at the platform entrance,
and it's returned to you only if there's unused fare on it still. Transfers within the metrô system are free, and for bus–metrô trips (one bus
only), you can buy a *bilhete integração* on buses or at metrô stations
for R$2.30. Maps of the metrô system are available from the Depar-
tamento de Marketing Institucional, or you can pick up the *Guia São
Paulo* at newsstands and bookstores.
➤ METRÔ INFORMATION: **Departamento de Marketing Institucional**
(✉ Av. Paulista 1842, 19th floor, ☎ 011/283–4933). **Metrô** (☎ 011/
286–0111 for general information).

MONEY MATTERS

Avenida Paulista is the home of many banks (generally open 10–4),
including Citibank. For currency exchange services without any extra

fees, try Action. In Centro, you can exchange money at Banco do Brasil and at Banespa. Several banks have automatic-teller machines (ATMs) that accept international bank cards and dispense reais.

➤ BANKS: **Banco do Brasil** (⊠ Av. São João 32, Centro, ☎ 011/234–1646). **Banespa** (⊠ Rua Duque de Caxias 200, República, ☎ 011/222–7722). **Citibank** (⊠ Av. Paulista 1111, Jardins, ☎ 011/5576–1190).

➤ EXCHANGE SERVICE: **Action** (⊠ Guarulhos Airport, TPS2 arrival floor, ☎ 011/6445–4458; ⊠ Rua Melo Alves 357, Jardins, ☎ 011/3064–2910; ⊠ Shopping Paulista, Rua 13 de Maio 1947, Paraíso, ☎ 011/288–4222).

SAFETY

Stay alert and guard your belongings at all times, especially at major sights. Avoid wearing shorts, expensive running shoes, or flashy jewelry—all of which attract attention. Also beware of the local scam in which one person throws a dark liquid on you and another offers to help you clean up while the first *really* cleans up!

TAXIS

Taxis in São Paulo are white. Owner-driven taxis are generally well maintained and reliable as are radio taxis. Fares start at R$3.40 and run R$.75 for each kilometer (½ mi) or R$.40 for every minute sitting in traffic. After 8 PM and on weekends fares rise by 20%. You'll also pay a tax if the taxi leaves the city, as is the case with trips to Cumbica Airport. Good radio-taxi companies include Chame Taxi, Ligue-Taxi, and Paulista.

➤ TAXI COMPANIES: **Chame Taxi** (☎ 011/3865–3033). **Ligue-Taxi** (☎ 011/3672–2633). **Paulista** (☎ 011/3746–6555).

TELEPHONES

Phone booths are bright green and yellow. Most operate using prepaid cards, but some still use tokens. Both cards and tokens are sold at newsstands. Cards with 30 credits are sold for R$3. Each credit allows you to talk for 3 minutes on local calls and 17 seconds on long-distance calls.

International calls can be made at special phone booths found in Telesp offices around the city. You can choose your own long-distance company. After dialing 0, dial a two-digit company code, followed by the country code and/or area code and number. To call Rio, for example, dial 0, then 21 (for Embratel, a major long-distance and international provider), then 21 (Rio's area code), and then the number. To call the United States, dial 00 (for international calls), 23 (for Intelig, another long-distance company), 1 (country code), and the area code and phone number. For operator-assisted (in English) international calls, dial 000111. To make a collect long-distance call (which will cost 40% more than normal calls), dial 9 + the area code and the number. São Paulo's area code is 11; phone numbers in the city and state have six, seven, or eight digits. Most cellular phone numbers have eight digits (a few have seven) and start with the number 9.

TOURS

You can hire a bilingual guide through a travel agency or hotel concierge (about R$15 an hour with a four-hour minimum), or you can design your own walking tour with the aid of information provided at Anhembi booths around the city. Anhembi also offers Sunday tours of museums, parks, and Centro that are less expensive than those offered in hotels. The tourist board offers three different half-day Sunday bus tours: of the parks, of the museums, and of historic downtown. Officially, none of their guides speaks English; however, they may be able to arrange something on request.

Gol Tour Viagens e Turismo and Opcional Tour and Guide Viagens e Turismo offer custom tours as well as car tours for small groups. A half-day city tour costs about R$40 a person (group rate); a night tour—including a samba show, dinner, and drinks—costs around R$100; and day trips to the beach or the colonial city of Embu cost R$80–R$90. The English-speaking staff at Savoy specializes in personalized tours.

Canoar is one of the best rafting tour operators in São Paulo State. Trilha Brazil arranges treks in forests around São Paulo. Reputable operators that offer rain-forest, beach, and island excursions include Biotrip, Pisa Trekking, and Venturas e Aventuras.

➤ TOUR-OPERATOR RECOMMENDATIONS: **Biotrip** (✉ Rua Gama Cerqueira 187, Cambuci, ☎ 011/278–1122). **Canoar** (✉ Rua Caetés 410, Sumaré, ☎ 011/3871–2282). **Gol Tour Viagens e Turismo** (✉ Av. São Luís 187, Basement, Loja 12, Centro, ☎ 011/256–2388). **Opcional Tour and Guide Viagens e Turismo** (✉ Av. Ipiranga 345, 14th floor, Suite 1401, Centro, ☎ 011/259–1007). **Pisa Trekking** (✉ Alameda dos Tupiniquins 202, Moema, ☎ 011/5571–2525). **Savoy** (✉ Rua James Watt 142, Suite 92, Itaim Bibi, ☎ 011/5507–2064 or 011/5507–2065). **Tourist board** (☎ 011/6971–5000). **Trilha Brazil** (✉ Rua Professor Rubião Meira 86, Jardim América, ☎ 011/3082–7089). **Venturas e Aventuras** (✉ Rua Minerva 268, Perdizes, ☎ 011/3872–0362).

TRAIN TRAVEL

Most travel to the interior of the state is done by bus or automobile. Still, a few places are served by trains. Trains from Estação da Luz, near 25 de Março, run to some metropolitan suburbs and small interior towns. Trains from Estação Barra Funda serve towns in the west of the state. Estação Júlio Prestes, in Campos Eliseos, has trains to the southeast and some suburbs. Estação Roosevelt serves the suburbs only.

➤ TRAIN INFORMATION: **Estação Barra Funda** (✉ Rua Mário de Andrade 664, Barra Funda, ☎ 011/3612–1527). **Estação Júlio Prestes** (✉ Praça Júlio Prestes 148, Campos Elíseos, ☎ 011/220–8862). **Estação da Luz** (✉ Praça da Luz 1, Luz, ☎ 011/227–7605). **Estação Roosevelt** (✉ Praça Agente Cícero, Brás, ☎ 011/266–4455).

VISITOR INFORMATION

The most helpful contact is the São Paulo Convention and Visitors Bureau, open 9–6. The sharp, business-minded director, Roberto Gheler, speaks English flawlessly and is extremely knowledgeable. Branches of the city-operated Anhembi Turismo e Eventos da Cidade de São Paulo are open daily 9–6.

The bureaucracy-laden Secretaria de Esportes e Turismo do Estado de São Paulo, open weekdays 9–6, has maps and information about the city and state of São Paulo. SEST also has a booth at the arrivals terminal in Cumbica airport; it's open daily 9 AM–10 PM.

➤ TOURIST INFORMATION: **Anhembi Turismo e Eventos da Cidade de São Paulo** (✉ Anhembi Convention Center, Av. Olavo Fontoura 1209, Santana, ☎ 011/6971–5000; ✉ Praça da República at Rua 7 de Abril, Centro, ☎ 011/231–2922; ✉ Av. São Luís at Praça Dom José Gaspar, Centro, ☎ 011/257–3422); ✉ Av. Paulista, across from MASP, Cerqueira César, ☎ 011/251–0970; ✉ Av. Brigadeiro Faria Lima, in front of Shopping Center Iguatemi, Jardim Paulista, ☎ 011/3031–1277). **São Paulo Convention and Visitors Bureau** (✉ Rua Dom José de Barros 17, Centro, ☎ 011/289–7588). **Secretaria de Esportes e Turismo do Estado de São Paulo** (SEST; ✉ Praça Antônio Prado 9, Centro, ☎ 011/239–5822).

SIDE TRIPS FROM SÃO PAULO

Several destinations just outside São Paulo are perfect for short get-aways. Embu's weekend crafts fair and many furniture stores are famous. Although paulistanos often come for a weekend, you can see all the sights in an afternoon. Northwest of the city, water flows in abundance. Soak up the healing properties at the spas and springs of Águas de São Pedro. In Brotas you can go white-water rafting or hike past waterfalls. If you like mountains, try Campos de Jordão; its cafés and clothing stores are often crowded with oh-so-chic paulistanos. For beach lovers, Ilhabela is off the coast from São Sebastião, on the state's North Shore. The island is part of the Mata Atlântica (Atlantic Rain Forest) and is known for its many waterfalls, trails, and diving spots.

Embu

27 km (17 mi) west of São Paulo.

Embu is a Portuguese colonial town of whitewashed houses, old churches, wood-carvers' studios, and antiques shops. A huge downtown handicrafts fair is held every Saturday and Sunday (on Sunday the streets are so crowded you can barely walk). Embu also has many stores that sell handicrafts and wooden furniture; most of these are close to where the street fair takes place.

The baroque **Igreja Nossa Senhora do Rosário** was built in the 18th century. The church contains many images of saints as well as a museum of sacred art. ⊠ *Largo dos Jesuítas 67,* ☎ *011/494–5333.* 🖃 *Free.* ⊙ *Tues.–Sun.*

In the Mata Atlântica you can visit the ᗷ **Cidade das Abelhas** (City of the Bees), a bee farm with a small museum. You can buy honey while your kids climb the gigantic model of a bee. It's about 10 minutes from downtown; just follow the signs. ⊠ *Estrada da Ressaca 9,* ☎ *011/493–6460.* 🖃 *R$3.* ⊙ *Tues.–Sun. 8–6.*

Dining

$–$$$$ ✕ **Celas.** Pull up one of the wooden chairs and prepare to feast on the food of either Minas Gerais or Bahia. ⊠ *Largo 21 de Abril 75,* ☎ *011/494–5791. No credit cards.*

$–$$ ✕ **Os Girassóis Restaurante e Choperia.** Right downtown, this restaurant serves a great variety of dishes, including the recommended *picanha brasileira* (barbecued steak with french fries and manioc flour.) ⊠ *Rua Nossa Senhora do Rosário 3,* ☎ *011/4781–2247. AE, DC, MC, V.*

$ ✕ **Churrascaria Gaúcha.** This roadside barbecue place is inspired by the *churrascarias* of Brazil's south. If meat isn't your thing, check out the large all-you-can-eat salad bar. ⊠ *Via Régis Bittencourt, Km 280,* ☎ *011/494–2961. AE, DC, MC, V.*

Shopping

Atelier Lustres Medieval (⊠ Largo 21 de Abril 183, ☎ 011/494–2903) specializes in decorator light fixtures. The place is 25 years old and has different kinds of table lamps, floor lamps, and ceiling lamps.
Cantão Móveis e Galeria (⊠ Largo dos Jesuítas 169, ☎ 011/4781–2247) is a good place to buy ceramics, colonial-style furniture, and antique decorations.
Choupana Móveis Rústicos (⊠ Av. Elias Yazbek 2800, ☎ 011/494–6177) is one of the biggest places to buy furniture in town. The store makes the items it sells.
Cigana Móveis Rústicos (⊠ Rua Joaquim Santana 16, ☎ 011/494–3501) manufactures some of the furniture, curtains, and cushions it sells.

São Paulo State

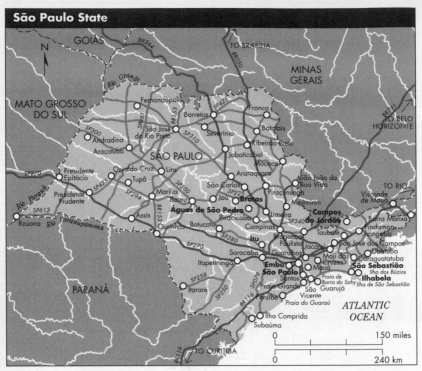

Fenix Galeria de Artes (⊠ Rua Marechal Isidoro Lopes 10, ☎ 011/494–5634) is a good place to find oil paintings and wood and stone sculptures.

Galeria Jozan (⊠ Rua Nossa Senhora do Rosarío 59, ☎ 011/494–2600) sells unmounted Brazilian gemstones, such as *ametistas* (amethysts) and crystals, which you can have set as you wish.

Guarani Artesanato (⊠ Largo dos Jesuítas 153, ☎ 011/494–3200) sells handicrafts made of wood and stone, including sculptures carved from pau-brasil.

Águas de São Pedro

190 km (119 mi) northwest of São Paulo.

Sulfurous waters have made Águas de São Pedro famous countrywide. The healing hot springs were discovered by chance in the 1920s when technicians were drilling for oil. Fonte Junventude is the richest in sulfur and is often used to treat rheumatism, asthma, bronchitis, and skin ailments. The waters at Fonte Gioconda have minor radioactive elements (and yes, they are reportedly good for you). And the Fonte Almeida Salle's water has chlorine bicarbonate and sodium in it, which is said to alleviate the symptoms of diabetes and upset stomachs.

You can access the springs at the *balnéario publico* (public bathhouse) or through your hotel. You can pay to use hotel facilities whether or not you are staying there. Though a number of illnesses respond to the water, most visitors are just healthy tourists soaking in relaxation. Every July, classical music and song fill the air during the Festival de Julho.

A walk through the woods in **Bosque Municipal Dr. Octávio Moura Andrade** (⊠ Av. Carlos Mauro) is a chance to relax. Horseback riding costs R$10 for a half hour.

The **Torre de Petróleo Engenheiro Angelo Balloni** (⊠ Av. Joaquim de Moura Andrade) commemorates the discovery of the town's springs. The tower marks the spot where the city began.

Built in the Swiss style, **Capela Nossa Senhora Aparecidab** (⊠ Rua Izaura de Algodoal Mauro, Jardim Porangaba) perches atop the highest part of the city. Twelve pine trees were planted around this chapel to represent the Twelve Apostles.

Balneário Municipal Dr. Octávio Moura Andrade (⊠ Av. Carlos Mauro, ☎ 019/482–1333) offers immersion baths in sulfurous springwater. You can swim in the pool or sweat in the sauna while you wait for your private soak, massage, or beauty appointment. A snack bar and a gift shop round out the spa services.

Dining and Lodging

$–$$$ ✕ **Bier Haus.** Formerly just a pub, this is now the most popular restaurant in town. People flock in for the pizza and live music. For something more sophisticated, try *peixe na telha*, fish cooked on a ceramic tile. ⊠ *Av. Carlos Mauro 300,* ☎ *019/482–1445. DC, MC, V. Closed Mon.–Wed.*

$–$$ ✕ **Restaurante Avenida.** This simple restaurant offers tasty home cooking like the *filé Cubana* (steak with fried banana and pineapple), served with rice, vegetables, and french fries. The plastic chairs, along with the rest of the decor, leave something to be desired. ⊠ *Av. Carlos Mauro 246,* ☎ *019/482–1422. No credit cards. Closed Mon.*

¢ ✕ **Zuleica Doces.** Good coffee and very sweet deserts are found here. Indulge in the *bombom de maracujá trufado* (a chocolate ball with passion-fruit filling). ⊠ *Av. Carlos Mauro 388, Loja 11,* ☎ *no phone. No credit cards.*

$$–$$$ ▦ **Grande Hotel São Pedro.** In the 1940s this place was a casino. Nowadays it's a teaching hotel with all the comforts of a full-service spa. Many of the friendly, helpful staff members are students. Rest by the pool, have a massage, or a soak in the sulfurous waters. ⊠ *Parque Dr. Octavio de Moura Andrade,* ☎ *019/482–1211,* ℻ *019/482–1665,* 🌐 *www.sp.senac.br/ghp. 96 rooms, 16 suites. 2 restaurants, bar, room service, heated pool, beauty salon, massage, sauna, tennis court, exercise room, recreation room, business services, meeting room. AE, DC, MC, V.*

$ ▦ **Hotel Jerubiaçaba.** Recently updated, the rooms in this 30-year-old hotel are bathed in light colors and filled with simple furnishings. Spa services are offered, or you can float along in the regular swimming pool. ⊠ *Av. Carlos Mauro 168,* ☎ *019/482–1411,* 🌐 *www.jerubiacaba.com.br. 120 rooms, 8 suites. Restaurant, bar, room service, heated pool, beauty salon, massage, tennis court, recreation room, business services, meeting room. AE, DC, MC, V.*

¢ ▦ **Hotel Avenida.** Guests relax on the arcaded veranda of this hotel that resembles a large ranch house. Rooms are plain but spacious. ⊠ *Av. Carlos Mauro 246,* ☎ *019/482–1221,* ℻ *019/482–1224. 53 rooms. Restaurant, room service, pool. No credit cards.*

Shopping

Arte Brasil (⊠ Av. Carlos Mauro 348, ☎ 019/482–1260) sells gemstones, willow baskets, and wood ornaments. **Eldorado** (⊠ Av. Carlos Mauro 341, ☎ 019/482–1756) sells homemade sweets and liqueurs. The owners are very friendly and will give you a taste of the liqueur before you buy. Try the *doce de leite* (a spongy pudding), a typical Brazilian sweet.

Brotas

50 km (31 mi) from Águas de São Pedro, 242 km (151 mi) northwest of São Paulo.

No one is sure how the city of Brotas got its name. One theory is that its founder, Dona Francisca Ribeiro dos Reis, a Portuguese woman who was a devout Catholic, dedicated the site to her patron saint, Nossa Senhora das Brotas. Other people think the name originated in the abundant water springing from the landscape. (The verb *brotar* means "to sprout.") The region has approximately 30 *cachoeiras* (waterfalls), many rivers, and endless opportunities for outdoor diversion. Jacaré-Pepira is the main river, which crosses town from east to west. Nearby rafting, canyoning (rappelling down a waterfall), cascading (sliding down waterfalls), rappelling, biking, hiking, and *bóia cross* (floating down the river in an inner tube) are available.

Most visitors use Brotas as a base and branch out with an arranged agency tour. Admission to some of the sights is free; if not, the fee is included in the price of a tour. Those who choose to drive head toward the neighborhood and then follow the signs. Insect repellent is essential, especially on afternoon river excursions.

See both artwork and performances at the **Centro Cultural** (⊠ Av. Mário Pinotti 584, ☎ FAX 014/653–1107, ext. 233). This 19th-century house used to be a meeting place for the rich and famous.

Seventeen waterfalls are accessible and open to visitors. The **Cachoeira Água Branca** is on D. Calila Ranch, 22 km (13.6 mi) from town; ask for directions. Relax and bathe in the fall's collection pool. On-site is a small distillery were you can try the homemade liqueur. Like everything else in Brazil, it is crowded during summer (January and February).

An hour's walk in the beautiful native forest filled with *jequitibas* and *figueiras* (typical regional trees) brings you to one of the highest waterfalls, the 57-m (186-ft) **Cachoeira Santa Maria** (Bairro Pinheiro neighborhood, ☎ 014/973–6612). The site is 12 km (7.5 mi) from downtown Brotas.

At **Cachoeira Três Quedas** (Alto de Serra neighborhood, 22 km/14 mi from downtown Brotas, ☎ 014/973–6612) you can take a short walk to Cachoeira das Andorinhas for a waterfall shower, then follow the trail to Cachoeira da Figueira, a 40-m (131-ft) waterfall. On the way back stop at the smaller Cachoeirinha das Nascentes to bathe in a collection pool.

Cachoeira Bela Vista (Alto da Serra neighborhood, 28 km/17 mi from downtown Brotas, ☎ 014/978–3855) is one of three waterfalls formed by small streams. The Cachoeira Bela Vista and Cachoeira dos Coqueiros are easy to get to, but a longer trek is necessary to reach the Cachoeira dos Macacos. If you are lucky you may see *macacos* (monkeys) on the way.

On the Beneditos ranch, **Cachoeira do Escorregador** (⊠ Alto da Serra, 38 km/23 mi from downtown Brotas, ☎ 014/978–3855) can be reached by driving toward São Pedro city. The waterfall's natural pools are perfect for cooling off after a light hike. Camping and picnic spots are available, or stop at the snack bar for refreshment.

Dining and Lodging

$ ✕ **Restaurante Casinha.** A lake view adds ambience to this family-owned restaurant. Try the delicious *pintado na brasa*, a charcoal-grilled fish made with garlic, onions, and lemon. ⊠ *Av. Lorival Jaubert Braga 1875*, ☎ *014/653–1225. No credit cards. Closed Mon.–Wed.*

¢–$ ✗ **Malagueta.** Owned by a young couple from São Paulo, Malagueta serves grilled meat, salads, and sandwiches. A green and red color scheme gives the place a happy, modern look. *Salada portofino* (lettuce, sun-dried tomatoes, mozzarella, olives, and mustard dressing) is a noteworthy choice. ⊠ *Av. Mário Pinotti 243,* ☎ *014/653–2297. No credit cards. Closed Mon.*

¢–$ 🏨 **Hotel Estalagem Quinta das Cachoeiras.** Considered the best place in town, this Victorian-style hotel has a staff that prides itself on providing personal attention to their adult guests; no children allowed. ⊠ *Rua João Rebecca, 225 Parque dos Saltos,* ☎ *014/653–2497. 13 rooms. Air-conditioning, refrigerator, pool, sauna, recreation room.* V.

¢ 🏨 **Pousada Caminho das Águas.** The owners of the small inn live on-site, providing a friendly place to rest—and a good breakfast. Rooms are decorated in light colors, with cool ceramic-tile floors. ⊠ *Av. Mário Pinotti 1110, 13309-010,* ☎ *014/653–2428. 18 rooms. Fans, refrigerator, pool. No credit cards.*

Outdoor Activities and Sports

White-water rafting on the Jacaré-Pepira River is best from November to May. The 9-km (5.6-mi) course ranges in difficulty from Class III to Class IV rapids, with drops from 1 to 3 m (3 to 9 ft).

Mata'dentro Ecoturismo e Aventura (⊠ Av. Mário Pinotti 230, ☎ 014/653–1915, WEB www.matadentro.com.br) is the oldest rafting operator in town. It also offers canyoning, rappelling, and hiking excursions. An hour of rafting is about R$48.

You can change in the **Vias Naturais** (⊠ Rua João Rebecca 195, ☎ 014/653–1855 or 014/653–4050, WEB www.viasnaturais.com.br) dressing rooms—or buy a souvenir at the gift shop—before heading out on a river tour. Horseback riding, hiking, and canyoning are also available.

Campos do Jordão

184 km (114 mi) northeast of São Paulo.

Set in the Serra da Mantiqueira at an altitude of 1,690 m (5,576 ft), Campos do Jordão and its fresh mountain air have attracted visitors for years. In July the temperatures drop as low as 32°F (0°C), though it never snows; in warmer months, temperatures linger in the 13°C–16°C (55°F–60°F) range. Some people come for their health (the town was once a tuberculosis treatment area), others for inspiration, including such Brazilian artists as writer Monteiro Lobato, dramatist Nelson Rodrigues, and painter Lasar Segall. The arts continue to thrive, especially during July's Festival de Inverno (Winter Festival), which draws classical musicians from around the world.

Boulevard Genéve, in the busy Vila Capivari district, is lined with cafés, bars, and restaurants, making it a nightlife hub. You'll also find many candy shops (many featuring chocolate) and clothing stores.

Palácio Boa Vista (⊠ Rua Dr. Adhemar de Barros 300, ☎ 012/262–1122), the official winter residence of the state's governor, has paintings by such famous Brazilian artists as Di Cavalcanti, Portinari, Volpi Tarsila do Amaral, and Malfatti. The associated **Capela de São Pedro** (São Pedro Chapel) has sacred art from the 17th and 18th centuries. Admission is free.

The **Horto Florestal** (⊠ Av. Pedro Paulo, ☎ 012/263–1977) is a natural playground for macacos-prego (nail monkeys), squirrels, and parrots, as well as people. The park has a trout-filled river, waterfalls, and trails all set among trees from around the world.

Close-Up

OS BANDEIRANTES

N THE 16TH AND 17TH CENTURIES, groups called *bandeiras* (literally "flags"; it's an archaic term for an assault force) set out on expeditions from São Paulo. Although the *bandeirantes* (bandeira members) are remembered as heroes, their objectives were far from noble. Their initial goal was to enslave Native Americans. Later, they were hired to capture escaped African slaves and destroy *quilombos*, communities these slaves created deep in the interior. Still, by heading inland at a time when most colonies were close to the shore, the bandeirantes inadvertently did Brazil a great service.

A fierce breed, they often adopted indigenous customs and voyaged for years at a time. Some went as far as the Amazon River; others only to what is today Minas Gerais, where gold was discovered; still others found deposits of precious gems. In their travels, they ignored the 1494 Treaty of Tordesillas, which established a boundary between Spanish and Portuguese lands. (The boundary was a vague north–south line roughly 1,600 km/1,000 mi west of the Cape Verde islands; the Portuguese were to control all lands—discovered and yet to be discovered—east of this line and the Spanish all lands to the west of it.) Other Brazilians followed the bandeirantes, and towns were founded, often in what was technically Spanish territory. These colonists eventually claimed full possession of the lands they settled, and thus Brazil's borders were greatly expanded.

Outside town, a chair-lift ride to the top of **Morro do Elefante** (Elephant Mountain) is a good way to enjoy the view. The athletically inclined can climb the 370-step iron staircase to the **Pedra do Baú** (Trunk Stone), north of the city. A trail starts in São Bento de Sapucaí.

Dining and Lodging

$$–$$$ ✕ **Baden-Baden.** One of the specialties at this charming German restaurant in the heart of town is fondue *misto* (with a variety of meats). ⊠ *Rua Djalma Forjaz 93, Vila Capivari,* ☎ *012/263–3610. AE, MC, V.*

$–$$ ✕ **Itália Cantina e Ristorante.** As its name suggests, this place specializes in Italian food. The pasta and the meat dishes are delicious. ⊠ *Av. Macedo Soares 306, Capivari,* ☎ *012/263–1140. AE, DC, MC, V.*

$–$$ ✕ **Sabor Café.** This pleasant place serves an all-you-can-eat sequence of fondues: cheese, meat, and, for dessert, chocolate. ⊠ *Rua Djalma Forjaz 100, Loja 15, Capivari,* ☎ *012/263–3043. AE, DC, MC, V.*

$$ 🏠 **Pousada Vila Capivary.** A stay at this cozy guest house puts you in the gastronomic and commercial center of Campos. The friendly staff is helpful and efficient. ⊠ *Av. Victor Godinho 131, Vila Capivari 12460-000,* ☎ *012/263–1746,* ℻ *012/263–1736,* 🕸 *www.capivari.com.br. 10 rooms, 5 suites. Hot tub. AE, DC, MC, V.*

$–$$ 🏠 **Lausanne Hotel.** Set on an enormous green 7 km (4 mi) outside town, this hotel offers plenty of solitude and the chance to commune with nature. ⊠ *Rodovia SP 50, Km 176, Vila Santa Cruz 12460-000,* ☎ *012/262–2900,* ℻ *011/262–2985. 26 rooms. Restaurant, bar, air-conditioning, pool, tennis court, game room. DC, MC, V.*

Shopping

Casa de Chocolates Montanhês (⊠ Av. Macedo Soares 123, Loja 08, Capivari, ☎ 012/263–3205) is a well-known chocolate shop. **Geléia**

dos Monges (⊠ Rua Tadeu Rangel Pestana 506, ☎ no phone) sells delicious jellies. You'll find handmade embroidered clothing at **Geneve Store** (⊠ Rua Djalma Forjaz 100, Lojas 01 and 03, Capivari, ☎ 012/263–2520). For knit items, try **Paloma Malhas** (⊠ Rua Djalma Forjaz 78, Loja 11, Capivari, ☎ 012/263–1218).

Ilhabela

São Sebastião is 210 km (130 mi) southeast of São Paulo; Ilhabela is 7 km (5 mi)—a 15-min boat ride—from São Sebastião.

Ilhabela is favored by those who like the beach and water sports; indeed, many championship competitions are held here. Beaches along the western shore are calm. The hotels are mostly at the north end, though the best sandy stretches are to the south. Scuba divers have six wrecks to explore, and hikers will appreciate the abundance of inland trails that often lead to a waterfall (the island has more than 300 of them). Note that mosquitoes are a problem; bring plenty of insect repellent.

There are two small towns on the island: one is where the locals live; the other is where most visitors stay because of its hotels, restaurants, and stores. Most businesses that cater to tourists—including restaurants—are open only on weekends during the winter months.

The best way to get around Ilhabela is by car, which you must rent on the mainland. The ferry from São Sebastião transports vehicles as well as passengers to the island.

Praia Grande is 6 km (4 mi) south of the ferry dock and has a long sandy strip with food kiosks, a soccer field, and a small church. At night, people gather 6 km (4 mi) south of Praia Grande at **Praia do Curral,** where there are many restaurants and bars—some with live music—as well as places to camp. The ship *Aymoré* is sunk off the coast of this beach, near the Ponta do Ribeirão.

A small church and many fishing boats add to the charm of **Praia da Armação,** 14 km (9 mi) north of the ferry dock. The beach was once the place for processing whales caught in the waters around the island. Today, windsurfers stick to capturing the wind and the waves.

To reach **Baía dos Castelhanos,** 22 km (14 mi) east of the ferry dock, you need a four-wheel-drive vehicle; if it rains, even this won't be enough. Consider arriving by sailboat, a trip of 1½–3 hours that can be arranged through local tour operators. With such an isolated location, you can see why slave ships once used the bay to unload their illicit cargo after slavery was banned in Brazil. If you're lucky, you might spot a dolphin.

Dining and Lodging

$–$$$ ✕ **Viana.** This restaurant serves *camarão* (shrimp) prepared in sundry
★ ways, as well as grilled fish. Reservations are recommended; there are only a few tables. ⊠ *Av. Leonardo Reale 1560,* ☎ *012/472–1089. AE, DC, MC, V. Closed Mon.–Thurs. Mar.–June and Aug.–Nov.*

$–$$ ✕ **Ilha Sul.** The best option on the menu is the grilled shrimp with vegetables. Fish and other seafood are also available. ⊠ *Av. Riachuelo 287,* ☎ *012/472–9426. AE, DC, MC, V. Closed Mon.–Thurs. Mar.–June and Aug.–Nov.*

$–$$$ 🏨 **Maison Joly.** On arrival, you're given a beach kit complete with
★ mosquito repellent and a hat. Each room is equipped with something that gives it a theme, such as a piano, a billiard table, or a telescope. ⊠ *Rua Antônio Lisboa Alves 278, Morro do Cantagalo,* ☎ *012/472–1201,* FAX *012/472–2364,* WEB *www.maisonjoly.com.br. 10 rooms. Restaurant, bar, air-conditioning, in-room safes, pool. AE, DC, MC, V.*

¢ ⚜ **Pousada dos Hibiscos.** North of the ferry dock, this red house of-
★ fers midsize air-conditioned rooms. The friendly staff serves up a good
breakfast and provides poolside bar service. ⊠ *Av. Pedro de Paula
Moraes 714,* ☎ FAX *012/472–1375. 13 rooms. Bar, air-conditioning,
refrigerator, pool, sauna. DC, MC.*

Outdoor Activities and Sports

BOATING AND SAILING
Because of its excellent winds and currents, Ilhabela is a sailor's mecca.
You can arrange boating and sailing trips through **Maremar Turismo**
(⊠ Av. Princesa Isabel 90, Ilhabela, ☎ 012/472–1418), one of the biggest
tour agencies in Ilhabela. They also offer sailing courses.

For information on annual boating competitions that Ilhabela hosts,
including a large Sailing Week, contact the **Iate Club de Ilhabela** (⊠
Av. Força Expedicionária Brasileira 299, ☎ 012/472–2300). If you'd
like to learn to sail, **Ilha Sailing Ocean School** (⊠ Av. Pedro de Paula
Moraes 578, Hotel da Praia, ☎ 012/472–1992) has 12-hour courses
that cost roughly R$380.

HIKING
The **Cachoeira dos Três Tombos** trail starts at Feiticeira Beach and leads
to three waterfalls. The **Trilha da Água Branca** (Park administration:
⊠ Rua do Morro da Cruz 608, Itaguaçú Beach, ☎ FAX 012/472–2660)
is an accessible, well-marked trail. Three of its paths go to waterfalls
that have natural pools and picnic areas. You can arrange a guided hike
through the park administration.

SCUBA DIVING
Ilhabela has several good dive sites off its shores. In 1894, the British
ship **Dart** sank near Itaboca, about 17 km (11 mi) south of the ferry
dock; it still contains bottles of wine and porcelain dishes. The **Ilha de
Búzios** is a good place to see a variety of marine life. Recommended
for beginners is the sanctuary (which has a statue of Neptune at a depth
of 22 ft) off the shore of **Ilha das Cabras,** a nearby islet.

You can rent equipment and arrange for a dive-boat trip through **Discover Dive** (⊠ Av. Força Expedicionária Brasileira 147, ☎ 012/472–
1999).

SURFING
One of the best places to surf is **Baía de Castelhanos** (22 km/14 mi
east of the ferry dock). **Pacuíba** offers decent wave action 20 km (12
mi) north of the ferry dock.

The **Associação de Surf de Ilhabela** (⊠ Rua Espírito Santo 170, Barra
Velha, ☎ 012/472–8798) promotes surfing events on the island.

WINDSURFING
Savvy windsurfers head to **Ponta das Canas,** at the island's northern
tip. **Praia do Pinto and Armação** (about 12 km/7 mi north of the ferry
dock) have favorable wind conditions.

You can take windsurfing and sailing lessons at **BL3** (⊠ Engenho
D'Água Beach, ☎ 012/472–1034; ⊠ Armação Beach, ☎ 012/472–
1271), the biggest school in Ilhabela. It costs about R$290 for a 12-
hour course.

Side Trips from São Paulo A to Z

BOAT AND FERRY TRAVEL
The ferry from São Sebastião to Ilhabela accepts reservations. It's
worth making them, particularly from December to February. Ferries

run every 20 minutes from 5:30 AM to 1 AM weekdays; weekends see 24-hour service. The fare is R$5 with a car.

➤ INFORMATION: **Ferry** (☎ 0800/55–5510).

BUS TRAVEL

São Pedro buses run daily to Águas de São Pedro from São Paulo's Tietê station. Expresso Prata buses run to Brotas three times a day from São Paulo's Barra Funda station. Viação Litorânea buses leave Tietê station five times daily for the trip to Ilhabela. Viação Mantiqueira buses travel to Campos do Jordão every two hours from Tietê. Every half hour Soamin buses depart for Embu from one of several São Paulo locations.

➤ BUS INFORMATION: **Expresso Prata** (☎ 011/3612–1717). **São Pedro** (☎ 011/6221–0038). **Soamin** (☎ 011/7947–1423). **Viação Litorânea** (☎ 011/6972–0244). **Viação Mantiqueira** (☎ 011/6972–0244).

CAR TRAVEL

Roads in São Paulo State are in good condition and are well marked; some of them are toll roads. To make the 30-minute drive from São Paulo to Embu, take Avenida Professor Francisco Morato to the Rodovia Régis Bittencourt and then follow the signs. Águas de São Pedro is about a 2½-hour drive on SP 330, SP 340, and SP 304. Brotas is three hours on SP 330 and SP 340, SP 310, and SP 225. To reach Campos do Jordão from the city (a 2½-hour drive), take the Rodovia Carvalho Pinto and SP 123. The drive from São Paulo to São Sebastião is about 2½ hours; take the Rodovia Ayrton Senna, followed by the Rodovia Tamoios to Caraguatatuba, and then follow the signs.

EMERGENCIES

➤ HOSPITALS AND CLINICS: **Fundação de Saúde** (✉ Rua Antônio Feijó 52, Águas de São Pedro, ☎ 019/482–1721). **Pronto Socorro Municipal** (✉ Av. Elias Yazbek 1415, Embu, ☎ 011/7822–5744). **Santa Casa** (✉ Rua Pe. Bronislau Chereck 15, Ilhabela, ☎ 012/472–1222). **Santa Teresinha** (✉ Av. Rua Barbosa 703, Brotas, ☎ 014/653–1200). **São Paulo** (✉ Rua Agripino Lopes de Morais 1100, Campos do Jordão, ☎ 012/262–1722).

➤ POLICE: (☎ 190).

ENGLISH-LANGUAGE MEDIA

Ponto das Letras, in Ilhabela, has a small café-bookstore with international magazines.

➤ BOOKSTORE: **Ponto das Letras** (✉ Rua Dr. Carvalho 146, ☎ 012/472–2104).

MONEY MATTERS

Embu has a branch of Bradesco, as does Águas de São Pedro. Brotas is served by Banco do Brasil. In Campos do Jordão, there's an ATM at the Parque Centro Shop; banks include Bradesco and Itaú. Ilhabela has both Banespa and Bradesco branches.

➤ BANKS: **Banco do Brasil** (✉ Av. Rodolfo Guimarães 673, Brotas). **Banespa** (✉ Rua Dr. Carvalho 98, Ilhabela). **Bradesco** (✉ Praça Cel. Julião M. Negrão 29 Ilhabela; Rua Boulevard Francisco P. Carneiro 28, Campos; Rua Maranhão 44, Embu; Rua João B. Azevedo, 269, Águas de São Pedro). **Itaú** (✉ Av. Pelinca 19 Campos).

TOURS

As its name suggests, Ilha Tour specializes in tours (by boat, bike, horse, or jeep) of Ilhabela. Another Ilhabela operator is Mare Mare, which offers scuba-diving, jeep, horseback-riding, and hiking tours. HS Turismo offers five tours in or around Campos do Jordão.

➤ TOUR-OPERATOR RECOMMENDATIONS: **HS Turismo** (✉ Rua Carlina Antonia Sirin 65, ☎ 012/262–2759). **Ilha Tour** (✉ Av. Pedro de Paula Moraes 149, ☎ 012/472–1083). **Mare Mare** (✉ Av. Princesa Isabel 90, ☎ 012/472–1418).

TRANSPORTATION AROUND TOWNS NEAR SÃO PAULO

On weekends, it's difficult to find a place to park in Embu, and parking lots can be expensive. Although you can easily walk to the town's main sights, the *bondinho* (a "train" whose cars are pulled by a truck) crosses Embu and stops at every main square. In Brotas, most natural attractions are outside town, making a car essential. Águas de São Pedro is compact, so it's possible to get around on foot.

Exploring Campos do Jordão without a car is very difficult. The attractions are far-flung, except for those at Vila de Capivari. Trains depart from the Estação Ferroviária Emílio Ribas on tours of the city and its environs (including the 47 km/29 mi trip to Reino das Águas Claras, where there's a park with waterfalls). In Ilhabela a car is the best option, although public buses do cross the island from north to south daily.

➤ CONTACTS: **Estação Ferroviária Emílio Ribas** (☎ 012/263–1531).

VISITOR INFORMATION

➤ TOURIST INFORMATION: **Embu Secretaria do Turismo** (✉ Largo 21 de Abril 139, ☎ 011/494–5333). **Águas de São Pedro Informações Turísticas** (✉ Av. Carlos Mauro, in front of Balneário, ☎ 019/482–1811). **Brotas Informações Turísticas–Centro Cultural** (✉ Av. Mário Pinotti 584, ☎ 014/653–1107). **Campos do Jordão Tourist Office** (✉ At entrance to town, ☎ 012/262–2755). **Ilhabela Secretaria do Turismo** (✉ Rua Bartolomeu de Gusmão 140, ☎ 012/472–1091).

3 THE SOUTH

Brazil's south is a mosaic of cultures and landscapes. *Gaúcho* (cowboy) traditions flourish in immense fields and rangelands near the borders of Uruguay and Argentina. The *colono* (German and Italian colonist) heritage is evident in the cool mountain climes. Spectacular beaches and lush rain forest line the Atlantic coast, vast canyons and eerie sandstone formations dot the interior, and the mighty Iguaçu Falls beckon with their watery chorus.

Updated by
Carlos G.
Tornquist

EXPECT THE UNEXPECTED IN THE SOUTHERN STATES of Paraná, Santa Catarina, and Rio Grande do Sul. The climate is remarkably cooler (the highest elevations even get a couple of inches of snow every year) and the topography more varied than in the rest of Brazil. Further, you're as likely to find people of German and Italian ancestry as Portuguese. And, as Brazil's breadbasket, the Região Sul (Southern Region) has a standard of living comparable to many developed nations.

The southern section of the Serra do Mar, a mountain range along the coast, stretches well into Rio Grande do Sul. It looks like one green wall—broken only by the occasional canyon or waterfall—separating the interior from the shore. Most mountainsides are still covered with the luxuriant Mata Atlântica (Atlantic Rain Forest), which is as diverse and impressive as the forest of the Amazon. The Serra do Mar gives way to hills that roll gently westward to the valleys of the *rios* (rivers) Paraná and Uruguay. Most of these lands were originally covered with dense subtropical forests interspersed with natural rangelands such as the Campos Gerais, in the north, and the Brazilian pampas, in the south.

Although Portugal controlled the continent's Atlantic coast from the Amazon to the Rio de la Plata delta for more than a century after discovering Brazil, the Spanish influence was greatly felt throughout the interior. In the late 1500s, Jesuit missionaries ventured into the valleys of the rios Paraná, Paraguay, and Uruguay, converting (and dominating) the region's native Guarani peoples. The Jesuits and their converts lived in self-sustaining *missões* (mission communities) built around magnificent churches. In the late 1600s, these settlements were increasingly attacked by *bandeirantes* (slave hunters and adventurers), who sought labor for the gold mines of Minas Gerais.

By the time the Treaty of Madrid was signed in 1750, recognizing Portuguese rule in what is roughly today's Brazil, the Jesuits were gone, the native peoples were either enslaved or dispersed in the wilderness, and most of the missões were in ruins. Border issues were more or less resolved, and Portuguese settlement increased. In these early days, cattle raising was the activity of choice. A large number of *charqueadas* (ranches where cattle were slaughtered, and the meat salted and sundried by slaves before export) evolved in the late 1800s. This business was so profitable that "cattle barons" turned small cities into bustling commercial hubs. Although not as significant today, cattle culture still dominates these southern areas.

Perhaps the greatest transformation in the region followed the arrival of German and Italian colonos. These immigrants brought along centuries of Old World farming and wine-making traditions. Many also contributed greatly to urbanization and industrialization, which in turn brought about socioeconomic improvements still evident today.

Pleasures and Pastimes

Dining
Compared with the dishes of northern Brazil, southern cuisine seems bland. It is, however, eclectic. Rice and beans, Brazilian staples, sit on southern tables beside Italian or German dishes. In the state capitals and larger cities, you can find a variety of international cuisines, though not as readily as you can in São Paulo or Rio. Seafood is very popular along the coast, but don't expect elaborate recipes or seasonings.

The *churrasco* (barbecue), by far the most renowned southern dish and now popular throughout the country, originated in Rio Grande do Sul.

A gaúcho's daily rations consisted of beef or mutton—charbroiled on skewers over pit fires—and *mate* (a tea made from the leaves of the *ilex paraguayensis* tree), also called *chimarrão* in Rio Grande do Sul. (Mate remains as popular as coffee in the south today.) This tradition is carried on in *churrascarias* (restaurants that specialize in grilled meats), where waiters bring skewers full of different meats to your table until you can eat no more—a system known as *espeto-corrido* (called *rodízio* in the north-central states). The *barreado* is a lesser-known dish from coastal Paraná. The original recipe called for stewing beef, bacon, potatoes, and spices for several hours in a clay pot made airtight with moistened manioc flour.

Café colonial is the elaborate 5 PM tea that's very popular among the Germans and a dieter's nightmare (the term is also used to refer to the establisment where it is served). Coffee and tea are served—for a set price—with a variety of breads, pies, German kuchen, honey, butter, and several kinds of jelly. For dessert there's ice cream and fruit creams (puréed fruit mixed with cream).

For price categories, *see* the chart *under* Dining *in* Smart Travel Tips A to Z.

Lodging
The south has a great variety of hotels and inns, though upscale facilities are limited. Except for in the smallest towns and most remote areas, however, you shouldn't have a problem finding comfortable accommodations. *Pousadas,* simple inns usually in vintage houses, are common, particularly in beach towns. A recent trend associated with ecotourism is the *hotel-fazenda,* a farm with guest facilities that often includes meals, horseback riding, and visits to local attractions in its rates.

Southern beaches attract many Argentine tourists, so seaside cities might become crowded from December through March, depending on the exchange rate between the currencies. There's usually enough lodging for this influx of visitors (though you'd be wise to reserve in advance), but traffic on highways and crowding on beaches can be nightmares.

For price categories, *see* the chart *under* Lodging *in* Smart Travel Tips A to Z.

Natural Wonders
You can see the power of nature at work at one of Brazil's best-known wonders: the Foz do Iguaçu (Iguaçu Falls), at the southwestern tip of Paraná. Vila Velha, a series of strange sandstone formations in the center of Paraná, might remind you of the eerily moving landscapes of the western United States. The Serra do Mar and Superagüí regions have Mata Atlântica and almost pristine marine ecosystems. In the Aparados da Serra region of Rio Grande do Sul, gargantuan canyons are the result of millions of years of erosion.

The coastline from Paraná to the city of Torres in Rio Grande do Sul has spectacular scenery dotted with great beaches. The landscape is dominated by bays, coves, and hills that end abruptly in the sea. There are a few offshore islands, of which the largest and most visited is Ilha de Santa Catarina. South of Torres, and extending well onto Uruguay, Brazil's southern neighbor, the coastline is basically a 644-km-long (400-mi-long) sandy stretch interrupted only by a few river deltas and lagoons.

Wine
The slopes of the Serra Gaúcha (a mountain district in Rio Grande do Sul) were settled by Italians whose wine-making traditions flourished

in the region's fertile soil. Recent agricultural and industrial developments have dramatically improved the quality of the wines from Rio Grande do Sul. The best varieties come from Caxias do Sul and Bento Gonçalves and can rightfully compete with their more renowned Chilean and Argentine counterparts.

Exploring the South

Touring this region—roughly the size of France—in a short time is a challenge, even though the transportation network is relatively efficient. The major hubs include Curitiba, capital of the region's northernmost state of Paraná, and the Foz do Iguaçu, way to the west; Florianópolis, the capital of the central Santa Catarina State; and Porto Alegre, capital of the southernmost state of Rio Grande do Sul.

The region can be divided into two large but more or less homogeneous areas—the coast and the interior— both of which should be visited. The coast offers great beaches, forested slopes, canyons, the peaks and valleys of the Serra do Mar, and Santa Catarina's German colonies. Trips to the interior can include Iguaçu, Vila Velha and Curitiba in Paraná, the missões and the mountains of Rio Grande do Sul.

Great Itineraries

IF YOU HAVE 5 DAYS

Spend two days in Florianópolis for a taste of life on the southern beaches. Then head to the remarkable Foz do Iguaçu—an hour's flight—for another two days. Return to Florianópolis for the flight home.

IF YOU HAVE 7 DAYS

Spend a day touring the city of Curitiba and take a one-day side trip by car to Vila Velha or by train to Paranaguá. Then head out for a two-day visit to Foz do Iguaçu. From here travel to Florianópolis for a day or two on the beach on the island or along the coast; a visit to the inland German communities could be included.

IF YOU HAVE 10 DAYS

To the seven-day itinerary detailed above add a day in the city of Porto Alegre. Then choose from a two-day visit to the Serra Gaúcha or use one day to visit the missões. If you're truly interested in the great outdoors, include one day at the fantastic canyons at Aparados da Serra.

When to Tour

December through March is invariably hot and humid. Rainfall is high and evenly distributed throughout the year, although some years have had extremely rainy, El Niño–related summers. January and February are top vacation months, so expect crowded beaches, busy highways, and higher prices. Winter (April–November) brings much cooler temperatures, sometimes as low as the upper 20s in the higher elevations at night. Cold fronts blowing in from Patagonia can bring gray, blustery days.

PARANÁ

The state of Paraná is best known for the Foz do Iguaçu, a natural wonder, and the Itaipú Dam, an engineering marvel. At one time the rolling hills of the state's plateau were covered with forests dominated by the highly prized Paraná pine, an umbrella-shape conifer. Most of these pine forests were logged by the immigrants half a century ago, and the cleared land of the immense interior is now where soybeans, wheat, and coffee are grown. (Still, be on the lookout for the occasional Paraná pine.) The state has a very short coastline, but the beaches and the Serra do Mar are spectacular. Curitiba, the upbeat capital, ranks

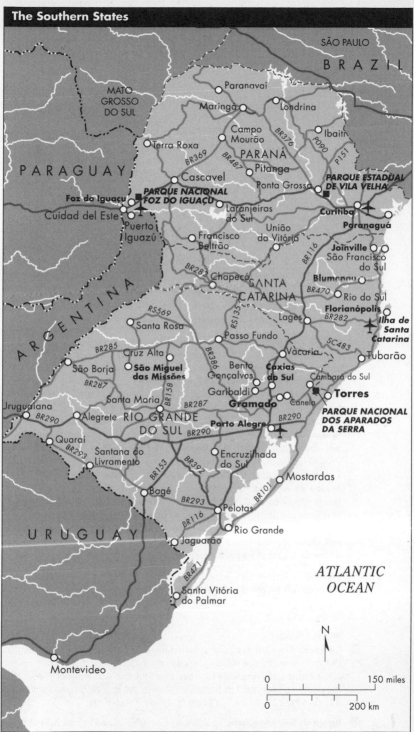

The Southern States

SÃO PAULO

B R A Z I L

MATO
GROSSO
DO SUL

Paranavaí

Maringá

Londrina

Campo
Mourão

Ibaiti

Terra Roxa

BR376

P090

P151

PARANÁ

Pitanga

BR369

BR487

P A R A G U A Y

Cascavel

Ponta Grossa

**PARQUE ESTADUAL
DE VILA VELHA**

**PARQUE NACIONAL
FOZ DO IGUAÇU**

Laranjeiras
do Sul

Curitiba

Foz do Iguaçu

Paranaguá

Cuidad del Este

Puerto
Iguazú

Francisco
Beltrão

União
da Vitória

BR116

Joinville
São Francisco
do Sul

BR283

Chapecó

SANTA

CATARINA

Blumenau

BR470

Rio do Sul

A R G E N T I N A

RS569

Santa Rosa

Lages

Florianópolis

BR282

**Ilha de
Santa
Catarina**

Passo Fundo

SC483

Vacaria

Tubarão

BR285

Cruz Alta

BR386

Caxias
do Sul

Cambará do Sul

São Borja

BR158

**São Miguel
das Missões**

Bento
Gonçalves

Torres

BR287

Garibaldi

Canela

BR290

**PARQUE NACIONAL
DOS APARADOS
DA SERRA**

Santa Maria

BR287

Gramado

Uruguaiana

BR290

Alegrete

RIO GRANDE

Porto Alegre

DO SUL

BR290

Quaraí

BR293

Santana do
Livramento

BR153

Encruzilhada
do Sul

BR392

Mostardas

Bagé

BR293

BR101

U R U G U A Y

BR116

Pelotas

Rio Grande

Jaguarão

*ATLANTIC
OCEAN*

BR471

Santa Vitória
do Palmar

N

Montevideo

0   150 miles

0   200 km

as a top Brazilian city in terms of efficiency, innovative urban planning, and quality of life.

Curitiba

408 km (254 mi) south of São Paulo, 710 km (441 mi) north of Porto Alegre.

A 300-year-old city, Curitiba is on the Paraná plateau, at an elevation of 2,800 ft. It owes its name to the Paraná pinecones, which were called *kur-ity-ba* by the native Guaranis. A large number of the 1.5 million inhabitants with European ancestry and a temperate climate (with a mean temperature of 16°C /61°F) make the city unique within a region that already differs considerably from the rest of the country.

The city is called the environmental capital, not only because of its geographical features but also because progressive city governments since the 1980s have been innovative in their urban planning—a process linked to the former mayor (currently second-term governor of Paraná) and architect, Jayme Lerner. The emphasis on protecting the environment has produced an efficient public transportation system, a comprehensive recycling program, and an array of parks that are being studied by cities around the globe.

Numbers in the text correspond to numbers in the margin and on the Curitiba Setor Histórico map.

Setor Histórico

A GOOD TOUR

Start your tour in the downtown Setor Histórico (Historic District) at the **Museu Paranaense** ①. Then circle the block and take Rua Monsenhor Celso north to the Praça Tiradentes. The **Catedral Metropolitana** ② will be on the opposite side of the square. Continue a couple of blocks north on Rua do Rosário to the Largo da Ordem, site of the **Igreja de São Francisco** ③ and its Museu de Arte Sacra. A block uphill you'll find **Società Giuseppe Garibaldi** ④ on the northern side of Praça Garibaldi. Right behind the society building are the ruins of São Francisco de Paula Church. Proceed from here on Rua Kellers to the **Museu de Arte do Paraná** ⑤. You can then retrace your steps to the Igreja São Francisco and walk three blocks east on Rua São Francisco and then north on Rua Presidente Faria to the **Passeio Público** ⑥. Alternatively, you can leave the Setor Histórico and explore the **Santa Felicidade** neighborhood—with its many restaurants and shops—or have a bite to eat on the **Rua 24 Horas.**

TIMING

You can follow the tour in two hours, but allow half a day to fully see the sights. Shopping or people-watching in a park can fill up the rest of the day.

SIGHTS TO SEE

② **Catedral.** The Cathedral, also called Basílica Nossa Senhora da Luz dos Pinhais, is on the site where the city was founded in 1693. The present neo-Gothic structure was finished in 1893 and was built according to the plan of a cathedral in Barcelona, Spain. ⊠ *Rua Barão do Serro Azul 31,* ☎ *041/222–1131.* ☜ *Free.* ☉ *Daily 7 AM–9 PM.*

③ **Igreja de São Francisco.** St. Francis, Curitiba's oldest church, was built in 1737 and was fully restored in 1981. Check out its gold-plated altar before ducking into the attached **Museu de Arte Sacra** (Sacred Art Museum), with its baroque religious sculptures made of wood and terracotta. ⊠ *Largo da Ordem s/n,* ☎ *church: 041/223–7545; museum: 041/ 322–1525, ext. 265.* ☜ *Free.* ☉ *Tues.–Fri. 9–6, weekends 9–2.*

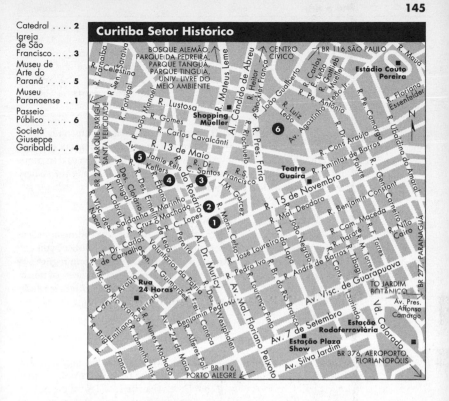

Curitiba Setor Histórico

⑤ Museu de Arte do Paraná. Set in what was once a residence, the Art Museum of Paraná displays works by prominent artists from throughout the state. ✉ *Rua Kellers 289, Setor Histórico,* ☎ *041/323–1617.* 🎟 *Free.* ⊙ *Weekdays 9–6, weekends 10–4.*

① Museu Paranaense. Founded in 1876, the State Museum of Paraná moved several times before installing its collections in this imposing art nouveau building, which served as city hall from 1916 to 1969. The permanent displays contain official documents, ethnographic materials of the native Guarani and Kaigang peoples, coins and photographs, and archaeological pieces related to the state's history. ✉ *Praça Generoso Marques s/n, Centro,* ☎ *011/323–1411.* 🎟 *Free.* ⊙ *Weekdays 9–5, weekends 10–4.*

⑥ Passeio Público. Opened in 1886, the Public Thoroughfare was designed as a botanical and zoological garden. It soon became a favorite place for the affluent to spend their weekend afternoons. The main gate is a replica of that at the Cimetière des Chiens in Paris. Although it's no longer the official city zoo, you can observe several Brazilian primates and birds still kept in the park, as well as majestic sycamores, oaks, and the famed Brazilian *ipê amarelo.* Main Gate: ✉ *Rua Pres. Faria at Pres. Carlos Cavalcanti,* ☎ *041/222–2742.* 🎟 *Free.* ⊙ *Tues.–Sun. 6 AM–7 PM.*

....

OFF THE
BEATEN PATH

RUA 24 HORAS – To satisfy your hunger head for Rua 24 Horas, a short downtown alley that's sheltered by a glass roof (with interior lighting) supported by a steel structure. The entrance is marked by stylish clocks that hint at the appealing ambience inside. You'll find shops and newsstands as well as coffeehouses, bars, and restaurants whose tables spill out onto the walkway. All are open 24 hours a day, seven days a week. ✉ *Rua Coronel Mena Barreto between Rua Visconde de Rio Branco and Rua Visconde de Nacar,* ☎ *041/225–1732.*

SANTA FELICIDADE – What was once an Italian settlement (it dates from 1878) is now one of the city's most popular neighborhoods. It has been officially designated as Curitiba's "Gastronomic District," and, indeed, you'll find some fantastic restaurants—as well as some wine and handicrafts shops—along Via Veneto and Avenida Manuel Elias. The area also has several colonial buildings, such as the Igreja Matriz de São José (St. Joseph Church).

❹ **Società Giuseppe Garibaldi.** The stately neoclassical mansion housing the Garibaldi Society—a philanthropic organization that once helped a great many Italian immigrants—was built with the help of donations from the Italian government and finished in 1890. Today the society sponsors a folkloric dance group and a choir. ⊠ *Praça Garibaldi s/n,* ☎ *041/222–8843.*

Parks, Gardens, and Forests

It would be a shame to visit Brazil's environmental capital without seeing one of its many parks. In addition to the Passeio Público, you can visit the **Bosque Alemão, Parque da Pedreira, Parque Tangüá, Parque Tingüi,** and **Universidade Livre do Meio Ambiente** (they're clustered northwest of Centro and the Setor Histórico). Tour **Jardim Botânico** (east from downtown) on your own or as part of the 2½-hour Linha Turismo bus tour.

PARKS TO SEE

🐦 **Bosque Alemão.** The 8-acre German Woods—which, as its name suggests, is a park honoring German colonos—is on a hill in the Jardim Schaffer neighborhood. On its upper side is the Bach Oratorium, a small concert hall that looks like a chapel; it's the site of classical music performances. The park also has a viewpoint with a balcony overlooking downtown, a library with children's books, and a path through the woods called Hanzel and Gretel Trail. Named after the Grimm Brothers' tale, the trail has the story depicted in 12 paintings along the way, ending at the Mural de Fausto, where there's a stage for music shows. ⊠ *Rua Nicolo Paganini s/n,* ☎ *041/338–6835.* ☜ *Free.* ♥ *Daily sunrise–sunset.*

Jardim Botânico. Although not as old and renowned as its counterpart in Rio, the Botanical Garden has become a trademark of Curitiba. Opened in 1991, its most outstanding feature is the two-story tropical greenhouse that resembles a castle. The Botanical Museum is also worth visiting, with a remarkable collection from the Brazilian flora. There are several paths for jogging or just wandering. ⊠ *Rua Eng. Ostoja Roguski s/n, Jardim Botânico,* ☎ *041/264–6994.* ☜ *Free.* ♥ *Daily 6 AM–8 PM.*

★ **Parque da Pedreira.** In 1992 a cultural complex opened in the abandoned João Gava quarry and adjacent wooded lot. The quarry itself was converted to an amphitheater that can accommodate 60,000 people. The 2,400-seat **Opera de Arame** (Wire Opera House), also on the grounds here, is built of tubular steel and wire mesh and is surrounded by a moat. National and international musical events have given this facility world renown. ⊠ *Rua João Gava s/n,* ☎ *041/354–2662.* ☜ *Park: free.* ♥ *Tues.–Sun. 8 AM–10 PM.*

Parque Tangüá. Tangüá Park may be the latest addition to Curitiba's recreational scene but it has become the most visited. Its interesting landscaping includes a pond in an abandoned quarry that creates the backdrop for a tunnel (dug 36 m/120 ft into the rock wall), an artificial waterfall, and a walkway over the water. ⊠ *Rua Eugenio Flor s/n, Pilarzinho,* ☎ *041/352–5404.* ☜ *Free.* ♥ *Daily sunrise–sunset.*

Parque Tingüí. One of the city's most pleasant parks was designed to protect the upper basin of the Rio Barigüí from urban encroachment. It's best known as the site of the Ukrainian Memorial; finished in 1995, this reproduction of a wooden church with onion domes was built by Ukrainian Catholic immigrants. There is also a shop with traditional Ukrainian handicrafts. ⊠ *Rua Fredolin Wolf s/n,* ☎ *041/ 336–8467.* 🎟 *Free.* ☉ *Daily sunrise–sunset.*

Universidade Livre do Meio Ambiente. The Free University of the Environment—set in the Bosque Zaninelli (Zaninelli Woods)—opened in 1992, the same year that the UN Conference on the Environment and Development was held in Rio. Its main objective is to promote environmentally sound principles through courses, conferences, and seminars. The impressive main structure is built of eucalyptus wood and has a scenic overlook on its top level. Several paths through the woods make this a popular place to wander. ⊠ *Rua Victor Benato 210, Pilarzinho,* ☎ *041/254–5548.* 🎟 *Free.* ☉ *Daily 6–6.*

Dining and Lodging

$$–$$$$
★
✕ **Boulevard.** The pleasant atmosphere and excellent wine selection of this highly regarded French restaurant won't fail to impress. The seafood cassoulet is an outstanding appetizer, and the *coté de veau* (veal steak) with lemon sauce and spinach is a fine entrée. ⊠ *Rua Voluntários da Pátria 539, Centro,* ☎ *041/224–8244. AE, DC, MC, V. Closed Sun. No lunch Sat.*

$–$$$
✕ **Marinheiro.** By far, this is the best seafood in town. The shrimp dishes or the *garoupa* flambé—served with a spicy cream sauce—deserve your attention. ⊠ *Av. Bispo D. José 2315, Batel,* ☎ *041/243–3828. AE, V. Closed Mon. No dinner Sun.*

$–$$
✕ **Estrela da Terra.** Set in an old colonial house on the Praça Garibaldi, this is *the* place to try the local barreado. The menu also contains choices from other regions. ⊠ *Rua Kellers 95, Setor Histórico,* ☎ *041/225–5007. AE, DC, MC, V.*

$–$$
✕ **Schwarzwald.** Recognized as one of the city's best German restaurants, Schwarzwald has also carved a name for itself with great draft beer. Try the house version of *eisbein* (pig's leg served with mashed potatoes) and *kassler* (beef fillet with a cream sauce). ⊠ *Largo da Ordem 63, Setor Histórico,* ☎ *041/223–2585. AE, DC, MC, V.*

$
✕ **Devon's Baby Beef.** The service is excellent at this rodízio-style churrascaria. It's very popular with businesspcople and visitors to the administrative building in the Centro Cívico area. ⊠ *Rua Lysimaco Ferreira da Costa 436, Centro,* ☎ *048/254–7073. DC, MC, V. No dinner Sun.*

$
✕ **Madalosso.** An enormous, hangerlike building (seating 4,500) houses the best-known restaurant in Santa Felicidade. The prix-fixe Italian menu includes a similarly large selection of pasta and sauces, meat dishes, and salads. ⊠ *Rua Manoel Ribas 5875, Santa Felicidade,* ☎ *041/372–2121. AE, DC, MC, V. No dinner Sun.*

¢–$
✕ **Baviera.** Set in an imposing house on a hillside, this popular, affordable restaurant requires you to enter through the cellar. Baviera is essentially a pizzeria, but the menu also includes Brazilian-style steak, grilled chicken, and hamburgers. ⊠ *Rua Augusto Stellfeld 18, Setor Histórico,* ☎ *041/232–1995. AE, DC, MC, V.*

$$–$$$
★
🏨 **Grand Hotel Rayon.** A spacious lobby welcomes you to Curitiba's most sophisticated hotel. Superbly furnished standard rooms have soundproof windows and two phone lines, which are a blessing for the business traveler. Service is impeccable, and the location—in the heart of the financial district and right next to Rua 24 Horas—is convenient. ⊠ *Rua Visconde de Nacar 1424, Centro 80411-201,* ☎ *041/322–6006 and 800/ 41–8899,* 🖷 *041/322–4004,* 🖳 *www.rayon.com.br. 136 rooms, 11 suites.*

2 restaurants, bar, coffee shop, room service, outdoor pool, sauna, exercise room, business services, meeting room. AE, DC, MC, V. CP.

$–$$ ☷ **Bourbon & Tower.** Much like its counterpart in Foz do Iguaçu, this hotel is recommended for the sophisticated business or leisure traveler. The decor is sober, with custom antique-style furniture and textured wallpaper. The restaurant Le Bourbon serves French-Swiss dishes, but the Brazilian *feijoada* is the Saturday special. ⊠ *Rua Candido Lopez 102, Centro 80010-050,* ☎ *041/322–4001 and 0800/11–8181,* ℻ *041/ 322–2282,* WEB *www.bourbon.com.br. 165 rooms, 10 suites. Restaurant, bar, coffee shop, business services, convention center, exercise room, sauna. AE, DC, MC, V. CP.*

$–$$ ☷ **Duomo Park Hotel.** Everything is shiny and new at the small Duomo Park Hotel. The apartments and suites are unusually spacious. Bathrooms are heated—hard to find in Brazil—but welcome in the cold Curitiba winters. Another draw is the location: one step from Rua 24 Horas. ⊠ *Rua Visconde de Rio Branco 1710, Centro, 80420-200,* ☎ *041/224–7095 or 0800/41–1816,* ℻ *041/224–7095. 48 rooms. Restaurant, bar, business services, meeting room, airport shuttle. AE, DC, MC, V. CP.*

$–$$ ☷ **Slaviero Braz Hotel.** The last renovation brought this 50-year-old hotel up to date. Rooms are large, with wood paneling and matching furniture. Beds are king-size, with colorful spreads and cushions that invite you to relax. Note that rooms in the east wing are smaller and oddly shaped, and elevators are cramped because of the original building plan. The second-floor Getúlio bar-café has a balcony overlooking the walkway of Rua das Flores and is a popular gathering spot for businesspeople. ⊠ *Av. Luiz Xavier 67, Centro, 80020-020,* ☎ *041/322–7271 or 800/41-3311,* ℻ *041/322–2398,* WEB *www.slaviero-hotels.com. 89 rooms, 2 suites. Restaurant, bar, meeting rooms, business center. AE, DC, MC, V. CP.*

¢ ☷ **Condor Hotel.** Location is the main draw of this basic, low-budget option a block from the bus and rail terminal. The nondescript rooms are showing their age but are comfortable enough to be recommended for those en route to other southern destinations. ⊠ *Av. 7 de Setembro 1866, Centro 80060-070,* ☎ *041/262–0322,* ℻ *041/262–0322. 95 rooms. AE, DC, MC, V. CP.*

¢ ☷ **Íbis Curitiba.** A recent and welcome addition to the city's roster of budget lodging, the hotel combines comfort and efficiency in cream-color rooms with a no-frills approach to the extras. Be prepared to carry your own luggage. The reception desk and the restaurant are detached from the main building, in restored historic houses. Íbis is one of the few hotels to offer rooms for guests with disabilities. ⊠ *Rua Mateus Leme 358, Centro Cívico 80020-050,* ☎ *041/324–0469 or 800/11–1790,* ℻ *041/324–3404,* WEB *www.ibis-brasil.com.br. 80 rooms. Restaurant, bar. AE, DC, MC, V.*

Nightlife and the Arts

Curitiba has a bustling cultural scene, a reflection of the European background of many of its citizens. Complete listings of events are published in the *Gazeta do Povo*, the major daily newspaper.

The **Estação Plaza Show** has something for everyone—night and day. What was once a railway terminal is now a 210,000-square-m (700,000-square-ft) covered area with a colorful and noisy collection of bars and restaurants, amusement parks, and more than 100 shops. The small Museu Ferroviário (Railway Museum), a cineplex, and daily live musical shows add to the center's charm. ⊠ *Av. 7 de Setembro 2775, Centro,* ☎ *041/322–5356.* ☜ *Free.* ☉ *Daily 10 AM–2 AM.*

The **Teatro Guaíra** (⊠ Rua 15 de Novembro s/n, Centro, ☎ 041/322–2628), formerly the Teatro São Teodoro (circa 1884), was totally rebuilt in its present location and reopened in 1974. It has a modern, well-equipped 2,000-seat auditorium, as well as two smaller rooms. Shows include plays, popular music concerts, and the occasional full-fledged opera.

Outdoor Activities and Sports

Curitiba has three professional soccer clubs: Coritiba, Atlético Paranaense, and Paraná Clube. Check local newspaper listings for upcoming game times and locations. Many of the area's parks have paths for jogging and bicycling.

Arena da Baixada (⊠ Rua Eng. Rebouças 3113, Água Verde, ☎ 041/333–4747) was opened in early 1999 as the new stadium of Atlético Paranaense. It's the most modern (and safest) sports facility in the country, with a 32,000-seat capacity to be expanded to 50,000 in the future. **Estádio Couto Pereira** (⊠ Rua Ubaldino do Amaral 37, Alto da Glória, ☎ 041/362–3234) is the 60-year-old home of Coritiba FC and holds 40,000 fans.

Parque Barigüi (⊠ Av. Candido Hartmann at Av. Gen. Tourinho; Km 1 of BR 277, ☎ 041/244–8778) contains soccer fields, volleyball courts, and paths spread throughout 310 acres.

Shopping

Curitiba Outlet Center (⊠ Rua Brigadeiro Franco 1916, Batel, ☎ 041/224–1900) has a large array of clothing shops with rock-bottom prices.

Buy traditional crafts made of wicker, clay, and leather at **Feito Aqui-Artesanato do Paraná** (⊠ Alameda Dr. Muricy 950, Centro, ☎ 041/222–6361). Interact directly with the artisans every Sunday at the **Feira de Artesanato,** held in the Praça Garibaldi from 9 to 3.

Shopping Center Müller (⊠ Rua Candido de Abreu 127, São Francisco, ☎ 041/224–0510) is the city's prime shopping location, with branches of national chains, upscale fashion and jewelery stores, as well as small handicraft shops, restaurants and cafés, bookstores, and movie theaters.

Paranaguá

90 km (56 mi) southeast of Curitiba.

Most of Brazil's coffee and soybeans are shipped out of Paranaguá, the nation's second-largest port, which also serves as chief port for land-locked Paraguay. Downtown holds many examples of colonial architecture and has been designated an official historic area. The city, founded in 1565 by Portuguese explorers, is 30 km (18 mi) from the Atlantic on the Baía de Paranaguá. The northern side of this bay has a great swatch of Mata Atlântica; several islands in the bay also have rain forests as well as great beaches. You'll find other attractive sandy stretches farther south, toward the Santa Catarina border.

Although you can reach Paranaguá on BR 277, consider taking the more scenic Estrada da Graciosa, which follows the route taken by 17th-century traders up the Serra do Mar. This narrow, winding route—paved with rocks slabs for most of its length—is some 30 km (18 mi) longer than BR 277, but the breathtaking peaks and slopes covered with rain forest make the extra travel time worthwhile.

Igreja Nossa Senhora do Rosário, the city's first church, was destroyed, sacked, and rebuilt several times, but its facade (circa 1578) is original. ⊠ *Largo Monsenhor Celso s/n, ☎ no phone. ☎ Free. ☺ Daily 7 AM–9 PM.*

The **Museu de Arqueologia e Etnologia** (Archaeology and Ethnology Museum) occupies a building that was part of a Jesuit school founded in 1752. It closed in 1759 when the Marques de Pombal from Portugal, trying to eliminate the power of the Church, forced the Jesuits to be expelled from Brazil. The collection includes pieces found in excavations in the area, most belonging to the Sambaqui, a native, coastal-dwelling people. ⊠ *Rua General Carneiro 66,* ☎ *041/422–8844.* ☜ *R$1.50.* ◷ *Tues.–Sun. noon–5.*

★ The 10-km-long (6-mi-long) **Ilha do Mel** (Honey Island), a state park in the Baía de Paranaguá, is the most popular destination on Paraná's coast. It's crisscrossed by hiking trails—cars aren't allowed and the number of visitors is limited to 5,000 at any one time—and has two villages, Encantadas and Nova Brasília, and several pristine beaches. Local lore has it that the east shore's Gruta das Encantadas (Enchanted Grotto) is frequented by mermaids. On the south shore, check out the great views from Farol das Conchas (Lighthouse of the Shells) and the Forte de Nossa Senhora dos Prazeres (Fort of Our Lady of Pleasures), built in 1767. Ferries leave regularly from Pontal do Sul, 49 km (30 mi) east of Paranaguá; the boat ride takes 30 minutes and costs R$10. To ensure admission in the high season (December–March), it's best to book a tour to the island in Curitiba. ⊠ *Ferry dock: Pontal do Sul, Pontal do Paraná,* ☎ *041/455–1316.*

The northern shore of Baía de Paranaguá is also home to the 53,000-acre **Parque Nacional de Superagüi** and its complex system of coves, saltwater marshes, and forested islands—including Ilha Superagüi and Ilha das Peças. These pristine settings contain animal and bird species unique to the Mata Atlântica. You can visit the continental part of the park from the fishing village of Guaraqueçaba (on the bay's far northern side), a three-hour ferry ride from Paranaguá's harbor, though it's best to explore the islands on an organized boat tour. *Park Admininstration, 2 km N of Guaraqueaba,* ☎ *041/422–6045.*

Dining and Lodging

$ ✕ **Casa do Barreado.** As its name suggests, this small, homey, family-run restaurant specializes in the traditional barreado. You'll also find *galinha na púcura,* an unusual chicken barreado. Although the restaurant is officially open only on weekends, you can call ahead to arrange a dinner during the week. ⊠ *Rua Antônio Cruz 9, Paranaguá,* ☎ *041/423–1830. Reservations essential. No credit cards. Closed weekdays.*

$ ✕🛏 **Camboa.** In the historic district, Camboa has comfortable facilities and a dedicated staff. Modern architecture and cheerful colors blend with the colonial surroundings. Ask to be on the north side for a bay view. Continental cuisine, with an emphasis on French, is served in the restaurant. ⊠ *Rua João Estevão s/n, Paranaguá 83203-020,* ☎ *041/423–2121,* ℻ *041/423–2121,* 🌐 *www.hotelcamboa.com.br. 114 rooms, 6 suites. Restaurant, 2 bars, coffee shop, indoor pool, pool, sauna, 2 tennis courts, exercise room, shops, recreation room, business services, meeting room. AE, DC, MC, V. CP.*

¢ ✕🛏 **Dantas Palace.** Simple but clean rooms in a quiet quarter make this hotel a good-value choice. The on-site restaurant, Le Bistrô, serves excellent international cuisine and attracts residents from the whole region. ⊠ *Rua Visconde de Nacar 740, Paranaguá 83203-430,* ☎ *041/423–1555,* ℻ *041/422–7075. 45 rooms. Restaurant, bar. AE, DC, MC, V. CP.*

Parque Estadual de Vila Velha

97 km (60 mi) northwest of Curitiba.

The 22 towering rock formations of the 7,670-acre Vila Velha State Park stand in sharp contrast to the green rolling hills of the Campos

Gerais, Paraná's central plains. Three hundred million years of rain and wind have carved these sandstone formations, whose names—the Lion, the Cup, the Mushroom—reflect their shapes. You can visit these natural monuments on foot or in a tractor-pulled wagon along a well-marked, 2½-km (1½-mi) trail that starts a mile from the visitor center. Traversing the path and viewing the formations on foot takes about two hours. ✉ *Km 511 on BR 376, 20 km (12 mi) before Ponta Grossa,* ☎ *042/228–1138.* 🎫 *R$2.* ☉ *Daily 8–6.*

Dining and Lodging

$ ✗ **Pampeana.** This busy, espeto-corrido-style churrascaria is the perfect place to satisfy a hearty appetite acquired after a day of touring Parque Estadual de Vila Velha. It has a great salad bar for those not too crazy about the meat excesses of churrasco. ✉ *Km 373 on BR 376,* ☎ *042/229–2881. DC, MC, V. No dinner Sun.*

¢–$ ✗🏨 **Vila Velha Palace.** Considering that this hotel is *the* luxury option in the city and one of the largest in Paraná, the amenities are limited, but service is friendly and efficient. Rooms have standard decor, with large beds. The house restaurant serves Brazilian fare. ✉ *Rua Balduino Taques 123, 84040-000,* ☎ *042/225–2200,* 🖷 *042/225–2200,* WEB *www.convoy.com.br/~hvvelha. 94 rooms, 2 suites. Restaurant, bar, sauna, meeting rooms. AE, DC, MC, V. CP.*

¢–$ 🏨 **Hotel Fazenda Capão Grande.** The 150-year-old Fazenda Capão Grande is a fully functional ranch that breeds *criollo* horses. You can fully experience cowboy traditions—a great way to round out your visit to Vila Velha—riding classes are available, too. There are trails and waterfalls to explore within the farm. ✉ *19 km (12 mi) along an unpaved road off BR 276 (entrance near Km 500 marker),* ☎ *042/228–1198,* 🖷 *042/225–4348. 7 rooms. Dining room, horseback riding. No credit cards. FAP.*

¢ 🏨 **Planalto Palace.** Although you'll find few facilities here, it's a clean, reliable choice for the budget traveler. ✉ *Rua 7 de Setembro 652, 84010-350,* ☎ *042/225–2122,* 🖷 *042/225–2122. 66 rooms. Bar. AE, DC, MC, V. CP.*

Foz do Iguaçu

637 km (396 mi) west of Curitiba, 544 (338 mi) west of Vila Velha.

The Foz do Iguaçu cascade in a deafening roar at a bend in the Rio Iguaçu, where southwestern Paraná State meets the borders of both Argentina and Paraguay. This Brazilian town, and the Argentine town of Puerto Iguazú are the hubs for exploring the falls (the Paraguayan town of Ciudad del Este is also nearby).

The avalanche of water actually consists of some 275 separate falls (in the rainy season, they can number as many as 350) that plunge 80 m (250 ft) onto the rocks below. The backdrop is one of dense, lush jungle, ubiquitous red earth, and rainbows and butterflies. The falls and the lands around them are protected by Brazil's Parque Nacional Foz do Iguaçu and Argentina's Parque Nacional Iguazú (where the falls are referred to by their Spanish name, the Cataratas de Iguazú).

The Brazilians are blessed with the best panoramic view (allow one full day to explore); the Argentine side—where most of the falls are actually situated—offers better up-close experiences. Local tour operators offer trips that will take you to both. To set your own pace, you can take a taxi or one of the regularly scheduled buses across the international bridge, Ponte Presidente Tancredo Neves, to Argentina. If you're a Canadian, U.K., or U.S. citizen crossing into Argentina from Brazil (or Brazil from Argentina or Paraguay), you don't need a visa for a short visit to the falls. You must, however, pay an entry fee and have your passport stamped. Immigration authorities keep the region under close watch.

The summer months (November–March) are hot and humid, so if you're bothered by the heat, plan to visit between April and October. Be aware, however, that high waters due to heavy rainfall on the upper Iguaçu River basin might restrict access to some catwalks. Whatever time of year you visit, bring rain gear: some of the paths take you right to the falling water, where the spray can leave you drenched.

★ The **Parque Nacional do Iguaçu** extends 25 km (16 mi) along a paved highway southwest of downtown Foz do Iguaçu. Park administration has recently been handed over to a private operator, which has implemented several changes. An ATM, a currency exchange, and information are available at the entrance. You can no longer drive into the park, you must park at the entrance and take a double-decker shuttle from there. A small museum sits is 1 km (½ mi) away; a restaurant and souvenir kiosks with souvenirs are at the falls (11 km/7 mi). Near the trailhead is the luxurious, historic Hotel das Cataratas. The path to the falls is 2 km (1 mi) long, and its walkways, bridges, and stone staircases lead through the rain forest to concrete and wooden catwalks. (Much of the park's 457,000 acres is protected rain forest—off-limits to visitors and home to the last viable populations of jaguars as well as rare bromeliads and orchids).

Salto Macuco (Macuco Falls) is an optional stop within the park. The crystal-clear waters of the Rio Macuco, a tributary of the Iguaçu, fall 18 m (60 ft) into a natural pool within the forest. The only way to visit this little gem is on a tour that takes about two hours and costs roughly R$70 per person. The trip requires a 7-km (5-mi) ride in a four-wheel-drive vehicle, followed by a short hike through the forest; it includes a boat ride to the main falls.

Highlights of the Brazilian side of the falls include first the Salto Santa Maria, from which catwalks branch off to Salto Deodoro and Salto Floriano, where you'll be doused by the spray. The end of the catwalk puts you right at tallest and most popular falls, Garganta do Diabo (Devil's Throat), which extend for 3 km (1½ mi) in a 270-degree arch; the water thunders down 54 m (180 ft). On the last section of the main trail, there's a building with facilities, including a panoramic elevator (open daily 8:30–6) for which a very small fee is charged. ⊠ *Km 17, Rodovia das Cataratas,* ☎ *045/523–8383.* ⬚ *R$5. Mon. 1–6, Tues.– Sun. 8–6.*

In Argentina's **Parque Nacional Iguazú** (☎ 0757/20180), there are a couple of major *circuitos* (routes). The Circuito Inferior (Lower Circuit) is a loop trail that leads to the brink of several falls. It starts off the main path leading from the visitor center, which is open daily from 7 AM to 8 PM. Wear your bathing suit on this route so you can take a dip in the calm pools at the trail's edge. The Circuito Superior (Upper Circuit) is a 900-m-long (3,000-ft-long) path that borders the ridge on the river's south side, along the top of the falls.

The Argentina side offers the chance to view Devil's Throat from a different perspective. From Puerto Canoas, 4 km (2½ mi) up river from the visitor center, a small fleet of zodiacs will take you to the remnants of the ½-km-long (¼-mi-long) catwalk that once spanned the river to the falls. Much of this structure was washed away by floods. An overlook lets you watch the mighty waters of the Iguaçu disappear right in front of you.

There are other notable sights near the Foz do Iguaçu, including the privately funded **Parque das Aves** (Bird Park). Here, on 36 acres of mostly untouched tropical forest right outside the national park, are 8-m-high (25-foot-high) aviaries with 170 species of birds. A butterfly collection, a gift shop, and a restaurant round out the facilities. ⊠ *Km 10.5, Rodovia das Cataratas,* ☎ *045/523–1007.* ☞ *R$10.* ☉ *Daily 9–6.*

About 21 km (13 mi) up the Rio Paraná (which flows into the Rio Iguaçu just below the falls) is a great achievement of Brazilian civil engineering: the mighty **Hidrelétrica de Itaipú.** The main structure of the world's largest hydroelectric power plant is 8 km (5 mi) long; its powerhouse (which provides electricity for much of the country) alone is 2 km (1 mi) long. An hour-long guided bus tour of the complex leaves from the visitor center, where you can also watch a 30-minute video about the dam's construction. ⊠ *Km 11, Av. Tancredo Neves,* ☎ *045/520–5252.* ☞ *Free.* ☉ *Daily 8–6.*

At the **Ecomuseu de Itaipú,** with six biological refuges, you can learn about attempts to preserve local flora and fauna. ⊠ *Km 10, Av. Tancredo Neves,* ☎ *045/520–5817.* ☞ *Free.* ☉ *Daily 8–6.*

Dining and Lodging

Near the borders of two other countries, the town of Foz do Iguaçu has a cosmopolitan atmosphere that's reflected in the cuisine. For a city of its size, the options are great. There's also one noteworthy hotel on the Argentina side—the Internacional Cataratas de Iguazú. For convenience, most visitors stay in the establishments that line BR 469 (Rodovia das Cataratas), the highway that runs from the city of Foz do Iguaçu to the national park and the falls.

$–$$$ ✕ **Zaragoza.** In a quiet neighborhood on a tree-lined street, this cozy
★ restaurant is owned by Paquito, a Spanish immigrant. The fare includes the seafood paella, the house specialty (order serves two), as well as several delicious fish options. The *surubi,* a regional fish, definitely merits a try. ⊠ *Rua Quintino Bocaiúva 882,* ☎ *045/574–3084. AE, V.*

$–$$ ✕ **Cantina 4 Sorelle.** The atmosphere at this Italian restaurant is warm and cheerful—and it's very popular among the locals. The staff serves the pasta dishes and pizzas efficiently. ⊠ *Rua Alm Barroso 1336,* ☎ *045/523–1707. AE, DC, MC, V.*

$ ✕ **Bufalo Branco.** The restaurant is the city's finest and largest churrascaria. The picanha and surubi fillets stand out among the 20-plus meat varieties. The salad bar is well stocked, a boon for those on the vegetarian side of the gourmet spectrum. ⊠ *Av. Rebouças 530,* ☎ *045/523–9744. AE, V.*

$$ ✕▥ **Bourbon Foz do Iguaçu Resort & Convention Center.** This hotel is both a great choice for the leisure traveler and a preferred location for conventions. The decor is elegant in light yellow tones, and the upper floors let you enjoy a view of the national park's lush rain forest. Most of the spacious rooms and guest facilities are in the main building; suites occupy the top floors of an adjacent tower. On the lower floors is a small shopping center. Hotel grounds have a jogging path that runs through a patch of rain forest. The highly regarded restaurant, Tarobá, serves international fare. ⊠ *Km 2½, Rodovia das Cataratas, 85863-000,* ☎ *045/523–1313 or 0800/11–8181,* 𝔽𝔸𝕏 *045/574–1110. 298 rooms, 13 suites. 3 restaurants, 2 bars, coffee shop, 3 pools, 2 tennis courts, soccer, sauna, health club, jogging, shops, convention center, travel services, car rental. AE, DC, MC, V. MAP.*

$$ ✕▥ **Internacional Cataratas de Iguazú.** Half the rooms in this top-notch
★ Argentina-side hotel have direct views of the falls, so be sure to ask for a view when you make a reservation. Floor-to-ceiling windows let

the inspiring scene into the lobby, restaurants, and bars; even the pool has a vista. The handsomely decorated main restaurant serves a memorable trout maître d'hôtel wrapped in pastry. ⊠ *Km 4, Ruta 12, Parque Nacional Iguazú, Puerto Iguazú, Argentina,* ☎ *0757/21100,* FAX *0757/21090. 180 rooms, 4 suites. 2 restaurants, 2 bars, pool, 3 tennis courts, meeting room. AE, DC, MC, V. CP.*

$-$$ ✕▥ **Hotel das Cataratas.** Not only is this stately hotel *in* the national
★ park (with wonderful views of the falls), but it also provides the more traditional comforts—large rooms, terraces, vintage furniture, hammocks—of a colonial-style establishment. This pink building is surrounded by galleries and gardens; its main section has been declared a Brazilian national heritage site. The Itaipú restaurant serves a traditional Brazilian dinner, featuring feijoada with a variety of side dishes. Anything featuring fish from the Paraná basin is also recommended. ⊠ *Km 25, Rodovia das Cataratas, 85850-970,* ☎ *045/574–7000 or 0800/15–0006,* FAX *045/574–1688,* WEB *www.tropicalhotel.com.br. 200 rooms. 2 restaurants, bar, coffee shop, pool, 2 tennis courts, shops. AE, DC, MC, V. CP.*

$$ ▥ **Iguaçu Golf Club and Resort.** Even the most demanding visitors will
★ find a stay at the Iguaçu Golf Club unforgettable. The resort has an 18-hole, par-72 course, a driving range, and a practice green. Accommodations are spacious and plush with plenty of tropical vegetation to preview what lies beyond in the national park. If you're traveling with family or a group of friends, ask for one of the separate guest houses. ⊠ *Km 7, Rodovia das Cataratas 6845, 85863-000,* ☎ *045/523–4749,* FAX *045/523–5737,* WEB *www.iguassugolf.com.br. 67 rooms, 5 guest houses. Restaurant, 2 bars, pool, golf course, health club, shops. AE, DC, MC, V. CP.*

¢ ▥ **Foz Plaza.** This downtown hotel is a reliable budget choice. Although the rooms are standard—and the decor isn't really tasteful—they're clean. ⊠ *Rua Mal, Deodoro 1819, 85851-030,* ☎ *045/523–1448 or 0800/ 11–6768,* FAX *045/523–1448. 64 rooms. Restaurant, bar, pool, sauna. AE, DC, MC, V, CP.*

SANTA CATARINA

The state of Santa Catarina has almost 485 km (300 mi) of coastline (with many gorgeous beaches) and a small interior countryside. Its capital, Florianópolis, is on Ilha de Santa Catarina, an island with 42 beaches and many world-class hotels and resorts. Santa Catarina is also home to the German settlements of Blumenau and Joinville, in the valley of the Rio Itajaí. This highly industrialized district still retains some of its German flavor, including a popular Oktoberfest.

Florianópolis and Ilha de Santa Catarina

300 km (187 mi) southeast of Curitiba, 476 km (296 mi) northeast of Porto Alegre.

It's no wonder that every summer around 300,000 Argentines travel more than 960 km (600 mi) to enjoy the breathtaking beaches and warm waters off the shore of the Ilha de Santa Catarina. They add to a constant influx of Brazilians, making this one of the country's top tourist destinations. Called Magic Island by locals and enthusiastic visitors, Ilha de Santa Catarina is joined to the mainland by two bridges: the modern multi-lane Ponte Colombo Sales, and the 60-year old Ponte Hercilio Luz—the later now condemned. The island has more than 42 charming, easy-to-reach beaches. Lovers of the outdoors will find not only plenty of opportunities for scuba diving, surfing, sailing, and jet skiing but also plenty of chances to view nature along trails through tropical forests, from beaches (the whale-watching is good), or even from the sky strapped into a hang glider.

But the island isn't only a place of natural wonders. The city of Florianópolis played an important part in history. It was the southernmost post of Portuguese rule for some time, and it was the site of several skirmishes with the Spanish before the border disputes were settled.

Although you might be lured by the beaches, downtown Florianópolis offers worthwhile attractions.

The **Alfândega** (Old Customs House), which dates from 1875, is the city's best example of neoclassical architecture. It now houses an artists' association and a handicrafts shop that sells *rendas de bilro* (hand-woven tapestries) and pottery. ⊠ *Rua Cons. Mafra 141, Centro,* ☎ *048/224–6082.* ☞ *Free.* ⊙ *Weekdays 9–7, Sat. 9–noon.*

Beyond the Alfândega is the picturesque, 100-year old **Mercado Público** (Public Market), a Portuguese colonial structure with a large central patio. A recent renovation managed to restore the market—which is filled with stalls selling fish, fruit, and vegetables—while preserving its Arabian-bazaar atmosphere. ⊠ *Rua Cons. Mafra 255, Centro,* ☎ *048/225–3200.* ⊙ *Mon.–Sat. 7 AM–9 PM.*

NEED A
BREAK?

Despite being small and cramped, **Box 32** (⊠ Rua Cons. Mafra 255, Mercado Público, Centro, ☎ 048/224–5588) is *the* meeting place for everyone from businesspeople to students. You'll find more than 100 kinds of liquor, including the Brazilian mainstay, *cachaça* (a sugarcane-based alcohol). Be sure to try the house specialty, *bolinho de bacalhau* (a cod appetizer).

The **Museu Histórico** is housed in the 18th-century Palácio Cruz e Souza (once the governor's home and office), a boxy, rose-color structure whose stairways are lined with Carrara marble. The sidewalks around the building are still paved with the original stones brought from Portugal. The museum's collection includes documents, personal items, and artwork that belonged to former governors. Sections of the museum are undergoing renovation. ⊠ *Praça 15 de Novembro 227, Centro,* ☎ *048/221–3504.* ☞ *Free.* ⊙ *Weekdays 10–6, weekends 10–4.*

Another great sight to visit by sailboat is the **Baía dos Golfinhos** (Dolphin Bay). A few nautical miles up the coast from the island, this bay is home to hundreds of *botos-cinza* (gray dolphins). They tolerate sailboats moving in very close to them.

The SC 404 highway travels through the eastern hills to the **Lagoa da Conceição** (Our Lady of Conception Lagoon), 12 km (8 mi) east of downtown Florianópolis. The region provides a combination of fresh- and saltwater environments where there are plenty of opportunities for water sports. The village has a busy nightlife and dining district, and most of its streets are packed with people on weekend evenings.

Beaches

The island's northern *praias* (beaches) are considered the best—and are therefore the busiest—because of to their warm waters. Impressive seascapes dominate the Atlantic beaches, and southern beaches have fewer sun worshipers and a much more laid-back atmosphere.

You're strongly advised to explore the sophisticated **Praia do Canasvieiras** at the end of SC 401. **Praia Jurerê** normally has bigger waves than its neighbors. The increased development of beachfront hotels, restaurants, and shops has attracted many out-of-state visi-

Ilha de Santa Catarina

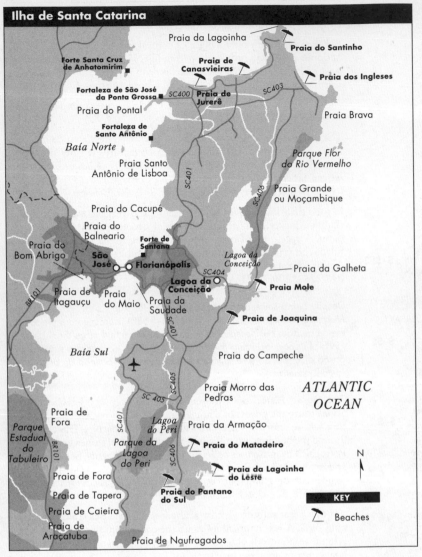

Praia da Lagoinha
Praia do Santinho
Praia de Canasvieiras
Praia dos Ingleses
Forte Santa Cruz de Anhatomirim
Fortaleza de São José da Ponta Grossa
SC400
Praia de Jurerê
SC403
Praia do Pontal
Praia Brava
Fortaleza de Santo Antônio
Baía Norte
Parque Flor do Rio Vermelho
Praia Santo Antônio de Lisboa
SC401
Praia Grande ou Moçambique
SC403
Praia do Cacupé
Praia do Balneario
Forte de Santana
Lagoa da Conceição
Praia do Bom Abrigo
São José
Florianópolis
Praia da Galheta
SC404
Lagoa da Conceição
Praia Mole
BR101
Praia de Itagauçu
Praia do Maio
Praia da Saudade
Praia de Joaquina
SC401
Baía Sul
Praia do Campeche
SC405
Praia Morro das Pedras
ATLANTIC OCEAN
SC 405
Praia da Armação
Praia de Fora
SC401
Lagoa do Peri
Praia do Matadeiro
Parque Estadual do Tabuleiro
BR101
Parque da Lagoa do Peri
SC406
Praia da Lagoinha do Leste
N
Praia de Fora
Praia do Pantano do Sul
Praia de Tapera
KEY
Praia de Caieira
Beaches
Praia de Araçatuba
Praia de Naufragados

tors. **Praia dos Ingleses,** English Beach, acquired its name because a British sailboat sank here in 1700. Although it is a narrow beach, the unparalleled line-up of hotels and restaurants for all budgets makes it one of the most popular beaches on the island. In summer, Spanish with an Argentine accent is the local language. **Praia do Santinho** is a mile-long stretch of sand backed by green hills at the far northeastern corner of the island. It was a secluded, laid back neighborhood until a major resort opened in the 1990s.

Surfers have staked claims to **Praia da Joaquina,** the beach where several surfing events take place, including one round of the world professional circuit. Nudism is tolerated at **Praia Mole,** with white sands that attract mostly surfers and foreign tourists. A paragliding platform on the hill and beachfront bars add to the eclectic atmosphere. **Praia do Matadeiro,** also quite popular among surfers, is a small beach surrounded by breathtaking hills. It can only be reached by a footpath from the Armação village.

If you're seeking peace (and you don't mind colder waters), make your first stop **Pântano do Sul.** This small beach community in the south of the island is surrounded by hills. Secluded **Praia da Lagoinha do Leste** is a breathtaking beach that you can only reach by boat or by way of a steep, 5-km (3-mi) path that starts at Pântano do Sul.

Forts

In the early days of the colony, the Portuguese built forts on the Baía Norte and Baía Sul to protect their investment. Today some of the forts can only be reached by taking a sailboat tour.

One of the best-preserved forts open to the public is **Fortaleza de São José. Forte Santa Cruz de Anhatomirim** was built in 1744, opposite Fortaleza de São José at the entrance to the Baía Norte. It has a historical photo exhibit as well as a small aquarium. **Fortaleza de Santo Antônio** has marked trails to follow up to the fort. Check out the tropical vegetation along the way. The **Forte de Santana,** under Hercílio Luz bridge, houses a firearms museum run by the state military police.

Dining and Lodging

$–$$$$ ✕ **Arante.** This rustic beachfront restaurant has a 40-year track record. The menu—mostly Brazilian seafood dishes—is flawless; don't pass up the *pirão de caldo de peixe* (black beans cooked with a fish sauce). Weekend reservations are advised, and you'll most likely have to park on the beach. ⊠ *Rua Abelardo Gomes 254, Pântano do Sul,* ☎ *048/237-7022. No credit cards. Closed Mon.*

$–$$$$ ✕ **Marina Ponta da Areia.** This bar and restaurant, part of the marina
★ complex, offers a grand view of the Lagoa da Conceição, with surrounding green hills as the backdrop. The fare, organized by Chef Fedoca, a diver himself, includes a wide variety of seafood. ⊠ *Rua Sen. Ivo D'Aquino Neto 133, Lagoa da Conceição,* ☎ *048/232-0759. MC, V. Closed Mon.*

$–$$$$ ✕ **La Pergoletta.** A variety of fresh pasta dishes is the highlight. Try
★ the one with shrimp, *kani kama* (ground crabmeat), and white-wine sauce. ⊠ *Trv. Careirão 62, Centro, Florianópolis,* ☎ *048/224-6353. Reservations essential. AE. Closed Mon.*

$–$$ ✕ **Martim Pescador.** The restaurant is very popular among the Argentine tourists and surfers that take over nearby Joaquina Beach every summer. In tune with this setting, seafood is the main fare—you can appreciate basic appetizers like *siri na casca* (crabmeat served in the shell) as well as full meals such as *camarão* (fried shrimp). ⊠ *Beco do Surfista (Km 17, Estrada da Joaquina), Lagoa da Conceição, Florianópolis,* ☎ *048/232-5560. AE, DC, MC, V. Closed Mon.*

$ ✕ **Ataliba.** With 20-odd years in the business, you can expect nothing less than excellent service at this rodízio-style churrascaria. The meat selection—more than 20 kinds, from beef to mouton and rabbit—and the salad bar are both outstanding. ⊠ *Rua Irineu Bornhausen 5050, Agronomica, Florianópolis,* ☎ *048/333-0990. AE, DC, MC, V. No dinner Sun.*

$$–$$$$ ▨ **Jurerê Praia.** On the sophisticated Jurerê Beach, this hotel is a prime destination for South American visitors, especially those from Argentina. The four- to eight-person guest houses usually require a minimum stay of one week in high season (December to March). The world-class facilities and efficient staff make the guest feel like a homeowner at Jurerê. And all this is just one step from the sand. ⊠ *Alameda Carlos Nascimento 200, Praia de Jurerê, 88053-000,* ☎ *048/282-1108 or 0800/48-1530,* FAX *048/282-1644,* WEB *www.jurere.com.br. 40 guest houses. Restaurant, bar, kitchenette, 2 pools, tennis court, health club, soccer, volleyball, beach, jet skiing, marina, snorkeling. AE, DC, MC, V. CP.*

$$–$$$ 🏨 **Cabanas da Praia Mole.** With the Lagoa da Conceição on one side and Praia da Joaquina on the other, the location is superb. Neatly decorated rooms with pastel tones, colonial-style furnishings, and paintings by local artists contrast with the casual atmosphere. An unending lineup of amenities in a 16-acre wooded lot make this a prime choice for the visitor looking for relaxation. ⊠ *Estrada Geral da Barra da Lagoa 2001, Praia Mole, 88062-970,* ☎ *048/232–5231,* 𝔽𝔸𝕏 *048/ 232–5482,* 𝕎𝔼𝔹 *www.iacess.com.br/cabanas. 74 rooms, 18 chalets. Restaurant, bar, 2 pools (1 indoor), massage, sauna, spa, tennis court, aerobics, paddle tennis, marina, convention center. AE, DC, MC, V. BP.*

$$ 🏨 **Lexus Internacional Ingleses.** Although it has much to offer, this midsize hotel's main attraction is its location on the popular (therefore crowded) Praia dos Ingleses, 34 km (21 mi) northeast of downtown Florianópolis. The pools are one step from the beach, making the Lexus a great place to enjoy the warm northern waters. Choose the bay-facing apartments with balconies to hang your hammock on and feel the sea breeze. Each has a small kitchen, and some have a barbecue grill. ⊠ *Rua Dom João Becker 859, Praia dos Ingleses, 88058-601,* ☎ *048/269–2622,* 𝔽𝔸𝕏 *048/269–2622. 63 rooms. Restaurant, bar, 2 pools, sauna, volleyball, beach. AE, DC, MC, V. CP.*

$–$$$ 🏨 **Costão do Santinho Resort.** The island's most sophisticated resort
★   offers many facilities and a terrific location on Santinho Beach, 35 km (22 mi) north of Florianópolis. The ocean view from rooms that face north is one reason to stay here; the surrounding 100-acre Atlantic forest is another (a trail leads to petroglyhs on the hill). Full apartments with kitchens are available for longer stays. ⊠ *Rua Ver. Onildo Lemos 2505, Praia do Santinho, 88001-970,* ☎ *048/261–1000 or 0800/48–1000,* 𝔽𝔸𝕏 *048/261–1236,* 𝕎𝔼𝔹 *www.costao.com.br. 228 rooms. 3 restaurants, 2 bars, lounge, 6 pools, hot tub, massage, sauna, 4 tennis courts, exercise room, soccer, volleyball, beach, hiking, snorkeling, shopping, recreation room, children's programs, playground, business services, travel services, airport shuttle. AE, DC, MC, V. MAP.*

¢–$ 🏨 **Baia Norte Palace.** Lush suites for more discerning guests were added in a recent renovation of this centrally located hotel. Rooms are carefully furnished, and those facing west have a grand view of the bay and bridge. ⊠ *Av. Beira-Mar Norte 220, Centro, Florianópolis 88000-000,* ☎ *048/225–3144 or 0800/48–0202,* 𝔽𝔸𝕏 *048/225–3227. 90 rooms, 12 suites. Restaurant, bar, coffee shop, pool, exercise room, meeting room. AE, DC, MC, V. CP.*

Outdoor Activities and Sports

Associação de Vôo Ingleses/Santinho (Escola da AVIS; ⊠ Rua João Jose Luz 240, Praia do Santinho, ☎ 048/9983–6770). This flight club maintains a hang-gliding and parasailing school—popular sports on this mountainous, windy island. A lesson including a tandem flight with an instructor costs about R$87.

Marina Ponta da Areia (⊠ Rua Sen. Ivo D'Aquino Neto 133, Lagoa da Conceição, ☎ 048/232–2290) is the place for sailing classes and jet-ski rentals. Snorkeling and scuba diving are very popular on the northern beaches; check out **Sea Divers** (⊠ Av. Luiz B. Piazza 6562, Ponta das Canas, ☎ 048/284–1535) for diving lessons and equipment rentals. The cost to rent basic gear is about R$160 a day.

Turismo Vida, Sol e Mar (⊠ Rua Manuel de Araújo 200, Centro, Garopaba, ☎ 048/254–4199, 𝕎𝔼𝔹 www.vidasolemar.com.br) is a tour operator working in conjunction with Projeto Baleia Franca—a nongovernmental environmental organization—to offer whale-watching boat trips. The warm waters around the island attract whales from Patagonia (especially from Pensinsula Valdéz), July through October. Surfing classes are also available.

Shopping

For modern shops in a world-class mall, try **Beira-Mar Shopping** (✉ Rua Bocaiúva 2468, Centro, ☎ 048/224–1563). The Arte Catarinense store has a large assortment of traditional tapestries and pottery.

Blumenau

250 km (156 mi) northwest of Florianópolis.

Blumenau—the cradle of the prosperous Vale do Itajaí region—is a pleasant place, with clean streets and friendly people who take great pride in their community. The name of this city of more than 240,000 is indicative of its German origins. Downtown has been restored to preserve its early German architectural style, *enxaimel* (half-timber construction), and the annual Oktoberfest has attracted crowds from all over the south since its inception in 1984. Events spill from the festival site into downtown (around Rua 15 de Novembro) for three weeks, when almost 100,000 gallons of beer are consumed.

For insight into the history of German immigration, check out the **Museu da Família Colonial** (Colonial Family Museum). The house, which was built in 1864 for the Gaertner family, contains a collection of everyday objects that belonged to the city's first residents; its garden has many examples of regional flora. ✉ *Rua das Palmeiras 64,* ☎ *047/322–1676.* 🎟 *R$2.* ⊙ *Tues.–Fri. 8–6, Sat. 9–4, Sun. 9–noon.*

The Blumenau area is home to a growing glassware industry, with high-quality products aimed at the discriminating customer. At **Glaspark** you can see artisans at work, learn about the industry at a museum, and buy designer glassware at reasonable prices. ✉ *Rua Rudolf Roedel 147, Salto Weisbach,* ☎ *047/327–1261.* 🎟 *Free.* ⊙ *Mon.–Sat.*

Dining and Lodging

$–$$ ✕ **Abendbrothaus.** A must for German cuisine with a Brazilian flair, this restaurant is 26 km (17 mi) from Florianópolis. The building is a typical enxaimel-style German immigrant house. *Marreco recheado* (stuffed duck served with mashed potatoes, cassava, and red cabbage) is a regional specialty. ✉ *Rua Henrique Konrad, 1194, Vila Itoupava,* ☎ *047/378–1157. No credit cards. Reservations essential weekdays. No dinner.*

$ ✕🏨 **Plaza Blumenau.** Check in if you're looking for upscale accommodations, spacious rooms, and great facilities. The Terrace restaurant serves international cuisine with an emphasis on things German. ✉ *Rua 7 de Setembro 818, Centro 89010-200,* ☎ *047/231–7000 or 0800/47–1213,* 🖷 *047/231–7001,* 🌐 *www.plazahoteis.com.br. 123 rooms, 8 suites. Restaurant, bar, pool, exercise room, business services, meeting room. AE, DC, MC, V. CP.*

¢ ✕🏨 **Hotel Glória.** This best-buy has rooms that are basic but comfortable, and attentive staff. The elegant British-style lobby—with wood paneling, wrought-iron lamps, and large leather chairs—is unique in Brazil. What really makes the place popular is the on-site KaffeHaus Glória, which serves the traditional, lavish *café colonial,* with 50 kinds of pies and cakes. ✉ *Rua 7 de Setembro 954, Centro 89010-280,* ☎ *047/326–1988,* 🖷 *047/326–5370,* 🌐 *www.hotelgloria.com.br. 94 rooms, 3 suites. Bar, restaurant, coffee shop, meeting rooms. AE, DC, MC, V. CP.*

Shopping

Hering Presentes (✉ Rua 15 de Novembro 759, Centro, ☎ 047/326–3593) sells its own glassware and china, all at below-market prices.

Flamingo (✉ Rua 15 de Novembro 367, Centro, ☎ 047/326–0277) offers a great variety of table, bedding, and bathroom articles from the textile factories in the Itajaí, also at bargain prices.

Joinville

105 km (65 mi) northeast of Blumenau, 195 km (121 mi) north of Florianópolis.

Founded by German immigrants 150 years ago, Joinville is today Santa Catarina's largest city. It's a bustling convention, industrial, and international trade center that relies on the nearby seaport of São Francisco do Sul. Although the city itself isn't particularly attractive, its surrounding rain-forested hills provide opportunities for some interesting excursions.

The **Museu Nacional da Colonização e Imigração** has a fine collection of objects and crafts from the first immigrants. ✉ *Rua Rio Branco 229, Centro,* ☎ *047/433–3736.* ✑ *Free.* ☉ *Tues.–Sun. 9–5.*

Dining and Lodging

$ ★ ✕☎ **Tannenhof.** This hotel reigns absolute as the region's best and largest, with emphasis on serving the business traveler. Some executive rooms are outfitted with desktop computers and two phone lines. The architecture imitates the traditional, German enxaimel style. Rooms are decorated accordingly, with classic Alpine furnishings and lush velvet curtains. You can dine on German fare in the 11th-floor Weishof restaurant, which also serves up a panoramic view of the city and the nearby hills. Or try a late afternoon café colonial. ✉ *Rua Visconde de Taunay 340, Centro, 89201-420,* ☎ *047/433–8011 or 0800/99–8011,* ☒ *047/433–8011,* 🌐 *www.tannenhof.com.br. 100 rooms, 3 suites. Restaurant, bar, pool, exercise room, meeting room. AE, DC, MC, V. CP.*

¢–$ ☎ **Anthurium Park Hotel.** Rooms are small in this former bishop's residence, built in 1938, and the decor can be sober. Thankfully, colorful bedding makes it more pleasant. The charm of the setting, which includes a nearby cathedral and a park, won't disappoint. ✉ *Rua São José 336, Centro, 89202-010,* ☎ *047/433–6229,* ☒ *047/433–6229,* 🌐 *www.joinville.com.br/anthurium. 45 rooms, 4 suites. Restaurant, bar, pool, sauna, hot tub, meeting rooms. AE, DC, MC, V.*

RIO GRANDE DO SUL

The state of Rio Grande do Sul is almost synonymous with the gaúcho, the South American cowboy who is glamorized as much as his North American counterpart. There's more to this state, however, than the idyllic cattle-country lifestyle of early days. As it is one of Brazil's leading industrial areas, its infrastructure rivals that of any country in the northern hemisphere. Its mix of Portuguese, German, and Italian cultures is evident not only in the food and architecture. Indeed, to be gaúcho (which is a term for all people and things from this state) may mean to be a vintner with Italian heritage from Caxias do Sul or an entrepreneur of German descent from Gramado as much as a cattle rancher with Portuguese lineage out on the plains.

The state capital, Porto Alegre, is a sophisticated metropolis of 1.3 million that rivals Curitiba in terms of quality of life. This important industrial and business center has universities, museums, and convention centers. The slopes of the Serra Gaúcha were settled by Italian immigrants; thanks to their wine-making skills, the state now produces a couple of nice varieties, particularly in the Caxias do Sul and Bento Gonçalves areas. Along the coast, basaltic cliffs drop into a raging At-

THE SOUTH'S GERMAN SETTLERS

I N THE EARLY 1820S, Austrian-born Empress Dona Leopoldina, wife of Dom Pedro I (Brazil's first emperor), envisioned the vast, sparsely populated Brazilian countryside settled with the kind of farmers she knew from Europe. Although European farmers had a poor track record in the tropics, it was felt that southern Brazil's cooler, subtropical climate wouldn't be so inhospitable. Agents hired by the Brazilian crown were dispatched to central Europe, where they touted the wonders of Brazil and the abundance of its "farmland" (actually covered by dense forest, home to native peoples—such as the Guarani and Kaigang—and wild animals like the South American puma). Beginning in 1824 and continuing for more than 50 years, thousands of Europeans—many of them German—were lured to central and eastern Rio Grande do Sul and to eastern Santa Catarina.

High-end estimates place the number of German colonos in the 200,000–300,000 range (exact figures are hard to come by owing to poor record keeping on the part of Brazilian authorities and the tendency for colonists to indicate the region—Hunsrück, Pommern, Pfalz—from which they came rather than simply "Germany," which only became unified in 1871). Most of those who came were poor or landless farmers who faced famine in their homelands. Some were craftsmen who provided the goods and services needed to truly create settlements. The first New World community was established in São Leopoldo (named after Dona Leopoldina), 31 km (19 mi) north of Porto Alegre on the Rio dos Sinos (Bells River). This and the valley of the Rio Itajaí in Santa Catarina became cradles of Brazil's German immigrants.

The Germans brought their unswerving work ethic, their knowledge of intensive, cash-crop agriculture, and their rich culture—much of which still thrives. Recent studies indicate that at least 500,000 Brazilians speak some German (usually dialects that speakers of the standard language would find hard to understand). Further, the Lutheran religion is still practiced by many people with German ancestry. Researchers of Rio Grande do Sul's rich folklore are keen to acknowledge that the rhythms of some regional music can be traced back to German polkas. German cuisine is so much a part of the region that hardly anyone here can conceive of a churrasco without pork sausages and *Kartofelln Salat* (potato salad). And pastries are an essential part of the German-bred café colonial. Although most small local breweries have been incorporated into large national companies, prior to the 1970s the southern states had a long list of them. In addition, German immigrants and their descendants were behind such internationally renowned Brazilian companies as Varig Airlines, the steel company Gerdau, and the jeweler H. Stern.

If you visit such communities as Blumenau, Joinville, São Leopoldo, Novo Hamburgo, Gramado, Lageado, and Santa Cruz do Sul, you'll certainly experience a bit of Europe in Brazil. Indeed, Blumenau and Santa Cruz host large Oktoberfests. Crowds of Brazilian-Germans flock to these festivals to dance to their traditional rhythms (polkas and waltzes) and indulge in sausages, sauerkraut, and beer.

lantic and provide an impressive backdrop for the sophisticated sea-side resort of Torres. Farther inland the Aparados da Serra National Park straddles the state's highest elevations and contains several canyons with breathtaking views.

Porto Alegre

476 km (296 mi) southwest of Florianópolis, 760 km (472 mi) south-west of Curitiba, 1,109 km (690 mi) southwest of São Paulo.

Porto Alegre's hallmark is the hospitality of its people, a trait that has been acknowledged over and over by visitors, earning it the nickname Smile City. The capital of one of Brazil's wealthiest states, it has many streets lined with *jacarandá* trees that create violet tunnels when in full spring bloom.

The city was founded on the banks of the Rio Guaíba by immigrants from the Azores in 1772. The Guaíba is actually a 50-km-long (31-mi-long) lagoon formed by four rivers that merge a few miles up-stream from the city. The city's port, connected to the Atlantic by the Lagoa dos Patos, has become increasingly active in recent years.

Exploring

From Morro de Santa Teresa (Santa Teresa Hill), you get a grand view of the skyline as it confronts the expanse of the Rio Guaíba. From this spot and the numerous riverfront parks, the great spectacle of Porto Alegre's sunset is inspirational. As local poet Mário Quintana put it: "Skies of Porto Alegre, how could I ever take you to heaven?" For an-other great perspective of Centro, consider taking a riverboat tour of the Rio Guaíba and its islands, which are part of a state park.

The heart of Porto Alegre lies within a triangle formed by Praça da Alfândega, the Mercado Público, and the Praça da Matriz. Not only is this the main business district, but it's also the site of many cultural and historical attractions. Outside this area, Casa de Cultura Mário Quintana and Usina do Gasômetro are very active cultural centers, with movies, live performances, art exhibits, and cafés.

Numbers in the text correspond to numbers in the margin and on the Porto Alegre Centro map.

A GOOD WALK

On the side of Praça da Alfândega facing the river are two neoclassi-cal structures: the **Museu de Arte do Rio Grande do Sul** ① and the **Memo-rial do Rio Grande do Sul** ②. From the square, head north on Avenida 7 de Setembro to the open space in front of the Prefeitura (the Fonte Talavera de la Reina was donated by the Spanish community of Rio Grande do Sul in 1935). On the opposing side of Avenida Borges de Medeiros is the **Mercado Público** ③. Follow Avenida Borges de Medeiros south to the Viaduto Otávio Rocha, the city's first overpass, and climb the stairway to Avenida Duque de Caxias. One block to your right is the **Museu Júlio de Castilhos** ④, where you can catch a glimpse of gaú-cho culture. A couple of blocks west, on Praça da Matriz, are the **Cat-edral Metropolitana Nossa Senhora Madre de Deus** ⑤ and the adjacent **Palácio Piratini** ⑥. Finish your tour at **Theatro São Pedro** ⑦.

TIMING

You can follow this tour—and visit the museums—in about four and a half hours.

SIGHTS TO SEE

❺ **Catedral Metropolitana Nossa Senhora Madre de Deus.** Although con-struction began in 1921, this cathedral wasn't completed until 1986.

Its predominant style is Italian Renaissance, but note the twin bell towers, which were inspired by 17th-century Jesuit missions. The facade's mosaic panels were made in the Vatican ateliers. ⊠ *Praça Marechal Deodoro s/n,* ☎ *051/3228–6001.* ⊡ *Free.* ☉ *Daily 7–noon and 2–7.*

❷ **Memorial do Rio Grande do Sul.** Built at the turn of the 20th century, the building was declared a national architectural landmark in 1981, when it housed the main post office. Then in 2000 work was completed that transformed it into a state museum. Although the style is neoclassical overall, the German-baroque influences are strong; the asymmetrical corner towers with their bronze rotundas are said to resemble Prussian army helmets. A permanent exhibit focuses on the state's history and the lives of important gaúchos, and on the second floor there's a small collection of artifacts from the state's native peoples. ⊠ *Praça da Alfândega s/n,* ☎ *051/3221–5214.* ⊡ *Free.* ☉ *Daily 9–5.*

❸ **Mercado Público.** The neoclassical Public Market was constructed in 1869. It has undergone repeated renovations, the last of which (in 1996) added the glass roof that now covers the central, inner plaza. With these changes, some of the produce stalls have been replaced by cafés and restaurants—taking away a bit of the boisterous bazaar ambience. ⊠ *Largo Glenio Peres s/n.* ☉ *Mon.–Sat. 7 AM–11 PM.*

❶ **Museu de Arte do Rio Grande do Sul.** In 1997, the old, neoclassical customs building was restored, and it now houses an art museum. German immigrant Theo Wiederspahn designed this and several other of the city's early buildings. A collection of his sketches and blueprints is also on display. You can also see paintings, sculptures, and drawings by Brazilian artists (in a variety of styles and from several periods). Two works of Di Cavalcanti—one of the country's most renowned painters—are exhibited. ⊠ *Praça da Alfândega s/n,* ☎ *051/3227–2311.* ⊡ *Free.* ☉ *Tues.–Sun. 10–5.*

❹ **Museu Júlio de Castilhos.** The small Júlio de Castilhos Museum displays an impressive collection of gaúcho documents, firearms, clothing, and household utensils. The home belonged to Governor Julio de Castilhos, who lived here at the turn of the 20th century, before the Palácio Piratini was built. ⊠ *Rua Duque de Caxias 1231,* ☎ *051/3221–3959.* ⊡ *Free.* ☉ *Tues.–Fri. 10–5, weekends 1–5.*

❻ **Palácio Piratini.** The Piratini Palace is the stately governor's mansion, which also houses executive offices. The structure's Roman columns convey a solidity and permanence uncommon in official Brazilian buildings. Duck into the main room to see the murals (depicting gaúcho folktales) by Italian artist Aldo Locatelli. ⊠ *Praça da Matriz s/n,* ☎ *051/3210–4100.* ⊡ *Free.* ☉ *Daily 9–5.*

❼ **Theatro São Pedro.** In a 130-year-old building that was thoroughly renovated in the 1980s, São Pedro is run by a private foundation. Tickets to stage and musical performances—including those of the theater's own chamber orchestra (March–December)—vary in price. The popular Café Orquestra das Panelas, on the balcony above the lobby, has an ample view of the Praça da Matriz, the cathedral and Palácio Piratini. ⊠ *Praça da Matriz s/n,* ☎ *051/3227–5100.* ⊡ *Free.*

Dining and Lodging

$$–$$$$ ✕ **Barranco.** One of Porto Alegre's oldest churrascarias has several dining rooms, but most people head for a table on the tree-shaded patio. The dishes featuring Argentine beef (tenderer than the local product) are popular, as are the pork ribs au gratin. ⊠ *Rua Protásio Alves 1578, Petrópolis,* ☎ *051/3331–6172. AE, DC, MC, V.*

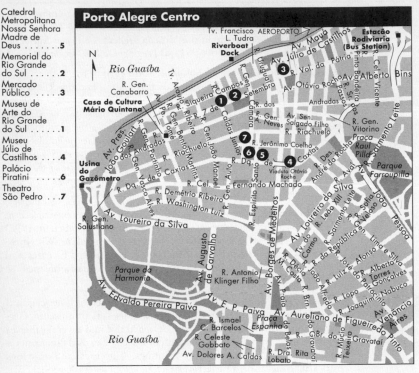

Porto Alegre Centro

$$\text{---}$$

$$–$$$$ ✕ **Al Dente.** This small restaurant features northern Italian cuisine. Try the *garganelli* (a variety of pasta from Napoli) with salmon and wine sauce or the fettuccine *negro* (black) with caviar sauce. ✉ *Rua Mata Bacelar 210, Auxiliadora,* ☎ *051/3343–1841. AE, D, MC, V. Closed Sun.*

$–$$$$ ✕ **Il G.** For several years, Il Gattopardo (now with an abbreviated trade
★ name) has been a trendy lunch and dinner spot. It now caters to the business crowd, with an essentially international fare leaning to the Italian—obviously pasta dishes reign supreme. ✉ *Rua 24 de Outubro 1585, Moinhos de Vento,* ☎ *051/3330–1972. AE, DC, MC, V. Closed Sun. No lunch Sat.*

$–$$$ ✕ **Gambrinus.** Generations of politicians, artists, and journalists have flocked to this old-fashioned Mercado Público establishment to debate the city's past and present. The German brauhaus decor is in tune with the Mercado Público's down-to-earth atmosphere. The fare is regional with an emphasis on seafood: try the stuffed *tainha* (a tasty southern Atlantic fish) with shrimp. The *rabada* (cow's tail stewed with vegetables) is also recommended. ✉ *Mercado Público, Lojas 85–89, Centro,* ☎ *051/3226–6914. Reservations essential weekdays. No credit cards. Closed Sun.*

$–$$ ✕ **Galpão Crioulo.** This churrascaria is near the Guaíba riverfront, within
★ a park that emulates a typical ranch—complete with gaúchos, cattle, and sheep. The setting is perfect for indulging in the espeto-corrido or in *carreteiro* (rice cooked with beef cubes and onions). Gaúcho music and dance performances liven up the evenings. ✉ *Parque da Harmonia s/n, Centro,* ☎ *051/3226–8194. AE, V.*

¢–$$ ✕ **Café do Porto.** This mainstay in the city roster of fine cafés not only serves several different types of coffee, but also drinks, sandwiches, and pastries. Highly recommended is the *antipasto sott'olio* (Italian rolls with dried tomatoes and red and yellow peppers). Combine this a with glass of chardonnay from the regional vineyard, Casa Valduga, or with the house cappuccino. ⊠ *Rua Padre Chagas 293, Moinhos de Vento,* ☎ *051/3346–8385. No credit cards.*

$$ ✕🏨 **Holiday Inn Porto Alegre.** The first member of the Holiday Inn family in Southern Brazil is in the booming business district of Bela Vista, which not too long ago was a purely residential neighborhood. The decor is modern; rooms have king-size beds. Chef's Grill, the house restaurant with Italian leanings, has quickly carved a name for itself. ⊠ *Av. Carlos Gomes 565, Bela Vista 90450-000,* ☎ *051/3378–2727 or 0800/99–3366,* FAX *051/3378–2727. 173 rooms. Restaurant, coffee shop, bar, business center, exercise room, meeting rooms. AE, DC, MC, V.*

$$ ✕🏨 **Plaza San Rafael.** Conveniently located in Centro, the Plaza has long been one of the city's most sophisticated hotels; recent renovations have brought even more improvements. The restaurant, Le Bon Gourmet, has the best French cuisine in town and is very popular with international visitors. One highlight is the juicy fillet Camembert with a mushroom sauce. ⊠ *Rua Alberto Bins 514, Centro 90030-040,* ☎ *051/3220–7000 or 0800/51–2244,* FAX *051/3220–7001,* WEB *www.plazahoteis.com.br. 261 rooms, 23 suites. Restaurant, bar, pool, sauna, health club, business services. AE, DC, MC, V. CP.*

$$$$ 🏨 **Sheraton Porto Alegre.** Opened in July 2000 in the fashionable neighborhood of Moinhos de Vento, the Sheraton sets the city's new standard of luxury. The level of comfort is outstanding, from the lobby to the top-floor rooms. In the Brazil suite, you'll find 18th-century-style wooden furniture and copies of paintings by the French artist Debret, whose works depict rural scenes of colonial Brazil. Other suites include one with a Tahitian decor and another with an Argentine theme. The in-house restaurant, Clos du Moulin, offers Mediterranean fare, which is accompanied by live piano performances each evening. Shoppers take note: the hotel is in the same complex as the Moinhos de Vento Mall. ⊠ *Rua Olavo Barreto Viana 18, 90570-010,* ☎ *051/3323–6000,* FAX *051/3323–6010. 156 rooms, 22 suites. Restaurant, bar, in-room data ports, in-room safes, minibar, health club, concierge, business services, convention center, meeting rooms. AE, DC, MC, V. CP.*

$–$$ 🏨 **Everest Palace Hotel.** This unassuming hotel has an excellent downtown location and recently renovated rooms. The staff is well trained and can help you find tours and activities. The top-floor restaurant offers a commanding view of the Guaíba riverfront. ⊠ *Av. Duque de Caxias 1357, Centro, 90010-283,* ☎ *051/3228–3133,* FAX *051/3228–4792,* WEB *www.everest.com.br. 153 rooms. Restaurant, bar, pool, business center, meeting rooms. AE, DC, MC, V.*

¢–$$ 🏨 ★ **Blue Tree Porto Alegre.** This hotel has set new standards to lure well-traveled guests. Rooms are spacious with modern decor—those at the back have superb views of downtown and the Guaíba. You can ask that a basic office be set up in them. The on-site Joomon restaurant serves up food with a Japanese accent. ⊠ *Rua Lucas de Oliveira 995, Mont Serrat 90940-011,* ☎ *051/3333–0333, 0800–150500,* FAX *051/3330–5233,* WEB *www.bluetree.com.br. 130 rooms, 2 suites. Restaurant, bar, pool, sauna, health club, business services, meeting rooms. AE, DC, MC, V. CP.*

¢–$ 🏨 **Umbú.** Although it retains some of its original splendor, location is this traditional, 40-year-old hotel's primary draw. It's close to the bus terminal, and access to the airport is quick and easy. ⊠ *Av. Farrapos 292, Centro 90035-050,* ☎ *051/3228–4355,* FAX *051/3228–4355. 70 rooms. Restaurant, bar. AE, DC, MC, V.*

Nightlife and the Arts

Porto Alegre has a very active cultural life. Complete listings of entertainment and cultural events are published in the daily papers *Zero Hora* and *Correio do Povo.*

The **Casa de Cultura Mário Quintana** (⊠ Rua dos Andradas 736, ☎ 051/3221–7147) occupies what was Porto Alegre's finest hotel at the turn of the 20th century, the Majestic. The building has two art-film cinemas, one theater, and several exhibit rooms. The popular Café Concerto Majestic, on the seventh floor, has regular music performances.

Dado Bier (⊠ Av. Nilo Peçanha 3228, ☎ 051/3328–5111) started off as the city's first microbrewery. Its success among the fashionable led to expansions that have transformed it into an entertainment center open daily 10 AM–3 AM, with a R$20 cover charge. On-site are two restaurants (one serving Japanese cuisine, the other international) and a live-music venue, Dado Tambor.

The **Usina do Gasômetro,** with its conspicuous 90-m (300-ft) brick smokestack, was the city's first coal-fired powerhouse—built in the early 1920s, when the city experienced rapid growth. Today it's a cultural center housing theaters, meeting rooms, and exhibit spaces right on the bank of the Rio Guaíba. A terrace café overlooking the river—the perfect place to take in a sunset—is the center's newest addition. ⊠ *Av. João Goulart 551,* ☎ *051/3212–5979.* ⊙ *Daily 8 AM–midnight.*

Outdoor Activities and Sports

Clube Veleiros do Sul (⊠ Av. Guaíba 2941, Asunção, ☎ 051/3346–4382) takes advantage of the great expanse of the Guaíba waters to offer sailing classes and boat rentals.

Estádio Beir-Rio (⊠ Av. Padre Cacique 891, Praia de Belas, ☎ 051/3231–4411), with a capacity of 70,000, is home of Internacional—one of the city's major *futebol* (soccer) clubs. **Estádio Olímpico** (⊠ Largo dos Campeões s/n, Azenha, ☎ 051/3217–4466) is the stadium of Grêmio Football Portoalegrense, the city's other major soccer team. It seats 60,000 fans.

Shopping

At the **Brique da Redenção,** on Rua José Bonifácio (southeast side of Parque Farroupilha), you can find antiques and crafts. The entire street is closed to vehicles and taken over by dealers and artisans every Sunday from 10 to 3.

Moinhos Shopping (⊠ Rua Olavo Barreto Vianna 36, Moinhos de Vento, ☎ 051/3346–6013) recently opened in the trendy Moinhos de Vento neighborhood. It's the smallest of the city's malls and caters to the sophisticated consumer. A Sheraton hotel is attached.

Shopping Center Iguatemi (⊠ Rua João Wallig 1831, Três Figueiras, ☎ 051/3334–4545), the oldest of the world-class malls in the city, was extensively expanded in the late '90s. It includes branches of large chain stores as well as high-end specialty shops.

Look for traditional leather crafts, gaúcho apparel, and souvenirs at **Rincão Gaúcho** (⊠ Rua dos Andradas 1159, Centro, ☎ 051/3224–1004). If you don't have the time to venture into Brazilian wine country, look for a sample to buy at **Vinhos do Mundo** (⊠ Rua João Alfredo 557, Cidade Baixa, ☎ 051/3226–1911).

Caxias do Sul

150 km (93 mi) north of Porto Alegre.

Caxias do Sul is the heart of the state's Italian region, where the first immigrants set foot in 1875. The mild climate and fertile soil helped spur development through agriculture. The city and such neighboring communities as Bento Gonçalves and Garibaldi produce 90% of Brazil's wine, which has received international recognition in recent years.

The **Museu da Casa de Pedra** (Stone House Museum) was the residence (circa 1878) of the Lucchesi family, one of the first Italian families to arrive in the region. The basalt walls and hewn-wood window frames and doors are testaments to the hardiness of the early days. ⊠ *Rua Ludovico Cavinatto s/n.* 🖾 *Free.* ⊘ *Tues.–Sun. 9–5.*

Igreja São Pelegrino, finished in 1953, has 14 religious murals, including 12 depicting the *via crucis* (stations of the cross) painted by Italian classical painter Aldo Locatelli, who came to Rio Grande do Sul on a Vatican assignment and eventually became one of the state's most renowned artists. Another highlight is the replica of Michelangelo's *Pietá*, donated in 1975 by the Italian government to celebrate the centennial of immigration (1975). ⊠ *Rua Itália 50,* ☎ *no phone.* 🖾 *Free.* ⊘ *Daily 7 AM–9 PM.*

Wineries

Casa Cordelier (⊠ Km 65, RS 470, Bento Gonçalves, ☎ 054/453–2333) offers guided tours through the facilities that end in a wine-tasting session. There's a restaurant on the premises that's open weekends; the winery is open weekdays 9 to 4 and weekends 9 to 5.

Casa Valduga (⊠ Km 6, RS 444, Vale dos Vinhedos, Bento Gonçalves, ☎ 054/462–2499) is run by Luiz Valduga and his sons. Together they produce Selecum Wines (the 1997 cabernet sauvignon is highly regarded). During the summer (December to February) you can take a tour of the family-owned vineyards. Year-round you can stop by the winery for a tasting weekdays 8 to 11 and 2 to 6; weekends 9 to 5.

International heavyweight **Moët et Chandon** (⊠ Km 61.5, RS 470, Garibaldi, ☎ 054/462–2499) has a branch in Garibaldi, a few miles south of Bento Gonçalves. Guided tours are lead by an enologist who explains the science of wine and champagne production before offering you a taste.

In recent years the Miolo family has carved a name for itself in the Brazilian wine industry with the **Vinícola Miolo** (⊠ Km 9, RS 444, Vale dos Vinhedos, Bento Gonçalves, ☎ 054/459–1233). A tour that includes the vineyards and the on-site restaurant is one of the best in the region. Taste the award-winning Miolo Reserva wines—which include outstanding chardonnays and cabernet sauvignons—daily from 9 to 5.

Dining and Lodging

$–$$$$ ✗ **Osteria Mamma Miolo.** This restaurant is connected to the Miolo Winery. In addition to local versions of Italian fare, you'll also find such game as wild boar on the menu. Try the Miolo Reserva Chardonnay as an accompaniment. ⊠ *Km 68.5, RS 470, Vale dos Vinhedos, Bento Gonçalves,* ☎ *054/221–1696. MC, V.*

$–$$ ✗ **La Vindima.** In business since 1962, this restaurant is nationally recognized for the *galeto al primo canto* (young fried chicken served with an herb cream sauce). The pasta is made "like in the olden days." If you're not driving, try the house wine; if you are driving, the house grape juice is also good. ⊠ *Rua Borges de Medeiros 446, Caxias do Sul,* ☎ *051/3221–1696. No credit cards. Closed Sun.*

$ 🏬 **Reynolds International.** Impeccable service has become a hallmark at this small establishment, and a downtown location adds to the convenience. Because of this, it is attracting more and more international businesspeople. Rooms are spacious, with an emphasis on functionality. ⊠ *Rua Dr. Montaury 1441, Caxias do Sul 95100-970,* ☎ *054/ 223–5844,* 🖷 *054/223–5843,* 🌐 *www.reynolds.com.br. 47 rooms. Restaurant, bar, health club, business services, meeting rooms. AE, DC, MC, V. CP.*

168

Close-Up

BRAZILIAN WINE

ALTHOUGH THE FIRST GRAPE VINES were brought to Brazil in 1532 by early Portuguese colonists, the Jesuits who settled in the south decades later were the first to establish true vineyards and wineries (to produce the wine needed for the Catholic mass). It wasn't until Italian immigrants arrived that Brazil's viticulture gained any importance. With the blessing of Italian-born empress Teresa Cristina, wife of Dom Pedro II, the first group of immigrants from northern Italy arrived in 1875. In the next decades, at least 150,000 Italians came to settle the mountainous region of Rio Grande do Sul—the Serra Gaúcha. These newcomers were the first to produce significant quantities of wine, thereby establishing a truly Brazilian wine industry.

Although the region is suitable for growing grapes, the rainfall is often excessive from January to March—when the grapes reach maturity. This has traditionally made local winegrowers true heroes for being able to produce decent wines in spite of difficult conditions. Traditional grapes such as Bordeaux, merlot, and cabernet were grown to some extent, but most of the wine produced originated from less impressive American stock—Concord and Niagara grapes. These average wines are still produced for local markets.

In recent years, such international industry heavyweights as Moët et Chandon, Almadén, and Heublein, in cooperation with state agricultural authorities, have brought modern viticulture to the area. New agricultural techniques and hybridization have enabled European grapes to thrive, dramatically improving wine quality. (Wines from Rio Grande do Sul have even received prizes in international contests.) In the 1980s, Almadén established new vineyards in the hills near the city of Santana do Livramento (about 480 km/300 mi southwest of Porto Alegre, on the Uruguay border), where climate and soils are more apt to produce high-quality grapes. In addition, Brazil's wine producers' association (UVIBRA) is working on a system similar to that used in European countries for controlled-origin wines.

Today, there are more than 100 *cantinas* (wine makers), primarily around the cities of Caxias do Sul and Bento Gonçalves in Rio Grande do Sul. Many of these offer tours or tastings. Only a few produce wines of superior quality. The following wines have received mentions in recent contests supervised by the Office International de la Vigne e du Vin (International Bureau of Wine): Chardonnay Brut and Gewürztraminer (from Casa Valduga); Miolo Reserva Cabernet (from Vinícola Miolo); Grand Philippe Cabernet and Grand Philippe Merlot (from Moët et Chandon).

Gramado

115 km (72 mi) northeast of Porto Alegre.

It was no doubt Gramado's mild mountain climate that attracted German settlers to the area in the late 1800s. They left a legacy of German-style architecture and traditions that attract today's travelers. Ample lodging options and a seemingly endless choice of restaurants and café colonials have given this city a reputation with convention-eers and honeymooners. Every August the city hosts the Festival de Cinema da Gramado, one of Latin America's most prestigious film festivals. At Christmastime the city is aglow with seasonal decorations and schedules choral music performances. During peak periods it can be difficult to find lodging if you haven't made arrangements in advance.

Near Gramado's sister city, Canela (20 km/13 mi on RS 020), is the **Parque Estadual do Caracol** (Caracol State Park; ⊠ Rua Godofredo Raymundo 1747, Estrada Parque do Caracol, ☎ 054/282–3035). An impressive 120-m (400-ft) waterfall flows straight down into a horseshoe-shape valley carved out of the basaltic plateau. The park also includes 50 acres of native forests with several well-marked paths, dominated by Paraná pine.

Dining and Lodging

$$$–$$$$ ✕ **Gasthof Edelweiss.** The rustic atmosphere at this superb German restaurant is the ideal setting for duck *à la viennese* (with an orange-flavored cream sauce)—the house specialty. ⊠ *Rua da Carriere 1119, Gramado,* ☎ *051/3286–1861. DC, MC, V.*

¢–$ ✕☵ **Bavária.** If you're looking for a peaceful, natural setting, this is a good choice—the hotel is within a private park just off the busy shopping district. A small restaurant of the same name serves German fare and is highly recommended. ⊠ *Rua da Bavária 543, Gramado 95670-000,* ☎ *051/3286–1362,* ☒ *051/3286–1362. 56 rooms. Restaurant, bar, pool, sauna, paddle tennis. AE, DC, MC, V.*

$–$$ ☵ **Serra Azul.** This prestigious hotel's name is almost synonymous with
★ Gramado. It's the preferred choice of Brazilian TV and movie stars during the winter film festival. Location is prime for browsing the myriad clothing shops and enjoying cafés colonials and restaurants. Recently the owners bought a ranch outside the city, where you can experience the gaúcho lifestyle. ⊠ *Rua Garibaldi 152, Gramado 95670-000,* ☎ *054/286–1082,* ☒ *054/286–3374. 151 rooms, 18 suites. Restaurant, bar, indoor pool, massage, sauna. AE, DC, MC, V.*

$ ☵ **Laje de Pedra.** Built near a cliff, this hotel offers impressive views
★ of the Vale do Quilombo from its west wing. On weekends it regularly hosts a variety of musical performances. Rooms in the main building are rather small and somewhat outdated. ⊠ *Av. Pres. Kennedy s/n, Canela 95680-000,* ☎ *054/282–4300, 0800/51–2153,* ☒ *054/282–4400,* ☒☒☒ *www.lajedepedra.com.br. 250 rooms, 8 suites. Restaurant, bar, theater, pool, massage, sauna, tennis court, health club, children's program. AE, DC, MC, V.*

¢ ☵ **Pousada Zermatt.** Tired of budget hotels that lack charm? This old inn offers a cozy atmosphere with affordable rates and is recommended if you want to stay away from the noisy downtown district. ⊠ *Rua da Fé 187, Gramado 95670-000,* ☎ *051/3286–2426,* ☒ *051/3286–2426. 9 rooms. Bar. No credit cards.*

Parque Nacional dos Aparados da Serra

★ *47 km north(29 mi) of Gramado, 145 km (91 mi) north of Porto Alegre.*

This national park was created to protect the great canyons—of which Itaimbezinho is the most famous—that dissect the plateau in the north

of Rio Grande do Sul State. Winter (June to August) is the best time
to take in the spectacular canyon views as there's less chance of fog.
The park's main entrance, the Portaria Gralha Azul, is 20 km (13 mi)
southeast of Cambará do Sul, the small town that serves as the park's
hub. A visitor center provides information on regional flora and fauna,
as well as the park's geology and history. Beyond the entrance, you'll
come to grassy meadows that belie the gargantuan depression ahead.
A short path (a 45-minute walk, no guide necessary) takes you to the
awesome Itaimbezinho Canyon, cut deep into the basalt bedrock to
create the valley 7,500 m (2,500 ft) below. The longest path takes you
into the canyon's interior. Hire a guide, as it's impossible to navigate
the longest trails without one. They can also make arrangements for
other trips in the region. The park allows only 1,500 visitors each day,
so it's best to arrive early, especially in the summer months. ⊠ *20 km
(12 mi) southeast of Cambará do Sul on unpaved road,* ☎ *051/3251–
1262 or 051/3251–1277, 051/3251–1265 for tour guides.* ⊡ *R$6 per
person, R$5 per vehicle.* ⊙ *Wed.–Sun. 9–5.*

Dining and Lodging

$ ✕ **Churrascaria Pampa.** After a day on the trails in the Parque Nacional,
most visitors flock to the only full-fledged churrascaria in Cambará
do Sul. The cool evenings make a *caipirinha* (a drink made with
cachaça, crushed lime, and crushed ice) and espeto-corrido the order
of choice. ⊠ *Rua J. F. Ritter 584, Cambará do Sul,* ☎ *051/3251–1279.
No credit cards.*

¢   🏨 **Pousada das Corucacas.** Step into the gaúcho's world by staying at
this inn housed in an old ranch (Fazenda Baio Ruano). Guest rooms
are small, and facilities are basic (though breakfast and dinner are included in the rates), but all this seems in tune with the region's rugged
spirit. There are waterfalls and woods in the area: consider exploring
them on horseback and perhaps venturing to the canyons beyond. ⊠
Km 1, Estrada Ouro Verde, 95481-970, ☎ *054/251–1128. 7 rooms.
Dining room, horseback riding. No credit cards. MAP.*

Torres

205 km (128 mi) northeast of Porto Alegre.

The beaches around the city of Torres are Rio Grande do Sul's most
exciting. The sophistication of the seaside areas attracts international
travelers, particularly those from Argentina and Uruguay. The best
beaches include Praia da Cal, Praia da Guarita, and Praia Grande. They're
separated by outcroppings from which locals like to fish. The Parque
da Guarita (Watchtower Park), 3 km (2 mi) south of downtown, was
set aside to protect the area's unique vegetation as well as the basalt
hills that end abruptly in the Atlantic. A mile off Praia Grande, Ilha
dos Lobos (Seawolf Island) is a way station for sea lions in their annual migrations along the south Atlantic coast.

Dining and Lodging

$–$$$$ ✕ **Restaurante Parque da Guarita.** The thatched roof and tropical gar-
den of this restaurant blend in perfectly with its beach setting. Seafood
is the specialty here, and you can partake of your meal while enjoying
the magnificent view of the surf with the cliffs as a backdrop. ⊠
Estrada do Parque da Guarita, Km 2, ☎ *051/3664–1056. DC, MC,
V. No dinner Mar.–Nov.*

$ 🏨 **Solar da Barra Hotel.** In one of the newest hotels in the city the decor
is not distinguished but rooms are ample and comfortably furnished.
The highlight is services normally found only in larger resorts. Sight-
seeing boat trips to Ilha dos Lobos can be arranged by the hotel. ⊠
Rua Plínio Kroeff 465, Mampituba, 95560-000, ☎ *051/3664–1811,*

0800/6100, FAX *051/3664–1090,* WEB *www.solardabarra.com.br. 179 rooms. Restaurant, bar, 2 pools (1 indoor), sauna, nightclub, meeting room. AE, DC, MC, V.*

São Miguel das Missões

482 km (300 mi) northwest of Porto Alegre on BR 285/BR 466.

Jesuit missionaries moved from Paraná Valley to the upper Uruguayan River basin around 1700. In the following decades the local Guarani peoples were converted to Christianity, abandoning their seminomadic lifestyle and congregating around the new missions. Seven of these existed in what is now Brazil and several more in Argentina—all linked by a closely knit trade and communication route. Historians have claimed that at the peak of their influence, the Jesuits actually had created the first de facto country in the Americas, complete with a court system and elections. This important historical period was depicted in *The Mission,* starring Robert De Niro. Later in the century, the missions were raided by slave hunters and Portuguese militia. The Jesuits fled, and the Guaranis were either taken as slaves or disappeared into unexplored country.

São Miguel das Missões is the best-preserved and -organized. Circa 1745 an impressive church was built of reddish basalt slabs brought by the Guaranis from quarries miles away. The ruins are a UNESCO World Heritage Site. There is a small museum on the grounds designed by by Lucío Costa (who was instrumental in the development of Brasília). It holds religious statues carved by the Guaranis, as well as other pieces recovered from archaeological digs. Admission to the site includes a sound and light show, which tells the mission's story at 8 PM in summer and 6 PM in winter.

Tours of the missions can be booked through any of the tour operators in Porto Alegre. Other mission sites with ruins are São Lourenço and São Nicolau; however, there is much less to be seen, and access is difficult. ⊠ *Parque Histórico de São Miguel,* ☎ *055/3381–3259.* ⊠ *R$3.* ☉ *Museum: daily 8–6; grounds: 8 AM–dusk.*

Dining and Lodging

$ ✕ **Churrascaria Barichello.** This typical gaúcho restaurant is the best option in town. Savor the espeto-corrido with more than a dozen different kinds of meat. ⊠ *Av. Borges do Canto 1519,* ☎ *055/381–1327. No credit cards.*

¢ 🏨 **Wilson Park Hotel Missões.** Opened in late 2000, the hotel filled a
★ gap in the regional tourism industry. You'll find large rooms painted in relaxing pastel colors, with colonial-style furnishings. Arched doorways echo the design of the mission a few blocks away. The well-trained staff is knowledgeable about attractions in the region. ⊠ *Rua São Miguel s/n, 98865-000,* ☎ *055/3381–2000. 80 rooms. Restaurant, bar, pool, horseback riding. AE, MC, V. CP.*

THE SOUTH A TO Z

To research prices, get advice from other travelers, and book travel arrangements, visit www.fodors.com.

AIR TRAVEL
CARRIERS

No international airlines serve Curitiba directly from Canada, the United Kingdom, or the United States. Domestic airlines that fly here include TAM, Transbrasil, Varig, and VASP. Foz do Iguaçu is served by Transbrasil, Varig, and VASP. TAM now serves destinations in

Paraguay, including Ciudad del Este. Domestic air carriers that serve the Santa Catarina region include TAM, Transbrasil, Varig/RioSul, and VASP. Airlines that serve Rio Grande do Sul include Aerolíneas Argentinas, TAM, Transbrasil, Varig, and VASP.

Several airlines have code-share agreements. So technically you can fly United or American Airlines to Porto Alegre, although the planes are owned by Varig or TAM. The closest airport to São Miguel das Missões is 60 km (38 mi) away in Santo Angelo. It's served daily by Varig flights from Porto Alegre and São Paulo.

➤ AIRLINES AND CONTACTS IN PARANÁ: **TAM** (☎ 041/381–1620 or 041/323–5201 in Curitiba; 045/523–8588 in Foz do Iguaçu). **Transbrasil** (☎ 041/381–1579 or 041/322–5655 in Curitiba; 045/523–5205 or 045/523–3836 in Foz do Iguaçu). **Varig** (☎ 041/381–1600 or 041/322–1343 in Curitiba; 045/523–2155 or 045/523–2111 in Foz do Iguaçu). **VASP** (☎ 041/382–0345 or 041/221–7422 in Curitiba; 045/523–8331 in Foz do Iguaçu).

➤ AIRLINES AND CONTACTS IN SANTA CATARINA: **TAM** (☎ 048/236–1812 or 041/323–5201). **Transbrasil** (☎ 048/236–1380 or 048/223–7777). **Varig/RioSul** (☎ 048/236–1121 or 048/236–1779). **VASP** (☎ 048/236–3033).

➤ AIRLINES AND CONTACTS IN RIO GRANDE DO SUL: **Aerolíneas Argentinas** (☎ 051/3371–3256 or 051/3221–3300). **TAM** (☎ 051/3371–2409 or 051/3337-3200). **Transbrasil** (☎ 051/3371–4111 or 051/3211–2800). **Varig** (☎ 051/3358–7200 or 051/3358–7999). **VASP** (☎ 051/3371–4496 or 051/3225–6111).

AIRPORTS AND TRANSFERS

Curitiba's Aeroporto Internacional Afonso Pena is 21 km (13 mi) east of the city. A cab ride to downtown is around R$27.

The Aeroporto Internacional Foz do Iguaçu is 13 km (8 mi) southeast of downtown. The 20-minute taxi ride should cost R$30, the 45-minute regular bus ride about R$.60. Note that several major hotels are on the highway to downtown, so a cab ride from the airport may be less than R$16.

The Aeroporto Internacional Hercílio Luz is 12 km (8 mi) south of downtown Florianópolis. Taking a cab into town will run about R$22. In addition, there's *amarelinho* (minibus) service for R$3.30.

Porto Alegre's Aeroporto Internacional Salgado Filho is in a new terminal only 8 km (5 mi) northeast of downtown. You can prepay (R$27) for a ride to town in special airport cars—full-size sedans painted white with a blue stripe—at a booth near the arrivals gate. Regular city cabs (painted a red-orange color) have meters; a ride to downtown should cost around R$16. There's also a minibus shuttle into town for R$1.30.

➤ AIRPORT INFORMATION: **Aeroporto Internacional Afonso Pena** (✉ Av. Rocha Pombo, São José dos Pinhais, Curitiba, ☎ 041/381–1515). **Aeroporto Internacional Foz do Iguaçu** (✉ Km 13, Rodovia das Cataratas, ☎ 045/523–4244). **Aeroporto Internacional Hercílio Luz** (✉ Km 12, Av. Deomício Freitas Florianópolis, ☎ 048/236–0879). **Aeroporto Internacional Salgado Filho** (✉ Av. dos Estados s/n, Porto Alegre, ☎ 051/3371–4110).

BUS TRAVEL

For the most part, each city is served by a different company. For long-distance trips it's best to opt for *executivo* buses, which have air-conditioning, reclining seats, and rest rooms. Regular buses are 20%–30% less but aren't nearly as comfortable.

PARANÁ

Curitiba's main bus station is the Estação Rodoferroviária. Catarinense buses travel to Blumenau (4 hrs) and Joinville (1½ hrs). Itapemirim buses run to and from São Paulo (5 hrs). For trips to Porto Alegre (12 hrs), try Pluma. Sulamericana buses make the 10-hour trip to Foz do Iguaçu.

Foz do Iguaçu's Terminal Rodoviário is 5 km (3 mi) northeast of downtown. For trips to Florianópolis (14 hrs), contact Catarinense. Pluma buses make the 16-hour journey to São Paulo. For trips to Curitiba (10 hrs), try Sulamericana.

➤ Bus Information: **Catarinense** (☎ 041/222–1298 in Curitiba; 045/223–2996 in Foz do Iguaçu). **Estação Rodoferroviária** (✉ Av. Afonso Camargo 330, ☎ 041/320–3232). **Itapemirim** (☎ 041/356–2338). **Pluma** (☎ 041/223–3641 in Curitiba; 045/522–2515 in Foz do Iguaçu). **Sulamericana** (☎ 041/223–6387 in Curitiba; 045/522–2050 in Foz do Iguaçu). **Terminal Rodoviário** (✉ Av. Costa e Silva s/n, ☎ 045/522–3633).

SANTA CATARINA

Several bus companies have regular service to and from Florianópolis's Terminal Rodoviário Rita Maria. For the 12-hour journey to São Paulo, the 3½-hour trip to Joinville, or the two-hour trip to Blumenau, try Catarinense. Pluma buses travel to Curitiba (5 hrs). For trips to Porto Alegre (6 hrs), try União Cascavel.

➤ Bus Information: **Catarinense** (☎ 048/222–2260). **Pluma** (☎ 048/223–1709). **Terminal Rodoviário Rita Maria** (✉ Av. Paulo Fontes 1101, ☎ 048/224–2777). **União Cascavel** (☎ 048/224–2080).

RIO GRANDE DO SUL

All bus lines to the interior—and to other states and countries—use the ugly, overcrowded Estação Rodoviária. Itapemirim/Penha has service to São Paulo (19 hrs). Pluma buses travel to Curitiba (12 hrs). Florianópolis (6 hrs) is served by Santo Anjo/Eucatur. To reach Foz do Iguaçu (14 hrs), try Unesul. Bus service to São Miguel das Missões is painfully slow and not designed for tourists.

➤ Bus Information: **Estação Rodoviária** (✉ Largo Vespasiano Veppo s/n, ☎ 145). **Itapemirim/Penha** (☎ 051/3225–0933). **Pluma** (☎ 051/3228–5112). **Santo Anjo/Eucatur** (☎ 051/3228–8900). **Unesul** (☎ 051/3228–2981).

BUS TRAVEL WITHIN THE SOUTHERN CITIES

Within the region's cities, the bus is the preferred form of public transportation. You can reach virtually any neighborhood, and the fares are modest. Still, you must use caution, as crime can be a problem on little-traveled routes or during off-peak hours.

In Curitiba, the Linha Turismo is a special bus line maintained by the city that follows a 2½-hour circular route. Buses depart every 30 minutes from 9 to 5:30 from the Praça Tiradentes, stopping at 22 attractions. There are taped descriptions of the sights (available in three languages—including English), and the fare is about R$7. You can contact the Prefeitura-Turismo for more information.

In Foz do Iguaçu, Linha Cataratas buses depart hourly (8–6) from the Terminal Urbano for the Hotel das Cataratas, right near the falls. The fare is about R$1 but does not include park admission. Buses for Puerto Iguazú, Argentina, and Ciudad del Este, Paraguay, depart from the same terminal.

In Florianópolis, a quick, convenient way to visit the beaches is by amarelinho, or express minibus. They leave regularly from the Terminal Urbano.

Porto Alegre has an extensive bus system (although there's not one central station) as well as *lotação* (express minibus) service. The lotaçãoes leave from several spots in Centro and cost about R$2 for most routes. For more information, call Informações Municipais.

➤ BUS INFORMATION: **Informações Municipais** (Porto Alegre, ☎ 051/3156). **Prefeitura-Turismo** (✉ Curitiba, ☎ 156 or 041/200–1511). **Terminal Urbano** (✉ Av. Juscelino Kubitschek s/n, across from army barracks, Foz do Iguaçu, no phone). **Terminal Urbano** (✉ Praça 15 de Novembro s/n, Centro, Florianópolis, ☎ 048/1517).

CAR RENTAL

Don't expect to find vehicles in the luxury range of the car spectrum. Automatic transmission is not normally available, and there's a surcharge for air-conditioning.

➤ MAJOR AGENCIES IN PARANÁ: **Avis** (✉ Aeroporto Internacional Afonso Pena, Av. Rocha Pombo, São José dos Pinhais, Curitiba, ☎ 041/381–1383; ✉ Av. Salgado Filho 1491, Curitiba, ☎ 041/278–8808; ✉ Km 10, Rodovia das Cataratas, Foz do Iguaçu, ☎ 045/523–1510). **Hertz** (✉ Aeroporto Internacional Afonso Pena, Av. Rocha Pombo, São José dos Pinhais, Curitiba, ☎ 041/381–1383; ✉ Av. Nossa Senhora Aparecida 3731, Curitiba, ☎ 041/342–4222).

➤ LOCAL AGENCY IN PARANÁ: **Localiza** (✉ Km 10, Rodovia das Cataratas, Foz do Iguaçu, ☎ 045/523–4800; ✉ Av. Juscelino Kubitschek 2878, Foz do Iguaçu, ☎ 045/522–1608).

➤ MAJOR AGENCIES IN SANTA CATARINA: **Avis** (✉ Aeroporto Internacional Hercílio Luz, Km 12, Av. Deomício Freitas, Florianópolis, ☎ 048/236–1426; ✉ Av. Silva Jardim 495, Florianópolis, ☎ 048/225–7777). **Hertz** (✉ Aeroporto Internacional Hercílio Luz, Km 12, Av. Deomício Freitas, Florianópolis, ☎ 048/236–9955; ✉ Rua Bocaiuva 2125, Florianópolis, ☎ 048/224–9955).

➤ LOCAL AGENCY IN SANTA CATARINA: **Localiza** (✉ Aeroporto Internacional Hercílio Luz, Km 12, Av. Deomício Freitas, Florianópolis, ☎ 048/236–1244; ✉ Av. Paulo Fonte 730, Florianópolis, ☎ 048/225–5558).

➤ MAJOR AGENCIES IN RIO GRANDE DO SUL: **Avis** (✉ Aeroporto Internacional Salgado Filho, Av. dos Estados s/n, Porto Alegre, ☎ 051/3371 4344; ✉ Av. Ceará 444, Porto Alegre, ☎ 051/3342–0400). **Hertz** (✉ Av. Sertório 976, Porto Alegre, ☎ 051/3337–7755).

➤ LOCAL AGENCY IN RIO GRANDE DO SUL: **Localiza** (✉ Aeroporto Internacional Salgado Filho, Av. dos Estados s/n, Porto Alegre, ☎ 051/3371–4326; ✉ Av. Carlos Gomes 230, Porto Alegre, ☎ 051/3328–6000; ✉ Km 13, Estrada Catuipe, Santo Angelo (60 km/38 mi from São Miguel das Missões), ☎ 055/312–1000)

CAR TRAVEL

The southern states have extensive highway systems connecting major cities and tourist destinations. Be prepared for stretches that aren't in top condition; some are being renovated, and there may be delays. When planning a road trip, ask at the nearest Polícia Rodoviária (Highway Patrol) station for guidance. These are by the main roads, usually a few kilometers out from major cities. Privatized toll roads in Rio Grande do Sul and Paraná are generally in good shape, but you'll have to pay R$2–R$6.

You can drive from Curitiba to Foz do Iguaçu on BR 277, which traverses Paraná State. It's a long drive, but the highway is in good shape. To visit Vila Velha State Park, a detour must be made on BR 376 toward Ponta Grossa. The BR 101 is the most direct route from Curitiba to other southern communities, but it's one of the country's busiest roads (there's lots of truck traffic night and day). There's a dramatic increase in traffic during the vacation months of January and February. It's also been under renovation for several years.

BR 116, the Mountain Route, runs from Curitiba to Porto Alegre. Built 40 years ago, it was the first highway connecting the region with the rest of the country. Although it's scenic for much of the way—and a little shorter than other routes—it's also narrow, with many curves and many trucks.

The 482-km (300-mile) route from Porto Alegre to São Miguel das Missões follows BR 386 to Carazinho, and then BR 285 to the São Miguel exit. From there, take BR 466 the short 11 km (7 mile) to the mission site. These roads are all single-lane but generally in good condition. Expect heavy truck traffic.

Traffic in Curitiba, Florianópolis, and Porto Alegre isn't as hectic as in São Paulo or Rio, so driving won't be overly daunting. Finding a place to park is relatively easy, except, of course, in the downtown districts during business hours. Parking lots are abundant in the cities, and one-hour tickets cost about R$4.

EMERGENCIES
➤ CONTACTS THROUGHOUT THE SOUTH: **Ambulance** (☎ 192). **Emergency** (☎ 100 in Curitiba). **Fire** (☎ 193). **Police** (☎ 190).
➤ CONTACTS IN PARANÁ: **FarmaRede** (⊠ Av. Brasil 46, Foz do Iguaçu, ☎ 045/523–1929). **Hospital Cajuru** (⊠ Av. São José 300, Curitiba, ☎ 041/362–1100). **Hospital Internacional** (⊠ Av. Brasil 1637, Foz do Iguaçu, ☎ 045/523–1404).
➤ CONTACTS IN SANTA CATARINA: **Farmácia Rita Maria** (⊠ Av. Paulo Fontes 1101, Terminal Rita Maria, Florianópolis, ☎ 048/224–3249. **Hospital Universitário** (⊠ Av. Beira-Mar Norte, Trindade, Florianópolis, ☎ 048/231–9100).
➤ CONTACTS IN RIO GRANDE DO SUL: **Hospital Pronto Socorro** (⊠ Av. Osvaldo Aranha s/n, Porto Alegre, ☎ 051/3316–9600). **Farmácia Pan-Vel** (⊠ Av. 24 de Outubro 722, Moinhos de Vento, Porto Alegre, ☎ 051/3222–0188).

ENGLISH-LANGUAGE MEDIA
Few bookstores stock English-language books. When they're available, expect only a limited selection of paperbacks. Foreign newspapers are rarely available; you might have more success with popular international magazines.

In Curitiba, try Livraria O Livro Técnico. Florianópolis has the Livraria Alemã. In Porto Alegre, good bets are Prosa i Verso, which has a limited selection of classics and run-of-the-mill paperbacks; and Saraiva Mega Store, which carries paperbacks, travel guides, and several popular magazines.
➤ BOOKSTORES: **Livraria Alemã** (⊠ Rua Felipe Schmidt 14, Florianópolis, ☎ 041/224–0178). **Livraria O Livro Técnico** (⊠ Shopping Center Itália, Rua João Negrão 129, Curitiba, ☎ 041/232–6621). **Prosa i Verso** (⊠ Quinta Avenida Shopping Center, Av. Mostardeiro 120, Porto Alegre, ☎ 051/3222–2409). **Saraiva Mega Store** (⊠ Shopping Center Praia de Belas, Av. Praia de Belas 1181, Porto Alegre, ☎ 051/3231–6868).

HEALTH
Here, in Brazil's most developed region, tap water is safe to drink in most areas. It's usually highly chlorinated, so you may prefer the taste of bottled water. As in the rest of Brazil, avoid eating unpeeled fruit.

MAIL, INTERNET, AND SHIPPING

➤ COURIER SERVICES: **FedEx** (✉ Rua Nossa Senhora da Penha 435, Curitiba, ☎ 041/362–5155; ✉ Rua Coronel Américo 912, Florianópolis, ☎ 048/240–6232; ✉ Av. Ceará 255, Porto Alegre, ☎ 051/3343–5424). **UPS** (✉ Rua Visc. Rio Branco 279, Porto Alegre, ☎ 051/3346–6655).

➤ INTERNET CAFÉ: **Saraiva Mega Store** (✉ Shopping Center Praia de Belas, Av. Praia de Belas 1181, Menino Deus, Porto Alegre, ☎ 051/3231–6868).

➤ POST OFFICES: **Correios** (✉ Av. Marechal Deodoro 298, Curitiba, ☎ 041/310–2100). **Correios** (✉ Praça Getúlio Vargas 72, Foz do Iguaçu, ☎ 045/574–2381). **Correios** (✉ Praça 15 de Novembro 242, Florianópolis, ☎ 048/159). **Correios** (✉ Rua Siqueira Campos 1100, Porto Alegre, ☎ 051/3228–9102).

MONEY MATTERS

In general, banks are open weekdays 10–4 in major cities, 10–3 in the countryside, though airport branches have extended hours for currency exchange (daily 8 AM–9 PM); some also have Saturday-morning hours. ATMs that dispense reais and work with international bank or credit cards are readily available. Banco 24 Horas ATMs are linked with Cirrus; Banco do Brasil ATMs are affiliated with Plus.

➤ BANKS IN PARANÁ: **Banco ABN-AMRO Real** (✉ Av. Candido de Abreu 304, Centro Cívico, Curitiba, ☎ 041/252–2233). **Banco do Brasil** (✉ Aeroporto Internacional Afonso Pena, Av. Rocha Pombo, São José dos Pinhais, Curitiba, ☎ 041/223–1350; ✉ Av. Brasil 1377, Foz do Iguaçu, ☎ 045/523–2288). **BankBoston** (✉ Av. Mal. Deodoro 869, Centro, Curitiba, ☎ 041/322–5052). **STTC** (✉ Av. das Cataratas 1419, Foz do Iguaçu, ☎ 045/574–2527).

➤ BANKS IN SANTA CATARINA: **Amplestur** (✉ Rua Jerônimo Coelho 293, Loja 01, Centro, Florianópolis, ☎ 041/224–9422). **Banco do Brasil** (✉ Praça 15 de Novembro 20, Florianópolis, ☎ 048/222–7000).

➤ BANKS IN RIO GRANDE DO SUL: **Banco do Brasil** (✉ Rua Uruguai 185, Centro, Porto Alegre, ☎ 051/3214–7777; ✉ Aeroporto Internacional Salgado Filho, Av. dos Estados s/n, Porto Alegre, ☎ 051/3371–1822). **Citibank** (✉ Praça Maurício Cardoso 176, Porto Alegre, ☎ 051/3222–4488). **Turispres** (✉ Rua dos Andradas 1091, Suite 104, Porto Alegre, ☎ 051/3225–3111; ✉ Estação Rodoviária, Largo Vespasiano Veppo s/n, Porto Alegre, ☎ 051/3225–3565).

SAFETY

Crime is low compared with the northern parts of the country. However, you should guard your belongings on city buses and in crowded public spaces—especially bus terminals, which are havens for pickpockets.

TAXIS

Taxis in Brazil are normally independently owned, and most are locally organized into cooperatives that maintain phone numbers and dispatchers (hence, the moniker "radio taxis"). These outfits have booths in all airports, with posted rates (regulated by city authorities) for specific destinations, and you pay up front for the ride to town. Although it's best to call for a cab in town to avoid delays, you can hail passing taxis. Cabs have meters, but ask for an estimate of the fare to your destination before departing to avoid surprises. In Foz do Iguaçu, independent tour operators (certified by the city government) offer their services outside hotel lobbies. These special cabs are usually large sedans with air-conditioning. The driver doubles as a tour guide and you can tailor the route and pace according to your interests. A half-day trip to the Argentinian side of the falls will cost about R$60.

➤ Taxi Companies: **Curitiba radio-taxi service** (☎ 041/262–6262 or 041/276–7676). **Foz do Iguaçu radio-taxi service** (☎ 045/523–4800). **Florianópolis radio-taxi service** (☎ 197). **Porto Alegre radio-taxi service** (☎ 051/3334–7444).

TELEPHONES

Area codes in the region are 41 for Curitiba, 45 for Foz do Iguaçu, 48 for Florianópolis, and 51 for Porto Alegre. Outside hotels, you can make long-distance calls from *posto telefônicos* (central phone offices), run by phone companies in all cities. Fax services and, more recently, Internet services are also provided at most of these offices.

In Porto Alegre, you can make long-distance calls from some phone booths, or try the CRT Phone Center open 7 AM–11 PM, with fax services.
➤ Contacts: **CRT Phone Center** (✉ Av. Sen. Salgado Filho 27, Porto Alegre, ☎ 051/3228–0505). **Posto Telefônico TELEPAR** (✉ Rua E. Barros s/n, Centro, Foz do Iguaçu, ☎ 045/523–2449). **Posto Telefônico TELESC** (✉ Praça Pereira Oliveira 20, Florianópolis, ☎ 048/106). **Teleposto TELEPAR** (✉ Av. Pres. Afonso Camargo 330, Centro, Curitiba, ☎ 041/322–9848).

TOURS

In Curitiba, try Best Ways for train tickets to Paranaguá and tours of the Paranaguá Bay, including the national park.

STTC Turismo in Foz do Iguaçu is reliable. Macuco Safari arranges Zodiac trips to Salto Macuco and on to the main falls. Helisul Táxi Aéreo offers helicopter tours of the falls between 9 and 6 and, if you like, of Itaipú dam. The shortest flight (10 min) costs R$135 per person.

In Florianópolis try Amplestur for bus tours of the city and destinations in Santa Catarina. Scuna Sul has three sailboats that give tours near the northern part of the island. Vento Sul operates a larger schooner outfitted for overnight trips around the island and along Santa Catarina's coast.

In Porto Alegre, tours of the city, to the Serra Gaúcha, of the coast, or to the missions can all be arranged by most operators. Cisne Branco runs day and night boat trips on the Guaíba. Caá-Etê Expeditions is a good choice for adventure trips—rafting, horseback riding, or hiking excursions—to the state parks.
➤ Contacts in Paraná: **Best Ways** (✉ Estação Rodoferroviária, Gate 8, Curitiba, ☎ 041/323–4007). **Helisul Táxi Aéreo** (✉ Km 16.5, Rodovia das Cataratas, Foz do Iguaçu, ☎ 045/523–1190. **Macuco Safari** (✉ Km 21, Rodovia das Cataratas, Foz do Iguaçu, ☎ 045/574–4244). **STTC Turismo** (✉ Av. Morenitas 2250, Padre Monti, Foz do Iguaçu, ☎ 045/523–1115, ℻ 045/523–3137, 🌐 www.sttcturismo.com.br).
➤ Contacts in Santa Catarina: **Amplestur** (✉ Rua Jerônimo Coelho 293, Loja 01, Centro, Florianópolis, ☎ 041/224–9422, 🌐 www.amplestur.com.br). **Scuna Sul** (✉ Rua Antonio Heil s/n, Canasvieiras, Florianópolis, ☎ 048/266–1810). **Vento Sul** (✉ Public Marina s/n, Canasvieiras, Florianópolis, ☎ 048/9982–2857).
➤ Contacts in Rio Grande do Sul: **Caá-Etê Expeditions** (✉ Av. Protásio Alves 2715, Suite 905, Porto Alegre, ☎ 051/3338–3323 or 051/3338–1888, 🌐 www.caa-ete.com.br). **Cisne Branco** (✉ Port of Porto Alegre, Main Gate, Av. Mauá 1050, Porto Alegre, ☎ 051/3224–5222). **Hamburguesa** (✉ Rua Alberto Bins 514, Suite 10 [Hotel Plaza San Rafael lobby], Porto Alegre, ☎ 051/3211–5088). **Unesul** (✉ Rua Vigário José Inácio 629, Porto Alegre, ☎ 051/3228–8111).

TRAIN TRAVEL

One of Brazil's few passenger rail lines runs from Curitiba to Paranaguá—a fabulous 110-km (69-mi) trip. Trains traverse the Serra do Mar slope from 1,000 m (3,300 ft) down to 5 m (17 ft) through bridges and tunnels. There are great views of the peaks, waterfalls, and Atlantic rain forest, which covers most of the slopes on the way. Two stops, at the historic towns of Morretes and Marumbi, complete this great route. Two kinds of trains operate: the faster *litorina* makes the trip in 3½ hours, departs from Curitiba at 9 AM (Fri.–Sun. and holidays), returns from Paranaguá at 3:30 PM, and costs R$45; the trip by regular train takes four hours, departs at 8 AM (except Monday), returns at 4 PM, and costs R$11. To make arrangements, contact Serra Verde Express.

➤ TRAIN INFORMATION: **Serra Verde Express** (✉ Estação Rodoferroviária, Gate 8, Curitiba, ☎ 041/323–4008).

VISITOR INFORMATION

➤ TOURIST INFORMATION IN PARANÁ: **FozTur** (✉ Rua Alm. Barroso 1300, 2nd floor, Foz do Iguaçu, ☎ 045/523–0222; ✉ Aeroporto Internacional Foz do Iguaçú, Km 13, Rodovia das Cataratas, ☎ 045/522–2590). **Paraná Turismo** (State Tourism Board; ✉ Rua Dep. Mário de Barros 290, Curitiba, ☎ 041/224-7273 or Teletur [24-hr hot line] 041/1516, WEB www.pr.gov.br/turismo).

➤ TOURIST INFORMATION IN SANTA CATARINA: **Portal Turístico** (✉ BR 262 [Via Expressa] s/n, mainland side of Ponte Colombo Sales (Colombo Sales Bridge), São José, ☎ 048/244–5822. **SanTur** (State Tourism Authority; ✉ Rua Felipe Schmidt 249, 9th floor, Florianópolis, ☎ 048/223–7796 or Disque Turismo [24-hr hot line] 048/1516, WEB www.sc.gov.br/turismo).

➤ TOURIST INFORMATION IN RIO GRANDE DO SUL: **Central Municipal de Informações Turísticas** (✉ Rua Vasco da Gama 253, Bom Fim, Porto Alegre, ☎ 051/3311–5289. **Centro de Informações Turísticas** (✉ Estação Rodoviária, Largo Vespasiano Veppo s/n, Porto Alegre, ☎ 051/3228–7377, ext. 247). **Secretaria de Turismo** (State Tourism Authority; ✉ Av. Borges de Medeiros 1501, 10th floor, Porto Alegre, ☎ 051/3225–8183; ✉ Aeroporto Internacional Salgado Filho, Av. dos Estados s/n, Porto Alegre, ☎ 051/3228–7377, ext. 248).

4 MINAS GERAIS

In the early 18th century, gold was discovered in the rich, red earth of Minas Gerais. The legacies of this discovery are historic cities with narrow cobblestone streets that wind past baroque churches; mineral-spa towns made mystical with therapeutic waters and mountainous surroundings; and a type of Brazilian like no other. The traditional, proud *mineiros* have sent forth some of the nation's most famous artists and politicians.

B RAZIL'S CENTRAL MOUNTAINOUS REGION is dominated by the
state of Minas Gerais, a name (meaning "general mines") inspired by the area's great mineral wealth. In the 18th century
its vast precious-metal reserves made the state, and particularly the city
of Ouro Preto (also seen as Ouro Prêto, an archaic spelling) the de facto
capital of the Portuguese colony. That period of gold, diamond, and
semiprecious-stone trading is memorialized in the historic towns scattered across the mountains, and remains a tremendous source of pride
for the *mineiros* (inhabitants of the state). Minas Gerais is a calmer,
more conservative, more thoughtful Brazil. Yet it has also been a
hotbed for movements that have triggered political, economic, and cultural development.

Updated by
Ana Lúcia
do Vale

Exploration of Minas Gerais began in the 17th century, when *bandeirantes* (bands of adventurers) from the coastal areas came in search
of slaves and gold. Near the town of Vila Rica, they found a black stone
that was later verified to be gold (the coloring came from the iron oxide
in the soil). Thus Vila Rica came to be called Ouro Preto (Black Gold),
and at the beginning of the 18th century Brazil's first gold rush began.
Along with the fortune seekers came Jesuit priests, who were later exiled by the Portuguese (for fear that they would try to manipulate the
mineral trade) and replaced by *ordens terceiros* ("third," or lay, orders). By the middle of the century, the Gold Towns of Minas were gleaming with new churches built first in the baroque-rococo style of Europe
and, later, in a baroque style unique to the region.

Minas was also blessed with a local artistic genius, Antônio Francisco
Lisboa. The son of a Portuguese architect and a former slave, Lisboa
was born in 1738 in what is today Ouro Preto. As an adult he acquired
the nickname Aleijadinho, "the little cripple," because of an illness that
left him deformed. Working in cedarwood and soapstone, Aleijadinho
carved the passion of his beliefs in sculptures that grace churches
throughout the state.

By the end of the 18th century the gold had begun to run out, and Ouro
Preto's population and importance decreased. The baroque period
ended at the start of the 19th century, when the Portuguese royal family, in flight from the conquering army of Napoléon Bonaparte, arrived
in Brazil, bringing with them architects and sculptors with different
ideas and artistic styles. Ornate twisted columns and walls adorned with
lavish carvings gave way to simple straight columns and walls painted
with murals or simply washed in white.

Though you'll always be awed by the Gold Towns, Minas Gerais has
other attractions. Roughly six hours south of Belo Horizonte, the state
capital, several mineral-spa towns form the Circuito das Águas (Water
Circuit). Thought to have healing powers, the natural springs of places
like São Lourenço and Caxambu have attracted the Brazilian elite for
more than a century. Close by is the unusual town of São Tomé das
Letras—a place where UFOs are said to visit, and where mystics and
bohemians wait for the dawn of a new world.

Although justifiably proud of their state's artistic accomplishments,
mineiros are also passionate about their politics. Minas Gerais has produced many of Brazil's most famous leaders, including Tiradentes, who
led Brazil's first attempt at independence; Juscelino Kubitschek, the president who made Brasília happen; and Tancredo Neves, who helped re-
store Brazilian democracy in the mid-1980s.

Today Minas is Brazil's second most industrialized state, after São Paulo. The iron that darkened the gold of Ouro Preto remains an important source of state income, along with steel, coffee, and auto manufacturing. Although some of its once heavily wooded areas have been stripped bare, Minas still has diverse and amazingly pristine ecosystems, including Atlantic forests, rain forests, wetlands, and grasslands. The traffic that the mines brought here in the 17th century thrust Brazil into civilization, and now, well into the wake of the gold rush, a steady sense of progress and a compassion for the land remain.

Pleasures and Pastimes

Architecture

In the 17th century, to ensure their control of the mining industry when gold was discovered in Minas Gerais, the Portuguese exiled the traditional religious orders, which led to the formation of third orders. Attempts by these lay brothers to build churches on European models resulted in improvisations (they had little experience with or guidance on such matters) and, hence, a uniquely Brazilian style of baroque. Many churches from this period have simple exteriors that belie interiors whose gold-leaf-encrusted carvings are so intricate they seem like filigree.

As the gold supply diminished, facades became more elaborate—with more sophisticated lines, elegant curves, and large round towers—and their interiors less so, as murals were used more than carvings and gold leaf. Today you can see several outstanding examples of baroque architecture, many of them attributed to the legendary Aleijadinho, in Ouro Preto (where there are 13 such churches) and the other Gold Towns of Minas.

Dining

Comida mineira (Minas cuisine) offers distinctive flavors and specialties. Pork, particularly *lombo* (pork tenderloin), is used in many dishes and is often served with white rice and/or corn porridge. Typical specialties include *tutu à mineira* (mashed beans with roast pork loin, pork sausage, chopped collard greens, and boiled egg), *feijão tropeiro* (beans mixed with manioc flour, roast pork loin, fried egg, chopped collard greens, and thick pork sausage), *frango com quiabo* (chicken cooked in broth with chopped okra), and *frango ao molho pardo* (chicken cooked in a black sauce—the chicken's blood). Of course, *caipirinhas* (drinks of crushed ice, crushed lime, sugar, and *cachaça*, a sugarcane-based liquor) go well with all the regional dishes.

Mineiros tend to eat dinner after 8 (often closer to 10). Restaurants are busiest on weekends and may require reservations; many close on Monday. For price categories, *see* the chart *under* Dining *in* Smart Travel Tips A to Z.

Gemstones

Minas Gerais produces most of the world's colored gemstones, including the grande dame of them all, the imperial topaz, which is found nowhere else. It comes in shades of pink and tangerine, and the clearer the stone the better the quality. The state's mines also produce amethysts, aquamarines, tourmalines, and emeralds.

The stones are cut, polished, and incorporated into jewelry in cities like Ouro Preto and Belo Horizonte, where you can buy authenticated pieces—often at heavily discounted prices—from top jewelers. Note that gems vary widely in quality and value; don't buy them on the streets, and be wary about buying them from smaller shops (get recommendations first).

Shopping

Hand-carved wood and soapstone figures and other objects are sold by street vendors in all the historic cities. Other typical handicrafts include pottery and tapestries, in particular the handwoven *arraiola* tapestries for which the area around Diamantina is famous. Of course, you should always be on the lookout for interesting jewelry.

Lodging

Mineiro hotel, *pousada* (inn), and *fazenda* (farm) owners are paying more and more attention to the quality of their rooms and service. That said, most hotels remain small, lack English-speaking staffs, and have few of the amenities common in American and European chains. When you book, you'll likely be given a choice between a standard and a luxury room; the *apartamento de luxo* (luxury room) may be slightly larger, offer air-conditioning, and have a better-equipped bathroom. In most cases, breakfast is included in the rate. Significant weekend discounts are common in Belo Horizonte. For price categories, *see* the chart *under* Lodging *in* Smart Travel Tips A to Z.

Exploring Minas Gerais

The peaks of the Serra do Mantiqueira separate Minas from Rio de Janeiro and give way to the Paraíba Valley. Although Minas is large, its major attractions, including Belo Horizonte, Ouro Preto, and the mineral-spa towns, are in the state's southeast, within driving distance of one another. The key historic cities—called the Gold Towns—are in the Serra do Espinhaço range, with Ouro Preto at 1,220 m (4,000 ft) above sea level.

Great Itineraries

IF YOU HAVE 5 DAYS

Rest from your journey by staying overnight in Belo Horizonte, the gateway city and hub for trips to the Gold Towns. On the second day, head to Sabará, a short local bus ride away. On the third day, travel to Ouro Preto, a two-hour drive or bus ride from the capital, for two days of exploring its rich architecture, shopping for its unique handicrafts, and absorbing its folklore.

IF YOU HAVE 7 DAYS

Spend a day in Belo Horizonte. On the second day, rent a car and head to Ouro Preto for two days of sightseeing. On the fourth day, visit neighboring Mariana, the state's oldest city. For your remaining days you can either head north to Diamantina or south through Congonhas and on to the charming town of Tiradentes.

IF YOU HAVE 10 DAYS

Follow the seven-day itinerary above. On the eighth day head to the spa towns south of Belo Horizonte for the remainder of your trip. Be aware that innkeepers in places like São Lourenço and Caxambu will do their best to convince you that a few days in their towns aren't nearly enough—the waters' curative properties are said to only take effect after 20 or so days.

When to Tour

The busiest and often most exciting times to travel are during the Christmas, Easter, and Carnaval (Carnival) periods—although Carnaval is much more subdued here than in Bahia or Rio. July, when the weather is cool and dry, is winter break month and another peak season. To avoid crowds, travel from April to June or August to December. Discounts may be available during these months, although fewer services will be offered.

Minas Gerais

BELO HORIZONTE AND THE HISTORIC CITIES

Brazil's first planned state capital, Belo Horizonte (often called the Garden City or simply Belo) has tree-lined streets and an intimate small-town atmosphere that belies its size. Although it has few attractions, it's the gateway to the region's historic cities, and its citizens are warm, gracious, and helpful.

Two hours southeast of Belo is Ouro Preto, a UNESCO World Heritage Site. The country's de facto capital during the gold-boom years, it was also the birthplace of Brazil's first independence movement: the Inconfidência Mineira. Today a vibrant student population ensures plenty of year-round activity, and there are plenty of lodging, dining, and shopping options.

All the Gold Towns are characterized by winding cobblestone streets, brilliant baroque churches, impressive mansions and museums, and colorful markets. Smaller but no less charming than Ouro Preto is Tiradentes, which truly seems to have stopped in time about midway through the 18th century. Between Ouro Preto and Tiradentes lies Congonhas, whose basilica is guarded by Aleijadinho's extraordinary sculptures of the 12 Old Testament prophets. In each of the towns you visit, from Sabará to Mariana to Diamantina, you'll discover a rich cultural history that sheds considerable light on colonial Brazil.

Belo Horizonte

444 km (276 mi) northwest of Rio, 741 km (460 mi) southeast of Brasília.

With a population of just over 2 million, Belo Horizonte is Brazil's third-largest city and the capital of Minas Gerais, a state renowned as much

for its love of tradition as for its mineral wealth. For visitors, the city
is primarily a jumping-off point for trips to the surrounding region, as
it offers little of historic value. (It is, in fact, a relatively young city,
having been founded in 1897.)

The well-maintained **Parque Municipal** is in the heart of the business
district and close to several hotels. Its tree-lined walks, small lakes, and
rustic bridges make it an example of the passion for orderliness that's
characteristically mineiro. This same trait has helped make Belo Horizonte one of the cleanest and safest of Brazil's leading cities. Within
the park is the **Palácio das Artes** (Palace of the Arts; ⊠ Av. Afonso Pena
1537, ☎ 031/3237–7333), a cultural center with a theater, a library,
art galleries, exhibition halls, and the Centro de Artesanato Mineiro,
with such contemporary Minas handicrafts as carvings of wood and
soapstone, pottery, and tapestries—all for sale. Admission is free; it's
open daily 10–8.

Ironically, though most people come to Belo for the nearby historic region, one of the city's principal attractions is the Pampulha neighborhood, famed for its examples of modern Brazilian architecture. Foremost
among these is the **Igreja de São Francisco de Assis** (Church of St. Francis of Assisi), completed in 1943 and considered one of the most important works of Brazil's famed architect Oscar Niemeyer. Inside the
small but distinctive chapel, with its undulating roof, are frescoes—of
St. Francis and of the stations of the cross—by Cândido Portinari, a
famous Brazilian modernist. To reach the chapel, take a taxi or Bus
2004 (it goes north on Avenida Presidente Antônio Carlos). The chapel
is on the edge of an artificial lake a half hour from downtown; the drive
here is lovely. ⊠ *Av. Otacílio Negrão de Lima, Km 12, Pampulha,* ☎
031/3491–2319. ⊡ *Free.* ⊙ *Weekdays 8:30–noon and 1:30–5, weekends 9–6.*

Dining

$$$–$$$$ ✕ **Splêndido Ristorante.** The food and the service at this cosmopoli-
tan restaurant are exceptional; the prices are also on the "splendid"
side. The kitchen blends northern Italian and French cuisines, and it's
assured that anyone who's anyone will show up here at some point
during a visit to Belo Horizonte. ⊠ *Rua Levindo Lopes 251, Savassi,*
☎ *031/3227–6446. AE, DC, MC, V.*

$$$–$$$$ ✕ **Vecchio Sogno.** What is widely considered Belo Horizonte's best Ital-
★ ian restaurant attracts a well-heeled clientele. Tuxedo-clad waiters
serve selections from the extensive wine list as well as steak, seafood,
and pasta dishes. Consider the grilled fillet of lamb with saffron risotto
in a mushroom-and-garlic sauce; the gnocchi *di mare*, with spinach and
potatoes and served with a white-clam and scallop sauce; or the *badejo*,
a local white fish baked and dressed in a seafood sauce. Reservations
are highly recommended. ⊠ *Rua Martim de Carvalho 75, Santo
Agostinho,* ☎ *031/3292–5251 or 031/3290–7585. AE, DC, MC, V.
No lunch Sat. No dinner Sun.*

$–$$$ ✕ **Chalezinho.** There's only one reason to come here: romance. The
★ dimly lit chalet, with its elegant piano music (accompanied by the oc-
casional saxophone), is a magical retreat in the hills above town. The
specialty is fondue; the filet mignon cooked in a bowl of sizzling oil
and paired with any one of eight delicious sauces is a treat. Afterward,
order a chocolate fondue, which comes with a mouthwatering selection of fruits waiting to be dipped. When you finish, step outside to
the Praça dos Amores (Lovers' Plaza) for a kiss under the moonlit sky.
⊠ *Alameda da Serra 18, Vale do Soreno–Nova Lima,* ☎ *031/3286–
3155. AE, DC, MC, V. No lunch.*

$-$$ ✕ **Amici Miei.** This casual Italian eatery is popular with Brazilians cel-
★ ebrating the end of the workday. The restaurant is often packed both
inside and on the large outdoor patio; you may need to wait a minute
for the staff to find you a table. Start with the *champignon Recheado*
(a large mushroom stuffed with shrimp and prosciutto), followed by
tournedo Amici Miei (filet mignon wrapped in bacon and marinated
in garlic and olive oil). ⊠ *Rua Tome de Souza 1331, Funcionários,* ☎
031/3282–4992. DC, MC, V.

$-$$ ✕ **Chico Mineiro.** Dining Minas Gerais–style means ample portions of
★ such hearty dishes as tutu à mineira, the local equivalent of meat and
potatoes. Nowhere is it better prepared than at this traditional restaurant in the Savassi neighborhood, home to Belo's liveliest nightspots.
Lunch sees a self-service mineira buffet for a fixed price of R$13, in-
cluding dessert. ⊠ *Rua Alagoas 626, Savassi,* ☎ *031/3261–3237. AE,
DC, MC, V.*

$-$$ ✕ **Restaurante Varandão.** On the 25th floor of the Othon Palace
hotel, this romantic restaurant offers spectacular urban vistas. Start off
with a cocktail at one of the outdoor candlelit tables before coming
inside for dinner, where a generous buffet serves as the dining room's
centerpiece. On weekends, the chef serves an innovative "soapstone
barbecue," where you choose thinly sliced meats to grill on a hot soapstone; your meal also comes with potatoes, sauces, and toast. Live Brazilian music accompanies dinner nightly. ⊠ *Av. Afonso Pena 1050,
Centro,* ☎ *031/3213–0000. AE, DC, MC, V.*

$ ✕ **Casa dos Contos.** The menu at this gathering place for local jour-
nalists, artists, and intellectuals is unpretentious and varied, ranging
from fish and pasta to comida mineira. In keeping with its bohemian
clientele, Casa dos Contos serves well past midnight. ⊠ *Rua Rio
Grande do Norte 1065, Funcionários,* ☎ *031/3261–5853. AE, DC,
MC, V.*

$ ✕ **Dona Lucinha II.** Roughly 35 traditional Minas dishes are offered in
this cafeteria-style eatery. Though there's not much charm, the self-service concept helps to keep the price—which is fixed—down. Families
will appreciate the deep discounts for children. ⊠ *Rua Sergipe 811,
Savassi,* ☎ *031/3261–5930. AE, DC, MC, V.*

$ ✕ **Restaurante Top Beer.** This trendy restaurant-bar makes an ideal
launching pad for your evening. The large outdoor patio offers great
people-watching, as students and executives alike plan their night out
while sipping caipirinhas. The inside dining room is an inviting tropical enclave, with fountains and trees surrounding the tables. The
pasta dishes and grilled steaks are commendable. ⊠ *Rua Tomé de Souza
1121, Savassi,* ☎ *031/3221–1116. AE, DC, MC, V.*

Lodging

$$-$$$$ ⊞ **Ouro Minas Palace Hotel.** Though not centrally located, this hotel
★ truly deserves a star. Rooms are comfortable and appealing, with large
beds and well-appointed bathrooms; minibars and modem hookups are
standard. The hotel offers numerous amenities uncommon in Belo Hor-
izonte: a pool with waterfalls, a fitness center, tennis courts, and a mul-
tilingual staff. ⊠ *Av. Cristiano Machado 4001, Ipiranga, 31910-810,*
☎ *031/3429–4001,* FAX *031/3429–4002,* WEB *www.ourominas.com.br.
343 rooms, 44 suites. Restaurant, bar, café, in-room data ports, mini-
bars, pool, massage, Turkish baths, 2 tennis courts, health club, busi-
ness services, car rental. AE, DC, MC, V. BP.*

$$-$$$ ⊞ **Othon Palace.** The Othon has the best location of any hotel in Belo
Horizonte. Although aging (it opened in 1978), renovations are on-
going, and the level of service remains high. Rooms have very little char-
acter, but are comfortable and enjoy spectacular city views, including
the tree-lined Parque Municipal. The rooftop pool and bar are the best

in town, and the on-site Restaurante Verandão is excellent. ✉ *Av. Afonso Pena 1050, Centro 30130-002,* ☎ *031/3213–0000 or 0800/313844,* FAX *031/3213–1050,* WEB *www.hoteis-othon.com.br. 266 rooms, 19 suites. Restaurant, bar, pool, massage, sauna, tennis court, health club, concierge floor, business services, meeting room. AE, DC, MC, V. BP.*

$ 🏨 **Brasilton Contagem.** This modern member of the Hilton chain is popular with business travelers because of its proximity to the Contagem industrial district (it is, however, quite far from the center of town). Guest rooms face a central courtyard with a pool and tropical gardens, creating an atmosphere of total relaxation. ✉ *BR 381, Km 3.65, Contagem 32241-410,* ☎ *031/3399–4000,* FAX *031/3399–4040,* WEB *www.hilton. com.br. 141 rooms. Restaurant, bar, pool. AE, DC, MC, V. BP.*

$ 🏨 **Grandarrel Minas Hotel.** The lobby of this centrally located hotel, one of the city's older establishments, is often crowded with conventioneers. Rooms are comfortable, if a bit dark; many, however, have the same view of the city and surrounding mountains that you'll find from the small rooftop pool and bar. ✉ *Rua Espírito Santo 901, Centro 30160-031,* ☎ *0800/31–1188 or 031/3248–1000,* FAX *0800/33–1188,* WEB *www. grandarrel.com.br. 247 rooms, 8 suites. Restaurant, bar, pool, sauna, health club, business services, meeting room. AE, DC, MC, V. BP.*

$ 🏨 **Merit Plaza.** Located downtown, this hotel offers excellent value,
★ particularly for business travelers in need of modern amenities and a convenient location. Granite covers the contemporary atrium lobby, and guest rooms have soundproof walls, large beds, well-appointed bathrooms, and phones equipped for computer and fax use. ✉ *Rua dos Tamoios 341, Centro 30130-002,* ☎ *031/3201–9000,* FAX *031/3271– 5700,* WEB *www.meritplaza.com.br. 115 rooms, 2 suites. Restaurant, bar, café, in-room data ports, business services. AE, DC, MC, V. BP.*

$ 🏨 **Palmeiras da Liberdade.** Although it's in the chic Savassi neighborhood, this comfortable hotel is very affordable. Rooms count cable TV and direct-dial phones among their many amenities, all of which make this place a good bet if you lack deep pockets. Discounts of as much as 25% off the usual rates aren't unheard-of. ✉ *Rua Sergipe 893, Savassi 30130-171,* ☎ FAX *031/3261–7422. 62 rooms. Restaurant, bar, air-conditioning, minibars, refrigerator. AE, DC, MC, V. BP.*

$ 🏨 **Wembley Palace.** This aging high-rise offers clean (albeit small) rooms, reliable service, and a central location. ✉ *Rua Espírito Santo 201, Centro 30160-031,* ☎ *031/3273–6866,* FAX *031/3273–1601,* WEB *www. hotelwembley.com.br. 105 rooms, 2 suites. Restaurant, bar, minibars. AE, DC, MC, V. BP.*

¢–$ 🏨 **Hotel Wimbledon.** An elegant yet warm atmosphere and a central
★ location are two of this hotel's draws. Guest rooms have polished hardwood floors, local artwork, and modern bathrooms; luxury rooms have Jacuzzis. Attentive service makes this hotel feel more like a bed-and-breakfast. There's a rooftop pool and bar—the perfect spot for an afternoon drink. ✉ *Av. Afonso Pena 772, Centro 30130-002,* ☎ *031/ 3222–6160,* FAX *031/3222–6510,* WEB *www.wimbledon.com.br. 69 rooms, 1 suite. Restaurant, bar, pool, sauna. AE, DC, MC, V. BP.*

¢ 🏨 **Amazônas.** You'll find clean, simply furnished, reasonably priced rooms at this downtown hotel. There's a good restaurant on the 11th floor. ✉ *Av. Amazônas 120, Centro 30160-031,* ☎ *031/3201–4644,* FAX *031/3212–4236. 76 rooms. Restaurant, bar. AE, DC, MC, V. BP.*

Nightlife and the Arts

The center of cultural life in Belo Horizonte is the downtown **Palácio das Artes** (✉ Rua Afonso Pena 1537, Parque Municipal, ☎ 031/ 3237–7286 or 031/3237–7219, WEB www.palaciodasartes.com.br), where ballet companies and symphony orchestras sporadically perform. The box office is open only when performances are coming up.

Much of Belo's nightlife is in the Savassi neighborhood, with its inviting cafés and bars, as well as a handful of clubs with live Brazilian music. For some of Brazil's best cachaças and one of the city's best views, try **Alambique** (✉ Av. Raja Gabaglia 3200, Chalé 1D, São Bento, ☎ 031/3296–7188). **Arrumação** (✉ Av. Assis Chateaubriand, 524, Floresta, ☎ 031/3224–8399) is a traditional bar that's owned by Brazilian comedian and actor Saulo Laranjeira.

The oh-so-chic **Café** (✉ Rua Cláudio Manoel 583, Funcionários, ☎ 031/3261–6019) is open late every night but Monday (when it's closed completely). A popular bar for "GLS" (gays, lesbians, and sympathizers) is **Excess Mix Club** (✉ Rua Antônio de Albuquerque 729, Savassi, ☎ 031/3225–2307). **Idaho** (✉ Alameda das Acácias 1371, Trevo das Seis Pistas, Vila da Serra, ☎ 031/3286–7858) is just one of the city's popular nightclubs.

A contemporary crowd gathers at **A Obra** (✉ Rua Rio Grande do Norte, 1168, Savassi, ☎ 031/3261–9431), which is situated in a basement. **Restaurante Top Beer** (✉ Rua Tomé de Souza 1121, Savassi, ☎ 031/3221–1116) is an ideal spot to begin your evening. A good nightclub is **Swingers** (✉ Rodovia MG 030, 20, Trevo das Seis Pistas, Vila da Serra, ☎ 031/3286–3384).

Outdoor Activities and Sports

FUTEBOL

The **Estádio Mineirão** (✉ Av. Antônio Abrão Carão 1001, Pampulha, ☎ 031/3499–1100) is Brazil's third-largest stadium and the home field for Belo's two professional *futebol* (soccer) teams: Atletico Mineiro and Cruzeiro. Admission to the stadium for a look around (there are no guided tours) is R$1; it's open daily 9–5, except when there's a match. Prices for match tickets vary depending on the type of seat and how important the match is. Expect to pay R$10–R$30 or more for a big game.

HORSEBACK RIDING

Nossa Tropa (☎ 031/9972–8505, 031/9952–7152, or 031/3583–7105) arranges day treks on horseback into the mountains surrounding Belo.

RUNNING

Most of the city's parks offer good, if small, jogging paths, and running is common during the day. The best place to jog is probably the Parque Municipal, with its shaded lawns and sparkling lake.

SPELUNKING

For amateur spelunkers, the mountains of Minas are replete with caves to be explored, though they must be seen with a guided tour. The largest and most popular cavern is the **Maquiné Gruta** (☎ 031/3715–1078), 113 km (70 mi) northwest of Belo Horizonte near the town of Cordisburgo, with six large chambers. Admission is R$6, and the cavern is open daily 8–5. The **Lapinha Gruta** (☎ 031/3681–1958) is only 36 km (22 mi) north of Belo, near the city of Lagoa Santa, on the road leading from Confins Airport. You can tour the cave any day 9–4:30; the entry fee is R$3.

Shopping

In the fashionable Savassi and Lourdes neighborhoods you'll find the city's best antiques, handicrafts, and jewelry stores. For clothing, head to one of the major shopping centers. On Saturday morning, Avenida Bernardo Monteiro (between Rua Brasil and Rua Otoni) is the site of an antiques fair and food market, offering a taste of mineiro cuisine. On Sunday morning, head for the large (nearly 3,000 vendors) arts-and-crafts fair in front of the Othon Palace hotel, on Avenida Afonso Pena.

ANTIQUES

Arte Sacra Antiguidades (⊠ Rua Alagoas 785, Savassi, ☎ 031/3261–7256) offers a fine selection of Minas antiques.

CLOTHING

The centrally located **Bahia Shopping** (⊠ Rua de Bahia 1022, Centro, ☎ 031/3201–7966) is a good place to shop for clothing. Many shops sell designer togs for men and women in Belo Horizonte's most exclusive mall, **BH Shopping** (⊠ BR 040, Belvedere, ☎ 0800/319001).

HANDICRAFTS

Brasarts (⊠ Rua Curitiba 2325, Lourdes, ☎ 031/3291–5220) has a good selection of handicrafts. The **Centro de Artesenato Mineiro** (⊠ Av. Afonso Pena 1537, Parque Municipal, ☎ 031/3222–2400), in the Palácio das Artes, offers a wide range of regional crafts.

JEWELRY AND GEMSTONES

Gems are the obvious focus in an area famous for its mines; just be sure to buy only from reputable dealers. (If you're going to Ouro Preto, wait to buy until you get there.) **Amsterdam Sauer** (⊠ Av. Afonso Pena 1050, Centro, ☎ 031/3273–3844) is a good place to begin your search for jewelry. The **Gem Center** (⊠ Av. Afonso Pena 1901, 5th Floor, Centro, ☎ 031/3222–8189) is another good jewelry bet. **H. Stern** (⊠ BH Shopping Center, Loja 105–106, BR 040, Belvedere, ☎ 031/3286–1568) is one of Brazil's leading names for gems. **Raymundo Vianna** (⊠ BH Shopping Center, BR 040, Belvedere, ☎ 031/3286–6635; ⊠ Rua Bernardo Guimarães 2412, ☎ 031/3292–2655) has a fine reputation for jewelry.

Parque Nacional Serra do Cipó

96 km (60 mi) northeast of Belo Horizonte.

Highlights of the Serra do Cipó National Park include the roaring Cachoeira da Farofa, a waterfall, and the sprawling Canyon das Bandeirantes. Numerous bird species as well as wolves, jaguars, anteaters, monkeys, and the poisonous *sapo de pijama* (colored pajama frog) make up the area's wildlife. Although difficult to reach and lacking in infrastructure, the park's beautiful landscape and ecological wealth make it worth the trip along MG 010 north from Belo toward Lagoa Santa.

The park is open daily 8–5, and admission is R$3. Facilities are poor, so consider visiting the area as part of an organized tour. If you're an intrepid traveler, you can rent a car, call the park's **visitor center** (☎ 031/3683–5117) for some information, and head out on your own.

Lodging

Come expecting basic, rustic—though clean—accommodations that accept most major credit cards. The area's best hotel is **Cipó Veraneio** (⊠ MG 010, Km 95, Jaboticatubas, ☎ 031/3651–4000). The cost for a double is R$110, including all meals. Bed and board at the **Fazenda Monjolas Pousada** (⊠ MG 010, Km 100, Santana do Riacho, ☎ 031/3221–4253) runs R$150 a night. Camping facilities are available at **Véu da Noiva** (⊠ MG 010, Km 101, Santana do Riacho, ☎ 031/3790–1177). Rates are R$14 a night per person.

Diamantina

290 km (180 mi) northeast of Belo Horizonte.

Diamantina took its name from the diamonds that were extracted in great quantities here in the 18th century. Perhaps because of its remote setting in the barren mountains close to the *sertão* (a remote, arid region), Diamantina is extremely well preserved, although its churches lack the grandeur of those in other historic towns. Its white-wall structures stand in pristine contrast to the iron red of the surrounding mountains. The principal attraction in Diamantina is the simple pleasure of walking along the clean-swept cobblestone streets surrounded by colonial houses—note the overhanging roofs with their elaborate brackets.

The city was the home of two legendary figures of the colonial period: diamond merchant João Fernandes and his slave mistress, Xica da Silva, today a popular figure in Brazilian folklore. According to legend, Xica had never seen the ocean, so her lover built her an artificial lake and then added a boat. Two area attractions are linked with her; to see them, you should contact the Casa da Cultura to arrange a guided tour.

The **Casa de Xica da Silva** was the couple's official residence from 1763 to 1771, and contains colonial furniture and Xica's private chapel. ⊠ *Praça Lobo Mesquita 266,* ☎ *038/3531-2491.* ▭ *Free.* ☉ *Tues.–Sat. noon–5:30, Sun. 9 –noon.*

The **Igreja Nossa Senhora do Carmo** is a church built in 1751 as a gift from Fernandes to his mistress. Supposedly, Xica ordered that the bell tower be built on the back of the building so the ringing wouldn't disturb her. The altar has gold-leaf paneling, and the organ has 514 pipes. ⊠ *Rua do Carmo,* ☎ *no phone.* ▭ *Free.* ☉ *Tues.–Sat. 1–5, Sun. 9–noon.*

The **Museu do Diamante,** the city's diamond museum, is in a building that dates from 1789 and displays equipment used in colonial-period mines. Other items on exhibit include instruments made to torture slaves and sacred art that date from the 16th to the 19th centuries. There are guided tours of the rooms where diamonds were classified and separated. ⊠ *Rua Direita 14,* ☎ *038/3531-1382.* ▭ *R$1.* ☉ *Tues.—Sat. noon–5:30, Sun. 9–noon.*

The **Casa de Juscelino Kubitschek** was the childhood home of one of Brazil's most important 20th-century presidents and the man who built Brasília. ⊠ *Rua São Francisco 241,* ☎ *038/3531-3607.* ▭ *Free.* ☉ *Tues.–Sun. 9–5.*

On Rua da Glória, notice the covered wooden **footbridge** connecting the second stories of two buildings that once served as the headquarters of the colonial governors.

Dining and Lodging

¢–$ ✕ **Cantina do Marinho.** This well-respected restaurant specializes in comida mineira. Favorites are pork steak with tutu and pork tenderloin with feijão tropeiro. There's an à la carte menu as well as a self-service buffet for a fixed price of R$7.50, including dessert. ⊠ *Rua Direita 113,* ☎ *038/3531-1686. No credit cards.*

¢ ▥ **Tijuco.** Surprisingly, this historic-district inn is housed in an Oscar Niemeyer–designed structure. It's considered the best hotel in town; the views from it are certainly outstanding. ⊠ *Rua Macau do Meio 211, 39100,* ☎ *038/3531-1022. 26 rooms. Restaurant, bar. AE, DC, MC, V. BP.*

Nightlife

Diamantina enjoys a special distinction as Brazil's center of serenading. At night, particularly on the weekends, romantics gather in a downtown alley known as Beco da Mota, the former red-light district and now home to several popular bars frequented by students and young professionals. Strolling guitar players also gather on Rua Direita and Rua Quitanda.

Sabará

19 km (12 mi) east of Belo Horizonte.

Sabará's churches drive home the enormous wealth of Minas Gerais during the gold rush days. In this former colonial town, today a sprawling suburb of 90,000, historic buildings are scattered about, requiring you either to join a tour or drive. The interiors of the baroque churches are rich in gold-leaf paneling.

In the main square sits the unfinished **Igreja de Nossa Senhora do Rosário dos Pretos** (Church of Our Lady of the Rosary of the Blacks; circa 1767), which was built, like its counterpart in Ouro Preto, by slaves. Here, however, they ran out of gold before the project could be completed. When slavery was abolished in 1888, the church was left as a memorial. ⊠ *Praça Melo Viana s/n,* ☎ *031/3671–1523.* ☑ *R$1.* ⊙ *Daily 9–noon and 2–6.*

The ornate **Igreja de Nossa Senhora da Conceição** (Our Lady of the Immaculate Conception), though small, is Sabará's main church and an outstanding example of Portuguese baroque architecture combined with elements of Asian art. Its simple exterior gives no indication of the wealth inside, typified by its luxurious gold altar and lavishly decorated ceiling. ⊠ *Praça Getúlio Vargas s/n,* ☎ *031/3671–1724.* ☑ *R$1.* ⊙ *Wed.–Fri. 10–noon and Sun. mass.*

Igreja de Nossa Senhora do Ó (Our Lady of Ó), one of Brazil's oldest and smallest churches, contains paintings said to have been completed by 23 Chinese artists brought from the former Portuguese colony of Macau. Other signs of Asian influence include the Chinese tower and the gilded arches. At press time, the church was undergoing renovations. ⊠ *Largo do Ó s/n,* ☎ *031/3671–1724.* ⊙ *Wed.–Sat. 9–noon and 2–5, Sun. 9–1 and 3–5.*

In the **Igreja de Nossa Senhora do Carmo** (Church of Our Lady of Carmel) are pulpits, a choir loft, and a doorway all designed by the famed Aleijadinho. This is one of several Minas churches that were a collaboration between Aleijadinho and painter Manuel da Costa Ataíde, a brilliant artist in his own right. ⊠ *Rua do Carmo s/n,* ☎ *031/ 3671–1523.* ☑ *R$1.* ⊙ *Wed.–Sun. 9–noon and 1–5.*

Ouro Preto

97 km (60 mi) southeast of Belo Horizonte.

The former gold-rush capital is the best place to see the legendary Aleijadinho's artistry. Now a lively university town, it has been preserved as a national monument and a World Heritage Site. The surrounding mountains, the geometric rows of whitewashed buildings, the cobblestone streets and red-tile roofs that climb the hillsides, and the morning mist and evening fog—all give Ouro Preto an evocative air, as if at any moment it could be transported back three centuries.

In its heyday, Ouro Preto was one of Brazil's most progressive cities and the birthplace of the colony's first stirrings of independence. A movement called the Inconfidência Mineira was organized to overthrow the Portuguese rulers and establish an independent Brazilian republic. It was to have been led by a resident of Ouro Preto, Joaquim José da Silva Xavier, a dentist known as Tiradentes (Tooth Puller). But the Minas rebellion never got off the ground. In 1789, word of Tiradentes's intentions reached the capital of Rio de Janeiro; he was hanged, drawn, and quartered, and his followers were either imprisoned or exiled.

THE PASSION OF ALEIJADINHO

IT'S A TESTAMENT to the creative spirit that Brazil's most famous artist couldn't use his hands or feet. Born in 1738 in Vila Rica (today's Ouro Preto) to a Portuguese architect and a black slave, Antônio Francisco Lisboa developed a passion for art through exposure to his father's projects. In his mid-thirties, he developed an illness (some say leprosy, others syphilis; most assume it was arthritis) that led to a life of torment. Nicknamed Aleijadinho (Little Cripple), he shunned human contact, going out only at night or before dawn. With the help of some assistants, he traveled between towns, sculpting and overseeing church construction. He died on November 18, 1814, and was buried in the church he attended as a child.

There's no hint of Aleijadinho's pain in the delicate, expressive features of his soapstone and cedarwood figures. Indeed, his art is distinguished by a striking liveliness and deep religious faith. His most cherished works, such as the larger-than-life Old Testament prophets at the church in Congonhas, were created with a hammer and chisel strapped to his wrists, a feat often compared to the suffering of Christ. After those in Congonhas his best works are in Ouro Preto, where he designed the brilliant Igreja São Francisco de Assis, among other things.

Exploring Ouro Preto

Ouro Preto has several museums as well as 13 colonial *igrejas* (churches) that are highly representative of mineiro baroque architecture. The Minas style is marked by elaborately carved doorways and curving lines. Most distinctive, though, are the interiors, richly painted and decorated lavishly with cedarwood and soapstone sculptures. Many interiors are unabashedly rococo, with an ostentatious use of gold leaf, a by-product of the region's mineral wealth.

All the town's sights are within easy walking distance of the central square, Praça Tiradentes, which teems with gossiping students, eager merchants, and curious visitors. From here, the longest walk you'll make takes about 15 minutes. Note that many museums and churches are closed on Monday.

Numbers in the text correspond to numbers in the margin and on the Ouro Preto map.

A GOOD WALK

Begin at Praça Tiradentes. Two blocks east stands the distinctive twin-tower **Igreja de São Francisco de Assis** ①. Two blocks farther east is the **Igreja de Nossa Senhora da Conceição** ② and its small Aleijadinho museum. From here, head east on Rua da Conceição, which becomes Rua Santa Efigênia, to the **Igreja de Santa Efigênia** ③. Retrace your steps to Praça Tiradentes, and visit the **Museu do Oratório** ④ and its neighboring **Museu da Inconfidência** ⑤. Walk north across the plaza to **Museu da Mineralogia e das Pedras** ⑥, inside the Escola de Minas.

West of Praça Tiradentes and off Rua Brigadeiro Musqueira is the **Teatro Municipal** ⑦. Next door is the **Igreja de Nossa Senhora do Carmo** ⑧,

Ouro Preto

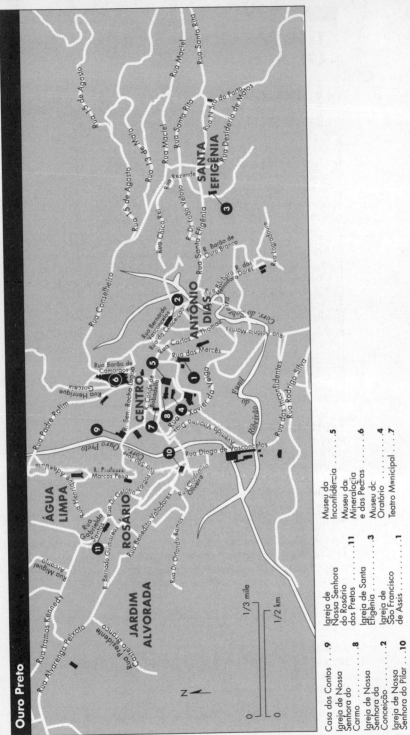

Casa dos Contos . . . **9**
Igreja de Nossa
Senhora do
Carmo **8**
Igreja de Nossa
Senhora da
Conceição **2**
Igreja de Nossa
Senhora do Pilar . . **10**

Igreja de
Nossa Senhora
do Rosário
dos Pretos **11**
Igreja de Santa
Efigênia **3**
Igreja de
São Francisco
de Assis **1**

Museu da
Inconfidência **5**
Museu da
Mineralogia
e das Pedras **6**
Museu do
Oratório **4**
Teatro Municipal . . . **7**

with major works by Aleijadinho and Ataíde. Ouro Preto's original mint, the **Casa dos Contos** ⑨, is a short distance northwest on Rua São José. Continuing south on the same street, which becomes Rua Randolfo Bretas, you'll come to the **Igreja de Nossa Senhora do Pilar** ⑩ with its baroque interior. Head northwest on Rua Randolfo Bretas followed by Rua Dr. Getúlio Vargas to the less ornate but equally intriguing **Igreja de Nossa Senhora do Rosário dos Pretos** ⑪.

TIMING

This is an all-day tour. Start out early, as some churches are only open in the morning. Unless you're an ecclesiastic, plan to spend about 20 minutes in each church and 30–45 minutes in each museum.

SIGHTS TO SEE

⑨ **Casa dos Contos.** The colonial coinage house contains the foundry used to mint the coins of the gold-rush period as well as examples of coins and period furniture. The museum building is considered one of the best examples of Brazilian colonial architecture. ⊠ *Rua São José 12,* ☎ *031/3551–1444.* ⌷ *R$1.* ☼ *Tues.–Sat. 12:30–5:30, Sun. 9–3.*

⑧ **Igreja de Nossa Senhora do Carmo.** Completed in 1772, the impressive Our Lady of Carmel Church contains major works by Aleijadinho and Ataíde. It was originally designed by Aleijadinho's father, himself an architect, but was later modified by Aleijadinho, who added additional baroque elements, including the characteristic soapstone sculptures of angels above the entrance. ⊠ *Praça Tiradentes s/n,* ☎ *031/ 3551–4735.* ⌷ *R$1.* ☼ *Tues. and Thurs.–Sun. 1:30–5.*

❷ **Igreja de Nossa Senhora da Conceição.** The lavishly gilded Our Lady of the Conception Church, completed in 1760, contains the tomb of Aleijadinho as well as a small museum dedicated to the artist. ⊠ *Praça Antônio Dias s/n,* ☎ *031/3551–3282.* ⌷ *R$3.* ☼ *Tues.–Sun. 8–11:30 and 1–5.*

⑩ **Igreja de Nossa Senhora do Pilar.** Built around 1711 on the site of an earlier chapel, this is the most richly decorated of Ouro Preto's churches and one of Brazil's best examples of baroque religious architecture. It's said that 400 pounds of gold leaf were used to cover the interior. ⊠ *Rua Brigador Mosqueira Castilho Barbosa s/n,* ☎ *031/3551–4735.* ⌷ *R$3.* ☼ *Tues.–Sun. noon–4:30.*

⑪ **Igreja de Nossa Senhora do Rosário dos Pretos.** The small, intriguing Our Lady of the Rosary of the Blacks was built by slaves, some of whom bought freedom with the gold they found in Ouro Preto. According to legend, the church's interior is bare because the slaves ran out of gold after erecting the baroque building. ⊠ *Largo do Rosário s/n,* ☎ *031/3551–1209.* ⌷ *Free.* ☼ *Tues.–Sun. noon–4:30.*

❸ **Igreja de Santa Efigênia.** On a hill east of Praça Tiradentes, this interesting slave church was built over the course of 60 years (1730–90) and was funded by Chico-Rei. This African ruler was captured during Brazil's gold rush and sold to a mine owner in Minas Gerais. Chico eventually earned enough money to buy his freedom—in the days before the Portuguese prohibited such acts—and became a hero among slaves throughout the land. The clocks on the facade are the city's oldest, and the interior contains cedar sculptures by Francisco Xavier de Brito, Aleijadinho's teacher. ⊠ *Just off Rua de Santa Efigênia,* ☎ *031/ 3551–5047.* ⌷ *R$2.* ☼ *Tues.–Sun. 8–noon.*

★ ❶ **Igreja de São Francisco de Assis.** Considered Aleijadinho's masterpiece, this church was begun in 1766 by the Franciscan Third Order and not completed until 1810. In addition to designing the structure, Aleijadinho was responsible for the wood and soapstone sculptures on the portal, high altar, side altars, pulpits, and crossing arch. The panel on the nave ceiling representing the Virgin's glorification was painted by Ataíde. Cherubic faces, garlands of tropical fruits, and allegorical characters carved into the main altar are still covered with their original paint. ⊠ *Largo de Coimbra s/n,* ☎ *031/3551–3282.* ⌑ *R$3.* ⊙ *Tues.– Sun. 8–11:30 and 1:30–4:45.*

★ ❺ **Museu da Inconfidência.** A former 18th-century prison as well as the one-time city hall, this museum commemorates the failed Inconfidência Mineira rebellion with many artifacts. Among the displays are furniture, clothing, slaves' manacles, firearms, books, and gravestones, as well as works by Aleijadinho and Ataíde. The museum also holds the remains of the unlucky revolutionaries. ⊠ *Praça Tiradentes 139,* ☎ *031/3551–1121.* ⌑ *R$4.* ⊙ *Tues.–Sun. noon–5.*

★ ❻ **Museu da Mineralogia e das Pedras.** Housed opposite the Museu da Inconfidência in the former governor's palace and inside the current Escola de Minas (School of Mines), the Museum of Minerals and Rocks contains an excellent collection of precious gems (including diamonds), gold, and crystals. The minerals have been organized according to their rarity, color, and crystallization. ⊠ *Praça Tiradentes 20,* ☎ *031/3559–1530 or 031/3559–1531.* ⌑ *R$3.* ⊙ *Weekdays noon–4:45, weekends 9–1.*

❹ **Museu do Oratório.** Established in the old house of the St. Carmel Novitiate, this museum celebrates sacred art from the 18th and 19th centuries. Some of the oratories, which reflect ideas of religious beauty from the period, have been displayed at the Louvre. ⊠ *Rua Costa Senna and Rua Antônio Pereira,* ☎ *031/3551–5369.* ⌑ *R$2.* ⊙ *Daily 9:30– 11:50 and 1:30–5:30.*

❼ **Teatro Municipal.** The former opera house, built between 1746 and 1769, still presents shows and plays, making it Latin America's oldest municipal theater still in operation. There's no regular schedule for performances, however; check with the Associação de Guias de Turismo for information on events. ⊠ *Rua Brigadeiro Mosqueira s/n,* ☎ *031/ 3551–1544 Ext. 224.* ⌑ *R$1.* ⊙ *Daily 1–6.*

Dining

$$–$$$$ ✕ **Le Coq d'Or.** The finest restaurant in Minas Gerais and one of the
★   best in Brazil is in Ouro Preto's Solar Nossa Senhora do Rosário hotel. An elegant atmosphere with formal place settings, attentive service, and soft Brazilian music make it ideal for a quiet, romantic dinner. The executive chef trained in Paris at the renowned Cordon Bleu culinary institute before introducing creative, French-inspired cuisine to Brazilian gourmands. The ever-changing menu always includes an innovative selection of meat and fish dishes, and the wine list is excellent. ⊠ *Rua Dr. Getúlio Vargas 270,* ☎ *031/3551–5200. AE, DC, MC, V.*

$–$$$ ✕ **O Profeta.** The friendly staffers at this cozy restaurant serve up
★   mineira and international dishes. On weekends there's also live MPB (*música popular brasileira,* or Brazilian popular music). ⊠ *Rua Conde de Bobadela 65,* ☎ *031/3551–4556. MC, V.*

$–$$ ✕ **Casa do Ouvidor.** Atop a jewelry store in the heart of the historical
★   district, this popular restaurant has garnered several awards for such regional dishes as tutu à mineira, feijão tropeiro, and frango com quiabo. Portions are huge, so come with an empty stomach and be prepared for a noisy, ever-crowded dining room. ⊠ *Rua Conde de Bobadela 42,* ☎ *031/3551–2141. AE, DC, MC, V.*

$ ✕ **Café Geraes.** This cozy bilevel café is at the center of Ouro Preto's
★   artistic and intellectual life. Students sip wine and feast on delicious

sandwiches, soups, and other snacks. The pastries and the coffees are equally appealing. ⊠ *Rua Direita 122,* ☎ *031/3551–1405. DC, MC.*

$ **✗ Chafariz.** Regional cuisine is served buffet style in this informal
★   eatery near the Casa dos Contos. The small, colorful dining room has hardwood floors, wood-beam ceilings, and wooden tables draped with blue, green, or white tablecloths. ⊠ *Rua São José 167,* ☎ *031/3551–2828.* ⊘ *No dinner. AE, DC, MC.*

Lodging

Some families in Ouro Preto rent rooms in their homes, although usually only during Carnaval and Easter, when the city's hotels fill up. For a list of rooms to rent, contact the Associação de Guias de Turismo. The association also provides information on places to camp.

$$ 🏨 **Estalagem das Minas Gerais.** As it's near a nature preserve, this place is perfect for those who like to hike or walk in the woods. Rooms are modern, and those in front have wonderful views of the valley. The luxury chalets have two floors and granite details. Each can accommodate as many as five people with a double bed upstairs, single beds downstairs, and two bathrooms. The restaurant serves regional fare. ⊠ *Rodovia dos Inconfidentes, Km 90, 35400,* ☎ *031/3551–2122,* 𝖥𝖠𝖷 *031/3551–2709. 114 rooms, 32 chalets. Restaurant, bar, pool, sauna, recreation room. AE, DC, MC, V. BP.*

$–$$ 🏨 **Luxor Ouro Preto Pousada.** With stone walls that date back 200 years, beautiful wood floors, and gracious antique furnishings, this hotel has the feeling of a 19th-century lodge. The lobby leads to a small, romantic restaurant: typical mineira cooking is served to the lucky few at tables. Guest rooms enjoy views of the city, and some have original paintings by famous Minas artist Chanina. ⊠ *Rua Dr. Alfredo Baeta 16, 35400,* ☎ 𝖥𝖠𝖷 *031/3551–2244,* 𝖶𝖤𝖡 *www.luxor.hotels.com. 16 rooms. Restaurant, bar. AE, DC, MC, V. BP.*

$–$$ 🏨 **Pousada do Mondego.** This small, intimate inn is next to the Igreja
★   de São Francisco de Assis in a house that dates from 1747. You'll find period furnishings, a colonial ambience, and highly personalized service. The hotel also offers two-hour city tours in a minibus from the 1930s, and it has its own antiques store and art gallery. ⊠ *Largo de Coimbra 38, 35400,* ☎ *031/3551–2040, 021/2287–1592, ext. 601, reservations in Rio;* 𝖥𝖠𝖷 *031/3551–3094;* 𝖶𝖤𝖡 *www.roteirosdecharme.com.br. 23 rooms. Restaurant, bar, travel services. AE, DC, MC, V. BP.*

$ 🏨 **Solar Nossa Senhora do Rosário.** Superior service and the world-
★   class Le Coq d'Or restaurant are among this hotel's draws. The beautiful 19th-century building feels like a bed-and-breakfast, with elegant yet comfortable decor, quiet floors, and charming guest rooms. When you're not exploring the town, have a swim in the luxurious hilltop pool or stop by the atrium for afternoon tea. The hotel even has its own section of an original mine, discovered during renovations. ⊠ *Rua Dr. Getúlio Vargas 270, 35400,* ☎ *031/3551–5200,* 𝖥𝖠𝖷 *031/3551–4288,* 𝖶𝖤𝖡 *www.hotelsolardorosario.com.br. 28 rooms, 9 suites. Restaurant, bar, pool, sauna, business services, convention center. AE, DC, MC, V. BP.*

¢–$ 🏨 **Grande Hotel de Ouro Preto.** As its name suggests, the Grande is Ouro Prêto's largest hotel (it's actually immense by local standards). It's also the town's premier modernist structure—a curving two-story building on concrete pillars designed by world-acclaimed architect Oscar Niemeyer. Cultural purists and aesthetes, however, consider it an eyesore. ⊠ *Rua Senador Rocha Lagoa 164, 35400,* ☎ 𝖥𝖠𝖷 *031/3551–1488,* 𝖶𝖤𝖡 *www.hotelouropreto.com.br. 35 rooms. Restaurant, bar. AE, DC, MC, V. BP.*

¢ ⊞ **Colonial.** Close to the main square, this is a good example of the small, no-frills inns found in most historic cities. What you'll get is a very basic, clean room for a low price. Room 1 has a loft and can sleep up to five people. ⊠ *Rua Camilo Veloso 26, 35400,* ☎ *031/3551–3133,* FAX *031/3551–3361. 18 rooms. AE, DC, MC, V. BP.*

¢ ⊞ **Pousada Ouro Preto.** Popular with backpackers, this pousada has
★ small rooms individually decorated with local art. Its open-air halls have flowers and paintings of Ouro Preto; the terrace in front of the lobby offers a peaceful view of the city center. The English-speaking staff will do laundry for free. ⊠ *Largo Musicista José dos Anjos Costa 72, 35400,* ☎ FAX *031/3551–3081. No credit cards. BP.*

¢ ⊞ **Pousada Recanto das Minas.** Its hilltop location at the edge of town is both a blessing and a curse. A stay at this comfortable pousada affords lovely views, but the walk to and from it is a somewhat strenuous one. It's a popular place with families and other groups. For more privacy and peace, opt for a simple but cozy chalet instead of a room in the main building. ⊠ *Rua Manganês 287, São Cristóvão, 35400,* ☎ FAX *031/031/3551–3003. 11 rooms, 25 chalets. Bar, pool, sauna. AE, DC, MC, V. BP.*

¢ ⊞ **Pousada Toledo.** You'd be hard-pressed to tell that this simple inn was a recent addition to Ouro Preto's selection of lodgings. The architecture is strictly 18th century, the furnishings are all colonial style, and the service is solid. If the surroundings put you in the mood for authentic antiques, head for the shop next door. ⊠ *Rua Conselheiro Quintiliano 395, Centro, 35400,* ☎ *031/3551–3366,* FAX *031/3551–5915. 13 rooms. Bar, pool, sauna. V. BP.*

Nightlife and the Arts

Even if the food and the barman at **Acaso 85** (⊠ Largo do Rosário, ☎ 031/3551–2397) don't impress you, the incredibly high ceilings, stone walls, and medieval ambience will. It's popular with the late-night crowd. **Bardobeco** (⊠ Trv. do Arieira 15, ☎ no phone) is the city's best *cachaçaria,* with more than 40 brands of cachaça, including the owner's own Milagre de Minas.

The best place for information about theater, arts, and musical performances is the Associação de Guias de Turismo. **Fundação das Artes de Ouro Preto** (FAOP; ⊠ Rua Dr. Getúlio Vargas 185, ☎ 031/3551–2014), the local arts foundation, hosts various art and photographic exhibitions throughout the year.

Outdoor Activities and Sports

The best source of information about hiking and hiking tours in the region is the Associação de Guias de Turismo. The association also rents sports equipment.

Shopping

HANDICRAFTS

There are numerous handicrafts stores on Praça Tiradentes and its surrounding streets. At the daily **handicrafts fair,** in front of the Igreja de São Francisco de Assis, vendors sell soapstone and wood carvings, paintings, and other goods.

For sculpture, head to **Bié** (⊠ Praça Professor Amadeu Barbosa 129, ☎ 031/3551–2565). **Beco da Mãe Chica** (⊠ ☎ 031/3551–2511) has a good selection of unique sculptures. For authentic Minas antiques and handicrafts, visit **Bureau d'Art** (⊠ Largo do Rosário 41). If you're looking for religious souvenirs, don't miss **Ciríaco** (⊠ Largo do Rosário 41, ☎ 031/3551–5279). **Z Nelson** (⊠ Rua Randolfo Bretas, 65, ☎ 031/3551–2624) sells crafts and religious objects.

JEWELRY AND GEMSTONES

Amsterdam Sauer (☎ 031/3551–3383) has a branch in Praça Tiradentes. One of the best places in Brazil to purchase gems, especially the rare imperial topaz, is **Ita Gemas** (✉ Rua Conde de Bobadela 139, ☎ 031/ 3551–4895). An excellent store for authenticated gems—including imperial topazes, emeralds, and tourmalines—is **Luiza Figueiredo Jóias** (✉ Rua Conde de Bobadela 48, ☎ 031/3551–2487).

En Route Between Ouro Preto and Mariana lies **Mina de Ouro de Passagem,** Brazil's oldest gold mine. During the gold rush, thousands of slaves perished here owing to its dangerous, back-breaking conditions. Although the mine is no longer in operation, you can ride an old mining car through 11 km (7 mi) of tunnels and see exposed quartz, graphite, and black tourmaline. Buses travel here from Ouro Preto (catch them beside the Escola de Minas) and cost about R$2.25; taxis are less than R$23. ✉ *4 km (3 mi) from Ouro Preto on road to Mariana,* ☎ *031/3557–1255 or 031/3557–5000.* ▣ *R$15.* ☉ *Mon.–Sat. 9–5:30, Sun. 9–5.*

Mariana

11 km (7 mi) east of Ouro Preto.

The oldest city in Minas Gerais (founded in 1696) is also the birth-place of Aleijadinho's favorite painter, Manuel da Costa Ataíde. Mariana, like Ouro Preto, has preserved much of the appearance of an 18th-century gold-mining town. Its three principal churches showcase examples of the art of Ataíde, who intertwined sensual romanticism with religious themes. The faces of his saints and other figures often have mulatto features, reflecting the composition of the area's population at the time. Today Mariana is most visited for the weekly organ concerts at its cathedral.

The **Catedral Basílica da Sé,** completed in 1760, contains paintings by Ataíde, although it's best known for its 1701 German organ, transported by mule from Rio de Janeiro in 1720. This unique instrument—there are only two of its kind in the world—was a gift from Dom João V. Concerts take place Friday at 11 AM and Sunday at 12:15 PM. ✉ *Praça Cláudio Manoel s/n,* ☎ *031/3557–1216.* ▣ *Suggested donation R$1.* ☉ *Tues.–Sun. 8–noon and 2–6:30.*

Behind the cathedral is the **Museu Arquidiocesano,** which claims to have the largest collection of baroque painting and sculpture in the state, including wood and soapstone carvings by Aleijadinho and paintings by Ataíde. ✉ *Rua Frei Durão 49,* ☎ *031/3557–2516.* ▣ *R$3.* ☉ *Tues.– Sun. 8–noon and 1:30–5.*

Although the 1793 **Igreja de São Francisco de Assis** (Church of St. Francis) features soapstone pulpits and altars by Aleijadinho, its most impressive works are the sacristy's ceiling panels, which were painted by Ataíde. They depict, in somber tones, the life and death of St. Francis and are considered by many to be the artist's masterpiece. Sadly, however, they've been damaged by termites and water. ✉ *Praça João Pinheiro,* ☎ *031/3557–1023.* ▣ *R$2.* ☉ *Daily 8–noon and 1–5.*

The **Igreja da Nossa Senhora do Carmo** (Our Lady of Carmel Church), with works by Ataíde and Aleijadinho, is noteworthy for its impressive facade and sculpted soapstone designs. Ataíde is buried at the rear of the church. At press time, it was closed because of reconstruction work after an enormous fire. ✉ *Praça João Pinheiro,* ☎ *031/3557– 1635.* ☉ *Daily 8–5.*

Congonhas do Campo

50 km (31 mi) west of Mariana; 94 km (58 mi) south of Belo Horizonte.

★   To see Aleijadinho's crowning effort, head to the small Gold Town of Congonhas do Campo. Dominating Congonhas is the hilltop pilgrimage church **Igreja Bom Jesus do Matosinho,** built in 1757 and the focus of great processions during Holy Week. At the churchyard entrance, you'll see Aleijadinho's 12 life-size Old Testament prophets carved in soapstone, a towering achievement and one of the greatest works of art from the baroque period. The prophets appear caught in movement, and every facial expression is unforgettable. Leading up to the church on the sloping hillside are six chapels, each containing a scene from the Stations of the Cross. The 66 figures in this remarkable procession were carved in cedar by Aleijadinho and painted by Ataíde. ⊠ *Praça da Basílica s/n,* ☎ *031/3731–1590.* ☜ *Free.* ☼ *Tues.–Sun. 10–5.*

Tiradentes

129 km (80 mi) south of Congonhas do Campo.

Probably the best historic city to visit after Ouro Preto, Tiradentes was the birthplace of a martyr who gave it its name (it was formerly called São José del Rei) and retains much of its 18th-century charm. Life in this tiny village—nine streets with eight churches set against the backdrop of the Serra de São José—moves slowly. This quality attracts wealthy residents of Belo Horizonte, Rio, and São Paulo, who have sparked a local real estate boom by buying up 18th-century properties as weekend getaways.

Besides the excellent selection of handicrafts—some 20 shops line Rua Direita in the town center—the principal attraction is the **Igreja de Santo Antônio.** Built in 1710, it contains extremely well-preserved, gilded carvings of saints, cherubs, and biblical scenes. The church's soapstone frontispiece—a celebration of baroque architecture—was sculpted by Aleijadinho. ⊠ *Rua Padre Toledo,* ☎ *no phone.* ☜ *Suggested donation.* ☼ *Daily 9–noon and 2–5.*

Dining and Lodging

$$ ✕ **Canto do Chafariz.** This center of regional cuisine is rated tops for its tutu. All the dishes, such as feijão tropeiro and frango ao molho pardo, have the same price and are big enough for two. ⊠ *Largo do Chafariz 37,* ☎ *032/3355–1377. Reservations not accepted. No credit cards. Closed Mon.*

$$ ✕ **Theatro da Villa.** On the site of an old Greek-style amphitheater, this restaurant offers dinner theater Tiradentes style. The menu features international fare, including meat and fish dishes. Most performances involve local folk music and dance. ⊠ *Rua do Sol 157,* ☎ *032/3355–1275. No credit cards. Closed weekdays.*

$ ✕ **Estalagem.** The Estalagem draws rave reviews for its feijão tropeiro
★   and frango ao molho pardo, just two of the dishes that are part of the self-service, fixed-price buffet. Although it's small and cozy, its atmosphere is elegant. Light music and a quiet, attentive staff make for a relaxing meal. ⊠ *Rua Gabriel Passos 280,* ☎ *032/3355–1144. No credit cards. Closed Mon.*

$ 🛏 **Pousada Alforria.** Alforria enjoys a quiet, peaceful location with a
★   fabulous view of the São José Mountains. The light-filled lobby—with its stone floors, high ceilings, and beautiful Brazilian artwork (some of it from Bahia)—leads to a charming breakfast space and courtyard. Rooms have considerable natural light and are individually decorated;

mattresses are firm and bathrooms modern. ⊠ *Rua Custódio Gomes 286, 36325,* ☎ ℻ *032/3355–1536. 9 rooms. Pool. MC. BP.*

$ ⛱ **Pousada Três Portas.** This pousada is in an adapted colonial house—with hardwood floors and locally made furniture and artwork—in the historic center of Tiradentes. The owner runs a small puppet theater adjacent to the breakfast room. Rooms are clean and modern. Note that prices jump dramatically on weekends. ⊠ *Rua Direita 280A, 36325,* ☎ *032/3355–1444,* ℻ *032/3355–1184. 8 rooms, 1 suite. Pool, steam room. No credit cards. BP.*

$ ⛱ **Solar da Ponte.** In every respect—from the stunning antiques to the
★ comfortable beds to the elegant place settings—this inn is a faithful example of regional style. Breakfast and afternoon tea (included in the rate) are served in the dining room, overlooking well-tended gardens. With advance notice, the English owner and his Brazilian wife can arrange historical, botanical, and ecological tours on foot or horseback. ⊠ *Praça das Mercês s/n, 36325,* ☎ *032/3355–1255 or 021/2287–1592 reservations in Rio,* ℻ *032/3355–1201. 12 rooms. Bar, dining room, pool, sauna. AE, DC, MC, V. BP.*

The Arts

Cultural life in Tiradentes revolves around the **Centro Cultural Yves Alves** (⊠ Rua Direita 168, ☎ 032/3355–1503), which has theatrical performances, films, concerts, and art exhibitions. On weekends, the **Theatro da Villa** (Rua do Sol 157, ☎ 032/3355–1275) has musical shows that accompany dinner.

Shopping

Local artwork is the biggest draw here, with painters and sculptors famous throughout Brazil working in their gallerylike studios. The main street for galleries and antiques shops is Rua Direita.

ART

Atelier Fernando Pitta (⊠ Beco da Chácara s/n, ☎ 032/3355–1475) is set up like Michelangelo's studio, with wild, abstract variations on religious themes. **Atelier José Damas** (⊠ Rua do Chafariz 130, ☎ 032/9961–0735) belongs to Tiradentes's most famous artist. He paints local scenes—such as a train winding through the mountains or a dusty afternoon street—on canvas and on stones.

JEWELRY AND GEMSTONES

Although not as upscale as the stores in Ouro Preto, **Artstones** (⊠ Rua Ministro Gabriel Passos 22, ☎ 032/3464–4595) carries imperial topazes, emeralds, quartz, and tourmalines, and it also has some finished jewelry.

THE MINERAL-SPA TOWNS

Known for the curative properties of their natural springs, a collection of mineral-spa towns in southern Minas Gerais forms the Circuito das Águas (Water Circuit). For more than a century, people in need of physical, mental, and spiritual rejuvenation have flocked to these mystical towns, bathing in the pristine water parks and drinking from the bubbling fountains. Today, they're especially popular among older, wealthier Brazilians, who come to experience the fresh air and beautiful landscapes and to relieve their hypertension, arthritis, allergies, diabetes, and various stomach problems.

You'll be told that a minimum of three weeks drinking the waters is required for their healing powers to take hold (don't try drinking three weeks' worth of water in a day, unless you want to leave with more ailments than when you arrived). Usually, a one- or two-day visit is enough to experience a helpful placebo effect.

São Lourenço

387 km (240 mi) south of Belo Horizonte.

The most modern of the mineral-spa towns is a good base from which to visit the other Circuito das Águas communities. From here, taxis and tour operators will happily negotiate a day rate for the circuit, usually around $50.

São Lourenço's **Parque das Águas** (Water Park) includes a picturesque lake with art deco pavilions, fountains, and gorgeous landscaping. The center of activity is its *balneário,* a hydrotherapy spa where you can immerse yourself in bubbling mineral baths and marble surroundings. There are separate bath and sauna facilities for men and women, and you can also get a massage. ⊠ *Praça Brasil s/n,* ☎ *035/3332–3066.* ᛜ *R$2.* ⊙ *Park: daily 8–6. Balneário: daily 8:30–11:30 and 2–5.*

If your experience at the park fails to rid you of all physical and mental illness, head to the **Templo da Eubiose,** the temple of a spiritual organization dedicated to wisdom and perfection through yoga. It's open to the public only on weekend afternoons. In any case, get yourself here before the end of the world—the Eubiose believe this will be the only place to survive. ⊠ *Praça da Vitória s/n,* ☎ *035/3331–1333.* ᛜ *Suggested donation.* ⊙ *Weekends 2–4.*

Dining and Lodging

$ ✕⊡ **Fazenda Emboaba.** About a half hour's walk from the Parque das
★ Águas, this gracious fazenda is more like a private estate than a rural farm. Its carefully decorated rooms have bucolic views; at night, the only sounds you'll hear will be those of various animals roaming through the countryside. Occasional performances are offered in the fazenda's theater, and there are numerous other activities, such as horseback riding, to keep you amused. The restaurant offers fixed-price buffets of at least three regional dishes as well as salads and dessert. ⊠ *Rua Jorge Amado 350, Solar dos Lagos, 37410,* ☎ *035/3332–4600,* FAX *035/3332–4392. 20 rooms. Restaurant, massage, sauna, tennis court, horseback riding, soccer, theater. MC, V. FAP.*

$ ✕⊡ **Hotel Brasil.** This luxury hotel is just across from the Parque das Águas at the Praça Duque de Caxias. It has its own pools, fountains, and mineral waters, and the rate includes full board. Ask for a room with a park view. The restaurant's fixed-price buffet serves regional fare. ⊠ *Alameda João Lage 87, 37440,* ☎ *035/3332–1313,* FAX *035/ 3331–1536,* WEB *www.hotelbrasil.com.br. 145 rooms. Restaurant, bar, pool. AE, DC, MC, V. FAP.*

¢–$$ ✕⊡ **Pousada Le Sapê.** The restaurant's eclectic menu includes mineira food, as well as pizza, pasta, and fondue selections. The pousada's six tiny rooms are reasonable, low-budget options for a night or two. ⊠ *Av. Comendador Costa 589,* ☎ *035/3331–1142. 6 rooms. Restaurant. No credit cards. BP.*

Caxambu

30 km (19 mi) northeast of São Lourenço.

A 19th-century town once frequented by Brazilian royalty, Caxambu remains a favorite getaway for wealthy and retired *cariocas* (residents of Rio). Although most people spend their time here relaxing in bathhouses and drinking curative waters, you can also browse in the markets where local sweets are sold or take a horse-and-buggy ride to a fazenda.

In Caxambu's **Parque das Águas,** you'll find towering trees, shimmering ponds, and fountains containing various minerals—each believed to cure a different ailment. Lavish pavilions protect the springs, and the balneário, a beautiful Turkish-style bathhouse, offers saunas and massages. In addition, hundreds of thousands of liters of mineral water are bottled here daily and distributed throughout Brazil. ⊠ *Town center,* ☎ *035/3341–3999.* ☞ *R$2.* ⊙ *Park: daily 7–6. Balneário: Wed.–Sat. 8:30–noon and 3–5.*

Overlooking the springs is the **Igreja Isabel da Hungria.** The small Gothic church was built by Princess Isabel, daughter of Dom Pedro II, after the springs were believed to restore her fertility. ⊠ *Rua Princesa Isabel s/n,* ☎ *035/3341–1582.* ☞ *Suggested donation.* ⊙ *Daily 9–4.*

Horse-and-buggy rides start at the water park's entrance and explore the streets of Caxambu as well as old farms in the surrounding area. The best of these fazendas is Chácara Rosalan, with its beautiful flower and fruit orchards. Rides cost about R$45.

You could take a **chairlift** (it operates daily 7–6 and costs R$5) from near the bus station to the peak of Cristo Redentor, where there's a small restaurant and an impressive city view.

Dining and Lodging

$–$$$$ ✕ **La Forelle.** The best restaurant in town is Danish, not Brazilian. The
★ filet mignon, the salmon, and the trout are among the extensive menu's stellar entrées. You'll also find delicious fondues and freshly made breads. ⊠ *Vale Formoso, Caxambu,* ☎ *035/3343–1900. AE, DC, MC, V. No lunch.*

$$ ▥ **Hotel Glória.** Although it's just across from Caxambu's Parque das Águas, this luxury resort has its own rehabilitation pool and sauna as well as a variety of sports amenities. Rooms are well equipped and have marble baths; the rate includes full board, and meals are served in an antiques-filled dining room. ⊠ *Av. Camilio Soares 590, 37440,* ☎ FAX *035/3341–3000. 120 rooms. Bar, dining room, minibars, pool, sauna, tennis court, basketball, health club. AE, DC, MC, V. FAP.*

São Tomé das Letras

54 km (33 mi) northwest of Caxambu.

With its tales of flying saucers, its eerie stone houses that resemble architecture from outer space, and its 7,500 inhabitants who swear by years of friendship with extraterrestrials, São Tomé das Letras may be one of the oddest towns on earth. Set in a stunning mountain region, it attracts mystics, psychics, and flower children who believe they've been spiritually drawn here to await the founding of a new world. Most visitors make São Tomé a day trip from Caxambu, smartly escaping nightfall's visiting UFOs.

A center of religious activity and one of the few nonstone buildings in São Tomé, **Igreja Matriz** is in São Tomé's main square and contains frescoes by Brazilian artist Joaquim José de Natividade. Next to the Igreja Matriz is the **Gruta de São Tomé,** a small cave that, in addition to its shrine to São Tomé, features some of the mysterious inscriptions for which the town is famous. Just 3 km (2 mi) from São Tomé, two **caverns,** Carimbado and Chico Taquara, both display hieroglyphs. A short walk from the caves will put you in view of Véu da Noiva and Véu da Eubiose, two powerful waterfalls.

MINAS GERAIS A TO Z

To research prices, get advice from other travelers, and book travel arrangements, visit www.fodors.com.

AIR TRAVEL

Belo Horizonte, with its two airports, is the gateway to Minas Gerais.

CARRIERS

American Airlines flies from Miami to Rio and on to Confins. TAM has domestic flights to and from Pampulha. Transbrasil has domestic service to both airports. In addition to connecting Belo Horizonte with other Brazilian cities, Varig has service to Confins from New York. VASP also offers domestic flights into both airports.

➤ AIRLINES: **American Airlines** (☎ 0800/12–4001). **TAM** (☎ 0800/12–3100 or 031/3490–5500). **Transbrasil** (☎ 031/3273–6722, 031/3689–2480, or 0800/15–1151). **Varig** (☎ 031/3339–6000 or 0800/99–7000). **VASP** (☎ 031/3689–5360 or 0800/99–8277).

AIRPORTS

Aeroporto Internacional Tancredo Neves—also known as Aeroporto Confins—is 39 km (24 mi) north of Belo Horizonte and serves domestic and international flights. Taxis from Confins to downtown cost about R$50 and take roughly a half hour. There are also *executivo* (air-conditioned) buses that leave every 45 minutes and cost R$10. Aeroporto Pampulha is 9 km (5 mi) northwest of downtown and serves domestic flights. Taxis from here to downtown cost about R$10.

➤ AIRPORT INFORMATION: **Aeroporto Internacional Tancredo Neves** (☎ 031/3689–2700). **Aeroporto Pampulha** (☎ 031/3490–2001).

BUS TRAVEL

Belo Horizonte's municipal bus system is safe and efficient, although buses are crowded during rush hour (7–9 and 5–7). They're clearly numbered, and you can get route information in the *Guia do Ônibus,* a guide that's available in bookstores. All city buses have a chord to pull or a button to press to request a stop. Fares depend on the distance traveled but are always less than R$2.

Frequent buses (either air-conditioned executivos or warmer, less comfortable, but cheaper coaches) connect Belo Horizonte with Rio (R$60–R$90; 7 hrs), São Paulo (R$60–R$113; 9 hrs), and Brasília (R$60–R$90; 12 hrs). Advance tickets are recommended at holiday times. All buses arrive at and depart from (punctually) the Rodoviária. Bus companies include Cometa, for Rio and São Paulo; Gontijo, for São Paulo; Itapemirim, for Brasília; Penha, for Brasília; and Útil, for Rio and São Paulo.

Coaches connect Belo Horizonte with Ouro Preto (R$16; 2–3 hrs), Diamantina (R$41; 6 hrs), and São João del Rei (R$25; 4 hrs). Mariana can be reached from Ouro Preto (R$2.25; 30 mins), Tiradentes from São João del Rei (R$4.50; 30 mins). From Belo Horizonte, a bus to São Lourenço or Caxambu takes roughly 6½ hours and costs about R$23. To reach São Tomé das Letras, you must change buses in Três Coracões; the entire journey takes 5½ hours.

Companies with regular service from Belo Horizonte include Cisne, for Sabará; Gardênia, for São Lourenço; Pássaro Verde, for Ouro Preto, Diamantina, and Mariana; and Sandra for Congonhas.

➤ BUS INFORMATION: **Cisne** (☎ 031/3201–8660). **Cometa** (☎ 031/3201–5611). **Gardênia** (☎ 031/3271–2111). **Gontijo** (☎ 031/3201–6130).

Itapemirim (☎ 031/3271–1027). Pássaro Verde (☎ 031/3272–1811). Penha (☎ 031/3271–5621). **Rodoviária** (✉ Av. Afonso Pena at Av. do Contorno, Belo Horizonte, ☎ 031/3201–8111 or 031/3271–3000). **Sandra** (☎ 031/3201–2927). **Útil** (☎ 031/3201–7744).

CAR RENTAL
Rental cars cost between R$45 and R$113 per day, depending on whether mileage is included. Agencies include Localiza and Lokamig.
➤ AGENCIES: **Localiza** (✉ Aeroporto Confins, Belo Horizonte, ☎ 031/ 3689–2070; ✉ Rua Bernardo Monteiro 1567, Belo Horizonte, ☎ 0800/99–2000 or 031/3247–7957). **Lokamig** (✉ Aeroporto Confins, Belo Horizonte, ☎ 031/3689–2020; ✉ Av. Contorno 8639, Belo Horizonte, ☎ 031/3335–8977).

CAR TRAVEL
BR 040 connects Belo Horizonte with Rio (444 km/276 mi), to the southeast, and Brasília (741 km/460 mi), to the northwest; BR 381 links the city with São Paulo (586 km/364 mi). The roads are in good condition, although exits aren't always clearly marked.

Belo Horizonte's rush-hour traffic can be heavy, and parking can be difficult (for on-street parking you must buy a sticker at a newsstand or bookshop). Narrow cobblestone streets inside the historical cities, however, weren't designed for cars, and some alleys can make for a tight squeeze. Parking isn't a problem in the smaller communities, except during holidays.

The historic cities and spa towns are, for the most part, connected by fairly decent minor routes to one of the region's main highways. There's no ideal direct route from Belo Horizonte to Diamantina; your best bet is north on BR 040 and then east on BR 259. Sabará is slightly east of Belo, just off BR 262. From Belo you can take BR 040 south and BR 356 (it becomes MG 262) east to Ouro Preto and beyond to Mariana. To reach Tiradentes from Belo, take BR 040 south (Congonhas do Campo is on this route) and then BR 265 west. São Lourenço, Caxambu, and São Tomé das Letras are south of Belo off BR 381, parts of which are under construction. As an alternative, you can take BR 040 south to BR 267 west.

CONSULATES
The United States has no consulate in Belo Horizonte, but it does have the U.S. Commercial Service, which assists companies that are doing business in Minas Gerais. It's open weekdays 8–5.
➤ CONTACTS: **British Consulate** (✉ Rua Inconfidentes 1075, Funcionários, Belo Horizonte, ☎ 031/3261–2072). **U.S. Commercial Service** (✉ Rua Timbiras 1200, 7th floor, Funcionários, Belo Horizonte, ☎ 031/3213–1571).

EMERGENCIES
➤ GENERAL EMERGENCIES: **Ambulance or Police** (☎ 190). **Fire** (☎ 193).
➤ HOSPITAL: **Hospital João XXIII** (✉ Av. Alfredo Balena 400, Sta. Efigênia, Belo Horizonte, ☎ 031/3239–9200).
➤ 24-HR PHARMACY: **Drogaria Araújo** (☎ 031/3270–5000 in Belo Horizonte).

HEALTH
There are no major health concerns in Minas Gerais, although you should drink bottled rather than tap water. (Despite the curative properties

of the mineral waters in the spa towns, don't drink too much when you first arrive unless you want to cleanse your system thoroughly.)

MAIL AND INTERNET

Belo Horizonte's main post office is open weekdays 9–7, weekends 9–1. Internet service is slowly making its way to the region and may be available at your hotel's business center. In Belo Horizonte, the Internet Club Café lets you hook up for about R$20 an hour.

➤ INTERNET CAFÉ: **Internet Club Café** (✉ Rua Fernandes Tourinho 385, Savassi, ☎ 031/3282–3132, WEB www.iclubcafe.com.br).

➤ POST OFFICE: **Belo Horizonte** (✉ Av. Afonso Pena 1270, Centro, ☎ 031/3201–9833).

MONEY MATTERS

Outside Belo Horizonte, currency exchange can be challenging and/or expensive, so change money before you arrive or plan to do it at your hotel. You can change money at Confins Airport weekdays 10–6 and Saturday 10–4 (you're out of luck if you arrive on Sunday). Banco Sudameris has good exchange rates. Banco do Brasil also offers exchange services, though the rates aren't the best.

➤ BANKS: **Banco do Brasil** (✉ Rua Rio de Janeiro 750, Centro, Belo Horizonte, ☎ 031/3217–3000). **Banco Sudameris** (✉ Av. João Pinheiro 214, Centro, Belo Horizonte, ☎ 031/3277–3134).

SAFETY

Petty crime is an issue in Belo Horizonte, though not as much as it is in Rio or São Paulo. Use common sense: avoid waving your money around or wearing expensive jewelry. The historic cities and mineral-spa towns are among Brazil's safest places.

TAXIS

Taxis in Belo Horizonte are white and can be hailed or called. The meter starts at about R$2 and costs about R$1 for every kilometer traveled (slightly higher at night and on weekends). Two reputable companies are BH Taxi and Rádio Taxi.

In the historic towns it's hard to drive along narrow cobblestone streets, so taxis aren't abundant. Besides, these towns are small enough to explore on foot. You'll find plenty of eager taxis in both Caxambu and São Lourenço waiting to take you around the Circuito das Águas. A taxi between São Lourenço and Caxambu runs about R$100; R$200 to São Tomé das Letras.

➤ TAXI COMPANIES: **BH Taxi** (☎ 031/3215–8081). **Rádio Taxi** (☎ 0800/31–2288 or 031/3421–505).

TELEPHONES

The area code for the region is 031. If you don't want to place long-distance calls from your hotel, you can make them from the *posto telefônicos* (phone offices), found in airports and bus stations throughout Minas. Office hours are generally 7 AM–10 PM. In Belo Horizonte, the main TELEMIG office is open 24 hours.

➤ CONTACT: **TELEMIG** (✉ Av. Afonso Pena 744, Centro).

TOURS

CLN Tourism and Transportation Services offers exceptional tours of Ouro Preto and the historic cities. CLN's Cláudio Neves speaks fluent English, knows a great deal about the region's history, and can arrange airport pickup and other transportation.

AMETUR, the Association of Rural Tourism, is a group of respected, trustworthy ranch owners who have converted their fazendas into accommodations with luxurious yet down-home surroundings. You can visit one or more of these ranches, where relaxation, swimming, horse-back riding, walks in the woods, and home-cooked meals are the orders of the day. Suzana Sousa Lima runs AMETUR as well as her own fazenda, Boa Esperança, which has been rated among the top accommodations in the country.

AMO-TE, Minas's Association of Ecological Tourism, offers many fascinating tours. A great way to get acquainted with the history and topography of Minas is on a one- to five-day horseback trip with AMO-TE's Tulio. His English is perfect, his knowledge impressive, and his horses—native Mineiros themselves—have a unique step (not unlike the lambada) that makes extensive trips more comfortable than you might imagine.

Companhia Trekking organizes spelunking, hiking, rafting, and mountain-biking trips throughout Minas. The Associação de Guias, formed by Ouro Preto's professional tour guides, can provide general information on the city weekdays 8–6. Its well-informed, courteous guides also conduct six- to seven-hour walking tours (in English) of the historic area. Be prepared for some stiff hiking up and down numerous hills.

➤ CONTACTS: **AMETUR** (✉ Rua Alvarenga Peixoto 295/102, Lourdes, Belo Horizonte, ☎ FAX 031/3275–2139). **AMO-TE** (✉ Rua Professor Morais 624, Apartamento 302, Centro, Belo Horizonte, ☎ 031/3344–8986). **Associação de Guias** (✉ Rua Padre Rolim s/n, São Cristóvão, Ouro Preto, ☎ 031/3551–2655; ✉ Praça Tancredo Neves s/n, Mariana, ☎ 031/3557–9000). **CLN Tourism and Transportation Services** (✉ Rua Dr. Antônio Ibrahim 103A, Ouro Preto, ☎ FAX 031/3551–6311 or 031/9961–1220). **Companhia Trekking** (✉ Rua Pernambuco 1389, Funcionários, Belo Horizonte, ☎ 031/3281–6618).

TRAVEL AGENTS

Sangetur is an all-purpose agency that can help you rent a car, make travel arrangements or hotel reservations, and book city tours. YTUR Turismo can arrange hotel bookings, transportation plans, and tours of Belo Horizonte and beyond.

➤ TRAVEL AGENCIES: **Sangetur** (✉ Rua Inconfidentes 732, Funcionários, Belo Horizonte, ☎ 031/3261–1055). **YTUR Turismo** (✉ Av. do Contorno 8000, Lourdes, Belo Horizonte, ☎ 031/3275–3233).

VISITOR INFORMATION

In Belo Horizonte, Belotur, the municipal tourist board, is open daily 8 AM–10 PM at the airports and weekdays 8–7 elsewhere. Turminas, the state tourism authority, has been undergoing administrative changes, and its future is uncertain. At press time, however, it was still supplying information on the historic cities and other attractions weekdays 12:30–6:30.

Diamantina's Casa da Cultura has information on the town, including all cultural events. It's open weekdays 8–6, Saturday 9–5, and Sunday 9–noon. In Ouro Preto contact the Associação de Guias (open daily 8 AM–10 PM), which has an office on the edge of town, or the tourist information desk (open daily 8–6) in the center of town. In Mariana, contact the Associação de Guias for general information on the city. Its hours are Tuesday–Saturday noon–5:30. In Tiradentes, the Secretária de Turismo is the best place to go for information weekdays 8–6.

São Lourenço has a small tourist kiosk in front of the water park. It's open weekdays 8–11 and 1–6. In Caxambu, there's an equally small tourist desk that's open weekdays 8–6.

➤ BELO HORIZONTE VISITOR INFORMATION: **Belotur** (✉ Rua Pernambuco 284, Funcionários, ☎ 031/3277–9797; ✉ Mercado das Flores at Av. Afonso Pena and Rua da Bahia, Centro, ☎ 031/3277–7666; ✉ Rodoviária, Av. Afonso Pena at Av. do Contorno, Centro, ☎ 031/3277–6907; ✉ Confins Airport, ☎ 031/3689–2557). **Turminas** (✉ Praça Rio Branco 56, Lourdes, Belo Horizonte, ☎ 031/3212–2134 or 031/3272–8573).

➤ HISTORIC TOWNS VISITOR INFORMATION: **Caxambu Tourist Desk** (✉ Praça Cônego José de Castilho Moreira s/n, ☎ 035/3341–3977. **Diamantina Casa de Cultura** (✉ Praça Antônio Eulálio 53, ☎ 038/3531–1636). **Posto de Informação Turística** (✉ Praça Tiradentes 41, Centro, Ouro Preto, ☎ 031/3559–3269). **São Lourenço Tourist Kiosk** (✉ Praça João Lage s/n, ☎ 033/3332–4455). **Tiradentes Secretária de Turismo** (✉ Rua Resende Costa 71, ☎ 032/3335–1212).

5 BRASÍLIA AND THE WEST

In 1960, when Brasília replaced Rio de Janeiro as the capital, Brazil finally turned from its coastline to face its interior. The temperate climate and government jobs have attracted many people to this futuristic city. West of it are the sparsely populated states of Goiás, Mato Grosso, and Mato Grosso do Sul, which are best known for their frontier feel and for the Pantanal— South America's largest swamp.

V ISITING BRASÍLIA IS LIKE LEAPING HEADLONG into the late 21st
century. Rising from the red earth of the 914-m (3,000-ft)
Planalto Central (Central Plateau) and surrounded by the *cerrado* (Brazilian savanna) is one of the world's most singular cities. Its
structures crawl and coil along the flat landscape and then shoot up
in shafts of concrete and glass that capture the sun's rays.

Updated by
Carlos G.
Tornquist

The idea of moving the capital to the interior dates from the early days
of Brazil's independence, but it wasn't until 1955 that the scheme became more than just a possibility. Many said Brasília couldn't be built;
others simply went ahead and did it. The resolute Juscelino Kubitschek
made it part of his presidential campaign platform. On taking office,
he organized an international contest for the city's master plan. A design submitted by urban planner Lúcio Costa was selected, and he and
his contemporaries—including architect Oscar Niemeyer and landscape
artist Roberto Burle Marx—went to work. With a thrust of energy, the
new capital was built less than five years later quite literally in the middle of nowhere.

Costa once mused, "The sky is the sea of Brasília." He made sure that
the city had an unhindered view of the horizon, with buildings whose
heights are restricted, wide streets and avenues, and immense green
spaces. The sky here is an incredible blue that's cut only by occasional
clusters of fleecy clouds. The earth is such an amazing shade of red
that it seems to have been put here just for contrast. At night it's hard
to tell where the city lights end and the stars begin. On a visit to Brazil,
the renowned contemporary architect Frank O. Gehry said "It's a different city. I call it holy land, an untouchable icon of architecture."

All around this wonderland of modernity nestles the old Brazil—the land
of soybean plantations, beef cattle, and sluggish rivers. Nevertheless, those
who flock to the rugged yet beautiful west have their eyes on the future.
The surreal collection of migrants includes opportunists with get-rich-
quick schemes; frontier folk with hopes of a solid, stable tomorrow; mystics and prophets who swear by the region's spiritual energy; and
dreamers who are convinced that extraterrestrials visit here regularly. For
most earthly visitors, however, the high point of the west is the Pantanal,
a flood plain the size of Great Britain that's home to an amazing array
of wildlife and the ever-present possibilities for adventure.

Pleasures and Pastimes

Design
Urban planning, engineering, architecture, and landscape design were
applied so harmoniously in Brasília that the city seems like one gigantic
sculpture. Costa had a simple, original concept: "Brasília was conceived
by the gesture of those who mark a place on a map: two axes intersecting at a right angle, that is, the sign of a cross mark." From above,
his original Plano Piloto (Pilot, or Master, Plan) portion of the city looks
like an airplane (it has also been described as a bow and arrow).

Costa had several objectives, among them: do away with a central downtown, where all the commercial and government facilities were separate from residential areas; design highways that were as accident-free
as possible; and ensure that the vast horizon would always be visible.
The latter goal complemented Oscar Niemeyer's idea of architecture
as "a manifestation of the spirit, imagination, and poetry." Though his
buildings are often massive, they're generally low, linear, and set in grand
spaces—conveying a sense of both light and lightness. Such structures
epitomize functionality and simplicity (of design) and economy (of build-

ing materials); they also embody the vastness of Brazil. Many are set upon huge concrete *pilotis* (pillars), leaving large open areas beneath them. Enormous glass facades and reflecting pools often add to the sense of space; organic-looking sculptures—either as plump and curvaceous as a cluster of coconuts or as willowy and elongated as palm fronds—add touches of softness. To complete the package, the Plano Piloto's most important gardens (some are more like "waterscapes") were planned by landscape designer Roberto Burle Marx, who emphasized the use of Brazilian vegetation in natural arrangements. The works of Costa, Niemeyer, and Burle Marx fully articulate the longing expressed by Brazilian leaders in the mid-20th century to portray Brazil as a "nation of the future."

Dining

As the capital, Brasília attracts citizens from throughout the country as well as dignitaries from around the world. Hence, you'll find restaurants offering a variety of regional cuisines—particularly that of the northeast—as well as international fare. In the west, the dishes aren't as interesting or as flavorful as those found elsewhere in the country. That said, however, the food is hearty, and the meals are large; affordable, all-you-can-eat buffets are ubiquitous. For price categories, *see* the chart *under* Dining *in* Smart Travel Tips A to Z.

Lodging

Brasília's master plan called for its hotels to be built amid commercial areas. As they cater primarily to businesspeople and government officials, few hotels fall into budget categories. Such budget options as *pousadas* (inns) are far from these hubs; many are in neighboring *cidades-satélite* (satellite cities), the communities where many city workers reside. A recent ordinance has allowed new development along the shores of Lago Paranoá; at press time, several upscale hotels were in the works here.

The frontier towns west of Brasília have few deluxe accommodations. Inside the Pantanal, the *fazendas* (farms) where most people stay are quite spartan; pack a pillow and bug spray (not all fazendas have netting for their beds). If roughing it doesn't thrill you, there are a few jungle lodges that are full-blown resorts with all expected amenities. For price categories, *see* the chart *under* Lodging *in* Smart Travel Tips A to Z.

Natural Wonders

Brazil's vast cerrado has small trees, shrubs, and grasses that are adapted to the harshness of the dry season, when temperatures in some parts rise well above 38°C (100°F) and humidity drops to a desert low of 15%. Several palm species grow around natural springs. Cacti and bromeliads are also abundant. Look also for the *pequi*, a shrub that produces berries used in local cuisine. Since development, it has become harder to spot such cerrado wildlife as deer, emus, and jaguars. In the lush Pantanal wetlands, on the other hand, it's easy to see birds (more than 600 species flock here), monkeys, *jacarés* (caiman alligators), and fish—including the famous piranha. You may also catch a glimpse of *capivaras* (capybaras, the world's largest rodents), wild boar, giant anteaters, and many types of snakes (including the *sucuri*, or anaconda). Of the elusive panthers, jaguars, and pumas, however, the most you'll probably see are some tracks.

Exploring Brasília and the West

Brasília is 1,600 km (1,000 mi) from the Atlantic, on the flat plateau known as the Planalto Central. This is the domain of the vast cerrado, whose climate and vegetation are akin to those of the African savanna. The capital is actually in the Distrito Federal (Federal District), a 55,000 square km (21,000 square mi) administrative region. Also in this district are the cidades-satélite, which originated as residential areas for Brasília workers but which now qualify as cities in their own right.

The Distrito Federal is flanked by Goiás State, part of the country's agricultural heart and the starting point for two massive Amazon tributaries, the rios Araguaia and Tocantins. Here, civilization consists of small towns. Although a few date from colonial times, many have sprung up in recent years as farmers from Brazil's south have settled in the region. Still farther west, the states of Mato Grosso and Mato Grosso do Sul have their share of Brazil's agribusiness. They also contain the Pantanal, an area whose watery terrain and rich, unique wildlife have escaped being paved over by the modern world—for now.

Great Itineraries

IF YOU HAVE 5 DAYS
Spend two days exploring Brasília's Plano Piloto, including the Eixo Monumental, the Praça dos Três Poderes, the shores of the Lago Paranoá, and the Parque da Cidade. On the third morning, fly to Cuiabá and sign up for an overnight trip into the Pantanal to spot wildlife and maybe to fish for piranha.

IF YOU HAVE 7 DAYS
For Brasília, set aside two days to explore the Plano Piloto and to tour the Parque Nacional da Brasília, the Jardim Botânico, and the Catetinho. On the third day, make an early departure to Pirenópolis, a colonial town just outside the capital. On the following day, fly from Brasília to Cuiabá and spend the remaining time exploring the Pantanal.

IF YOU HAVE 10 DAYS
Spend four leisurely days in Brasília exploring the Plano Piloto and visiting the Parque Nacional, the cult communities, and Pirenópolis. On the fifth day, fly to either Cuiabá or Campo Grande and schedule a four-day (three-night) trip into the Pantanal. Such treks include riverboat rides, horseback rides, fishing, bird-watching, and cooking your very own piranha stew.

When to Tour

In Brasília and much of the west you can count on clear days and comfortable temperatures from March to July (the mean temperature is 22°C/75°F). The rainy season runs from December to February; in August and September, the mercury often rises to 38°C (100°F). When congress adjourns (July and January–February), the city's pulse slows noticeably.

In the Pantanal, peak season is synonymous with the dry season (July–October; which coincides with southern Brazil's winter, though temperatures rarely drop below 27°C (80°F). At this time, the rivers have receded, the roads (what few there are) are passable, the mosquito population has dwindled, and the birds are nesting. You won't see as much wildlife during the wet season, but you will experience the swamp in all its impenetrable glory.

BRASÍLIA

Brazil's capital was moved from Salvador to Rio in 1763 so that the Portuguese court could be near the center of all the mining and exporting activity. In 1960 it was moved from coastal Rio to Brasília in an attempt to awaken the center of this sleeping giant.

As far back as 1808, Brazilian newspapers ran articles discussing Rio's inadequacies and proposing a new interior capital: "Our present capital is in a corner of Brazil and contact between it and Pará or other far removed states is extremely difficult. Besides, Rio subjects the government to enemy invasion by any maritime power." In 1892 congress authorized the overland Cruls Expedition to find a central locale where "a city could be constructed next to the headwaters of big rivers" and where "roads could be opened to all seaports." Within three months the expedition leaders had chosen one of the plateaus in the southeastern Goiás region. Despite this and several other attempts to establish a location and to move the capital, nothing was done for more than 60 years.

In the mid-1950s, a sharp politician named Juscelino Kubitschek made the new capital part of his presidential campaign agenda, which was summarized in the motto "Fifty Years in Five." When he was elected president in 1956, he set the wheels in motion. After a site was selected (in Goiás, as proposed by the 1892 expedition), President Kubitschek flew to the inhospitable Planalto Central, had mass said on the building site, stayed the night, set up work committees, and put Niemeyer in charge of architectural and urban development. Lúcio Costa's master plan was chosen through an international contest, but when work on his project officially began in February 1957—with Kubitschek's deadline only 38 months away—3,000 workers were already at the site building the airport and Niemeyer's design for the Palácio do Planalto, the president's palace.

To build a new seat of power for Latin America's largest nation, complete with a modern infrastructure, was a monumental undertaking. In the first days of the construction, few of the necessary materials could be obtained on the Planalto Central. Before paved roads were built, supplies were flown in from the eastern cities. Thousands of workers came to the region; most came from the poor northeast, which was perennially stricken by droughts, making plenty of cheap labor available. Immigrants were unskilled; all were willing to face any hardship for a paycheck. They learned fast and worked hard. Wooden shacks and army tents sprang up around the construction site. The largest settlement, known as Freetown (now the cidade-satélite called Nucleo Bandeirante), was home to close to 15,000 workers and their families. It was a rough place where anything went as long as there was money to pay for it.

Back in Rio, opposition to the new capital was loud and heated. Debates in the senate turned into fist fights, and committees were continuously conducting investigations into all the spending. Government employees were unhappy about the impending move. Some feared that Rio's business would drastically decline and its real-estate values would drop dramatically once the city ceased to be the capital. Others simply didn't want to leave the glorious beaches and the many and familiar services. Kubitschek's government countered all this with inducements: 100% salary increases, tax breaks, earlier-than-usual retirement ages, free transportation and moves to the capital, ridiculously low rents on Brasília's new residences, and even discounts on new home furnishings.

Despite all the odds, Kubitschek's deadline was met, and on April 21, 1960, the city was inaugurated. The day began with mass in the uncompleted cathedral and ended with a fireworks display, during which the president's name burned in 5-m-high (15-ft-high) letters.

In spite of its high cost and the initial criticism, Brasília has become a comfortable, functional capital. Highways run directly from it to several regions, including the farther-flung states that once were so isolated from the capital. Kubitschek's vision of a nation looking westward from the coast became a reality. His project set off a new era of pioneering and colonization.

Exploring Brasília

Addresses in the airplane-shape Plano Piloto might make even surveyors scratch their heads. There are the usual streets, avenues, and plazas with numbers or letters. There are sometimes compass points: *norte* (north), *sul* (south), *este* (east), *oeste* (west). And there are also such things as *setors* (S.; sectors), *trechos* (sections), *quadras* (Q.; squares), *blocos* (Bl.; blocks, but really more akin to buildings), *lotes* (Lt.; lots), *lojas* (Lj.; literally, "shops" or "stores," but here a type of subdivision within a larger building), and *conjuntos* (Cj.; yet another type of building subdivision). Although the original layout is very logical, it can be hard to get chapter-and-verse addresses, making them seem illogical.

The Eixo (pronounced *ay*-shoo) Monumental, the city's "fuselage," is lined with government buildings, museums, and monuments as well as banks, hotels, and shops. It runs roughly from the Praça do Cruzeiro to the Esplanada dos Ministérios, at the tip of which is the Praça dos Três Poderes. Intersecting the Eixo Monumental, near the Esplanada dos Ministérios, is the Eixo Rodoviário. It and the areas just off it form the city's "wings." The Asa Sul, or South Wing, is almost totally built up; the Asa Norte, or North Wing, still has spaces for development.

The Eixo Rodoviário has a double line of *superquadras* (supersquares) made up of two (usually) quadras numbered from 100 to 399 and consisting of eight six-story blocos. New quadras numbered 400 and above have been added outside the initial plan. In and around the two main axes are streets and avenues that connect still more residential and commercial areas, parks and gardens, and the Lago Paranoá (formed by a dam built about 16 km/10 mi southeast of the Plano Piloto and divided into Lago Sul and Lago Norte shores/districts). Along the outer shores of this lake are several residential areas. These include the Setores de Habitações Individuais (Individual Habitation Sectors) and the Setores de Mansões (Mansion Sectors).

It's best to tackle the Eixo Monumental and the Esplanada dos Ministérios first and then visit the Praça dos Três Poderes. The sights in these areas are easy to reach by bus, cab, or organized tour. Staying at a hotel in the nearby Setor Hotel Norte or Setor Hotel Sul (SHN or SHS; Hotel Sector North or South) will keep traveling time to a minimum. If you have time, get a taxi to the *Entorno* (literally, "surroundings"), the city's suburbs and cidades-satélite. Before heading out, get as detailed an address as possible, check that your cabbie knows where to go, and agree on a fare up front.

Eixo Monumental

Most of the Plano Piloto's major sights are along or just off the grand, 8-km-long (5-mi-long) Eixo Monumental and its multilane boulevards. The distances are too far to see everything on foot, so if you want to explore on your own rather than as part of a tour, you'll have to combine walking with bus and/or cab rides.

Numbers in the text correspond to numbers in the margin and on the Brasília map.

A GOOD TOUR

Start at the **Praça do Cruzeiro** ① at the Eixo Monumental's northwestern end. It's an easy 180-m (200-yard) walk to Niemeyer's **Memorial JK** ②, where you can learn about the man who made Brasília happen. From here, it's another short walk to the **Memorial dos Povos Indígenas** ③, a round structure containing indigenous artifacts. If you're interested in history and geography, hop a cab for the **Instituto Histórico e Geográfico** and then take a break in the nearby **Parque da Cidade.** Alternatively, you can continue (by taxi or bus) to the other Eixo Monumental sights, starting with the **Torre de TV** ④.

Head southeast and cross the Eixo Rodovíario to the pyramid that houses the **Teatro Nacional Cláudio Santoro** ⑤. At the other side of the Eixo Monumental and a little farther southeast is the unique **Catedral Metropolitana de Nossa Senhora da Aparecida** ⑥, a Niemeyer masterpiece. You're just a few steps from the Esplanada dos Ministérios, a gigantic corridor formed by 17 identical government buildings lined up along either side of the Eixo Monumental. The buildings that face each other at the far end of the Esplanada (just before the Praça dos Três Poderes) are two more world-renowned Niemeyer works: the **Palácio do Itamaraty** ⑦ and **Palácio da Justiça** ⑧.

TIMING AND PRECAUTIONS

You need at least a day (6–8 hours) to visit and fully appreciate all the sights. Although you'll probably ride as well as walk, wear comfortable shoes and drink plenty of water, particularly if you're exploring in the hotter months. Note that all government buildings frown on shorts, tank tops, and the like, so dress comfortably but conservatively.

SIGHTS TO SEE

★ ⑥ **Catedral Metropolitana de Nossa Senhora da Aparecida.** The city's cathedral is a Niemeyer masterpiece that was finished in 1967. The circular structure consists of 16 reinforced concrete "fingers" that arch skyward. They support huge panes of glass that shelter a subterranean church awash in natural light. Inside, *Os Anjos* (*The Angels*)—an aluminum sculpture by Brazilian modern artist Alfredo Ceschiatti—hovers above the altar. The *cruzeiro* (cross) used at the city's first mass is also here. Above ground, the cathedral resembles a crown of thorns and is surrounded by a reflecting pool. Its entrance is guarded by four majestic bronze statues, also by Ceschiatti, *Os Evangelistas* (*The Evangelists*). The outdoor carillon is a gift of the Spanish government. ⊠ *Esplanada dos Ministérios,* ☎ *061/224–4073.* 🎫 *Free.* ☉ *Daily 8–6.*

OFF THE
BEATEN PATH

INSTITUTO HISTÓRICO E GEOGRÁFICO – The small collection of photographs and memorabilia in the saucer-shape History and Geography Institute document the city's story with emphasis on the period from the demarcation of the area to the inauguration. The exhibition includes a vintage Jeep used by Kubitschek to visit the construction site in the late '50s. ⊠ *Av. W-5, SEPS 703/903,* ☎ *061/226–7753.* 🎫 *Free.* ☉ *Tues.–Sun. 8–noon and 2–6.*

★ ❷ **Memorial JK.** This Niemeyer structure is a truncated pyramid and has a function similar to its Egyptian counterpart: it's the final resting place of former president Juscelino Kubitschek (JK), the city's founding father, who died in 1981. The mortuary chamber has a lovely stained-glass roof by local artist Marianne Peretti. JK's office and library from his apartment in Rio have been moved to the memorial's north wing. The bronze statue of JK—his hand raised as if in blessing—surrounded by a half-shell (a trademark of Brasília) looks down upon the Eixo Monumental and makes this one of the capital's most moving monuments. Permanent and changing exhibits here document the city's construction. ⊠ *Praça do Cruzeiro at Eixo Monumental Oeste,* ☎ *061/6778.* 🎫 *R$2.* ☉ *Tues.–Sun. 9–6.*

Brasília

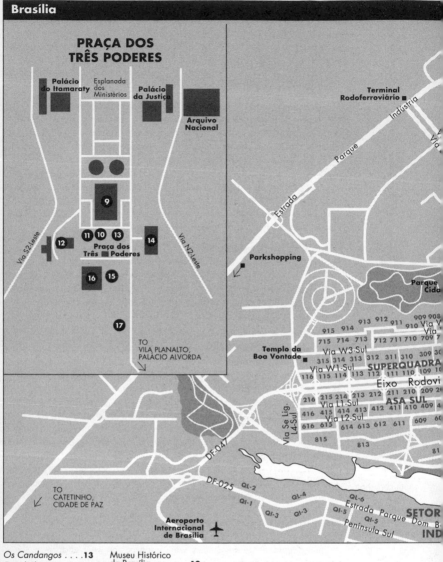

PRAÇA DOS TRÊS PODERES

Palácio do Itamaraty
Esplanada dos Ministérios
Palácio da Justiça
Arquivo Nacional
Terminal Rodoferroviário ■
Indústria
Via
Parque
Estrada
Via S2-Leste
Via N2-Leste
Praça dos Três Poderes ■
Parkshopping
Parque Cida
Templo da Boa Vontade ■
Via W3-Sul
Via W1-Sul
SUPERQUADRA
Eixo Rodovi
ASA SUL
Via L1-Sul
Via L2-Sul
Via Sc Lig. L4-Sul
TO VILA PLANALTO, PALÁCIO ALVORDA
TO CATETINHO, CIDADE DE PAZ
DF-047
DF-025
QL-2
QL-4
QL-6
QL-1
QL-3
QL-3
QL-5
QL-5
Estrada Parque Dom B
Península Sul
SETOR
IND
Aeroporto Internacional de Brasília ✈

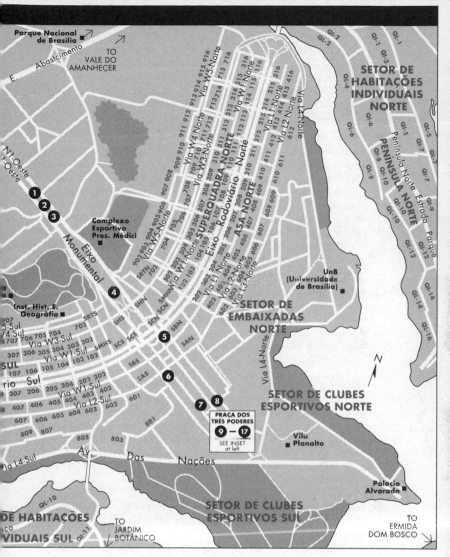

Parque Nacional
de Brasília

TO
VALE DO
AMANHECER

E. Abastecimento

**SETOR DE
HABITAÇÕES
INDIVIDUAIS
NORTE**

QI-2
QI-2

QI-1 QI-1

QI-3 QI-1

QI-4

QI-5 QI-5

QI-6 QI-6

QI-7 QI-7

QI-8 QI-7

QI-9

QI-10 QI-10

QI-10

QI-12 QI-12

QI-14

QI-14

QI-16

**PENÍNSULA
NORTE**

Península Norte Estrada Parque

N1-Oeste
1-Oeste

Eixo Monumental

Complexo
Esportivo
Pres. Médici

Via W5-Norte
Via W4-Norte
Via W3-Norte

913 914 915 916
909 910 911 912
907 908
905 906
903 904
902 905
SRTN 701
702 703 704 705 706 707 708
709 710 711 712 713 714 715 716

Via W2-Norte
301 302 303 304 305 306 307 308 309
310 311 312 313 314 315 316

SUPERQUADRA NORTE

Eixo Rodoviário Norte

ASA NORTE

Via W1-Norte
201 202 203 204 205 206 207 208 209
210 211 212 213 214 215 216

Via L1-Norte
111 112 113 114 115 116

Via L2-Norte
411 412 413 414 415 416

Via L3-Norte
611 610 609 608 607 606 605 604 603 602 601

401 402 403 404 405 406 407 408 409 410

Via L4-Norte

① ② ③

④

Inst. Hist. E.
Geografia

SRTS

SHS SHN

SGN SCN

SBN

SAN

⑤

SBS

SCS SGS

SMHS

SMHN

② 307
② 306 305 304 303 302
② 107 106 105 104 103 102
③ 207 206 205 204 203 202
④ 407 406 405 404 403 402
⑤ 607 606 605 604 603 602
⑥ 809 807

907
5-Sul
4-Sul
707 706 705 704 702
Via W3-Sul
Via W1-Sul
rio Sul
Via W1-Sul
Via L2-Sul
601
801

805 803

**SETOR DE
EMBAIXADAS
NORTE**

UnB
(Universidade
de Brasília)

**SETOR DE CLUBES
ESPORTIVOS NORTE**

⑥

⑦ ⑧

┌─────────────────┐
│ **PRAÇA DOS** │
│ **TRÊS PODERES**│
│ ⑨ — ⑰   │
│ SEE INSET   │
│ at left   │
└─────────────────┘

Vila
Planalto

Via 14-Sul

Av. Das Nações

QI-10

DE HABITAÇÕES

VIDUAIS SUL QI-11

TO
JARDIM
BOTÂNICO

**SETOR DE CLUBES
ESPORTIVOS SUL**

N

Palácio
Alvorada

TO
ERMIDA
DOM BOSCO

❸ Memorial dos Povos Indígenas. Another Niemeyer project, slated to contain a memorial to native peoples, was transformed into an art museum at completion by the city government. A popular uproar ensued, and the building was overtaken by indigenous peoples' organizations. The cylindrical structure has a spiraling ramp around a center plaza and houses a small museum with crafts by such peoples as the Kayapó and the Xavante, who once lived on the cerrado and now dwell in the Xingu area of the Amazon. ⊠ *Eixo Monumental Oeste,* ☎ *061/223–3760.* 🎟 *Free.* 🕐 *Tues.–Sun. 9–5.*

★ **❼ Palácio do Itamaraty.** For the home of the Foreign Ministry, Niemeyer designed a glass-enclosed rectangular structure with a detached concrete shelter whose facade is a series of elegant arches. The whole complex rests amid a Burle Marx–designed reflecting pool that augments the sense of spaciousness and isolation. The building and the water create a perfect backdrop for the *Meteoro* (*Meteor*), a round, abstract Carrara-marble sculpture by Brazilian-Italian artist Bruno Giorgi. On the guided tour of the interior, you'll see an astounding collection of modern art—including paintings by Brazilian artists like Candido Portinari—and a Burle Marx tropical garden. ⊠ *Esplanada dos Ministérios,* ☎ *061/411–6640.* 🎟 *Free.* 🕐 *Tours weekdays at 4.*

❽ Palácio da Justiça. The front and back facades of Niemeyer's Justice Ministry have waterfalls that cascade between its arched columns. Inside there's an important library (not open to the public) that contains one of the few complete original sets of Shakespeare's works—a gift from Queen Elizabeth to Kubitschek. ⊠ *Esplanada dos Ministérios,* ☎ *061/429–3877.* 🕐 *Weekdays 8–noon and 2–6.*

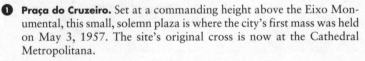

OFF THE BEATEN PATH **PARQUE DA CIDADE –** A few blocks from the Instituto Histórico and Geográfico, you can relax in the shade of City Park, a collaborative effort by Costa, Niemeyer, and Burle Marx. Recent improvements include a state-of-the-art lighting system and more security guards, making an evening walk, run, or bike ride along a path more agreeable than ever. There's also a go-cart racetrack. ⊠ *Entrances at Q. 901 S and Q. 912 3,* ☎ *061/225 2451; 061/223–0702 for park administration office.* 🕐 *Daily 5 AM–midnight.*

❶ Praça do Cruzeiro. Set at a commanding height above the Eixo Monumental, this small, solemn plaza is where the city's first mass was held on May 3, 1957. The site's original cross is now at the Cathedral Metropolitana.

❺ Teatro Nacional Cláudio Santoro. Another of Niemeyer's "pyramid projects," this theater is adorned with an array of concrete cubes and rectangles designed by Brazilian architect Athos Bulcão. Its three stages host a variety of performances, and its several small art galleries offer changing exhibits. ⊠ *SBN, Via N2,* ☎ *061/325–6240.* 🎟 *Free.* 🕐 *Tues.–Sun. 2–6.*

❹ Torre de TV. The *salão panorâmico* (observation room) of this 204-m (670-ft) TV tower offers spectacular views, particularly at night. On a lower level, the small **Museu Nacional das Gemas** has an impressive collection of Brazilian gems as well as a shop that sells stones and crafts and a café with a view of the Eixo. ⊠ *Eixo Monumental,* ☎ *061/322–3227 (museum).* 🎟 *Deck: free. Museum: R$3.* 🕐 *Deck: Mon. 2–9, Tues.–Sun. 9–9. Museum: Tues.–Sun. 10–6.*

Praça dos Três Poderes

Buildings housing the government's three branches symbolically face each other in the Plaza of the Three Powers, the heart of the Brazilian republic. Here both power and architecture have been given balance as well as a view of Brasília and beyond. Indeed, the cityscape combined with the planalto's endless sky have made the plaza so unusual that Russian cosmonaut Yuri Gagarin once remarked, "I have the impression of landing on a different planet, not on Earth!"

A GOOD TOUR

Start at the plaza's western end, where twin high-rises and two bowl-shape structures make up the **Congresso Nacional** ⑨. Directly in front of it is the **Museu Histórico de Brasília** ⑩, whose facade is adorned with a sculpture of Kubitschek. To one side of the museum and beneath the plaza is the **Espaço Lúcio Costa** ⑪, with exhibits depicting the planner's ideas for the city, beyond which you'll find the **Supremo Tribunal Federal** ⑫. To the other side of the museum is Giorgi's famous sculpture **Os Candangos** ⑬, which sits in front of the **Palácio do Planalto** ⑭, the executive office. Heading eastward across the plaza, you'll come to the **Mastro da Bandeira** ⑮ and the **Panteão da Pátria** ⑯. Head eastward along the path in the lawn to the **Espaço Cultural Oscar Niemeyer** ⑰, where several of the renowned architect's projects are displayed and explained. From here you can head beyond the plaza by cab to the **Vila Planalto** neighborhood and on to the **Palácio da Alvorada**.

TIMING

All the plaza's sights are close to one another, so you can easily complete this tour on foot in about four hours. Trips by taxi or bus to the Vila Planalto and the Palácio da Alvorada will make this a full-day tour.

SIGHTS TO SEE

⑬ **Os Candangos.** This 8-m-tall (25-ft-tall) bronze sculpture by Giorgi has become the symbol of Brasília. The laborers, many from the northeast, who built the city from scratch were called *candangos*. The statue, which consists of graceful, elongated figures holding poles, is right across from Palácio do Planalto.

⑨ **Congresso Nacional.** One of Niemeyer's most daring projects consists of two 28-story office towers for the 500 representatives of the Câmara dos Deputados (House of Representatives) and the 80 members of the Senado (senate); a convex structure, where the Câmara meets; and a concave structure, where the Senado convenes. The complex is connected by tunnels to several *anexos* (office annexes) and contains works by such Brazilian artists as Di Cavalcanti, Bulcão, and Ceschiatti as well as French designer Le Corbusier. The indoor gardens were done by Burle Marx. An hourly guided tour takes you through major sites within the building. ⊠ *Praça dos Três Poderes,* ☎ *061/318–5107.* ⊡ *Free.* ⊙ *Weekdays 9–noon and 2–5, weekends 10–2.*

⑰ **Espaço Cultural Oscar Niemeyer.** This branch of the Oscar Niemeyer Foundation—which is based in Rio and was created to preserve and present the architect's work—houses a collection of sketches and drafts as well as a database with texts and images from Niemeyer's archives. The small auditorium hosts a variety of presentations, which have included talks by the architect himself—after all, this is also the site of his Brasília office. ⊠ *Praça dos Três Poderes, Lt. J,* ☎ *061/224–3255.* ⊡ *Free.* ⊙ *Weekdays 10-6.*

⑪ **Espaço Lúcio Costa.** As a tribute to the urban planner who masterminded Brasília, this underground complex was added to the plaza in the late '80s. It has a 139-sq-m (1,500-sq-ft) display of the city's blueprint, and you can read Costa's original ideas for the project (the text is in Portuguese and English). ⊠ *Praça dos Três Poderes,* ☎ *061/321–9843.* ⊡ *Free.* ⊙ *Daily 9–6.*

⑮ **Mastro da Bandeira.** This structure, a 92-m (300-ft) steel flagpole that supports a 242-sq-m (2,600-sq-ft) Brazilian flag, is the only element of Praça dos Três Poderes that was not designed by Niemeyer. At noon on the first Sunday of the month, members of the armed forces take part in a *troca da bandeira* (flag change) ceremony. This is a good spot to contemplate the Brazilian flag's elements. The green background symbolizes the forests that once spanned much of the country. The yellow diamond represents the gold-mining period that so influenced the nation's history. The blue circle in the center is a homage to the great blue skies that dominate the territory; inside it are 26 stars—one for each state—from the southern skies and a white band with the national motto, *"Ordem e Progresso"* ("Order and Progress").

⑩ **Museu Histórico de Brasília.** Brasília's first museum has a small collection of pictures of the city and writings about it by such luminaries as Pope Pius XII, Kubitschek, and Niemeyer. The statue of Kubitschek on its facade is a 1960 work of Brazilian sculptor José Pedrosa. ⊠ *Praça dos Três Poderes*, ☎ *061/325–6244.* ☞ *Free.* ⊙ *Weekdays 9–6.*

OFF THE
BEATEN PATH   **PALÁCIO DA ALVORADA –** At the tip of a peninsula projecting into Lago Paranoá, the president's official residence—with its trademark slanting supporting columns of white marble—was Niemeyer's first project and was finished in June 1958. Incredible as it may seem, many presidents chose not to live here, preferring other government buildings in the city. You can't go inside, but you can appreciate the grand view of the palace and gardens from the reflecting pool next to the gate. ⊠ *SHTN, Via Presidencial s/n,* ☎ *061/411–4000.* ⊙ *Dawn–dusk.*

⑭ **Palácio do Planalto.** Although you can't enter the executive office building, you should pause to study its facade. Niemeyer gave the highly acclaimed structure an unusual combination of straight and slanting lines, a variation of the design from Palácio da Alvorada. The access ramp to the main entrance is part of the national political folklore because of the many slips and falls it has provoked. ⊠ *Praça dos Três Poderes*, ☎ *061/411–2317.*

★ ⑯ **Panteão da Pátria.** Designed by Niemeyer in 1985, this building honors the nation's heroes, including the beloved Tancredo Neves (it's also known as the Panteão Tancredo Neves), whose untimely death prevented him from being sworn in as Brazil's first democratically elected president after the military dictatorship ended. Inside the curved structure, which resembles a dove, you'll find works by Bulcão and João Camara. One set of panels, *Os Inconfidentes,* depicts the martyrs of the 18th-century Inconfidência Mineira movement, which was organized in Minas Gerais State to overthrow the Portuguese and establish an independent Brazilian republic. ⊠ *Praça dos Três Poderes*, ☎ *061/325–6244.* ☞ *Free.* ⊙ *Daily 8–5.*

⑫ **Supremo Tribunal Federal.** The Brazilian Supreme Court has the structural lightness that is the backbone of Niemeyer's work. The Tribunal Pleno, the highest court in Brazil, convenes on the ground floor. The top floor houses an 80,000-volume library, which you can visit on a guided tour. The 3-m (10-ft) granite statue set to the left of the main entrance is *The Justice,* by Ceschiatti. ⊠ *Praça dos Três Poderes*, ☎ *061/316–5859.* ☞ *Free.* ⊙ *Weekends 10–5.*

OFF THE
BEATEN PATH   **VILA PLANALTO –** Not far from the Palácio da Alvorada, this neighborhood was where the architects, engineers, topographers, accountants, and other professionals stayed while Brasília was under construction. They all lived in prefabricated wooden houses, which are representative

of a architectural trend within Modernism called *racionalismo carioca* (Rio's rationalism), which was based on Le Corbusier's work. Some of the houses still can be seen along Avenida dos Engenheiros (Avenue of the Engineers). Vila Planalto is a down-to-earth middle- to low-income residential area that maintains a boomtown spirit. It's the perfect place to find a *buteco* (bar) for a late-evening *seresta* (impromptu musical soirée).

Beyond the Plano Piloto

If you have the time, head beyond the Plano Piloto and explore Lago Paranoá's outer perimeter, where you'll find parks, gardens, and several interesting neighborhoods. You'll also encounter the cult communities that reflect Brasília's mystical side. In 1883, an Italian priest named Dom Bosco (St. John Bosco) had a vision of a new civilization rising around a lake between the 15th and 20th parallels. "This will be the promised land," he proclaimed. The futuristic architecture; the location between the 15th and 16th parallels in the vast, eerie cerrado; and the fantastic sky views, reinforced by the flatness of the region have led many to believe that Brasília is the realization of Bosco's vision. (Bosco never actually set foot in Brazil, making his vision seem even more mysterious.) Since its inception, the city has attracted a variety of religious groups.

★ **Catetinho.** When Rio was the capital, the president resided in the Palácio Catete. Although the new capital was being built, Kubitschek's temporary lodging was called the Catetinho (Little Catete). The barrackslike wooden edifice was built in 10 days during the summer of 1956. A nearby landing strip allowed the president to fly in from Rio for his frequent inspections. The building, which is 16 km (10 mi) southeast of the bus terminal in the Plano Piloto, was abandoned for several years. A recent renovation, however, has transformed it into a must-see museum for those interested in the city's history. It's surrounded by woods in which there's a small springwater pool where the president and his entourage once bathed. ✉ *Km 0, BR 040,* ☎ *061/380–1921.* ☞ *Free.* ☉ *Tues.–Sun. 9–5.*

Cidade da Paz. Partly subsidized by the Federal District government, the City of Peace is home to a branch of the Universidade Holística Internacional (International Holistic University), whose goal is to "contribute to the awakening of a new conscience and a new world view." The community occupies the 500-acre Granja do Ipé, 26 km (16 mi) southeast of the Plano Piloto and once the country manor of General Golbery do Couto e Silva, whom many consider the éminence grise behind the military regime (1964–85). The buildings on the grounds now accommodate university offices, meditation rooms, art galleries, and artisans shops. There are also three thermal pools and waterfalls. ✉ *Km 30, BR 040,* ☎ *061/380–1202.* ☞ *Free.* ☉ *Weekdays 9–noon and 3–6.*

Ermida Dom Bosco. This lakefront sanctuary 24 km (15 mi) east of the Plano Piloto is dedicated to the saint who inspired so many of those who settled in the new capital. The project is attributed to Niemeyer, though he denies it vehemently. It's adjacent to the impressive postmodern architecture of the Mosteiro São Bento (São Bento Monastery). A scenic overlook with a view of the Plano Piloto and a tranquil Burle Marx–designed garden make it an ideal place to watch the sun set. There's an environmental preserve on the monastery grounds; the entrance is before the ermida's gate. ✉ *Lago Sul, S. de Mansões Dom Bosco, Cj. 12,* ☎ *061/366–2141.* ☞ *Free.* ☉ *Tues.–Sun. 9–5.*

Jardim Botânico. The Botanical Gardens are in a 9,000-acre ecological reserve 27 km (17 mi) south of the Plano Piloto that's only partially open to the public. Three marked trails educate you about Brazilian vegetation, and there's an herb garden with almost 100 types of native medicinal plants. ⊠ *Lago Sul, Km 12 Estrada de Unaí,* ☎ *061/366–2141.* 🎫 *Free.* ⊙ *Tues.–Sun. 9–5.*

Parque Nacional de Brasília. The 60,000-acre Brasília National Park is in the northeastern area of the Federal District. The typical cerrado vegetation includes grasslands, woodland savannas, and taller gallery woods on the bottomlands. A 5-km (3-mi) trail through mostly flat terrain starts at the visitor center, where you can pick up maps and brochures. The park also has two pools (fed by natural springs), dressing rooms, and picnic and barbecue areas. ⊠ *EPIA, 9 km (6 mi) from bus terminal,* ☎ *061/233–5322.* 🎫 *R$3.* ⊙ *Daily 8–4.*

Templo da Boa Vontade. This temple 8 km (5 mi) south of the Eixo Monumental is adjacent to the national headquarters of the Legião da Boa Vontade (Goodwill Legion), a philanthropic organization. The pyramid-shape building is open to all denominations for worship or meditation. At the top of it sits a 21-kilogram (46-pound) quartz crystal, the largest ever found in Brazil. ⊠ *SGAS 915, Lt. 75/6,* ☎ *061/245–1070.* 🎫 *Free.* ⊙ *Daily 24 hrs.*

Vale do Amanhecer. The most famous of the cult communities, the Valley of the Dawn, is near Planaltina, a cidade-satélite 40 km (25 mi) north of the Plano Piloto. The community was established in 1969 by Neiva Zelay, known as Tia Neiva, a onetime truck driver who died in 1985 and who reportedly had extrasensory powers. Each day, the community's grounds are the site of rituals conducted by followers of a variety of faiths and philosophies. About 1,000 people live here. ⊠ *Km 10, DF 15,* ☎ *061/389–1258.* 🎫 *Donation suggested.* ⊙ *Grounds: daily 10–midnight. Services: daily 12:30–2:30.*

Dining

Brazilian

$-$$ ✕ **Antigamente.** This colonial house was brought stone by stone from
★   the town of Diamantina in Minas Gerais. The restaurant's location—not far from the shore of Lago Paranó—is less of a draw these days as construction on the lakefront somewhat taints the scenery, but the *comida mineira* (food typical of Minas Gerais) is reason enough to come. Try the *galinha á D. Carlota Joaquina* (chicken with red sauce) or the *ouro velho de Goiás* (butter-fried chicken nuggets). There's a fixed-price buffet option at lunch. At dinner, Brazilian music performances accompany your meal. ⊠ *Lago Sul, SCS, Trecho 4, Cj. 5, Lt. 1-B,* ☎ *061/316–6967. DC, MC, V. Closed Mon. No dinner Sun.*

$-$$ ✕ **Cumê na Roça.** The specialty is lunch (dinner is served only on Friday) at this farm-side restaurant outside the Plano Piloto, 16 km (10 mi) north of the bus terminal. The fare is comida mineira; try the *leitão pururuca* (roasted piglet with regional seasonings) while you take in the view of the Lago Norte. ⊠ *Fazenda Brejo, Chácara 8T, Ólhos d'Água,* ☎ *061/500–1600. Reservations essential. No credit cards.*

$ ✕ **Churrascaria do Lago.** At this rodízio-style *churrascaria* (barbecue restaurant), waiters bring meats to your table until you tell them to stop. As the name indicates, it's on the lakefront; it has been here, near the Palácio da Alvorada, since the city's early days. Reservations are advised. ⊠ *Lago Norte, SHTN, Cj. 1-A,* ☎ *61/223–9266. AE, DC, MC, V. No dinner Sun.*

Eclectic

$$-$$$$ ✕ **O Convento.** From the outside O Convento doesn't look like a restaurant, mainly because the residential area it's in forbids outdoor signs, hence the small plaque near its doorbell. Its name comes from its location—in a house built with material from a convent. The fur-

nishings are 18th century, and the waiters are dressed as monks. The fare is international, with a Brazilian accent—the *camarão rosa grelhado* (grilled shrimp with butter sauce and tropical fruits) is highly recommended. ⊠ *SHIS, QI. 9, Cj. 9, Casas 4, Lago Sul,* ☎ *061/248–1211. Reservations essential. AE, DC, MC. Sun.–Mon.*

$$–$$$$ ⚹ ★ ✕ **La Via Vecchia.** The powers-that-be favor this restaurant in the Bonaparte Hotel for its quiet atmosphere and superb decor. Chefs Dudu and Eduardo will do all they can to please even the most demanding customer. Specialties include the *piccole cotolette di agnello* (mutton with a cream sauce made with cassis and port) and the grilled seafood combination served with a fruit risotto. It's best to make reservations for dinner. ⊠ *SHS Q. 02, Bl. I,* ☎ *061/322–2288. AE, DC, MC, V. Closed Sun. No lunch Sat.*

$–$$$ ✕ **The Falls.** As its name suggests, this restaurant, in the basement of the Naoum Plaza Hotel, has a decor that includes artificial waterfalls that cascade amid vegetation. The ambience is as much of a draw as the food, which includes such exquisite dishes as the *sinfonia de peixes,* the "fish symphony" of Brazilian seafood, rice, and *pirão* (beans and cassava flour). ⊠ *SHS, Q.05, Bl. H/I,* ☎ *061/322–4545. AE, DC, MC, V.*

French

$$–$$$ ★ ✕ **La Chaumière.** The atmosphere of this highly regarded 30-year-old restaurant won't fail to impress. The fare is classical French, the fillet of beef with green pepper sauce and grilled fillet with Roquefort sauce are mainstay entrées. ⊠ *SCLS, Q. 408, Bl. A, Lt. 13,* ☎ *61/242–7599. AE. Closed Mon. No lunch Sat.; no dinner Sun.*

German

$–$$ ✕ **Fritz.** In business for decades, this restaurant is synonymous with German cuisine. Try the *Eisbein* (pig's leg with mashed potatoes) or *Ente mit Blaukraut und Apfelpurée* (duck cooked in wine served with red cabbage and applesauce). ⊠ *SCLS, Q. 404, Bl. D, Lj. 35,* ☎ *061/ 223–4622. AE, DC, MC, V. No dinner Sun.*

Italian

$–$$$ ✕ **Villa Borghese.** The cantina ambience and fantastic cuisine (including many freshly made pastas) make you feel as if you're in Italy. The *tagliatelli negro* (pasta with squid ink), served with a garlic, herb, and shrimp sauce, is divine. ⊠ *SCLS, Q. 201, Bl. A, Lj. 33,* ☎ *061/ 226–5650. AE, DC, MC, V. Closed Mon.*

Spanish

$$–$$$ ✕ **Salamanca.** Don't let looks fool you at this restaurant. The decor may not be very sophisticated, but the paella certainly is. ⊠ *SCLS 112, Bl. B, Lj. 37,* ☎ *061/346–8212. AE, MC, V. Closed Mon. No dinner Sun.*

Lodging

$$$ ★ 🏨 **Bonaparte Hotel Residence.** A sober granite lobby with sophisticated accent lighting make the Bonaparte an appealing choice. All rooms could be considered small apartments, with plush carpeting, king-size beds, and large bathtubs in every bathroom (quite rare in Brazil). The business services here are outstanding, and the on-site restaurant, La Via Vechia, is one of the best in town. ⊠ *SHS, Q. 02, Bl. J, 70322-900,* ☎ *061/218–6600 or 0800/61–9991,* FAX *061/322– 9092,* WEB *www.bonapartehotel.com.br. 128 rooms. 2 restaurants, bar, coffee shop, room service, pool, sauna, exercise room, business services, convention center. AE, DC, MC, V.*

$$$ ★ 🏨 **Naoum Plaza Hotel.** Brasília's most sophisticated hotel attracts heads of state (Prince Charles, Nelson Mandela, and Fidel Castro have stayed in the Royal Suite) and their diplomats. Rooms have tropical-wood fur-

niture and beige color schemes. The service is impeccable. Two upscale restaurants, the Falls and Mitsubá (with Japanese fare), add to the hotel's appeal. ✉ *SHS, Q. 05, Bl. H/I, 70322-914,* ☎ *061/322–4545 or 0800/61–4844,* FAX *061/322–4949,* WEB *www.naoumplaza.com.br. 171 rooms, 16 suites. 2 restaurants, bar, coffee shop, room service, pool, sauna, exercise room, business services, meeting room, travel services. AE, DC, MC, V.*

$$–$$$ 🏨 **Kubitschek Plaza.** High-caliber service and upscale amenities are the
★ hallmarks here. The lobby is decorated with antiques, Persian rugs, and original paintings by renowned Nippo-Brazilian artist Tomie Otake. Rooms are comfortable and have a sedate, modern decor. After a hard day conducting affairs of state and/or business, many people head for the on-site Plaza Club, a restaurant-bar with a dance floor. ✉ *SHN, Q. 02, Bl. E, 70710-908,* ☎ *061/329–3333 or 0800/61–3995,* FAX *061/328–9366,* WEB *www.kubitschek.com.br. 246 rooms. 2 restaurants, bar, coffee shop, room service, indoor pool, sauna, exercise room, business services, meeting rooms, travel services. AE, DC, MC, V.*

$–$$ 🏨 **Academia de Tênis Resort.** What was once merely a tennis club on the shore of Lago Paranoá has, over the course of 30 years, become a resort with all the usual amenities. Rooms are in chalets that dot the gardens and woods of the grounds, which also contain several restaurants and bars. ✉ *SCES, Trecho 4, Cj. 5, Lt. 1-B, 70200-000,* ☎ *061/ 316–6252,* FAX *061/316–6268. 228 rooms. 6 restaurants, 3 bars, coffee shop, room service, 6 outdoor pools, indoor pool, sauna, 21 tennis courts, exercise room, business services, meeting room. AE, DC, MC, V.*

$–$$ 🏨 **Eron Brasília Hotel.** This hotel offers such high-tech in-room amenities as Internet connections and complete stereo systems; you can even have a desktop computer installed. Rooms are carefully decorated in pastel color schemes. Request a room above the ninth floor to avoid traffic noise. The Restaurante Panorâmico and its piano bar afford a grand view of the Eixo Monumental and are popular with political types. ✉ *SHN, Q. 05, Bl. A, 70710-300,* ☎ *061/329–4100,* FAX *061/ 326–2698,* WEB *www.eronhotel.com.br. 170 rooms, 10 suites. Restaurant, bar, in-room data ports, nightclub, meeting room, travel services. AE, DC, MC, V.*

$–$$ 🏨 **Hotel Nacional.** Echoing Brasília's modernist architecture, the Hotel Nacional, though slightly outdated, is still one of the city's best options. It has accommodated any number of distinguished guests, including Queen Elizabeth. The Taboo Grill is a great place for grilled meat or seafood, and the Tropical Coffee shop offers a different buffet table for each day of the week. ✉ *SHS, Q. 01, Bl. A 70322-900,* ☎ *061/321–7575,* FAX *061/223–9213,* WEB *www.hotelnacional.com.br. 346 rooms. Restaurant, bar, coffee shop, room service, indoor pool, sauna, exercise room, business services, meeting room, travel services. AE, DC, MC, V.*

$–$$ 🏨 **Metropolitan Hotel Residence.** This low-key hotel has a lower price tag than its sister property, the Bonaparte. The rooms are also fully furnished apartments. It's convenient to the Brasília Shopping mall and offers special rates for extended stays. The Francisco Norte restaurant is highly recommended. ✉ *SHN Q. 02, Bl. J, 80020-020,* ☎ *061/327–3939 or 0800/61–3939,* FAX *061/327–3738,* WEB *www. metropolitanflat.com.br. 115 rooms. Restaurant, bar, pool, sauna, exercise room, meeting rooms. AE, DC, MC, V.*

$–$$ 🏨 **San Marco.** If you're looking for functionality and reliability, stay at the San Marco. You can bask in the central Brazilian sun, taking in the Eixo Monumental, beside its rooftop pool. The adjacent restaurant, La Gondola, serves international fare. ✉ *SHS, Q. 05, Bl. C, 70710-300,* ☎ *061/321–8484,* FAX *061/223–6552,* WEB *www.sanmarco.com.br.*

191 rooms, 4 suites. Restaurant, bar, pool, sauna, exercise room, meeting room, travel services. AE, DC, MC, V.

$ ⊞ **Aracoara Hotel.** One of Brasília's oldest and most traditional hotels played a role in the country's history: João Figueiredo made this the *de facto* presidential residence for a while in the late '70s. Although it's starting to show its age, it's still a worthy choice. The restaurant combines international fare with live Brazilian music. ⊠ *SHN, Q. 05, Bl. C, 70710-300,* ☎ *061/328–9222 or 0800/61–4881,* FAX *061/328–9067,* WEB *www.aracoara.com.br. 114 rooms, 16 suites. Restaurant, bar, coffee shop, sauna. AE, DC, MC, V.*

$ ⊞ **Hotel das Nações.** You can spend some of the money you save by staying at this budget hotel, which has been around since the city's early days, at the nearby Patio Brasil mall. (After all, who needs abundant facilities and imaginative decor when you can go shopping?) ⊠ *SHS, Q. 04, Bl. I, 70300-300,* ☎ *061/322–8050,* FAX *061/225–7722. 126 rooms. Bar. AE, DC, MC, V.*

$ ⊞ **Península Hotel.** Although it has few frills, this new hotel is a good budget choice. Rooms have a tasteful decor that makes them feel cozy, bathrooms are large, and the staff is dedicated. ⊠ *SHN, Q. 03, Bl. B, 71710-911,* ☎ *061/328–4144,* FAX *061/328–4144. 99 rooms. Restaurant, bar. AE, DC, MC, V.*

¢–$ ⊞ **SAN Park.** This hotel is a convenient budget option for those en route to other destinations who do not need to stay downtown. Bathrooms are small, and facilities are basic but up to date. ⊠ *SAAN, Qd. 3, Bl. D, 70300-300,* ☎ *061/361–0077,* FAX *061/361–0088. 56 rooms. Restaurant, sauna. AE, DC, MC, V.*

Nightlife and the Arts

Nightlife

BARS

Beirute (⊠ SCLS 109, Bl. A, Lj. 02/04, ☎ 061/244–1717), an eclectic bar-restaurant with an Arabian flair, has been in business since 1966. During its first decade, it drew politicians for postsession discussions; today, it attracts intellectuals and the alternative-minded. Embassy personnel gather at the stylish **Café Cassis** (⊠ SCLS 214, Bl. B, Lj. 22, ☎ 061/346–7103). For a classical ambience, try **Café Colonial à Capitú,** (⊠ SCLS 403, Bl. D, Lj. 20, ☎ 061/223–0080), which has performances of baroque music. **Gates Pub** (⊠ SCLS 403, Bl. B, Lj. 34, ☎ 061/322–9301) is popular with those who appreciate jazz and blues.

DANCE CLUBS

In Brasília's clubs, some nights are devoted to such northeastern Brazilian rhythms as *forró*—the result of the large number of northeasterners who settled here. A mixed clientele gathers at the **Music Hall Caffé** (⊠ SCLS 411, Bl. B, Lj. 28/34, ☎ 061/346–5214), where local bands and DJs display their varied repertoire. The **Universal Diner** (⊠ SCLS 210, Bl. B, Lj. 30, ☎ 061/443–2089) caters to a young, trendy crowd.

The Arts

THEATER

The main building of the **Fundação Brasileira de Teatro** (Brazilian Theatrical Foundation; ⊠ SDS, Bl. C, Lj. 30, ☎ 061/226–0182) has two theaters for plays and concerts: the Teatro Dulcina de Moraes and the Teatro Conchita de Moraes. The **Teatro Nacional Cláudio Santoro** (⊠ SBN, Via N2, ☎ 061/325–6105 for symphony ticket information; 061/325–6109) has three stages and several practice rooms used by the Orquestra Sinfônica do Teatro Nacional, which performs here from March through November.

Outdoor Activities and Sports

Participant Sports

GOLF

At the tip of Eixo Monumental, not far from the Palácio da Alvorada, you can golf on the 18-hole course at the **Clube de Golfe de Brasília** (✉ SCES, Trecho 2, Lt. 2, ☎ 061/223–6029 or 061/224–2718). Guests at some hotels have free access to the course; all others pay R$40 on weekdays R$60 on weekends.

HIKING

If you just want to wander along a trail, head to the **Parque Nacional de Brasília** (✉ EPIA, 9 km/6 mi from bus terminal, ☎ 061/233–4055). If you're interested in learning about local vegetation while you walk, try one of the three trails at the **Jardim Botânico** (✉ Lago Sul, S. de Mansões Dom Bosco, Cj. 12, ☎ 061/245–5003). You can arrange long guided treks into the cerrado.

SWIMMING

Some 35 km (22 mi) south of the Eixo Monumental is the **Cachoeira da Saia Velha** (✉ BR 040, Saída Sul, ☎ 061/627–0000), a natural preserve with cerrado vegetation and several waterfalls. Admission is free. The **Parque Nacional de Brasília** (✉ EPIA, 9 km/6 mi from bus terminal, ☎ 061/233–4055) has pools filled with mineral water. It is best to take your dip in the morning to beat the crowds.

TENNIS

You can get in a match or take classes at the **Academia de Tênis Resort** (✉ SCES, Trecho 4, Lt. 1-B, ☎ 061/316–6161) daily from 8 to 4. Court fees are about R$46 an hour (equipment included); lessons cost R$58 an hour.

Spectator Sports

Most sporting events are held in the Centro Desportivo Presidente Medici complex, on the north side of the Eixo Monumental. The **Autódromo Internacional Nelson Piquet** (☎ 061/273–6586), named after three-time Formula I champion and Brasília native Nelson Piquet, has a 5-km (3-mi) racetrack that hosts such events as Formula III and stock car races. The modern, 66,000-seat **Estádio Mané Garrincha** (☎ 061/225–9860) is where Gama FC plays, a second-tier *futebol* (soccer) team that has occasionally risen to the major league. **Ginásio Cláudio Coutinho** (☎ 061/225–5977) is a small, 6,000-seat facility used mostly for practice by national teams. **Ginásio Nilson Nelson** (☎ 061/225–4775) is a large arena with 17,000 seats right on Eixo Monumental. It's used for volleyball and basketball games as well as for musical events.

Shopping

There are two major shopping districts along the Eixo Monumental: the Setor Commercial Norte (SCN; Northern Commercial Sector) and the Setor Commercial Sul (SCS; Southern Commercial Sector). In addition, almost every superquadra has its own commercial district.

Centers and Malls

Brasília Shopping. Housed in an odd, arch-shape building, Brasília's most sophisticated mall has several international chain stores, as well as movie theaters, restaurants, and snack bars. ✉ SCN, Q. 05, ☎ 061/328–2122. ⏰ Mon.–Sat. 10–10, Sun. 2–10.

Conjunto Nacional Brasília. The Conjunto is one of the nation's first malls. Its central location (across from the Teatro Nacional and bus terminal) and glitzy neon facade make it one of the most visited, though you won't find many international brand names here. ✉ *SDN, Cj. A,* ☎ *061/316–9700.* ⊙ *Mon.–Sat. 10–10.*

Parkshopping. Brasília's largest shopping center has 183 shops as well as a Burle Marx–designed central garden, the site of many cultural events. The annual Verão Cultural (Cultural Summer) program, for example, attracts major Brazilian musical talents. ✉ *SAI/Sudoeste, Q. A-1,* ☎ *0800/61–4444.* ⊙ *Mon.–Sat. 10–10.*

Crafts

The **Feira de Antiguidades** (Antiques Fair; ✉ Centro Comercial Gilberto Salomão, SHIS, QI. 5) is held on the last weekend of each month from 8 to 6. At the **Feira de Artesanato** (Artisans' Fair) you'll find semiprecious-stone jewelry, bronze items, wood carvings, wicker crafts, pottery, and dried flowers. It's held at the foot of the Torre de TV on the Eixo Monumental weekend days from 9 to 6. A few stalls might open during the week.

Gemstones

For quality stones head to the **Museu Nacional das Gemas** at the Torre de TV (✉ Eixo Monumental, ☎ 061/322–3227, ext. 201). Its shop is open Tuesday–Friday 10–6.

THE WEST

The virtually untamed west consists of the frontier states of Goías, Mato Grosso, and Mato Grosso do Sul. Although the settlers were mostly after gold and precious stones, agriculture and ranching are the mainstays now. The cerrado is Brazil's bread basket, and the landscape is one large chess board of crops and pastures. The main hubs—such as Goiânia, Cuiabá, and Campo Grande—are, for the most part, sophisticated trading outposts for farmers and ranchers. Tourism has begun to flourish as more and more people discover the charms of the colonial towns of Pirenópolis, Goiás, and Campo Grande; the quasi-mystical mesa of Chapada dos Guimarães; the haven of Bonito, with its great water sports; and, of course, the wildlife paradise of the Pantanal.

Goiânia

209 km (130 mi) southwest of Brasília.

Much like Brasília, Goiânia is a planned metropolis, though it was built in the 1930s. The capital of the important farming state of Goiás, today it is one of Brazil's 10 largest cities, with more than 1 million people. Although the city might never make it to UNESCO's list of World Heritage Sites, it's an important gateway to the west. It has also acquired a reputation for its nightlife.

The **Museu Antropológico da UFG** (University Anthropology Museum) has a large collection of indigenous artifacts. *Praça Universitário 1166, S. Universitário,* ☎ *062/261–6898.* 🎟 *Free.* ⊙ *Tues.–Fri. 9–5.*

Near the middle of town is the **Bosque dos Buritis,** a large wooded park. Stroll beside its man-made lakes, sit by its fountains (wear bug spray as the mosquitoes can be fierce), or visit the small **Museu de Arte** (Art Museum) in its northwestern corner. Note that the park isn't safe at night. ✉ *S. Oeste,* ☎ *062/824–1190 for museum.* 🎟 *Free.* ⊙ *Park: daily 9–6. Museum: Tues.–Sun. 9–6.*

OFF THE
BEATEN PATH

POUSADA DO RIO QUENTE RESORTS/HOTEL TOURISMO – This resort complex 175 km (109 mi) south of Goiânia in the municipality of Rio Quente (Hot River) consists of two hotels and a water park. The park itself makes a nice day trip from Goiânia (a day pass costs R$25). On a

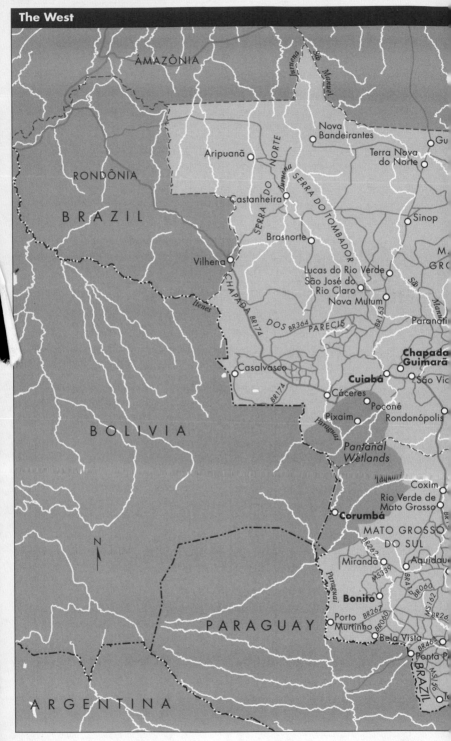

AMAZÔNIA

RONDÔNIA

BRAZIL

Nova Bandeirantes

Aripuanã

Terra Nova do Norte

Gu

SERRA DO NORTE

Castanheira

Sinop

Brasnorte

SERRA DO TOMBADOR

M.
GRO

Vilhena

Lucas do Rio Verde

São José do Rio Claro

Nova Mutum

Sa

Manuel

Paranat

Itenes

CHAPADA BR174

DOS PARECIS

BR364

BR 63

Chapada
Guimarã

Casalvasco

Cuiabá

São Vic

BR174

Cáceres

Poconé

Rondonópolis

Pixaim

BOLIVIA

Paraguai

Pantanal
Wetlands

Taguan

Coxim

Rio Verde de
Mato Grosso

BR

Corumbá

MATO GROSSO
DO SUL

N

Miranda

Aquidau

BR262

MS339

BR1

BR060

BR16

Bonito

Porto
Murtinho

BR267

BR060

BR26

Bela Vista

PARAGUAY

BR4

Ponta P

BRAZIL

MS136

ARGENTINA

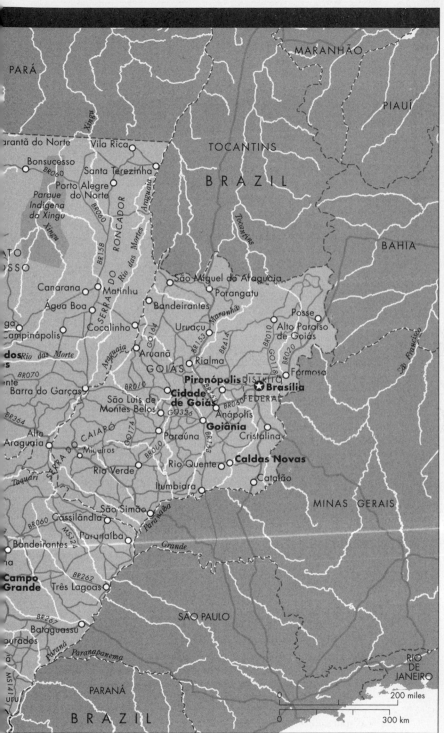

longer stay, you can take advantage of the hotels' ($$$–$$$$) many activities, such as tennis, horseback riding, and fishing; there are also on-site restaurants and bars. Consult the well-informed staff about transportation options. ⊠ *Off GO 507,* ☎ *062/452–8000,* FAX *062/452–8575. AE, DC, MC, V.*

Dining and Lodging

$–$$$ ✕ **Aroeiras.** The main draw of Aroeiras is *tartaruga a moda Araguaia* (Araguaian-style turtle served in its shell, with a spicy sauce and rice), a delicacy from the Araguaia River basin. The brick house is built in the style of Goiás's country houses, with a tile roof and high ceilings, and the brick walls are hung with paintings by local artists. You can also dine on the patio, where water winds around a miniaqueduct. ⊠ *Rua 146 No. 570, S. Marista,* ☎ *062/241–5975. AE, DC, MC, V.*

$–$$$ ✕ **Piquiras.** This popular, upscale eclectic restaurant is best known for its *peixe na telha* (fried surubi fish fillet, served with *pirão*—beans in a thick sauce—and rice). It has two locations: the original is in the quiet Piquiras neighborhood down the street from the Castro's Park hotel; the other branch is in the Marista section of town. Be prepared for the automatic spritzer, designed to help keep you cool during the day; at night, your biggest concern will be making reservations. ⊠ *Av. República do Líbano 1758, S. Oeste,* ☎ *062/251–8168. AE, DC, MC, V;* ⊠ *Rua 146, 464, S. Marista,* ☎ *062/281–4344. AE, DC, MC, V.*

$–$$ ✕🏨 **Castro's Park.** Goiânia's top-of-the-line hotel caters to wealthy busi-
★ nesspeople during the week; on weekends there are more families by the pool. Rooms are modern, though small and nondescript. The Ipê, one of the on-site restaurants, serves a great *feijoada* (traditional Brazilian stew of pork, black beans, rice, and spices) on Saturday. ⊠ *Av. República do Líbano 1520, S. Oeste, 74115-30,* ☎ *062/223–7766,* FAX *062/225–7070,* WEB *www.castrospark.com.br. 161 rooms, 16 suites. 2 restaurants, bar, minibars, pool, sauna, business services, convention center, travel agency. AE, DC, MC, V.*

$ 🏨 **Bandeirantes.** The rooms in this hotel—which is cheaper than it ought to be because it doesn't have a pool—are pleasant enough and have TVs and decent bathrooms. Its location is both a draw and a disadvantage: it's near the center of town, but it's in a neighborhood that can be noisy and unsafe at night. ⊠ *Av. Anhangüera 5106, S. Central,* ☎ FAX *062/212–0066. 70 rooms, 3 suites. Restaurant, bar, meeting room. AE, DC, MC, V.*

Nightlife

Goiânia has a vibrant nightlife: the Setor Marista and Setor Oeste harbor several bars, restaurants, and dance clubs where crowds of all ages take advantage of the cool evenings. **Cervejaria Goyaz** (⊠ Rua T-5 at Av. 85, S. Marista, ☎ 062/281–0770) has a good beer selection and live music on weekends. **Draft Casual Bar** (⊠ Rua 22 at Rua 23, Setor Oeste, ☎ 062/214–4455) is a great choice for drinks and dancing.

Shopping

Across from the Estação Rodoviária (bus station), you'll find the massive **Centro de Tradições e Artesanato** (⊠ Av. Goiás at Praça do Trabalhador, S. Norte Ferroviário, ☎ 062/229–3676), which has a wide selection of locally made ceramics, baskets, and wood carvings as well as stall upon stall of semiprecious stones. It's open daily 8–8. On Saturday a crafts market, the **Feria da Lua,** is held in the Praça Tamanadré. On Sunday, you can shop at the **market** in the Praça Cívica.

Pirenópolis

131 km (81 mi) north of Goiânia, 159 km (99 mi) west of Brasília.

Settled in the 18th century at the height of the Goiás gold rush, Pirenópolis was abandoned by the early 19th century after most of its gold was mined. Some locals say that the years of isolation were a blessing, as they've helped to preserve the town's character: most streets in the historic downtown district retain the original pavement, which has slivers of quartzite, an abundant mineral that's still quarried north of town. In 1989, the federal government gave what was once virtually a ghost town national monument status, drawing attention from the tourism industry. On weekends, people flee from the modern concrete and glass of nearby Goiânia and Brasília to immerse themselves in Pirenópolis's colonial flavor. The town has several blocks of historic houses, churches, charming restaurants, and quaint resorts, along with several well-respected jewelers.

Slightly above town is the **Praça da Matriz,** with several historic structures. The handsome, colonial **Igreja Nossa Senhora do Rosário–Matriz** (circa 1728–32) is the oldest church in Goiás. Across the plaza is the restored theater with the odd spelling **Teatro de Pyrenópolis** (circa 1899).

Just down the street from the Praça da Matriz is the **Museu das Cavalhadas,** with displays of the outlandish medieval costumes worn by participants in the Festa do Divino Espírito Santo. First celebrated in 1891, this three-day event, which has the atmosphere of a Renaissance fair, takes over the town six weeks after Easter Sunday. Among the roster of activities is a staged battle between Moors and Christians (the Christians win every year). The museum is in a private home—Dona Maria Eunice, the owner, will guide you. ☒ *Rua Direita 39,* ☎ *062/ 331–1166.* ☒ *R$2.* ☉ *Fri.–Sun. 9–5.*

The most striking of all the town's churches is the **Igreja Nosso Senhor do Bonfim** (circa 1750–54). Its stunning interior (the altars and Christ statue are particularly beautiful) was brought from Salvador by slaves in 1755. ☒ *Rua do Bonfim near intersection of Rua Aurora,* ☎ *no phone.* ☒ *Free.*

Dining and Lodging

¢–$ ✕ **Aravinda.** This eatery is also a "spiritual" center—the raspy-voiced, aging-hippie owner is the town's mother figure. The food is colorful and tasty with an emphasis on vegetarian fare; the highlight is delicious fish dishes, particularly the peixe na telha. There's live music—anything from blues to salsa—on weekends. ☒ *Rua do Rosário 25,* ☎ *062/9991–6083. No credit cards. Closed Mon.–Tues.*

¢–$ ✕ **Pireneus.** Lunch options at this outstanding eatery include Goiás-style barbecue (beef is roasted over coals or on a grill, instead of using riodizio-style skewers). At dinner time, the restaurant takes advantage of its traditional brick stove and becomes a pizzeria. ☒ *Rue do Rosário 31,* ☎ *062/969–3039. MC, V. Closed Mon.–Tues.*

¢ ✕ **As Flor.** Popular with locals because of the affordable buffet-style service, As Flor serves traditional Brazilian fare—both the lunch and the dinner menu consist mostly of cured meats with rice and beans. ☒ *Sizenando Jaime 16,* ☎ *062/331–1276. No credit cards. Closed weekends.*

¢ ✕▦ **Hotel Quinta de Santa Bárbara.** Across from the Igreja Nosso Senhor do Bonfim sits this family-oriented resort with colonial-style bungalows. Each has two rooms with TVs, comfortable beds, and fantastic flagstone floors; a veranda offers views of the town that are particularly beautiful at sunset. The open-air all-you-can-eat restaurant serves excellent Goiás specialties cooked in a massive kilnlike stove. ☒ *Rua* *do Bonfim 1,* ☎ FAX *062/331–1304. 20 rooms. Restaurant, bar, mini-bars, 2 pools, sauna, fishing. V.*

$ ⊞ **Pousada dos Pireneus.** Some people come here on weeklong quests
★ to lose weight; others bring their families for weekend retreats. The
main lodge—which is reminiscent of an adobe structure from the
southwestern United States—contains the restaurant and bar, which
looks out at the pools, tennis courts, and beyond the landscaped
grounds to town. Rooms are in what can only be described as a 17th-
century condo complex; ground-floor quarters have decks and hammocks. ⊠ *Chácara Mata do Sobrato,* ☎ *062/331–1345,* FAX *062/331–
1462. 103 rooms. Restaurant, bar, 2 pools, massage, sauna, spa, tennis court, aerobics, horseback riding, bicycles, shops, recreation room,
convention center. AE, DC, MC, V. MAP*

$ ⊞ **Pousada Walkeriana.** This pousada is named after *Cattleya walk-
eriana*—one of the several rare Brazilian orchids on display in the garden. The main building housed different city government offices over
the years before it was declared an architectural heritage site in 1990.
There is an antiques shop specializing in furniture in the west wing,
and the pousada's small, comfortable rooms are furnished with pieces
from the shop. ⊠ *Praça do Rosário 2, Centro,* ☎ FAX *062/331–1260.
16 rooms. Bar, pool, shop. V. CP.*

Nightlife

Most nightlife is along or just off the **Rua do Rosário,** which is closed
to vehicular traffic on weekends, when bar and restaurant tables take
over the narrow sidewalks and the street proper. The liveliest bars are
Lanchonete da Chiquinha, Varanda, and Choperia Santo Graal.

Leve Encanto (⊠ Rua do Rosário 23, ☎ no phone) has French-style
crepes and pancakes—perfect pick-me-ups after a long night. For a late-
night snack, head to **Pizza Trotramundos** (⊠ Rua do Rosário 32, ☎
062/331–1559) for the house special (pizza with olives, mushrooms,
and ham).

Outdoor Activities and Sports

Cachoeiras Bonsucesso (⊠ Rua do Carmo, 7 km/4 mi north of town,
☎ 062/321–1217) are the most popular of the several waterfalls and
swimming holes in the Rio das Almas because they're the closest to
town. There's a campsite, soccer fields, beach volleyball courts, and
trails. The area is open daily 8–6, and an admission of R$3 is charged.

The historic sugar mill and farm house, **Fazenda Babilônia** (⊠ GO 431,
24 km/15 mi west of town, ☎ 062/9974–0026) has been a national
heritage site since 1965. Peek into Brazil's agricultural past—dominated
by the sugar and molasses trade for more than a century—and try the
café colonial goiano (Goiás brunchlike version of southern Brazil's café
colonial, an elaborate 5 PM tea). You can also go horseback riding on
the grounds. Note that the site is open only on weekends and holidays
from 8–5. Admission is R$2.

There are several parks right outside Pirenópolis, some with wonderful waterfalls, swimming holes, and trails. **Fazenda Vagafogo** (⊠ Rua
do Carmo, 6 km/4 mi north of town center, ☎ 062/9969–3090) is a
57-acre ecological preserve with a medium-size waterfall that crashes
into a natural pool, a small forest, hiking trails, and a little café near
the visitor center at the entrance (admission is R$3). The preserve is
open Tuesday through Sunday 8–5; the owner, Eduardo Ayer, serves
a highly recommended brunch of fruits and farm produce Friday
through Sunday.

The **Museu das Lavras de Ouro** (⊠ Km 2, Estrada dos Pireneus, ☎ no
phone) isn't a museum in the usual sense: a 1½-km (1-mi) trail on a

small farm winds along the wooded banks of the Rio das Almas (River of Souls). More than 200 years ago the whole area (more than 5 acres) was sifted and panned thoroughly by Portuguese gold seekers with the help of hundreds of Indian slaves. Aqueducts brought water downstream to aid the miners. You can still see the intricate maze of ditches, embankments, and rubble piles amid the vegetation. The owners of the small farm will guide you (admission is R$3) and know a lot about the history of the *lavras* (diggings) and the region's plants and wildlife. There's a swimming hole on Rio das Almas for when you need a break after walking the trail.

The **Reserva Ecológica Vargem Grande** (⊠ 11 km/7 mi along road to Parque Estadual da Serra dos Pireneus, ☎ 062/331–1171) is slightly out of the way, but this private nature preserve, open daily from 8:30 to 5, is worth the trip, with two incredible waterfalls as well as swimming holes in Ribeirãao do Inferno (Hell's Creek, a tributary of Rio das Almas). Admission is R$4.

Shopping
The number of art and antiques shops in Pirenópolis keeps growing, but the jewelry shops around the commercial district still remain the highlight of the town. **Ateliê Cláudia Azeredo** (⊠ Rua Direita 58, ☎ 62/331–1328) sells designer furniture and tapestries. **Galleria** (⊠ Rua do Bom Fim 18, ☎ 062/331–1483) sells jewelry made from gold, silver, and semiprecious stones. **Pica Pedra** (⊠ Beira Rio at Rua do Rosário, ☎ no phone) specializes in silver and stones, especially emeralds, amethysts and quartz. At **Shanti** (⊠ Rua do Bonfim 20, ☎ 62/9969–3161), you can shop for local handicrafts and indulge in an ice cream or an espresso.

Cidade de Goís

150 km (93 mi) northwest of Goiânia, 320 km (200 mi) west of Brasília.

The city of Goiás, better known as Goiás Velho, was founded in 1727 by the *bandeirantes* (explorers whose initial goals were to enslave Indians and, later, to capture African slaves who had escaped into the interior), who settled here when they found gold and diamonds. By order of the king of Portugal, a mint was built here in 1774 to process the large amounts of gold found in the Serra Dourada (Golden Sierra)—a mountain range surrounding the city. The town kept growing well into the 1800s, but became stagnant as the gold, silver, and gemstones disappeared.

It was the state's capital until 1937, when the government moved to a more central location in the new planned city of Goiânia; Goías seemingly lost its importance overnight. Thanks to this sudden downfall, most of the baroque-colonial architecture in the downtown area was preserved. The town has also completed a restoration project in which all the power lines in the area were buried and the stone pavement and several buildings were refurbished; UNESCO World Heritage Site status is forthcoming.

Cidade de Goiás is the site of the Procissão do Fogaréu (Fire Procession), a popular Holy Week celebration. Hooded participants toting burning stakes reenact Christ's descent from the cross and burial. In addition, much like Pirenópolis, Goiás is an important handicrafts center.

The **Chafariz de Cauda,** a baroque fountain, was built around 1778 to provide water for the population and the horses and mules that hauled supplies and gold. Water was drawn from the Chapéu de Padre mine and carried by ingenious pipes carved in stone blocks—some are on display at the Palácio Conde dos Arcos. ⊠ Praça Brasil Caiado s/n.

The handsome baroque **Igreja São Francisco de Paula,** built in 1761, is the oldest church in Goiás. The murals, depicting the life of St. Francis, were painted by local artist André da Conceição in 1870. You can view the church's interior Wednesday through Friday 1–5 and weekends 9–1. ⊠ *Praça Zacheu Alves de Castro s/n.* 🎟 *Free.* ☉ *Wed.–Fri. 1–5, weekends 9–1.*

The imposing two-story **Museu das Bandeiras** (circa 1766) housed the regional government, court, and jail for almost 200 years. There is a 20-minute guided tour that shows a cell, as well as a collection of vintage furniture, church relics, and indigenous artifacts. ⊠ *Praça Brasil Caiado s/n,* ☎ *062/371–1087.* 🎟 *R\$3.* ☉ *Tues.–Sat. 1–5, Sun. 8–noon.*

The **Palácio Conde dos Arcos** housed the Goiás executive government from 1755 until the capital moved to Goiânia in 1937. Now, the government returns here for three days every July in recognition of the city's historical importance. A guided tour highlights the state's and the city's history. ⊠ *Praça Tasso Camargo 1,* ☎ *062/371-1200.* 🎟 *R\$2.*

Casa de Cora Coralina. Cora Coralina (1889–1985), Goiás's most important poet, started writing at 19 but only published her first book when she was 75. The museum—a collection of her belongings, writings, and letters from fellow poets—is in the house owned by her family since 1784. ⊠ *Rua D. Cândido 20,* ☎ *062/371–1990,* ☉ *Tues.– Sat. 9–5, Sun. 8–noon.*

Dining and Lodging

¢–\$ ✕ **Flor do Ipê.** This simple, homey restaurant may be nondescript when it comes to decor, but it is the best place to experience *comida goiânia: arroz com pequi* (rice with berries) and *galinhada* (chicken and rice with spices and pequi). ⊠ *Rua Boa Vista 32-A,* ☎ *062/372–1133. No credit cards. Closed Mon. No dinner Sun.*

\$ 🏠 **Vila Boa.** On a hill outside town, this pousada has great views. Although accommodations are standard, this is the best option in town, and the staff makes every possible effort to make your stay comfortable. ⊠ *Av. Dr. Deusdete Ferreira de Moura, Morro do Chapéu de Padre,* ☎ *062/371–1000,* 🖷 *062/371–1000. 33 rooms. Restaurant, bar, pool, bicycles. No credit cards.*

Outdoor Activities and Sports

The hills of Serra Dourada are covered with dense forest and are a great place to hike. There are also waterfalls and swimming holes in the creeks and the Rio Vermelho (Red River). **Balneário Santo Antônio** (⊠ Km 125, GO-070) is a popular bathing spot near town. The Rio Vermelho also has rapids and a first-come-first-served camping site that is free. **Pé no Chão Excursionismo** (☎ 062/372–1782) organizes guided tours and rafting trips.

Shopping

Associação dos Artesãos de Goiás (⊠ Largo do Rosário, s/n, ☎ 062/ 371-1116) sells pottery, wicker, and terra-cotta pieces, all by local artists.

Cuiabá

934 km (580 mi) west of Goiânia.

The capital of Mato Grosso State is almost in the middle of nowhere. To give you an idea of how isolated the city really is: São Paulo is 1,615 km (1,000 mi) to the southwest; Brasília 1,130 km (700 mi) to the west; Porto Velho 1,456 km (900 mi) to the northeast. Originally settled in

THE PANTANAL

RIGHT IN THE MIDDLE of South America, the gigantic flood plain of the Rio Paraguay and its tributaries covers about 225,000 square km (140,000 square mi), two-thirds of which are in Brazil. Most land is still owned by ranching families who have been here for generations. The Portuguese began colonizing the area about 200 years ago; today it's home to more than 21 million head of cattle and some 4 million people. Yet there's still abundant wildlife in this mosaic of swamp, forest, and savanna. From your hub of an area *fazenda* (ranch) or lodge—where air-conditioning, swimming pools, and well-cooked meals are possibilities—you can experience the *pantaneiro* lifestyle, yet another manifestation of the cowboy culture. Folklore has it that the pantaneiro can communicate with the Pantanal animals.

It's widely held that the Pantanal is the best place to view wildlife in all of South America, and it is slated to become a UNESCO Biosphere Reserve. More than 600 species of birds live in the Pantanal during different migratory seasons, including *araras* (hyacinth macaws), fabulous blue-and-yellow birds that can be as long as 1 m (3 ft) from head to tail; larger-than-life rheas, which look and walk like aging modern ballerinas; the fantastically colored *tuiuiú*, an icon of the Pantanal, which build an intricate assemblage of nests (*ninhais*) on trees; as well as cormorants, ibises, herons, kingfishers, hawks, and egrets, to name a few. You're also sure to spot *capivaras* (capybaras; large South American rodents), tapirs, giant anteaters, marsh deer, maned wolves, otters, and one of the area's six species of monkey.

The countless *jacarés* (caiman alligators) would never dream of attacking, unless provoked. Blind, deaf, and lacking a sense of smell, caimans catch the fish they eat by following vibrations in the water. Poaching put these creatures on the verge of extinction—it takes four animals to make one pair of shoes—but intensive control by wildlife authorities has allowed the population to recover. Although it's hard to spot jaguars and pumas—one native guide reported having spotted no more than six big felines in his life—finding their tracks isn't uncommon. Though all trade in wild species has been illegal since 1967, poachers still prize these cats for their skins. Don't let scary tales about *sucuri* (anacondas), which can grow up to 9 m (30 ft) in length, worry you. They've only eaten a couple of humans since people started keeping track.

October is the beginning of the Pantanal's rainy season, which peaks in February but lasts through March. The land is much greener and more ravishing than at other times of the year, but the wildlife is harder to spot. In the dry season (July–October), when leaves fall and grasses die, land animal sightings are more frequent. As the waters continue to disappear, fish get caught in the remaining pools and attract a great variety of birds. The best fishing season is May through October, and considering the more than 240 varieties of fish in the area, anglers won't be disappointed. *Piraputanga* and *dourado* are the most prized catches, but the abundant *pacú*, *pintado*, and *traíra* are also popular. *Piranhas* are endemic to the area, but much like caymans, they seldom cause trouble. Just remember to check with locals before venturing into unknown waters.

the 18th century, when gold was found nearby, Cuiabá is now mostly known as the southernmost gateway to the Amazon and, more importantly, as the northern gateway to the Pantanal. You can visit one of several museums while you're waiting for a tour into these wetlands (arrangements usually take about a day).

The **Museu História Natural e Antropologia e Museu Histórico,** close to the center of town, is really a complex of museums with everything from ancient Indian artifacts to contemporary art. ⊠ *Palácio da Instrução, Praça da República,* ☎ *065/321–3391.* 🎫 *R$3.* ⊙ *Weekdays 12:30–5:30.*

Northeast of the town's main square is the **Museu de Pedras Ramis Bucair,** with a stunning collection of area fossils and stones (including what's purportedly a meteorite). ⊠ *Rua Galdino Pimentel 195.* 🎫 *R$5.* ⊙ *Weekdays 7–11 and 1–4.*

Slightly outside town is the **Museu do Indio/Museu Rondon.** Its displays include photos of and objects from the indigenous peoples—the Bororo, Pareci, Xavante, and Txukarramae—of Mato Grosso. The museum is at a university, whose grounds also contain a zoo populated by Pantanal wildlife. ⊠ *Av. Fernando Correia da Costa, 4 km/2 mi east of town,* ☎ *065/615–8489.* 🎫 *R$2.* ⊙ *Weekdays 8–11 and 2–5.*

Dining

$–$$ ✕ **Morro de St. Antônio.** This surf-and-turf place has a Polynesian vibe and caters to a yuppie crowd. Many entrées are enough for two people. Dinner is served nightly until 1 AM; on weekends, this is a good place to drink and be merry into the wee hours. ⊠ *Av. Isaac Póvoas 1167, Centro, Cuiabá,* ☎ *065/622–0502. AE, DC, MC, V.*

$ ✕ **Regionalíssimo.** Set in the same building as the Casa do Atesão, a shop filled with indigenous artifacts, this self-service eatery offers regional cuisine. After a hearty meal you can browse for ceramics, baskets, and wood handicrafts. ⊠ *13 de Junho 314, Porto, Cuiabá,* ☎ *065/322–4523. AE, DC, MC. Closed Mon. No dinner.*

¢–$$ ✕ **Papagaio Grill.** The menu here has some decent regional fare of simple meat and fish dishes, but the pasta is the big draw. The drinks are good, too—particularly the *caipirinhas* (cachaça, crushed lime, crushed ice, and sugar)—which may be why this place hops until almost dawn on weekends. (Dinner is served nightly until 2 AM.) The huge TV screen that looms over the tables, however, makes conversation difficult. ⊠ *Av. Mato Grosso 764, Centro, Cuiabá,* ☎ *065/621–1020. AE, DC, MC, V.*

¢–$ ✕ **Peixaria Popular.** This is the place for Pantanal fish; don't miss the
★ delicious *piraputanga,* either prepared in a stew or fried. Other options are the *pintado* (a large freshwater fish) and *pacu* (a small fish that resembles a piranha). All orders have a side serving of *pirão* and *banana frita* (fried bananas). ⊠ *Av. São Sebastião 2324, Goiabeiras, Cuiabá,* ☎ *065/322–5471. No credit cards.* ⊙ *No dinner weekends.*

¢ ✕ **Peixaria do Jairo.** This little *comida-por-quilo* (food-by-the-kilo) joint is good for a filling, affordable lunch or dinner. Its buffet has one regional specialty after another, and you pay (by weight) only for what you eat. Don't be shy about asking a staffer to explain the dishes to you. ⊠ *Rua Cândido Mariano at Comandante Costa, Centro, Cuiabá,* ☎ *065/321–7485. MC, V.* ⊙ *No dinner Sat.–Mon.*

Lodging

CUIABÁ

$–$$ 🏨 **Eldorado Cuiabá.** A vision of glass and brass (no gold, as the name would suggest), this hotel in the center of town has some of the best rooms. You'll appreciate the pleasant decor, air-conditioning, and cable TV—particularly after staying at a sparse Pantanal fazenda. Don't miss the giant birdcage beside the pool; it's an easy way to see toucans and macaws up close. ⊠ *Av. Isaac Póvoas 1000, Centro 78045-640,* ☎ *065/624-4000 and 0800/17-1888,* FAX *065/624-1480. 141 rooms, 6 suites. Restaurant, bar, air-conditioning, pool, shops, convention center. AE, DC, MC, V.*

$ 🏨 **Paiaguás Palace.** Rooms are simple and rather small but charming. The top-floor restaurant is highly regarded by local businesspeople and has good views—on clear nights you can see the plains. Location is one of its main draws; it's right in the business district with easy access to the airport. ⊠ *Av. Rubens de Mendonça 1718, Bosque da Saúde,* ☎ *065/642-5353,* FAX *065/642-5910,* WEB *www.hotelpaiaguas.com.br. 121 rooms. Restaurant, bar, gym, business services, travel agency. AE, DC, MC, V. CP.*

¢ 🏨 **Jaguar Palace.** Location is key at this high-rise: it's close enough to everything but far enough removed to offer a peaceful night's sleep. Rooms are small and somewhat outdated, but everything is well kept by the attentive staff. Another highlight here is the lavish breakfast buffet. ⊠ *Av. Getúlio Vargas 600, Centro,* ☎ *065/624-4404,* FAX *065/623-7798. 82 rooms, 9 suites. Restaurant, bar, pool, meeting room, travel agency. AE, DC, MC, V. CP*

THE PANTANAL

$ 🏨 **Cabanas do Pantanal.** This Pantanal resort offers two- to three-night packages that include transportation to and from Cuiabá; its main draw is its fishing trips. Though not very charming, the cabins are fairly modern and have private baths. The resort's location makes it an excellent base for exploring the wetlands and for spotting wildlife. ⊠ *42 km/26 mi south of Poconé (144 km/90 mi south of Cuiabá) on Porto Cercado road,* ☎ *065/721-1924 in Cuiabá,* FAX *065/623-8880. 18 cabins. Restaurant, pool, hiking, boating, fishing, horseback riding. MC, V. FAP.*

$ 🏨 **Pantanal Mato Grosso.** On the Transpantaneira Highway, this member of the local Mato Grosso chain is one of the northern Pantanal's more upscale choices. Its rooms may be sparsely decorated, but they're comfortable enough (all are air-conditioned) to make your stay pleasant. The hotel can arrange fishing expeditions, guided treks on horseback or on foot, and trips by small airplane for a bird's-eye view of the wetlands. Two- to four-night packages are available; just be sure to book ahead, particularly in high season. ⊠ *Km 65, Rodovia Transpantaneira, Pixaim,* ☎ FAX *065/968-6205 and 065/614-7500. 35 rooms. Restaurant, pool, hiking, horseback riding, boating, marina, fishing, private airstrip, airport shuttle. AE, DC, MC, V. FAP.*

¢ 🏨 **Pousada Pixaim.** This small, low-key pousada is a great choice for budget travelers. Halfway to Porto Jofre at the end of Transpantaneira Highway, the inn makes a great stopover on a bumpy adventure through the Pantanal. The wooden cabins, which are on stilts, sleep three people and are far from deluxe (though they do have private baths). Guided boat and horseback riding excursions are available. ⊠ *Km 61, Rodovia Transpantaneira, Pixaim,* ☎ *065/721-2091; 065/721-1172 reservations in Cuiabá,* FAX *065/623-5329. 8 cabins. Restaurant, horseback riding, boating. No credit cards. CP.*

Nightlife

On weekends, two restaurants, Morro de St. Antonio and Papagaio Grill, stay open late just to serve drinks and encourage revelry. Toward the newer part of the city, along Avenida C.P.A. and sidestreets, you'll find many sports bars and nightclubs. If you're looking for a wholesome evening, try one of the many ice-cream parlors, such as **Alaska** (⊠ Rua Pedro Celestino 215). Check out **Entrentanto** (⊠ Av. Lava-Pés 500), which is set up like a biergarten and has daily performances of Brazilian and international pop music.

Shopping

For Indian handicrafts, try the **Casa do Artesão** (⊠ 13 de Junho at Rua Senador Metello, ☎ 065/321–0603). If you're beginning to feel the power of South America's geodesic center radiating from the Chapada dos Guimarães, head for **Flora Guarani** (⊠ Av. Duarte 689-B, ☎ 067/983–7109). The proprietor, Everaldo, sells candles, herbal remedies, and concoctions that seem an awful lot like magic potions. For rocks, visit the shop inside the **Museu de Pedras Ramis Bucair** (⊠ Rua Galdino Pimentel 195).

Chapada dos Guimarães

74 km (40 mi) north of Cuiabá.

This quasi-mystical mesa is the area's most popular attraction after the Pantanal, and much of it is protected by a national park. Along the road to the town from Cuiabá you'll pass the **Portão do Inferno** (Hell's Gate), a scenic viewpoint over the chasm that was created when the mesa was formed. Beyond the Portão do Inferno, you'll come to the park's visitor center (⊠ Km 13, MT 251, ☎ 065/791–1133), which is open daily 8–5. One step from the visitor center, the **Cachoeira Véu de Noiva** (Bridal Veil Falls), with a 250-ft freefall, is the most impressive of the five falls. You can enjoy lunch at the nearby open-air restaurant. Beyond this point there are hills, caves, more falls, and archeological sites. Admission to the park is R$3.

In the town of Chapada dos Guimarães, the **Igreja de Nossa Senhora de Santana do Sacramento** (⊠ Praça Central) is a handsome colonial church (circa 1779) with some exceptional gold-plated interior flourishes. Just 8 km (5 mi) beyond the center of town you'll come to a site that has made this chapada a spiritual mecca for the New Age set, the **Mirante do Ponto Geodésico.** In 1972, a satellite photograph proved that the continent's true center was not in Cuiabá, where a monument had been built, but right here, on the mesa's edge. If the geodesic center doesn't hold spiritual meaning for you, come for the fantastic vista; on a clear day, you can see as far as the Pantanal. If you have time, arrange a guided visit to **Caverna Aroe Jari,** 45 km (30 mi) to the east on the gravel road to Campo Verde. The cave's name means "home of souls" in the Bororo language. This mile-long sandstone cave (one of Brazil's largest) can only be reached after a 4.8-km (3-mi) hike through the cerrado.

Dining and Lodging

$ ✕ **O Mestrinho.** Both day-trippers and locals pack this self-service, all-you-can-eat restaurant, making it the liveliest place in town. Everyone in the split-level dining room seems to get up at once whenever something new is brought from the kitchen (try to avoid a table near the buffet). The feijoada here is especially tasty. Obviously, Pantanal fish is available. ⊠ *Rua Quinco Caldas 119,* ☎ *065/791–1181. V. No dinner Sun.–Tues.*

$ ✕ **Nivo's Tour Restaurant.** The restaurant is true to its motto, "*Qualidade: Ingrediente Fundamental de Boa Cozinha*" ("Quality: the Basic Ingredient of Good Cooking"). The fish entrées such as pacu and *dourado* are delicious, always served with pirão. ⊠ *Praça Dom Wunibaldo 63,* ☎ *065/791–1284. V. Closed Mon. No dinner.*

$ 🏠 **Pousada Penhasco.** Clinging to the mesa's edge, this small resort may be far from the Chapada dos Guimarães's town center, but it has tremendous views of the cerrado. The sunny rooms are in cabins scattered about the property. All rooms have access to verandas with great vistas. The staff frequently arranges soccer matches at the on-site field and en masse outings to area sights. If you want to explore on your own, you can borrow a bike. ⊠ *Av. Penhasco s/n, Bom Clima,* ☎ *065/ 624–1000 in Cuiabá;* ☎ FAX *065/301–1555,* WEB *www.penhasco.com.br. 18 rooms. Restaurant, bar, pool, sauna, hiking, soccer, bicycles, meeting rooms. AE, DC, MC, V. CP.*

Campo Grande

1025 km (638 mi) west of São Paulo, 694 km (430 mi) south of Cuiabá.

Nicknamed the Cidade Morena (Brunette City) because of the reddish-brown earth on which it sits, this relatively young city (founded in 1899) was made the capital of Mato Grosso do Sul in 1978, when the state separated from Mato Grosso. Campo Grande's economy traditionally relied on ranching, but in the 1970s farmers from the south settled in the region, plowed the flat lands, and forever changed the landscape. Now ecotourism is booming in the region: as the gateway to the southern Pantanal and the town of Bonito, Campo Grande receives a growing number of foreign and Brazilian visitors each year.

The **Museo Dom Bosco (Museu do Índio)** has taxidermy exhibits and more than 5,000 indigenous artifacts. Don't miss the bug room, whose walls are covered from floor to ceiling with insects of every type. If you find these critters more horrifying than fascinating, retreat to the room filled only with butterflies. ⊠ *Rua Barão do Rio Branco 1843, facing Praça do República,* ☎ *067/721–1090.* ☜ *R$2.* ☉ *Weekdays 8–6, Sat. 8–5, Sun. 8–11:30 and 1:30–5.*

To get acquainted with Mato Grosso's indigenous population—which numbers more than 50,000—visit the **Memorial da Cultura Indigena,** a 25-ft-high maloca (Indian hut) built in the middle of a modern-day urban Indian reservation (Aldeia Marçal de Souza). You can watch children from the reservation school perform traditional dances, and shop for pottery and tapestries. ⊠ *Road to Três Lagoa, Tiradentes,* ☎ *067/ 725–4822.*

OFF THE BEATEN PATH — **CORUMBÁ –** Eight hours by bus from Campo Grande, and just 11.2 km (7 mi) from Bolivia on the Rio Paraguai's banks, is the port city of Corumbá. The city can be rightfully called the the "capital of the Pantanal," where you can arrange river trips or wetland treks upon arrival. Consider staying at the reasonably priced **Nacional Palace** (⊠ Rua América 936, ☎ 067/231–6868, FAX 067/231 6202, WEB www.brum.com.br/ nacional.html AE, DC, MC, V), which has all the amenities you could want in a steamy swamp town. The **Santa Mônica Palace** (⊠ Rua Antônio Maria Coelho 345, ☎ 067/231–3001, FAX 067/231–7880, WEB www.pantanalnet.com.br/stmonica/ AE, DC, MC, V) is another good hotel with all the necessary comforts. The staffs at both hotels can make arrangements for trips into the wetlands.

Dining

$–$$ ✕ **Centurion.** Campo Grande's best restaurant, in a colonial-style ★ house, serves eclectic fare with a strong leaning toward the regional cuisine. The standout here is the *pintado grelhado ao molho de laranja* (grilled pintado with orange sauce). The shrimp with curry sauce is also recommended. ⊠ *Rua Pedro Celestino 1641,* ☎ *067/725–8339. AE, DC, MC, V.*

$ ✕ **Costelaria Gaúcho Gastão.** Once you've had your fill of Pantanal fish, this popular rodízio-style churrascaria provides the perfect contrast. One meal and you'll see why the state has a such a reputation for its high-quality lean beef. ⊠ *Rua Allan Kardec 238,* ☎ *067/724– 8851. No credit cards.*

Close-Up

OTHERWORLDLY VISITORS

MANY BELIEVE THAT THE CERRADO and the Chapada dos Guimarães (south of the 15th parallel) are landing spots of choice for UFOs. This assertion goes back to Brasília's early days, when an air force officer claimed that his weekend home just outside the city was one such spot. A popular story in the Chapada tells of a bus left powerless for several minutes after being encircled by beams of colored light.

In 1996, officials in Barra do Garças, 420 km (260 mi) northwest of Brasília on the Goiás–Mato Grosso border, designated 12 acres for the world's first UFO "airport"—the Interspace Aerodrome. Though the aerodrome was never built, the publicity it received fueled the notion that the cerrado is a hotbed of UFO activity.

In mid-1997, members of a small farming community 258 km (160 mi) northeast of Cuiabá were convinced that a local farmer and his son were hiding aliens after a fiery ball was seen to crash on their property. The next year people all over the west, from Campo Grande to Cuiabá, reported seeing a large, shiny cylinder pass silently overhead. Other mass and individual sightings have been reported, as have alien abductions. Many cerrado residents will warn you to be wary of nighttime attacks . . . not by jaguars, but by aliens.

¢–$$ ✕ **Radio Clube.** One of the fancier places in town, this restaurant-nightclub adds some energy to the somewhat lifeless Praça da República. You can stop by for a drink or a meal of Continental fare. ✉ *Rua Pedro João Cripa 1280,* ☎ *067/721–0131. AE, DC, MC, V. Closed Mon.*

Lodging

CAMPO GRANDE

$ ☷ **Campo Grande Hotel.** This futuristic concrete structure has the friendliest staffers in town (they *love* to practice their English). Rooms are as comfortable and appealing as any in the more expensive hotels. ✉ *Rua 13 de Maio 2825, 79002-351,* ☎ *067/384–6061 or 067/384–6961,* FAX *067/724–8349. 84 rooms, 4 suites. Restaurant, bar, air-conditioning, minibars, business services, meeting room. AE, DC, MC, V.*

$ ☷ **Jandaia.** The Jandaia is so thoroughly modern that it almost seems out of place in this wild-west town. Though it has little character—it's geared toward businesspeople, so convenience wins over aesthetics—it does have all the facilities and amenities you'd expect of a deluxe hotel. The upscale Imperium restaurant, on the second floor, serves international fare with Brazilian options. ✉ *Rua Barão do Rio Branco 1271, 79002-174,* ☎ *067/721–7000,* FAX *067/721–1401,* WEB *www.jandaia.com.br. 130 rooms, 10 suites. 2 restaurants, bar, pool, gym, meeting room. AE, DC, MC, V.*

¢ ☷ **Hotel Internacional.** Though modest, this budget option is clean and well maintained; what's more, management doesn't feel compelled to jack up the rates just because there's a pool. The dormitorylike rooms have firm single beds, TVs, and en-suite bathrooms. The only problem here is the location near the bus station—a part of town that can be dangerous at night. ✉ *Rua Allan Kardac 223, 79008-330,* ☎ *067/*

784–4677, FAX *067/721–2729. 100 rooms. Restaurant, bar, pool. AE, DC, MC, V.*

THE PANTANAL

$$–$$$ 🏨 **Caiman Ecological Refuge.** This 100,000-plus-acre ranch pioneered
★ the idea of sustainable land use and ecological awareness in the early
1980s, and it remains one of the Pantanal's top lodges. The service is
excellent—from the professional manner of the kitchen and bar staffs
to the knowledgeable guides, all of whom hold a degree in biology or
a related science and most of whom speak English. What's more, they
clearly love what they do and are sincerely interested in your well-being.
Rooms, which have such amenities as private baths and air-conditioning,
are in one of four lodges. Opt for a room in the Sede Lodge (main lodge),
which has the nicest common areas and the best location. Pousada Ba-
iazinha, the lodge that's surrounded almost entirely by water, has its
charms, too. Activities include horseback rides through the wetlands,
boat trips to islands on the refuge's vast holdings, night rides in open
vehicles to see nocturnal animals, and video and slide shows. Excursions are accompanied by at least one multilingual staffer who can answer most questions about flora and fauna, and a local guide who knows
the terrain. The schedule of activities also allows ample time for relaxation and dips in the pool. Though steep, the price includes meals
and bus transfers in and out of Campo Grande's airport. A minimum
two-day stay is recommended though not required. ⊠ *North of Miranda, 235 km (146 mi) west of Campo Grande,* ☎ *067/687–2102;
011/3079–6622 reservations in São Paulo,* FAX *067/687–2103; 011/3079–
6037 in São Paulo,* WEB *www.caiman.com.br. 29 rooms. Restaurant,
bar, pool, hiking, horseback riding, boating, private airstrip. AE, DC,
MC, V. FAP.*

$$ 🏨 **Fazenda Rio Negro.** The good regional food is only one of the high-
lights of this rustic but charming century-old farmhouse. Although fa-
cilities aren't up to international hotel standards, all rooms have baths.
The abundant wildlife, knowledgeable guides, and the chance to ex-
perience the *pantaneiro* (Pantanal cowboy) lifestyle are the true draws.
The only way to reach this 25,000-acre property is by plane (a roughly
R$650 flight) from either Campo Grande or Corumbá. ⊠ *About 200
km (125 mi) northwest of Campo Grande,* ☎ FAX *067/751–5191; 067/
751–5248 for reservations in Campo Grande,* WEB *www.rio-negro.com.
9 rooms. Restaurant, hiking, horseback riding, boating, private airstrip.
No credit cards. FAP.*

Nightlife

Campo Grande is wilder than Cuiabá; parts of town (particularly the
area near the bus station) are downright dangerous and best avoided
at night. On the better side of the tracks is **4 Mil** (⊠ Av. Afonso Pena
4000, ☎ no phone), a bar frequented by young hipsters. **Iris** (⊠ Av.
Afonso Pena 1975, ☎ 067/784–6002) is one of the few cybercafés in
the west. You can surf the Web (for about R$14 per hour) every night
'til 10, or leaf through one of the week-old English-language maga-
zines. The nightclub **Nix** (⊠ Av. Afonso Pena near corner of 25 de Dezem-
bro, ☎ no phone) is a hot spot in the safe part of town.

Shopping

For baskets of all shapes, beautiful wood handicrafts, and interesting
ceramics made by Pantanal Indians, head to **Casa de Artesão** (⊠ Rua
Calógeras 2050 at Av. Afonso Pena, ☎ 067/383–2633). It's open
weekdays 8–6 and Saturday 8–noon. The **Feria Indígena,** adjacent to
the Mercado Central and just across Avenida Afonso Pena from the
Casa de Artesão, is also a good place to shop for locally made crafts.
It operates Tuesday–Sunday 8–5. The massive **Shopping Campo Grande**

(⌧ Av. Afonso Pena 4909) has everything you'd expect in an American- or European-style mall—from a Carrefours department store to a food court with McDonald's. The many boutiques are what make this place shine, though.

Bonito

277 km (172 mi) southwest of Campo Grande.

The region around this small town of 15,000 (literally and rightfully named "Beautiful") is a great stopover before you head out to the overland stretch west from Campo Grande and on to the southern Pantanal. Here you can swim and snorkel among schools of colorful fish in the headwaters of several Pantanal rivers, which has some of the world's clearest waters. Rafting and spelunking are other options.

At **Parque Ecológico Baía Bonita,** you can go snorkeling along a 900-yard section of the Baía Bonita River, where you can see an incredible diversity of fish. ⌧ *Km 7, Estrada para Jardim.* ☞ *R$45 (equipment rental included).*

The 160-ft-deep **Gruta do Lago Azul** (Blue Lagoon Grotto) has a crystal-clear freshwater lake where you can see a rare type of bottom-feeding albino shrimp. The best time to visit is from mid-December to mid-January, when sunlight beams down the entrance, reflecting off the walls to create a staggering spectacle of lights. ⌧ *Fazenda Jaraguá, 20 km/12.4 mi from Bonito on the road to Campo dos Índios.* ☞ *R$10.*

Dining and Lodging

$–$$ ✕🖫 **Resort Hotel Zagaia.** This resort has international-class facilities that
★   are welcome both for short and longer stays. The rooms are large and cozy, with colorful furnishings. Be sure to ask for a room with a view of the gardens and forest-covered hills that lie beyond the complex. The restaurants serve international fare, but Pantanal fish is also available. ⌧ *Km 0, Rodovia Bonito–Três Morros,* ☎ *067/255–1280; 0800/6777 for reservations,* FAX *067/255–1710,* WEB *www.zagaia.com.br. 36 rooms, 30 suites. 2 restaurants, bar, 3 pools, hair salon, massage, sauna, tennis court, gym, hiking, horseback riding, soccer, volleyball, bicycles, shops, meeting rooms, travel services, helipad. AE, DC, MC, V. FAP.*

BRASÍLIA AND THE WEST A TO Z

To research prices, get advice from other travelers, and book travel arrangements, visit www.fodors.com.

AIR TRAVEL

CARRIERS

Airlines that serve Brasília include American Airlines, British Airways, Canadian Airlines, Rio-Sul/Nordeste, and TAM. Three regional carriers serve the West: TAM, Varig, and VASP.

➤ AIRLINES AND CONTACTS: **American Airlines** (☎ 061/321–3322). **British Airways** (☎ 061/327–2333). **Canadian Airlines** (☎ 061/328–9203). **Rio-Sul/Nordeste** (☎ 061/242–4099). **TAM** (☎ 061/365–1000 in Brasília, 062/207–4539 in Goiânia, 065/682–3650 in Cuiabá, or 067/763–4100 in Campo Grande). **Transbrasil** (☎ 061/365–1188 or 061/365–1618). **Varig** (☎ 061/327–3455 in Brasília, 062/207–1743 in Goiânia, 065/682–1140 in Cuiabá, 067/763-0000 in Campo Grande, or 0800/99–7000 nationwide). **VASP** (☎ 061/365–1425 in Brasília, 062/207–1350 in Goiânia, 065/682–3737 in Cuiabá, 067/763–2389 in Campo Grande, or 0800/99–8277 nationwide).

AIRPORTS AND TRANSFERS

The Aeroporto Internacional de Brasília, 12 km (7 mi) west of the Eixo Monumental, is considered South America's first "intelligent" airport, with computer-controlled communications and baggage-handling operations.

Major western airports are Aeroporto Santa Genoveva, 6 km (4 mi) northeast of Goiâna; Aeroporto Marechal Rondon, 7 km (4 mi) south of Cuiabá; and Aeroporto International de Campo Grande, 7 km (4 mi) west of Campo Grande.

➤ AIRPORT INFORMATION: **Aeroporto Internacional de Brasília** (☎ 061/365–1224). **Aeroporto International de Campo Grande** (☎ 067/763–2444). **Aeroporto Marechal Rondon** (☎ 065/682–2213). **Aeroporto Santa Genoveva** (☎ 062/265–1500).

AIRPORT TRANSFERS

To get from the international airport in Brasília to the city center, taxis are your only real option (city buses, which cost about R$1, don't have room for your luggage). Trips to the hotel sectors along the Eixo Monumental take roughly 15 minutes and cost about R$23. Double-check costs at the dispatcher booth near the arrival gate, and reconfirm the fare with your driver.

The western airports are all close to their respective cities, so a taxi is your best bet. The fare into Goiânia and Campo Grande is about R$11; into Cuiabá it's R$16. Though buses (about R$1.16) serve the airports, they don't have space for luggage and often pull up well away from the terminals. To use them, you need to understand each city's layout fairly well.

BUS TRAVEL

BRASÍLIA

The interstate bus station, the Estação Rodoferroviária, is at the westernmost tip of the Eixo Monumental. For trips to Goiânia (3 hrs), try Araguaina. Expresso São Luiz buses make the 12-hour journey to Cuiabá. To make the 14-hour trip to São Paulo, try Real. Itapemirim buses run to and from Rio de Janeiro (17 hrs) and Belo Horizonte (11 hrs).

Within the city itself, virtually all buses depart from Estação Rodoviária at the Eixo Monumental. Route names (usually coinciding with the final destination) and departing times appear on digital displays. Rides within the Plano Piloto cost about R$1. There are also a few air conditioned express buses, which make fewer stops and cost about R$2.50. Of these, the Terminal Rodoferroviária and Palácio da Alvorada buses are good for sightseeing along the Eixo Monumental.

➤ BUS INFORMATION: **Araguaina** (☎ 061/233–7566 or 0800/62–1011). **Estação Rodoferroviária** (☎ 061/233–7200). **Expresso São Luiz** (☎ 061/233–7961). **Itapemirim** (☎ 061/361–4505 or 0800/99–2627). **Real** (☎ 061/361–4555).

THE WEST

Although the distances in the west are great, buses remain the primary mode of transportation owing to high airfares and limited air service. Goiânia's rodoviária is in the Norte Ferroviário sector. Cuiabá's rodoviária is in the Alvorada neighborhood north of the city center. Campo Grande's rodoviária is at the corner of Dom Aquino and Joaquim Nabuco.

A dazzling array of companies offers regular bus service connecting Brasília and Goiânia (3 hrs/R$23), Goiânia and Cuiabá (13 hrs/R$70), Goiânia and Cidade de Goiás (2½ hrs/R$16), Cuiabá and Campo Grande (10 hrs/R$50), Cuiabá and Chapada dos Guimarães (2 hrs/R$9), and Campo Grande and Corumbá (7 hrs/R$46). There's less frequent service between Brasília and Pirenópolis (2½ hrs/$3) and Pirenópolis and Goiânia (2 hrs/R$16).

Andorinha has frequent service between Campo Grande and Corumbá. Auto Viação Goinésia operates most of the buses between Pirenópolis and both Brasília and Goiânia.

The major western cities are fairly compact, so you won't need to worry about taking a bus except perhaps to the airport or the interstate bus depot. The one exception is Campo Grande, where the shopping area is quite a distance east along Avenida Afonso Pena. Bus fares in all the western cities are about R$1.20. Try to have the exact fare available when you board because the space between the door and the area where the conductor takes your money quickly gets crowded and claustrophobic.
➤ Bus INFORMATION: **Andorinha** (⊠ Corner of Dom Aquino and Joaquim Nabuco, upstairs inside Rodoviária, Campo Grande, ☎ 067/383–5314). **Auto Viação Goinésia** (⊠ Terminal Rodoviário "L" Norte, Brasília, ☎ 061/562–0720). **Campo Grande's Rodoviária** (⊠ ☎ 067/783–1678). **Cuiabá's Rodoviária** (⊠ Av. Marechal Deodoro, ☎ 065/621–2429). **Goiânia's Rodoviária** (⊠ Av. Goiás, ☎ 062/224–8466).

CAR RENTAL
In Brasília, a compact car with air-conditioning and insurance will cost about R$116 a day. Area rental agencies include Avis, Hertz, Localiza, and Unidas. Rental companies with offices in the western region include Avis, Hertz, Localiza, and Unidas.
➤ MAJOR AGENCIES: **Avis** (☎ 061/365–2344 in Brasília or 0800/55–8066 nationwide). **Hertz** (☎ 061/365–2816 in Brasília or 0800/14–7300 nationwide).
➤ LOCAL AGENCIES: **Localiza** (☎ 061/365–2782 in Brasília or 0800/99–2000 nationwide). **Unidas** (☎ 061/365–2266 in Brasília or 0800/12–1211 nationwide).

CAR TRAVEL
BRASÍLIA
Brasília is connected with the rest of the country by several major highways. BR 050 is the shortest way south to São Paulo (1,015 km/632 mi). From the city of Cristalina (113 km/70 mi south of Brasília), it's another 612 km (380 mi) to Belo Horizonte on BR 040. The westbound route, BR 060, runs to Goiânia and the Pantanal and intersects with BR 153, the north–south Transbrasiliana Highway, which stretches another 1,930 km (1,200) mi north to Belém in the Amazon. BR 020 runs northeast from Brasília to Salvador (1,450 km/900 mi).

The capital was originally designed for cars. Until recently, wide north–south and east–west multilane highways—with their nifty cloverleafs, overpasses, and exits—allowed quick access to all major points. Nowadays, you can expect traffic jams at rush hour. Parking is easy in the residential areas but can be tricky in the commercial sectors.

THE WEST
Driving isn't recommended in most western cities, as Brazilian drivers are frightening in their disregard for signs, stop lights, and basic rules of the road. If you do rent a car, expect to pay about R$92–R$137 per day for a VW Golf (very popular in Brazil) with unlimited mileage. Insurance is necessary, so be sure to ask about it when getting a quote, and opt for the most comprehensive coverage possible. Note that many of the large urban hotels have free parking.

Most routes within the west aren't paved, and Brazilian drivers usually pack onto those that are. Further, getting around on your own by car is difficult without a very good working knowledge of Portuguese. Outside the cities, few people speak English, making it hard to get directions if you get lost. In short, it's best to avoid traveling to and within the west by car. With the exception of the paved BR 163, which skirts the Pantanal's eastern edge from Cuiabá to Campo Grande and is in fairly good condition, the roads near the Pantanal aren't in great shape. The Transpantaneira Highway goes well into the Pantanal, from Cuiabá to Porto Jofre, a dead-end smack in the middle of the wetlands. This "highway" is mostly a dirt road with at least 126 log bridges that allow the annual floods to flow without washing away the road. Even during dry season, traversing the Transpantaneira is time-consuming and dangerous. Whole bridges have caved in while cars pass over them. It's best to join an organized tour with experienced guides.

EMBASSIES

In Brasília, embassies have their own sectors (Setores das Embaixadas), and most of them are south of the Eixo Monumental, hence the abbreviation *SES* in their addresses.

➤ CONTACTS: **Australia** (✉ SHIS, Q. 9, Cj. 01, Casa 1, ☎ 061/248–5523 or 061/248–5569). **Canada** (✉ SES, Av. da Nações, Lt. 16, ☎ 061/321–2171). **United Kingdom** (✉ SES, Av. da Nações, Q. 801, Cj. K, Lt. 8, ☎ 061/225–2710 or 061/225–2625). **United States** (✉ SES, Av. da Nações, Q. 801, Lt. 3, ☎ 061/321–7272).

EMERGENCIES

In Brasília, Drogaria Rosário is open 24 hours a day and has delivery service. There's a late-night pharmacy in Cuiabá near the corner of Avenida Getúlio Vargas and Rua Joaquim Murtinho. In Campo Grande, try the late-night pharmacy at the corner of Avenida Afonso Pena and Rua 14 de Julho. Elsewhere in the region, use the 24-Hour Pharmacy Hotline.

➤ CONTACTS IN BRASÍLIA: **Drogaria Rosário** (✉ SHCS 102, Bl. C, Lj. 05, ☎ 061/323–5901 or 061/323–1818 for deliveries). **Hospital de Base do Distrito Federal** (✉ S. Hospitalar Sul, ☎ 061/225–0070).

➤ CONTACTS IN THE WEST: **Hospital Ernestina Lopes Jayme** (✉ Rua dos Pirineus, Pirenópolis, ☎ 062/331–1530). **Hospital Santo Antônio** (✉ Rua Quinco Caldas, Chapada dos Guimarães, ☎ 065/791–1116). **Hospital Santa Casa** (✉ Rua Eduardo Santos Pereira 88, Campo Grande, ☎ 067/721–5151). **Hospital Santa Casa** (✉ Praça Seminário 141, Cuiabá, ☎ 065/624–4222). **Hospital Santa Helena** (✉ Rua 95 No. 99, S. Sul, Goiânia, ☎ 062/219–9000).

➤ GENERAL NUMBERS: **Ambulance** (☎ 192). **Fire** (☎ 193). **Police** (☎ 190). **Tropical Disease Control Hotline** (☎ 061/225–8906). **24-Hour Pharmacy Hotline** (☎ 132).

ENGLISH-LANGUAGE MEDIA

In Brasília, Livraria Saraiva has the best selection of English-language books, magazines, and newspapers. Livraria Sodiler is also a good choice for magazines and paperbacks. Elsewhere in the west, English-language reading material is hard to come by, but try newsstands at the airports.

➤ BOOKSTORES: **Livraria Saraiva** (✉ SCS, Q. 1, Bl. H, Lj. 28, ☎ 061/323–4115). **Livraria Sodiler** (✉ Aeroporto Internacional, Upper Concourse, EC 14, ☎ 061/365–1967).

HEALTH

In Brasília and throughout the west, stick to bottled water (and check that restaurants use it to make juice and ice). You should have a long chat with your doctor before heading to the west. Malaria is a concern, yellow fever even more so. It's best to get a yellow fever shot before arriving, but if you decide to travel at the last minute, there's a clinic in Cuiabá's airport that offers free vaccinations. (It's on the second floor, right near the stairwell, and is open 8:45–5). Dengue fever—for which there is no vaccination or preventive medication—is also a concern in the cities around the Pantanal. Taking Vitamin B supplements a few days before and during your stay will help to fend off mosquitoes. Also, be sure to use insect repellant with DEET at all times, preferably from home (word is that area mosquitoes aren't deterred by local sprays).

MAIL, INTERNET, AND SHIPPING

Fax services are available at major *correio* (post office) branches. Although Brazil has more people on the Internet than any other single country in South America, most of them don't live in the west. The few hotels with business centers have only the slowest Internet dial-up connections; cybercafés are virtually nonexistent (there is one in Campo Grande).

Each of the region's major cities has a post office. Goiânia's post office is northeast of the civic center, just off Avenida Tocantins. The Cuiabá post office is in the middle of town, just south of the tourist office; there's also a small branch on the second floor of the airport. There are two centrally located branches of the Campo Grande post office.

➤ Major Shipping Service: **DHL** (✉ SCS, Q. 06, Bl. A, Suite 1A, Brasília, ☎ 061/225–9263).

➤ Post Offices: **Brasília post office** (✉ SBN, Q. 1, Bl. A, Brasília). **Campo Grande post office** (✉ Av. Calógeras 2309, at corner of Rua Dom Aquino; ✉ Rua Barão do Rio Branco, across from bus depot). **Cuiabá post office** (✉ Praça da República). **Goiânia post office** (✉ Praça Civica 11).

MONEY MATTERS

You'll find major banks equipped with ATMs (dispensing reais) in the capital and most parts of the west (Chapada dos Guimarães is a notable exception). Note, however, that they run primarily on the Plus network; if your card is only affiliated with Cirrus, plan accordingly. Banco do Brasil is the best for cashing traveler's checks, with relatively low fees and decent exchange rates. Throughout the region, the better hotels will either exchange money for you (though rates aren't always great) or tip you off to the area's best *casas de câmbio* (exchange houses).

In Goiânia, the BankBoston across from the Castro's Park Hotel has an ATM. Goiânia's main Banco do Brasil is open weekdays 10–6; there's also one at the airport. In Pirenópolis, Banco do Brasil has 24-hour ATMs.

Banco do Brasil's main Cuiabá branch is in the middle of town and is open weekdays 10–4, with 24-hour ATMs; there are also ATMs at the airport. Several little câmbios line Rua Cândido Mariano, including Guimel He Tour, which is open weekdays 8:30–6 and offers good rates.

All the major banks have offices in the center of Campo Grande, along Avenida Afonso Pena. Try Banco do Brasil, which is open weekdays 10–5; there are also a branch and several ATMs at the airport.

➤ Contacts: **American Express** (✉ Beltour, CLS 410, Bl. A, Lj. 29, Brasília, ☎ 061/244–5577). **Banco do Brasil** (✉ SBN, Q. 01, Bl. A, Brasília, ☎ 061/310–2000; ✉ Aeroporto Internacional, Brasília, ☎ 061/365–1183; ✉ Av. Afonso Pena at Rua 13 de Maio, Campo Grande; ✉ Av. Getúlio Vargas and Rua Barão de Melgaço, Cuiabá; ✉ Av. Goiás 980, Centro, Goiânia; ✉ Av. Sizenando Jayme 15, Centro, Pirenópolis). **BankBoston** (✉ SCS, Q. 06, Bl. A, Lj. 200, Brasília, ☎ 061/321–7714 or 0800/55–1784). **Citibank** (✉ SCS, Q. 06, Bl. A, Lj. 186,

Brasília, ☎ 061/225–9250). **Guimel He Tour** (✉ Rua Cândido Mariano 402, Cuiabá). **Kammoun Câmbio** (✉ SHS, Q. 3, Bl. J, Brasília, ☎ 061/321–1983).

SAFETY

Although Brasília doesn't have as much crime as Rio and São Paulo, be cautious at night and at any time on buses or in bus terminals. For the most part, the western cities are safe, but—as in Brasília—you should always be cautious when going out at night, particularly near bus terminals. The southern and western parts of Goiânia are safest. In Cuiabá, steer clear of the embankment at night.

TAXIS

BRASÍLIA

Fares in Brasília are lower than in the rest of the country, and most cabs are organized into cooperatives with dispatchers. It's best to call for one of these "radio taxis," particularly in the evening; unlike those in other Brazilian cities, some offer discounted rates for cabs ordered by phone—inquire when calling.

➤ TAXI COMPANIES: **Rádio Táxi** (☎ 061/325–3030). **Rádio Táxi Cidade** (☎ 061/321–8181).

THE WEST

As most of the tourist areas in western cities are compact, you'll rarely need a cab except for trips to the airport, the bus depot, or to and from your hotel at night. Cabs in the region are somewhat expensive, but they're all metered, so you shouldn't have to haggle. They're safe and comfortable, and you can generally hail them on the street. Tips aren't expected, though a small gratuity (less than 10%) is greatly appreciated.

TELEPHONES

Area codes in the region are as follows: Brasília, 061; Goiânia and Pirenópolis, 062; Cuiabá, 065; and Campo Grande, 067. You can make long-distance calls from TeleBrasília's *postos telefônicos* (phone centers) on the lower concourse at the airport (open 24 hours) and at the Terminal Rodoferroviária. For long-distance calls, you can choose from two companies: Embratel (access code 021) and Telebrasília (access code 014).

Brazil recently deregulated its phone system, resulting in marginally lower rates for domestic calls and an increase in confusion for visitors: before making a long-distance call from a pay phone in the west, you must dial 014 or 021 to connect to a carrier. Goiânia's phone office is at the corner of Rua 3 and Rua 7. In Cuiabá, you'll find such an office on Rua Barão de Melgaço, near the Praça Jaudy. Campo Grande's phone office is at the corner of Rua Rui Barbosa and Rua Dom Aquino.

TOURS

BRASÍLIA

Most hotels have an associated travel agency that will arrange tours. Popular excursions include a basic day trip along the Eixo Monumental, a shorter night version with stops at clubs, and an uncanny "mystical tour" to the cult communities around town. ESAT Aero Táxi can arrange helicopter tours of the Plano Piloto and other Distrito Federal sights. The shortest flight (10 mins) costs R$80 per person (minimum four people per flight). MS Turismo offers city tours as well as trips into the cerrado. VoeTur offers a variety of tours.

➤ BRASÍLIA TOUR OPERATORS: **ESAT Aero Táxi** (✉ Monumental Axis at TV Tower, ☎ 61/323–8777). **MS Turismo** (✉ SHCS/EQS 102/103, Bl. A, Lj. 04/22, ☎ 061/224–7818). **VoeTur** (✉ Brasília Shopping, SCN, Q. 05, Bl. A, Lj. 235-A, ☎ 061/327–1717).

In Pirenópolis, Estação Aventura has bus, bike, or horseback tours of the ecological spots surrounding the town. Diniz of Ecotur is another good Pirenópolis guide who offers similar "ecological" trips. In Goiânia, check with Pireneus Tour for in-state tours to Caldas Novas, Pirenópolis, and Goís.

Arriving in one of the Pantanal's gateway cities without having a tour already booked isn't a problem. Just be careful when choosing a guide upon arrival—some budget travelers have had bad experiences. To avoid being overcharged, compare prices. Also be sure your guide has adequate equipment, sufficient knowledge about area wildlife, and good English-language skills. Anaconda runs large tours into the Pantanal and around Cuiabá—including longer trips upriver in their popular "hotel-boats," which are equipped with comfortable air-conditioned cabins. In Cuiabá many guides will vie for your attention, but none will be as persistent or as personable as Joel Souza of Joel Safari Tours. Although he does treks to the Chapada dos Guimarães, he specializes in taking groups of four to six people on three- to four-day Pantanal tours. You'll stay in various fazendas and travel by horseback, car, boat, and on foot—whatever it takes to get the best animal sightings. The cost is about R$92 per person per day, everything included.

The owner of Impacto Turismo, Adnésio Junior (call him Junior), speaks serviceable English and offers four different trips into the Pantanal or on to Bonito. In the Campo Grande area, Geni Barbier of Panbratour really does take your budget and interests into account when planning a tour. In Corumbá, Corumbátur and Pantanal Tours are recommended operators that can arrange fishing and sightseeing trips on the Rio Paraguay or van trips into the wetlands.

➤ Tour Operators: **Anaconda** (✉ Rua Commandante Costa 649, Cuiabá, ☎ 065/624–4142 or 065/624–5128). **Corumbátur** (✉ Rua Antônio Maria Coelho 852, Corumbá, ☎ 067/231–1532). **Ecotur** (✉ Rua Emílio 21, Pirenópolis, ☎ 062/331–1392). **Estação Aventura** (✉ Rua da Prata 9, Pirenópolis, ☎ 062/331–1069). **Impacto Turismo** (✉ Rua Padre João Crippa 686, Campo Grande, ☎ FAX 067/725–1333). **Joel Safari Tours** (✉ Av. Getúlio Vargas 155-A, Cuiabá, ☎ 065/623–4696). **Panbratour,** (✉ Rua Estevão Alves Corrêa 586, Aquidauana, ☎ FAX 067/241–3494). **Pantanal Tours** (✉ Rua Manoel Cavassa 6, Porto Geral, Corumbá, ☎ 67/231–1559). **Pireneus Tour** (✉ Rua 87 560, Suite 106, S. Sul, Goiânia, ☎ 062/281–8111, FAX 062/281–8116, wwww.pireneustour.com.br).

VISITOR INFORMATION

Visit the main office of the Federal District Tourism Dvelopment Agency (ADETUR). At press time, the branch at the airport was being renovated. There's a small information kiosk at Praça dos Três Poderes (across from the Panteão da Pátria).

➤ Brasília Tourist Info: **ADETUR** (✉ SDC, Centro de Convenções Ulisses Guimarães, 1st floor, ☎ 061/325–5730).

Goiás's AGETUR has a lot of information, but it's far from comprehensive. In Pirenópolis, you can collect information at PIRETUR. The staff members in Campo Grande's Centro de Informação Turística e Cultura can give you information about everything under the sun in Campo Grande and environs, but don't look for any smiles. In Cuiabá, the staffers at SEDTUR try to be helpful, but they don't have much information.

➤ TOURIST INFORMATION IN THE WEST: **AGETUR** (✉ Rua 30 at Rua 4, Centro de Convenções, Goiás, ☎ 062/217–1000). **Centro de Informação Turística e Cultura** (✉ Av. Noroeste at Av. Afonso Pena, Campo Grande, ☎ 067/724–5830). **PIRETUR** (✉ Rua do Bom Fim, s/n, Pirenópolis, ☎ 062/331–1299, ext. 119). **SEDTUR** (✉ Praça da República 131, Cuiabá, ☎ 065/624–9060).

6 SALVADOR, RECIFE, AND FORTALEZA

These colonial cities are the triple crown of Brazil's northeast. Salvador at once startles you with its African rhythms and soothes you with its salty breezes. Recife, cut by rivers and edged by an ocean laden with reefs, is called the "Venice of Brazil." Fortaleza is set on a coast blessed with constant cooling breezes and amazingly warm waters.

Updated by
Joan Gonzalez

THE NORTHEASTERN CITIES ARE IMBUED WITH BRAZIL'S ESSENCE. Churches, villas, and fortresses in Salvador, Recife, and Fortaleza tell the tale of Portuguese settlers who fought Dutch invaders and amassed fortunes from sugar. The beaches in and around these cities evoke Brazil's playful side and its love affair with sun, sand, and sea. West of the cities, the rugged, often drought-stricken *sertão* (bush) seems a metaphor for Brazil's darker side—one where many people struggle for survival. This warp and weave of history and topography is laced with threads of culture: indigenous, European, African, and the unique blend of all three that is essentially Brazilian.

The area known as the northeast begins in the state of Bahia and extends to the edge of the Amazon. In addition to Bahia, the region is composed of the states of Sergipe, Alagoas, Pernambuco, Paraiba, Rio Grande do Norte, Ceará, Piauí, and Maranhão. In Bahia, the historical and cultural influence is predominately African; northward, it's more European. Throughout the region, the influence of native peoples is a mere shadow of long-ago days when they first worked with the Portuguese to harvest *pau-brasil* (brazilwood) trees. Later the indigenous tribes either fled inland to escape slavery or were integrated into the European and African cultures.

Although the Spanish and Portuguese had established rough territorial boundaries in the New World with the 1494 Treaty of Tordesillas, the French, English, and Dutch weren't inclined to respect the agreement, which was made by Papal decree. In the 16th century, the Portuguese Crown established 15 "captaincies" (the forerunners of today's states) as a way to protect Brazil from invaders. Each captaincy was assigned a "captain," who governed the territory and collected taxes while also defending it and ensuring its colonization. During this period, many northeasterners made huge profits either from sugar grown on plantations they had established or in the trade of African slaves, who were forced to work the cane fields and *engenhos* (mills).

Under the leadership of Duarte Coelho, the northeastern captaincy of Pernambuco thrived. Coelho adeptly established good relations with the area's native people and was among the first to employ African labor. At one point, Pernambuco had more sugar engenhos than any other captaincy. Olinda, its capital, was filled with the elegance and luxury that only true sugar barons could finance. Recife, the capital of what is now Pernambuco State, also began to evolve as a major port.

By 1549 it became clear to Portugal's monarch, Dom João III, that his New World captaincies were failing for the most part. He appointed Tomé de Sousa as Brazil's first governor general and ordered him to establish a colonial capital in the central captaincy of Bahia. Hence the city of Salvador was established on a bluff overlooking the vast Baía de Todos os Santos (All Saints' Bay).

In 1611 Martim Soares Moreno was dispatched from Portugal to a captaincy farther in the northeast, with orders to fend off the French who were threatening the area. Captain Moreno fell in love with the place—parts of which became the state of Ceará and its capital, Fortaleza—as well as its people. He was especially taken with a native woman, whom he married. (The love affair was immortalized in the 19th-century classic Brazilian novel *Iracema,* named for the Indian woman, by José de Alencar. Contemporary Fortaleza's Mucuripe Bay has a famous statue of Iracema by Corbiano Lins, a sculptor from Pernambuco.)

Although the French had posed an early threat to Brazil, it was the Dutch who truly tested its mettle. In 1602, they set up the powerful Dutch East India Company, which demolished Portugal's Asian spice-trade monopoly. Soon the Dutch began to look toward Brazil and its profitable sugar enterprises (they even sent botanists to catalog the nation's flora). In 1621, after the Dutch West India Company was established, Dutch attacks in northeastern Brazil began. They invaded and took over several captaincies, but the Portuguese drove them from one after another, finally ousting them entirely in 1654.

The coveted northeast still has much to offer explorers, and though it's experiencing a renaissance, the changes strike a balance between preservation and progress. Some of Salvador's buildings have been spruced up, but the city is still alive with the music, art, dance, religions, and cuisine of Africa. Farther north, Recife remains a place of beautiful waters, and nearby Olinda is still a charming enclave of colonial architecture—though bohemians have long since replaced sugar barons. And on Ceará State's 570-km-long (354-mi-long) coast Fortaleza continues to thrive against a backdrop of fantastic beaches with both new amenities and timeless white dunes.

Pleasures and Pastimes

Beaches
Urban sands are often lined by wide walkways and filled with beachgoers as well as vendors hawking coconut drinks and renting chairs and colorful umbrellas. The Atlantic waters throughout the region are warm year-round, and many beaches, particularly those near Fortaleza, have dunes high enough to ski down. The 193-km (120-mi) Costa dos Coqueiros, named after the graceful coconut palms that dot its pristine shores, stretches from Salvador to the border of Sergipe state. The BA 099 highway, called the Linha Verde (Green Line), links cities and beaches and is part of an effort to protect Brazil's green spaces.

Carnaval
IN SALVADOR
As Bahia's distinctive *axé* music has gained popularity around the country, Salvador's Carnaval (Carnival) has begun to compete with Rio de Janeiro's more traditional celebrations. In Salvador, Carnaval means dancing night after night in the street to the earsplitting, bone-rattling music of *trios elétricos* (bands on special sound trucks). It means watching parades of groups such as the Filhos de Gandhi (Sons of Gandhi), a Carnaval association founded by striking stevedores in 1949, whose members dress in white tunics and turbans—the relics of Africa's Muslim conversions. And it means ridding yourself of your inhibitions and moving freely to ancient, mesmerizing rhythms produced by such famous percussion groups as Ilê Aiyê and Casa do Olodum. This movable feast formally lasts a week in February or March but begins in spirit at New Year's and continues even into Lent in small towns outside Salvador, with street festivals called *micaretas*.

IN RECIFE AND OLINDA
Recife's citizens attend Carnaval *bailes* (dances) and *bloco* (percussion group) practice sessions for two months prior to the main festivities. Here the beat of choice is *frevo* (a fast-paced, frenetic music that normally accompanies a lively dance performed with umbrellas). Galo da Madrugada, the largest of Recife's estimated 500 blocos, officially opens Carnaval and has been known to draw 20,000 costumed revelers. Throughout the festivities the blocos are joined by *escolas de samba* (samba schools or groups), escolas de frevo, the *caboclinhos* (who dress in traditional Indian garb and bright feathers), and the *maracatus* (African processions

The Northeast Coast

accompanied by percussionists). In Olinda, Carnaval lasts a full 11 days. Highlights include the opening events—led by a bloco of more than 400 "virgins" (men in drag)—and a parade of huge dolls (likenesses of famous northeasterners) made of Styrofoam, fabric, and papier-mâché.

Dining

African culture was the catalyst for much of the region's cuisine, particularly that of Bahia. When the slaves arrived, they brought their own knowledge of how to cook using tropical ingredients. Coconut milk, *dendê* (palm) oil, and hot spices were insinuated into Portuguese and Indian dishes, transforming them into something quite new. Regional dishes often feature seafood; most are well seasoned if not fiery hot.

Moqueca is a regional seafood "stew" made with fish and/or shellfish, dendê oil, coconut milk, onions, and tomatoes. Other classics include *vatapá* (a thick, puréelike stew made with fish, shrimp, cashews, peanuts, and a variety of seasonings) and *ximxim de galinha* (chicken marinated in lemon or lime juice, garlic, and salt and pepper, and then cooked with dendê and peanut oil, coconut milk, tomatoes, and seasonings).

For details on price categories, *see* the chart *under* Dining *in* Smart Travel Tips A to Z.

Lodging

Lodging options range from modern high-rises with an international clientele and world-class service to cozy, family run *pousadas* (inns) on remote beaches or in fishing villages. "Flat" or apartment hotels—where guest quarters have kitchens and living rooms as well as bedrooms—are also options. For details on price categories, *see* the chart *under* Lodging *in* Smart Travel Tips A to Z.

Exploring Bahia, Fortaleza, and Recife

Several good main and secondary roads, some of them right along the coast, run north–south through the region. Still, considering the distances, it's best to fly between the cities. From each, you can rent a car, take a bus, or sign up for a guided tour and explore other coastal communities or inland areas.

Great Itineraries

IF YOU HAVE 5 DAYS

For such a short stay, you'll have to pick one of the cities and explore it and its environs. Your best bet is Salvador. Spend two days seeing the in-town sights and touring Ilha de Itaparica or the Península Itapagipe. On the third day visit Praia do Forte, where you can lounge on the beach, shop for handicrafts, and tour the Tamar sea-turtle project. On the fourth day, head west to Cachoeira. Built in the 16th century, it was Brazil's economic capital in the heyday of sugarcane; it's now the site of a religious order whose members are descendants of slaves. Either spend a night in a pousada here or return to Salvador for your flight out the next day.

IF YOU HAVE 7 DAYS

Fly into Salvador and spend two days exploring the city. On the third day fly to Recife for a two-day tour of it's historic areas as well as of Olinda. Spend the sixth day on the beach, followed by an evening boat trip through the rivers of Recife. On the seventh day catch your return flight home.

IF YOU HAVE 10 DAYS

Fly into Salvador and spend two days there. On the third day, take a trip to one of the beaches outside town. Fly to Recife on the fourth day, and spend the next two days exploring the in-town sights and visiting Olinda. On the seventh day, fly to Fortaleza; spend a day in town and another shopping for lace in nearby Aquiraz or sunbathing on the beach at Canoa Quebrada. Fly home on the 10th day.

When to Go

Peak seasons are November–April (the South American summer) and the month of July, when schools have breaks. Make reservations far in advance for stays during these months, especially if you plan to visit during Carnaval (February or March). As the weather is sunny and warm year-round, consider a trip in the off-season, when prices are lower and the beaches less crowded.

SALVADOR

Bahia's state capital is a city of 2 million people, at least 70% of whom are Afro-Brazilian. African rhythms roll forth everywhere—from buses and construction sites to the rehearsals of percussion groups. The scents of coriander, coconut, and palm oil waft around corners, where turbaned women in voluminous lace-trimmed white dresses cook and sell local delicacies.

Churches whose interiors are covered with gold leaf were financed by the riches of the Portuguese colonial era, when slaves masked their religious beliefs under a thin Catholic veneer. And partly thanks to modern-day acceptance of those beliefs, Salvador has become the fount of Candomblé, a religion based on personal dialogue with the *orixás,* a family of African deities closely linked to both nature and the Catholic saints. The influence of Salvador's African heritage on Brazilian music has also turned this city into one of the most stirring places to spend Carnaval, the bacchanalian fling that precedes Lent and only one of more than 20 festivals punctuating the local calendar.

Exploring Salvador

Salvador, Brazil's capital for 200 years, was founded in 1549 along the northeast coast of the Baía de Todos os Santos. The contemporary city now sprawls across a peninsula surrounded by the bay on one side and the Atlantic Ocean on the other. The original city, referred to as the Cidade Histórica (Historic City), is divided into *alta* (upper) and *baixa* (lower) districts.

The Cidade Alta neighborhood of Pelourinho, or just Peló, is on UNESCO's list of World Heritage Sites and contains some of the most significant examples of colonial architecture in the Americas. Along streets whose cobbles were laid by slaves, restored 17th- and 18th-century buildings now house museums, galleries, shops, and cafés. The Cidade Baixa is a commercial area—known as Comércio—that runs along the port and is the site of Salvador's largest market, Mercado Modelo. You can move between the upper and lower cities on foot, by *comum* (common) taxi, or via the landmark Lacerda Elevator behind the market.

From the Cidade Histórica you can travel north along the bay to the fort of Monte Serrat and the hilltop Igreja Nossa Senhora do Bomfim, a church attended by people of all faiths. You can also head south to the point, guarded by the Forte Santo Antônio da Barra, where the bay waters meet those of the Atlantic. Salvador's southern tip is home to the trendy neighborhoods of Vitória, Barra, Ondina, and Rio Vermelho, which are full of museums, theaters, shops, and restaurants. The beaches that run north from the tip and along the Atlantic coast are among the city's cleanest. Many are illuminated at night and have bars and restaurants that stay open late.

Numbers in the text correspond to numbers in the margin and on the Salvador Cidade Histórica map.

Cidade Alta

A GOOD WALK

Begin your walk at the most famous of the city's 176 churches, the 18th-century baroque **Igreja de São Francisco** ① and its neighboring **Igreja da Ordem Terceira de São Francisco** ②. From here, cross Rua Inácio Accioli (which becomes Rua São Francisco) and head through the Praça Anchieta to Rua da Oracão João de Deus and the **Igreja São Domingos de Gusmão da Ordem Terceira** ③. Just beyond this church is the large square called **Terreiro de Jesus** ④. At its northwest end is the 17th-century **Catedral Basílica** ⑤. From the cathedral head up to Rua Francisco Muniz Barreto and take a left onto Rua Alfredo de Brito. Two blocks up this street on your right is the **Fundação Casa de Jorge Amado/Museu da Cidade** ⑥, where you can see memorabilia of the

Salvador Cidade Histórico

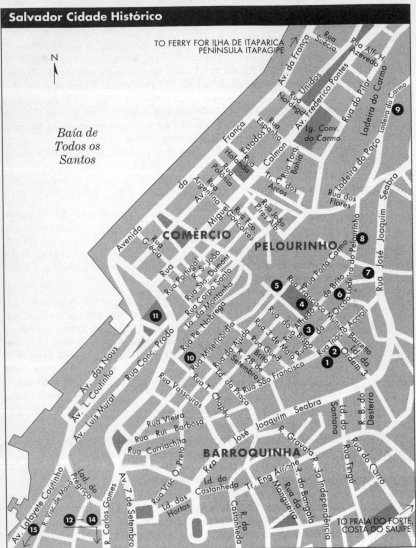

Baía de Todos os Santos

COMÉRCIO

PELOURINHO

BARROQUINHA

TO FERRY FOR ILHA DE ITAPARICA
PENÍNSULA ITAPAGIPE

TO PRAIA DO FORTE,
COSTA DO SAUÍPE

Catedral Basílica . . .**5**

Elevador Lacerda . .**10**

Forte de
Santo Antônio
da Barra **15**

Fundação Casa
de Jorge
Amado/Museu
da Cidade **6**

Igreja e Museu do
Convento do
Carmo **9**

Igreja de
Nossa Senhora
do Rosário
dos Pretos **8**

Igreja da Ordem
Terceira de São
Francisco **2**

Igreja São
Domingos de
Gusmão da
Ordem Terceira **3**

Igreja de São
Francisco **1**

Largo do
Pelourinho **7**

Mercado
Modelo **11**

Museu de Arte
Moderna da
Bahia **13**

Museu de
Arte Sacre **12**

Museu Carlos
Costa Pinto **14**

Terreiro de Jesus **4**

author of such famous titles as *Dona Flor e Seus dos Maridos* (*Dona Flor and Her Two Husbands*), as well as exhibits on Candomblé.

Rua Alfredo de Brito leads into the famed **Largo do Pelourinho** ⑦. To the north stands the baroque **Igreja de Nossa Senhora do Rosário dos Pretos** ⑧. Walk up the hill past ancient pastel-color houses and African handicrafts shops to the **Igreja e Museu do Convento do Carmo** ⑨.

TIMING

Simply walking this route will take about three hours. Pelourinho, with its music, cafés, restaurants, and shops, is a place that can be explored several times over a period of days and yet always seem new.

SIGHTS TO SEE

⑤ Catedral Basílica. Hints of Asia permeate this 17th-century masterpiece: Note the intricate ivory and tortoiseshell inlay from Goa on the Japiassu family altar, third on the right as you enter; the Asian facial features and clothing of the figures in the transept altars; and the 16th-century tiles from Macao in the sacristy. A Jesuit who lived in China painted the ceiling over the cathedral entrance. ⊠ *Terreiro de Jesus, Pelourinho,* ☎ *no phone.* ⊑ *Free.* ⊙ *Tues.–Sat. 8–11 and 3–6, Sun. 5–6:30.*

⑥ Fundação Casa de Jorge Amado/Museu da Cidade. The Jorge Amado House contains the writer's photos and book covers as well as a lecture room. Amado lived in the Hotel Pelourinho when it was a student house, and he set many of his books in this part of the city. Next door is the Museu da Cidade, with exhibitions on Candomblé's orixás. ⊠ *Rua Alfredo Brito and Largo do Pelourinho, Pelourinho,* ☎ *071/ 321–0122.* ⊑ *Free.* ⊙ *Fundação: weekdays 9:30 AM–10 PM. Museum: Tues.–Fri. 10–5, weekends 1–5.*

⑨ Igreja e Museu do Convento do Carmo. The 17th-century Carmelite Monastery Church and Museum is famous for its restored French organ and the carved cedar figure of Christ that's kept in the sacristy. Studded with tiny Indian rubies to represent blood, the figure was once carried through the streets on a silver-handled litter during Holy Week but is now too fragile to be moved. The monastery, which was occupied by the Dutch when they invaded in 1624, has a small church built in 1580 and a chapel with Portuguese *azulejos* (tiles) that recount the story of the Jesuit order. ⊠ *Largo do Carmo s/n, Pelourinho,* ☎ *071/ 242–0182.* ⊑ *Free.* ⊙ *Church: Daily for mass only, 7 AM, but accessible from museum. Museum: Mon.–Sat. 8–noon and 2–6, Sun. 8–noon.*

⑧ Igreja de Nossa Senhora do Rosário dos Pretos. Guides tend to skip over the Church of Our Lady of the Rosary of the Blacks, which was built in a baroque style by and for slaves between 1704 and 1796. It's worth a look at the side altars to see statues of the Catholic church's few black saints. Each has a fascinating story. ⊠ *Ladeira do Pelourinho s/n, Pelourinho,* ☎ *no phone.* ⊑ *Free.* ⊙ *Weekdays 8–5, weekends 8–2.*

② Igreja da Ordem Terceira de São Francisco. The Church of the Third Order of St. Francis has an 18th-century Spanish plateresque sandstone facade—carved to resemble Spanish silver altars made by beating the metal into wooden molds—that's unique in all Brazil. The facade was hidden for decades under a thick coat of plaster until, the story goes, a drunk electrician went wild with a hammer in the 1930s. ⊠ *Praça Anchieta s/n, Pelourinho,* ☎ *071/242–7046.* ⊑ *Free.* ⊙ *Mon.–Sat. 8–noon and 2–5, Sun. 8–noon.*

③ Igreja São Domingos de Gusmão da Ordem Terceira. The baroque Church of the Third Order of St. Dominic (1723) houses a collection of carved processional saints and other sacred objects. Such sculptures often had hollow interiors used to smuggle gold into Portugal to avoid government taxes. You'll see Asian features and details in the church decoration, evidence of long-ago connections with Portugal's Asian colonies of Goa and Macao. Upstairs are two impressive rooms with carved wooden furniture used for lay brothers' meetings and receptions. ⊠ *Terreiro de Jesus, Pelourinho,* ☎ *071/242–4185.* ⊒ *Free.* ☉ *Mon.– Sat. 8–noon and 2–5.*

★ ❶ **Igreja de São Francisco.** The famous 18th-century baroque Church of St. Francis has an active monastery. Listen for the sound of African drums in the square outside as you appreciate the ceiling painted in 1774 by José Joaquim da Rocha, a mulatto who founded Brazil's first art school. The ornate cedar-and-rosewood interior writhes with images of mermaids, acanthus leaves, and caryatids—all bathed in gold leaf. Guides will tell you that there's as much as a ton of gold here, but restoration experts say there's much less, as the leaf used is just a step up from a powder. A Sunday-morning alternative to crowded beaches is to attend mass here (9–11 and 11–11:45); stay until the end, when the electric lights go off, to catch the wondrous subtlety of gold leaf under natural light. ⊠ *Praça Padre Anchieta, Pelourinho,* ☎ *no phone.* ⊒ *Free.* ☉ *Mon.–Sat. 8–noon and 2–5, Sun. 8–noon.*

★ ❼ **Largo do Pelourinho.** Named for the pillory where slaves were whipped, this plaza is now the setting for one of the largest and most charming groupings of Brazilian colonial architecture and a thriving cultural renaissance. There are four public stages in Pelourinho, at least two of which have music nightly, all named after characters in Jorge Amado novels. The **Dia & Noite** (☎ 071/322–2525) association organizes Largo do Pelourinho's music shows; it publishes a monthly schedule that's available in tourist offices and hotels.

❹ **Terreiro de Jesus.** A large square with three churches and a small crafts fair, Terreiro de Jesus opens the way to historic Salvador. Where nobles once strolled under imperial palm trees you'll now see men practicing *capoeira*—a stylized, dancelike foot fight with African origins—to the *thwang* of the *berimbau,* a rudimentary bow-shape musical instrument.

Cidade Baixa and Beyond

You can travel between the Cidade Alta and the Cidade Baixa aboard the popular **Elevador Lacerda** ⑩. Exiting the elevator in the lower city, cross the Praça Visconde de Cairú to the **Mercado Modelo** ⑪ for some shopping and people-watching. From here you have several options. If you head north along the bay and past the port, you'll come to the terminal where you can catch a ferry or hop a schooner for **Ilha de Itaparica.** Or you can head due south by cab to one of several museums: the **Museu de Arte Sacra** ⑫, with its religious paintings; the **Museu de Arte Moderna da Bahia** ⑬, whose modern works are displayed in a colonial house; or the **Museu Carlos Costa Pinto** ⑭, with art and artifacts gathered by private collectors. Another option is to visit the tip of the peninsula, which is marked by the **Forte de Santo Antônio** ⑮ as well as a lighthouse, a nautical museum, and a popular beach.

TIMING

You could start late in the morning and make a relaxed day of this tour. Navigating the elevator and the market takes a little more than an hour, though you'll probably want to spend more time browsing. The trip to either Ilha de Itaparica or to one or more of the museums will fill up a leisurely afternoon.

SIGHTS TO SEE

❿ **Elevador Lacerda.** Costing only a few centavos and covering 72 m (236 ft) in a minute, the elevator runs between the Praça Municipal, in the
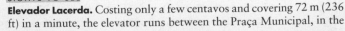

upper city, and Praça Visconde de Cairú and the Mercado Modelo. Built in 1872, the elevator ran on hydraulics until its 1930 restoration, when it was electrified. Bahians joke that the elevator is the only way to "go up" in life.

 Forte de Santo Antônio da Barra. Fort St. Anthony has guarded Salvador since 1583. The nearby Farol da Barra (Barra Lighthouse) wasn't built until 1696, after many a ship was wrecked on all the coral reefs and sandbanks. The fort now houses the **Museu Nautico**, with exhibitions of old maps, navigational equipment, artillery, model vessels, and remnants of shipwrecks found by Brazil's first underwater archaeological research team. There's also a café and a gift shop. Although the beaches here are popular with locals, particularly on weekends, their waters are too dangerous for swimming. ⊠ *Av. 7 de Setembro s/n, Barra,* ☎ *071/264–3296.* ☞ *R$2.* ⊙ *Tues.–Sat. 1–6.*

OFF THE
BEATEN PATH

ILHA DE ITAPARICA – The largest of 56 islands in the Baía de Todos os Santos, Itaparica was originally settled because its ample supply of fresh mineral water was believed to have rejuvenating qualities. Its beaches are calm and shallow, thanks to the surrounding reefs. The ferry ride here takes 45 minutes; another option is a slightly longer but very pleasant schooner cruise and tour, which can include lunch and a music show. You can always take a schooner to the island, opt out of the tour group lunch, and take a taxi to the restaurant of your choice. Then you can enjoy an afternoon stroll before catching the ferry back to Salvador.

⑪ **Mercado Modelo.** This enclosed market (closed Sunday afternoon) may not be the cheapest place to buy handicrafts—and you do have to bargain—but it must be experienced. It assaults the senses, with its *cachaça* (a strong Brazilian liquor made from sugarcane), cashew nuts, pepper sauces, cigars, the dried shrimp that are an integral part of Bahian cooking, manioc flour, leather goods, hammocks, lace, musical instruments, African sculptures, and gems. Outside, you'll hear the nasal-voiced *repentistas,* folk singers who make up songs on the spot. Notice the blue azulejos on the building with Gothic-style windows. Just inside the back door on the right is a tourist office where you can pick up maps and brochures.

⑬ **Museu de Arte Moderna da Bahia.** A mid-16th-century waterfront mill set between the upper and lower cities houses the Bahian Museum of Modern Art's permanent collection of work by some of Brazil's top painters, including Cândido Portinari, Alfredo Volpi, Siron Franco, and Hector Carybé. The museum is part of a complex that includes the Solar do Unhão, a former sugar mill that dates from the 18th century. ⊠ *Av. Contorno s/n, Solar do Unhão,* ☎ *071/329–0660.* ☞ *Free.* ⊙ *Tues.–Fri. 1–9, Sat. 11–9, Sun. 2–7.*

⑫ **Museu de Arte Sacra.** Housed in a former Carmelite monastery near the upper city, the Sacred Art Museum and its adjoining Igreja de Santa Teresa (St. Theresa Church) are two of Salvador's best-cared-for repositories of religious objects. An in-house restoration team has worked miracles that bring alive Bahia's 1549–1763 golden age as Brazil's capital and main port. See the silver altar in the church, moved here from the demolished Sé church, and the blue-and-yellow-tiled sacristy replete with a bay view. ⊠ *Rua do Sodré 276, Centro,* ☎ *071/243–6310,* ☞ *R$1.* ⊙ *Weekdays 11:30–5:30.*

⑭ **Museu Carlos Costa Pinto.** The collection is the fruit of one wealthy couple's fascination with art and antiques. Among the 3,000 objects fashioned around the world over the last three centuries are examples of oversize gold and silver *balangandãs* (or *pencas*), chains of large

SPIRITUAL SALVADOR

EVIDENCE THAT BRAZIL is officially a Roman Catholic country can be found everywhere. There are beautiful churches and cathedrals—from the colonial to the baroque to the modern—across the nation. Most Brazilians wear a religious medal or two, bus and taxi drivers place pictures of St. Christopher prominently in their vehicles, and two big winter celebrations (in June) honor St. John and St. Peter. For many Brazilians, however, the real church is that of the spirits.

When Africans were forced aboard slave ships, they may have left their families and possessions behind, but they brought along an impressive array of gods. Foremost among them were Olorum, the creator; Iemanjá, the goddess of the rivers and water; Oxalá, the god of procreation and the harvest; and Exú, a trickster spirit who could cause mischief or bring about death. Of lesser rank but still very powerful were Ogun, Obaluayê, Oxôssi, and Yansan, to name but a few.

The Catholic Church, whose spiritual seeds were planted in Brazil alongside the rows of sugarcane and cotton, was naturally against such religious beliefs. As a compromise, the slaves took on the rituals of Rome but kept their old gods. Thus, new religions—Candomblé in Bahia, Macumba in Rio, Xangó in Pernambuco, Umbanda in São Paulo— were born.

Iemenjá had her equivalent in the Virgin Mary, and was queen of the heavens as well as queen of the seas; the powerful Oxalá became associated with Jesus Christ; and Exú, full of deception to begin with, became Satan. Other gods were likened to saints: Ogun to St. Anthony, Obaluayê to St. Francis, Oxôssi to St. George, Yansan to St. Barbara. On their altars, crosses and statues of the Virgin, Christ, and saints sat beside offerings of sacred white feathers, magical beads, and bowls of cooked rice and cornmeal.

Salvadorans are eager to share their rituals with visitors, though often for a fee (you can make arrangements through hotels or tour agencies). The Candomblé temple ceremony, in which believers sacrifice animals and become possessed by gods, is performed nightly except during Lent.

Temples, usually in poor neighborhoods at the city's edge, don't allow photographs or video or sound recordings. You shouldn't wear black (white is preferable) or revealing clothing. The ceremony is long and repetitive, and there's no air-conditioning and often no chairs; men and women are separated.

A *pãe de santo* or *mãe de santo* (Candomblé priest or priestess) can perform a reading of the *búzios* for you; the small brown shells are thrown like jacks into a circle of beads—the pattern they form tells about your life. Don't select your mãe or pãe de santo through an ad or sign, as many shell readers who advertise are best not at fortune-telling but at saying "One hundred dollars, please" in every language.

charms—in the shape of tropical fruits, fish, perhaps a berimbau—worn by slave women around the waist. Prized slaves were initially given the chain and the clasp by their masters, who, over time, continued to reward loyalty and service with gifts of the charms (many jewelry and crafts stores sell replicas of these pieces). The balangandã usually includes a *figa,* a closed fist with a thumb sticking out of the top. According to African legend, the figa can increase warriors' fertility. In Brazil it's simply considered a good-luck charm (for it to work, though, it must always be a gift). It's also used as a good-luck gesture, sort of like crossing your fingers. ⊠ *Av. 7 de Setembro 2490, Vitória,* ☎ *071/ 336–6081.* ◱ *R$11.* ☉ *Mon. and Wed.–Fri. 2:30–7, weekends 3–6.*

Península Itapagipe

A GOOD DRIVE

A 20-minute taxi ride northwest along the Baía de Todos os Santos from the Mercado Modelo is the **Igreja de Nosso Senhor do Bonfim.** Here or in the square facing the church you'll be accosted by someone selling a printed ribbon, willing to tie it around your wrist with three knots (and sell 20 more to take home to friends), each good for one wish if you wear the ribbon until it falls off and throw it into the ocean. Each color stands for a paired Catholic saint and Candomblé deity. A five-minute drive from the church is the dazzling white **Forte Mont Serrat.**

TIMING

One and a half hours ought to suffice for a visit to the church and the fort. The morning mass on the first Friday of the month draws a huge congregation, most wearing white, with practitioners of Candomblé on one side and Catholics on the other.

SIGHTS TO SEE

Igreja de Nosso Senhor do Bonfim. A procession of women dressed in petticoat-puffed Empire-waist white dresses and adorned with turbans and ritual necklaces comes here the Thursday before the third Sunday in January to wash the steps with holy water. Built in the 1750s, the simple church has many ex-votos—wax, wooden, and plaster replicas of body parts—objects of devoted prayer believed to be capable of miraculous cures. Many figures in Catholicism have a counterpart deity in Candomblé; Nosso Senhor do Bonfim's is Oxalá, the father of all the gods and goddesses. Thus the seemingly bizarre mixture of figurines found in the shops opposite the church: St. George and the Dragon, devils, Indians, monks, sailors, and warriors, plus ex-votos that include house keys and Volkswagens for the devotees of consumerism. ⊠ *Praça do Senhor do Bonfim, Alto do Bonfim, Itapagipe,* ☎ *071/316–2196.* ◱ *Free.* ☉ *Tues.–Sun. 8–noon and 2:30–6:30.*

Forte Mont Serrat. Built in 1500 and named for the shrine of the Black Virgin at Montserrat, near Barcelona, the white fort is still used by the Brazilian military. It's not open to the public. There's a church by the same name nearby, rarely open, with a renowned carving of St. Peter.

Beaches

Beaches are wall-to-wall people on the weekends. If you don't mind a crowd, it's fun to soak up both sun and beach culture, which includes live music, sand sports, firewater drinks, spicy seafood snacks (don't miss the *acarajé,* a deep-fried bean cake with dried shrimp and an onion-and-pepper sauce), and the briefest of swimwear.

At most beaches the food and drink kiosks provide chairs and umbrellas for free; you pay only for what you consume. Some also offer patrons rudimentary bathroom, changing, and shower facilities free of charge. Aside from these, there are no functioning bathrooms on the beaches, though some have public showers that run on one-minute tokens that cost only a few centavos. Don't leave belongings unattended.

The comfortable *ônibus executivo* (executive bus; marked ROTEIRO DAS PRAIAS) runs from Praça da Sé to Flamengo Beach, stopping at all the beaches along the way. As a rule, the farther away from the port the better the beach.

Barra do Jacuípe. A river runs down to the ocean at this long, wide, pristine beach lined with coconut palms, about 40 km (25 mi) north of Salvador. There are beachfront snack bars, and the Santa Maria/Catuense bus company operates six buses here daily.

Guarajuba. With palm trees and calm waters banked by a reef, this is the nicest beach of them all, though it's 60 km (38 mi) north of Salvador and lined with condos. The bus to Barra do Jacuípe continues on to Guarajuba, which has snack kiosks, fishing boats, surfing, dune buggies, and a playground.

Itapuã. Frequented by artists who live nearby, Itapuã is about a half-hour drive from downtown. Although it's polluted in some places, it has a terrific atmosphere. Around K and J streets there are food kiosks, music bars, and amusement park rides. It was once a whale cemetery, and bones are still an occasional find. A mystical freshwater lagoon, the Lagoa de Abaeté, lies inland from Itapuã. Its black depths provide a startling contrast with the fine white sand of its shores. No one knows the source of these waters. City buses going to the lagoon leave from Campo Grande or Estação da Lapa. If you're driving, take the Orla Marítima north to Itapuã. At the Largo da Sereia (a square with a mermaid statue), follow signs for the lagoon. Tour operators include the lagoon on their beach tours, which cost about R$55.

Piatã. Heading north and leaving the more built-up areas of the city behind, the first truly clean beach you'll come to is the wide oceanside Piatã (20 km/13 mi from downtown). Its calm waters and golden sand attract families.

Porto da Barra and Farol da Barra. Some Salvadorans, especially singles, swear by these urban beaches, which are frequented by a colorful mix of people who live nearby and tourists staying at neighboring hotels. To avoid large crowds, don't go on weekends. Regardless of when you go, keep an eye on your belongings; petty thievery has been reported. There are no bathrooms or kiosks, but you can rent a beach chair for about R$2. The corner of Porto da Barra closest to the Grande Hotel da Barra is a gay hangout. Toward the other end, around the corner from the lighthouse, lie the hotel districts of Ondina and Rio Vermelho, where the beaches intermittently suffer pollution problems.

Stella Maris. Stella Maris (18 km/11 mi north of downtown), *the* beach in Salvador, is popular with surfers and beautiful girls, but it's most famous for its kiosks.

Dining

You can easily find restaurants serving Bahian specialties in Barra, a neighborhood full of bars and sidewalk cafés. There are also many good spots in bohemian Rio Vermelho and a slew of places along the beachfront drive beginning around Jardim de Alah. It's wise to order meat only in *churrascarias* (barbecued-meat restaurants), avoiding it in seafood places.

Brazilian

$$$$ ✕ **Casa da Gamboa.** A longtime favorite of Bahian writer Jorge
   Amado, this is a Bahian cooking institution. *Casquinha de siri* (breaded crab in the shell) comes as a complimentary starter; then try the *peixe com risoto de ostras* (grilled fish with oyster risotto), followed by a

traditional dessert. ✉ *Rua João de Deus 32, Pelourinho,* ☎ *071/321–3393. AE, MC, V. No lunch.*

$$$–$$$$ ✕ **Trapiche Adelaide.** You may want to call for a reservation at this popular restaurant near the Mercado Modelo in downtown Salvador. It's known for its excellent Bahian and seafood dishes. ✉ *Praça dos Tupinambás 02, Conforno,* ☎ *071/326–1942. MC, V.*

$$$ ✕ **Maria Mata Mouro.** At this intimate restaurant you almost feel as if you're at a friend's house for dinner. The Bahian food is served with an extra creative twist, and you're assured of a good meal. The *badejo* (grouper) in ginger is delicious. ✉ *Rua Inácio Acciole 8, Pelourinho,* ☎ *071/321–3929. AE, V. Closed Sun.*

$–$$ ✕ **Dona Celina.** This Bahian restaurant offers alfresco as well as indoor dining, and a good selection of vegetarian dishes. The ambience will charm you. ✉ *Rua Francisco Muniz Barreto 15, Pelourinho,* ☎ *071/321–1721. No credit cards.*

$–$$ ✕ **Uauá.** You'll find cuisine representative of many Brazilian regions here. The clientele, which includes most of the city, is devoted. There are two locations, one in Pelourinho and one at Itapuã Beach. ✉ *R. Gregório de Matos 36, Pelourinho,* ☎ *071/321–3089;* ✉ *Av. Dorival Caymi 46, Itapuã,* ☎ *071/249–9579. AE, DC, MC, V. Closed Mon.*

Eclectic

$$$–$$$$ ✕ **Boi Preto.** Although this restaurant specializes in steaks, it serves all kinds of food, including Japanese. ✉ *Av. Otávio Mangabeira s/n, Boca do Rio,* ☎ *071/362–8844. AE, MC, V.*

$$$ ✕ **Extudo.** Young professionals and singles jam-pack this bar and restaurant just about every night. Bahian and international dishes include camarão *comodoro,* shrimp and prunes gratinéed in a creamy tomato sauce; Finnegan's steak with black-pepper sauce; and *frango flambado,* flambéed chicken. ✉ *Rua Lídio Mesquita 4, Rio Vermelho,* ☎ *071/334–4669. No credit cards. Closed Mon.*

French

$$$$ ✕ **Chez Bernard.** Discerning *soteropolitanos* (the pompous but nonetheless correct term for natives of the city) say this is undoubtedly the best French restaurant in town, as well as one of the oldest. There are no particular specialties: everything is worth trying. ✉ *Gamboa de Cima 11, Aflitos,* ☎ *071/329–5403. AE, V. Closed Sun.*

Seafood

$$$$ ✕ **Bargaço.** Although it's in a shed—albeit a large, brightly lit one—and now caters mostly to tour groups, this old favorite still offers good, typical Bahian seafood dishes. Starters such as *pata de caranguejo* (vinegared crab claw) are hearty and may do more than take the edge off your appetite for the requisite moqueca de *camarão* (shrimp) or moqueca *de siri mole* (soft-shell crab); try the *cocada baiana* (sugar-caked coconut) for dessert, if you have room. ✉ *Rua P, Lote 1819, Quadra 43, Jardim Armação, Boca do Rio,* ☎ *071/231–5141 or 071/231–3900. AE, DC, MC.*

$$$–$$$$
★ ✕ **Yemanjá.** A bubbly underwater atmosphere—replete with aquariums and sea goddess murals—sets the tone for meals of traditionally prepared seafood dishes. The service is somewhat slow, and there's no air-conditioning, but most patrons don't seem to mind, concentrating instead on plowing through enormous portions of moqueca or ensopado. ✉ *Av. Otávio Mangabeira 929, Jardin Armação,* ☎ *071/231–3036. No credit cards.*

Lodging

There are only a few hotels in the Cidade Histórico. Going south into the Vitória neighborhood along Avenida 7 de Setembro there are many inexpensive establishments, convenient both to beaches and to sights. In the yuppie Barra neighborhood, many hotels are within walking distance of cafés, bars, restaurants, and clubs. The resorts in the beach areas of Ondina and Rio Vermelho are a 20-minute taxi ride from downtown.

$$$–$$$$ ⊞ **Catussaba Hotel.** Close to the airport and 40 km (25 mi) from the
★ city, the Catussaba's rooms all have balconies with hammocks and ocean views and all open directly onto a beach that's good for swimming. If you tire of saltwater and sand, head for the large, attractive pool area. ⊠ *Alameda da Praia, Itapuã 41600-270,* ☎ *071/374–0555,* FAX *071/374–4749,* WEB *www.catussaba.com.br. 186 rooms, 4 suites. Restaurant, bar, pool, sauna, tennis court, health club, meeting room. AE, MC, V.*

$$–$$$$ ⊞ **Tropical Hotel da Bahia.** Owned by Varig Airlines and often included in package deals, this centrally located hotel is a bit tattered, but it's practical for those whose priority is Salvador's history and culture, not beachcombing (although there's a free beach shuttle). Some rooms overlook the square where Carnaval begins; the Concha Acústica do Teatro Castro Alves, site of many big musical shows, is within walking distance, and performers there often stay here. ⊠ *Praça Dois de Julho 2, Campo Grande 40080-121,* ☎ *071/336–0102,* FAX *071/336–9725,* WEB *www.tropicalhotel.com.br. 282 rooms, 10 suites. Restaurant, bar, coffee shop, 2 pools, massage, sauna, dance club. AE, DC, MC, V.*

$$–$$$ ⊞ **Bahia Othon Palace Hotel.** A short drive from most sights, nightspots, and restaurants, this busy, modern hotel sits on a cliff overlooking Ondina Beach. Top local entertainers often perform at the hotel's outdoor park, and in high season the friendly staff organizes poolside activities and trips to better beaches. ⊠ *Av. Presidente Vargas 2456, Ondina 40170-010,* ☎ *071/247–1044,* FAX *071/245–4877,* WEB *www.hoteis-othon. com.br. 300 rooms, 25 suites. Restaurant, bar, coffee shop, pool, sauna, health club, dance club, concierge floor. AE, DC, MC, V.*

$$ ⊞ **Fiesta Bahia Hotel.** In the city's financial district and close to the convention center, the Fiesta offers rooms with direct phone lines, fax and PC terminals, and queen-size beds—amenities that distinguish it from its competitors. ⊠ *Av. Antônio Carlos Magalhães 711, Itaigara 41125-000,* ☎ *071/352–0000,* FAX *071/352–0050,* WEB *www.fiestahotel.com.br. 239 rooms. Restaurant, bar, coffee shop, room service, 2 pools, health club, shops, nightclub, business services. AE, DC, MC, V.*

$$ ⊞ **Hotel Sofitel Salvador.** Just beyond the city's northern perimeter, this resort and convention hotel near good beaches is a world unto itself, decorated with local art and oversize, old-fashioned farm implements. The green-and-blue-accented rooms all have a view of the spacious grounds and the ocean beyond. Amenities include a gallery, on-site boutiques, crafts demonstrations, and free minibus service to downtown. ⊠ *Rua da Pasárgada s/n, Farol de Itapuã 48280-000,* ☎ *071/374–9611 or 800/763–4835 in U.S.,* FAX *071/374–6946,* WEB *www.sofitel-brasil. com.br. 197 rooms, 9 suites. 2 restaurants, 3 bars, room service, 2 pools, beauty salon, massage, 9-hole golf course, 3 tennis courts, health club, boating, shops. AE, DC, MC, V.*

$$ ⊞ **Ondina Apart-Hotel Residência.** In the resort hotel district, a short
★ drive from the sights, nightlife, and restaurants, this outstanding beachside apartment-hotel complex has simple, modern furniture and kitchenettes. Businesspeople and families opt for this hotel when they're staying in Salvador for extended periods. ⊠ *Av. Presidente Vargas 2400, Ondina 40170-010,* ☎ *071/203–8000,* FAX *071/203–8112,* WEB *www.stn. com.br/ondapart. 100 apartments. Restaurant, bar, coffee shop, beauty salon, 2 tennis courts, health club, dance club. AE, DC, MC, V.*

$ ⊞ **Blue Tree Caesar Towers.** Although you won't find any sea views, you will appreciate the central location. The rooms are comfortable and have a tropical motif, with wicker furniture and tile floors From here it's only 8 km (5 mi) to downtown, 15 km (10 mi) to the best beaches, and a short way to the many restaurants and bars of the Barra district. The breakfast buffet, included in the room price, is famous. ⊠ *Av. Oceânica 1545, Ondina 41140-131,* ☎ *071/331–8200,* FAX *071/237– 4668,* WEB *www.bdh.com/br/reserva.htm. 120 rooms. Restaurant, coffee shop, pool, sauna, health club, meeting room. AE, DC, MC, V. BP.*

$ ☷ **Grande Hotel da Barra.** In front of the Porto da Barra Beach and convenient to the historic center, the Grande has comfortable, well-maintained rooms with pink-and-green floral bedspreads, latticework screens, and lots of wood carvings. The front rooms have verandas. Though not all rooms have an ocean view, they do all have VCRs. ⊠ *Av. 7 de Setembro 3564, Porto da Barra 40130-001,* ☎ *071/247–6506,* FAX *071/264–6011,* WEB *www.svn.com.br/grandehotelbarra. 112 rooms, 5 suites. Restaurant, bar, pool, beauty salon, sauna. AE, DC, MC, V.*

$ ☷ **Hotel Bahia do Sol.** It may be simple, but this hotel has a prime lo-
★ cation close to museums and historic sights. Front rooms have a partial ocean view, but those in the back are quieter. ⊠ *Av. 7 de Setembro 2009, Vitória 40080-002,* ☎ *071/336–7211,* FAX *071/336–7776. 86 rooms, 4 suites. Restaurant, bar, meeting room, free parking. AE, DC, MC, V.*

$ ☷ **Hotel Catharina Paraguaçu.** The sleeping areas at this intimate
★ hotel—set in a 19th-century mansion—are small but comfortable and include six split-level suites. It's family-run and in a neighborhood of good restaurants and bars. ⊠ *Rua João Gomes 128, Rio Vermelho 40210-090,* ☎ *071/334–0089,* ☎ FAX *071/247–1488. 23 rooms, 6 suites. Minibars. MC, V.*

¢ ☷ **Pousada das Flores.** A great location (within walking distance of
★ Pelourinho) combined with charming, helpful owners and simple elegance conspire to make this one of the city's best budget options. Rooms are large and have high ceilings, a stylish blue-and-white decor, and hardwood floors. For peace and quiet as well as an ocean view, opt for a room on an upper floor. If you feel like splurging, request the penthouse, which has a fantastic view of the harbor. ⊠ *Rua Direita de Santo Antônio 442, Cidade Histórico,* ☎ FAX *071/243–1836. 6 rooms, 3 suites. AE, DC, MC, V.*

Nightlife and the Arts

Pelourinho is filled with music every night and has more bars and clubs than you can count. And most bars serve food as well as drink. Activity also centers along the seashore, mainly at Rio Vermelho and between the Corsário and Piatã beaches, where many of the hotels have bars or discos.

Salvador is considered by many artists as a laboratory for the creation of new rhythms and dance steps. As such, this city has an electric performing arts scene. See the events calendar published by Bahiatursa or local newspapers for details on live music performances as well as the rehearsal schedules and locations of the Carnaval blocos. In Pelourinho, groups often give free concerts on Tuesday and Sunday nights.

Gay and lesbian information is available from the **Grupo Gay da Bahia** (⊠ Rua do Sodré 45, Centro, ☎ 071/322–2552), where you can purchase the guide *Guia para Gays* for about R$10.

Nightlife

BARS

At **Casquinha de Siri** (⊠ Coqueiros de Piatã, s/n, Piata, ☎ 071/367–1234), you can enjoy live music and typical Bahian food. The two branches of the traditional bar **Habeas Copos** (⊠ Rua Marques de Leão 172, Barra, ☎ 071/247–7895; Praça Quincas Berro D'Agua, Pelour-

Close-Up

THE FIGHT DANCE

The sport of *capoeira*—dance and martial arts all in one—is purely Brazilian. The early days of slavery often saw fights between Africans from rival tribes who were thrust together on one plantation. When an owner caught slaves fighting, both sides were punished. To create a smoke screen, the Africans incorporated music and song into the fights. They brought a traditional *berimbau* "string-drum" instrument (a bow-shape piece of wood with a metal wire running from one end to the other, where there's a hollow gourd containing seeds) to the battles. Its mesmerizing reverberations were accompanied by singing and chanting, and when the master appeared, the fighters punched only the air and kicked so as to miss their opponent.

The fights have been refined into a sport that was once practiced primarily in Bahia and Pernambuco but has now spread throughout Brazil. Today's practitioners swing and kick—keeping their movements tightly controlled—to the mood and beat of the berimbau without touching their opponents. (Tapped with a stick or a coin, the berimbau's taut wire produces a throbbing, twanging sound, whose rhythm is enhanced by the rattling seeds.) The back bending all the way to the floor, the agile foot movements (to avoid an imaginary knife), and the compelling music make capoeira a fascinating sport to watch.

inho, ☎ 071/321–0430; Rua Marques de Leão 172, Barra, ☎ 071/ 247–7895) are famous for their chicken. **Sancho Pança** (✉ Av. Otávio Mangabeira 112, Pituba, ☎ 071/248–3571) is a great place for sangria and typical Spanish fare.

DANCE SHOWS
Shows at the **Moenda** (✉ Rua P, Quadra 28, Lote 21, Jardim Armação, ☎ 071/231–7915 or 071/230–6786) begin daily at 8 PM. There are Afro-Brazilian dinner shows (the entertainment is better than the food) at the **Solar do Unhão** (✉ Av. do Contorno 8, near Mercado Modelo, ☎ 071/321–5551), which opens from Monday to Saturday at 8 PM. The Afro-Bahian show at the **Teatro Miguel Santana** (✉ Rua Gregório de Mattos 47, Pelourinho, ☎ 071/321–0222) has the town's best folkloric dance troupes.

NIGHTCLUBS
Kalamazoo, an old favorite, has a new name—it's now called the **Manatee** (✉ Av. Otávio Mangabeira s/n, Patamares, ☎ 071/363–5151). The **Queops** disco (✉ Hotel Sol Bahia Atlântico, Rua Manoel Antônio Galvão 100, Patamares, ☎ 071/370–9000) has a large dance floor and weekly shows by local bands. **Rock in Rio Café** (✉ Av. Otávio Mangabeira 6000, Boca do Rio, ☎ 071/371–0979) is in the shopping and entertainment complex Aeroclube Plaza. The atmosphere here is more like Miami than Salvador.

The Arts
CAPOEIRA REHEARSALS
You can see capoeira, the hypnotic African sport-cum-dance accompanied by the berimbau on Tuesday, Thursday, and Saturday evenings

at 7 at the Forte de Santo Antônio. Two schools practice here. The more traditional is the Grupo de Capoeira Angola. Weekday nights are classes; the real show happens on Saturday.

CARNAVAL REHEARSALS

Afro-Brazilian percussion groups begin rehearsals—which are really more like creative jam sessions—for Carnaval around midyear. **Ilê Aiyê,** which started out as a Carnaval bloco, has turned itself into much more in its 25-year history. It now has its own school and promotes the study and practice of African heritage, religion, and history. The work this bloco is undertaking in the name of Afro-Brazilian pride and prosperity is both vast and inspirational. Practices are held every Saturday night at Forte de Santo Antônio and should not be missed. Olodum, Salvador's most commercial percussion group, has its own venue, the **Casa do Olodum** (⊠ Rua Gregório de Matos 22, Pelourinho, ☎ 071/321–5010).

MUSIC, THEATER, AND DANCE VENUES

Casa do Comércio (⊠ Av. Tancredo Neves 1109, Ramal, ☎ 071/341–8700) hosts music performances and some theatrical productions. All kinds of musicians play at the **Concha Acústica do Teatro Castro Alves** (⊠ Ladeira da Fonte s/n, Campo Grande, ☎ 071/247–6414 or 071/339–8000), a band shell with great acoustics. The **Teatro ACBEU** (⊠ Av. 7 de Setembro 1883, Victória, ☎ 071/247–4395 or 071/336–4411) has contemporary and classic music, dance, and theater performances by both Brazilian and international talent. You can see theatrical, ballet, and musical performances at the **Teatro Yemanjá** (⊠ Jardim Armacão s/n, Centro de Convenções da Bahia, ☎ 071/370–8494).

Outdoor Activities and Sports

Participant Sports

BICYCLING AND RUNNING

The park **Dique do Tororó** (⊠ Entrances at Av. Presidente Costa e Silva and Av. Vasco da Gama, Tororó) has a jogging track and a lake with luminous fountains and statues of African orixás. You can bike here, too. At **Jardim dos Namorados** (⊠ Av. Otavio Mangabeira, Pituba) you can rent bikes, play volleyball, or perhaps join a soccer game. The **Parque Metropolitano de Pituaçu** (⊠ Av. Otávio Mangabeira s/n, Pituaçu) is an ecological reserve with a lake, bike rentals and a track, bars, and restaurants as well as sculptures by artist Mário Cravo.

GOLF AND TENNIS

Hotel Sofitel Salvador (⊠ Rua Passárgada s/n, Itapuã, ☎ 071/374–9611) offers day passes to its golf course and its tennis courts.

Spectator Sport

FUTEBOL

Bahia and Vitória are the two best local teams, and they play year-round (except at Christmastime) Wednesday and Sunday at 5, in the **Estádio da Fonte Nova** (⊠ Av. Vale do Nazaré, Dique do Tororó, ☎ 071/243–3322, ext. 237). Tickets are sold at the stadium a day in advance. Avoid sitting behind the goals, where the roughhousing is worst. The best seats are in the *arquibancada superior* (high bleachers).

Shopping

Areas and Malls

For paintings, especially art naïf, visit the many galleries in the Cidade Alta and around the **Largo do Pelourinho.** For local handicrafts—lace, hammocks, wood carvings, musical instruments—the **Mercado Modelo** is your best bet.

There are two large malls with cinemas, restaurants, and local boutiques as well as branches of the major Rio, São Paulo, and Minas Gerais retailers. **Shopping Barra** (✉ Av. Centenário 2992), in the Barra neighborhood, offers a calm shopping experience. Top hotels provide free transportation to it. The more traditional of Salvador's malls, **Shopping Center Iguatemi** (✉ Av. Antônio Carlos Magalhães 148, Pituba), is near the bus station and is always crowded.

Specialty Stores

ART

Top local artists (many of whom use only first names or nicknames) include Totonho, Calixto, Raimundo Santos, Joailton, Nadinho, Nonato, Maria Adair, Carybé, Mário Cravo, and Jota Cunha. **Atelier Portal da Cor** (✉ Ladeira do Carmo 31, Pelourinho, ☎ 071/242–9466) is run by an artists' cooperative.

HANDICRAFTS

The **Casa Santa Barbara** (✉ Rua Alfredo de Brito s/n, Pelourinho, ☎ 071/244–0458) sells Bahian clothing and lacework of top quality, albeit at high prices. Note that it's closed Saturday afternoon and Sunday. **Kembo** (✉ Rua João de Deus 21, Pelourinho, ☎ 071/322–1379) carries native handicrafts. The owners travel to reservations all over the country and buy from the Pataxós, Kiriri, Tupí, Karajá, Xingú, Waiwai, Tikuna, Caipós, and Yanomami, among others.

Of Salvador's state-run handicrafts stores, the **Instituto de Artesanato Visconde de Mauá** (✉ Praça Azevedo Fernandes 2, Porto da Barra, ☎ 071/264–5440; ✉ R. Gregorio de Mattos 27, Pelourinho, ☎ 071/321–5638) is the best. Look for exquisite lace, musical instruments of African origin, and a variety of weavings and wood carvings.

JEWELRY AND GEMSTONES

Salvador has a branch (actually there are several, most of them in malls and major hotels) of the well-known, reputable **H. Stern** (✉ Largo do Pelourinho s/n, Pelourinho, ☎ 071/322–7353) chain. At **Simon** (✉ Rua Ignácio Accioli s/n, Pelourinho, ☎ 071/242–5218), the city's most famous jewelers, you can peer through a window into the room where goldsmiths work.

Side Trips from Salvador

Praia do Forte
72 km (45 mi) northeast of Salvador.

Praia do Forte was first settled in 1549 when Garcia D'Avila, a clerk for the Portuguese Crown, arrived with Brazil's first governor general, Tomé de Sousa. The clerk became a big landowner and introduced the young nation to cattle raising and coconut harvesting. To protect the coast here, he built a medieval-style castle that served as a fort—hence the town's name, which means "Fortress Beach." Today, it's turtles, rather than people, that need protection. The area's biggest attraction is a sea-turtle preservation project known as Projeto Tamar.

Although you can visit Praia do Forte on a day trip from Salvador, the town has several lodging options for longer stays. You'll also find restaurants that serve good, wholesome meals as well as nightlife that's toned down a few decibels from that in Salvador but still lively. You can book a trip here through any Salvador tour operator or travel agent. There's also a bus that travels here from the city.

The development in 1980 of **Projeto Tamar** (☎ 071/876–1045) on the beaches of Praia do Forte has turned what was once a small, struggling fishing village into a tourist destination with a mission—to save

Brazil's giant sea turtles and their hatchlings. During the nesting season (September through March), workers patrol the shore nightly to locate nests and move those found to be at risk to safer areas or to the open-air hatchery at the Tamar base on the beach end of the village's main street. At the base, you can watch an educational video, listen to lectures, and see the tanks that house the tiny turtles until they can be released to the sea.

Turning the village into a tourist attraction has not only helped fund the project but has also provided the villagers with a better source of income. Instead of killing turtles for their meat, eggs, and shells, fishermen are paid to protect them. Also a boon are all the jobs provided by the bars, restaurants, and shops that line the three unpaved streets.

On a relaxing day trip, you can visit Praia do Forte's village, stop by the turtle project, and swim or snorkel in the crystal-clear (and safe) waters of the **Papa Gente,** a 3-m-deep (10-ft-deep) natural pool formed by reefs at the ocean's edge.

If you have a couple of days to visit Praia do Forte, spend one of them on a jeep tour through the **Reserva de Sapiranga.** Its 1,482 acres of secondary Atlantic forest contain rare orchids and bromeliads and make up a sanctuary for endangered animals. Whitewater rafting is possible on the Rio Pojuca, which flows through the park, and Lago Timeantube, where more than 187 species of native birds have been sighted.

DINING AND LODGING

$$$ ✕ **Savor da Vila.** It isn't surprising that seafood, fresh from the ocean, is the speciality at this small, modest restaurant on Praia do Forte's main street. The staff is friendly, and the kitchen will prepare your meal any way you want it. ✉ *Alameda do Sol,* ☎ *no phone. No credit cards.*

$ ✕ **Bar do Souza.** One of Praia do Forte's many informal restaurants, this one is famous for its fish cakes. ✉ *Alameda do Sol,* ☎ *no phone. No credit cards.*

$-$$ ✕🏨 **Pousada Praia do Forte.** The thatched-roof bungalows here are spread around landscaped grounds right beside the ocean and the Tamar sea-turtle project. The pleasant restaurant offers international and Bahian cooking and is open to the public. ✉ *Av. do Farol s/n, Praia do Forte, Mata de São João, 48280-000,* ☎ *071/676–1010,* FAX *071/ 676–1033. 19 bungalows. Restaurant, beach. MC, V. MAP.*

$$$$ 🏨 **Praia do Forte Resort Hotel.** You can relax on a hammock and contemplate the sea from your own veranda at this beachfront resort, which is just around a curve in the beach from the Tamar sea-turtle project. If you feel the need to move about, activities include kayaking, sailing, and bird-watching. The restaurant and other facilities are open only to resort guests. ✉ *Rua do Farol s/n, Praia do Forte, Mata de São João 48280-000,* ☎ *071/676–1111,* FAX *071/676–1112,* WEB *www.praiadoforte.com. 250 rooms, 2 suites. 2 restaurants, 3 bars, 5 pools, 4 tennis courts, health club, beach, snorkeling, windsurfing, boating, dance club, children's programs. AE, DC, MC, V. MAP.*

$ 🏨 **Pousada Porto da Lua.** Directly on the palm-lined beach, this two-story pousada has a nice dining room and a large veranda complete with hammocks. ✉ *Praia do Forte, Mata de São João 48280-000,* ☎ *071/676–1372,* FAX *071/676–1446,* WEB *www.portodalua.com. 26 rooms, 4 suites. Restaurant, 2 bars, beach. AE, MC, V. BP.*

Costa do Sauípe
114 km (71 mi) northeast of Salvador.

An hour's drive north from Salvador along the Atlantic coast brings you to the Costa do Sauípe resort. Its five hotels, convention center, re-created local village, and sports complex are all part of a 500-acre development in an environmental protection area bordered by rain forest. Buses (private cars aren't allowed) transport you from the complex's entrance to your hotel. To get around during your stay, you can either hop the resort van or take a horse and carriage.

If you prefer small lodgings to grand resorts, opt for a stay in one of the six themed *pousadas* (inns) in Vila Nova da Praia. This re-creation of a typical northeastern village has cobblestone lanes, crafts shops, restaurants, bars, and entertainment in the streets. Vila Nova da Praia is also the perfect place to find gifts, especially at the Cores da Terra shop to the left of the village entrance. You'll need dark glasses when you look at all the brilliantly colored ceramics.

Regardless of where you stay, you'll have access to all the resort's amenities, including those of the sports complex, with its 18-hole PGA golf course, 15 tennis courts, equestrian center, and water-sports facilities.

LODGING

Rates at Costa do Sauípe's six pousadas are under R$200 ($100). Pousada Gabriela resembles a mansion on a coconut plantation in the coastal town of Ilhéus, south of Salvador. It's named after a character from a Jorge Amado novel. With its bright colors, the Pousada Carnaval captures the spirit of Bahia's pre-Lenten festivites. Pousada Maria Bonita re-creates regional festivals, on a small scale, through music and food. Art and antiques fill Pousada da Torre, giving you a real sense of Brazilian history. As its name implies, Pousada do Pelourinho is a replica of a house in Salvador's historic district. Pousada da Aldeia will make you feel as if you're staying in a 16th-century coastal village. To arrange a stay, contact the **pousada reservations office** (⊠ Km 76, BA 099, Linha Verde s/n, Costa do Sauíe, Mata de São João 48280-000, ☎ 071/353–4544, WEB www.costadosauipe.com.br).

$$$$ ▥ **Marriott Resort & Spa.** The view from your balcony is of the garden's swaying palm fronds and a clean sweep of beach. Inside your large room, the heaviness of the dark-wood furniture is offset by fabrics splashed with red floral patterns. You can enjoy drinks or a typical Brazilian meal at the poolside bar and restaurant or retreat inside to the lobby bar or a restaurant that offers Asian cuisine—*teppanyaki,* sushi, and Korean barbecue—served up with an ocean view. There's also a ballroom where you and as many as 749 other guests can dance the night away. ⊠ *Rodovia BA 099, Linha Verde, Costa do Sauípe, Mata de São João 48280-000,* ☎ *071/3069–2807,* FAX *071/3069–2045,* WEB *www.marriott.com. 239 rooms, 17 suites. 3 restaurants, 2 bars, pool, spa, health club. AE, DC, MC, V. BP.*

$$$$ ▥ **Sofitel Conventions & Resorts.** In the lobby, replicas of early sailing ships hang above a narrow pool, a hint that the hotel's theme involves not only sailing but also the discovery of Brazil. There are several cozy lobby sitting areas, each with its own TV. The Porão da Nau Pub & Club, off the lobby, is decorated in the style of a ship's hold, making it a unique place for drinks and dancing. If you'd rather enjoy a cocktail in the sun, head for the enormous poolside bar. The convention center has three restaurants, including one that specializes in Brazilian cuisine. The main Ile de France restaurant is named after a luxurious French ship and serves fine French cuisine. ⊠ *Rodovia BA 099, Linha Verde, Costa do Sauípe, Mata de São João 48280-000,* ☎ *071/ 467–2000,* FAX *071/467–2001,* WEB *www.sofitel-brasil.com.br. 392 rooms, 12 suites. 3 restaurants, bar, pub, pool, airport shuttle. AE, DC, MC, V. MAP.*

$$$$ ▥ **Sofitel Suites & Resort.** This hotel is evocative of the days when large coconut groves filled the Bahian landscape. Public spaces and rooms are done in subdued shades of brown and gold, and wood and natu-

ral fibers are used throughout. From the cozy lobby bar you can see the free-form pool—which surrounds small islands planted with coconut trees—and the Atlantic beyond. From the Tabuleiro bar-restaurant you can watch the chef prepare traditional Bahian dishes. The more sophisticated Casa Grande restaurant serves French and other international fare. ✉ *Rodovia BA 099, Linha Verde, Costa do Sauípe, Mata de São João 48280-000,* ☎ *071/468–2000,* FAX *071/468–2001,* WEB *www. sofitel-brasil.com.br. 198 suites. 2 restaurants, 2 bars, pool, airport shuttle. AE, DC, MC, V. BP.*

$$$$ 🔲 **SuperClubs Breezes.** The all-inclusive Breezes is SuperClubs's first Latin American venture. It's also the chain's first true family resort, a nod to the local culture. With such offerings as trapeze and circus workshops and a Kids' Club program, it's a cinch that children and their parents will have a great time. The spacious bilevel lobby and the main dining areas look out over a large free-form pool, the hotel's hub. Four floors of large rooms decorated with a tropical motif run beside the pool all the way to the ocean. In addition to the large buffet and grill, there are four themed restaurants: Japanese, Italian, Bahian, and Mediterranean. A large Brazilian tour operator, BBTUR, has an office in the lobby where you can arrange tours of Bahia or reconfirm airline tickets. ✉ *Rodovia BA 099, Linha Verde, Costa do Sauípe, Mata de São João 48280-000,* ☎ *071/463–1000,* FAX *071/463–1026,* WEB *www. superclubs.com.br. 308 rooms, 16 suites. 5 restaurants, 3 bars, pool, disco, health club, children's programs, travel services, airport shuttle. AE, DC, MC, V. All-inclusive.*

$$$ 🔲 **Renaissance Costa do Sauípe Resort.** Although the hotel's overall design is one of classic elegance, the open-air lobby has a casual atmosphere and a restaurant that looks out over sand dunes. If you opt to dine in the Mediterranean restaurant, your choices will include specialties from Provence and southern Italy; some of the dishes will even be cooked in a wood-burning oven. Fully equipped meeting rooms can accommodate gatherings of more than 300 people. ✉ *Rodovia BA 099, Linha Verde, Costa do Sauípe, Mata de São João 48280-000,* ☎ *071/ 676–1561,* FAX *071/676–1560,* WEB *www.marriott.com. 237 rooms, 11 suites. 2 restaurants, deli, pool, sauna, fitness center, meeting rooms, airport shuttle. AE, DC, MC, V. BP.*

OUTDOOR ACTIVITIES AND SPORTS

The **Costa do Sauípe Sports Complex** (✉ Rodovia BA 099, Linha Verde, Costa do Sauípe, Mata de São João, ☎ 071/353–4544) has an 18-hole golf course with a clubhouse, a tennis center with 15 courts, a water-sports center, an equestrian center that offers trail rides and ecological tours, a soccer field, and squash courts. Your hotel staff members can help you make arrangements to participate in the sport of your choice.

Cachoeira

109 km (67 mi) northwest of Salvador.

This riverside colonial town dates from the 16th and 17th centuries, when sugarcane was the economy's mainstay. It has been designated a national monument and is the site of some of Brazil's most authentic Afro-Brazilian rituals. One of the most interesting is a festival held by the Irmandada da Boa Morte (Sisterhood of Our Lady of Good Death). Organized by descendants of 19th-century slaves who founded an association of black women devoted to abolition, it's held on a Friday, Saturday, and Sunday in the middle of August.

Devotion to Our Lady of Good Death began in the slave quarters, the sites of discussions on abolition and prayer meetings honoring those who had died for liberty. The slaves implored Our Lady of Good

Death to end slavery and promised to hold an annual celebration in her honor should their prayers be answered.

The festival begins with a procession by the sisters who, heads held high, carry an 18th-century statue of their patron saint through the streets. The statue is adorned in a typical all-white Bahian dress, which signifies mourning in the Candomblé religion practiced by many of the sisters. Sunday, the festival's main day, sees a solemn mass followed by a joyful procession that begins with the traditional samba *de roda,* which is danced in a circle. Other festival events include community suppers featuring local delicacies.

On an excursion to Cachoeira you can walk through the colorful country market and see architecture preserved from an age when Cachoeira shipped tons of tobacco and sugar downriver to Salvador. Next to Cachoeira's oldest church, the Nossa Senhora da Ajuda (circa 1595), is the **Museu da Boa Morte** (⊠ Largo D'Ajuda s/n, ☎ 075/725–1343), with photos and ceremonial dresses worn by members of the Sisterhood of Our Lady of Good Death during their rituals and festivals. You may also meet some of the elderly but always energetic women whose ancestors protested slavery. It's recommended that you make a small donation; hours are weekdays 10–1 and 3–5.

¢–$ ✕🛏 **Pousada do Convento.** You can stay overnight or have a good lunch at this one-time Carmelite monastery. It dates from the 17th century. ⊠ *Praça da Aclamação s/n,* ☎ 𝖥𝖠𝖷 *075/725–1716. 26 rooms. Restaurant, air-conditioning, minibars, pool, playground, meeting room, free parking. AE, MC, V.*

Parque Nacional da Chapada Diamantina

318 km (198 mi) west of Cachoeira; 427 km (265 mi) west of Salvador.

A waterfall so clear it looks like glass, mysterious caves with ancient paintings, trails etched into the ground forever by *garimpeiros* (miners) who walked the same paths every day to the diamond mines, the tall peaks of the Sincorá Range, a cavern with a fossilized panther—these are just some of the sights in the 84,000-sqare-km (32,424-sqare-mi) Chapada Dimantina National Park.

Fortunes were made in the region when gold and diamonds were discovered in the early 17th century. The largest city was Lençóis, which became so important that it even had a French consulate. When the boom ended, the city was forgotten. Since the park was established in 1985, Lençóis has enjoyed a renaissance. More than 250 mansions are being restored, and new hotels, pousadas, and restaurants are opening as the town becomes the park's hub.

Tours from Salvador include transportation to and from the region as well as guides. You can also take a bus from the city and arrange for tours through agencies in Lençóis. Options for freelance guides range from local children who simply know the way in and out of the park to ecologists and other scientists. One interesting trek is a 3-day bus and hiking journey to the Cachoeira da Fumaça, also known as the Glass Waterfall. It's 400 m (1,312 ft) high, the tallest in Brazil and fifth highest in the world. The trip includes an overnight in a cave.

$ 🛏 **Pousada de Lençóis.** On the edge of Lençóis and next to the Parque Nacional da Chapada Diamantina is this homey pousada. A stay in one of its extra-large rooms (some sleep up to five people) truly makes you feel as if you're a guest in someone's country house. On-site amenities include a bar, a restaurant that serves lunch and dinner, a tour agency

AFRO-BRAZILIAN HERITAGE

There are few other countries with such a symphony of skin tones grouped under one nationality. This rich Brazilian identity began when the first Portuguese sailors were left to manage the new land. From the beginning, Portuguese migration to Brazil was predominantly male, a fact that unfortunately led to unbridled sexual license—ranging from seduction to rape—involving Indian women and, later, African women.

The first Africans arrived in 1532, along with the Portuguese colonizers, who continued to buy slaves from English, Spanish, and Portuguese traders until 1855. All records pertaining to slave trading were destroyed in 1890, making it impossible to know exactly how many people were brought to Brazil. Still, it's estimated that 3 to 4.5 million Africans were captured and transported from the Sudan, Gambia, Guinea, Sierra Leone, Senegal, Liberia, Nigeria, Benin, Angola, and Mozambique. Many were literate Muslims who were better educated than their white overseers and owners.

In Brazil, miscegenation and cohabitation between white men and women of other races was practiced openly. In the great houses of sugar plantations, which relied on slave labor, it was common for the master to have a white wife and slave mistresses. A master might free the mother of his mixed-race offspring and allow a son of color to learn a trade or inherit a share of the plantation. The legendary Xica da Silva—a slave concubine elevated to mistress of the manor by her wealthy master (and then consigned to oblivion and abandonment when he was ordered back to Portugal)—vividly demonstrates the nexus of Brazilian sexual and racial politics.

When the sugar boom came to an end, it became too expensive for slave owners to support their "free" labor force. Abolition occurred gradually, however. It began around 1871, with the passage of the Law of the Free Womb, which liberated all Brazilians born of slave mothers. In 1885, another law was passed freeing slaves over age 60. Finally, on May 13, 1888, Princess Isabel signed a law freeing all slaves.

Often unskilled, the former slaves became Brazil's unemployed and underprivileged. Although the country has long been praised for its lack of discrimination, this veneer of racial equality is deceptive. Afro-Brazilians still don't receive education on a par with that of whites, nor do they always receive equal pay for equal work. There are far fewer black or mulatto professionals, politicians, and ranking military officers than white ones.

Although a civil rights movement like that of the United States is unlikely, subtle activism to bring about racial equality and educate all races about the rich African legacy continues. For many people, the most important holiday isn't September 7 (Brazilian Independence Day) but rather November 20 (National Black Consciousness Day). It honors the anniversary of the death of Zumbi, the leader of the famous *quilombo* (community of escaped slaves) of Palmares, which lasted more than 100 years and was destroyed by *bandeirantes* (adventurers who tracked runaway slaves) in one final great battle for freedom.

that can arrange park trips, and a large pool that's surrounded by flower gardens. ✉ *Av. Tancredo Neves, 274, Bloco B, Sala 336, Lençóis 41820-020,* ☎ *071/358–9395,* FAX *071/358–0114,* WEB *www.svn.com. br/lencois/ingles02.html, 36 rooms. Air-conditioning, restaurant, bar, pool, travel services. V. BP.*

¢   Ⅲ **Pousada Sincorá.** Named after the mountain range in the Parque
★   Nacional da Chapada Diamantina, this pousada is in the foothill village of Andaraí, close to Lençóis as well as to several trails and remarkable scenery. It has an excellent library with English-language books
and magazines. The owners, Helder and Ana Maria Madeira, speak
English; he's a guide and she's the cook. Rooms (two double and three
triple) have private baths and TVs. You can get your laundry done on
request, get help hiring local guides, and arrange for transportation to
and from the park. ✉ *Av. Paraguaçu s/n, Andaraí, 46830-000. 5
rooms. Dining room, air-conditioning, laundry service. V. BP.*

RECIFE

Just over 3.2 million people call the capital of Pernambuco State home.
This vibrant metropolis, set 829 km (515 mi) north of Salvador, has
a spirit that's halfway between that of the modern cities of Brazil's south
and of the traditional northeastern centers. It offers both insight on
the past and a window to the future.

It was in Pernambuco State, formerly a captaincy, that the most violent battles between the Dutch and the Portuguese took place. Under
the Portuguese, the capital city was the nearby community of Olinda.
But beginning in 1637 and through the Dutch turn at the reins (under
the powerful count Maurício de Nassau), both Olinda and Recife
were greatly developed.

The Dutch had hoped that Brazilian sugar planters wouldn't resist their
rule, but many took up arms. In 1654, after a series of battles around
Recife, the Dutch finally surrendered. In the 17th century, Pernambuco
maintained much of the affluence of the earlier sugar age by cultivat-
ing cotton. With several rivers and offshore reefs, Recife proved to be
an excellent port and began to outgrow Olinda.

Today Recife is a leader in health care and design, among other things.
It's also Brazil's third-largest gastronomic center—it's almost impossible to get a bad meal here. Nearby Olinda has been recognized by
UNESCO as part of Humanity's Natural and Cultural Heritage. It has
attracted artists who display their canvases on easels behind the iron-
barred windows of well-preserved colonial homes.

Recife is built around three rivers and connected by 49 bridges. Its name
comes from the *arrecifes* (reefs) that line the coast. Because of this unique
location, water and light often lend the city interesting textures. In the
morning, when the tide recedes from Boa Viagem Beach, the rocks of
the reefs slowly reappear. Pools of water are formed, fish flap around
beachgoers, and the rock formations dry into odd colors. And if the
light is just right on the Rio Capibaribe, the ancient buildings of Recife Velho (Old Recife) are reflected off the river's surface in a water-
color display.

Exploring Recife

Recife is spread out and somewhat hard to negotiate. Centro—with
its mixture of high-rises, colonial churches, and markets—is always busy
during the day. The crowds and the narrow streets can make finding
your way around even more confusing.

Centro consists of three areas: Recife Velho; Recife proper, with the districts of Santo Antônio and São José; and the districts of Boa Vista and Santo Amaro. The first two areas are on islands formed by the Rivers Capibaribe, Beberibe, and Pina; the third is made into an island by the Canal Tacaruna.

Six kilometers (4 miles) south of Centro is the upscale residential and beach district of Boa Viagem, reached by bridge across the Bacia do Pina. Praia da Boa Viagem (Boa Viagem Beach), the Copacabana of Recife, is chockablock with trendy clubs and restaurants as well as many moderately priced and expensive hotels.

Numbers in the text correspond to numbers in the margin and on the Recife map.

A Good Tour

A visit to Santo Antônio's **Praça da República** ①—with its stately palms, fountains, and statues—is a pleasant way to start your day and get your bearings. In and around the square are several landmark buildings, including the Palácio da Justiça. Behind it, on the Rua Imperador Dom Pedro II, is the **Igreja da Ordem Terceira de São Francisco** ②. From this church, follow Rua Imperador for about nine blocks to Travessa do Macêdo. On your right is the **Mercado de São José** ③. Head west from the market, past the Praça Dom Vital, to Rua das Águas Verdes, where you'll find the Pátio de São Pedro and the **Catedral de São Pedro dos Clérigos** ④. From the cathedral, cross Avenida Dantas Barreto to the **Igreja e Convento do Carmo** ⑤. Take Rua Mq. de Herval toward the Rio Capibaribe and cross Rua Floriano Peixoto to the **Casa da Cultura** ⑥.

For a relaxing lunch, hop a cab to Rua do Bom Jesus in **Recife Velho** ⑦ and pick any restaurant. Afterward, if you're up for more sightseeing, you can take another taxi to one of the city's forts or museums. In Recife Velho, up Rua do Brum, is the **Fortaleza do Brum** ⑧. Across the Ponte 23 de Setembro and along Avenida Sul and the waterfront is the **Forte das Cinco Pontas** ⑨, in the São José district. Near the Rio Capibaribe as it curves northwest are the **Museu do Estado de Pernambuco** ⑩ and the **Museu do Homem de Nordeste** ⑪. On the other side of the Capibaribe and 15 km (9 mi) out of town by way of Avenida Caxangá is the **Oficina Cerâmica Francisco Brennand** ⑫.

TIMING AND PRECAUTIONS

The walking portion of this tour takes three to four hours, longer if you linger at a café. Add another two or three hours if you visit one of the farther-flung forts or museums. Although petty thievery has been greatly reduced in Recife, take the normal precautions—be on guard against pickpockets, keep a tight hold on purses and cameras, and leave jewelry in the hotel safe.

SIGHTS TO SEE

⑥ Casa da Cultura. In a 19th-century building that was once a prison, the old cells with their heavy iron doors have been transformed into shops that sell clay figurines, wood sculptures, carpets, leather goods, and articles made from woven straw. One of the cells has been kept in its original form to give you an idea of how the prisoners lived. There are areas for exhibitions and shows, such as the Monday, Wednesday, and Friday performances of local dances like the *ciranda,* the forró, and the *bumba-meu-boi.* There are also clean public rest rooms. ⊠ *Rua Floriano Peixoto s/n, Santo Antônio,* ☎ *081/3224–2850.* ⚏ *Free.* ☾ *Mon.–Sat. 9–7, Sun. 9–2.*

④ Catedral de São Pedro dos Clérigos. The facade of this cathedral, which was built in 1782, has fine wood sculptures; inside is a splen-

Recife

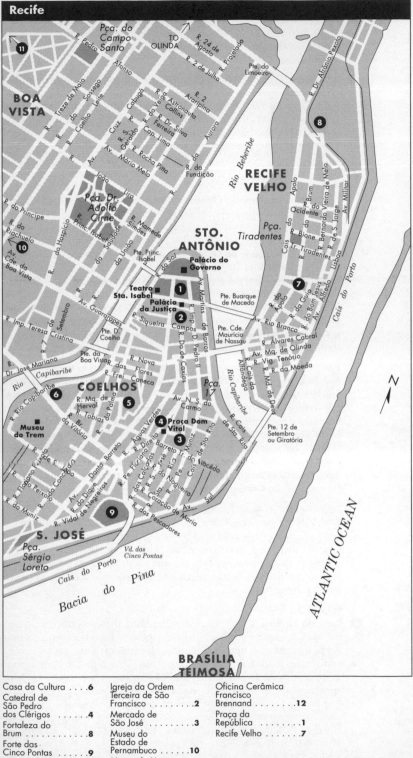

did trompe-l'oeil ceiling. The square surrounding the cathedral is a hangout for artists, who often read their poetry or perform folk music. It's lined with many restaurants, shops, and bars; you'll also find a museum containing exhibits on Carnaval and an art gallery. ⊠ *Pátio de São Pedro, São José,* ☎ *081/3224–2954.* ⊠ *Free.* ⊙ *Tues.–Sat. 9–5.*

❽ Fortaleza do Brum. To safeguard their control, the Dutch wisely yet futilely built more than one fortress. In this one (circa 1629) you'll find reminders of those precarious days, in the on-site **Army Museum,** with its collection of old cannons, infantry weapons, and soldiers' utensils; there's even a skeleton of a soldier that dates from 1654. On a lighter note, the fort also contains a restaurant. ⊠ *Praça Luso-Brasileiro, Recife Velho,* ☎ *081/3224–4620.* ⊠ *Free.* ⊙ *Tues.–Fri. 9–4, weekends 2–4.*

❾ Forte das Cinco Pontas. The Dutch built the original fort—which had five sides—using mud in 1630. It was rebuilt in 1677 with stone and mortar; it now only has only four sides, but it has retained its original name. Inside is the **Museu da Cidade,** where maps and photos illustrate Recife's history. Before becoming a museum, it was used as a military headquarters and a prison. ⊠ *Largo das Cinco Pontas, São José,* ☎ *081/3224–8492.* ⊠ *Free.* ⊙ *Weekdays 9–6, weekends 1–5.*

❺ Igreja e Convento do Carmo. The historic baroque-style church and convent are constructed of wood and white gold. The main altar has a life-size statue of Our Lady of Carmel. ⊠ *Praça do Carmo s/n, Santo Antônio,* ☎ *081/3224–3341.* ⊠ *Free.* ⊙ *Weekdays 6:30 AM–8 PM (mass at 6:30 AM, 6 PM, and 7 PM), Sat. 7 AM–8 PM (mass at 7 AM), Sun. 10 AM–8:30 PM (mass at 10 AM and 7 PM).*

❷ Igreja da Ordem Terceira de São Francisco. Built in 1606, this church has beautiful Portuguese tile work. Don't miss the adjoining Capela Dourada (Golden Chapel), which was constructed in 1697 and is an outstanding example of Brazilian baroque architecture. The complex also contains a convent, the Convento Franciscano de Santo Antônio, and a museum containing sacred art. ⊠ *Rua Imperador Dom Pedro II s/n, Santo Antônio,* ☎ *081/3224–0530.* ⊠ *Church: Free. Museum: R$2.40.* ⊙ *Weekdays 8–11:30 and 2–5, Sat. 8–11:30.*

❸ Mercado de São José. In the city's most traditional market, vendors sell handicrafts, produce, and herbs. It's housed in a beautiful cast-iron structure that was imported from France in the 19th century. ⊠ *Trv. do Macêdo s/n, São José.* ⊙ *Mon.–Sat. 6–6, Sun. 6–noon.*

❿ Museu do Estado de Pernambuco. The state historical museum is in a mansion once owned by a baron and seems more like a home filled with beautiful antiques than a museum. There's a grand piano, a dining-room table set with 18th-century china, an ornate 19th-century crib, and many beautiful paintings. ⊠ *Av. Rui Barbosa 960, Graça,* ☎ *081/3427–9322.* ⊠ *R$2* ⊙ *Tues.–Fri. 9–5:30, weekends 2–5:30.*

⓫ Museu do Homem do Nordeste. With three museums under one roof—one has displays about sugar, another anthropological exhibits, and the third regional handicrafts, the Museum of Northeastern Man offers great insight into Brazil's history. You'll find utensils made by indigenous peoples, European colonizers, and African slaves; religious articles used in Catholic and Candomblé rituals; and ceramic figurines by such artists as Mestre Vitalino and Mestre Zé. ⊠ *Av. 17 de Agosto 2187, Casa Forte,* ☎ *081/3441–5500.* ⊠ *Free.* ⊙ *Tues. and Fri. 11–6, Thurs. 8–6, weekends 1–6.*

⓬ Oficina Cerâmica Francisco Brennand. In the old São José sugar refinery, this museum-workshop houses more than 2,000 pieces by the great (and prolific) Brazilian artist Francisco Brennand. Having studied in France, he was influenced by Pablo Picasso and Joan Miró, among others, and his works include paintings, drawings, and engravings as well as sculptures and ceramics. Although it's 15 km (9 mi) from Recife Velho, the museum's location amid forest and fountains is almost as appealing as its displays. ⊠ *Av. Caxangá, Km 16, Várzea,* ☎ 081/ 3271–2466. ☜ *R$2.* ⊙ *Weekdays 8–6.*

❶ **Praça da República.** Republic Square was originally known as the Field of Honor, a nod to those who were drawn and quartered here during the Republican movement of 1817. The structures around the square showcase the city's architecture from the 19th through the 20th centuries. Highlights include the Teatro Santa Isabel (St. Isabel Theater, 1850); the Palácio do Campo das Princesas, also known as the Palácio do Governo (Government House, 1841); and the Palácio da Justiça (Court House, 1930).

❼ **Recife Velho.** Most of Old Recife's colonial public buildings and houses have been restored. The area between Rua do Bom Jesus and Rua do Apolo is full of shops, cafés, and bars, making it the hub of downtown life both day and night; on some weekends there's even dancing in the streets. A handicrafts fair is held every Sunday from 1–10 on Rua do Bom Jesus.

Beaches

Boa Viagem. Coconut palms line Recife's most popular beach, the 7-km-long (4-mi-long) Praia da Boa Viagem. A steady Atlantic breeze tames the hot sun, and reef formations create pools of warm water that are perfect for swimming. Sailors and fishermen beach their *jangadas* (handcrafted log rafts with beautiful sails), and vendors sell coconut drinks from kiosks. Avenida Boa Viagem separates a row of hotels and apartments from the beach, which is lined by a wide blue *calçadão* (sidewalk) that's perfect for runs, bike rides, or evening promenades. On weekend afternoons there's a handicrafts fair in Praça da Boa Viagem. Surfing seems to be the only beach activity that's forbidden here, owing to shark sightings.

Cabo de Santo Agostinho. About 35 km (22 mi) southeast of Recife is one of Pernambuco's finest beaches. It's good for swimming, though surfing has been banned owing to the danger of shark attacks. In the town of Cabo de Santo Agostinho you can walk around the ruins of the Forte Castelo do Mar.

Gaibu. Just 30 km (19 mi) south of Recife, quiet, beautiful Gaibu is surrounded by palm trees. Its blue waters are good for surfing, and it's also the site of volleyball competitions and fishing and sailing events.

Ilha de Itamaracá. This island is off the coast of the historic city of Igarassu, 39 km (24 mi) north of Recife. The best beach is Forte Orange, next to Coroa do Avião.

Maracaípe. Roughly 73 km (46 mi) southwest of Recife is secluded Maracaípe Beach, where surfing championships take place.

Porto de Galinhas. You'll find cool, clean waves and several resorts at Porto de Galinhas, 70 km (43 mi) south of Recife. The beach, which follows the curve of a bay lined with coconut palms and cashew trees, gets crowded on weekends year-round. There are plenty of jangadas for rent; other boats can take you to the island of Santo Aleixo.

Tamandaré. Although it's 110 km (68 mi) south of Recife and in the middle of an important nature reserve, developers have their eye on Tamandaré. Come quick, before its beaches—such as Praia dos Carneiros and Praia de Guadalupe—become one big resort area.

Dining

Brazilian

$–$$ ✕ **Oficina do Savor.** Everything is tasty at this regional restaurant, but do try the *abóbora com camarão* (pumpkin stuffed with shrimp and served with a *pitanga* sauce). ⊠ *Rua do Amparo 335, Amparo/Olinda,* ☎ *081/3429–3331. AE, DC, MC, V. Closed Mon.*

Eclectic

$–$$ ✕ **Leite.** Established in 1882, Leite is one of Brazil's oldest restaurants.
★ Some tables are filled by the same people each day, and several waiters are following in the footsteps of generations of family members who have worked here. Recent restorations added the coolness of air-conditioning to the already pleasant ambience. Roast lamb is a specialty. ⊠ *Praça Joaquim Nabuco 147, Santo Antônio,* ☎ *081/3224–7977. AE, DC, MC, V.*

Italian

$$$ ✕ **Famiglia Giuliana.** This is one restaurant where you can take your time and not risk having the place close. It's open from lunchtime until the last diner leaves. The seafood fettuccine is an excellent choice. ⊠ *Av. Eng. Domingos Ferreira 3980, Boa Viagem,* ☎ *081/3465–9922. AE, DC, MC, V.*

$–$$ ✕ **Barbarico Bongiovani.** A sophisticated setting and a high-quality Italian menu are among the draws here. Try the scallopini al Marsala. ⊠ *Av. Engenheiro Domingos Ferreira 2655, Boa Viagem,* ☎ *081/3325–4268. AE, DC, MC, V. No lunch.*

$–$$ ✕ **Buongustaio.** If you like lamb, head for this highly recommended establishment. ⊠ *Rua Santo Elias 350, Espinheiro,* ☎ *081/3241–1470. DC. Closed Sun.*

Portuguese

$$$ ✕ **Tasca.** The menu is perhaps more Portuguese than Brazilian, so one of the best dishes is *bacalhau* (codfish cooked with olive oil, onion, garlic, tomatoes, potatoes, and white wine). ⊠ *165 Rua Dom José Lopes, Boa Viagem,* ☎ *081/3326–6309. AE. Closed Mon.*

Seafood

$–$$ ✕ **Bargaço.** People come to this pleasant restaurant for moquecas *pernambucanas* (with onion, tomatoes, peppers, parsley, and coconut milk). ⊠ *Av. Boa Viagem 670, Pina,* ☎ *081/3465–1847. AE, DC, MC, V.*

$–$$ ✕ **Oamphitrião.** At least one dinner and evening out in Recife Velho
★ is a must on your trip. Although there are many good restaurants along Rua Bom Jesus, Oamphitrião stands out for its camarão Maurício de Nassau, a shrimp dish named after one of the bridges that was named after the Dutch head of the state before Recife was recaptured by Portuguese. Space is limited inside, but most diners opt for the sidewalk tables, where they can eat and watch the action. ⊠ *Rua do Bom Jesus 183, Recife Velho,* ☎ *081/3224–2143. V. No dinner Sun.–Tues.*

Lodging

Most of Recife's top hotels are about 20 minutes from the airport, across from the Boa Viagem and Pina beaches or along Piedade Beach, in the municipality of Jaboatão dos Guararapes.

$$$$ ⊞ **Mar Hotel Recife.** Location is one of this hotel's main draws: it's a five-minute drive from the airport, a 15-minute drive from Recife Velho, and very close to Boa Viagem. Rooms have desks with swivel chairs, two phone lines, and fax/modem lines. When you're ready to call it a day, you can relax by the pool—with its soothing waterfall—or feast on international, Italian, or Japanese cuisine at one of the three restaurants. Afterward, you can retire to the bar for drinks or maybe a little dancing on the small dance floor. ✉ *Rua Barão de Souza Leão 451, Boa Viagem 51030-300,* ☎ *081/3462–4444,* 🖷 *081/3462–4445,* WEB *www.marhotel.com.br. 207 rooms, 30 suites. 3 restaurants, bar, pool, sauna, health club, meeting room. AE, DC, MC, V.*

$$$ 🏨 **Recife Monte Hotel.** Just a block from Boa Viagem Beach, this hotel has all the amenities of a luxury hotel, including a lovely pool. A must during your stay here is the Sunday *feijoada* (Brazilian national dish consisting of black beans, smoked meats, oranges, and whatever else the chef may decide to throw in) in the Marruá restaurant. ✉ *Rua dos Navegantes 363, Boa Viagem 51021-010,* ☎ *081/3465–7422,* 🖷 *081/3465–8406,* WEB *www.recifemontehotel.com.br. 152 rooms, 21 suites. Restaurant, bar, pool, sauna, health club, beauty salon. AE, DC, V. BP.*

$$ 🏨 **Atlante Plaza Hotel.** Facing Recife's most popular beach, this highrise's blue-glass windows make even the sky look pale. All rooms, decorated in subdued shades of blue, have sea views, but be sure to take a ride in the glass-enclosed elevator for a truly memorable ocean panorama. If you tire of sand in your shoes but not of the sun, head for the pool. A buffet breakfast is served in the Brasserie restaurant, where you can also have a buffet or à la carte lunch. The Mirage restaurant serves international or Brazilian dinners. ✉ *Av. Boa Viagem 5426, 51030-000,* ☎ *081/3462–3333,* 🖷 *081/3302–3333,* WEB *www.atlanteplaza.com.br. 70 room, 29 suites. 2 restaurants, 2 bars, pool, health club, business services, meeting rooms. AE, DC, V. BP.*

$$ 🏨 **Parthenon Golden Beach.** At one of the best apartment hotels in town, each unit has one or two bedrooms, a living room, and a fully equipped kitchen. ✉ *Av. Bernardo Vieira de Melo 1204, Piedade, Jaboatão dos Guararapes 54410–001,* ☎ *081/3468–3002,* 🖷 *081/3468–1941. 175 apartments. 2 restaurants, 2 bars, air-conditioning, kitchenettes, pool, sauna, health club. AE, DC.*

$ 🏨 **Hotel do Sol.** This hotel faces Praia do Pina on Avenida Boa Viagem. Each simple but comfortable room has a TV, a minibar, and a phone. ✉ *Av. Boa Viagem 978, Pina, 50030-010,* ☎ *081/3465–9898,* 🖷 *081/3465–5278. 69 rooms. Bar, air-conditioning, minibars, pool. DC, MC, V.*

$ 🏨 **Recife Plaza.** Overlooking the Rio Capibaribe, this modern downtown hotel is simple and functional. Rooms count TVs and phones among their amenities. ✉ *Rua da Aurora 225, Boa Vista 50060-000,* ☎ 🖷 *081/3231–1200. 68 rooms. Restaurant, air-conditioning, minibars, pool, sauna. AE, DC, MC, V.*

Nightlife and the Arts

Nightlife

Pólo Pina, the calçadão in the Pina district, is a popular area near the beach for nighttime activities. In the streets off Rua Herculano Bandeira you'll find close to two dozen bars and restaurants. Between Rua do Apolo and Rua do Bom Jesus (or Rua dos Judeus) in Recife Velho, people gather in a seemingly endless variety of bars, cafés, and nightclubs. On Saturday, the market in Praça de Boa Viagem comes alive with forró dancers.

BARS

O Biruta (✉ Rua Bem-te-vi 15, Brasília Teimosa, ☎ 081/3325–5321) is a great spot to watch the moon rise over the beach. Chilled draft beer, tasty snacks, and excellent service make **Boteco** (✉ Av. Boa Viagem 1660, Boa Viagem, ☎ 081/3325–1428) one of the most popu-

lar bars in town. **Depois** (⊠ Av. Rio Branco 66, Recife Velho, ☎ 081/
3424–7451) is in an old building at the heart of a bohemian neighborhood. Hits from the '60s and '70s are a hit with an over-30 crowd.

CYBERCAFÉ

Just about anything you need can be found in the Guararapes shop-
ping center, including Internet services at **Cyber Café do Shopping
Guararapes** (⊠ Av. Barreto de Menezes 800, Piedade, Jaboatão dos
Guararapes, ☎ 081/3464–2488).

DANCE AND MUSIC CLUBS

The **Calypso Bar** (⊠ Rua do Bom Jesus 147, Recife Velho, ☎ 081/3224–
4855) is *the* place to dance to live music ranging from Caribbean
rhythms to forró. You can fortify yourself with appetizers as well as
drinks. **Downtown** (⊠ Rua Vigário Tenório 105, Recife Velho, ☎
081/3424–5731), a club with a London pub look, is a good place to
be on Wednesday night when local bands play. The club is popular with
a younger set. **Fashion Club** (⊠ Av. Fernando Simões Barbosa 266, Boa
Viagem, ☎ 081/3327–4040) is a hot spot Wednesday through Sunday,
with a DJ, a laser show, a great dance floor, and three pubs. Sometimes
there are live shows, too.

GAY AND LESBIAN BARS

Galeria Joana D'Arc (⊠ Rua Herculano Bandeira 500, Pina) is a cluster of small cafés and bars, among them Café Poire, Anjo Solto, Barn-
abé, and Oriente Médio.

The Arts

Closed for 30 years, the **Teatro Santa Isabel** (⊠ Praça da República
s/n, Santo António, ☎ 081/3224–1020), built in 1850, has reopened
after a complete restoration. The neoclassical theater is the setting for
operas, plays, and classical concerts.

Outdoor Activities and Sports

Participant Sports

SAILING

At Boa Viagem, fishermen with jangadas offer sailing or fishing trips.
The waters are shallow and calm at Maria Farinha Beach, on the
north coast at the mouth of the Rio Timbó. Here you can rent jet skis,
take ultralight flights, and enjoy motorboat and catamaran rides. The
bar-restaurant **Sea Paradise** (⊠ Rua Almir B. Cunha s/n, ☎ 081/
3435–1740) offers live music, a noteworthy fish stew, and day or night
catamaran rides.

SCUBA DIVING

For centuries, the treacherous offshore reefs that gave Recife its name
have struck fear into the hearts of sailors. Many a vessel has failed to
navigate the natural harbor successfully. Seventeen wrecks have been
identified as good and safe dives for underwater explorers of various
experience levels. The *Vapor de Baixo* is one such ship. Bombed by
the Germans during World War II, it's 20 m (65 ft) down and is crawl-
ing with lobsters and turtles. Though diving is practiced year-round,
visibility is best between October and May, when the wind and water
are at their calmest.

The **Seagate–Expedição Atlântico** dive operation (⊠ Cais de Santa Rita
s/n, ☎ 081/3426–1657 or 081/3469–3182) dive operation is off
Avenida Sul on Pina Bay, near the Forte das Cinco Pontas and just before the 12 de Setembro Bridge to Recife Velho. It offers courses, rents
equipment, and runs trips for certified divers.

Shopping

Vendors at the **Mercado de São José** (⊠ Trv. do Macedo, São José) sell clothes and handicrafts as well as produced. It's open Monday–Saturday 6–6 and Sunday morning 6–11:30. The **Feira Hippie** (Hippie Fair), held in the seafront Praça da Boa Viagem on weekend afternoons starting at 4, has handicrafts.

Shopping Center Guararapes (⊠ Av. Barreto de Menezes 800, Piedade, Jaboatão dos Guararapes, ☎ 081/3464–2211) has everything the Shopping Center Recife has but on a smaller scale. It's near Piedade Beach.

The enormous **Shopping Center Recife** (⊠ Rua Padre Carapuceiro 777, Boa Viagem, ☎ 081/3464–6000) is the perfect place for a day of shopping. In addition to a good variety of both Brazilian and international stores, you'll find restaurants, banks, a post office, pharmacies, and a business center. It's not far from the Boa Viagem Beach.

Side Trips from Recife

Olinda

7 km (4 mi) north from Recife.

The name of Pernambuco State's original capital means "beautiful," and this must have been what came to mind when the first Europeans stood atop the forested hills and gazed at ocean and beach spread out before them. Today the town's natural beauty is complemented by colonial buildings painted in every color found in the crayon box, making it a stunning slice of the old northeast.

Founded by the Portuguese in 1535, Olinda was developed further by the Dutch during their brief turn at running Pernambuco in the 1600s. The narrow cobblestone streets of this UNESCO World Cultural Site curve up and down hills that, at every turn, offer spectacular views of both Recife and the Atlantic. The scene is just as picturesque up close: many of the houses have latticed balconies, heavy doors, and stucco walls. The zoning laws are strict, resulting in a beautiful, compact city that artists, musicians, and intellectuals have made their own.

Although the city center is easy to explore on foot, the hills are steep and the attractions are spread out, so it's best to take a guided bus or van tour. Look for the official guides (they have ID cards) who congregate in the Praça do Carmo. They're former street children, and half the fee (R$45) for a full city tour goes to a home for street children.

On Olinda's southern edge is the **Centro de Convenções Pernambuco** (Pernambuco Convention Center; ⊠ Complexo de Salgadinho s/n, ☎ 081/3241–7966), one of the most modern in Latin America and the location of Empetur, the state tourism office. Cultural performances are often held in the center's theater and auditorium.

The main chapel of the **Mosteiro de São Bento,** a Benedictine monastery, is considered one of Brazil's most beautiful. It once housed the nation's first law school. The 10 AM Sunday mass features Gregorian chant. ⊠ *Rua de São Bento s/n, Varadouro,* ☎ *081/3429–3288.* ☞ *Free.* ☉ *Daily 7–11:30 and 2–6:30.*

The **Alto da Sé** is the most scenic spot for viewing Olinda, Recife, and the ocean. It's also a good place see some historic churches as well as to sample Pernambuco's famous tapioca cakes, thin pancakes filled with grated coconut and sour cheese. Have a seat at one of the outdoor tables here, or browse in the shops that sell handicrafts—including lace—and paintings.

Built in 1540 and restored in 1654, the **Igreja da Misericórdia** (Mercy Church) has rich sculptures of wood, gold, and silver. It's atop the Alto da Sé. ⊠ *Rua Bispo Coutinho s/n,* ☎ *081/3429–0627.* ☒ *Free.* ☽ *Daily 8–noon and 2–5.*

The last of many renovations to the 1537 **Igreja da Sé,** on the Alto da Sé, was in 1983. It has now been restored as much as possible to its original appearance. From its side terrace you can see the Old City and the ocean. ⊠ *Rua Bispo Coutinho s/n,* ☎ *081/3429–0677.* ☒ *Free.* ☽ *Daily 8–11 and 2–5.*

At the abbey affiliated with the 1585 **Igreja E Mosteiro Nossa Senhora do Monte,** the Benedictine nuns sell homemade cookies, liqueurs, and postcards. On weekend mornings and afternoons there's also Gregorian chant. ⊠ *Largo Nossa Senhora do Monte s/n,* ☎ *081/3429–0317.* ☒ *Free.* ☽ *Daily 8–11:30 and 1–5.*

At the **Museu do Mamulengo-Espaço Tirida,** everyday life and northeastern folk tales are the stuff of shows presented using some of the more than 300 puppets made of wood and cloth on display in this whimsical museum. ⊠ *Rua do Amparo 59,* ☎ *081/3429–6214.* ☒ *R$2.* ☽ *Tues.–Fri. 9–5, weekends 10–5.*

The collection of sacred art and other objects in the **Museu de Arte Sacra de Pernambuco** tell the story of Olinda. ⊠ *Rua do Bispo Coutinho 726,* ☎ *081/3429–0036.* ☒ *Free.* ☽ *Weekdays 9–1.*

Dining and Lodging

$–$$$ ✗ **Bella Via.** On the Alto da Sé, Bella Via offers great views and a terrific linguine *al funghi* (with mushrooms). Plus, you can always get a pizza. ⊠ *Rua Bispo Coutinho 799,* ☎ *081/3429–3756. No credit cards. Closed Mon.–Tues.*

$ 🏨 **Hotel 7 Colinas.** Olinda's newest hotel sits in an off-street hollow amid the trees and flowers of a tangled garden. From here it's just a short hike up to Alto da Sé. Rooms are comfortably furnished and all look out on the grounds. ⊠ *Ladeira de Sáo Francisco 307, Carmo 53120-070,* ☎ *081/3439–6065,* WEB *www.hotel7colinasolinda.com.br. 39 rooms. Restaurant, bar, air-conditioning, pool, meeting room. AE, DC, V.*

$ 🏨 **Hotel Pousada Quatro Cantos.** This recommended pousada is in a converted mansion within walking distance of the Mercado da Ribeira, the former slave market that now sells handicrafts and antiques. The spacious rooms have lovely antique furniture. ⊠ *Rua Prudente de Morais 441, Carmo 53020-140,* ☎ *081/3429–0220. 15 rooms. Air-conditioning, restaurant, bar. AE, DC, V. BP.*

$ 🏨 **Pousada do Amparo.** This lovely pousada is a member of the Brazilian Roteiros e Charme group and has many amenities. It's made up of two colonial houses with 12-m (39-ft) ceilings. Wood and brick details, original artwork, and an indoor garden lend considerable warmth to the cavernous spaces. ⊠ *Rua do Amparo 199, 53020-190,* ☎ *081/3439–1749,* FAX *081/3429–6889,* WEB *www.pousadadoamparo.com.br. 8 rooms. Restaurant, bar, air-conditioning, pool, sauna. AE, DC, V.*

¢–$ 🏨 **Pousada Peter.** You may wonder whether this patrician mansion is a pousada or an art gallery. Peter Bauer, whose paintings have hung in many galleries, is both the owner and the resident artist. The large guest rooms lead out to a terrace where you can enjoy a view of the gardens, Olinda, and Recife. During Carnaval, revelers dance along the street in front of the pousada, and Peter offers special packages. ⊠ *Rua do Amparo 215, 53020-170,* ☎ FAX *081/3439–2171,* WEB *www.pousadapeter.com.br. 8 rooms. Air-conditioning, minibars, pool. AE, DC, V. BP.*

For crafts, head to the **Casa do Artesão** (⊠ Rua de Sáo Bento 170, ☎ 081/3429–2979). It's open weekdays 9–6 and Saturday 9–1. The **Mercado Eufrásio Barbosa** (⊠ Largo do Varadouro s/n, ☎ 081/3439–1415) was once the site of the Royal Customs House, where goods from Europe were sold. It's now a tourist center—with handicrafts for sale and snack bars—that's open Monday–Saturday 9–6. The **Mercado da Ribeira** (⊠ Rua Bernardo Vieira de Melo s/n, Ribeira, ☎ 081/3439–1660) was once a slave market. Today you'll find more than a dozen handicrafts shops that are open daily 9–6.

Caruaru
134 km (83 mi) west of Recife.

Caruaru and its craft center, Alto do Moura (6 km/4 mi south of Caruaru), became famous in the '60s and '70s for clay figurines made by local artisan Mestre Vitalino. There are now more than 400 craftspeople working in Alto do Moura. All are inspired by Vitalino, whose former home is now a museum that's open Monday–Saturday 9–noon and 2–5 and Sunday 9–noon. At the crafts center, you can buy not only figurines, which depict northeasterners doing everyday things, but also watch the artisans work.

In Caruaru, a great open-air market, **Feira de Artesanato,** at Parque 18 de Maiois is held every Saturday, when, as the songwriter Luis Gonzaga put it, "It is possible to find a little of everything that exists in the world." Look for pottery, leather goods, ceramics, hammocks, and baskets.

$ 🏨 **Caruaru Park Hotel.** On the outskirts of town, the Caruru Park's rooms and chalets are sparsely decorated but neat and clean. ⊠ *BR 232, Km 128, 55000-000,* ☎ *081/3721–5120 or 081/3722–9191,* 𝔽𝔸𝕏 *081/3722-7397,* WEB *www.caruaruparkhotel.com.br. 40 rooms. Restaurant, pool. AE, V. BP.*

Fernando de Noronha Archipelago
322 km (200 mi) off the coast of Recife.

This group of 21 islands is part of the mid-Atlantic ridge, an underwater volcanic mountain chain more than 15,000 km (9,315 mi) long. It was discovered in 1503 by the Italian explorer Amérigo Vespucci, but was taken over by Fernando de Noronha of Portugal. It's attackers included the French, Dutch, and English, but the Portuguese built several fortresses and, with cannons in place, fought them off. In later years, the Brazilians took advantage of its isolated location and built a prison on one of the islands; it was later used as a military training ground. As word of its beauty and spectacular underwater life spread, however, it was turned over to Pernambuco State and designated a protected marine park. Today, fierce regulations protect the archipelago's ecology.

The mountainous, volcanic main—and only inhabited—island of Fernando de Noronha is ringed by beaches with crystal-clear, warm waters that are perfect for swimming, snorkeling, and diving. In summer, surfers show up to tame the waves. There are shipwrecks to explore and huge turtles, stingrays, and sharks (14 species of them) with which to swim. Diving is good all year, but prime time is December to March on the windward side (facing Africa) and July to October on the leeward side (facing Brazil).

If you're an experienced diver, be sure to visit the *Ipiranga,* a small Brazilian destroyer that sank in 1987. It sits upright in 60 m (200 ft) of water and is swarming with fish, and you can see the sailors' personal effects, including uniforms still hanging in closets. Another good site is the Sapata Cave, which has an antechamber so large that it has been used for marriage ceremonies, attended by giant rays, no doubt.

In 1998, trails were mapped out and guides trained to lead landlubbers over rough stone paths. You can also enjoy the landscape on a horseback trek to the fortress ruins and isolated beaches where hundreds of seabirds alight. In addition, Projeto Tamar has an island base for its work involving sea turtles. One of the most fascinating exploring experiences, however, is an afternoon boat trip to the outer fringes of the Baía dos Golfinos (Bay of the Dolphins), where dozens of spinner dolphins swim south each day to hunt in deep water.

Fernando de Noronha is a 60-minute flight from Recife (the airport is almost in the center of the island). Only 100 visitors are allowed here each day, and there's a daily tourist tax of R$28, including the day you arrive and the day you leave. Divers pay an additional R$20 a day. Although credit cards are generally accepted, bring enough reais to last the trip, as changing money here is difficult.

DINING AND LODGING

$$–$$$ ✕ **Ecologiku's.** Famous for seafood, especially lobster, this very small restaurant is open for lunch and dinner. ⊠ *Near airport,* ☎ *081/3619–1404. Reservations essential. AE, MC, V.*

$–$$$ ✕ **Tartarugão.** One of island's best restaurants also operates a little rent-a-buggy business on the side. The phenomenal steak is big enough for two people and comes with rice and a salad. ⊠ *Praia do Boldró (west side of island),* ☎ *081/3619–1331. Reservations essential. AE, MC, V.*

$$$ 🏨 **Hotel Esmeralda do Atlântico.** As you might expect of a former military base, the rooms here are plain. They are, however, large, clean, and comfortable. ⊠ *Vila do Boldró, next to Praia do Boldró, 53990-000,* ☎ *081/3619–1255,* 𝔽𝔸𝕏 *081/3619–1277. 40 rooms. Restaurant, air-conditioning. AE, MC, V. FAP.*

$$ 🏨 **Pousada Dolphin.** The island's newest hotel is also the only one with a pool. Rooms are large and attractively decorated. It's about a five-minute walk from the beach. ⊠ *Near Praia do Boldró, 53990-000,* ☎ *081/3465–7855. 18 rooms. Restaurant, bar, air-conditioning, pool, hot tub, sauna. AE, MC, V. MAP.*

$$ 🏨 **Pousada Zé Maria Paraiso.** Although this friendly, popular pousada isn't on the beach, you can see the ocean, which is a 15-minute walk away. It sits atop a hill, surrounded by vegetation. ⊠ *Rua Nicie Cordeiro 1, Floresta Velha, 53990-000,* ☎ 𝔽𝔸𝕏 *081/3619–1258. 3 rooms. Air-conditioning, restaurant. AE, MC, V. FAP.*

OUTDOOR ACTIVITIES AND SPORTS

For dive trips, **Atlantis Divers** (⊠ Fernando de Noronha, Caixa Postal 20, 53990-000, ☎ 𝔽𝔸𝕏 081/3619–1371) has excellent English-speaking staffers and good boats.

FORTALEZA

Called the "City of Light," Fortaleza claims that the sun shines on it 2,800 hours a year. And it's a good thing, too, as the coastline stretches far beyond city. To the east, along the Litoral Leste or the Costa Sol Nascente (Sunrise Coast), you'll find many fishing villages. To the west, along the Litoral Oeste or the Costa Sol Poente (Sunset Coast) there are pristine stretches of sand. The shores here are cooled by constant breezes and lapped by waters with an average temperature of 24°C/72°F.

The city originally sprang up around the Forte de Schoonemborch, a Dutch fortress built in 1649. After the Portuguese defeated the Dutch, the small settlement was called Fortaleza Nossa Senhora da Assunção (Fortress of Our Lady of the Assumption). It didn't fully burgeon until 1808, when its ports were opened and the export of cotton to the United Kingdom commenced.

Today Fortaleza, a large, modern state capital with more than 2 million inhabitants, is Brazil's fifth-largest city. It's also on the move with a modern airport, a new convention center, a huge cultural center with a planetarium, large shopping malls, several museums and theaters, and an abundance of sophisticated restaurants. At Praia de Iracema, you'll find a revitalized beachfront area of sidewalk cafés, bars, and dance clubs. Still, if you wander along the shore, you're bound to encounter fishermen unloading their catch from traditional jangadas—just as they've done for hundreds of years.

Numbers in the text correspond to numbers in the margin and on the Fortaleza Centro Histórico map.

Exploring Fortaleza

Fortaleza is fairly easy to navigate on foot because its streets are laid out in a grid. Its business center lies above the Centro Histórico (Historic Center) and includes the main market, several shopping streets, and government buildings. East of the center, urban beaches are lined with high-rise hotels and restaurants. Beyond are the port and old lighthouse, from which Praia do Futuro runs 5 km (3 mi) along Avenida Dioguinho.

A Good Walk (or Two)

For a tour of the Centro Histórico, start at the **Theatro José de Alencar** ①, at Praça do José Alencar, alongside Rua General Sampaio. The theater is a good jumping-off point for a cab ride to the **Museu da Cachaça.** As an alternative, you can continue on the walk, heading toward the waterfront on Rua Sampaio. Turn right at Rua Guilherme Rocha and onto Rua Floriano Peixoto. In a cluster between Rua Peixoto and Rua Sena Madureira (which becomes Rua Conde D'eu and then Avenida Alberto Nepomuceno as you walk toward the waterfront) are the **Palácio da Luz** ②, on your right; the **Igreja do Rosário** ③, on your left; the **Praça dos Leões** ④; and the **Museu do Ceará** ⑤, near Rua Dr. João Moreira. As you walk along Rua Conde D'eu and Avenida Nepomuceno, on your right you'll see the **Catedral Metropolitana** ⑥. Across the street is the **Mercado Central** ⑦, where you can relax over lunch before exploring the 500-plus shops. If you feel like more walking, turn left on Rua Dr. João Moreira. On your right is the **Fortaleza de Nossa Senhora da Assunção** ⑧. Continue on to the **Passeio Público** ⑨ and walk across the park to the **Centro de Turismo e Museu de Arte e Cultura Populares** ⑩, on Rua Senador Pompeu near the waterfront.

On another day, consider a stroll along the seaside, palm-lined walkway east of the Passeio Público. From Praia Formosa, you can walk to Praia de Iracema, which has some late-19th-century houses. Along the way you'll pass the Ponte Metálica (also called the Ponte dos Ingleses), a pier from which you might spot dolphins. Farther east are Praia do Meireles and Praia do Mucuripe, with the **Farol do Mucuripe** ⑪ and its Museu de Fortaleza. You can continue all the way to Praia do Futuro for a total seashore walk of 8 km (5 mi). Along the way, you'll pass the statue of **Iracema** ⑫.

TIMING AND PRECAUTIONS

The tour of the Centro Histórico will take three hours, much longer if you browse in the Mercado Central or explore the Centro de Turismo. Although a straight walk along the shore moving at a good clip

Fortaleza Centro Histórico

would take roughly three hours, you'll want to move at a more leisurely pace, stopping to enjoy the view and to rest. Be on guard against pickpockets—particularly in the historic district.

SIGHTS TO SEE

6 Catedral Metropolitana. Inspired by the cathedral in Cologne, Germany, the city cathedral was built between 1937 and 1963 and has a dominant Gothic look. Its two spires are 75 m (250 ft) high, and it can accommodate 5,000 worshipers, who are no doubt inspired by its beautiful stained-glass windows. ⊠ *Praça da Sé s/n, Centro,* ☎ *085/ 231–4196.* 🎫 *Free.*

10 Centro de Turismo. Originally a prison, this building was structurally changed in 1850 along simple, classical lines. It's now the home of the state tourism center, with handicraft stores as well as the Museu de Minerais (Mineral Museum) and the Museu de Arte e Cultura Populares (Popular Art and Culture Museum), whose displays of local crafts and sculptures are interesting. ⊠ *Rua Senador Pompeu 350, Centro,* ☎ *085/212–3566.* 🎫 *Museums: R$2 for entry to both.* ☉ *Weekdays 8– 6, Sat. 8–noon.*

11 Farol do Mucuripe. Erected by slaves and dedicated to Princess Isabel, the monarch who eventually put an end to slavery, this lighthouse was inaugurated in 1846. Surrounded by a system of battlements, it operated for 111 years and was not deactivated until 1957. In 1982, it underwent restoration and was designated a municipal historic monument. It now houses the Museu de Fortaleza, better known as the Museu do Farol, with exhibits on the city's history. ⊠ *Av. Vicente de Castro s/n, Mucuripe,* ☎ *085/263–1115.* 🎫 *Free.* ☉ *Weekdays 7–6, weekends 7–noon.*

8 Fortaleza de Nossa Senhora da Assunção. Built by the Dutch in 1649, this fort was originally baptized Forte Schoonemborch. In 1655 it was seized by the Portuguese and renamed after the city's patron saint, Nossa Senhora da Assunção. It was rebuilt in 1817 and is now a military headquarters. The city took its name from this fortress (*fortaleza*), which still has the cell where the mother of one of Ceará's most famous writers, José de Alencar, was jailed. ⊠ *Av. Alberto Nepomuceno s/n, Centro*, ☎ *085/231–5155.* ☜ *Free.* ⊘ *Open daily 8–4.*

③ Igreja Nossa Senhora do Rosário. Built by slaves in the 18th century, it's one of the city's oldest churches and has a typical Brazilian colonial design. As the slaves who built it also worshiped in it, it's an important piece of African heritage in Ceará, a state considered a pioneer in the liberation of slaves. ⊠ *Rua Rosário*, ☎ *085/231–1998* ☜ *Suggested donation.* ⊘ *Mon.–Sat. 7–6:30, Sun. 7:30 AM–10 PM.*

⑫ Iracema. Along the Praia do Mucuripe on Avenida Beira-Mar is the statue of *Iracema*, an Indian girl who waited at the port for her lover to return. Inspired by the work of Ceará writer José de Alencar, the statue shows Iracema with an arrow in her hand as she looks at Martinho, a Portuguese soldier seated in front of her, holding their son, Moacir.

⑦ Mercado Central. With four floors and more than 500 stores, this is *the* place to find handicrafts and just about anything else. It has elevators to take you from one floor to the next, but since it's built with an open style and has ramps that curve from one floor to the next, it's just as easy to walk. ⊠ *Av. Alberto Nepomuceno 199, Centro*, ☎ *085/454–8766 or 085/454–8273.* ⊘ *Weekdays 7:30–6:30, Sat. 8–4, Sun. 8–noon.*

OFF THE   **MUSEU DA CACHAÇA** – It's a toss-up whether coffee or cachaça is
BEATEN PATH   Brazil's national drink. This museum just west of Fortaleza offers tastings of the latter in a tavern. Of course, this happens after you tour the plant and learn the history of what has been a family business for four generations. In the tavern, you'll see a 374,000-liter (98,736-gallon) wooden barrel, the largest in the world. ⊠ *Turn left off CE 65 just before small town of Maranguape; look for signs*, ☎ *085/341–0407 or 085/9985–7982.* ☜ *R$5.* ⊘ *Tues.–Sat. 8–5.*

⑤ Museu do Ceará. Housed in the former Assembléia Provincial (Provincial Assembly Building), this museum's exhibits are devoted to the history and anthropology of Ceará state. ⊠ *Rua São Paulo s/n*, ☎ *085/251–1502.* ☜ *R$2.* ⊘ *Wed.–Fri. 8:30–5:30, Sat. 10–4, Sun. 2–5.*

② Palácio da Luz. What was originally the home of the Portuguese Crown's representative, Antônio de Castro Viana, was built by Indian laborers. In 1814, it became the property of the imperial government and served as the residence of the provincial president. The next important occupant was painter Raimundo Cefa. It now houses a display of his work and has been designated a historic landmark. ⊠ *Rua do Rosário*, ☎ *085/231–5600.* ☜ *Free.* ⊘ *Tues.–Fri. 8–6, Sat. 2–9.*

⑨ Passeio Público. Also called the Praça dos Mártires, this landmark square dates from the 19th century. In 1824 many soldiers were executed here in the war for independence from the Portuguese crown. It has a central fountain and is full of century-old trees and statues of Greek deities. Look for the ancient baobab tree.

④ Praça dos Leões (Praça General Tibúrcio). Built in 1817, this square is officially named after a Ceará general who fought in Brazil's war against Paraguay. However, it's also commonly referred to as the Praça de Leões owing to its bronze lions, which were brought over from Paris in the early 20th century.

1 **Theatro José de Alencar.** The José de Alencar Theater is a rather shocking example (especially if you come upon it suddenly) of the eclectic phase of Brazilian architecture. It's a mixture of neoclassical and art nouveau styles. The top of the theater, which looks as if it was designed by the makers of Tiffany lamps, really stands out against Ceará's perpetually blue sky. It was built in 1910 of steel and iron (many of its cast-iron sections were imported from Scotland) and was restored in 1989. It's still used for cultural events—including concerts, plays, and dance performances—and houses a library and an art gallery. If you'd like to take a tour, you'll find that some of the guides speak English; call ahead for reservations. ⊠ *Praça do José Alencar, Centro,* ☎ FAX *085/252–2324,* WEB *www.secult.ce.gov.br.* 🎫 *R$2.40.* ☻ *Weekdays 10–noon and 2–5.*

Beaches

Fortaleza's enchanting coast runs 22 km (14 mi) along the Atlantic between the Rio Ceará, to the west, and the Rio Pacoti, to the east. This great urban stretch of sand's scenery and feel vary as often as its names: Barra do Ceará, Pirambu, Formosa, Iracema, Beira-Mar, Meireles, Mucuripe, Mansa, Titanzinho, Praia do Futuro, Sabiazuaba.

In the city center and its immediate environs, feel free to soak up the sun and the ambience of the beaches, but stay out of the water—it is, unfortunately, too polluted for swimming. However, you'll find clean waters and amazing sands just a little way from Centro and beyond. Surfing is fine at several beaches, including those near the towns of Paracuru and Pecém, to the west of Fortaleza, and Porto das Dunas, to the east.

Canoa Quebrada. Hidden behind dunes 164 km (101 mi) east of Fortaleza, the stunning Canoa Quebrada Beach was "discovered" a little more than 30 years ago by French doctors working in the area. The spectacular scenery not only includes dunes with colored sands used to make pictures in bottles but also jangadas, red cliffs, and groves of palm trees. Carved into a cliff is the symbol of Canoa: a crescent moon with a star in the middle. Although it was originally settled by Italian hippies, the village itself has moved on with the times and now has good roads, several comfortable pousadas, and bars and restaurants. Although the best way to get here is on a trip offered by one of Fortaleza's many tour operators, bus companies have daily departures from Fortaleza.

Iguape. The white sand dunes at this beach, 50 km (31 mi) east of Fortaleza, are so high that people actually ski down them. The water is calm and clean. In the nearby village you'll find both fishermen and lace makers (lace is sold at the Centro de Rendeiras). There's also a lookout at Morro do Enxerga Tudo. Buses depart from Fortaleza for this beach several times daily.

Flexeiras (or Fleixeiras). The ocean is always calm at this beach 177 km (110 mi) northwest of Fortaleza. Coconut trees, lagoons, and sand dunes surround it. During low tide, the reefs surface, and you can see small fish and shells in the rocks. When the tide comes in and the natural pools form, you can grab your mask and go snorkeling. In a 5-km (3-mi) stretch between Flexeiras and Mundaú (another almost-deserted beach) there are several fishing villages and a working lighthouse. A river joins the ocean at Mundaú, forming a large S on the sand; on one side is a line of coconut trees and on the other, fishermen with their jangadas—the scene conveys the very essence of Ceará. Flexeiras is about a 90-minute drive from Fortaleza. You can take the Rendenção bus or arrange a trip here with a tour operator. As yet there are no luxury resorts here, but there are several simple, clean pousadas.

Porto das Dunas. Its water-sports options, including surfing, and its sand dunes are enough to draw many people to this beach just 22 km (14 mi) southeast of Fortaleza. But it has much more, including an all-suites hotel and a water park and entertainment complex that would make even Disney jealous. You can get here on the *jardineira* bus from Centro or from along Avenida Beira-Mar.

Dining

You'll find several good seafood restaurants along Praia de Iracema and Praia do Mucuripe. Be sure to try the *lagosta ao natural* (langouste simply cooked in water and salt and served with homemade butter). Sun-dried meat with *paçoca* (manioc flour seasoned with herbs and red onions) and *caldeirada* (shrimp soup with vegetables and strong spices and herbs) are also popular regional dishes.

Brazilian

$–$$$ ✕ **Colher de Pau.** Ana Maria Vilmar and her mother opened this restaurant 10 years ago in a small rented house in the Varjota district. It became so popular that they had to open in a larger building down the street. The original place still serves meals to faithful patrons who are mostly locals; the new branch is popular with visitors. At both branches, the sun-dried meat is served not only with paçoca but also with banana and *baião-de-dois* (rice and beans). The shellfish dishes, many prepared using regional recipes, are also standouts. ⊠ *Rua Frederico Borges 204, Varjota,* ☎ *085/267–3773; Rodovia dos Tabajaras 412, Praia de Iracema,* ☎ *085/219–4097. AE, DC, MC, V. No lunch at Iracema branch.*

$–$$ ✕ **Caçuá.** Regional objects decorate this restaurant and create an agreeable setting. The house specialty is sun-dried meat and paçoca, though dishes of chicken and lamb are also recommended. ⊠ *Av. Engenheiro Santana Jr. 970, Papicu,* ☎ *085/234–1915. AE, V.*

Eclectic

$$$–$$$$ ✕ **Le Dinner.** The savvy mix of French and Asian cuisine blends well with this restaurant's sophisticated ambience and personalized service. The menu includes beef, poultry, and seafood selections. Reservations are recommended, particularly on Friday and Saturday nights. ⊠ *Rua Afonso Celso 1020, Aldeota,* ☎ *085/224–2627. AE. Closed Sun. and last 2 wks Feb.*

French

$$$–$$$$ ✕ **Le Marine.** Candles flicker on each table, and violin and cello music fills the air-conditioned dining room and sitting room. The flambéed dishes are the best: try the King Jorge shrimp or the langouste in champagne. ⊠ *Av. Marechal Castelo Branco 400, Centro,* ☎ *085/252–5253. AE, DC, MC, V.*

$$–$$$$ ✕ **La Bohème.** If you like original art, you must have dinner at La Bo-
★   hème. Only one room inside this former colonial home is for dining; the others are part of an art gallery that you can wander through while waiting for your first course. Be sure to see the wall with photos from films of the 1930s. There's plenty of seating on the patio out front, where a small combo entertains, competing with a combo at a restaurant across the street. Although La Bohème specializes in French cuisine, it also offers a small selection of regional seafood dishes. ⊠ *Rua dos Tabajaras 380, Praia de Iracema,* ☎ *085/219–3311. AE, MC, V.*

Italian

$–$$$ ✕ **Pulcinella.** You can feast on this restaurant's classic Italian fare (sometimes given a regional twist) in either the air-conditioned dining room, which has a smoking section, or in the alfresco seating area.

Among the most popular dishes are spaghetti in garlic sauce with shrimp and pimiento and veal in a mushroom-and-herb sauce. ⊠ *Rua Osvaldo Cruz 640, Aldeota,* ☎ *085/261–3411. AE, DC, MC, V. Closed Sun.*

Seafood

$$–$$$$ ✕ **Cemoara.** A sophisticated decor with clean lines adds to the appeal
★ of this traditional seafood restaurant. Although the *bacalão* (salt cod) selections are fabulous, you can't go wrong with the grilled lobster in a caper sauce or any of the flambéed dishes. The piano in the corner is there for a purpose: a musician accompanies your dinner with nice, soft music. Air-conditioning and smoking/no-smoking areas ensure that your meal will be a comfortable one. ⊠ *Av. da Abolição 3340-A, Meireles,* ☎ *085/263–5001. AE, DC, MC, V.*

$$–$$$ ✕ **Al Mare.** Facing as it does out to the sea, it seems appropriate that the building housing this establishment is shaped like a ship. The grilled seafood *al mare*—a medley of fish, langouste, shrimp, octopus, and squid in an herb sauce—is the specialty. ⊠ *Av. Beira-Mar 3821, Mucuripe,* ☎ *085/263–3888. AE, DC, MC, V.*

$$–$$$ ✕ **La Nuit.** There's no end of good places to chow down in Praia de Iracema, and this 10-table establishment is one of the best. The specialty is seafood—whether you like fish, shrimp, or lobster. ⊠ *Rua dos Tabajaras 440, Praia de Iracema,* ☎ *085/219–3000. AE, DC, MC.*

¢–$ ⊞ **Picanha Iracema Bar E Restaurante.** Although the decor is sparse, the location—amid Praia de Iracema's hopping nightlife—is terrific, and you can eat shrimp, fish, or steaks here for very little money. Top your meal off with an espresso that costs the equivalent of 5 U.S. cents. ⊠ *Av. Historiador Raimundo Girão 574,* ☎ *085/219–0488. AE, DC, V.*

Lodging

Most hotels are along Avenida Beira-Mar (previously known as Avenida Presidente John Kennedy). Those in the Praia de Iracema are generally less expensive than those along Praia do Mucuripe. Iracema, however, is also a more interesting area to explore; it's also full of trendy restaurants and bars.

$$$$ ⊞ **Marina Park.** Designed to look like a huge ship, the resort overlooks a calm bay and is connected to a marina from which you can take boat trips. It has an enormous free-form pool and a top-notch staff. It is rather far from the center of everything, but it does have an uncrowded 5-km-long (3-mi-long) beach. ⊠ *Av. Presidente Castelo Branco 400, Praia de Iracema 60312-060,* ☎ *085/252–5253,* FAX *085/253–1803,* WEB *www. marina@park.com.br. 305 rooms, 10 suites. 6 restaurants, bar, coffee shop, air-conditioning, in-room data ports, in-room safes, minibars, room service, pool, beauty salon, massage, sauna, 4 tennis courts, volleyball, dock, shops, dance club, children's programs, playground, business services, meeting room, helipad, free parking. AE, DC, MC, V.*

$$$–$$$$ ⊞ **Imperial Othon Palace.** The Palace has a lively beachfront location at the center of Avenida Beira-Mar and right in front of *feirinha de artesanato* (artisans' fair). Standard rooms are large, conservatively decorated, and well equipped; suites face the sea. ⊠ *Av. Beira-Mar 2500, Meireles 60165-121,* ☎ *085/242–9177,* FAX *085/242–7777,* WEB *www. hotels-othon.com.br. 222 rooms, 14 suites. 2 restaurants, bar, coffee shop, air-conditioning, in-room safes, minibars, room service, pool, beauty salon, massage, sauna, children's programs, business services, meeting room, free parking. AE, DC, MC, V.*

$$$–$$$$ ⊞ **Meliá Confort.** The Meliá hotel sits on a small hill right where the
★ beach makes a big curve, affording guests a spectacular view of the beach and Mucuripe Bay. There's comfortable seating in the lobby. Nice

paintings of dolphins hang behind the desk, and a spiral staircase leads up to a sushi bar. Rooms are more like minisuites; they're decorated more for comfort than flash. ✉ *Av. Beira-Mar 3470, Mucuripe 60165-121,* ☎ *085/466–5500,* FAX *085/466–5501,* WEB *www.solmelia.com. 136 rooms. Restaurant, coffee shop, sushi bar, fitness center, business services, meeting rooms. AE, MC, V. BP.*

$$$ 🖫 **Holiday Inn.** Because of the way the Iracema Beach curves, all rooms
★   here have either ocean or harbor views. There isn't anything opulent about the hotel, but its location is great: a block off the beach and within walking distance of Centro Dragão do Mar, Ceará's largest cultural center. An innovative touch is a panic button in all rooms in case you need help in a hurry. The pool is on a top deck, and there's a coffee shop as well as a small French restaurant. ✉ *Av. Historiador Raimundo Girão 800, Praia de Iracema 60165-050,* ☎ *085/455–5000,* FAX *085/ 455–5055. 273 rooms. Restaurant, bar, coffee shop, pool, fitness center, business services, convention center. AE, DC, MC, V. BP.*

$$–$$$ 🖫 **Caesar Park Hotel Fortaleza.** On Praia do Mucuripe, just a 15-minute
★   drive from either the airport or Centro, this luxury hotel can certainly include "convenient location" in its list of features. Marble and black granite give the building a modern, sleek look, and all rooms have terrific sea views. One of the on-site restaurants serves Brazilian fare, another French; the third, Mariko, is noteworthy for Japanese food and buffets of lobster, shrimp, sushi, sashimi, and oysters. The view from the pool area on the 20th floor is fantastic. The hotel has facilities for travelers with disabilities. ✉ *Av. Beira-Mar 3980, Mucuripe, 60165-050,* ☎ *085/263–1133 or 085/800–2202,* FAX *085/263–1444,* WEB *www. caesarpark-for.com.br. 185 rooms, 45 suites. 3 restaurants, 2 bars, air-conditioning, in-room safes, minibars, room service, pool, hot tub, massage, sauna, steam room, health club, business services, convention center, free parking. AE, DC, MC, V.*

$$ 🖫 **Beach Park Suites Resort.** There's very little this pleasant, all-suite resort doesn't offer. It faces the beautiful Porto das Dunas Beach, and the Beach Park Acqua Center—the most fantastic facility of its kind in Latin America—is a five-minute walk away (hotel guests get a 30% discount on admission). All the spacious suites have have balconies, and the dozens of pots of flowers in the lobby give the whole place a cheerful atmosphere. A hotel shuttle regularly makes 10-km (6-mi) runs to and from Fortaleza. ✉ *Rua Porto das Dunas 2734, Aquiraz 61700-000,* ☎ *085/360–1150,* FAX *085/360–1413,* WEB *www.beachpark.com.br. 198 suites. Restaurant, bar, pool, health club, sauna, beauty salon, children's programs. AE, MC, V. BP.*

$$ 🖫 **Parthenon Golden Flat.** The comfortable apartments here are perfect for families and visitors in the city on a long stay. Each unit has one or two bedrooms, a living room, and a fully equipped kitchen. If you get tired of preparing your own meals, you can head for the restaurant or the coffee shop; kids will appreciate the pool and the playground. ✉ *Av. Beira-Mar 4260, Mucuripe 60165-121,* ☎ FAX *085/263–1413. 132 apartments. Restaurant, bar, coffee shop, pool, sauna, playground. AE, DC, MC, V.*

$$ 🖫 **Seara Praia.** There's plenty of action at the Meirles Beach across the street, which appeals to a younger crowd. The lobby is decorated with works by local artists. Rooms have tile floors; modern art; and furniture with clean, classic lines. For an ocean view, ask for a deluxe room or suite. Don't despair if such a room isn't available; simply head for the rooftop pool and deck and partake of the glorious sunsets. ✉ *Av. Beira-Mar 3080, Meireles 60165-121,* ☎ *085/242–9555,* FAX *085/ 242–5955,* WEB *www.hotelseara.com.br. 203 rooms, 14 suites. Restaurant, bar, pool, beauty salon. AE, DC, MC, V.*

$ ☷ **Esplanada Praia.** At this top-end Praia do Meireles hotel, rooms have hammocks on balconies that face the sea. You'll feel inclined to unwind amid beige-color linens and basic furnishings that offer all the comforts of home. The multilingual staff is very efficient. ☒ *Av. Beira-Mar 2000, Meireles 60165-121,* ☎ *085/248–1000,* FAX *085/248–8555. 224 rooms, 6 suites. Restaurant, bar, pool, beauty salon, shops, nightclub. AE, DC, MC, V.*

$ ☷ **Ponta Mar Hotel.** In addition to the popular beach across the street, a handicrafts fair, and a shopping plaza nearby, the hotel has two swimming pools and extra-large rooms. ☒ *Av. Beira-Mar 2200, Meireles. 60165-121,* ☎ *085/248–9000,* FAX *085/248–9001,* WEB *www.bdh.com.br. 260 rooms, 3 suites. Restaurant, bar, 2 pools, restaurant, bar, meeting rooms. AE, DC, MC V. BP.*

$ ☷ **Praiano Palace.** This hotel is a surprisingly affordable option in the chic Praia do Meirles area. Its rooms are simple but comfortable, and all have sea views. Windows alongside the lobby that look out on a small garden and a waterfall add a soothing touch. It also has a nice restaurant. ☒ *Av. Beira-Mar 2800, Meirles 60165-121,* ☎ *085/242–9333,* FAX *085/242–3333. 189 rooms. Restaurant, bar, pool. AE, DC, MC, V.*

Nightlife and the Arts

Nightlife

Fortaleza is renowned for its lively nightlife, particularly along Avenida Beira-Mar and Rua dos Tabajaras in the vicinity of Praia de Iracema. The action often includes live forró, the traditional and very popular music and dance of the northeast. As the story goes, U.S. soldiers based in Fortaleza during World War II always invited the townsfolk to their dances, saying they were "for all," which the Brazilians pronounced "forró."

BARS AND CLUBS

At **Alambique Cachaçaria** (☒ Rua dos Potiguares 192, Praia de Iracema, ☎ 085/219–0656) you'll find more than 400 types of cachaça. Line 'em up. For *música popular brasileira*, commonly referred to as MPB (popular Brazilian music), head to **Aldeia In** (☒ Av. Dom Luís 879, Aldeota, ☎ 085/261–3227). **Cais Bar** (☒ Av. Beira-Mar 696, Praia de Iracema, ☎ 085/219–4963) is a known hangout for artists and intellectuals. **Chico do Caranguejo** (☒ Av. Zezé Diogo 4930, Praia do Futuro, ☎ 085/234–6519) is the place to feast on crabs while enjoying live samba and axé music shows.

On Monday night—the most popular night for forró—check out the **Pirata Bar** (☒ Rua dos Tabajaras 325, Praia de Iracema, ☎ 085/219–8030), where as many as 2,000 people can move to the forró beat on the dance floor and in other areas inside or out. For exotic drinks, try **Siriguela Banana** (☒ Rua dos Tremembés 100, Loja 6, Praia de Iracema, ☎ 085/219–6111). Although **Spark & Smoke** (☒ Rua dos Tabaras 440, Loja 3, ☎ 085/219–2336) is actually a cigar bar and there are boxes and boxes of cigars for sale from all over the world, no one seems to be smoking. Stop in for a drink, select your favorite CD from the enormous collection, and ask a staffer to play it for you.

CYBERCAFÉ

You can plug into the Internet at **Mirante Cyber Bar** (☒ Av. Beira-Mar 4430, Mucuripe, ☎ 085/263–1006).

GAY BAR

Broadway (☒ Rua Carolina Sucupira 455, Aldeota, ☎ 085/261–2074) is Fortaleza's premier gay nightclub. A dance floor, bars, and seating areas both open and intimate fill its great space.

DANCE SHOWS AND RODEOS

Just outside Fortaleza, you'll find establishments that blend forró shows with *vaquejada,* a traditional rodeo in which farmhands try to wrangle bulls and wild horses. **Cajueiro Drinks** (⊠ BR 116, Km 20, Eusébio, ☎ 085/275–1482) is a highly recommended spot for rodeo shows. Sunday sees a forró show and performances of local country music.

For a lively mix of vaquejada with samba, reggae, forró, and other types of music, drop in at **Clube do Vaqueiro** (⊠ Quarto Anel Viário de Fortaleza, BR 116, Km 14, Eusébio, ☎ 085/278–2000), especially on Wednesday when there's usually a samba show. On Friday there's a forró show at **Parque do Vaqueiro** (⊠ BR 020, Km 10, after the loop in intersection, Caucaia, ☎ 085/296–1159).

NIGHTCLUBS

A young crowd grooves to MPB and rock and roll at **Boite Domínio Público** (⊠ Rua Dragão do Mar 212, Praia de Iracema, ☎ 085/219–3883). A sophisticated, over-25 clientele fills the two dance floors and the bars at **Boite Mustike** (⊠ Mucuripe Club, Av. Beira-Mar 4430, Mucuripe, ☎ 085/263–1006). In Praia do Futuro, Tuesday nights are hottest at **Oásis** (⊠ Av. Santos Dumont 6061, Papicu, ☎ 085/262–2326), when the live music from years past draws a crowd to the large dance floor.

The Arts

Not far from the Mercado Central, the large, white **Centro Dragão do Mar de Arte e Cultura** (⊠ Rua Dragão do Mar 81, Praia de Iracema, ☎ 085/488–8600) is a majestic cultural complex. Its architecture is an eccentric mix of curves, straight lines, and angular and flat roofs. What's inside is as diverse as the exterior. There's a planetarium as well as art museums with permanent exhibitions of Ceará's two most famous artists, Raimundo Cela and Antônio Bandeira. Another museum presents Ceará's cultural history, with exhibits of embroidery, paintings, prints, pottery, puppets, and musical instruments. Several theaters and an open-air amphitheater host live performances. There are also classrooms for courses in cinema, theater, design, and dance. When you need a break, head for the center's romantic Café & Cultura, which serves a variety of cocktails made with coffee as well as little meat or vegetarian pies. The center's bookstore has English-language titles as well as souvenirs and cards for the folks back home.

The **Centro Cultural Banco do Nordeste** (⊠ Rua Floriano Peixoto 941, Centro, ☎ 085/488–4100) often hosts plays, concerts, and art exhibitions.

The beautiful, early 19th-century **Theatro José de Alencar** (⊠ Praça José de Alencar, Centro, ☎ 085/252–2324) is still the site of many concerts, plays, and dance performances. Alongside the main theater is a smaller venue (it seats about 120 people) for more intimate events. There's also a small stage in the theater's garden.

Outdoor Activities and Sports

Participant Sports

The sidewalk along Avenida Beira-Mar is a pleasant place for a walk, run, or bike ride, and there's usually a pickup volleyball or soccer game in progress on the beach—don't hesitate to ask if they need another player. There are also running tracks and sports courts in the 25-km-long (16-mi-long) Parque do Cocó, on Avenida Pontes Vieira.

SCUBA DIVING

Off the coast of Ceará are some good dive sites with coral reefs, tropical fish, and wrecks. To rent equipment and arrange lessons and/or trips, contact **Projeto Netuno** (✉ Rua do Mirante 165, Mucuripe, ☎ 085/263–3009). If you're a novice, you'll benefit from its courses, which feature presentations on equipment and dive techniques as well as marine biology.

WATER PARK

Just 30 minutes from downtown on the idyllic Porto das Dunas Beach is the enormous **Beach Park Acqua Center,** an amusement park with an emphasis on water rides. Check out the 14-story-high water slide that dumps you into a pool at a speed of 105 kph (65 mph). If you prefer slow-paced attractions, visit its museum, which has the country's largest collection of jangadas, the wooden sailing rafts used by fishermen. An open-air restaurant at the beach serves excellent seafood dishes. You can get here on the jardineira bus from Centro or from along Avenida Beira-Mar. ✉ *Rua Porto das Dunas 2734,* ☎ *085/361–3000,* WEB *www.beachpark.com.br.* ✍ *R$58.* ☉ *July–mid-Dec., daily 10:30–5; mid-Dec.–June, Thurs.–Mon. 10:30–5.*

WINDSURFING

Open seas and constant trade winds make Ceará's beaches perfect for windsurfing. You can arrange lessons and rent equipment at **Windcenter/Hi-Winds** (✉ Av. Beira-Mar 3222, Loja 20, ☎ 085/242–2611). The **Windclub** (✉ Av. Beira-Mar 2120, Praia dos Diários, ☎ 085/982–5449) is a good bet for equipment and lessons.

Spectator Sport

FUTEBOL

Fortaleza's two futebol teams, Ceará and Fortaleza, haven't reached world-class status yet, but you can watch them play in the **Estádio Plácido Castelo** (✉ Av. Alberto Craveiro s/n, ☎ 085/295–2466), also known as Castelão. Fortaleza's other futebol venue is the **Estádio Presidente Vargas** (✉ Av. Marechal Deodoro s/n, ☎ 085/281–3225).

Shopping

Fortaleza is one of the most important centers for crafts—especially bobbin lace—in the northeast. You'll find shops that sell a good variety of handicrafts, and others offering clothing, shoes, and jewelry along Avenida Monsenhor Tabosa in Praia de Iracema. Shopping centers, both large and small, house branches of the best Brazilian stores. The biggest and most traditional center is **Shopping Center Iguatemi** (✉ Av. Washington Soares 85, Água Fria, ☎ 085/273–3577).

Markets and fairs are the best places to look for lacework, embroidery, leather goods, hammocks, and carvings. The large, warehouse-style **Central de Artesanato do Ceará** (CEART; ✉ Av. Santos Dumont 1589, Aldeota, ☎ 085/268–2970) sells all types of handicrafts, though at higher prices than elsewhere. The handicraft stores at **Centro de Turismo** (✉ Rua Senador Pompeu 350, Centro, ☎ 085/231–3566 or 085/253–1522) are good options. More than 600 artisans sell their work at the nightly **feirinha de artesanato** (✉ Av. Beira-Mar, in front of Imperial Othon Palace), on Praia do Meireles.

For lace aficionados, a trip to the town of **Aquiraz,** 30 km (19 mi) east of Fortaleza, is a must. Ceará's first capital (1713–99) is today a hub for artisans who create the famous *bilro* (bobbin) lace. On the beach called Prainha (6 km/4mi east of Aquiraz) is the Centro de Rendeiras Luiza Távora. Here, seated on little stools, dedicated and patient women lace makers explain how they create such items as bedspreads and tablecloths using the bilro technique.

Side Trips from Fortaleza

Vale Monumental do Ceará
158 km (98 mi) southwest of Fortaleza.

Brazil is very sports minded, and although water activities take precedence, away from the beaches there's an entirely different world, one centered on sports, in Vale Monumental do Ceará (Monumental Valley), Ceará's *sertão* (bush), a two-hour drive over good roads from Fortaleza. Within this area of nearly 247,100 acres are ecological parks and huge monoliths. Activities include mountain climbing, biking, hiking, horseback tours, paragliding, hang gliding, geology treks, and birding (400 species of birds have been identified).

LODGING

$ 🏨 **Fazenda Hotel Parelhas.** It's called a hotel, but it's really a working farm that also welcomes overnight guests. Horseback riding is free, and you can walk down a short path and fish in a small lake. There's also a very small pool. ✉ *Rodovia do Algodao, Km 133, Quixeramobim 63800-000,* ☎ *088/402–2847,* 🗚 *088/441–1326. 6 rooms. Pool. No credit cards. FAP.*

OUTDOOR ACTIVITIES AND SPORTS

You can hire guides to take you on hikes along the Trilha das Andorinhas (Andorinhas Trail). The valley is filled with giant rocks sculptured by the elements into unusual formations. Trails have been mapped out for moderate hikes to grottos, caves (some of which have prehistoric etchings), lagoons, canyons, and tunnels. Contact **Eco Turismo Fundação Maria Nilva Alves** (✉ Av. Monsenhor Tabosa 314, Fortaleza, ☎ 085/254–4011) to arrange a trek. **Trip Trekking** (✉ Rua Capitão Francisco Pedro 768, Loja 1, Rodolfo Teófilo, Fortaleza, ☎ 085/281–2869) offers a variety of hiking excursions.

Thermal wind conditions are just right for paragliding off a mountaintop near the towns of Quixadó and Quixeramobim, about two hours southwest of Fortaleza (BR 116 to BR 122). One person's excursion of 6½ hours in the air made it into the *Guinness Book of World Records.* Once you're harnessed up, it's just a short downhill run before the wind grabs you and off you go. The main month for competitions is November, because it's dry. Chico Santos at **Go Up Brazil** (✉ Estrada das Canoas 722, Bloco 4, Apto. 207, São Conrado, Rio de Janeiro, RJ, 22610-210, ☎ 021/3322–3165, 🌐 www.goup.com.br) can help you make arrangements for paragliding trips in the Vale Monumental. If you'd like to learn to paraglide, contact Claudio Henrique Landim, an instructor with **Escola de vôo Livre** (☎ 085/234–0494). The course is R$680 for 30 hours.

Jericoacoara
300 km (186 mi) northwest of Fortaleza

It could be the sand dunes, some more than 30 m (100 ft) tall; it could be the expanse of ocean that puts no limits on how far your eyes can see; or it could be that in the presence of this awesome display of nature everyday problems seem insignificant. Jericoacoara, a rustic paradise on Ceará State's northwest coast, affects everyone differently but leaves no one unchanged—just like the sand dunes that change their shape and even their colors as they bend to the will of the winds.

In Jericoacoara, or Jerí, time seems endless, even though in the back of your mind you know you'll be leaving in a day or two (or a week or two, if you're lucky). It's the ultimate relaxing vacation, and not because there isn't anything to do. You can surf down sand dunes or ride up and down them in a dune buggy. You can splash about in the surf or go fishing. And after all that activity you can roll into a hammock for a nap.

Jerí is said to be one of the 10 most beautiful beaches in the world, a classification you might think would bring hordes of tourists. Its remoteness has kept this from happening, and the Brazilian government has now listed it as an environmental protection area. The few pousadas, restaurants, and bars that have sprung up are mainly owned by former tourists, especially from Europe, who were lured back to stay, almost as if by a siren's call. The biggest industry seems to be fishing. As you watch the men set sail each morning you know the catches they make will keep you fed at dinner that evening.

You can visit Jerí on a day trip from Fortaleza, and many do, despite the distance and the poor condition of some of the roads. Contacting a tour operator and arranging a trip that includes transportation and at least three nights in a pousada is the wiser choice.

SALVADOR, RECIFE, AND FORTALEZA A TO Z

To research prices, get advice from other travelers, and book travel arrangements, visit www.fodors.com.

AIR TRAVEL

CARRIERS

Airlines that serve Salvador include Air France, American Airlines, Lufthansa, Rio-Sul, TAM, Transbrasil, Varig, and VASP. The main airlines operating in Recife are American Airlines, Rio Sul Nordeste, TAM, Transbrasil, Varig, and VASP. In addition to international flights, there is regular service to all major Brazilian cities from Fortaleza on the national carriers: Transbrasil, TAM, Varig, and VASP. Fernando de Noronha is a one-hour flight from Recife on Trip Airlines or Rio-Sul/Nordeste.

➤ SALVADOR AIRLINE CONTACTS: **Air France** (☎ 071/351–6631). **American Airlines** (☎ 071/245–0477). **Lufthansa** (☎ 071/341–5100). **Rio-Sul/Nordeste** (☎ 071/204–1253). **TAM** (☎ 071/204–1367). **Transbrasil** (☎ 071/377–2467). **Varig** (☎ 071/204–1070). **VASP** (☎ 071/377–2495).

➤ RECIFE AIRLINE CONTACTS: **American Airlines** (☎ 081/3465–2156 or 081/3465–2876). **Rio-Sul/Nordeste** (☎ 081/3465–6799 or 0800/710–737). **TAM** (☎ 081/3465–8800). **Transbrasil** (☎ 081/3423–1366 or 081/3423–4040). **Trip** (☎ 0800/558–747). **Varig** (☎ 081/3464–4440 or 081/3464–4499). **VASP** (☎ 081/3421–3611 or 081/3421–1427).

➤ FORTALEZA AIRLINE CONTACTS: **Transbrasil** (☎ 085/477–1800 or 085/477–1818). **TAM** (☎ 085/477–6261 or 085/477–1881). **Varig** (☎ 085/477–1710 or 085/477–1720). **VASP** (☎ 085/477–5353).

AIRPORTS AND TRANSFERS

The Aeroporto Deputado Luís Eduardo Magalhães, 37 km (23 mi) northeast of Salvador, accommodates international and domestic flights. The Aeroporto Internacional Guararapes is 10 km (6 mi) south of Recife, just five minutes from Boa Viagem, and 15 minutes from the city center. The Aeroporto Internacional Pinto Martins in Fortaleza is 6 km (4 mi) south of downtown.

➤ AIRPORT INFORMATION: **Aeroporto Deputado Luís Eduardo Magalhães** (☎ 071/204–1010). **Aeroporto Internacional Guararapes** (⊠ Praça Ministro Salgado Filho s/n, Imbiribeira, ☎ 081/3464–4188). **Aeroporto Internacional Pinto Martins** (⊠ Av. Senador Carlos Jereissati, ☎ 085/477–1200).

In Salvador, avoid taking comum taxis from the airport; drivers often jack up the fare by refusing or "forgetting" to turn on the meter. Opt for one of the prepaid *cooperativa* (co-op) taxis (they're white with a broad blue stripe); the cost is R$79–R$113 for the 20- to 30-minute drive downtown. The *ônibus executivo*, an air-conditioned bus, runs daily from 6 AM to 9 PM at no set intervals; it costs about R$9 and takes an hour to reach downtown, stopping at hotels along the way. (Drivers don't speak English, so write your hotel's address down to show to them). Several companies operate these buses, the largest being Transportes Ondina. The municipal Circular buses, operated by both Transportes Ondina and Transportes Rio Vermelho, cost mere centavos and run along the beaches to downtown, ending at São Joaquim, where ferries depart for Ilha de Itaparica.

In the lobby of Recife's airport, on the right just before the exit door, is a tourist information booth, and next to that a taxi stand. You can pay at the counter; the cost is about R$23 to Boa Viagem and R$34 to downtown. The ride from the airport to Olinda will cost R$34–R$45. There are also regular buses and microbuses (more expensive). The bus labeled AEROPORTO runs to Avenida Dantas Barreto in the center of the city, stopping in Boa Viagem on the way. To reach Olinda, take the AEROPORTO bus to Avenida Nossa Senhora do Carmo in Recife and then take the CASA CAIADA bus.

Fortaleza'a fixed-price *especial* (special) taxis charge about R$23 for trips from the airport to downtown on weekdays, R$41 on weekends. Highly recommended is the Guanabara Top-Bus, a *frescão* (air-conditioned bus) that loops from the airport through the center and on to Praia Iracema and Praia Meireles. It leaves the airport every 25 minutes, 7 AM–10 PM daily, and costs about R$9. City buses also run from here to the nearby bus station and Praça José de Alencar in Centro.

➤ SHUTTLES IN SALVADOR: **Transportes Ondina** (✉ Av. Vasco da Gama 347, ☎ 071/245–6366). **Transportes Rio Vermelho** (✉ Av. Dorival Caymmi 18270, ☎ 071/377–2587).

BOAT AND FERRY TRAVEL

SALVADOR

Itaparica and the other harbor islands can be reached by taking a ferry or a launch from Salvador, by hiring a motorized schooner, or by joining a harbor schooner excursion—all departing from the docks behind the Mercado Modelo. Launches cost about R$2 and leave every 45 minutes from 7 AM to 6 PM from Terminal Turístico Marítimo. The ferry takes passengers and cars and leaves every half hour between 6 AM and 10:30 PM from the Terminal Ferry-Boat. The fare is around R$2 for passengers, R$14–R$18 for cars, and takes 45 minutes to cross the bay.

➤ CONTACTS: **Terminal Ferry-Boat** (✉ Terminal Marítimo, Av. Oscar Ponte 1051, São Joaquim, ☎ 071/321–7100). **Terminal Turístico Marítimo** (✉ Av. França s/n, ☎ 071/243–0741).

RECIFE

Catamaran rides along the Rio Capibaribe pass Recife's grand houses, bridges, and mangrove swamps. There are two such excursions: The hour-long afternoon trip goes through the old rotating bridge and passes Recife Velho and São José, the customs quay, the Santa Isabel Bridge, and the Rua da Aurora quays to the area near the Casa da Cultura. The two-hour-long night tour is aboard a slower—though more lively—vessel. The trip is like a party, with live music, drinks, and snacks. It passes the quays of São José Estelita (a set of restored warehouses) and then goes back by the Calanga Iate Clube, passing the ruins of the

Casa de Banhos and running to the Rio Beberibe, from where there's a beautiful view of Olinda. Boats leave from near the Praça do Marco Zero in Recife Velho.

➤ CONTACTS: **Catamaran reservations** (☎ 081/3436–2220).

BUS AND METRÔ TRAVEL

SALVADOR

You can purchase bus tickets at the Terminal Rodoviário in Salvador. The Itapemirim Company has three buses a day to Recife (13 hrs, R$90–R$125), Fortaleza (19 hrs, R$150), and Rio (28 hrs, R$200–R$375).

The Santa Maria/Catuense Company has hourly service from the Terminal Rodoviário to Praia do Forte starting at 7:30 AM, with the last bus returning to the city at 5:30 PM; tickets cost about R$11. The Camurujipe Company has hourly service from the Terminal Rodoviário to Cachoeira between 5:30 AM and 7 PM. You can also reach Cachoeira by a combination of boat and bus: boats depart weekdays at 2:30 PM from the Terminal Turístico Marítimo for the three-hour trip to Maragojipe; you then board a bus for the bumpy half-hour ride.

Within Salvador, use the executive buses. Although other buses serve most of the city and cost a pittance (R$1.40), they're often crowded and dirty, and they're also favored by pickpockets. The fancier executivo buses (R$3.50) serve tourist areas more completely. The glass-sided green, yellow, and orange jardineira bus (marked PRAÇA DA SÉ)—which runs from the downtown Praça da Sé to the Stella Maris Beach along the beachfront Orla Marítima series of avenues—is fine for getting to the beach. The Santa Maria/Catuense company operates six buses (marked PRAIA DO FORTE) daily that stop at Barra do Jacuípe Beach.

➤ BUS INFORMATION: **Itapemirim** (☎ 071/358–0037). **Santa Maria/Catuense** (☎ 071/359–3474). **Terminal Rodoviário** (✉ Av. Antônio Carlos Magalhães, Iguatemi, ☎ 071/358–6633). **Terminal Turístico Marítimo** (✉ Behind Mercado Modelo, Av. França s/n, ☎ 071/243–0741).

RECIFE

The Terminal Integrado de Passageiros (TIP), a *metrô* (subway, although trains run above ground) terminal and bus station 14 km (9 mi) from the Recife city center, handles all interstate bus departures and some connections to local destinations. To reach it via metrô, a 30-minute ride, enter through the Museu do Trem, opposite the Casa da Cultura, and take the train marked RODOVIÁRIA. Several buses a day go to Salvador (12–14 hrs, R$90) and Fortaleza (12 hrs, R$100); there are also daily departures to Rio (40 hrs, R$270) and frequent service to Caruaru (2 hrs, R$23).

In Boa Viagem, you can take the PIEDADE/RIO DOCE bus to Olinda. Buses to Igarassu and Ilha de Itamaracá leave from the center of Recife, at Avenida Martins de Barros, in front of the Grande Hotel.

City buses cost R$1.10; they're clearly labeled and run frequently until about 10:30 PM. Many stops have signs indicating the routes. To reach Boa Viagem via the metrô, get off at the Joana Bezerra stop (a 20-min ride) and take a bus or taxi (R$34) from here. Combination bus-metrô tickets cost about R$4.50; routes are explained in a leaflet issued by CBTU Metrorec.

➤ BUS AND METRÔ INFORMATION: **CBTU Metrorec** (☎ 081/3251–5256). **Terminal Integrado de Passageiros** (TIP; ✉ Rodovia BR 232, Km 15, Curado, Jaboatão dos Guararapes, ☎ 081/3452–1999).

FORTALEZA

The main bus station, Terminal Rodoviário João Tomé, is 6 km (4 mi) south of Centro. In low season you can buy tickets at the station right before leaving. São Benedito runs five buses daily to Beberibe and Morro Branco Beach (2½ hrs; R$4.50), and three daily to Aracati and Canoa Quebrada (3½ hrs; R$23). Expresso Guanabara and Itapemirim have five daily buses to Recife (12 hrs; R$80–R$150), and three daily to Salvador (21 hrs; R$136); in addition, Itapemirim has daily buses to Rio de Janeiro. Penha also runs buses to Rio (48 hrs; R$305–R$375) and São Paulo (52 hrs; R$305–R$375).

The fare on city buses is R$1.70. Those marked 13 DE MAIO or AGUA-NAMBI 1 or 2 run from Avenida General Sampaio and pass the Centro de Turismo; from here (Rua Dr. João Moreira), you can take the bus labeled CIRCULAR to Avenida Beira-Mar and Praia de Iracema and Praia do Meireles. From Avenida Castro e Silva (close to Centro de Turismo), PRAIA DO FUTURO and SERVILUZ buses run to Praia do Futuro. For beaches west of the city, take a CUMBUCO bus from Praça Capistrano Abreu on Avenida Tristão Gonçalves or from along Avenida Beira-Mar. For the eastern beach of Porto das Dunas and the water park, take a BEACH PARK bus from Praça Tristão Gonçalves or from along Avenida Beira-Mar.

➤ BUS INFORMATION: **Expresso Guanabara** (☎ 085/227–0214 or 085/227–0215). **Itapemirim** (☎ 085/272–4511). **Penha** (☎ 085/272–4511). **São Benedito** (☎ 085/256–1999). **Terminal Rodoviário João Tomé** (✉ Av. Borges de Melo 1630, Fátima, ☎ 085/256–1566).

CAR RENTAL

Rental companies in Salvador include Avis, Hertz, Localiza, and VIP Rent a Car. The best companies in Recife are Interlocadora, Localiza, and Unidas. To rent a car in Fortaleza, contact Avis, Hertz, or Localiza.

➤ SALVADOR AGENCIES: **Avis** (☎ 071/237–0155 or 071/377–2276 at airport). **Hertz** (☎ 071/377–3633 at airport). **Localiza** (☎ 071/377–2272 at airport). **VIP Rent a Car** (☎ 071/461–8080).

➤ RECIFE AGENCIES: **Interlocadora** (☎ 081/3465–1041). **Localiza** (☎ 081/3341–2082 or 081/3341–0477). **Unidas** (☎ 081/3465–0200).

➤ FORTALEZA AGENCIES: **Avis** (☎ 085/261–6785). **Hertz** (☎ 085/242–5425). **Localiza** (☎ 085/242–4255).

CAR TRAVEL

SALVADOR

Two highways—BR 101 and BR 116—run between Rio de Janeiro and Salvador. If you take the BR 101, get off at the city of Santo Antônio/Nazaré and follow the signs to Itaparica, 61 km (38 mi) away. At Itaparica, you can either take the 45-minute ferry ride to Salvador or continue on BR 101 to its connection with BR 324. If you opt for the BR 116, exit at the city of Feira de Santana, 107 km (67 mi) from Salvador and take the BR 324, which approaches the city from the north. Follow the signs marked IGUATEMI/CENTRO for downtown and nearby destinations. To reach Praia do Forte by car, take the Estrada do Coco north and follow the signs; there's a short stretch of unpaved road at the end. To reach Cachoeira, take BR 324 north for about 55 km (34 mi), then head west on BR 420 through the town of Santo Amaro. The trip takes 1½ hours.

The dearth of places to park in Salvador makes rental cars impractical for sightseeing in the Cidade Alta. Further, many soteropolitanos are reckless drivers, making driving a dangerous proposition, especially if you don't know your way around. That said, cars are handy for visits to outlying beaches and far-flung attractions.

RECIFE

The main north–south highway through Recife is BR 101. To the north, it travels through vast sugar plantations; it's mostly straight, with only slight slopes. To travel south, you can also take the scenic coastal road, the PE 060, which passes through Porto de Galinhas Beach. To reach Caruaru, take BR 232 west; the trip takes 1½ hours. Because of horrible rush-hour traffic and careless drivers, it's best to rent a car only for side trips from Recife.

FORTALEZA

The main access roads to Fortaleza are the BR 304, which runs southeast to Natal and Recife and which is in good condition; the BR 222, which has a few poor sections and which travels west to the state of Piauí and on to Brasília; the BR 020 southwest, which goes to Picos, in Piauí State, and on to Brasília and is in decent shape; and the BR 116, which runs south to Salvador and has several stretches in poor condition. The CE 004, or Litoránea, links the coastal towns to the southeast as far as Aracati. Many of the secondary routes are paved, though there are also some dirt roads in fair condition.

Fortaleza is an easy city in which to drive. Major routes take you easily from one side of town to the other. Although rush hour sees traffic jams, they aren't nearly as bad as they are in other big cities.

CONSULATES

➤ SALVADOR: **British** (✉ Av. Estados Unidos 15, Comércio, ☎ 071/243–9222 or 071/243–7399). **United States** (✉ Rua Pernambuco 568, Pituba, ☎ 071/345–1545).

➤ RECIFE: **British** (✉ Av. Engenheiro Domingos Ferreira 4150, Boa Viagem, ☎ 081/3465–0230 or 081/3465–0247). **United States** (✉ Rua Gonçalves Maia 163, Boa Vista, ☎ 081/3421–2441).

➤ FORTALEZA: **British** (✉ Sede Grupo Edson Queiroz, Praça da Imprensa, ☎ 085/224–8888). **United States** (✉ Instituto Brasil Estados Unidos, Rua Nogueira Acioly 891, ☎ 085/252–1539).

EMERGENCIES

In Salvador, the office of the Delegacia de Proteção do Turista, the tourist police, is down the steps at the back of the Belvedere at the Praça da Sé. It deals as best it can (on a shoestring budget) with tourist-related crime after the fact. There are also military-police foot patrols; officers, some of whom have rudimentary second-language skills, wear armbands that say POLÍCIA TURÍSTICA.

➤ CONTACTS IN SALVADOR: **Aliança Hospital** (✉ Av. Juracy Magalhães Jr. 2096, ☎ 071/350–5600). **Delegacia de Proteção do Turista** (☎ 071/320–4103). **Hospital Jorge Valente** (✉ Av. Garibaldi 2135, ☎ 071/203–4333). **General emergencies** (☎ 192). **Hospital Português** (✉ Av. Princesa Isabel 2, Santa Isabel, ☎ 071/203–5555).

➤ CONTACTS IN RECIFE: **Ambulance** (☎ 081/3465–5566). **Centro Hospitalar Albert Sabin** (✉ Rua Senador José Henrique 141, Ilha do Leite, ☎ 081/3421–5411 or 081/3421–6155). **Farmácia Casa Caiada** (✉ Rua Padre Carapuceiro 777, Boa Viagem, ☎ 081/3465–1420). **Farmácia dos Pobres** (✉ Av. Conselheiro Aguiar 3595, Boa Viagem, ☎ 081/3325–5998). **Real Hospital Português** (✉ Av. Agamenon Magalhães, Derby, ☎ 081/3416–1122 or 081/3416–1112).

➤ CONTACTS IN FORTALEZA: **Ambulance** (☎ 085/254–5592, 085/221–2873, or 085/257–3322). **Hospital Antônio Prudente** (✉ Av. Aguanambi 1827, Fátima, ☎ 085/277–4000). **Hospital Batista** (✉ Rua Prof. Dias da Rocha 2530, Aldeota, ☎ 085/261–2999). **Hospital Génesis** (✉ Av. Santos Dumont 1168, Aldeota, ☎ 085/255–8500). **Surfing emergencies** (☎ 193).

ENGLISH-LANGUAGE MEDIA

SALVADOR

Graúna has many books in English. Livraria Brandão sells secondhand books in foreign languages. Livraria Planeta (Aeroporto Deputado

Luís Eduardo Magalhães) has English-language books, magazines, and newspapers.

➤ SALVADOR BOOKSTORES: **Graúna** (⊠ Av. 7 de Setembro 1448; ⊠ Rua Barão de Itapoã, Porto da Barra). **Livraria Brandão** (⊠ Rua Rui Barbosa 15B, Centro, ☎ 071/3243–5383).

RECIFE

Livraria Brandão has used English-language books; the shop also sells books from stalls on Rua do Infante Dom Henrique. Livro 7 is a large emporium with a huge stock, including many foreign-language titles. You can find English-language books, magazines, and newspapers at Sodiler, which has branches at the Guararapes Airport and in the Shopping Center Recife.

➤ RECIFE BOOKSTORES: **Livraria Brandão** (⊠ Rua da Matriz 22). **Livro 7** (⊠ Rua 7 de Setembro 329a). **Sodiler** (☎ (071/3467–5091 or 071/3464–6538).

FORTALEZA

You'll find English-language publications at Livros e Letras and Edésio.

➤ FORTALEZA BOOKSTORES: **Edésio** (⊠ Shopping Iguatemi, Av. Washington Soares 85, Loja 62, Água Fria, ☎ 085/273–1466). **Livros e Letras** (⊠ Avenida Shopping, Av. Dom Luís 300, Loja 232, Meireles, ☎ 085/264–9376).

MAIL, INTERNET AND SHIPPING

Salvador's main post office is in the Cidade Baixa's Praça Inglaterra. You'll also find branches on the Avenida Princesa Isabel in Barra and the Rua Marques de Caravelas in Ondina, at the Barra and Iguatemi shopping centers, and at the airport. The airport branch is open 24 hours; all others are open weekdays 8–5. All branches offer express-mail service.

Express-mail service is available at all Recife's post offices. The main branch is downtown; its *posta restante* (held mail) counter is in the basement. There are also branches at the airport, the TIP, and in Boa Viagem at Avenida Conselheiro Aguiar and Rua Coronel Sérgio Cardim.

For Internet service in Fortaleza, try Company Office Rede de Negócios, which also has fax and secretarial services. All branches of the post office offer express-mail services.

➤ INTERNET CAFÉ: **Company Office Rede de Negócios** (⊠ Av. Beira-Mar 3980, Mucuripe, Fortaleza, ☎ 085/263–1119).

➤ POST OFFICES: **Salvador** (☎ 071/243–9383). **Recife** (⊠ Av. Gurarapes 250). **Fortaleza** (⊠ Rua Senador Alencar 38, Centro; ⊠ Monsenhor Tabosa 1109, Iracema).

MONEY MATTERS

SALVADOR

Never change money on the streets, especially in the Cidade Alta. Major banks have exchange facilities, but only in some of their branches. Try Citibank, which has good rates; Banco Económico; and Banco do Brasil, which also offers exchange services at its branches in the Shopping Center Iguatemi and at the airport.

➤ SALVADOR BANKS: **Banco do Brasil** (⊠ Av. Estados Unidos 561, Comércio). **Banco Económico** (⊠ Rua Miguel Calmon 285). **Citibank** (⊠ Rua Miguel Calmon 555, Comércio).

RECIFE

Recommended *casas de câmbio* (exchange houses) in the city center include Mônaco Câmbio and Norte Câmbio Turismo. In Boa Viagem try Norte Câmbio Turismo or Colmeia Câmbio & Turismo. Banco do

Brasil offers exchange services in several in-town locations as well as at its airport branch.

➤ RECIFE BANKS AND EXCHANGE SERVICES: **Banco do Brasil** (⊠ Av. Dantas Barreto 541, Santo Antônio; ⊠ Av. Conselheiro Aguiar 3600, Boa Viagem). **Colmeia Câmbio & Turismo** (⊠ Rua dos Navegantes 784, Loja 4, Boa Viagem). **Mônaco Câmbio** (⊠ Praça Joaquim Nabuco 159). **Norte Câmbio Turismo** (⊠ Rua Mathias de Albuquerque 223, Sala 508; ⊠ Rua dos Navegantes 691, Loja 10, Boa Viagem).

FORTALEZA

The main Banco do Brasil branch is open weekdays 10–3; the Meireles branch on Avenida Abolição has the same hours. There are lots of casas de câmbio in Meireles as well.

➤ FORTALEZA BANK: **Banco do Brasil** (⊠ Rua Floriano Peixoto).

SAFETY

Discretion and a low-key approach will more than likely ensure a hassle-free trip to Salvador, Recife, or Fortaleza. Leave valuables at home, and don't wear jewelry or watches. Wear your purse bandolier style (with the strap across your front) and keep your wallet out of easy reach for thieves (a money belt isn't a bad idea). Never leave belongings unattended. Carry only a photocopy of your passport, leaving the original in the hotel safe.

TELEPHONES

Salvador's area code is 071. The area code for Recife is 081. For Fortaleza it's 085. Public phones take cards, which are sold in a variety of denominations at many shops.

TAXIS

SALVADOR

Taxis are metered, but you must convert the unit shown on the meter to reais using a chart posted on the window. Tipping isn't expected. You can hail a comum taxi (white with a red and blue stripe) on the street (they often line up in front of major hotels) or summon one by phone. If you bargain, a comum taxi can be hired for the day for as little as R$135. Try Ligue Taxi. The more expensive, though usually air-conditioned, *especial* (special) taxis also congregate outside major hotels, though you must generally call for them. Reliable companies include Cometas.

➤ SALVADOR TAXI COMPANIES: **Cometas** (☎ 071/244–4500). **Ligue Taxi** (☎ 071/357–7777).

RECIFE

Taxis are cheap (fares double on Sunday), but drivers seldom speak English. You can either hail a cab on the street or call for one. Recommended services are Coopertáxi, Radiotáxi Recife, and Teletáxi.

➤ RECIFE TAXI COMPANIES: **Coopertáxi** (☎ 081/3424–8944). **Radiotáxi Recife** (☎ 081/3423–7777). **Teletáxi** (☎ 081/3429–4242).

FORTALEZA

You can call cabs or hail them on the street. Fares are affordable, though they double on Sunday. Few drivers are English speakers. Reliable taxi services include Coopertáxi, Disquetáxi, Ligue Táxi, and Rádio Táxi.

➤ FORTALEZA TAXI COMPANIES: **Coopertáxi** (☎ 085/227–0480). **Disquetáxi** (☎ 085/287–7222). **Ligue Táxi** (☎ 085/231–7333). **Rádio Táxi** (☎ 085/287–5554).

TOURS

SALVADOR

Salvador's large group tours are cursory, and their guides often speak minimal English; such tours are also targeted by hordes of street vendors. Several travel agencies offer half-day minibus tours with hotel pickup and drop-off for about R$60–R$80. Agencies also offer day-long harbor tours on motorized schooners (R$80–R$90) and night tours (R$100–R$115) that include dinner and an Afro-Brazilian music and dance show. A beach tour that includes the Lagoa de Abaeté can be arranged as well, with a car and guide provided for about R$80 a head (minimum two people).

Another option is a private tour with a Bahiatursa guide (they carry the proper credentials), hired through your hotel, a travel agency, or at a Bahiatursa kiosk. Prices vary depending on the size of the group and include a car, which picks you up and drops you off at your hotel. Beware of guides who approach you at churches and other sights; they tell tall tales and overcharge you for the privilege.

Bahia Adventure can help you arrange jeep tours and other adventure treks to the Reserva de Sapiranga in the Praia do Forte area. BBTUR has excellent buses and vans; however, be sure to request an English-speaking guide ahead of time. The company has a full line of tours not only in Salvador but also to surrounding areas; there's also a branch in the lobby of the SuperClubs Breezes hotel in Costa do Sauípe. Odara Turismo, in the arcade at the Praia do Forte Resort Hotel arranges 4WD drive tours of the area plus horseback and hiking trips.

Though Tatur Tours specializes in African-heritage tours of Bahia, it also offers personalized special-interest city tours and arranges top-notch excursions from Salvador. Top Hilton Turismo offers the usual city tours and interesting boat cruises, including a trip around Baía de Todos os Santos in a trimaran and a schooner cruise to the islands. It also offers a tour to the nudist beach at Massarandupió, along the northern coast. For trips to Chapada Diamante, Trekking Tours is your best bet.
➤ SALVADOR TOUR OPERATORS: **Bahia Adventure** (☎ 071/876–1262). **BBTUR** (✉ Vila Nova da Praia, Loja 22/23, Costa do Sauípe, Mata de São João, ☎ 071/464–2121 or 71/341–8800 in Salvador). **Odara Turismo** (✉ Rua do Farol s/n, Praia do Forte, Mata de São João, ☎ 071/876–1080). **Tatur Tours** (✉ Av. Antônio Carlos Magalhães 2573, Edifício Royal Trade, ☎ 071/358–7216). **Top Hilton Turismo** (✉ Rua Fonte do Boi 05, Rio Vermelho, ☎ 071/334–5223,. **Trekking Tours** ✉ Bahia Praia Hotel, Av. Oceániana 2483, ☎ 071/332–5557).

RECIFE

Agência Luck's vans pick up from all the hotels for city tours. Make arrangements for these and excursions outside Recife with Andratur. Catamarã Tours books day and night river trips by catamaran and other small boats from its office at the port in Recife Velho on Praça Rio Branco (Marco Zero). You can make reservations for pousadas and land tours of Fernando de Noronha through Karitas Turismo Ltda.
➤ RECIFE TOUR OPERATORS: **Andratur** (✉ Av. Conselheiro Aguiar 3150, Loja 7, Boa Viagem, ☎ 081/3465–8588). **Agência Luck** (✉ Rua Jornalista Paulo Bittencourt 163, Casa A, Derby, ☎ 081/3421–3777. **Catamarã Tours** (☎ 081/3436–2220 or 081/3543–9117). **Karitas Turismo Ltda.** (✉ Rua Ribeiro de Brito 1002, ☎ 081/3466–4300, WEB www. karitas.com.br).

FORTALEZA

Recommended operators include Ernanitur, Lizatur Viagens e Turismo Ltda., Nettour Viagem e Turismo, and Beach Sun Serviços e Turismo LTDA. For trips to Flexeiras, Jericoacoara, or other beach areas outside Fortaleza, OceanView Tours and Travel is a solid choice.
➤ FORTALEZA TOUR OPERATORS: **Beach Sun Serviços e Turismo Ltda.**, (✉ Rua Silva Jatai 38, Meireles, ☎ FAX 085/248–2288). **Ernanitur** (✉

Av. Barão de Studart 1165, Aldeota, ☎ 085/244–9363). **Lizatur Viagens e Turismo Ltda.** (✉ Av. Dom Luiz 880, Sala 507, Aldeota, ☎ 085/ 244–7812). **Nettour Viagem e Turismo** (✉ Rua Tenente Benévolo 1355, Praia de Iracema, ☎ 085/268–3099). **OceanView Tours and Travel,** ✉ Av. Monsenhor Tabosa 1165, ☎ 085/219–1300.

VISITOR INFORMATION
SALVADOR
The main office of the state tourist board in Salvador, Bahiatursa, is far from tourist attractions. However, there are five other conveniently located branches: at the airport, the bus station, the downtown historic center, the Mercado Modelo, and the Cidade Alta. Emtursa, the municipal tourist board, is open weekdays 8–6.
➤ SALVADOR TOURIST INFORMATION: **Bahiatursa** (✉ Centro de Convenções, Jardim Armação s/n, ☎ 071/370–8400); (✉ Aeroporto Internacional, 2 de Julho s/n, ☎ 071/204–1244; ✉ Av. Antônio Carlos Magalhães s/n, Terminal Rodoviário, ☎ 071/358–0871; ✉ Terreiro de Jesus s/n, ☎ 071/321–0388 ✉ Mercado Modelo, Praça Visconde de Cairú s/n, ☎ 071/241–0240; ✉ Porto da Barra s/n, ☎ 071/247– 3195). **Emtursa** (✉ Largo do Pelourinho 12, ☎ 071/243–6555 or 071/ 243–5738; ✉ Trv. da Ajuda 2, 2nd floor, ☎ 071/321–4346 or 071/ 321–9307).

RECIFE
The state tourist board in Recife is Empetur. In Olinda contact the Secretaria de Turismo.
➤ RECIFE VISITOR INFORMATION: **Empetur** (✉ Guararapes Airport, ☎ 081/3462–4960; ✉ Centro de Convenções, Complexo Rodoviário de Salgadinho s/n, ☎ 081/3241–3119; ✉ TIP, Rodovia BR 232, Km 15, Curado, Jaboatão dos Guararapes, ☎ 081/3452–1999). **Secretaria de Turismo** (✉ Rua de São Bento 160, ☎ 081/3429–1927; ✉ Rua Bernardo Vieira de Melo, Mercado da Ribeira, Praça do Carmo, ☎ 081/3439–1660).

FORTALEZA
A tourist information hot line, Disque Turismo, operates weekdays 8– 6; English is spoken. You can also get information through the Secretaria de Segurança Pública do Estado do Ceará. Branches of Ceará State's tourist board, Setur, are open weekdays 8–6, except for the one at the airport, which is open 24 hours a day. The municipal tourist board, Fortur, has booths open weekdays 8 AM–10 PM and weekends 8–6.
➤ FORTALEZA VISITOR INFORMATION: **Disque Turismo** (☎ 1516). **Fortur** (✉ Av. Santos Dumont 5335, Papicu, ☎ 085/265–1177; ✉ Av. Beira-Mar, in front of Clube Náutico, ☎ 085/242–4447). **Secretaria de Segurança Pública do Estado do Ceará** (✉ Trv. José Napoleão 82, Meireles, ☎ 085/263–5904). **Setur** (✉ Centro Administrativo Virgílio Távora, Cambeba, ☎ 085/488–3900; ✉ Aeroporto Internacional Pinto Martins, Av. Senador Carlos Jereissati, ☎ 085/477–1667; ✉ Centro de Turismo, Rua Senador Pompeu 350, Centro, ☎ 085/212–3566 or 083/ 212–3966 or toll free in Brazil, 0800–991516).

7 THE AMAZON

Adventure awaits you in the Amazon.
You can travel by riverboat—perhaps
accompanied by pink dolphins—and bask
on the soft white sands of a river beach.
You can stay in a jungle lodge—fishing for
piranha by day, searching for alligators at
night. You can witness the violent meeting
of the world's most voluminous river with the
Atlantic. And you can dock in cities whose
mansions are a testament to the wealth and
ostentation of the bygone age of rubber.

Updated by
Rob Aikins

NOTHING IS MORE MEMORABLE THAN A FLIGHT OVER the Amazon region. The world's largest rain forest seems an endless carpet of green that's sliced only by the curving contours of rivers. Its statistics are as impressive: the region covers more than 10 million square km (4 million square mi) and extends into eight other countries (French Guiana, Suriname, Guyana, Venezuela, Ecuador, Peru, Bolivia, and Colombia). It takes up roughly 40% of Brazil in the states of Acre, Rondônia, Amazonas, Roraima, Pará, Amapá, and Tocantins. The rain forest produces a third of the world's oxygen and is home to a fifth of its freshwater supply, as well as 500,000 cataloged species of plants and animals. Yet it's inhabited by only 16 million people—that's less than the population of metropolitan São Paulo.

Life centers on the rivers, the largest of which is the Amazon itself. From its source in southern Peru, it runs 6,300 km (3,900 mi) to its Atlantic outflow. It's second in length only to the Nile, and of its hundreds of tributaries 17 are more than 1,600 km (1,000 mi) long. In places the Amazon is so wide you can't see the opposite shore, earning it the appellation of Rio Mar (River Sea). Although there has been increasing urbanization, 45% of the Amazon's residents live in rural settlements along the riverbanks, where the trees are full of fruit, the waters teem with fish, and the soil—whose nutrients are leached by heavy rainfall—is suited to the hearty, multipurpose manioc root.

The Spaniard Vicente Pinzón is credited with having been the first to sail the Amazon in 1500. But the most famous voyage was undertaken by Spanish conquistador Francisco de Orellano, who set out from Ecuador on a short mission to search for food in 1541. Orellano was also, no doubt, familiar with the legend of El Dorado (the Golden One), a monarch whose kingdom was so rich in gold he covered his naked body in gold dust each day. Instead of gold or a lost kingdom, however, Orellano ran into natives, heat, and disease. When he emerged from the jungle a year later, his crew told a tale of women warriors they called the Amazons (a nod to classical mythology). This captivating story lent the region its name.

Much later, Portuguese explorer Francisco Raposo claimed to have found the ruins of a lost civilization in the jungle. He wrote: "We entered fearfully through the gateways to find the ruins of a city. . . We came upon a great plaza, a column of black stone, and on top of it the figure of a youth was carved over what seemed to be a great doorway." Whatever Raposo saw was never again found. Unlike the highly organized Indian kingdoms and cities of Mexico and Peru, the Amazon natives were primarily nomadic hunter-gatherers.

Documented accounts indicate that early Portuguese contacts with the Indians were relatively peaceful. But it wasn't long before the peace ended, and the indigenous populations were devastated. Diseases brought by the Europeans and against which the Indians had no resistance took their toll; Portuguese attempts to enslave them did the rest. When the Portuguese arrived in Brazil, there were roughly 4.5 million Indians, many of them in the Amazon; today there are just over 300,000 in the nation, and fewer than 200,000 in the Amazon.

In the late 19th century, rubber—needed for bicycle and automobile tires—practically transformed Belém and Manaus from outposts to cities. Rubber barons constructed mansions and monuments and brought the most modern trappings of life into the jungle. The area attracted a colorful array of explorers, dreamers, and opportunists: in 1913, Brazilian adventurer Cândido Mariana da Silva Rondon (for whom the state of Rondônia is named) and former president Theodore Roosevelt came across a then-unknown river (Rondon named it for Roosevelt). In 1925, British adventurer Colonel Percy Fawcett, who had been seeking Raposo's lost city for years, disappeared into the jungle. In 1928, Henry Ford began to pour millions of dollars into vast rubber plantations. After much struggle and few results, the projects were scrapped 20 years later.

Since the rubber era, huge reserves of gold and iron have been discovered. Land-settlement schemes and development projects, such as hydroelectric plants and major roadworks, have followed. Conservation has not always been a priority. Vast portions of the "world's lung" have been indiscriminately deforested; tribal lands have again been encroached on; and industrial by-products, such as mercury used in gold mining, have poisoned wildlife and people. The 1988 murder (by a wealthy cattle rancher) of Brazilian activist Chico Mendes, who had made a name for himself lobbying for environmental issues abroad, brought still more global attention to the region. Although the Brazilian government has established reserves and made other efforts to preserve the territory, conservationists aren't satisfied.

And yet, 500 years after the first Europeans arrived, much of the Amazon has not been thoroughly explored by land. You can hear stories of lost cities and of unearthly creatures; stand on a riverboat deck and be astounded by the vastness of the mighty Rio Amazonas or charmed by wooden huts along a narrow waterway; hike through dense vegetation and gawk at trees that tower 35 m (150 ft). It's still a place where simple pleasures are savored and the mystical is celebrated.

Pleasures and Pastimes

Dining

Who needs regular old beef or poultry when you can have water-buffalo steak or wild Amazon duck? If you have even more intrepid taste buds, you can even try armadillo (beware of ordering alligator and turtle, which are still found on some menus although it's against the law). In addition to piranha, you'll find river fish with such exotic Indian names as *tucunaré, pirarucu, tambaquí, curimatá, jaraquí,* and *pacú.* The *pimenta-de-cheiro,* a local hot-pepper oil, seriously spices things up. Side dishes often include *farofa* (coarsely ground manioc), *farinha* (finely ground manioc), black beans, and rice.

For dessert, try some of the region's famed fruits, such as *cupuaçu* (a brown-skinned, fragrant fruit about the size of an eggplant), *guaraná* (a small, red fruit used in the popular Brazilian soft drink of the same name), and *açaí* (another small, red fruit; it's bitter but is commonly found in sweetened, energy-enhancing sorbets that are beloved by athletes). The region's most popular beers are Antarctica and Cerpa.

Reservations and dressy attire are rarely needed (indeed, reservations are rarely taken). Tipping isn't customary. For price categories, *see* the chart *under* Dining *in* Smart Travel Tips A to Z.

Handicrafts

Handicrafts made by indigenous groups include wooden furniture, woven items, bows and arrows, and jewelry and headdresses of seeds and feathers. (Note: U.S. Customs prohibits the import of certain feathers; ask the storekeeper about such items before you buy.) In Belém, you'll find *marajoara* pottery, which has the intricate designs used by the tribe of the same name. Vases and sculptures in Macapá often contain manganese—a black, shiny mineral mined locally.

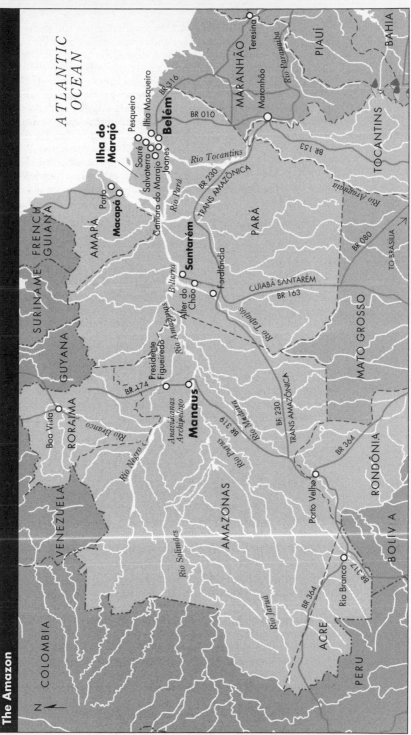

The Amazon

Lodging

Anyone going to Amazonia should be aware that it is still a very wild place and that most of the lodges and towns are remote with a capital "R." Don't expect to be pampered. Regardless of whether you stay in a resort, a hotel, a *pousada* (inn), or a jungle lodge, expect prices to be on the high side. Further, service and amenities may not match the price tags, and such extras as laundry service can be outrageously expensive (always ask about costs beforehand). All that said, there are bargains to be found, and most places include breakfast in their rates. Further, many establishments offer discounts of as much as 20%—don't be shy about asking for a reduced rate, especially in low season. Rooms in hotels, particularly in the cities, generally have air-conditioning, phones, and TVs. Unless otherwise noted, all rooms have baths, but jungle lodges and smaller hotels in outlying areas generally lack hot water and other common amenities.

For price categories, *see* the chart *under* Lodging *in* Smart Travel Tips A to Z.

Exploring the Amazon

Although there are regular flights throughout the Amazon, many visitors still opt for the area's primary mode of transportation—boat. The region encompasses hundreds of navigable rivers, but vessels tend to follow only a few well-charted waterways, mainly the Amazon, Negro, Solimões, Madeira, Pará, and Tapajós rivers. A trip along the Amazon itself—especially the 1,602 km (993 mi) four- to five-day journey between Belém and Manaus—is a singular experience. Averaging more than 3 km (2 mi) in width, but reaching up to 48 km (30 mi) in the rainy season, there are many spots where it's impossible to see either bank. At night, the moon and stars are the only sources of light, reinforcing the sense of being in true wilderness.

Cruises

Whatever your style of travel, your budget, or the length of your stay, there's a boat plying the river to suit your needs. You can sleep in a hammock on the deck of a thatch-roofed riverboat or in the air-conditioned suite of an upscale tour operator's private ship. Note that owing to the dense riverbank vegetation it's not easy to spot wildlife from a boat. Further, some craft travel far from shore, defeating any chance you have of seeing the flora or the fauna. It's best to plan a boat trip that includes a stop or two so you can explore the rain forest.

ENASA BOATS

The state-run Empresa de Navegação da Amazônia S/A (ENASA) has an enormous, first-rate catamaran that travels between Belém and Manaus once or twice a month. All of its 62 cabins have air-conditioning, music, phones, and baths with hot water. Other shipboard amenities include a pool, a bar, and a restaurant that serves regional food. The four- to five-day trip costs roughly R$770. Unfortunately, the schedule isn't regular, and you can't make reservations through travel agencies. ENASA has other ships that travel more frequently, but they don't offer the same standard of luxury.

OCEANGOING SHIPS

Some cruise ships call at Manaus as part of itineraries that may include stops in Santarém, Rio de Janeiro, and southern Caribbean islands. Most trips take place during the North American winter; they range in length from 11 to 29 days, and costs start at R$5,500. The major lines making such journeys are Princess Cruises and Royal Olympic Cruises.

SPEEDBOATS

Two high-speed catamarans run between Manaus and Santarém (12 hours, R$110) and between Macapá and Belém (seven hours, less than R$88). Traveling at 40–50 knots per hour, they arrive in about a third of the time as other boats, but they travel far from the riverbanks, so you won't see much on the journey. They have cushioned seats and air-conditioning.

STANDARD RIVERBOATS

If you think that comfort should take a backseat to adventure, consider a leisurely trip by standard double- or triple-decker boats, which carry both freight and passengers. Although you may not get a close-up view of the riverbank, you will get the real feel of life along the river. Frequent stops at small towns are opportunities for interesting interactions and observations.

You might be able to get a cabin, but expect it to be claustrophobic, costing from R$220 to R$440 between Manaus and Belém, and about half that to or from Santarém. The real adventure is out on the deck, where for R$110–R$165 most passengers sleep in hammocks with little or no space between them. You must bring your own (they're sold onshore for between R$11 and R$33), as well as a few yards of rope to tie it up with.

Clusters of booths sell tickets at the docks. Even if you don't speak Portuguese, there are easy-to-understand signs alongside the booths. Inspect the vessel you will travel on closely (sanitary conditions vary from boat to boat), and if you plan to sleep in a hammock, board early to secure a good spot (away from the engine and toilets). Travel as lightly as possible, and keep your gear secure at all times. Bring plenty of sunscreen and insect repellent. Nights can be surprisingly cool, so pack a light blanket. Food is served, but the quality ranges from okay to deplorable. At best, the diet of meat, rice, and beans can become monotonous. Most of the nicer boats have a small store at the stern where you can buy canned drinks and snacks. Fresh fruit is available at stops along the way (just be sure to peel or wash it thoroughly with bottled water before eating it). Experienced Brazilian travelers bring their own food, bottled water, small stoves, and pans.

TOURIST BOATS

Private groups can hire tourist boats that are more comfortable than standard riverboats. They generally travel close to the riverbank and have open upper decks from which you can observe the river and forest. The better tour operators have a regional expert on board—usually an ecologist or botanist—who's fluent in English. You can either sleep out on the deck in a hammock or in a cabin, which will usually have air-conditioning or a fan. Meals are generally provided.

Organized Trips

Most tour operators offer a variety of itineraries—from 3 to 19 days, from hammocks in the open air to luxurious wood-paneled boat cabins and/or jungle lodges, and from Belém to Manaus. Along the route you may visit indigenous villages, explore tributaries by small craft, and learn about the flora and fauna. For information on specific operators, *see* Tours *in* Smart Travel Tips A to Z.

CANOEING AND FISHING

Paddling local wooden canoes by day and camping at night, you may explore the rain forest that lines the banks of the Rio Negro (Negro River) and perhaps continue along smaller tributaries. En route, you'll see monkeys, iguanas, river dolphins, and alligators, and you'll visit with local river people. (Trips generally run 7–10 days.)

More than 2,000 species of fish inhabit the Amazon region. But it's the legendary peacock bass, described as the "ultimate adversary," that lures most anglers. Mobile safari camps allow you to reach obscure, unpopulated watersheds, or you can opt for an air-conditioned stateroom aboard a boat.

CULTURE

Although Brazil limits visits to Indian reservations to researchers, if you have an interest in indigenous cultures you can learn about the Yanomami people on 11- or 15-day itineraries with Swallows and Amazons. Small boats take you along the Rio Negro to visit Yanomami communities that aren't part of a reservation and to spend several days with the people of one village. Amizade Limited takes its cultural trips a step farther. You can help the organization's volunteers and Brazilian students in various community-related projects.

ECOLOGY

If you're interested in the flora and fauna of the region, you can join a professor from Dartmouth College with Ecotour Expeditions to study the wildlife of the rain forest as well as the history of medicinal plants. With Earthwatch, you can assist researchers in a variety of projects— including those involving studies of monkeys, beetles, or orchids. On bird-watching tours, you may spot the golden-wing parakeet—one of many exotic species inhabiting the Amazon.

TREKKING AND CAMPING

Inland jungle adventures last 3–15 days, and most begin with a boat trip up the Rio Negro from Manaus. Some trips are based at Ariaú Jungle Towers, where four-story accommodations, linked by catwalks, stand atop stilts. Other programs combine cruises with jungle lodge stays. All include rain-forest walks, usually led by a local guide. If you're more adventurous, consider a trip with Ecotour Expeditions or Swallows and Amazons. By day, you'll spend an average of six hours traveling through thick vegetation. At night, you'll no doubt sleep well—perhaps in a hammock and certainly serenaded by wildlife. Explorers Travel Group also offers a 15-day Green Hell Expedition—the physically demanding trip involves camping, hiking, and canoeing. Eldertreks' more gentle programs feature short, moderately easy walks in the Amazon Basin.

Great Itineraries

Even 10 days is a short time to explore the region. Still, during a weeklong stay you can see some urban highlights and spend a little time on the river as well. The following independent itineraries start in Belém and end in Manaus, but it's fine to follow them in reverse order.

IF YOU HAVE 7 DAYS

Fly into Belém and spend two days exploring the Cidade Velha and the natural reserves in and around the city. Then fly to Manaus for two days—enough time for the short boat ride to the meeting of the waters and to take a city tour that includes the Teatro Amazonas. Then head out for a stay of a day or two at one of the famed jungle lodges.

IF YOU HAVE 10 DAYS

Spend two days in Belém exploring the city and its environs. On your third day, travel by boat to Ilha do Marajó for a two-day *fazenda* (ranch) stay. Return to Belém for a flight to Manaus; two days is enough to see the urban sights and to see the meeting of the waters. Spend your last few days at a jungle lodge outside Manaus.

IF YOU HAVE 15 DAYS

After spending two days exploring Belém and a couple more on a fazenda in Ilha do Marajó, hop either a luxury or standard riverboat for the two-day journey to Santarém. Spend a day strolling the city before heading to Alter do Chão, an hour away. Then fly from Santarém into Manaus, where you should spend a day or two sightseeing before heading to a jungle lodge.

When to Tour

In summer (winter in the northern hemisphere) it's often brutally hot. During the winter it's hot but bearable. The average temperature is 80°F (27°C); nights are always cooler. The rainy season (high water) runs from December to June; the dry season (low water) is from July to November. "High water" means better access to some areas and superior wildlife spotting, but it also means that some river beaches will be flooded. Fishing is prime during low water, when the fish move from the forest back into areas more accessible by boat. Keep in mind that even the driest month has an average rainfall of 2 inches (compared with up to 13 inches during the wet season), so some kind of rain gear is always recommended.

BELÉM

The capital of Pará State, Belém is a river port of more than 1.5 million people on the south bank of the Rio Guamá—120 km (74 mi) from the Atlantic, and 2,933 km (1,760 mi) and 3,250 km (1,950 mi) north of Rio de Janeiro and São Paulo, respectively. The Portuguese settled here in 1616, using it as a gateway to the interior and an outpost to protect the area from invasion by sea. Because of its ocean access, Belém became a major trade center. Like the upriver city of Manaus, it rode the ups and downs of the Amazon booms and busts. The first taste of prosperity was during the rubber era. Architects from Europe were brought in to build churches, civic palaces, theaters, and mansions—often using fine, imported materials. When Malaysia's rubber supplanted that of Brazil in the 1920s, wood and, later, minerals provided the impetus for growth.

In the past 20 years, Belém has expanded rapidly, pushed by the Tucuruvi hydroelectric dam—Brazil's second-largest—and the development of the Carajás iron-ore mining region. High-rises are replacing the colonial structures. Recently, however, local governments have launched massive campaigns to preserve the city's rich heritage, at the same time promoting tourist-friendly policies.

Exploring Belém

Belém is more than just a jumping-off point for the Amazon. It has several good museums and restaurants and lots of extraordinary architecture. Several distinctive buildings—some with Portuguese *azulejos* (tiles) and ornate iron gates—survive along the downtown streets and around the Praça Frei Caetano Brandão, in the Cidade Velha (Old City). East of here, in the Nazaré neighborhood, colorful colonial structures mingle with new ones housing trendy shops.

Numbers in the text correspond to numbers in the margin and on the Belém map.

Cidade Velha

A GOOD WALK

Begin at the **Igreja Nossa Senhora das Mercês** ①, a large, pink church just northeast of the **Estação das Docas** ② and the **Ver-o-Peso** ③ market. Walking southwest through the market, you'll pass the small dock where fishermen unload the day's catch. Turn left on Avenida Portugal (past the municipal clock), which borders Praça Dom Pedro II. Follow it to the large, baby-blue Palácio Antônio Lemos, which houses the **Museu de Arte de Belém (MABE)** ④. Next door is the even larger white Palácio Lauro Sodré, in which you'll find the **Museu do Estado do Pará** ⑤. Just behind this museum looms the golden church, **Igreja de São João Batista** ⑥. From here, head back toward Praça Dom Pedro II along Rua Tomásia Perdigão, and turn left onto Travessa Félix Roque. This takes you to the rear of the **Catedral da Sé** ⑦ (the entrance faces Praça Frei Caetano Brandão). To your right as you exit is the **Museu de Arte Sacra** ⑧, and just beyond is the **Forte do Castelo** ⑨.

TIMING

This tour will take two to three hours—longer if you linger in museums. It's best to start at 8 or 9 and finish by lunchtime. Next to the Forte do Castelo is Círculo Militar restaurant, the perfect place to enjoy a meal and a view of Baía de Guajará (Guajará Bay). Or you can head back to Estação das Docas for a wider variety of food choices.

SIGHTS TO SEE

❼ **Catedral da Sé.** In 1771 Bolognese architect Antônio José Landi, whose work can be seen throughout the city, completed the cathedral's construction on the foundations of an older church. Carrara marble adorns the rich interior, which is an interesting mix of baroque, colonial, and neoclassical styles. The high altar was a gift from Pope Pius IX. ⊠ *Praça Frei Caetano Brandão.* 🍽 *Free.* 🕐 *Tues.–Fri. 8–noon and 2–5, Sat. 6 PM–8 PM, Sun. 4–9.*

❷ **Estação das Docas.** Next to Ver-o-Peso market on the river, three former warehouses have been artfully converted into a commercial/tourist area. All have one wall of floor-to-ceiling glass that provides a full river view when dining or shopping. The first warehouse is a convention center, the second is full of shops and kiosks selling crafts and snacks, and the third has a microbrewery and 14 upscale restaurants. The buildings are air-conditioned and connected by glass-covered walkways. Inside, you can view photos and artifacts from the port's heyday. A stroll outside along the docks provides a grand view of the bay. Tourist boats arrive and depart at the dock—a good place to relax both day and night. ⊠ *Boulevard Castilhos França s/n,* ☎ *091/212–5525.* 🍽 *Free.* 🕐 *10 AM–3 AM.*

❾ **Forte do Castelo.** Belém's birthplace was originally called Forte do Presépio (Fort of the Crèche). From here the Portuguese launched conquests of the Amazon. The fort's role in the region's defense is evidenced by the English- and Portuguese-made cannons. Renovations to this landmark will be completed in early 2002. ⊠ *Praça Frei Caetano Brandão,* ☎ *no phone.* 🍽 *Free.* 🕐 *Daily 8 AM–9 PM.*

❶ **Igreja Nossa Senhora das Mercês.** Our Lady of Mercy Church is another baroque creation attributed to Antônio Landi. Notable for its pink color and its convex facade, it's part of a complex that includes the Convento dos Mercedários, which has served both as a convent and, less mercifully, as a prison. ⊠ *Largo as Mercês.* 🍽 *Free.* 🕐 *Mon.–Sat. 8–1.*

❻ **Igreja de São João Batista.** Prodigious architect Antônio Landi finished the small, octagonal St. John the Baptist Church in 1777. It was completely restored in 1997 and is considered the city's purest example of baroque architecture. ⊠ *Rua Dr. Tomásia Perdigão at Largo de São João.* 🍽 *Free.*

❹ **Museu de Arte de Belém (MABE).** Temporary expositions on the bottom level of the Metropolitan Art Museum are free to view. Don't be surprised if a staff member hands you large, brown, furry objects

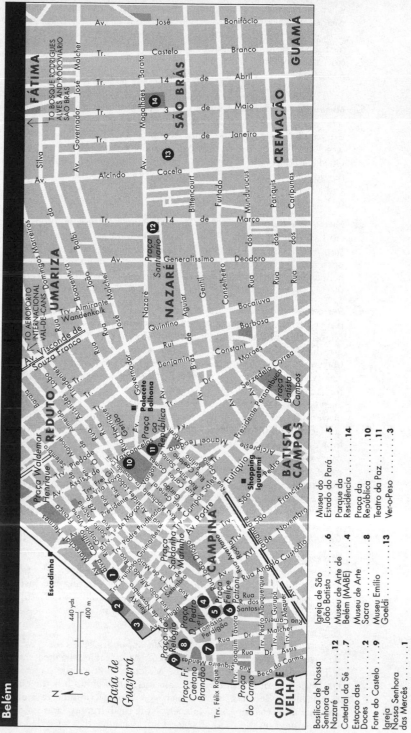

Belém

Basílica de Nossa
Senhora de
Nazaré 12
Catedral da Sé 7
Estacao das
Doces 2
Forte do Castelo ...9
Igreja
Nossa Senhora
das Mercés 1

Igreja de São
João Batista 6
Museu de Arte de
Belém (MABE) 4
Museu de Arte
Sacra 8
Museu Emílio
Goeldi 13

Museu do
Estado do Pará 5
Parque da
Residência 14
Praça da
República 10
Teatro da Paz 11
Ver-o-Peso 3

when you arrive on the second level—these are slippers that you must wear over your shoes to protect the wooden floors. The permanent collection of furniture and paintings dates from the 18th century through the rubber boom. The museum is housed in the recently renovated Palácio Antônio Lemos (circa 1883), a municipal palace built in the imperial Brazilian style with French influences. ⌂ *Praça Dom Pedro II s/n,* ☎ *091/241–1398.* ▭ *R$1.* ☉ *Tues.–Fri. 10–6, weekends 9–1.*

⑧ Museu de Arte Sacra. A guided tour (call 48 hours in advance to reserve an English-speaking docent) begins in the early 18th-century Amazon baroque Igreja de Santo Alexandre (St. Alexander's Church), which is distinguished by intricate woodwork on its alter and pews. On the second half of the tour, you'll see the museum's collection of religious sculptures and paintings. Temporary exhibitions, a gift shop, and a café are on the first floor. ⌂ *Praça Frei Caetano Brandão,* ☎ *091/225–1125.* ▭ *R$4, Tues. free.* ☉ *Tues.–Sun. 10–6.*

⑤ Museu do Estado do Pará. Pará State Museum is in the sumptuous Palácio Lauro Sodré (circa 1771), an Antônio Landi creation with Venetian and Portuguese elements. The first floor hosts consistently outstanding visiting exhibitions; the second floor contains the permanent collection of furniture and paintings. ⌂ *Praça Dom Pedro II,* ☎ *091/225–3853.* ▭ *R$2.* ☉ *Tues.–Sat. 10–6, Sun. and holidays 10–2.*

★ ③ Ver-o-Peso. Literally meaning "See the Weight" (a throwback to the time when the Portuguese weighed everything entering or leaving the region), this market is a hypnotic confusion of colors and voices. Vendors hawk tropical fruits and regional wares, as well as an assortment of tourist kitsch. Most interesting are the *mandingueiras,* women who claim they can solve any problem with "miracle" jungle roots and charms for the body and soul. They sell jars filled with animal eyes, tails, and even heads, as well as a variety of herbs—each with its own legendary power. The sex organs of the river dolphin are a supposedly unrivaled cure for romantic problems. In the fish market, you'll get an up-close look at pirarucu, the Amazon's most colorful species; the *mero,* which can weigh more than 91 kilos (200 pounds); and the silver-scale *piratema.* Across the street is a small arched entrance to the municipal meat market. Duck in and glance at the pink-and-green-painted ironwork, imported from Britain and done in a French style. Be sure to visit Ver-o-Peso before noon, which is when most vendors leave (they stay as long as they're selling), and be careful of pickpockets. ⌂ *Av. Castilhos França s/n, Comércio.*

Nazaré

Just east of the Cidade Velha, Nazaré's mango tree–lined streets create the sensation of walking through tunnels. Among the historic buildings there's a tremendous variety of pastel colors and European styles. Many of the newer buildings house elegant shops.

A GOOD TOUR

Begin at the south end of the **Praça da República** ⑩. Across Avenida da Paz is the large, pink **Teatro da Paz** ⑪. After leaving the theater, veer left onto Avenida Governador José Malcher; look for the sign for Lá em Casa, one of Belém's best restaurants. Just behind it is the elaborate Palacete Bolonha, from which you should continue east along Avenida Governador José Malcher. (Note the burgundy-and-gold designs painted on the road at several intersections; they're styled after those on marajoara pottery.) Turn right onto Travessa Benjamin Constant and then left onto Avenida Nazaré. Just beyond Avenida Generalíssimo Deodoro is the **Basílica de Nossa Senhora de Nazaré** ⑫. Avenida Nazaré becomes Avenida Magalhães Barata at this point.

TALES FROM THE MIST

THE IMMENSE AMAZON REGION is fertile ground not only for flora and fauna, but also for legends. They're an integral part of local culture and are remarkably consistent throughout the region. Many are based on strange creatures that inhabit the rivers and jungle. One of the most widespread legends is that of the *cobra grande* (giant snake), which strikes fear into the hearts of many a river dweller. Popularized by the movie *Anaconda* (filmed near Manaus), the story involves *sucuri* (anaconda) snakes of epic proportions that terrorize jungle creatures. They're said to cause shipwrecks and to eat fleeing passengers whole.

Another extremely popular (and considerably less gruesome) legend is that of *botos* (dolphins) that take human form. Always dressed immaculately in white, they appear at parties and dance with the youngest, most beautiful girls. They lure the girls outside, where they seduce them, and then return to the water just before dawn. You can always tell a boto from its slightly fishy smell and the hole in the top of its head, which is covered by a hat.

Curupira appears as a nude and savage indigenous child, about six or seven years old, whose feet are turned backward. He is said to lure people into the jungle—causing them to become irreversibly lost. As the story goes, white men cut off his feet before killing him; a god sewed Curupira's feet on backward and returned him to the forest to exact revenge. Some people claim that you can solicit Curupira's help for hunting and crop failures. As payment, you must bring him tobacco, matches, and a bottle of liquor—the latter of which he will down in one swig to seal the pact. If you ever

tell anyone about the agreement, Curupira will hunt you down and stab you to death with his long, sharp fingernails.

Several tales explain the origins of important fruits and vegetables. Guaraná, for example, was the name of a young child beloved by all. As the story goes, he was killed by the jealous god Jurupari, who disguised himself as a snake. Lightning struck as the village gathered around Guaraná's body and wept. At that moment the lightning god, Tupã, ordered the villagers to bury the child's eyes. The *guaraná* fruit (which actually resembles eyes) sprouted from the burial spot.

In the legend of Açaí, the chief of a starving tribe ordered all babies to be sacrificed to end the famine. The chief's daughter, Iaça, had a beautiful baby. Before its sacrifice, she found the child holding a palm tree, and then he suddenly vanished. The tree then became full of *açaí* (which is Iaça spelled backward) fruit, from which a wine was made that saved the tribe and ended the sacrifices.

The legend of the native water flower *vitória régia* begins with a beautiful girl who wished to become a star in the heavens. She trekked to the highest point in the land and tried in vain to touch the moon. Iaci—the god of the moon—was awed and enchanted by the girl's beauty. He knew that a mortal could never join the astral kingdom, so he decided to use his powers to immortalize the girl on earth instead. He transformed her into a stunning flower with an unmistakable, alluring scent. Realizing that he needed something fitting to help display this "star," he stretched a palm leaf and created a lily pad, and thus the vitória régia came to be.

Continue east three more blocks to the **Museu Emilio Goeldi** ⑬. After touring the museum, consider going east another three blocks to the **Parque da Residência** ⑭ for a relaxing break and lunch, or take a short (R$11) taxi ride northeast to the **Bosque Rodrigues Alves**—a chunk of jungle right in the middle of town.

TIMING

It should take about 1½ hours to reach the Museu Emilio Goeldi. Plan to spend an hour or two here owing to the quantity (and quality) of the displays. If you need a break, the museum has a restaurant and a snack bar. Count on at least an hour at Bosque Rodrigues Alves.

SIGHTS TO SEE

★ ⑫ **Basílica de Nossa Senhora de Nazaré.** It's hard to miss this opulent Roman-style basilica. Not only does it stand out visually, but there's an enormous tree filled with screeching parakeets in the plaza out front. Built in 1908 on the site where a *caboclo* (rural inhabitant) named Placido is said to have seen a vision of the Virgin in the early 1700s. The basilica's ornate interior is constructed entirely of European marble and contains elaborate mosaics, detailed stained-glass windows, and intricate bronze doors. In the small, basement-level Museu do Círio, displays explain the Círio de Nazaré festival, which is held each October to honor the city's patron saint. ⊠ *Praça Justo Chermont s/n,* ☏ *Museum: 091/ 224–9614.* ⌨ *Free.* ⊙ *Basilica Mon. 6–11 and 3–5, Tues.–Sat. 6–11 and 3–7, Sun. 3–7; museum Tues.–Fri. 9–6.*

OFF THE BEATEN PATH | **BOSQUE RODRIGUES ALVES –** In 1883 this 40-acre plot of rain forest was designated an ecological reserve. Nowadays you'll find an aquarium and two amusement parks as well as natural caverns, a variety of animals (some in the wild), and mammoth trees. ⊠ *Av. Almirante Barroso,* ☏ *091/226–2308.* ⌨ *R$1.* ⊙ *Tues.–Sun. 8–5.*

★ ⑬ **Museu Emílio Goeldi.** Founded by a naturalist and a group of intellectuals in 1866, this complex contains one of the Amazon's most important research facilities. Its museum has an extensive collection of Indian artifacts, including the distinctive and beautiful pottery of the Marajó Indians, known as marajoara. An adjacent tract of rain forest has reflecting pools with giant *vitória régia* water lilies. But the true highlight is the collection of Amazon wildlife, including manatees, rare blue alligators, sloths, and various species of monkeys. ⊠ *Av. Magalhães Barata 376,* ☏ *091/249–1233.* ⌨ *Park R$1, park and museum R$4.* ⊙ *Tues.–Thurs. 9–11:30 and 2–5, Fri. 9–11:30, weekends and holidays 9–5.*

⑭ **Parque da Residência.** Formerly the official residence of the governor of Pará, this park was recently opened to the public. It includes a 400-seat theater that hosts a variety of cultural events, a conservatory where orchids are grown, an ice-cream parlor, a restaurant, and a variety of shaded spots to relax and soak in the atmosphere. ⊠ *Av. Magalhães Barata 830, São Brás,* ☏ *091/219–1220.* ⊙ *Tues.–Sun. 9 AM– 10:30 PM.*

⑩ **Praça da República.** Here you'll find a large statue that commemorates the proclamation of the Republic of Brazil, an amphitheater, and several French-style iron kiosks. On Sunday, vendors, food booths, and musical groups create a festival-like atmosphere that attracts crowds of locals.

⑪ **Teatro da Paz.** A complete renovation of this neoclassical theater (1878) was finished in fall 2001. New concert pianos were acquired to facilitate production of operas like the ones presented during the Verdi festival that marked the grand reopening. Greek-style pillars line the front and sides; inside, note the imported details such as the Italian marble pillars and the French chandeliers. Classical music performances are also held in the theater, which seats more than 800 people. English-speaking guides are available to give 20-minute tours. ⊠ *Av. da Paz s/n, Praça da República,* ☎ *091/224–7355.* 🖃 *Call for prices.* ⊙ *Weekdays 9–noon and 2–5.*

Beaches

The closest ocean beach is a four-hour drive from Belém; river beaches are much closer. Depending on the season and time of day, they're either expansive stretches or narrow strips of soft, white sand. Currents are rarely strong, and there's usually a large area of shallow water. Although the beach at **Outerio** is an easy half-hour bus ride from town, it's not very scenic; it's generally crowded and a little dirty.

Most people head for one of 18 beaches on **Ilha Mosqueiro,** along the Rio Pará. Connected to the mainland by a large bridge, it's an hour from the city. Farol is crowded because it is close to the island's hub, Vila, but the beach is still pretty. At low tide, you can walk to tiny, rocky Ilha do Amor (Love Island). In October and March the waves are high enough for river-surfing competitions. Morubira Beach, also close to Vila, has beautiful colonial houses and many restaurants and bars. The water is clear and the shore clean at Marahú Beach, but no bus from Belém travels here directly. You have to disembark in Vila and hop another bus. Paraíso Beach is lined with trees and has soft white sands and clear emerald waters. If you can't bear to leave at day's end, consider a stay at the Hotel Fazenda Paraíso.

Dining

$–$$$ ✕ **Gringo Louco.** In a colonial-era house in Nazaré, Gringo Louco serves an eclectic array of Continental and regional specialties. Favorites are seafood dishes and buffalo steaks topped with mushrooms and cheese sauce. The bar is popular with locals and visitors alike, and the place has a reputation for serving food and drink until the last customer decides it's time to go. ⊠ *Trv. Benjamin Constant 1415, Nazaré,* ☎ *091/ 212–3344. AE, V.*

$–$$ ✕ **Miako.** Belém has a large Japanese community (second only to that of São Paulo), so there's no lack of Japanese restaurants. This one, however, is a tried-and-true favorite for excellent service, attractive wooden decor, and consistently good food. The sushi is terrific. ⊠ *Rua 1 de Março 76, Centro,* ☎ *091/242–2355. AE, DC, MC, V.*

$ ✕ **Rodeio.** Devoted carnivores take note: there's nothing like a meal in a *churrascaria* (a restaurant specializing in grilled meat) after a few days on a riverboat with little to eat but fish and rice. A reasonable fixed-price menu not only includes as many servings of grilled and roasted meats as you can eat but also salads and dessert. ⊠ *Trv. Padre Eutíqiu 1308, Batista Campos,* ☎ *091/212–2112. AE, DC, MC, V. No dinner Sun. and Mon.*

¢–$$$ ✕ **Casa Portuguesa.** Although it's in the heart of the commercial district, this restaurant does its best to replicate the charm of a Portuguese country home. Specialties include dishes with chicken and, of course, cod. ⊠ *Rua Senador Manoel Barata 897, Centro,* ☎ *091/242– 4871. AE, DC, MC, V.*

¢–$$$ ✕ **Lá em Casa.** Thirty years ago, the owners of this restaurant started
★ serving meals from their home. From inauspicious beginnings has emerged one of Belém's most popular restaurants. Regional cuisine, prepared to exacting specifications, helps them keep their reputation. Consider trying Belém's premier dish, *pato no tucupi,* duck in a yellow herb sauce

made from manioc root and served with the mildly intoxicating *jambu* leaf. *Casquinho de caranquejo* (crabs on the half shell, covered with farofa sautéed in butter) is another good choice, as is açaí fruit sorbet for dessert. Sitting on the covered patio fringed by various flora, you feel like you're dining in the middle of the forest. More formal, indoor seating can be enjoyed at **O Outro** on the same property. ✉ *Av. Governador José Malcher 247, Nazaré,* ☎ *091/223–1212. AE, DC, MC, V.*

¢–$$ ✕ **Círculo Militar.** The specialty here at the entrance of the Forte do Castelo is fresh fish. Try *filhote ao leite de coco* (river fish sautéed in a coconut milk). Come for lunch so that you can enjoy the river view. Live MPB music is featured in the evening Thurs.–Sun. ✉ *Praça Frei Caetano Brandão s/n, Cidade Velha,* ☎ *091/230–2548. AE, DC, MC, V.*

¢–$$ ✕ **Dom Giuseppe.** From gnocchi to ravioli, flawless preparation of the basics distinguishes this Italian eatery from others. Everyone in town knows this, so reservations are a good idea—particularly on weekends. Don't leave without ordering a scrumptious *dolce Paula* (ice cream and brownie dessert). ✉ *Av. Conselheiro Furtado 1420, Batista Campos,* ☎ *091/241–1146. AE, DC, MC, V.*

Lodging

$$$–$$$$ 🏨 **Hilton International Belém.** The Hilton's reliability and amenities are topped only by its location right on the Praça da República. Although not very distinguished, rooms are well equipped and comfortable. Executive rooms have the nicest views as well as access to a lounge with a VCR, a meeting area, and complimentary food and drink. ✉ *Av. Presidente Vargas 882, Centro 66017-000,* ☎ *091/242–6500; 800/445–8667 in U.S.,* 📠 *091/225–2942. 361 rooms. Restaurant, 2 bars, pool, beauty salon, sauna, health club, convention center. AE, DC, MC, V.*

$ 🏨 **Equatorial Palace.** Widely considered to be one of the nicest hotels in town, the Equatorial Palace was recently renovated and now lives up to its reputation. New decor in the common areas and new furnishings throughout have brought this hotel back to its former glory. The Nazaré location—within walking distance of the port and Cidade Velha—is ideal. ✉ *Av. Braz de Aguiar 612, Nazaré 66035-000,* ☎ *091/ 241–2000,* 📠 *091/223–5222. 204 rooms, 7 suites. 2 restaurante, bar, pool. AE, DC, MC, V.*

$ 🏨 **Hotel Regente.** This hotel offers excellent service and a prime location for a reasonable price. Stained-glass windows and soft leather couches welcome you in an attractive lobby. Rooms on the 12th floor are nicer and more modern than those on other floors, yet cost the same. ✉ *Av. Governador José Malcher 485, Nazaré 66035-100,* ☎ *091/241–1222,* 📠 *091/242–0343. 196 rooms, 6 suites. Restaurant, bar, pool. AE, DC, MC, V.*

$ 🏨 **Hotel Sagres.** One drawback to this fine hotel is that it is a bit far from the center of town, but the staff is professional and the facilities immaculate. Rooms on the upper floors command a great view of the city. ✉ *Av. Governador José Malcher, São Bráz, 66090-100,* ☎ *091/ 266–2222. 244 rooms, 1 suite. Restaurant, bar, swimming pool, sauna, workout room. AE, DC, MC, V.*

$ 🏨 **Itaoca Hotel.** It comes as no surprise that this small, reasonably priced hotel has the highest occupancy rate in town. Its rooms are extremely comfortable, well equipped, and modern, and most have a fantastic view of the dock area and river. ✉ *Av. Presidente Vargas 132, Centro 66010-902,* ☎ 📠 *091/241–3434. 32 rooms, 4 suites. Restaurant, in-room safes, meeting room. AE, DC, MC, V.*

¢ 🏨 **Hotel Fazenda Paraíso.** A few feet from one of the most beautiful beaches on Ilha Mosqueiro, this hotel is the ideal place to spend a day or two just outside the city. Wood-and-brick chalets with red-tile roofs accommodate as many as five people. Similarly designed apartments, which house up to three people, are more economical for singles and couples. The pool is configured in the shape of a clover. Be sure to make reservations—the hotel is very popular on weekends. ⊠ *Beira-Mar, Praia do Paraíso, Ilha Mosqueiro 66915-000,* ☎ *091/228–3950. 12 rooms, 10 chalets. Restaurant, pool, horseback riding, beach, boating. AE, DC, MC, V.*

¢ 🏨 **Manacá Hotel.** This small, bright-red hotel with a slanted brown-
★ tile roof looks like a cross between a Monopoly hotel piece and a pagoda. Cozy, artfully decorated common areas with soft lighting have more charm than those at larger places—for about a quarter of the price. It's a clean, simple alternative if you can live without a pool or a bar. Make sure to call ahead—its often booked during the week. ⊠ *Trv. Quintino Bocaiuva 1645, Nazaré 66033-620,* ☎ *091/223–3335. 16 rooms. AE, DC, MC, V.*

¢ 🏨 **Zoghbi Apart Hotel.** The only apartment hotel in town has suites with fully equipped kitchens that are great for families or for those who plan on staying a while. Already reasonable rates are reduced nearly 50% for stays exceeding 15 days. ⊠ *Rua Ferreira Cantão 100, Centro 66017-110,* ☎ *091/241–1800. 55 apartments. Kitchenettes. V.*

Nightlife and the Arts

Nightlife

Doca Boulevard, about eight blocks east of Escadinha (the dock area used for boat trips), has many bars and dance clubs. The main strip is Avenida Visconde de Souza Franco, but there are several places a few blocks off it as well.

A variety of live music is played nightly at the Estação das Docas. Weekdays it consists mostly of acoustic singer/guitarists. Weekends, full rock, jazz, and MPB bands play on one of two suspended stages that move back and forth on tracks about 8 m (25 ft) above patrons of the microbrewery and surrounding restaurants in the auditoriumlike space.

BARS

Baixo Reduto (⊠ Rua Quintino Bocaiúva s/n, Reduto, ☎ 091/242–6282) has live music in a variety of styles from Wednesday blues to Saturday jazz. It's not open Sunday. **Colarinho Branco** (⊠ Av. Visconde de Souza Franco 80, Reduto, ☎ 091/242–1007) serves ice-cold draft beers with live MPB as a chaser nightly. If you prefer your music in a relaxed environment, head to **Cosanostra Caffé** (⊠ Rua Benjamin Constant 1499, Nazaré, ☎ 091/241–1068), which offers live MPB and jazz. Catering to locals and expatriate foreigners alike, it serves food from an extensive menu until late in the night. **Roxy Bar** (⊠ Av. Senador Lemos 231, Umarizal, ☎ 091/224–4514) tops nearly everyone's list of hip spots to sip a drink and people-watch.

DANCE CLUBS

Bora Bora (⊠ Rua Bernal do Couto 38, Umarizal, ☎ 091/241–5848) attracts a dance crowd for country music on Thursday and fast-paced *pagode* dancing on Friday and Saturday. **Zeppelin Club** (⊠ Av. Senador Lemos 108, Reduto, ☎ 091/223–8936) is the undisputed king of *boates* (dance clubs), with prices to match. The cover charge on Friday and Saturday (the only nights the club is open) is R$15.

The Arts

For information about cultural events, contact the state-run **Secretaria de Cultura** (SECULT; ⊠ Av. Governador Magalhães Barata 830, São Brás, ☎ 091/219–1207), which prints a monthly listing of cultural events throughout the city. Outstanding theatrical productions (in Portuguese) are held at the **Teatro Experimental Waldemar Henrique** (⊠ Av. Pres-

idente Vargas s/n, Praça da República, Campina, ☎ 091/222–4762).
Teatro da Paz often hosts plays, Philharmonic concerts, and dance recitals.

Outdoor Activities and Sports

Participant Sports

FISHING

Pará state is renowned for the quality and variety of its fish. For information about fishing trips, contact the **Secretaria de Estado de Ciência, Tecnologia e Meio Ambiente** (SECTAM; ⊠ Trv. Lomas Valentinas 2717, Marco, ☎ 091/266–5000).

JUNGLE AND RIVER EXCURSIONS

On one- to several-day trips from Belém, you can explore the Guamá, Acará, and Mojú rivers. You can also catch a boat from the Escadinha at 4:30 AM, travel approximately 11 km (7 mi) northwest, and be at **Ilha dos Papagaios** (Parrot Island) by sunrise, when thousands of green *papagaios* (parrots) leave in an unforgettable flight. Larger tour operators can make all the necessary arrangements.

Spectator Sports

Belém's two *futebol* (soccer) teams are Payssandú and Remo—neither of which is currently in the premier league. Still, attending a Brazilian match, regardless of the quality of the team, is a memorable experience. For Remo games, head to **Estádio Evandro Almeida** (⊠ Av. Almirante Barroso s/n, Marco, ☎ 091/223–2847). Payssandú plays at **Estádio Leônidas de Castro** (⊠ Av. Almirante Barroso s/n, Marco, ☎ 091/241–1726).

Shopping

Areas and Malls

Belém's main shopping street is **Avenida Presidente Vargas,** particularly along the Praça da República. There are many boutiques and specialty shops in **Nazaré.** To shop in air-conditioning, head for the upscale **Shopping Center Iguatemi** (⊠ Trv. Padre Eutíquio 1078, Batista Campos), a mall in the truest sense of the word.

In **Icoaraci,** a riverside town 18 km (11 mi) northeast of Belém, shops make and sell marajoara pottery.

Specialty Shops

Artesanato Paruara (⊠ Rua Sezedelo Correo 15, Nazaré, ☎ 091/248–4555) specializes in oils, stones, and other "mystical" items. At **Artindia** (⊠ Av. Presidente Vargas 762, Loja 6, Campina, ☎ 091/223–6248) you'll find a good selection of jewelry, painted wooden shields, bows and arrows, and other crafts—all handmade by Indians. (Note: Be careful about items that have feathers; some are prohibited by U.S. Customs.) Marajoara pottery and traditional crafts are sold at **Cacique** (⊠ Av. Presidente Vargas 692, Campina, ☎ 091/242–1144). **Vitória Régia** (⊠ Av. Presidente Vargas 552, Campina, ☎ 091/241–1113) is a good place to buy jewelry and knickknacks.

BETWEEN BELÉM AND MANAUS

The smaller communities between the Amazon's two major cities give the best picture of pure Amazonian culture. Life tends to be even more intertwined with the river, and the center of activity is the dock area in village after village. Even a brief stop in one of these towns provides an interesting window into the region's day-to-day life.

Ilha do Marajó

Soure is 82 km (49 mi) northwest of Belém.

With an area of roughly 49,600 square km (18,900 square mi), Ilha do Marajó is reputedly the world's largest river island. Its unspoiled environment and abundant wildlife make it one of the few accessible places in the Amazon that seems truly isolated. The island was once inhabited by the Aruã tribes; only after attempts by both the British and the Dutch did the Portuguese, through trickery, finally conquer them.

Ilha do Marajó's western half is dominated by dense rain forest, its eastern half by expansive plains and savannah—ideal spots for raising cattle and the famous water buffalo. According to local lore, the arrival of the buffalo was an accident, the result of the wreck of a ship traveling from India to the Guianas. Today, the island has a half million of these creatures as well as more than a million head of cattle; the human head count is only 250,000. A day trip to a local ranch or a stay at Fazenda Carmo, the only ranch that currently hosts overnight guests, will give you a close-up look at the unique lifestyle of the island's people as well as the chance to view some of its animals—both domesticated and wild. You may see alligators, monkeys, and the *capybara* (the world's largest and most adorable rodent).

Camará is the island's most important port and is where most boats from Belém dock. With almost 20,000 people, picturesque **Soure,** on the northeast coast, is Ilha do Marajó's largest town. Its many palm and mango trees, simple but brightly painted houses, and shore full of fishing boats make it seem more Caribbean than Amazon. **Salvaterra,** a short boat ride south across the narrow Rio Paracauari, is smaller than Soure but equally charming. Near these two towns, you'll find enchanting river beaches—all a short (and cheap) taxi ride away.

Praia do Pesqueiro, 14 km (8 mi) north of Soure, is understandably the island's most popular beach. When you stand on the white-sand expanse, looking out at a seemingly endless watery horizon and feeling the waves lap your feet, it's hard to believe that you're not on the ocean. There are several thatch-roof restaurant-bars, making this an even more ideal place to spend an afternoon. You can travel here from Soure by taxi, moto-taxi (which holds only one passenger), or even bike.

The beach at **Caju Una,** a secluded fishing village, is breathtaking: a long strip of white sand with no vendors and few people. The village and its neighbor, Vila do Céu, are about a 45-minute drive (19 km/11 mi north) from Soure. Buses don't travel here, but for about R$33 you can hire a taxi for an afternoon; a moto-taxi costs about half that. A 20-minute, 4-km (2-mi) taxi ride northeast of Soure is **Praia do Araruna.** Rather than sandy stretches, it has a red-mangrove forest. In this eerie setting of twisted trees jutting from the misty swamp, you almost expect Yoda to appear. More likely, it will be a flock of scarlet ibis. **Joanes,** 23 km (14 mi) southwest of Soure, was the island's first settlement. Poke around the ruins of a 16th-century Jesuit mission, bask in the sun on a pretty beach, and have a meal in one of the good seafood restaurants. A taxi from Soure will cost about R$44.

Dining and Lodging

Local cuisine invariably involves the water buffalo, whether in the form of a succulent steak or in cheeses and desserts made with buffalo milk. There's also an array of local fish to try. Bring cash in small bills, as breaking large ones can be a challenge and credit cards are rarely accepted. (In a pinch, beer vendors can usually make change.)

¢ ✕🖭 **Hotel Ilha do Marajó.** This hotel offers solid creature comforts and excellent facilities, including a lovely pool. Rooms are clean, but during the rainy season mosquitoes tend to infiltrate. At the attractive outdoor restaurant, partake of decent, reasonably priced food and enjoy the river view. Every Saturday evening the hotel hosts a performance of *carimbo,* local music that combines African and Indian rhythms. Package deals, which you can arrange at any travel agency in Belém, are highly recommended. They include van transport to and from the dock in Camará and day trips to nearby fazendas and beaches. English-speaking guides are available for the excursions. ✉ *Trv. 2, No. 10, Soure 68870-000,* ☎ *091/741–1315. 32 rooms. Restaurant, bar, minibars, pool, tennis court, recreation room. No credit cards.*

¢ ✕🖭 **Pousada Bosque dos Aruãs.** This pousada offers very simple wooden bungalows with river views. The bungalows aren't long on comfort or ambience, but if your budget is tight, this isn't a bad bet. The small restaurant serves the usual fare of buffalo, fish, and *maniçoba* (a stew containing beef and pork). ✉ *Rua 2, at Av. Beira Mar, Salvaterra 68860-000,* ☎ *091/765–1115; 091/223–0628 in Belém. 10 bungalows. Restaurant, bar, bicycles. No credit cards.*

¢ ✕🖭 **Pousada dos Guarás.** With private bungalows and its own beach, this Salvaterra pousada has a serene, intimate atmosphere. Because of the isolated location, though, you're limited to meals at the on-site restaurant. Still, the pousada is a good deal, particularly if you opt for the package that includes transportation to and from the docks and trips to Soure shops, local fazendas, and beaches; it's best to make arrangements with a travel agent in Belém. ✉ *Av. Beira-Mar (Praia Grande), Salvaterra 66860-000,* ☎ 🖷 *091/242–0904. 20 rooms. Restaurant, bar, air-conditioning, minibars, pool, horseback riding, beach, game room. AE, DC, MC, V.*

$$$$ 🖭 **Fazenda Carmo.** Reading through the guest book, it seems as if a
★ spiritual awakening is the standard result of a stay here. As a guest in the small, antiques-filled farmhouse, you're privy to simple comforts, wonderful hospitality, outstanding home-style meals prepared with farm-fresh ingredients, and fascinating activities galore. You can take an early-morning canoe trip in search of howler monkeys; set off on horseback through wildlife-rich pastures; hop in a jeep for a muddy ride to an archaeological site; or take a dip in the small lake surrounded by hundreds of large, affectionate fish. The fazenda can accommodate 8–10 people, and stays are generally part of a package that includes meals, transportation to and from the fazenda (a half-hour van ride and an hour boat ride from Camará), and accompaniment by an English-speaking guide. A minimum stay of three days, two nights with meals costs R$420 per person. ✉ *Contact Amazon Star Tours: Rua Henrique Gurjão 236, Belém 66053-360,* ☎ *091/212–6244. AE, MC, V. FAP.*

Nightlife

The carimbo group that performs at the Hotel Ilha do Marajó on Saturday sometimes puts on a show in Soure on Wednesday or Friday. Ask a staffer at your hotel or a taxi driver for details. On Friday night, there's usually live music at **Badalué** (✉ Trv. 14, Soure). One of the most popular types of music in the region is *brega,* which means "tacky." The name for this accordion-influenced music is appropriate, but don't be surprised if the music grows on you.

Shopping

There are a few stores that sell sundries along Travessa 17 and Rua 3 in Soure. For marajoara pottery and ceramic figurines, try **Arte Caboclo** (✉ Trv. 5 between Rua 8 and Rua 9, Soure). You can even see how the ceramics are made in the workshop at the back of the store, which is open daily 8–6.

For sandals, belts, and other leather goods, head to **Curtume Marajó** (⌂ Rua 1, Bairro Novo, ☎ no phone), a five-minute walk from the center of Soure (and next to the slaughterhouse). The workers here will be happy to give you a tour that demonstrates the month-long process of turning cowhide into tanned leather. The shop's hours are 7–11 and 1–5 Monday through Saturday.

At **Núcleo Operário Social Marilda Nunes** (⌂ Rua 3 between Trv. 18 and Trv. 19, Soure), you'll find stalls with everything from marajoara pottery and woven items to T-shirts and liquor. In theory, the hours are daily 7–noon and 2:30–6; the reality may be something else entirely.

Macapá

330 km (198 mi) northwest of Belém.

Macapá is on the northern channel of the Amazon Delta and, like Belém, was built by the Portuguese as an outpost from which to explore and protect the region. Today it's the capital of and largest city (150,000 people) in Amapá State. It's also one of only five metropolises in the world that sit on the equator.

Macapá's main lure, however, is as a base for trips to see an extraordinary phenomenon—the *pororoca* (meeting of the waters). Each day from March to May, when the Amazon is in flood stage, the incoming ocean tide crashes against the outflowing waters of the Rio Araguari 200 km (120 mi) north of Macapá. The violent meeting of the waters produces waves as high as 4 m (15 ft); the final stage of this event sounds like thunder. It gradually builds in intensity until the waters sweep into the forest along the riverbanks. The trip to the site of the pororoca takes nearly two days by boat and costs about R$444 per person (which gets you a private cabin, meals, and an English-speaking guide).

Macapá's top man-made attraction is Brazil's largest fort, **Fortaleza de São José de Macapá.** Completed in 1782 after 18 grueling years, it's constructed of stones brought from Portugal as ship ballast. The well-preserved buildings house a visitor center, an art gallery, a meeting room, and a dance/music recital room. ⌂ *Av. Cândido Mendes s/n,* ☎ *096/212–5118.* ◻ *Free.* ☉ *Daily 4–7.*

The **Marco Zero do Equador** is a modest monument to the equatorial line that passes through town. Although it consists of only a tall, concrete sundial and a stripe of red paint along the equator, there's a distinct thrill to straddling the line or hopping between hemispheres. The soccer stadium across the street uses the equator as its centerline. ⌂ *Av. Equatorial 0288,* ☎ *096/241–1951.* ◻ *Free.* ☉ *Daily 7:30–6.*

Dining and Lodging

$–$$$ ✕ **Café Aymoré.** This is a local favorite for regional specialties such as maniçoba and *vatapá* (shrimp in coconut oil). For those with more exotic tastes, it's the only restaurant in town with government permission to serve *tartaruga* (turtle) and *jacaré* (alligator). ⌂ *Av. Iracema Carvão Nunes 92,* ☎ *096/223-2328. No credit cards.*

$–$$ ✕ **Cantinho Baiano.** Due to the conservative tastes of the locals, the Salvador-born owner is phasing in famed specialties from the state of Bahia. These dishes, especially the seafood or shrimp *moquecas* (fish stews), are a highlight. The excellent river view, soft music, and colorfully clad waiters add to the pleasure of the meal. ⌂ *Av. Acelino de Leão 01,* ☎ *096/223–4153. MC, V. No dinner Sun.*

$ ⌂ **Hotel Atalanta.** Painted a garish pink and supported by towering Roman columns, this hotel seems out of place in its surroundings. Inside, you'll find such charming details as stained-glass windows, small pink columns, and immaculate, comfortable guest rooms. The inconvenient location—10 blocks from the river in an otherwise nondescript residential neighborhood—is its only drawback. ⊠ *Av. Coaracy Nunes 1148, 68900-010,* ☎ FAX *096/223–1612. 33 rooms, 3 suites. Air-conditioning, minibars, sauna, exercise room. AE, DC, MC, V.*

$ ☎ **Novotel Macapá.** Partially obscured by palm trees, this three-story, white, colonial-style hotel—topped by a classic red-tile roof—is set on well-manicured grounds. The interior, however, is slightly worn, and the guest rooms aren't very impressive—despite modern amenities. Opt for one of the suites, which have balconies with exceptional river views. ⊠ *Av. Francisco Azarias Neto 17, 68900-080,* ☎ *096/217–1350,* FAX *096/223–1115. 74 rooms, 2 suites. Restaurant, bar, air-conditioning, in-room safes, minibars, pool, tennis court. AE, DC, MC, V.*

¢   ☎ **Frota Palace Hotel.** A clean, spacious alternative for those on a budget, the rooms have modern amenities—air-conditioning, minibars, and phone in the room—which aren't always easy to come by in this area. Conveniently located in Centro, it has a friendly and helpful staff. A discount of up to 20% is offered for cash customers. ⊠ *Rua Tiradentes 1104, 68906-420,* ☎ *096/223–3999. 33 rooms. Restaurant, bar. MC, V.*

Nightlife and the Arts

Macapá has a surprisingly active nightlife. If you like to bar-hop, head for the riverfront, where about 10 bars—some with music—are busy nearly every night. True night owls will appreciate the **Arena** nightclub (⊠ Rua Hamilton Silva s/n, ☎ no phone), which doesn't open until midnight. To get the most out of the $10 cover charge, come on Saturday, the most popular night.

Most weekends there's a play (in Portuguese), a Philharmonic concert, or a dance recital in the **Teatro das Bacabeiras** (⊠ Rua Cândido Mendes 368, ☎ 096/212–5121).

Shopping

Although Macapá has a free-trade zone, neither the prices nor the selection is anything to write home about. The largest concentration of shops is on Rua Cândido Mendes and Rua São José.

The **Núcleo Artesanal** (⊠ Av. Engenheiro Azarias Neto 2201, ☎ 096/ 212–8528), an outstanding arts center, has two distinct parts. The Casa do Artesáo sells works by local craftspeople and artists—everything from tacky souvenirs to exquisite paintings and pottery. It's open 9–9 Monday–Saturday and 8 AM–10 PM Sunday; Visa is accepted. The Associação dos Povos Indígenas do Tumucumaque (APITU) has an excellent selection of textiles, baskets, and other objects made by Indian tribes. Its hours are 8–noon and 2–6 every day but Sunday, when it's open 5–9. In addition, an artisan fair is held outside the center on Sunday from 8 AM to 10 PM.

Santarém

836 km (518 mi) west of Belém, 766 km (475 mi) east of Manaus.

Since its founding in 1661, Santarém has ridden the crest of many an economic wave. First wood, then rubber, and today mineral wealth have been the lures for thousands of would-be magnates hoping to carve their fortunes from the jungle. The most noteworthy of these may well have been Henry Ford. Although he never actually came to Brazil, Ford left his mark on it in two rubber plantations southwest of Santarém—Fordlândia and Belterra. Today, Santarém, a laid-back city of 242,000, is a traditional port of call.

The city is at the confluence of the aquamarine Rio Tapajós and the muddy brown Amazon. Seeing the meeting of these waters is second only to witnessing the pororoca outside Macapá. It's best viewed from the **Praça Mirante do Tapajós,** on the hill in the center of town and just a few blocks from the waterfront.

To learn more about Santarém's culture and history, head for the **Centro Cultural João Fona** (João Fona Cultural Center). This small museum has a hodgepodge of ancient ceramics, indigenous art, and colonial-period paintings, as well as a library for more in-depth studies. ⊠ *Praça Barão de Santarém,* ☎ *091/522–1383.* 🎟 *Free.* ⊙ *Weekdays 8–5.*

★ You can take several cruises from Santarém on specially outfitted boats. The trip down the Rio Tapajós to the village of **Alter do Chão,** on the Lago Verde (Green Lake), is one of the best. The area has been called "the Caribbean of the Amazon," and when you see its clear green waters and its white-sand beach it's easy to understand why. Buses also make the hour-long journey from Santarém to Alter do Chão regularly. From the village, it's a short canoe ride across a narrow channel to the beach. (Note that from April to July, when the water is high, the beach disappears.)

While you're in the village, be sure to visit the outstanding **Centro de Preservação das Culturas Indígenas** (Center for the Preservation of Indigenous Cultures). An American expat sculptor has assembled a collection of more than 1,700 remarkable pieces from 57 Amazon tribes. Videos and photo displays help to teach you more about the indigenous cultures and their plight, and an on-site cooperative store sells indigenous art. ⊠ *Rua Dom Macêdo Costa 500,* ☎ *091/527–1176.* 🎟 *R$5.* ⊙ *Tues.–Fri. 9–noon and 2–5, weekends 10–noon and 2–4.*

Dining and Lodging

$-$$ ✕ **Alter Nativo.** Despite its name, this Alter do Chão establishment doesn't offer alternative dishes. Rather, it prepares typical fish dishes as well as, if not better than, many of the town's fish restaurants in town. Try the tucunaré or pirarucu with the *molho de escabeche,* a savory tomato-and-onion sauce. ⊠ *Praça da Nossa Senhora da Saude s/n, Alter do Chão,* ☎ *091/527–1160.* V. ⊙ *Weekdays 9 AM–midnight, weekends 9 AM–3 AM.*

¢-$$ ✕ **Lumi.** The cuisine and decor of this open-air restaurant are an interesting mix of Japan and Pará State. The *pratos econômicos* (economical dishes)—cheap, tasty (and large) portions of fried fish or steak accompanied by rice and vegetables—come on a sizzling metal platter that helps to keep the food warm. ⊠ *Av. Cuiabá 1683,* ☎ *091/523–1207. No credit cards.* ⊙ *Closed Mon.*

¢-$$ ✕ **Mascote.** Since 1934, this has been one of the most popular and famous restaurants in town. Inside, you'll find an enchanting dining area, but the palm-lined patio is well lighted, inviting, and offers the best view of both the river and the plaza. An extremely varied menu includes pizzas, sandwiches, steaks, and seafood. Generally, the food is good, but the service is lackadaisical at times. ⊠ *Praça do Pescador s/n,* ☎ *091/523–2844. AE, DC, V.*

¢-$ ✕ **Santo Antônio.** You can fill up at this restaurant tucked away behind a gas station with *churrasco* (grilled meat) or with one of its regional specialties. The fish is always fresh, and a single portion is enough for two persons with normal appetites. The tucunaré, served on a searing-hot marble platter, is incredible. ⊠ *Av. Tapajós 2061,* ☎ *091/523–8505. MC, V.*

¢ ✕ **Mutunuy II.** This meat lover's paradise is a quick taxi ride from the center of town and is a great place for a bargain meal. Try the *churrasco misto,* a grilled beef-, chicken-, and sausage-filled skewer ac-

Close-Up

FORD'S IMPOSSIBLE DREAM

HENRY FORD SPENT MILLIONS of dollars to create two utopian company towns and plantations to supply his Model T's with rubber tires. In 1927 he chose an area 15 hours southwest of Santarém. A year later, all that was needed to build a small town and its infrastructure was transported from Michigan to the Amazon by boat. Small Midwestern-style houses were built in row after row. *Seringueiros* (rubber harvesters) were recruited with promises of good wages, health care, and schools for their children. Fordlândia was born. Despite all the planning, the scheme failed. The region's climate, horticulture, and customs weren't taken into account. Malaria and parasites troubled the workers; erosion and disease plagued the trees.

Convinced that he had learned valuable lessons from his mistakes, Ford refused to give up. In 1934 he established another community in Belterra, just 48 km (30 mi) outside Santarém. Although some rubber was extracted from the plantation, production fell far short of original estimates. World War II caused further disruptions as German boats cruised the Brazilian coast and prevented food and supplies from arriving. Advancements in synthetic rubber struck the final blow. Today, some rusted trucks and electric generators, a few industrial structures, and many empty bungalows are all that remain of Ford's impossible dreams.

companied by rice, farofa, potato salad, and a garden salad—all for about R$8. If you still have room for dessert, the *creme de cupuaçu* (a frozen pudding similar to ice cream) is highly recommended. ⊠ *Trv. Turiano Meira 1680,* ☎ *091/522–7909.* V.

$ ☷ **Amazon Park Hotel.** The only "luxury" hotel in town has a decent location (a short taxi ride from Centro), a gorgeous pool, and such in-room amenities as TVs and minibars. Still, with little in the way of competition, it doesn't seem to have much incentive to improve, as evidenced by the aging facilities and the scantily furnished rooms. ⊠ *Av. Mendonça Furtado 4120, 68040-050,* ☎ *091/523–2800,* ℻ *091/522–2631. 122 rooms. Restaurant, bar, air-conditioning, minibars, pool. AE, DC, MC, V.*

¢ ☷ **Pousada Tupaiulândia.** If you're planning an overnight visit to Alter do Chão, this pousada three blocks from the beach is one of the best places to stay. Large rooms are comfortable and air-conditioned. (As this hotel is popular but small, reserve as far in advance as possible.) ⊠ *Rua Pedro Teixeira s/n, Alter do Chão 68109-000,* ☎ *091/527–1157. 7 rooms. Restaurant, air-conditioning, minibars. V.*

¢ ☷ **Rio Dourado.** Reasonable rates get you simple but attractive ac-
★ commodations, a convenient location, and friendly service in this peach-color hotel. ⊠ *Rua Floriano Peixoto 799, 68005-080,* ☎ ℻ *091/523–2174. 27 rooms. Air-conditioning, airport shuttle. AE, DC, MC.*

¢ ☷ **Santarém Palace.** The front of the hotel is on a busy street with lots of bus traffic; better to request a room in the back—which is quieter and may just have a view of the meeting of the waters. Facilities are clean and well maintained. ⊠ *Av. Rui Barbosa 726, 68005-080,* ☎ *091/523–2820,* ℻ *091/522–1779. 44 rooms. Restaurant, air-conditioning, minibars, meeting room. No credit cards.*

Nightlife

On Friday, **La Boom** (⊠ Av. Cuiabá 694, Liberdade, ☎ 091/522–3632) is *the* place to dance. One of the best places in town to get a drink, and certainly the best for people-watching, **Mascotinho** (⊠ Praça Manuel de Jesus Moraes s/n, ☎ 091/523–2399) has passable food and is right on the river. Friday and Saturday nights are filled with MPB.

Sygnus (⊠ Av. Borges Leal 2712, Santa Clara, ☎ 91/522–4119), with a mix of Brazilian and international music, is popular on Saturday night. Sunday afternoon can be sleepy in Santarém, but **Zoom** (⊠ Av. Presidente Vargas 1721, Santa Clara, ☎ 091/522–1787) is where everyone goes to dance off all the energy they saved up during their day of rest.

Shopping

There are several artisan shops in Santarém, but by far the best place for gifts and souvenirs is the **Centro de Preservação das Culturas Indígenas** (⊠ Rua Dom Macêdo Costa 500, Alter do Chão, ☎ 091/527–1176). The prices are on the high side, but it offers the region's best selection of authentic indigenous artwork. If you can't make it to Alter do Chão, try **Loja Muiraquitã** (⊠ Rua Senador Lameira Bittencourt 131, ☎ 091/522–7164), which sells an incredible variety of regional items including native musical instruments, locally mined minerals, and wood carvings.

MANAUS

Manaus, the capital of Amazonas State, is a sprawling, hilly city of more than 1 million. It's on the banks of the Rio Negro, surrounded by dense jungle, 766 km (475 mi) southwest of Santarém, 1,602 km (993 mi) southwest of Belém. The city, founded in 1669, took its name, which means "mother of the Gods," from the Manaó tribe. It has long flirted with prosperity. Of all the Amazon cities and towns, Manaus is most identified with the rubber boom. In the late 19th and early 20th centuries the city supplied 90% of the world's rubber. The immense wealth that resulted was monopolized by rubber barons, never numbering more than 100, who lived in the city, spent enormous sums on ostentatious lifestyles (and structures to match), and dominated the region like feudal lords. *Seringueiros* (rubber tappers) were recruited; a few were from indigenous tribes, but most were transplants from Brazil's crowded and economically depressed northeast. Thousands flocked to the barons' huge plantations, where they lived virtually as slaves. As work progressed, conflicts erupted between barons and indigenous workers over encroachment on tribal lands. Stories of cruelty abound: one baron is said to have killed more than 40,000 native people during his 20-year "reign." Another boasted of having slaughtered 300 Indians in a day.

The 25-year rubber era was brought to a close thanks to Englishman Henry A. Wickham, who smuggled rubber-tree seeds out of Brazil in 1876. The seeds were planted in Malaysia, where new trees flourished; within 30 years, Asian rubber ended the Brazilian monopoly. Although several schemes were launched to revitalize the Amazon rubber industry, and many seringueiros continued to work independently in the jungles, the high times were over. Manaus entered a depression that lasted until 1967, when it was made a free-trade zone. The economy was revitalized, and its population jumped from 200,000 to 900,000 in less than 20 years. Today it's the Amazon's most popular destination, due in large part to the many accessible jungle lodges in the surrounding area. Manaus's principal attractions are its lavish, brightly colored houses and civic buildings—vestiges of an opulent time when the wealthy sent their laundry to be done in Europe and sent for Old World artisans and engineers to build their New World monuments.

Exploring Manaus

Manaus is a fairly spread-out city with few true high-rises. Although many hotels and sights are in the city center, it lacks a truly concentrated downtown like that found in Belém. Centro isn't particularly large and is set on a slight hill above the river. The biggest problem getting around town is that many streets don't have signs—especially in the free-trade zone. Despite the income generated by the zone, many of the historic sites are in disrepair. There are beautiful fountains in many of its plazas; none is in working order or has water.

Numbers in the text correspond to numbers in the margin and on the Manaus Centro map.

Centro

A GOOD WALK

Begin as early in the day as possible at the **Mercado Adolfo Lisboa** ①. Exit at its northeast end and continue along the waterfront. You'll pass fishing and trading boats until you reach the Porto Flutuante, the British-made floating dock where most large ships anchor. To the right of the dock, a path runs to the **Alfândega** ②. Avenida Eduardo Ribeiro continues where the path leaves off; follow it to the municipal clock, on your left, and the stairs that lead to the **Catedral da Nossa Senhora da Conceição** ③. From here, you can turn right on Avenida 7 de Setembro and visit one of several interesting museums, including the **Palácio Rio Negro** ④ and the **Museu do Índio** ⑤.

Alternatively, you can continue north from the cathedral on Avenida Eduardo Ribeiro to the pink **Teatro Amazonas** ⑥. Turn right, just before the theater, onto Rua José Clemente and follow it to the plaza dominated by the **Igreja São Sebastião** ⑦. From here, head around the other side of the theater, along Rua 10 de Julho, and back onto Avenida Eduardo Ribeiro to the Praça do Congress. Cross the plaza and Avenida Ramos Ferreira and turn left; follow Ramos Ferreira to the **Praça da Saudade** ⑧—a good place to relax, eat, and people-watch.

TIMING

Plan to spend 3–4 hours following the walk from start to finish. The tour that continues to Avenida 7 de Setembro will probably take 1½ hours; if you opt to veer off from the rest of the walk here, count on spending up to three hours reaching and visiting the museums.

SIGHTS TO SEE

❷ **Alfândega.** The Customs House was built by the British in 1902 with bricks imported as ship ballast. It stands alongside the floating dock that was built at the same time to accommodate the annual 12-m (40-ft) rise and fall of the river. It's now home to the regional office of the Brazilian tax department; although it's not officially open to the public, the guards may let you in. ✉ *Rua Marquês de Santa Cruz s/n,* ☎ *092/234–5481.*

❸ **Catedral da Nossa Senhora da Conceição.** Built originally in 1695 by Carmelite missionaries, the Cathedral of Our Lady of the Immaculate Conception (also called Igreja Matriz) burned down in 1850 and was reconstructed in 1878. It's a simple, predominantly neoclassical structure with a bright, colorful interior. ✉ *Praça da Matriz,* ☎ *no phone.*

❼ **Igreja São Sebastião.** Neoclassical St. Sebastian's (circa 1888), with its charcoal-gray color and medieval characteristics, seems foreboding. Its interior, however, is luminous and uplifting, with an abundance of white Italian marble, stunning stained-glass windows, and beautiful ceiling paintings. The church has a tower on only one side. Explanations for this asymmetrical configuration include that the second tower

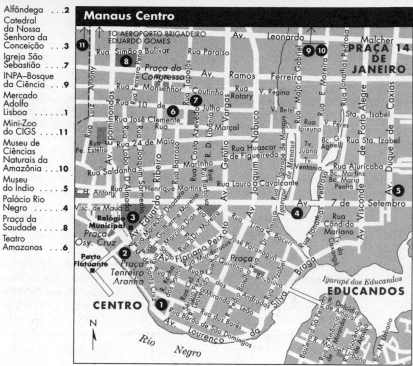

Manaus Centro

wasn't built as a result of lack of funds, that it was intentionally not added as a symbolic gesture toward the poor, and that the ship with the materials for its construction sank. As you stroll through the plaza that fronts this church and the Teatro Amazonas, note the black-and-white patterns on the ground. Done in Portuguese granite, they are said to represent Manaus's meeting of the waters. ⊠ *Praça São Sebastião,* ☎ *no phone.*

❶ **Mercado Adolfo Lisboa.** This market, built in 1882, is a wrought-iron replica of the original Parisian Les Halles (now destroyed); the iron-work is said to have been designed by Gustave Eiffel himself. Vendors sell Amazon food products and handicrafts daily from around dawn until noon. ⊠ *Rua dos Barés 6,* ☎ *092/234–8441.*

❺ **Museu do Índio.** The Indian Museum was constructed and is maintained by Salesian Sisters, an order of nuns with eight missions in the upper Amazon. It displays handicrafts, weapons, ceramics, ritual masks, and clothing from the region's tribes. ⊠ *Rua Duque de Caxias 356,* ☎ *092/ 635–1922.* ▦ *R$4.* ☉ *Weekdays 8:30–11:30 and 2–4:30, Sat. 8:30– 11:30.*

❹ **Palácio Rio Negro.** The extravagant Rio Negro Palace was built at the end of the 19th century as the home of a German rubber baron. Later it was used as the governor's official residence. Today it houses some of the city's finest art exhibits and a cultural center. The Museu da Imagem e do Som, on the same property, shows art films and documentaries at three daily screenings Tuesday through Friday, four on weekends. ⊠ *Av. 7 de Setembro 1546,* ☎ *092/633–2850.* ▦ *Free.* ☉ *Tues.–Sun 3–9.*

❽ **Praça da Saudade.** This bustling, energetic square is a great place to sit back and soak up the local culture. There's a small amusement park, some open grass, and several food stalls that serve such dishes as vat-apá and *tacacá* (shrimp stew). A crumbling amphitheater no longer in use is scheduled for repairs.

★ ❻ **Teatro Amazonas.** The city's lavish opera house was completed in 1896 after 15 years. The Italian Renaissance–style interior provides a clear idea of the wealth that marked the Amazon rubber boom: marble doorways, crystal chandeliers, and handblown glass sconces from Italy; wrought-iron banisters from England; and striking panels of French tiles. Italian frescoes depict Amazon legends. Operas and other events are presented regularly. Monday-evening performances are free events, usually featuring local artists from a variety of musical genres. The Amazonas Philharmonic Orchestra plays Friday night and can also be seen and heard practicing in the theater weekdays from 9 to 2. Recently, a wide variety of foreign entertainers—from José Carreras to the Spice Girls—have performed here. Half-hour tours are conducted daily between 9 and 4. ✉ *Praça São Sebastião s/n*, ☎ *092/622–2420.* ☞ *R$5.* ☉ *Mon.–Sat. 9–4.*

Elsewhere In and Around Manaus

If you have a little energy left after your Centro tour, you can take a cab to one of several far-flung in-town sights. The **INPA–Bosque da Ciência** ⑨ is northeast of the center, and beyond it is the **Museu de Ciências Naturais da Amazônia** ⑩. To the center's northwest is the **Mini-Zoo do CIGS** ⑪. If you have another day or two, consider an excursion to the **Amazon Ecopark** or the town of **Presidente Figueiredo,** both outside the city limits.

OFF THE   **AMAZON ECOPARK** – It's a half-hour boat ride from the Tropical Hotel
BEATEN PATH   along the Tarumã Bayou to the Amazon Ecopark, with its monkey jun-
               gle, waterfalls, and Amazon birds. The park offers half- and full-day
               tours (R$66 and R$132, respectively) with professional guides. *Reserva-*
               tions: ☎ *092/234–0939.*

❾ **INPA–Bosque da Ciência.** Used as a research station for the INPA (In-stituto Nacional de Pesquisa da Amazônia), this slice of the rain forest is home to a great diversity of flora and fauna. Some highlights include manatee tanks, alligator ponds, a botanical garden with an *orquidar-ium* (a greenhouse where orchids are grown), and nature trails. ✉ *Rua Otávio Cabral s/n, Aleixo,* ☎ *092/643–3293.* ☞ *R$2.* ☉ *Tues.–Fri. 9–11 and 2–4, weekends 9–4.*

⓫ **Mini-Zoo do CIGS.** At this zoo, you can see some 300 animals native to the Amazon. The Brazilian army also operates a jungle-survival training school here. Soldiers from around the globe come to participate in the two-year program. At the end of it, men (no women yet) are tested by being air-dropped into the jungle with only a pack of matches, a gun, and five bullets. ✉ *Estrada do São Jorge 750, São Jorge,* ☎ *092/ 671–6903.* ☞ *R$2.* ☉ *Tues.–Sun. 9–4:30.*

⓾ **Museu de Ciências Naturais da Amazônia.** The Natural History Museum of the Amazon has displays of insects and butterflies. You can also view Amazon river fish in large tanks. ✉ *Estrada Belém s/n, Aleixo,* ☎ *092/644–2799.* ☞ *Free.* ☉ *Mon.–Sat. 9–5.*

OFF THE   **PRESIDENTE FIGUEIREDO** – One of the Amazon's best-kept secrets is a
BEATEN PATH   two-hour, 107-km (64-mi) drive north of Manaus. This small, 12-year-old
               town has been the jumping-off point for mineral exploration and extrac-
               tion in recent years. Expeditions for these minerals have led to the dis-
               covery of such natural wonders as waterfalls (there are 45 in the area,
               some as high as 32 m/140 ft) and caves and caverns—some with pre-

THE VANISHING INDIANS

I N 1500, WHEN THE PORTUGUESE arrived in Brazil, the Indian population was 4.5 million, and there were an estimated 1,400 tribes. From the beginning, the Portuguese fell into two camps reflecting different attitudes toward the natives: the missionaries, who wanted to "tame" them and convert them to Catholicism, and the colonizers, who wished to first exploit and then enslave them. The missionaries lost, and when it became apparent that the Indians couldn't be enslaved, the infamous *bandeirantes* (members of *bandeiras,* or assault forces) relentlessly persecuted the Indians to "liberate" tribal lands. Although many Indians lost their lives defending their way of life, the greatest killers were smallpox and influenza—European diseases against which they had no immunity. A slow but steady integration into Portuguese society also caused the native population to dwindle.

Today, of Brazil's 328,000 remaining Indians, about 197,000 live in the Amazon. There are about 220 societies, each with its own religious beliefs, social customs, and economic activities. The larger groups include the Manaó, Yanomami, Marajó, Juma, Caixana, Korubo, and Miranha. They speak one of 170 distinct languages; Tupi (with seven in-use derivations, including Tupi-Guarani) is the most widely spoken, followed by Macro Jê, Aruák, Karíb, and Arawá.

Throughout Brazil's history, sporadic efforts were made to protect the Indians, but it was only in 1910 that the government established an official advocacy agency. Founded by Cândido Mariana da Silva Rondon, the Service for the Protection of the Indians (SPI) supported Indian autonomy, ensured that traditional practices were respected, and helped indigenous peoples to acquire Brazilian citizenship. In 1930, however, the SPI was abolished after funds were exhausted and administrative corruption became apparent. It was replaced in 1967 by the current governmental Indian advocacy group, FUNAI (Fundação Nacional do Indio, or the National Indian Foundation). Although it has been highly criticized, FUNAI helped to get the first (and, thus far, only) Indian elected into office: Mario Juruna, a FUNAI member and Indian chief, served as federal deputy from 1983 to 1987. The foundation has also defended the rights of Indians to protect their lands (it allows only legitimate researchers to visit reservations), which are increasingly targeted for logging, rubber extraction, mining, ranching, or the building of industrial pipelines and hydroelectric plants.

The Indians have always respected and understood their environment; hence, it's easy to understand how their plight and that of the rain forest have become linked. On his worldwide 1989 tour with the rock musician Sting, Chief Raoni of the Megkroniti garnered support for Brazil's Indians and raised overall environmental consciousness. At the same time, conservation efforts to preserve the rain forest have called attention to some of FUNAI's issues. For the Brazilian government, however, the issue is complicated: rainforest conservation often takes second place to economic development. Further, the Indians still lack many basic human rights, and violence (such as the 1998 murder of prominent activist Francisco de Assis Araujó) still sporadically occurs as the Indians continue to defend their way of life against outsiders.

— By Melisse Gelula and Althia Gamble

historic drawings and pottery fragments. There's also an archaeology museum near town. Call the tourist office ahead of time to arrange for an English-speaking guide. The office is next to the bus station. ⊠ *Secretaria de Turismo: Rua Das Araras 1,* ☎ *092/324–1158.* ⊙ *Mon.–Fri. 8–12 and 2–6.*

Beaches

Known as the Copacabana of the Amazon, **Praia do Ponta Negra** is next to the Tropical Hotel and has numerous restaurants, bars, and sports and nightlife facilities (including an amphitheater). Crescent-shape **Praia da Lua** is 23 km (14 mi) southwest of Manaus. You can only reach it by boat on the Rio Negro, so it's clean and less crowded than other beaches. **Praia do Tupé,** another Rio Negro beach accessible only by boat, is 34 km (20 mi) northwest of Manaus. It's popular with locals and tends to fill up on Sunday and holidays, when a special ship makes the trip from the city.

Dining

$–$$ ★ ✕ **Canto da Peixada.** Few eateries can claim to be fit for a pope; when Pope John Paul II came to Manaus in 1981, this restaurant was chosen to host him. The dining areas aren't elegant, but the fish dishes are outstanding. One platter feeds two. ⊠ *Rua Emilio Moreira 1677, Praça 14,* ☎ *092/234–3021. V. No dinner Sun.*

$–$$ ✕ **Suzuran.** For more than 20 years this festive restaurant has served the town's best Japanese food. If you can't decide between raw fish and fried favorites, don't. The *suzuran teishoku* has sushi, sashimi, shrimp and vegetable tempura, and fried fish. ⊠ *Boulevard Álvaro Maia 1683, Adrianópolis,* ☎ *092/633–3570. No credit cards. Closed Tues.*

$ ★ ✕ **Churrascaria Búfalo.** Twelve waiters, each offering a different cut of chicken, beef, or goat, scurry around this large, crowded restaurant. As if all the delectable meats weren't enough, the table is also set with about 10 side dishes, including two types of manioc root, pickled vegetables, and caramelized bananas. ⊠ *Rua Joaquim Nabuco 628-A, Centro,* ☎ *092/633–3773,* WEB *www.churrascariabufalo.com.br. AE, DC, MC, V.*

¢–$$ ✕ **Fiorentina.** The green awning and red-and-white-check tablecloths are hints that this restaurant serves authentic Italian. Pasta dishes are delicious, especially the simple lasagna *fiorentina* (with a marinara and ground-beef sauce). Saturday, there's a *feijoada* (black beans, rice, meats, and farofa or farinha) that costs about R$22. ⊠ *Praça da Polícia 44, Centro,* ☎ *092/232–1295. AE, DC, MC, V.*

¢–$ ✕ **Açai & Cia.** A local hangout as much for the atmosphere as for the food, this restaurant offers live MPB Thursday through Sunday. Regional dishes such as maniçoba and tacacá fill the menu and delight your senses. ⊠ *Rua Acre 98, Vieiralves,* ☎ *092/635–3637. AE, V.*

¢–$ ✕ **Coqueiro Verde.** Don't bother asking for a menu—everybody orders the *carne de sol* (beef cured in the sun for a day or two). This delicious, affordable treat is served with rice, beans, farofa, and salad. All this, and you can even pet the restaurant's mascot—a cute, woolly monkey—out in the garden. ⊠ *Rua Ramos Ferreira 1920, Centro,* ☎ *092/ 232–0002. AE, DC, MC, V. No dinner Sun.*

Lodging

Although there are several decent in-town hotels, the jungle lodges outside town—actually small hotels—offer far more opportunity for adventure. Whether you choose a treetop lodge, a floating barge, or a cabana on a scenic lake, they usually have guides on staff and offer swimming, nature walks, alligator "hunts" (they shine flashlights into the alligators' eyes, momentarily transfixing them, after which they grab the reptiles, hold them for photographs, and release them), piranha fishing, and canoe trips. Many lodges are near the Rio Negro, where mosquitoes aren't a problem because of the water's acidity level. Unless otherwise noted, prices are for two day/one night packages, which generally include transport to and from the lodge, meals (not drinks), and a variety of activities that will depend on the length of your stay.

Hotels

$$$–$$$$ ⊞ **Tropical.** Nothing in the Amazon can match the majesty of this resort. The sprawling complex is 20 km (12 mi) northwest of downtown and overlooks the Rio Negro, with a short path that leads to the beach. In addition to the on-site zoo, numerous sports facilities, and two gorgeous pools, the Tropical also has its own dock. The remote location, far from the center of town, can be a drawback. Book rooms through Varig Airlines, and if you fly Varig you'll receive a 20% room discount. The discount is 50% if you pay with American Express. Tarumã restaurant is a reliable choice for dinners of regional and international fare. ⊠ *Av. Coronel Teixeira 1320, Ponta Negra 69029-120,* ☎ *092/ 659–5000,* ℻ *092/658–5026. 601 rooms, 8 suites. 2 restaurants, bar, coffee shop, in-room safes, 2 pools, sauna, 4 tennis courts, basketball, exercise room, jogging, beach, dock, boating, shops, dance club, recreation room, travel services, helipad. AE, DC, MC, V.*

$$–$$$ ⊞ **Taj Mahal.** When this hotel became a member of the Holiday Inn chain it was a mixed blessing. Meeting the strict new quality standards transformed it into a more modern, more luxurious hotel than before. But much of the original, charming East Indian artwork—some of which you can still see in the lobby—didn't make the cut. Although the Taj Mahal seems more standardized now, it's still a pleasant option with a rooftop pool, a revolving restaurant, and convenient location. Request a room with a river view. ⊠ *Av. Getúlio Vargas 741, Centro 69020- 020,* ☎ ℻ *092/633–1010. 144 rooms, 26 suites. Restaurant, bar, pool, beauty salon, massage, sauna, meeting room. AE, DC, MC, V.*

$ **Ana Cássia.** The rooftop pool and most rooms at this 10-story hotel offer the city's best river and market views. Entering the lobby—with red-leather couches, highly polished green-and-white floors, and multiple mirrors—you may feel as if you've stepped into the early '80s. The well-equipped rooms aren't nearly as distinguished. ⊠ *Rua dos Andradas 14, Centro 69005-180,* ☎ *092/622–3637,* ℻ *092/622–4812. 88 rooms, 12 suites. Restaurant, pool, meeting room. AE, DC, MC, V.*

$ ⊞ **Lord Best Western.** Although it's clean and comfortable, this hotel in the heart of the free-trade zone shows signs of wear. Request a room on the recently renovated fourth floor, which has much nicer, more modern furnishings and novel amenities such as electronic DO NOT DISTURB signs. The staff is helpful and efficient. On Wednesday, the restaurant has live jazz and a feijoada. ⊠ *Rua Marcílio Dias 217, Centro 69005- 270,* ☎ *092/622–2844,* ℻ *092/622–2576. 95 rooms, 8 suites. Restaurant, bar. AE, DC, MC, V.*

$ ⊞ **St. Paul.** If you're planning an extended stay, this apartment-hotel (or "flat hotel," as they're called in Brazil) in Centro is your best bet. Accommodations are immaculate and have living rooms and fully equipped modern kitchens. For stays of more than a week you can get a discount of as much as 30%. ⊠ *Av. Ramos Ferreira 1115, Centro, 69010-120,* ☎ *092/622–2131,* ℻ *092/622–2137. 45 apartments. Pool, sauna, exercise room. AE, DC, MC, V.*

¢–$ ⊞ **Lider Hotel.** Although far from luxurious, this hotel is clean, comfortable, and conveniently located in Centro. It's a good base from which to branch out on city tours. ⊠ *Av. 7 de Setembro 827, Centro 69005-140,* ☎ *092/234–1966. 58 rooms, 2 suites. Restaurant, bar. AE, DC, MC, V.*

¢ 🏨 **Central.** In the free-trade zone, this hotel is it if you're on a tight budget. Rooms are simple and clean with standard amenities. ⊠ *Rua Dr. Moreira 202, Centro, 69005-250,* ☎ *092/622–2600,* FAX *092/622–2609. 50 rooms. Minibars. AE, DC, MC, V.*

Jungle Lodges

$$$$ 🏨 **Acajatuba Jungle Lodge.** Situated on Acajatuba Lake 80 km (50 mi) up the Rio Negro by boat from Manaus, this thatch-hut lodge will make you forget that the city is a mere four hours away. Twenty individual cabins are elevated 1 m (3.3 ft) above ground and connected to the rest of the lodge by walkways. Lighting is provided by 12-volt batteries (generators would keep wildlife away) and there is no hot water, but what it lacks in luxury, it more than makes up for by putting you in the middle of the rain forest. ⊠ *Contact: Anaconda Turismo,* ☎ *092/233–7642. 40 rooms. MC. FAP.*

$$$$ 🏨 **Amazon Lodge.** Nearly four hours by boat from Manaus, this lodge consists of rustic floating cabins with air-conditioning and baths. Because of its remote location, the chances for spotting moneys, and birds are terrific. The English-speaking guides are knowledgeable and friendly. The shortest package available is three days/two nights. ⊠ *Contact: Nature Safaris, Conjunto Parque Aripuanã, Rua 12, Casa 02, Planalto, Manaus 69040-180,* ☎ *092/656–6033,* FAX *092/656–6101. 14 rooms. Restaurant, fishing, hiking. No credit cards. FAP.*

$$$$ 🏨 **Ariaú Amazon Towers.** Undoubtedly the most famous of the Ama-
★ zon jungle lodges, these four-story wooden towers are on stilts and are linked by catwalks. The effect is more dramatic in the rainy season, when the river covers the ground below. Although the idea is to make you feel integrated with nature, the size of this complex generally prevents such a sense—or much contact with wildlife. The exceptions are brightly colored macaws and adorable, semiwild monkeys that often visit and inevitably make mischief. One hour by boat from Manaus on the Rio Ariaú, the lodge offers excellent food (although lacking in variety) and comfortable, albeit small, rooms. Its most popular accommodation—sought by honeymooners and celebrities alike—is the Tarzan House, in the treetops 30 m (100 ft) up, which can be had for a mere R$2,300 above the price of any package. ⊠ *Mailing address: Rua Silva Ramos 41, Centro, Manaus 69010-180,* ☎ *092/622–5000,* FAX *092/233–5615. 410 rooms, 10 suites. Restaurant, bar, 2 pools, hiking, dock, fishing, helipad, shops. AE, DC, MC, V. FAP.*

$$$ 🏨 **Jungle Palace.** It's quite a sight to cruise down the Rio Negro and see the neoclassical columns of this "flotel" looming on the horizon. Combining remote location with luxury, this lodge is built on a steel barge. Explore the region by day and return to your air-conditioned cabin for a hot shower and to watch some cable TV, or take a stroll on the observation deck. Thirty-five kilometers (20 miles) west of Manaus, it's the place for those who like to take their adventure with a splash of comfort. ⊠ *Rua Saldanha Marinho 700, Centro,* ☎ *092/633–6200. 42 rooms. Restaurant, bar, swimming pool, health club, conference room. AE, MC, V. FAP.*

$$$ 🏨 **Lago Salvador.** Although it's only a 45-minute boat ride from Man-
★ aus, this lodge still offers a serene, secluded atmosphere. Four cabanas with three apartments each are set on the shore of the lake from which the lodge takes its name. During the highwater season the lake flows over its shores to join the Rio Negro. Rooms are simple and comfortable, with fans and running water. All have trails leading to them, but your guide will probably use the most direct route—rowing a canoe across the lake—to get you there. ⊠ *Contact Amazônia Expeditions: Tropical Hotel, Estrada da Ponta Negra, Manaus,* ☎ *092/659–5119,* FAX *092/658–4221. 12 apartments. Restaurant, room service, hiking, boating. V. FAP.*

Nightlife and the Arts

The nighttime highlight is the *boi-bumbá*: pulsating live music plays while men and women in Indian costumes tell stories and perform a fascinating, sensual dance at clubs (or occassionaly the amphitheater). Many bars also have live music or a DJ.

The large amphitheater at Praia do Ponta Negra holds regular boi-bumbá performances. In addition, the Teatro Amazonas still draws some of the biggest names in theater, opera, and classical music. Pick up a copy of *Manaus Em Tempo* at any newsstand for event listings in Portuguese.

For a traditional boi-bumbá experience in a nightclub environment, head to **Boiart's** (⊠ Rua José Clemente 500, Centro, ☎ 092/637–0807), which is just across from the Teatro Amazonas. **Coração Blue** (⊠ Estrada da Ponta Negra 3701, Km 6, ☎ 092/984–1391) is an outdoor bar with a boi-bumbá show every night. Weeknights it's often the busiest place in town. A popular but somewhat high-brow dance club is the Tropical Hotel's **Studio Tropical** (⊠ Av. Coronel Teixeira 1320, Ponta Negra, ☎ 092/659–5000), which plays a variety of high-energy dance music for a well-dressed clientele but is open only Thursday through Saturday. **Tukannu's** (⊠ Av. do Turismo 3156, Tarumã, ☎ 092/658–3543) keeps the crowd dancing with a mix of pagode and carioca funk (originating in Rio) Tuesday through Saturday.

Outdoor Activities and Sports

Participant Sports

JET SKIING

How many of your friends can say they've been jet skiing in the Amazon? **Clube do Jet** (⊠ Rua Praiana 13, access through Av. do Turismo, Ponta Negra, ☎ 092/245–1332) rents equipment for about R$88 an hour on the Rio Negro.

JUNGLE AND RIVER EXCURSIONS

The most common excursion is a half- or full-day tourist-boat trip 15 km (9 mi) east of Manaus, where the jet-black water of the Rio Negro flows beside the yellowish-brown water of the Rio Solimões for 6 km (4 mi) before merging into one as the Rio Amazonas. (It's also common to see pink dolphins in this area.) Many of these meeting-of-the-waters treks include motorboat side trips along narrow streams or through bayous. Some also stop at the Parque Ecológico do Janauary, where you can see Amazon birds and a lake filled with giant *vitória régia* water lilies.

Overnight boat trips into the rain forest follow the Rio Negro, exploring flooded woodlands and narrow waterways, and stop for a hike on a trail. At night, guides take you by canoe on an alligator "hunt." Longer trips to the Negro's upper reaches—where the river is narrower and life along the banks easier to observe—are also options. Such trips usually stop at river settlements where you can visit with local families. They can also include jungle treks; fishing (with equipment supplied by boat operators); and a trip to Anavilhanas, the world's largest freshwater archipelago. It contains some 400 islands with amazing Amazon flora. Because of the dense vegetation, however, you won't see much wildlife other than birds and monkeys. To arrange any of these excursions, contact an area tour operator.

Spectator Sport

Manaus's professional soccer teams, Rio Negro and Nacional, play at **Estádio Vivaldo Lima** (⊠ Av. Constantino Nery, Parque 10, ☎ 092/236–1640). A taxi ride to the stadium and tickets should each cost about R$22.

Shopping

Areas and Malls
If you're not from South America, you probably won't find too much of interest in the free-trade zone. Still, you might want to duck into a couple of the endless shops scattered throughout the downtown district—just to have a look. The largest, most upscale mall is **Amazonas Shopping** (⌧ Av. Djarma Batista 482, Parque 10, ☎ 092/642–3555).

Specialty Stores
Ecoshop (⌧ Rua 10 de Julho 509-A, Centro, ☎ 092/234–8870) sells a variety of indigenous crafts, as well as regional art. **Museu do Índio** (⌧ Rua Duque de Caxias 356, Centro, ☎ 092/234–1422) has a gift shop that sells traditional crafts such as baskets, and necklaces made from seeds and feathers. **Selva Artesanato** (⌧ Rua Dos Barés 46, Centro, ☎ 092/232–7434), inside the Mercado Adolfo Lisboa, sells reasonably priced examples of indigenous and caboclo arts and crafts.

THE AMAZON A TO Z

To research prices, get advice from other travelers, and book travel arrangements, visit www.fodors.com.

AIR TRAVEL
BELÉM
All flights are served by Aeroporto Internacional Val-de-Cans, which is 11 km (7 mi) northwest of the city. Varig has three flights a week to and from Miami and daily flights to and from Rio, São Paulo, Brasília, and Manaus. Other domestic carriers fly daily to Rio, São Paulo, Brasília, and Manaus including TAM, Transbrasil, and VASP. Regional flights to smaller airports are offered by carriers such as Penta or Meta.

The easiest route from the airport is south on Avenida Julio Cesár and then west on Avenida Almirante Barroso. The 20-minute taxi ride costs R$25. There are also buses; look for those labeled MAREX/PRES. VARGAS (for the Hilton and other hotels), MAREX/PRAÇA KENNEDY (Paratur and the docks), or MAREX/VER-O-PESO (Cidade Velha).

BETWEEN BELÉM AND MANAUS
Although plans for a new Ilha do Marajó airport—one that can handle planes from large domestic carriers—are in the works, 30-minute flights between Belém and the existing airport are infrequent and expensive. For now, it's best to contact Amazon Star Tours to arrange a flight, or plan to take a boat.

Macapá is a 40-minute flight from Belém; VASP and Varig offer regular service. Between Santarém and both Belém and Manaus, Varig offers daily hour-long flights. Tavaj flies three times a week.

Aeroporto de Macapá is 4 km (2 mi) northwest of town. Although buses make the journey regularly, hopping a taxi for the short, inexpensive ride is your best bet. Aeroporto Maria José is 14 km (23 mi) west of Santarém. Buses and taxis are plentiful.

MANAUS
The international Aeroporto Brigadeiro Eduardo Gomes is 17 km (10 mi) south of downtown. TAM has daily nonstop flights to and from Miami, and Varig has a direct flight once per week. It may be cheapest to connect on LAB via La Paz or Aeropostale via Caracas. Transbrasil and VASP offer daily flights to and from Santarém, Belém, Brasília, Rio, and São Paulo.

The trip to Centro takes about 20 minutes and costs R$33–R$44 by taxi. A trip on one of the city buses, which depart regularly during the day and early evening, costs less than R$2.

➤ AIRLINES AND CONTACTS: **Aeropostal** (☎ 092/233–7685). **LAB** (☎ 092/633–4200). **Meta** (☎ 091/522–1697 in Belém). **Penta** (☎ 091/222–7777 in Belém; 091/523–2220 in Sanatarém). **TAM** (☎ 091/210–6400 in Belém; 092/652–1381 in Manaus, WEB www.tam.com.br). **Tavaj** (☎ 092/652–1166). **Transbrasil** (☎ 091/212–6977 in Belém; 092/622–1705 in Manaus, WEB www.transbrasil.com.br). **Varig** (☎ 091/224–3344 in Belém; 096/223–4612 in Macapá; 091/522–2488 in Santarém; 092/622–3161 in Manaus, WEB www.varig.com.br). **VASP** (☎ 091/212–2661 in Belém; 096/224–1016 in Macapá; 092/622–3470 in Manaus, WEB www.vasp.com.br).

➤ AIRPORT INFORMATION: **Aeroporto Brigadeiro Eduardo Gomes** (✉ Av. Santos Dumont s/n, Manaus, ☎ 092/652–1510). **Aeroporto de Macapá** (✉ Rua Hildemar Maia s/n, Santa Rita, Macapá, ☎ 096/223–2323). **Aeroporto Internacional Val-de-Cans** (✉ Av. Julio Cesár s/n, Belém, ☎ 091/210–6000). **Aeroporto Maria José** (✉ Rodovia Fernando Guilhon, Praça Eduardo Gomes s/n, Santarém, ☎ 091/523–1990).

BIKE TRAVEL

On Ilha do Marajó one of the best ways to reach the beaches or to explore Soure is to use a bike as the locals do. Rates are less than R$2 an hour.

➤ BIKE RENTAL: **Bimba** (✉ Rua 4, between Trv. 18 and Trv. 19, Soure, ☎ no phone).

BOAT AND FERRY TRAVEL

BELÉM

Most ships arrive and depart in the general dock area called the Escadinha. ENASA ships and standard riverboats head upriver from here to Santarém and Manaus. The docks are quite close to the town center. A taxi ride shouldn't cost more than R$11. The new tourist-boat terminal, 20 minutes south of town on Avenida Alcindo Cacela (Praça Princesa Isabel), is where many excursions start.

BETWEEN BELÉM AND MANAUS

Boats (including ENASA vessels) travel daily between Belém and Camará, on Ilha do Marajó. Arapari also operates boats between Belém and Camará twice daily Monday through Saturday; although they're slightly more expensive than other lines, they cut the time down to three hours. The ferry allows you to take cars to Ilha do Marajó, or vans run from Camará to Soure and cost about R$9. ENASA goes to Soure, making the four-hour, R$8 trip twice a week.

Although Macapá is very close to Ilha do Marajó's western side, all boats traveling to Macapá originate in Belém. Standard riverboats regularly make the 24-hour trip. If time is an issue, high-speed boats cut the journey down to seven hours and cost only R$88. Another option is the "party boat," which makes the run five times a week. Its restaurant, bars, and many decks make the 24-hour trip very enjoyable. You can rent hammock space for R$57 (hammocks aren't provided), or to reserve a fairly luxurious cabin in advance for R$92, contact Bom Jesus. Boats dock in the nearby port town of Santana, where taxis await. The fare to Macapá will range from R$12 to R$34, depending on how many other passengers the driver can gather. Buses, which cost R$2, run hourly.

Only standard riverboats make the trip from Macapá to Santarém and onward to Manaus (a two-day journey); travel on a standard riverboat from Belém to Santarém also takes roughly two days. Taxis are always at the docks in Santarém; the cost to anywhere in town will be less than R$12.

In front of the Porto Flutuante there's a group of stands where people sell tickets for everything from high-speed cruisers to standard riverboats. ENASA also has a reservation office in town. The docks are in Centro, so most hotels are quite close. A taxi, if necessary, shouldn't be very expensive.

To reach most Manaus-area beaches, catch a boat from the Porto Flutuante. Sunday is the only day with regularly scheduled trips; boats transport great crowds for about R$7 per person. You can hire small craft to the beaches and other attractions—such as the meeting of the waters. Look for people wearing the green vests of the Associação dos Canoeiros Motorizados de Manaus near the Porto Flutuante or in the Escadinha area closer to the market; they can set you up with local boat trips at reasonable prices. You can also make arrangements through tour operators.

➤ BOAT AND FERRY INFORMATION: **Arapari** (☎ 091/212–2492). **Bom Jesus** (✉ Av. Mendonça Junior 12, Macapá, ☎ 096/223–2342). **ENASA** (✉ Av. Artur Bernardes 1000, Icoaraci, Belém, ☎ 091/211–6613 or 091/257–0299; ✉ Rua Marechal Deodoro 61, Centro, Manaus, ☎ 092/622—3280). **Ilha do Marajó Vans** (☎ 091/741–1441).

BUS TRAVEL

The bus station in Belém, Rodoviário São Brás, is east of Nazaré. Reservations for buses are rarely needed. Boa Esperança makes the 209-km (125-mi) journey to Salinas Beach three times a day. The slow bus (4 hrs) costs R$12; the faster bus (3 hrs) costs $R34. Beira-Dão leaves every half hour on the 60-km (36-mi), two-hour, R$5 journey to Ilha Mosqueiro. Clearly marked buses to Outeiro Beach and the town of Icoaraci pass the bus station regularly and cost about R$1. Belém's local bus service is safe, efficient, and comprehensive, but a little confusing—ask a resident for guidance. You board buses at the rear, where you pay an attendant the equivalent of 50¢ and pass through a turnstile to take your seat.

All buses in the region between Belém and Manaus are entered from the rear and cost R$1–R$2. In Soure, buses to Camará pass by the riverside fairly regularly. In Macapá, there's an outdoor terminal on Rua Antônio Coelho de Carvalho, a block from the fort. Catch the bus labeled B. NOVO/UNIVERSIDADE to the Marco Zero, a 20-minute ride. Buses from Santarém to Alter do Chão depart from Praça Tiradentes in the city center or from Avenida Cuiabá (near the Amazon Park Hotel). They make the journey back and forth five or six times a day.

The bus station in Manaus, Terminal Rodoviário Huascar Angelim, is 7 km (4 mi) north of the center. You'll probably only use it to get to Presidente Figuereido: take the bus labeled ARUANÃ, which runs regularly and costs R$12. The city bus system is extensive and fairly easy to use. The fare is about R$1. Most of the useful buses run along Avenida Floriano Peixoto, including Bus 120, which goes to Ponta Negra and stops near the Tropical Hotel. The Fontur bus, which costs about R$12, travels between Centro and the Tropical several times a day.

➤ BUS INFORMATION: **Beira-Dão** (☎ 091/226–1162). **Boa Esperança** (☎ 091/266–0033). **Rodoviário São Brás** (✉ Av. Almirante Barroso s/n, São Brás, Belém). **Terminal Rodoviário Huascar Angelim** (✉ Rua Recife 2784, Flores, Manaus, ☎ 092/642–5805).

CAR RENTAL

In Belém, rental cars cost between R$91 and R$162 a day. Several companies have offices at the airport and in town. There aren't any car rental companies on Ilha do Marajó, but you can rent a car in Belém and transport it to the island on the ferry that leaves from Icoaraci. In Macapá, rent from Locvel, and in Santarém, from Sanvel Locadora. You can rent a car at the Manaus airport through Unidas Rent a Car.
➤ LOCAL AGENCIES: **Localiza** (✉ Av. Pedro Álvares Cabral 200, Umarizal, Belém, ☎ 091/212–2700). **Locvel** ✉ Av. Fab 2093, Macapá, ☎ 096/223–7999). **Norauto** (✉ Av. Gentil Bittencourt 2086, Nazaré, Belém, ☎ 091/249–4900). **Sanvel Locadora** (✉ Av. Mendonça Furtado 2085, Santarém, ☎ 091/522–3428). **Unidas Rent a Car** (✉ Aeroporto Brigadeiro Eduardo Gomes, Av. Santos Dumont s/n, Manaus, ☎ 092/621–1575).

CAR TRAVEL

The BR 316 begins on the outskirts of Belém and runs eastward toward the coast and then south, connecting the city with Brazil's major northeastern hubs. To reach the beaches at Ilha Mosqueiro outside Belém, take BR 316 and then head north on PA 391. To reach Salinas Beach, take BR 316 to PA 324 and head north on PA 124. From Manaus, BR 174 runs north to Boa Vista, and BR 319 travels south to Porto Velho. Unfortunately, both routes are in terrible condition and are often closed, especially during the rainy season.

Although Belém has the most traffic of any Amazon city and what seems like more than its fair share of one-way streets, in-town driving is relatively easy. Parking is only tricky in a few areas, such as Avenida Presidente Vargas and the Escadinha. Traffic and parking problems don't exist in the region between Belém and Manaus or in Manaus proper.

CONSULATES

➤ CONTACTS: **United Kingdom** (✉ Av. Governador José Malcher 815, Rooms 410–411, Nazaré, Belém, ☎ 091/223–0990 or 091/222– 0762; ✉ Rua Poraquê 240, Distrito Industrial, Manaus, ☎ 092/613– 1819). **United States** (✉ Rua Osvaldo Cruz 165, Campina, Belém, ☎ 091/223–0800; ✉ Rua Recife 1010, Adrianópolis, Manaus, ☎ FAX 092/ 232–4546 or 092/633–4907).

EMERGENCIES

Big Ben is a 24-hour pharmacy in Belém with many branches. Farmácia Teixeira may be one of the Soure pharmacies that's open 24 hours (they rotate 24-hour duty). In Macapá, Farmácia Globo is open 24 hours a day, and Santarém's only 24-hour pharmacy is Drogaria Droga Mil.
➤ EMERGENCY CONTACTS: **Ambulance** (☎ 192 in Belém; 1520 in Macapá; 192 in Manaus). **Fire** (☎ 193 in Belém; 193 in Macapá; 091/ 522–2530 in Santarém; 092/611–5040 in Manaus). **Police** (☎ 190 in Belém; 190 in Macapá; 091/523–2633 in Santarém; 190 in Manaus).
➤ HOSPITALS: **Hospital e Maternidade Dom Luiz I** (✉ Av. Generalíssimo Deodoro 868, Umarizal, Belém, ☎ 091/241–4144). **Hospital e Maternidade Sagrada Familia** (✉ Av. Presidente Vargas 1606, Santarém, ☎ 091/522–1988). **Hospital e Pronto Socorro Municipal 28 de Agosto** (✉ Rua Recife s/n, Adrianópolis, Manaus, ☎ 092/236–0326). **Pronto Socorro** (✉ Rua Milton Silva s/n, Macapá, ☎ 096/421–1499 or 192). **Santa Severa** (✉ Rua 8 and Trv. 17, Soure, Ilha do Marajó, ☎ 091/ 741–1459).
➤ 24-HOUR PHARMACIES: **Big Ben** (✉ Av. Gentil Bittencourt 1548, Nazaré, Belém, ☎ 091/241–3000). **Drogaria 24h** (✉ Boulevard Álvaro Maio 744, Centro, Manaus, ☎ 092/633–6040). **Drogaria Droga Mil** (✉ Av. Magalhães Barata 674, Santarém, ☎ 091/523–1000). **Farmá-**

cia Globo (⊠ Rua Leopoldo Machado 1902, Macapá, ☎ 096/223–1378). Farmácia Teixeira (⊠ Rua 2 s/n, Soure, Ilha do Marajó, ☎ 091/741–1487).

HEALTH

Dengue and malaria exist in the Amazon, although they aren't common concerns. Malaria is generally found in the jungle, while dengue primarily occurs in urban areas. Both are spread by mosquitoes. The best prevention is to take measures to avoid being bitten by mosquitoes. Throughout the region, avoid drinking tap water and using ice made from it. In the cities, most restaurants buy ice made from purified water. Bottled water is generally easy to find.

MAIL, SHIPPING, AND INTERNET

In Belém, Arlen Keuffer provides Internet service for R$5 an hour and is open Monday through Saturday 10–10 and Sun. 3–9. The central branch of the Belém post office is open weekdays 8–noon and 2–6. You can send faxes, and as in all Brazilian post offices, SEDEX international courier service is available.

On Ilha do Marajó, the Soure post office is on Rua 2 between the Travessa 13 and Travessa 14. The Macapá central post office is open weekdays 9–noon and 2–5. You can mail a letter at the Santarém post office weekdays 8–4.

In Manaus, Cybercity has 21 computers and charges R$6 per hour for Internet access. The owners are always friendly and always have relaxing music—usually in English—playing in the background. The most central Manaus post office is open weekdays from 9 to 5 and on Saturday from 9 to 1. In Santarém, NetSan is open from Monday through Saturday 9 to 6 and has a dozen computers available with Internet access for R$5 per hour.

➤ INTERNET CAFÉS: **Arlen Keuffer** (⊠ Shopping Iguatemi, Trv. Padre Eutíquio 1078, Loja 303, Batista Campos, Belém, ☎ 091/250–5595). **Cybercity** (⊠ Av. Getúlio Vargas 188, Centro, Manaus, ☎ 092/633–1236). **NetSan** (⊠ Trv. Silvino Pinto 470, Loja B, Santarém, ☎ 091/523–1223).

➤ POST OFFICES: **Belém post office** (⊠ Av. Presidente Vargas 498, Campina, ☎ 091/212–1155). **Macapá central post office** (⊠ Av. Coroliano Jucá 125, ☎ 096/223–0196). **Manaus post office** (⊠ Rua Marechal Deodoro 117, Centro, ☎ 092/622–2181). **Santarém post office** (⊠ Praça da Bandeira 81, ☎ 091/523–1178). **Soure post office** (⊠ Rua 2 s/n, ☎ 091/741–1207).

MONEY MATTERS

In Belém, the airport branch of the Banco do Brasil charges a hefty commission to cash traveler's checks. In town, you'll find the best rates at Banco Amazônia, which is open weekdays 10–4. Casa Francesa Câmbio e Turismo is one of several exchange houses that offer comparable rates. ATMs are available at most bank branches in major cities. In smaller towns, neither ATMs nor change is easy to come by: bring cash and lots of small bills.

There are no exchange facilities on Ilha do Marajó. In Macapá, you can exchange money at Banco do Brasil, which is open weekdays 11–2:30. You'll probably get a better rate at Casa Francesa Câmbio e Turismo. In Santarém, you can exchange money at Banco do Brasil, which is open weekdays 10–1.

At the airport in Manaus, you can exchange money at Banco do Brasil and Banco Real. In town, you'll probably get the best rates at Cortez Câmbio.

➤ BANKS: **Banco Amazônia** (✉ Av. Presidente Vargas 800, Comércio, Belém, ☎ 091/216–3252). **Banco do Brasil** (✉ Aeroporto Internacional Val-de-Cans, Av. Júlio César s/n, ☎ 091/257–1983; ✉ Rua Independência 250, Macapá, ☎ 096/223–2155; ✉ Av. Rui Barbosa 794, Santarém, ☎ 091/523–2600). **Casa Francesa Câmbio e Turismo** (✉ Trv. Padre Prudêncio 40, Batista Campos, Belém, ☎ 091/241–2716; ✉ Rua Independência 232, Macapá, ☎ 096/224–1418). **Cortez Câmbio** (✉ Av. 7 de Setembro 1199, Centro, Manaus, ☎ 092/622–4222).

SAFETY

In Belém, watch out for pickpockets at Ver-o-Peso market and avoid walking alone at night, particularly in the Cidade Velha. Manaus also has some crime problems; again, solitary nighttime walks aren't recommended—especially around the port. On the sleepy Ilha do Marajó, the greatest personal safety concern may well be getting hit on the head by a falling mango.

TELEPHONES

The area code for Belém is 091. Public phones, operated with cards (sold in newsstands), are found on many corners. You can make long-distance calls at Telepará, which is open daily 7 AM–midnight.

Santarém's area code is 091; in Macapá, it's 096. Throughout the region, there are a number of card-operated public phones. In Santarém, you can make long-distance calls at Telepará, which is open weekdays 7 AM–9:30 PM and Sunday 8 AM–9 PM.

In Manaus, the area code is 092. Public phones, which take cards, are plentiful in Centro but aren't easy to find elsewhere in town. For long-distance calls, go to Telamazon, which is open weekdays 7–6:30 and Saturday 8–2.

➤ CONTACTS: **Telamazon** (✉ Av. Getúlio Vargas 950, Centro, Manaus, ☎ 092/621–6339). **Telepará** (✉ Av. Presidente Vargas 610, Campina, Belém; ✉ Av. Rua Siqueira Campos 511, Santarém, ☎ 091/523–2974).

TAXIS

There are plenty of taxis in Belém, and they're easy to flag down on the street (you only need to call for one at odd hours). All have meters; tips aren't necessary. Reliable companies include Coopertaxi and Taxi Nazaré.

Between Belém and Manaus, except on Ilha do Marajó, where you have to bargain for a price, taxis have meters. In Soure, you can call for either a regular cab or a moto-taxi, which only fits one person but is much cheaper. In Macapá and Santarém, taxis are plentiful, and you can hail them on the street, or call Rádio Táxi in Macapá and Rádio Táxi Piauí in Santarém.

Taxis in Manaus, all equipped with meters, are easy to flag down on the streets. At odd hours, you can call Tucuxi.

➤ TAXI COMPANIES: **Coopertaxi** (☎ 091/257–1041 or 091/257–1720). **Rádio Taxi** (☎ 096/223–5656). **Rádio Táxi Piauí** (☎ 091/523–2725). **Soure Taxis** (☎ 091/741–1336). **Taxi Nazaré** (☎ 091/242–7867). **Tucuxi** (☎ 092/800–5050 or 092/622–4040).

TOURS

For excursions in Belém as well as help with plane and hotel reservations, contact Angel Turismo. Valeverde Turismo has a tour boat and office at the Estação das Docas.

Tour operators that arrange trips to Ilha do Marajó are based in Belém. Amapá Tours offers city and river tours and is the only company that arranges trips to see the pororoca. Santarém Tur can arrange boat trips of varying lengths on the Amazon and Arapiuns rivers, day trips to Alter do Chão, and city tours. Amazon Tours, run by a knowledgeable, friendly American, Steven Alexander, offers tailor-made river, city, and Alter do Chão tours; he also conducts half-day trips to a patch of forest he owns a half hour's drive southeast of Santarém.

In Manaus, Amazônia Expeditions can book the usual fare such as stays at jungle lodges, tours to the meeting of the waters, piranha fishing, and alligator hunting, but also has a float plane, with half-hour flights starting at R$222. Fontur arranges boat and city tours. Another operator, Tarumã, can help with hotel arrangements and transportation around the city or on the river.

➤ Tour-Operator Recommendations in Belém: **Amazon Star Tours** (✉ Rua Henrique Gurjão 236, Campina, ☎ 091/212–6244). **Angel Turismo** (✉ Hilton International Belém, Av. Presidente Vargas 882, Praça da República, Campina, ☎ 091/224–2111). **Fontenele** (✉ Av. Assis de Vasconcelos 199, ☎ 091/241–3218). **Lusotur** (✉ Av. Brás de Aguiar 471, Nazaré, ☎ 091/241–1011). **Valeverde Turismo** (✉ Boulevard Castilhos França s/n, Campina, ☎ 091/212–3388).

➤ Tour-Operator Recommendations between Belém and Manaus: **Amapá Tours** (✉ Hotel Macapá, Av. Azarias Neto 17, Macapá, ☎ 096/ 223–2553). **Amazon Tours** (✉ Trv. Turiano Meira 1084, Santarém, ☎ 091/522–1928). **Santarém Tur** (✉ Rua Adriano Pimentel 44, Santarém, ☎ 091/522–4847).

➤ Tour-Operator Recommendations in Manaus: **Anaconda Tours** (✉ Rua Dr. Almínio 36, Centro, ☎ 092/233–7642). **Amazon Explorers** (✉ Rua Nhamundá 21, Centro, ☎ 092/633–3319). **Amazônia Expeditions** (✉ Tropical Hotel, Av. Coronel Teixeira 1320, Ponte Negra, ☎ 092/658–4221). **Fontur** (✉ Tropical Hotel, Av. Coronel Teixeira 1320, Ponta Negra, ☎ 092/658–3052). **Tarumã** (✉ Av. Eduardo Ribeiro 620, Centro, ☎ 092/633–3363).

VISITOR INFORMATION
Belemtur, the city tourist board, is open weekdays 8–noon and 2–6. Para State's tourist board, Paratur, is open weekdays 8–6. Both agencies are well organized and extremely helpful. On Ilha do Marajó, contact the Secretaria Municipal de Turismo. For information in Macapá, contact the state tourism authority, DETUR. In Santarém, contact SANTUR.

Amazonas State's tourism authority, the Secretaria de Estado da Cultura e Turismo, is open weekdays 8–6. The Manaus tourism authority, Manaustur, is open weekdays 8–2.

➤ Tourist Information in Belém: **Belemtur** (✉ Av. Governador José Malcher 592, Nazaré, ☎ 091/242–0900 or 091/242–0033). **Paratur** (✉ Praça Maestro Waldemar Henrique s/n, Reduto, ☎ 091/212–0669, WEB www.paratur.pa.gov.br).

➤ Tourist Information between Belém and Manaus: **DETUR** (✉ Rua Raimundo Álvares da Costa 18, Macapá, ☎ 096/223–0627). **SANTUR** (✉ Rua Floriano Peixoto 777, Santarém, ☎ FAX 091/523–2434). **Secretaria Municipal de Turismo** (✉ Rua 2 between Trv. 14 and Trv. 15, Soure, ☎ 091/741–1326).

➤ Tourist Information in Manaus: **Manaustur** (✉ Av. 7 de Setembro 157, Centro, ☎ 092/622–4986 or 092/622–4886). **Secretaria de Estado da Cultura e Turismo** (✉ Av. 7 de Setembro 1546, Centro, ☎ 092/234–2252, WEB www.visitamazonas.com.br).

8 BACKGROUND AND ESSENTIALS

Portraits of Brazil

Further Reading

Chronology

Map of South America

Map of Brazil

Map of World Time Zones

Smart Travel Tips A to Z

Portuguese Vocabulary

A LAND OF CONTRAST AND DIVERSITY

ON NEW YEAR'S EVE 2001, Brazilians who had never seen a tennis ball cheerfully acclaimed Gustavo "Guga" Kuerten as their first tennis world champion. Many of them, however, were still feeling the pangs of a 2½-year-old nightmare involving other heroes, a larger ball, and a stunned nation. It was a lazy afternoon in June 1998. The match against France to decide the World Cup was about to start when the news hit that *futebol* (soccer) superstar Ronaldo had had an epileptic seizure and wouldn't play. Brazilians reacted as though an earthquake had hit. During the crisis, Brazilian sports commissioners rushed to the locker room in the packed Parisian stadium and came out seconds later with new plans. Ronaldo played, but Brazil lost, and the country's dream of winning the World Cup for the fifth time went down the drain. A national catastrophe, the incident monopolized public and private attention in Brazil for several months, eliciting media analyses and solemn discussions on radio programs and TV talk shows.

In Brazil, sports heroes are like royalty. They rivet the country's attention, forming an emotional chain across this spread-out land, linking its 170 million people. Even lesser princes, such as the bearers of a beach volleyball crown, are met by cheering crowds throughout the country. In 1994, when race-car driver Airton Senna died in a crash, the president declared three days of official mourning. The funeral in São Paulo was attended by a record 1 million people, and the whole country seemed to fall into a deep depression.

Brazilians rarely unite in so passionate a manner behind weightier issues, but when they do, the effects are awesome. No one who was in the country in 1984 can forget the months of nationwide marches that nudged the military regime toward holding democratic elections for a president after 20 years of dictatorship. Little more than a decade later, the movement to impeach the corrupt president, Fernando Collor de Mello, brought out similar crowds, not only politically organized groups but also citizens going about their everyday affairs. Housewives donned black as a sign of protest when they did their weekly shopping, and students made up their faces using Indian war paint when they attended classes. Involving very little direct confrontation—and even less violence—these events seemed more like Carnaval (Carnival) than political revolution. But this is a style that makes sense in Brazil.

In this gigantic territory, larger than the continental United States and 250 times the size of Holland, contrasts are overwhelming. Brazil is a fabulously rich land, but it's full of inequalities. You're as apt to see five-star hotels and resorts as you are shantytowns. Shopping malls, McDonald's restaurants, and international banks stand side by side with street vendors peddling homemade foods and herbal medicines. Brazil's GNP is nearly US$795 billion (more than half that of Latin America as a whole), yet it also has a relatively high infant mortality rate (out of 1,000 babies born, 34 don't make it to their first birthday) and one of the world's worst distributions of wealth. The nation has more than 100 million acres of arable land; unequaled reserves of iron, bauxite, manganese, and other minerals; and mammoth hydroelectric power plants. Yet reckless mining and agricultural procedures—particularly in the Amazon—-have poisoned rivers, created deserts, and dislodged entire Indian tribes. Further, the racial democracy for which Brazil is often praised is more evident in the bustling downtown markets than in the plush salons of suburban socialites.

It has been said that in this radiant land live a sad people, and certainly the feeling of *saudade* (nostalgia) is latent in much Brazilian poetry and music. Yet this plaintive tone vanishes as soon as the Carnaval season begins. In the heat of the South American summer (February or March, depending on the date of Easter) the country explodes in gaiety. From such cities as Rio de Janeiro, Salvador, and Recife—where hundreds of thousands dance in street parades—to the small towns of Pará or Goiás, Brazil comes alive. Carnaval season involves not only the days right before Lent (Friday through Ash Wednesday), but also months of rehearsal beforehand. And the sparks of passion flow over into other events throughout the year: religious festivals, ball games, weekend dances.

If you examine Brazil's demographics, you'll find other stark contrasts. You can drive through vast regions in the central *cerrados* (savannas), the southern pampas, or the northeastern *sertão* (arid interior) without seeing a soul, and then, paradoxically, spend hours stuck in traffic in a major city. The bloated urban areas harbor nearly 80% of the population. They're like cauldrons containing a stew of many races that's seasoned by regional customs and accents. Although Brazil is considered a Latin country—and the Portuguese language does, indeed, help to unify it—any type of person can fit the Brazilian "mold." The country's racial composition reflects the historical contact between native peoples, Portuguese colonizers, African slaves; and immigrants from Germany, Italy, Japan, and even the United States.

In terms of diversity, religion runs a close second to ethnicity. Although the almanac will tell you that Brazil is 70% Catholic, the people's spiritual lives are much more eclectic. Some estimates put the number of spiritualists—many followers of the 19th-century Belgian medium Alan Kardec—at 40 million. Candomblé,

Macumba, Umbanda, and other cults inspired by African religions and deities abound. And, recently, Pentecostal sects have opened one church after another, performing exorcisms and miraculous cures in front of packed auditoriums. Most of these churches and cults welcome visitors of any creed or culture. Brazilians, it seems, are anything but sectarian.

Brazil is truly a land of contrasts, and any visit here is likely to be a sensuous adventure. A variety of cultures, beliefs, and topographies makes this warm nation a showcase of diversity. An array of nature's bounty—from passion fruit and papaya to giant river fish and coastal crabs—has inspired chefs from all over the world to come and try their hands in Brazilian restaurants (adding lightness and zest to the country's already exquisite cuisine). Spas—with bubbling mineral water and soothing hot springs—all over the land offer the best that both nature and technology can offer. Whether you travel to the Amazon rain forest, the mountain towns of Minas Gerais, the urban jungle of São Paulo, or the immense central plateau surrounding Brasília, you'll plunge into an exotic mix of colors, rhythms, and pastimes.

Historical Notes

Colonial Days

Brazil was officially "discovered" in 1500, when a fleet commanded by Portuguese diplomat Pedro Álvares Cabral, on its way to India, landed in Porto Seguro, between Salvador and Rio de Janeiro. (There is, however, strong evidence that other Portuguese adventurers preceded him. Duarte Pacheco Pereira, in his book *De Situ Orbis,* tells of being in Brazil in 1498, sent by King Manuel of Portugal.)

Brazil's first colonizers were met by Tupinamba Indians, one group in the vast array of the continent's native population. Lisbon's early goals were simple: monopolize the lucrative trade of *pau-brasil,* the red wood (valued for making dye) that gave the colony its name, and establish permanent settlements. There's evidence that the Indians and Portuguese initially worked together to harvest trees. Later, the need to head farther inland to find forested areas made the pau-brasil trade less desirable. The interest in establishing plantations on cleared lands increased and so did the need for laborers. The Portuguese tried to enslave the indigenous peoples, but, unaccustomed to toiling long hours in fields and overcome by European diseases, many natives either fled far inland or died. (When Cabral arrived, the indigenous population was believed to have been more than 3 million; today, the number is scarcely more than 200,000.) The Portuguese then turned to the African slave trade for their workforce.

Although most settlers preferred the coastal areas (a preference that continues to this day), a few ventured into the hinterlands. Among them were Jesuit missionaries, determined men who marched inland in search of Indian souls to "save," and the infamous *bandeirantes* (flag bearers), tough men who marched inland in search of Indians to enslave. (Later they hunted escaped Indian and African slaves.)

For two centuries after Cabral's discovery, the Portuguese had to periodically deal with foreign powers with designs on Brazil's resources. Although Portugal and Spain had the 1494 Treaty of Tordesillas—which set boundaries for each country in their newly discovered lands—the guidelines were vague, causing the occasional territory dispute. Further, England, France, and Holland didn't fully recognize the treaty, which was made by papal decree, and were aggressively seeking new lands in pirate-ridden seas. Such competition made the Lusitanian foothold in the New World tenuous at times.

The new territory faced internal as well as external challenges. Initially, the Portuguese Crown couldn't establish a strong central government in the subcontinent. For much of the colonial period, it relied on "captains," low-ranking nobles and merchants who were granted authority over captaincies, slices of land often

as big as their motherland. By 1549 it was evident that most captaincies were failing. Portugal's monarch dispatched a governor-general (who arrived with soldiers, priests, and craftspeople) to oversee them and to establish a capital (today's Salvador) in the central captaincy of Bahia.

At the end of the 17th century, the news that fabulous veins of emeralds, diamonds, and gold had been found in Minas Gerais exploded in Lisbon. The region began to export 30,000 pounds of gold a year to Portugal. Bandeirantes and other fortune hunters rushed in from all over, and boatloads of carpenters, stonemasons, sculptors, and painters came from Europe to build cities in the Brazilian wilderness.

In 1763, the capital was moved to Rio de Janeiro for a variety of political and administrative reasons. The country had successfully staved off invasions by other European nations and it had roughly taken its current shape. It added cotton and tobacco to sugar, gold, and diamonds on its list of exports. As the interior opened so did the opportunities for cattle ranching. Still, Portugal's policies tended toward stripping Brazil of its resources rather than developing a truly local economy. The arrival of the royal family, which was chased out of Portugal by Napoléon's armies in 1808, initiated major changes.

The Empire and the Republic

As soon as Dom João VI and his entourage arrived in Rio, he began transforming the city and its environs. Building projects were set in motion, universities as well as a bank and a mint were founded, and investments were made in the arts. The ports were opened to trade with other nations, especially England, and morale improved throughout the territory. With the fall of Napoléon, Dom João VI returned to Portugal, leaving his young son, Pedro I, behind to govern. But Pedro had ideas of his own: he proclaimed Brazil's independence on September 7, 1822, and established the Brazilian Empire. Nine years later, following a period of internal unrest and costly foreign wars, the emperor stepped aside in favor of his five-year-old son, Pedro II. A series of regents ruled until 1840, when the second Pedro was 14 and Parliament decreed him "of age."

Pedro II's daughter, Princess Isabel, officially ended slavery in 1888. Soon after, disgruntled landowners united with the military to finish with monarchy altogether, forcing the royal family back to Portugal and founding Brazil's first republican government on November 15, 1889. A long series of easily forgettable presidents, backed by strong coffee and rubber economies, brought about some industrial and urban development during what's known as the Old Republic. In 1930, after his running mate was assassinated, presidential candidate Getúlio Vargas seized power via military coup rather than elections. In 1945, his dictatorship ended in another coup. He returned to the political scene with a populist platform and was elected president in 1951. However, halfway through his term, he was linked to the attempted assassination of a political rival; with the military calling for his resignation, he shot himself.

The next elected president, Juscelino Kubitschek, a visionary from Minas Gerais, decided to replace the capital of Rio de Janeiro with a grand, new, modern one (symbolic of grand, new, modern ideas) that would be built in the middle of nowhere. True to the motto of his national development plan, "Fifty years in five," he opened the economy to foreign capital and offered credit to the business community. When Brasília was inaugurated in 1960, there wasn't a penny left in the coffers, but key sectors of the economy (such as the auto industry) were functioning at full steam. Still, turbulent times were ahead. Kubitschek's successor Jânio Quadros, an eccentric, spirited carouser who had risen from high-school teaching to politics, resigned after seven months in office. Vice-president João "Jango" Goulart, a Vargas man with leftist leanings, took office only to be overthrown by the military on March 31, 1964, after frustrated attempts to impose socialist reforms. Exiled in Uruguay, he died 13 years later.

Military Rule and Beyond

Humberto Castello Branco was the first of five generals (he was followed by Artur Costa e Silva, Emílio Médici, Ernesto Geisel, and João Figueiredo) to lead Brazil in 20 years of military rule that still haunt the nation. Surrounded by tanks and technocrats, the military brought about the "economic miracle" of the 1970s. However, it did not last. Their pharaonic projects—from hydroelectric and nuclear power plants to the conquest of the Amazon—never completely succeeded, and inflation soared. Power was to go peacefully back to civil hands in 1985.

All hopes were on the shoulders of Tancredo Neves, a 75-year-old democrat chosen to be president by an electoral college. But just before his investiture Neves was hospitalized for routine surgery; he died of a general infection days later. An astounded nation followed the drama on TV. Vice-president José Sarney, a former ally of the military regime, took office. By the end of his five-year term, inflation was completely out of hand. Sarney did, however, oversee the writing of a new constitution, promulgated in 1988, and Brazil's first free presidential elections in 30 years.

Fernando Collor de Mello, a debonair 40-year-old from the state of Alagoas, took office in March 1990. Dubbed "the maharajah hunter" (an allusion to his promises to rid the government of idle, highly paid civil servants), Mello immediately set about trying to control inflation (his first step was to block all savings accounts in Brazil). His extravagant economic plans only became clear two years later with the discovery of widespread corruption involving his friend and campaign manager Paulo César "P. C." Farias. After an impeachment process, Collor was ousted in December 1992, and Brazil's leadership fell to Vice-President Itamar Franco. With his Plano Real, Franco brought inflation under control.

In 1994, Franco was replaced by Fernando Henrique Cardoso, the former secretary of the treasury. Following the dictates of the International Monetary Fund, Cardoso brought about relative economic stability, but at the price of recession, cuts in health and educational programs, and a soaring national debt. His policy of selling state-owned industries—from banks to mines to phone companies—was riddled with irregular practices.

In October 1998, taking advantage of a constitutional amendment that he personally engineered allowing for reelection, Cardoso won a second term, running against Workers Party candidate Luis Inácio "Lula" da Silva. He based his campaign on propaganda that promised a return to economic growth and an end to unemployment. Cardoso managed to avoid draconian economic measures and a 35% currency devaluation until the day after the election. Then, new taxes and budget cuts were announced, recession settled in, and unemployment soared. In 1999, Cardoso's popularity was at a record low, causing nationwide calls for his resignation. He held on—ruling with more gusto than his military prede-cessors—by churning out endless "temporary" executive decrees, which bypassed normal legislative procedures. Before the first quarter of 2001 was over, Cardoso had signed 48,000 such decrees in a seven-year period.

As the local saying goes, patience and chicken soup harm no one. Brazilians know how to be patient and resilient under stress. Many of them saw the news of significant growth in the 2000 GNP as a good omen. Economic recovery may be slow and political healing difficult, but it's almost impossible to lose faith in such a rich land. The dream is not over. Between a tennis crown, presidential elections, and the soccer World Cup, winning something in 2002 will be a cinch.

— by José Fonseca

Born and raised in Minas Gerais, José Fonseca left Brazil at the start of the military dictatorship, earned a master's in journalism from the University of Kansas, and then spent more than 10 years in Europe and West Africa before returning to Brazil. Working as a freelance environmental journalist, translator, and writer, and refreshed by a wonderfully cool year in Canada, he is now back in Porto Alegre, where he lives with his anthropologist wife, his children, and his cats and dogs.

BRAZILIAN MUSIC: THE HEARTBEAT OF THE COUNTRY

Nothing in the world sounds like the music of Brazil. Whether you're listening to a rousing samba on a restaurant radio, a soothing bossa nova in a beachside café, or an uplifting Afro-Brazilian spiritist song on the street, you know instantly that you're hearing the country's beating heart. And even a short list of musical styles—which are as often linked to rhythms and dances as they are to tunes and lyrics—rolls off the tongue like an ancient chant: *axé, bossa nova, forró,* *frevo, samba, tropicalismo.* Many of these are divided into subcategories, with varying types of lyrics, singing styles, arrangements, and instrumentation. Some also fall into the super-category of *música popular brasileira* (MPB; Brazilian popular music). All fill the ear with a seamless and enchanting blend of European, African, Indian, and regional Brazilian sound.

History explains the eclecticism. The Portuguese colonists brought the Western tonal system and the music of the church with them to Brazil. When they arrived, they encountered the music of the Indians, which was almost exclusively percussive. The African slaves added fresh, varied rhythms and a love for choral singing to the mix. In a country this large, it isn't surprising that different regions would develop their own styles as well. From the northeast alone come forró, which uses the accordion to its best and most rhythmic advantage; axé, a Bahian blend of samba and reggae; and frevo, a fast-paced dance music most associated with Recife's Carnaval.

Although varied, Brazilian music is always characterized by complex rhythms and layers of textured sounds. Performers often embrace the use of violins, accordions, and flutes in their compositions. Some, such as Hermeto Pascoal, have innovative keyboard styles; others, such as Milton Nascimento, incorporate moving choral arrangements. Very often, musical groups have a percussionist armed with chimes, rattles, and shells, all used so subtly as to belie the word *noisemaker.* Most distinctive of all is the squeaking sound of the *cuíca,* and a solo on this instrument, made from a metal can, will always bring an audience to its feet.

Samba: The Spirit of Carnaval

The music for which Brazil is perhaps most famous is believed to have its roots in *lundu,* a Bantu rhythm reminiscent of a fandango yet characterized by a hip-swiveling style of dance, and *maxixe,* a mixture of polka as well as Portuguese and African rhythms. The earliest references to samba appear in the late 19th century, and one theory suggests the term comes from the Bantu word *semba,* meaning "gyrating movement." "Pelo Telefone" ("On the Telephone"), the first song actually designated a samba, was recorded in 1917. By the 1930s, the samba was being played in Rio de Janeiro's Carnaval parades, and by the 1960s it was the indisputable music of Carnaval. Today its many forms include the pure samba *de morro* (lit-

erally, "of the hill"; figuratively, "of the poor neighborhood"), which is performed using only percussion instruments, and the samba *canção* (the more familiar "samba song").

Samba evokes the spirit of Carnaval, regardless of when it's played. In cities such as Rio, Salvador, and Recife entire neighborhoods are divided into *escolas de samba* (samba schools), which work all year on costumes, floats, dances, and music to prepare for the pre-Lenten festivities. Composers who might have remained humble, such as Carlos Cachaça and the legendary Cartola, have become revered *sambistas* thanks to Carnaval and its escolas. Some schools also recruit well-known samba singers such as Martinho da Vila to perform what they hope will be the winning composition in the Carnaval competitions. Although today's Carnaval is big business, it manages to remain honest to this great country's soul. Costumed dancers still swirl, drums still thunder, and sweating faces still smile through it all. The opening line of one samba from the Portela School says it all: "Samba suffers, but it never dies."

Bossa Nova and Beyond

Although Brazilian music has a long, rich history, it wasn't until the 1959 film *Black Orpheus* that it reached the outside world in a big way. The movie retells the Greek legend of Orpheus and Eurydice, only this time, the tragic love story is set amid Rio de Janeiro's Carnaval. It's a great film, but what most people treasure is the beauty of its music, by Antônio Carlos Jobim (known affectionately as "Tom") and Luis Bonfa.

In the early 1960s, things happened that caused the world to listen ever more closely to Brazilian music. Artists and intellectuals began gathering in the cafés and apartments of Rio's chic Zona Sul neighborhoods of Copacabana, Ipanema, and Leblon. From the mix of personalities and the air of creative freedom arose a sound never heard before. It came first from the voice and the guitar of a young songwriter named João Gilberto. He sang in an understated, breathy way, and when he recorded the song "Desafinado," he virtually stated a new philosophy of music. The title means "out of tune," and, indeed, a few listeners thought he was. Melodic lines went in unexpected directions and ended in surprising places, and under those melodies was a cool, intricate rhythm.

During this period, Tom Jobim and his frequent collaborator, Vinicius de Moraes (former diplomat, lifelong poet and lyricist, and later singer), met daily at a corner café in Ipanema. And every day, while seated at their preferred table, they saw the same beautiful teenage girl pass along the street between the beach and her home. They felt compelled to pay tribute both to her beauty and to the way she made them feel; so they composed a song. Tom wrote the music, Vinicius the lyrics, and the "The Girl from Ipanema" was born. Today, that café is known as Garota de Ipanema, the song's title in Portuguese, and the street that it's on has been renamed in honor of Vinicius.

Already influenced by Miles Davis and the cool California jazz made popular by Chet Baker, Gerry Mulligan, and others, American jazz musicians began heading to Rio. The great saxophonist Stan Getz was among the first to arrive. He teamed up with Tom Jobim and João Gilberto to record an album. At the last minute, it was decided that João's wife, who wasn't actually a singer, would perform both the Portuguese and English versions of "The Girl from Ipanema." Soon, Astrud Gilberto was a star, and the song became the quintessential bossa nova hit.

Loosely translated, the term "bossa nova" means "new thing," and its greatest songs are recorded time and again, presenting ever-new challenges to each generation of performers. Very often a bossa nova song has a cool but rather bouncy rhythm that supports a long melodic line and lyrics that discuss the transitory nature of both love and loss. The tension between the two makes the music subject to shifting interpretations. Such feelings are often expressed by Brazilians with the word *saudade*. When a Brazilian feels saudades, he may be smiling or even singing, but his heart is breaking with longing for something or someone missing in his life.

The politically turbulent late 1960s and 1970s saw the development of the tropicalismo movement. Musicians and intellectuals like Caetano Veloso, Chico Buarque, and Gilberto Gil began using such contemporary instruments as the electric guitar and keyboard in their works. They also combined rock-and-roll and avant-garde experimentation with samba and other traditional rhythms. Often the tunes were upbeat though the lyrics, which were frequently written in double and triple entendres, were critical of social and political injustices.

Tropicalismo sparked such heated debate that an angry Veloso once harangued a São Paulo audience for being unwilling to accept anything new. Despite this controversy, the music gained a strong enough following that it brought about the attention and disapproval of the military regimes. Some of its performers were arrested; others had to live abroad for several years.

Eclecticism is the hallmark of Brazilian music. During the latter half of the 20th century, Brazilian musicians collaborated with or influenced several U.S. performers. Tom Jobim recorded two classic albums with Frank Sinatra and appeared again on Sinatra's *Duets* album. Wayne Shorter introduced Milton Nascimento to North America as a vocalist on his 1975 album, *Native Dancer*. Paul Simon found inspiration in the music of Bahia for his *Rhythm of the Saints* album. David Byrne has championed many Brazilian singers with his compilations of Brazilian music. And James Taylor has recorded and often performed with Nascimento. The song "Only a Dream in Rio" appears on albums by each man, and they made a memorable appearance together at the 2001 Rock in Rio music festival.

Of late, Jamaican reggae has been added to the Brazilian mix. Gilberto Gil's recordings of classic Bob Marley songs, including "No Woman, No Cry," honor their source and yet have a richness all their own. The dreadlocked singer Carlinhos Brown and his group, Timbalada, blend reggae sounds with the traditional rhythms of northeastern Brazil.

Brazilian Voices

One of the greatest strengths of Brazilian music is its numbers of extraordinary female vocalists. Although Carmen Miranda may always have a special place in many hearts, by general agreement the country's greatest woman singer was Elis Regina, who died in 1982 at the age of 37. Her pure voice, perfect diction, and wonderful melodic sense made her unique. Among her many great albums, those recorded with Tom Jobim and Milton Nascimento are considered the best. For samba the recordings made by Clara Nunes are *the* classics for most Brazilians.

Today, Gal Costa, Maria Bethânia (Caetano Veloso's sister), Beth Carvalho, Elba Ramalho, Alcione, Joyce, Simone, and Nara Leão fill concert halls at home and abroad. In the early 1990s Marisa Monte shot to stardom. In the late 1990s she was followed by Daniela Mercury. Virginia Rodrigues applies a voice of operatic quality to both beautiful ballads and impassioned songs in praise of the *orixás* (African spiritual dieties). In 2000, Bebel Gilberto, daughter of João Gilberto, released her album, *Tanto Tempo (So Much Time)*, which topped the charts in both Brazil and the United States.

Many a Brazilian musician or singer has made his or her voice heard in forms of expression other than popular music. Several have written film scores. Milton Nascimento has composed a mass. Chico Buarque and Vinicius de Moraes are highly regarded poets; Buarque is also a novelist. Caetano Veloso has written a lengthy memoir and meditation on music called *Verdade Tropical (Tropical Truth)*. Gilberto Gil has served as the minister of culture for the state of Bahia and has held a seat on Salvador's city council. Brazil's greatest artists are often more than mere pop stars, and the country acknowledges their efforts. Vinicius de Moraes isn't the only one with a street named in his honor. And though many Brazilians still refer to Rio's international airport as Galeão, after the death of Antônio Carlos Jobim it was renamed for him.

A Few Notes of Your Own

The following anthologies provide good samplings of Brazilian singers, composers, and styles. If you like these, you can seek out CDs by individual artists.

Brazil Classics 1: Beleza Tropical (Sire). The 18 tracks, compiled by David Byrne, include songs by Milton Nascimento, Caetano Veloso, Jorge Ben, Maria Bethânia and Gal Costa, and Chico Buarque.

Brazil Classics 2: O Samba (Sire). David Byrne compiled these 15 tracks that include sambas by Alcione, Clara Nunes, Beth Carvalho, Martinho da Vila, and others.

Canta Brasil: The Great Brazilian Songbook (Verve). This compilation's 16 tracks include three by Elis Regina, two by Maria Bethânia, and singles by Djavan and others.

–by Alan Ryan

Novelist and journalist Alan Ryan has written extensively about Brazilian music, literature, and culture for many newspapers and magazines. He lives in the Zona Sul of Rio de Janeiro and in New York.

FURTHER READING

On the nonfiction front, Joseph A. Page provides a fascinating, highly readable overview of Brazilian history and culture in his book *The Brazilians*. Along the same lines is Marshall C. Eakin's *Brazil: The Once and Future Country*. A short but good new history by Brazilian scholar Boris Fausto is *A Concise History of Brazil*. Social anthropologist Claude Lévi-Strauss discusses his research of Amazonian peoples in *Tristes Tropiques*, a book that's part travelogue, part scientific notebook—with many interesting observations and anecdotes.

Chris McGowan's *The Brazilian Sound: Samba, Bossa Nova, and the Popular Music of Brazil* provides an overview of the country's 20th-century music. Also recommended is *Bossa Nova: The Story of the Brazil-ian Music That Seduced the World*, by Ruy Castro. Christopher Idone's *Brazil: A Cook's Tour* has more than 100 color photos and 100 recipes. *Eat Smart in Brazil*, by Joan and David Peterson, is a good introduction to Brazilian food, with history, color photos, recipes, and a detailed glossary

Fiction lovers should try John Grisham's captivating *The Testament*, in which a lawyer voyages to the Pantanal Wetlands to search for a missionary who has inherited a fortune. Several Jorge Amado titles, which are usually set in his native Bahia, are available in English, including *Dona Flor and Her Two Husbands*; *Gabriela, Clove and Cinnamon*; and *The War of the Saints*.

BRAZIL AT A GLANCE

1494 The Treaty of Tordesillas divides lands to be discovered in the New World between Spain and Portugal.

1500 On April 22, a Portuguese fleet commanded by 30-year-old Pedro Álvares Cabral lands on Brazil's easternmost point, near present-day Porto Seguro in the state of Bahia.

1502 On January 1, a Portuguese fleet commanded by Amerigo Vespucci first sights Guanabara Bay. Thinking it the mouth of a mighty river, he names it Rio de Janeiro (River of January).

1503 The name *Brasil* is used for the first time, taken from the Indian name of *pau-brasil* (brazilwood), valued for its red dye.

1532 The first Portuguese colony, called São Vicente, is established in the southern part of the land.

1549 A government seat is established in Salvador in the northeast to administer the colony as a whole and the unsuccessful system of 15 captaincies into which it had been divided in 1533. In the same year, the first Africans are imported as slaves.

1554 A Jesuit mission is established at São Vicente, giving birth to the city of São Paulo.

1555–65 French forces hold Guanabara Bay.

1567 The Portuguese governor general establishes the city of Rio de Janeiro on Guanabara Bay.

1621 Dutch attacks on northeastern Brazil begin. These continue—with the Dutch gaining, holding, and then losing territory—for the next 30-odd years.

1633 Work begins on Rio's Benedictine monastery of São Bento, famed for its elaborate gold-leaf interior.

1654 The Dutch are completely ousted from the northeastern regions.

1694 Colonial forces find and destroy Palmares, the largest of the *quilombos* (communities formed in the forest by runaway slaves). Palmares and its leader, Zumbi, still appear in modern stories, films, and songs.

1695 Gold is discovered in Minas Gerais. Great inland colonial cities and churches are built with the sudden new wealth, and for the next century Brazilian gold enriches and supports the government of Portugal.

1720 Rio's landmark Glória church is built. Named Nossa Senhora da Glória do Outeiro (Our Lady of Glory on the Hill), the small baroque beauty stands on a low rise and looks out across Guanabara Bay.

1750 Ther Treaty of Madrid recognizes Portuguese rule of what is roughly today's Brazil.

1759 Jesuit priests are expelled from Brazil after 200 years of conflict with both colonial factors and the Portuguese government.

1763 With a shift away from wealth and power in the northeast, which had been based on sugar, to a newer center of influence in the southeast, based on gold, the capital is moved from Salvador to Rio de Janeiro.

1792 The Inconfidência Mineira, an independence movement based in Minas Gerais and spurred by repressive taxation policies, comes to an end when its leader, Tiradentes (Tooth Puller), is hanged in Rio de Janeiro.

1807 Portugal is conquered by Napoléon, and King João VI goes into exile in Brazil. With his court in Rio de Janeiro and with a new understanding of the colony from which he now directs all Portuguese affairs, he introduces reforms and permits Brazil to trade with other countries.

1814 Aleijadinho dies, leaving behind a timeless treasure of religious art in the churches of his native state of Minas Gerais.

1821 King João returns to Portugal. His son, Dom Pedro, is named Prince Regent of Brazil.

1822 On September 7, Pedro I proclaims the Brazilian Empire and independence from Portugal, partly to establish his own position and partly to continue the reforms begun by his father. The United States recognizes the new nation in 1824; Portugal does so in 1825.

1824 Austrian-born Empress Dona Leopoldina, wife of Pedro I, begins a campaign to populate the southern Brazilian countryside with European farmers. For the next 30 years, colonists from Germany, Italy, and elsewhere settle in this region.

1831 Hoping to regain the throne of Portugal for himself, Pedro I abdicates in favor of his son, Pedro II, who is only five. Until 1840, the country suffers through a period of unrest and rebellion under a regency of political leaders.

1840–89 The reign of Pedro II brings further reforms and economic stability and earns the king the respect of Abraham Lincoln. But territorial skirmishes with neighboring countries bring the military to prominence.

1850 The importation of African slaves comes to an end.

1855 The first Carnaval celebration is held in Rio de Janeiro.

1871 All children of slaves are declared free.

1881 The Teatro Amazonas, modeled on the Paris Opera, opens in Manaus, capital of the Amazon.

1884 The first railway line takes passengers to the top of Corcovado, overlooking Rio de Janeiro.

1885 All slaves over the age of 60 are freed.

1888 On May 13, all remaining slaves (nearly a million people) are freed. Brazil begins to even more aggressively recruit agricultural laborers from Germany, Italy, Portugal, and Spain.

1889   A bloodless military coup overthrows Pedro II and sends him into exile in France. On November 15, the Republic of Brazil is founded.

1890–1910   Manaus and the Amazon region produce tremendous wealth in the rubber trade. At the same time, the wealth of coffee growers shifts power from Rio de Janeiro to São Paulo.

1894   Prudente de Morais is elected as Brazil's first nonmilitary president.

1906   Alberto Santos-Dumont brings glory to Brazil with the first self-propelled, heavier-than-air plane flight.

1908   The first Japanese immigrants arrive in Brazil to work on coffee plantations. Today, most of their descendants are settled in São Paulo, which has the largest Japanese population of any city outside Tokyo.

1910   The government's first official Indian advocacy agency, the Service for the Protection of the Indians (SPI), is founded by adventurer Cândido Mariana da Silva Rondon, for whom the state of Rondônia was later named.

1912   The first cable car carries passengers to the top of Sugarloaf, at the mouth of Rio's Guanabara Bay.

1913   Rondon and former U.S. president Theodore Roosevelt mount the Rondon-Roosevelt Expedition into the Amazon.

1917   Ernesto dos Santos, known as Donga, records "Pelo Telefone" ("On the Telephone"), the first song designated a samba. It's the hit of the year and forever changes the music of Carnaval.

1922   A "Week of Modern Art" is held in São Paulo, celebrating the latest ideas in painting and poetry. It crystallizes and legitimizes the newest styles and trends and encourages artists to find a truly Brazilian way to adopt them.

1923   The Copacabana Palace opens on Rio's famed beachfront and continues for decades as a mecca for gamblers (until 1946, when gambling is outlawed in Brazil), international high society, and countless celebrities and heads of state.

1927   Henry Ford makes the first of two unsuccessful attempts to establish his own rubber plantation in Brazil.

1930   With the support of the military, Getúlio Vargas becomes president and assumes dictatorial powers, but he introduces many social reforms and is initially extremely popular.

1931   The monumental statue of Cristo Redentor (Christ the Redeemer) is unveiled atop Corcovado, rising 30 m (100 ft) above the 701-m (2,300-ft) granite peak.

1938   Brazil is the first country in Latin America to send a national soccer team to the World Cup finals.

1942   Brazil declares war on Germany and sends 25,000 troops to fight in Italy.

1945   Getúlio Vargas is forced out of office by the military.

1950   Vargas becomes president again, this time elected by the people.

1951   In Rio during the early 1950s, Ipanema's dirt roads and beach cottages are replaced with fashionable, expensive apartments and shops.

1954   Again threatened by a military coup, Vargas commits suicide in the presidential palace.

1956   The new president, Juscelino Kubitschek, announces plans to attract foreign investments and develop Brazilian industry. He also promises to make real an old Brazilian dream of a new capital city.

1958   With Pelé on the team, Brazil wins the World Cup.

1959   João Gilberto's first album, *Chega de Saudade* (*No More Sadness*), which includes his famous "Desafinado" ("Out of Tune"), firmly establishes bossa nova as Brazil's most popular new music. In the same year, the film *Orfeu Negro* (*Black Orpheus*) brings to the world the colors of Rio's Carnaval and the brilliance of Brazilian music.

1960   On April 19, after four years of furious work, President Kubitschek inaugurates the new capital city of Brasília, designed by Oscar Niemeyer and Lúcio Costa.

1964   *Getz/Gilberto,* the album that includes Astrud Gilberto's famous vocals on "The Girl from Ipanema," is released and becomes an instant classic around the world. In the same year, a military coup ousts President João Goulart, and the generals begin a 20-year period of repression, runaway inflation, and enormous national debt.

1967   The current governmental Indian advocacy group, FUNAI (Fundação Nacional do Indio, or the National Indian Foundation), is established.

1970   Copacabana's beach is widened and the now-famous mosaic sidewalks designed by Roberto Burle Marx are installed on Avenida Atlântica.

1973   Singer-songwriter Chico Buarque releases "Cálice," a song whose title means "chalice" but sounds the same as "shut up" in Portuguese, turning it into a song of protest against governmental repression. From 1969 until 1972, just prior to its release, Buarque and fellow musician Caetano Veloso had been in exile.

1981–83   Following a brief economic boom in the late 1970s, a period of deep recession leads to the downfall of the military government.

1984   Rio's Sambadrome, designed by Oscar Niemeyer, opens for Carnaval.

1985   José Sarney becomes president. His Cruzado Plan fails to control inflation.

1988   A new constitution returns freedoms, ends censorship, and guarantees rights for Indians. In the same year, Chico Mendes, a spokesman for the rain forest and its rubber tappers, is murdered.

1989 In this year's election, Luís Inácio da Silva, known as Lula, a trade union leader, comes to national prominence, but he loses to Fernando Collor de Mello. Chief Raoni of the Megkroniti tribe embarks on a worldwide tour with the rock musician Sting to garner support for Brazil's Indians and to raise overall environmental consciousness.

1990 The day after he takes office, Collor de Mello orders harsh fiscal constraints that only briefly stem the growth of inflation.

1991 Brazil takes the lead in forming MERCOSUL, a trade alliance that includes Argentina, Paraguay, and Uruguay.

1992 The United Nations holds the Earth Summit in Rio de Janeiro. In December, Collor de Mello, brought down by corruption scandals, resigns the presidency on the brink of impeachment.

1994 Fernando Henrique Cardoso is elected president. His Plano Real finally stabilizes the economy and curbs inflation. Brazil takes the lead in building more trade alliances and expands its role in international affairs.

1999 After a constitutional amendment, Cardoso is permitted to run for a second term and wins. Despite bumps in the road, the Brazilian economy appears stable and progress continues.

2001 An economic crisis in Argentina, a major trading partner, causes the real to fall in relation to the dollar, but the Brazilian economy remains strong and on track.

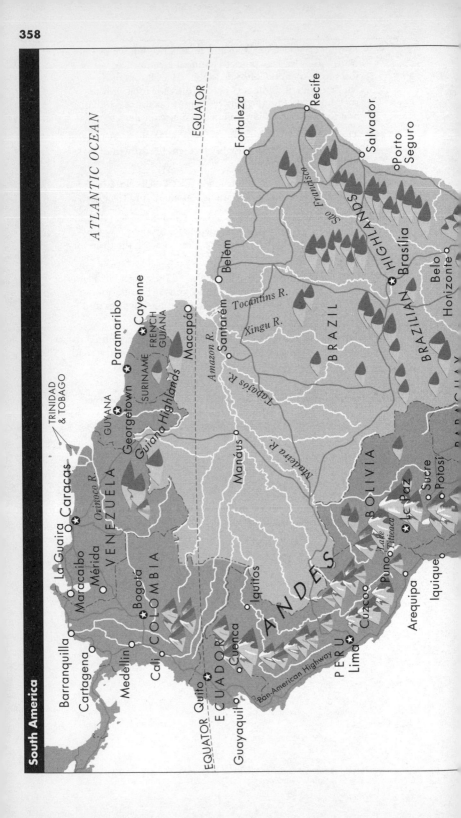

South America

ATLANTIC OCEAN

EQUATOR

Recife

Fortaleza

Salvador

Porto
Seguro

São Francisco

Belém

Belo
Horizonte

BRAZILIAN HIGHLANDS

Brasília

BRAZIL

Cayenne

Paramaribo

Macapáo

Santarém

Tocantins R.

Xingu R.

Amazon R.

Tapajós R.

FRENCH
GUIANA

SURINAME

Georgetown

GUYANA

Guiana Highlands

Manáus

Madeira R.

PARAGUAY

TRINIDAD
& TOBAGO

La Guaira Caracas

Maracaibo

Mérida

VENEZUELA

Orinoco R.

Bogotá

COLOMBIA

Barranquilla

Cartagena

Medellín

Cali

BOLIVIA

La Paz

Sucre

Potosí

Lake
Titicaca

Puno

ANDES

Iquitos

Cuzco

Arequipa

Iquique

PERU

Lima

Pan-American Highway

EQUATOR

Quito

ECUADOR

Cuenca

Guayaquil

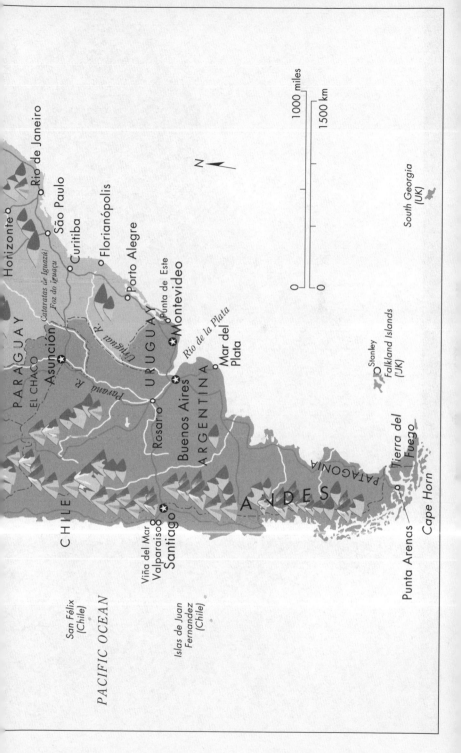

PACIFIC OCEAN

San Félix
(Chile)

Islas de Juan
Fernandez
(Chile)

CHILE

Viña del Mar
Valparaíso
Santiago

PARAGUAY

EL CHACO

Asunción

Cataratas de Iguazú
Foz do Iguaçu

Paraná R.

Rosario

Buenos Aires

ARGENTINA

ANDES

PATAGONIA

Punta Arenas

Tierra del
Fuego

Cape Horn

Río de Janeiro

Horizonte

São Paulo

Curitiba

Florianópolis

Porto Alegre

Uruguay R.

URUGUAY

Punta de Este

Montevideo

Río de la Plata

Mar del
Plata

N

1000 miles

1500 km

0

0

Stanley

Falkland Islands
(UK)

South Georgia
(UK)

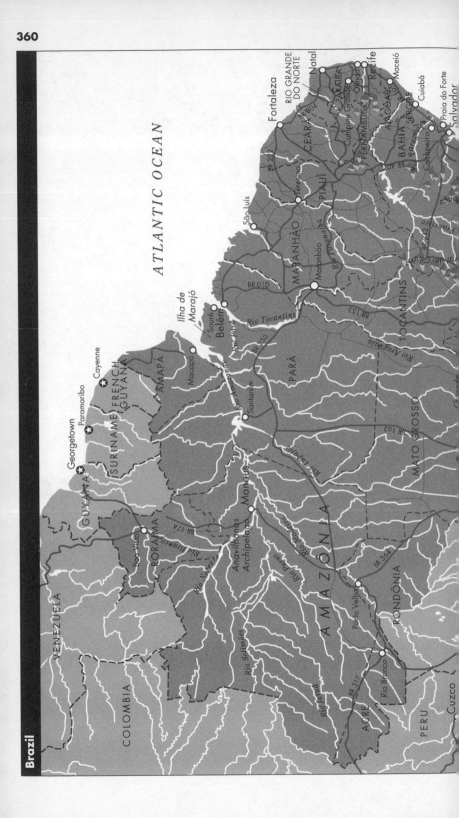

ATLANTIC OCEAN

VENEZUELA

COLOMBIA

Georgetown

Paramaribo

Cayenne

GUYANA

SURINAME

FRENCH GUYANA

Boa Vista

RORAIMA

Rio Branco

Rio Negro

A M A Z Ô N I A

Rio Solimões

Rio Juruá

Rio Purus

ACRE

Rio Branco

BR 317

PERU

Cuzco

Anavilhanas Archipelago

Manaus

BR 174

Rio Madeira

Porto Velho

RONDÔNIA

BR 364

Macapá

AMAPÁ

Ilha de Marajó

Souré

Belém

Rio Pará

Santarém

Rio Amazonas

BR 230

PARÁ

Rio Tapajós

Rio Xingu

Rio Araguaia

MATO GROSSO

BR 163

São Luís

BR 010

Rio Tocantins

TOCANTINS

BR 153

Teresina

PIAUÍ

MARANHÃO

Rio Tutuiuçu

Maranhão

Rio Parnaíba

Fortaleza

CEARÁ

RIO GRANDE DO NORTE

Natal

PARAÍBA

Campina Grande

Recife

Olinda

PERNAMBUCO

Maceió

ALAGOAS

SERGIPE

BAHIA

Cuiabá

Praia do Forte

Salvador

Cachoeira

Rio São Francisco

BR 242

BR 101

Rio Grande

BR 407

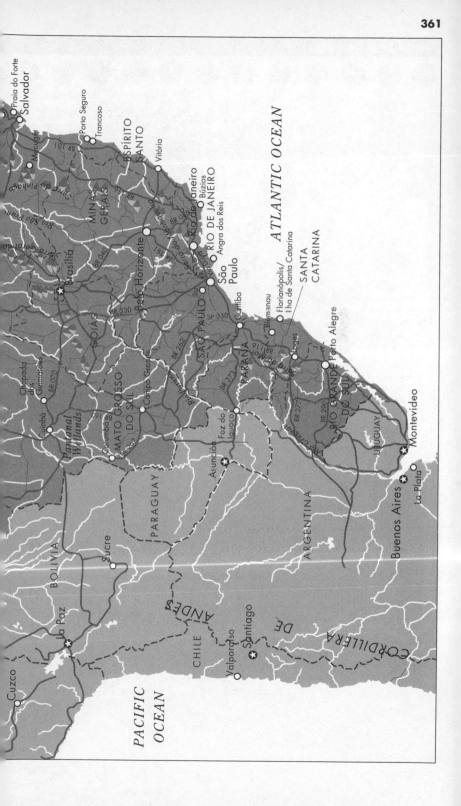

World Time Zones

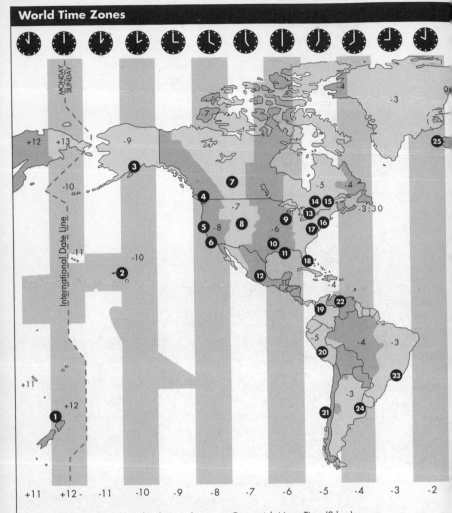

Numbers below vertical bands relate each zone to Greenwich Mean Time (0 hrs.).
Local times frequently differ from these general indications,
as indicated by light-face numbers on map.

Algiers, **29**	Berlin, **34**	Delhi, **48**	Jerusalem, **42**
Anchorage, **3**	Bogotá, **19**	Denver, **8**	Johannesburg, **44**
Athens, **41**	Budapest, **37**	Dublin, **26**	Lima, **20**
Auckland, **1**	Buenos Aires, **24**	Edmonton, **7**	Lisbon, **28**
Baghdad, **46**	Caracas, **22**	Hong Kong, **56**	London
Bangkok, **50**	Chicago, **9**	Honolulu, **2**	(Greenwich), **27**
Beijing, **54**	Copenhagen, **33**	Istanbul, **40**	Los Angeles, **6**
	Dallas, **10**	Jakarta, **53**	Madrid, **38**
			Manila, **57**

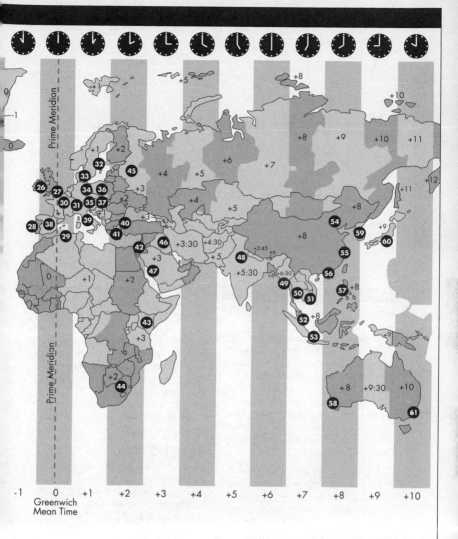

ESSENTIAL INFORMATION

ADDRESSES

In Portuguese *avenida* (avenue) and *travessa* (lane) are abbreviated (as *Av.* and *Trv.* or *Tr.*), while other common terms such as *estrada* (highway) and *rua* (street) often aren't. Street numbers follow the names; postal codes are widely used. In some places street numbering doesn't enjoy the wide popularity it has achieved elsewhere; hence, you may find the notation "s/n," meaning "no street number."

AIR TRAVEL

Atlanta, Chicago, Houston, Los Angeles, Miami, Newark, New York, and Toronto are the major gateways for flights to Brazil from the United States and Canada. Several airlines fly directly from London, but there's no direct service from Australia or New Zealand. The two biggest Brazilian gateways are Rio de Janeiro and São Paulo. For details on airports in these and other Brazilian cities, *see* chapter A to Z sections.

There's regular jet service between all the country's major cities and most medium-size cities. Remote areas are also accessible—as long as you don't mind small planes. Flights can be long, lasting several hours on trips to the Amazon, with stops en route. The most widely used service is the Ponte Aérea (Air Bridge), the Rio–São Paulo shuttle, which departs every half hour from 6 AM to 10:30 PM (service switches to every 15 minutes during morning and evening rush hours). Plane tickets (one-way) for the Rio–São Paulo shuttle service cost R$50–R$190 ($23–$88); reservations aren't necessary.

AIRPORT TRANSFERS

Getting to and from the airport may not be the most pleasant aspect of your Brazilian journey. Subway transit to the airports is nearly non-existent, and bus service, while often cheap, can require a serious time commitment. Taxi fares to city centers vary from the reasonable to a steep R$50–R$76 ($23–$35). To ensure your city destination is understood, write it down on a piece of paper and present it to bus or taxi drivers, most of whom don't speak English.

BOOKING YOUR FLIGHT

When you book, **look for nonstop flights** and **remember that "direct" flights stop at least once.** Try to avoid connecting flights, which require a change of plane. Within a country as big as Brazil, it's especially important to plan your itinerary with care. Book as far in advance as possible, particularly for weekend travel. Planes tend to fill up on Friday, especially to or from Brasília or Manaus. For more booking tips and to check prices and make on-line flight reservations, log on to www.fodors.com.

CARRIERS

Major U.S. carriers serving Brazil include American Airlines (which flies nonstop from New York and Miami to Rio and São Paulo), Continental Airlines (nonstop from Houston to São Paulo and then on to Rio and nonstop from Newark to Rio and São Paulo), and United Airlines (nonstop from Chicago, New York, and Miami to São Paulo and from Miami to Rio). Delta offers nonstop service from Atlanta to São Paulo; some of Delta's Atlanta–Rio flights are nonstop. Air Canada has nonstop service between Toronto and São Paulo six days a week. This carrier is a Star Alliance partner with Varig (a Brazil-based airline) and United.

From London's Heathrow Airport you can take American or United and fly to Brazil via Miami or New York. Varig has nonstop flights from Heathrow to São Paulo with continuing service to Rio. British Airways has nonstop service from both Heathrow and Gatwick Airports to Rio and São Paulo. Continental flies from Gatwick and Heathrow to Newark and Houston with connecting flights to Rio and São Paulo.

From Sydney, Australia, you can fly to Los Angeles, then continue to Brazil on Varig. Another option is to fly Qantas to Buenos Aires, Argentina, where you connect to either Varig or Transbrasil. From Buenos Aires, Varig flies to São Paulo, Rio, Porto Alegre, Florianópolis, Salvador, and Brasília; while Transbrasil flies to São Paulo, its hub, and on to most other Brazilian destinations. Air New Zealand offers flights to major Brazilian cities through its partnership with Varig. Direct flights to Los Angeles— where you transfer to Varig—depart from Auckland once or twice a day.

TAM, Transbrasil, and Varig are Brazil-based international carriers. TAM, which has an agreement with American Airlines that allows passengers to accumulate AA miles and awards, flies nonstop from Miami to São Paulo, with continuing service to Rio and connections to other cities. TAM also offers nonstop service between Miami and Manaus. Transbrasil offers daily service from Orlando via Miami from which it continues nonstop to São Paulo. From there, you can catch connecting flights on Transbrasil to virtually all major Brazilian cities. Its regional carrier, Interbrasil, flies to smaller but growing cities in the southeast. Transbrasil code-shares with Delta Airlines

Varig, Latin America's largest carrier, has service to Rio and São Paulo from Los Angeles, Miami, and New York. Varig also serves Manaus, Recife, Fortaleza, and Belém from Miami. From São Paulo, you can connect to Varig flights throughout Brazil.

➤ BRAZILIAN CARRIERS: **TAM** (☎ 888/235–9826 in the U.S. or 305/406–2826 in Miami). **Transbrasil** (☎ 800/872–3153 in the U.S.). **Varig** (☎ 800/468–2744 in the U.S.).

➤ NORTH AMERICAN CARRIERS: **Air Canada** (☎ 888/247–2262 in North America). **American Airlines** (☎ 800/433–7300 in North America). **Continental Airlines** (☎ 800/231–0856 in North America). **Delta Airlines** (☎ 800/241–4141 in North America). **United Airlines** (☎ 800/241–6522 in North America).

➤ FROM AUSTRALIA AND NEW ZEALAND: **Air New Zealand** (☎ 13–24–76 in Australia; 0800/737–000 in New Zealand). **Qantas** (☎ 13–13–13 in Australia; 357–8900 in Auckland; 0800/808–767 rest of New Zealand).

➤ FROM THE U.K.: **American Airlines** (☎ 0845/778–9789). **British Airways** (☎ 0845/773–3377). **Continental Airlines** (☎ 0800/776–464). **TAM Airlines** (☎ 0207/707–4586. **United Airlines** (☎ 0845/844–4777). **Varig** (☎ 0207/478–2114).

CHECK-IN & BOARDING

Assuming that not everyone with a ticket will show up, airlines routinely overbook planes. When everyone does, airlines ask for volunteers to give up their seats. In return, these volunteers usually get a certificate for a free flight and are rebooked on the next flight out. If there are not enough volunteers, the airline must choose who will be denied boarding. The first to get bumped are passengers who checked in late and those flying on discounted tickets, so **get to the gate and check in as early as possible,** especially during peak periods.

Always **bring a government-issued photo ID to the airport.** You may be asked to show it before you're allowed to check in. **Be prepared to show your passport when leaving Brazil and to pay a hefty departure tax,** which runs about R$78 ($36) for international flights. A departure tax also applies to flights within Brazil. Although the amount varies, figure on R$11–R$22 ($5–$10). Although some airports accept credit cards as payment for departure taxes, it's wise to **have the appropriate amount in reais.**

CUTTING COSTS

The least expensive airfares to Brazil must usually be purchased in advance and are nonrefundable. It's smart to **call a number of airlines, and when you are quoted a good price, book it on the spot**—the same fare may not be available the next day. Always **check different routings** and look into using different airports. Travel agents, especially low-fare specialists (☞ Discounts & Deals, *below*), are helpful.

Consolidators are another good source. They buy tickets for scheduled international flights at reduced rates from the airlines, then sell them at prices that beat the best fare available directly from the airlines, usually without restrictions. Sometimes you can even get your money back if you need to return the ticket. Carefully read the fine print detailing penalties for changes and cancellations, and **confirm your consolidator reservation with the airline.**

When you **fly as a courier,** you trade your checked-luggage space for a ticket deeply subsidized by a courier service. There are restrictions on when you can book and how long you can stay. The International Association of Air Travel Couriers (IAATC) has trips from New York, Miami, Los Angeles, San Francisco, Washington, D.C., Chicago, Auckland, London, and Toronto to destinations around the world, including Rio de Janeiro and São Paulo. The company sends information via e-mail and posts a list of available flights twice daily on its Web site, which also has tons of information about courier travel. There's a $45 annual membership fee. Air Facility has trips to Rio de Janeiro and São Paulo from New York.

Look into discount passes. If you plan to travel a lot within Brazil, buy an air pass from TAM, Transbrasil, or Varig before you leave home (these can only be purchased outside Brazil). Such passes can save you hundreds of dollars. Varig's Brazil AirPass costs $530 for five coupons, which are valid for 21 days on flights to more than 100 cities within Brazil on Varig or its affiliates, Rio-Sul or Nordeste. You can buy up to four additional coupons (for a total of nine) for $100 each. TAM's 21-day Brazilian AirPass also runs $530 for five coupons, with additional coupons at $100 each. Transbrasil's domestic pass comes in four versions. Airpass I offers unlimited coupons for travel anywhere in Brazil at a cost of $590 or $540, depending on the season (high season runs June 26–August 5 and December 14–January 10). Airpass II runs $490 or $440 for up to five coupons valid anywhere in the country.

Airpass III, at $350 or $300, is good for travel in Brazil's southern states, and Airpass IV, at $290 or $250, is valid for flights in the northeastern states. With Airpass I and II, you also can fly to Buenos Aires, Argentina, for an additional $80.

If you plan to visit more than one of the Mercosur (southern common market) countries—Argentina, Brazil, Paraguay, and Uruguay—the Mercosur Pass presents the greatest savings. It's valid on Aerolineas Argentinas, Transbrasil, Varig, and several other carriers. You must visit at least two countries within a minimum of seven days and a maximum of 30 days. Pricing is based on mileage.

Eight versions of the pass are offered, ranging from $225 for flights totaling between 1,450 and 2,300 km (1,200 and 1,900 mi) to $870 for flights totaling more than 8,450 km (7,000 mi). Contact participating airlines or tour operators and travel agents who specialize in South American travel for information and purchase.

➤ CONSOLIDATORS: **Cheap Tickets** (☎ 800/377–1000). **Discount Airline Ticket Service** (☎ 800/576–1600). **Unitravel** (☎ 800/325–2222). **Up & Away Travel** (☎ 212/889–2345). **World Travel Network** (☎ 800/409–6753).

➤ COURIER SERVICES: **Air Facility** (☎ 718/712–1769 in New York or 305/418–2035 in Miami, ᴡᴇʙ www.airfacility.com). **IAATC** (☎ 561/582—8320, ᴡᴇʙ www.courier.org).

ENJOYING THE FLIGHT

For more legroom, **request an emergency-aisle seat.** Don't sit in the row in front of the emergency aisle or in front of a bulkhead, where seats may not recline. If you have dietary concerns, **ask for special meals when booking.** These can be vegetarian, low-cholesterol, or kosher, for example. On long flights, try to maintain a normal routine to help fight jet lag. At night, **get some sleep.** By day, **eat light meals, drink water** (not alcohol), and **move around the cabin** to stretch your legs. For additional jet-lag tips consult *Fodor's FYI: Travel Fit & Healthy* (available at bookstores everywhere).

Travel between the Americas is a bit less wearing than to Europe or Asia because there's far less jet lag. (Rio is three hours behind Greenwich mean time: if it's 5 PM in London, it's noon in New York, and it's 2 PM in Rio; Manaus is an hour behind Rio.) Flights to Rio de Janeiro generally depart after dark; you're in luck if you sleep well while flying. Southbound, the best views are usually out windows on the left side of the plane.

FLYING TIMES

The flying time from New York is 8½ hours to Rio, 9½ hours to São Paulo. From Miami, it's seven hours to Rio, eight hours to São Paulo. Most flights from Los Angeles go through Miami, so add five hours to the Miami times given; direct flights to São Paulo from Los Angeles take about 13 hours. From London, it's seven hours to São Paulo.

Within Brazil, it's one hour from Rio to São Paulo or Belo Horizonte, 1½ hours from Rio to Brasília, two hours from Rio to Salvador, and 2½ hours from Rio to Belém or Curitiba. From São Paulo it's four hours to Manaus and 1½ hours to Iguaçu Falls.

HOW TO COMPLAIN

If your baggage goes astray or your flight goes awry, complain right away. Most carriers require that you **file a claim immediately.**

➤ AIRLINE COMPLAINTS: U.S. Department of Transportation **Aviation Consumer Protection Division** (✉ C-75, Room 4107, Washington, DC 20590, ☎ 202/366-2220, WEB www.dot.gov/airconsumer). **Federal Aviation Administration Consumer Hotline** (☎ 800/322-7873).

RECONFIRMING

Always **reconfirm your flights,** even if you have a ticket and a reservation. This is particularly true for travel within Brazil and throughout South America, where flights tend to operate at full capacity—usually with passengers who have a great deal of baggage to process before departure.

BIKE TRAVEL

Riding a bike will put you face to face with the people and landscapes of Brazil. However, the oft-rugged terrain and varying road conditions pose considerable challenges. **Consider a mountain bike,** because basic touring bikes are too fragile for off-road treks.

In Brazil, bike maps are nonexistent, and there are few rental shops. The establishments that do exist are usually in major cities and offer only short-term (an hour or two) rentals. If you're a hard-core cyclist, **bring your own bike and gear or sign up for a bike trip through a tour operator.** Many operators within South America offer trips—sometimes including equipment rental—that range in length from a half-day to several days.

Always remember to **lock your bike when you make stops.** Although some cities, such as Rio, have places that are perfect for a bike ride, in general, **avoid riding in congested urban areas,** where it's difficult (and dangerous) enough getting around by car let alone by bike.

BIKES IN FLIGHT

Most airlines accommodate bikes as luggage, provided they are dismantled and boxed. Airlines sell bike boxes, which are often free at bike shops, for about $5 (it's at least $100 for bike bags). International travelers can sometimes substitute a bike for a piece of checked luggage at no charge; otherwise, the cost is about $100. Domestic and Canadian airlines charge $25–$50.

BUS TRAVEL

The nation's *ônibus* (bus) network is affordable, comprehensive, and efficient—compensating for the lack of trains and the high cost of air travel. Every major city can be reached by bus as can most small-to medium-size communities.

Lengthy bus trips anywhere will involve travel over some bad highways, an unfortunate fact of life in Brazil today. Trips to northern, northeastern, and central Brazil tend to be especially trying; the best paved highways are in the south and southeast, so trips to and within this region may go more smoothly. When traveling by bus, **bring water, toilet paper, and an additional top layer of clothing** (the latter will come in handy if it gets cold, or it can serve as a pillow). Travel light, dress comfortably, and **keep a close watch on your belongings**—especially in bus stations.

CLASSES

Various classes of service are offered, with each increase in price buying plusher seats and more leg room (if you're over 5'10", buy the most expensive ticket available and try for front-row seats).

Buses used for long trips are modern and comfortable (bathrooms and air-conditioning are common amenities), and they stop regularly at reasonably clean roadside cafés. Sleeper buses have fewer seats, permitting the seats to recline more. Note that regular buses used for shorter hauls may be labeled AR CONDICIONADO (AIR-CONDITIONED) but often are not.

CUTTING COSTS

Bus fares are substantially cheaper than in North America or Europe. Between Rio and São Paulo (6½–7 hours), for example, a bus departs every ½ hour and costs about R$33–R$43 ($15–$20); a night sleeper will run about R$61–R$87 ($30–$40). Sometimes competing companies serve the same routes, so it can pay to shop around.

PAYING AND RESERVATIONS

Tickets are sold at bus-company offices and at city bus terminals. Note that larger cities may have different terminals for buses to different destinations, and some small towns may not have a terminal at all (you're picked up and dropped off at the line's office, invariably in a central location). **Expect to pay with cash,** as credit cards aren't accepted everywhere. Note that reservations or advance-ticket purchases generally aren't necessary except for trips to resort areas during high season—particularly on weekends—or during major holidays (Christmas, Carnaval, etc.) and school-break periods. In general, **arrive at bus stations early, particularly for peak-season travel.**

BUSINESS HOURS

BANKS & OFFICES

Banks are, with a few exceptions, open weekdays 10–4. Office hours are generally 9–5.

GAS STATIONS

Within cities and along major highways, many gas stations are open 24 hours a day, seven days a week. In smaller towns, they may only be open during daylight hours Monday–Saturday.

MUSEUMS

Many museums are open from 10 or 11 to 5 or 6 (they may stay open later one night a week). Some museums, however, are open only in the afternoon, and many are closed on Monday. Always check ahead.

SHOPS

Generally, small shops are open weekdays from 9 to 6 and on Saturday from 9 to 1 or 2. Centers and malls are often open from 10 to 10. Some centers, malls, and pharmacies are open on Sunday.

CAMERAS & PHOTOGRAPHY

Brazil, with its majestic landscapes and varied cityscapes, is a photographer's dream. Brazilians seem amenable to having picture-taking visitors in their midst, but you should always **ask permission before taking pictures in churches or of individuals.** If you're bashful about approaching strangers, **photograph people with whom you interact**: your waiter, your desk clerk, the vendor selling you crafts. Even better, have a traveling companion or a passerby photograph you *with* them.

To avoid the blurriness caused shaky hands, **buy a minitripod**—they're available in sizes as small as 6 inches. **Get a small beanbag to support your camera on uneven surfaces.** If you plan to take photos on some of the country's many beaches, **bring a skylight (81B or 81C) or polarizing filter** to minimize haze and light problems. If you're visiting the Amazon or Pantanal, **bring high-speed film** to compensate for low light under the tree canopy and **invest in a telephoto lens** to photograph wildlife; standard zoom lenses in the 35–88 range won't capture enough detail.

Casual photographers should **consider using inexpensive disposable cameras** to reduce the risks inherent in traveling with sophisticated equipment. One-use cameras with panoramic or underwater functions are also nice supplements to a standard camera and its gear.

The *Kodak Guide to Shooting Great Travel Pictures* (available at bookstores everywhere) is loaded with tips.

➤ PHOTO HELP: **Kodak Information Center** (☎ 800/242–2424).

EQUIPMENT PRECAUTIONS

Don't pack film and equipment in checked luggage, where it's much more susceptible to damage. X-ray machines used to view checked luggage are becoming much more powerful and therefore are much more likely to ruin your film. Always **ask for hand inspection of film,** which becomes clouded after successive exposures to airport X-ray machines, and **keep videotapes away from metal detectors. Carry an extra supply of batteries,** and **be prepared to turn on your camera or camcorder** to prove to security personnel that the device is real.

Always **keep your film and tape out of the sun** and on jungle trips **keep your equipment in resealable plastic bags** to protect it from dampness. As petty crime is a problem throughout Brazil, particularly in the cities, **keep a close eye on your gear.**

FILM

Bring your own film. It's expensive in Brazil and is frequently stored in hot conditions. Plan on shooting a minimum of one 36-exposure roll per week of travel. If you don't want the hassle of keeping a shot log, **make a quick note whenever you start a new roll**—it will make identifying your photos much easier when you get home.

VIDEOS

The system used in Brazil is PAL-M. The average price of a blank VHS tape is R$4 ($2) for 60 minutes and R$6.50 ($3) for 120 minutes. A DV tape (60 minutes) costs about R$43 ($20). Tapes, batteries, cables, and other equipment are readily available in electronics shops, convenience stores, gas stations, newsstands, and even some street-side stalls.

CAR RENTAL

Driving in cities is chaotic at best, mortally dangerous at worst; in the countryside, the usually rough roads, lack of clearly marked signs, and language difference are discouraging. Further, the cost of renting can be steep. All that said, certain areas are most enjoyable when explored on your own in a car: the beach areas of Búzios and the Costa Verde (near Rio) and the Belo Horizonte region; the North Shore beaches outside São Paulo; and many of the inland and coastal towns of the south, a region with many good roads.

Always **give the rental car a once-over** to make sure the headlights, jack, and tires (including the spare) are in working condition.

➤ MAJOR AGENCIES: **Alamo** (☎ 800/ 522–9696; 020/8759–6200 in the U.K.). **Avis** (☎ 800/331–1084; 800/ 879–2847 in Canada; 02/9353–9000 in Australia; 09/525 1982 in New Zealand; 0870/606–0100 in the U.K.). **Budget** (☎ 800/527–0700; 0870/607– 5000 in the U.K., through affiliate Europcar). **Dollar** (☎ 800/800–6000; 0124/622–0111 in the U.K.; 02/9223– 1444 in Australia). **Hertz** (☎ 800/ 654–3001; 800/263–0600 in Canada; 020/8897–2072 in the U.K.; 02/9669– 2444 in Australia; 09/256–8690 in New Zealand). **National Car Rental** (☎ 800/227–7368; 020/8680–4800 in the U.K., where it is known as National Europe).

CUTTING COSTS

Fly/drive packages are rare in Brazil. To make arrangements before you leave home, **book through a travel agent who will shop around.** Although international car-rental agencies have better service and maintenance track records than local firms (they also provide better breakdown assistance), your best bet at getting a good rate is to **rent on arrival, particularly from local companies.** Only reserve ahead (and check that a confirmed reservation guarantees you a car) if you plan to rent during a holiday period. (For details on local agencies, *see* chapter A to Z sections.)

Consider hiring a car and driver through your hotel concierge, or make a deal with a taxi driver for extended sightseeing at a long-term rate. Often drivers charge a set hourly rate, regardless of the distance traveled. You'll have to pay cash, but you may actually spend less than you would for a rental car.

Do **look into wholesalers,** companies that do not own fleets but rent in bulk from those that do and often offer better rates than traditional car-rental operations. Payment must be made before you leave home.

➤ WHOLESALER: **Kemwel Holiday Autos** (☎ 800/678–0678, 𝖥𝖠𝖷 914/825–3160, 𝖶𝖤𝖡 www.kemwel.com).

INSURANCE

When driving a rented car you are generally responsible for any damage to or loss of the vehicle as well as for any property damage or personal injury that you may cause. Before you rent, see what coverage your personal auto-insurance policy and credit cards provide.

REQUIREMENTS & RESTRICTIONS

In Brazil, the minimum driving age is 18. Your own driver's license is acceptable—sort of. An international driver's license, available from automobile associations, is a *really* good idea. If you do plan to drive in Brazil, find out in advance from a car rental agency what type of proof of insurance you need to carry.

SURCHARGES

Before you pick up a car in one city and leave it in another, **ask about drop-off charges or one-way service fees,** which can be substantial. Note, too, that some rental agencies charge extra if you return the car before the time specified in your contract. To avoid a hefty refueling fee, **fill the tank just before you turn in the car,** but be aware that gas stations near the rental outlet may overcharge.

CAR TRAVEL

Brazil has more than 1.65 million km (1.02 million mi) of highway, about ¹/₁₀ of it paved. Recent developments and construction are improving the situation, but independent land travel in Brazil definitely has its liabilities. In addition, Brazilian drivers are, to say the least, daredevils. For these reasons, you may find it easier to rely on taxis and buses for short distances and on planes for longer journeys.

Some common-sense rules of the road: before you set out, **establish an itinerary** and **ask about gas stations.** Be sure to **plan your daily driving distance conservatively** and **don't drive after dark.** Always **obey speed limits and traffic regulations.**

EMERGENCY SERVICES

The Automóvel Clube do Brasil (Automobile Club of Brazil) provides emergency assistance to foreign motorists in cities and on highways, but only if they're members of an automobile club in their own nation.

➤ CONTACT: **Automóvel Clube do Brasil** (✉ Rua do Passeio 90, Rio de Janeiro ☎ 021/2240–4060 or 021/2240–4191).

GASOLINE

Gasoline in Brazil costs around R$1.90 (88¢) a liter. Unleaded gas, called *especial,* costs about the same. Brazil also has an extensive fleet of ethanol-powered cars. Ethanol fuel is sold at all gas stations and is priced a little less than gasoline. However, such cars get lower mileage, so they offer little advantage over gas-powered cars. Stations are plentiful both within cities and on major highways, and many are open 24 hours a day. In smaller towns, few stations take credit cards, and their hours are more limited.

PARKING

Finding a space in most cities—particularly Rio, São Paulo, Belo Horizonte, and Salvador—is a major task. It's best to **head for a garage or a lot** and leave your car with the attendant. Should you find a space on the street, you'll probably have to pay a fee. There are no meters; instead, there's a system involving coupons that allow you to park for a certain time period (usually two hours) and that you post in your car's window. You can buy them from uniformed street-parking attendants or at newsstands.

No-parking zones are marked by a crossed-out capital letter *E* (which means *estacionamento,* the Portuguese word for "parking"). These zones are, more often than not, filled with cars, which are rarely bothered by the police.

ROAD CONDITIONS

Brazil's federal highways were built between 1964 and 1976, and maintenance on them was nearly nonexistent in the 1980s. The country's highway department estimates that 40% of the federal highways (including those with either the designation *BR* or a state abbreviation such as *RJ* or *SP*), which constitute 70% of Brazil's total road system, are in a dangerous state of disrepair. Evidence of this is everywhere: potholes, lack of signage, inadequate shoulders. Landslides and flooding after heavy rains are frequent and at times shut down entire stretches of key highways. Increasing traffic adds to the system's woes, as does the fact that neither speed limits nor basic rules of safety seem to figure in the national psyche. The worst offenders are bus and truck drivers. For these reasons, if you drive, do so with the utmost caution.

ROAD MAPS

Quatro Rodas offers atlases, books, and maps of different sizes for states, regions, and cities. It is *the* name for maps of Brazil. If you're a beach aficionado, look for this company's four-color book of topographical maps of all the nation's beaches.

RULES OF THE ROAD

Brazilians drive on the right, and in general, traffic laws are the same as those in the United States. The use of seat belts is mandatory. The national speed limit is 80 kph (48 mph) but is seldom observed. In theory, foreign driver's licenses are acceptable. In practice, however, police (particularly highway police) have been known to claim that driving with a foreign license is a violation in order to shake down drivers for bribes. It's best to **get an international driver's license,** which is seldom challenged. If you do get a ticket for some sort of violation—real or imagined—don't argue. And plan to spend longer than you want settling it.

CHILDREN IN BRAZIL

Brazilians love children, and having yours along may prove to be your ticket to meeting locals. Children are welcomed in hotels and restaurants, especially on weekends, when Brazilian families go out for brunch or lunch in droves.

Large hotels often offer a range of supervised activities—picnics, movies, classes, contests—for children of all ages. Brazil is a country of a great cultural diversity, so try to **attend one of the many festivals** held all over the country throughout the year. These often feature music and dance performances that transcend language barriers and will acquaint children with Brazilian folklore. Older kids and teenagers may well be captivated by Brazil's plants and animals. **Take a guided tour of an urban park or a trek into a national preserve.** Such expeditions are a safe, easy way to experience nature.

Let older children join in on planning as you outline your trip. **Scout your library for picture books, story books, and maps about places you'll be going.** Try to **explain the concept of foreign language**; some kids, who may have just learned to talk, are thrown when they can't understand strangers and strangers can't understand them. On sightseeing days try to **schedule activities of special interest to your children.** If you are renting a car, don't forget to **arrange for a car seat** when you reserve. For general advice about traveling with children, check out *Fodor's FYI: Travel with Your Baby* (available in bookstores everywhere).

FLYING

If your children are two or older, **ask about children's airfares.** As a general rule, infants under two not occupying a seat fly at greatly reduced fares or even for free. When booking, **confirm carry-on allowances** if you're traveling with infants. In general, for babies charged 10% of the adult fare you are allowed one carry-on bag and a collapsible stroller; if the flight is full, the stroller may have to be checked or you may be limited to less.

Experts agree that it's a good idea to use safety seats aloft for children weighing less than 40 pounds. Airlines set their own policies: U.S. carriers usually require that the child be ticketed, even if he or she is young enough to ride free, since the seats must be strapped into regular seats.

Do **check your airline's policy about using safety seats during takeoff and landing.** And since safety seats are not allowed everywhere in the plane, get your seat assignments early.

When reserving, **request children's meals or a freestanding bassinet** if you need them. But note that bulkhead seats, where you must sit to use the bassinet, may lack an overhead bin or storage space on the floor.

LODGING

Many hotels in Brazil allow children under a certain age to stay in their parents' room at no extra charge. Others charge for them as extra adults; be sure to **find out the cutoff age for children's discounts.**

PRECAUTIONS

Any person under the age of 18 who isn't traveling with both parents or legal guardian(s) must provide a notarized letter of consent signed by the nonaccompanying parent or guardian. The notarized letter must be authenticated by the Brazilian embassy or consulate and translated into Portuguese.

Children must have all their inoculations up to date (those between the ages of three months and six years must have an international polio vaccination certificate) before leaving home. **Make sure that health precautions, such as what to drink and eat, are applied to the whole family.** Not cramming too much into each day will also keep everyone healthier while on the road.

SIGHTS & ATTRACTIONS

Places that are especially appealing to children are indicated by a rubber-duckie icon (🦆) in the margin.

SUPPLIES & EQUIPMENT

Pack things to keep your children busy while traveling. For children of reading age, **bring books from home;** locally, literature for kids in English is hard to find. Inexpensive art supplies such as crayons (*giz de cera*), paint (*tinta*), and coloring books (*livros de pintar*) are sold in stationery stores, bookstores, newsstands, and some supermarkets and street stalls.

You'll find international brands of baby formula (*leite nan*) and diapers (*fraldas*) in drugstores, supermarkets, and convenience shops. The average cost of a 450-gram (16-ounce) container of formula is R$9 ($4). The average price for a package of diapers is R$9 ($4).

COMPUTERS ON THE ROAD

If you're traveling with a laptop, carry a spare battery, a universal adapter plug, and a converter if your computer isn't dual voltage. **Ask about electrical surges** before plugging in your computer. **Keep your disks out of the sun** and **avoid excessive heat for both your computer and disks.** In Brazil, carrying a laptop computer signals wealth and could make you a target for thieves; **conceal your laptop in a generic bag, and keep it close to you at all times.**

Internet access is surprisingly widespread. In addition to business centers in luxury hotels and full-fledged cybercafés, look for computers set up in telephone offices. Rates range from R$6.50 ($3) to R$22 ($10) an hour. Dial-up speeds are variable, though they tend toward the sluggish.

CONCIERGES

Concierges, found in many urban hotels, can help you with theater tickets and dinner reservations. A good one with connections—which are always key in Brazil—may be able to get you seats for a hot show or a table at the restaurant of the moment. You can also turn to your concierge for help with travel arrangements, sightseeing plans, services ranging from aromatherapy to zipper repair, and emergencies. **Always tip** a concierge who has been of assistance.

CONSUMER PROTECTION

Whenever shopping or buying travel services in Brazil, **pay with a major credit card,** if possible, so you can cancel payment or get reimbursed if there's a problem. If you're doing business with a particular company for the first time, **contact your local Better Business Bureau and the attorney general's offices** in your state and (for U.S. businesses) the company's home state as well. Have any complaints been filed? Finally, if you're buying a package or tour, always **consider travel insurance** that includes default coverage (☞ Insurance, *below*).

➤ BBBs: **Council of Better Business Bureaus** (✉ 4200 Wilson Blvd., Suite 800, Arlington, VA 22203, ☎ 703/276–0100, FAX 703/525–8277, WEB www.bbb.org).

CRUISE TRAVEL

Cruise itineraries to Brazil change from ship to ship, from line to line (or tour operator to tour operator), and from year to year, so contact a travel agent or a cruise company to get the most recent information. Popular Brazilian ports of call include Belém, Fortaleza, Manaus, Recife, Rio, Salvador, and Vitória. The following examples suggest the wide range of cruises that include or feature Brazil.

The tour operator Abercrombie & Kent typically offers several cruises along the Amazon that last from 11 to 18 days; longer trips begin in Belém and end in Iquitos, Peru. Among the South American itineraries scheduled by Clipper Cruise Lines is a 13-day Colonial Brazil program, which calls at Rio, Búzios, Vitória, Pôrto Seguro, Salvador, Recife, Natal, Arquipélago de Fernando de Noronha, and Fortaleza. Recent itineraries from Crystal Cruises have included 16-day voyages from Fort Lauderdale to Buenos Aires, with Fortaleza, Salvador, and Rio among the ports of call, and from Buenos Aires to Manaus, with visits to Rio, Fortaleza, Santarém, and Parintins.

If time (and money) are no object, consider one of the 69-day voyages that have been offered by Fred. Olsen Cruises. These have begun in in Southampton, England, with calls in Portugal and Senegal before reaching South America at Recife, Brazil. Following calls at Salvador and Rio, the vessel has continued around South America, visiting various ports in Argentina, the Falkland Islands, Chile, Peru, Ecuador, and Colombia, before continuing to Jamaica, Cuba, the Turks and Caicos Islands, Bermuda, and the Azores en route back to Southampton. A transit of the Panama Canal and a visit to Panama's San Blas Islands have also been featured.

Lindblad Expeditions typically offers cruises to Brazil and other parts of South America. A 15-day sailing by this operator has included Salvador, Ilhéus, the Abrolhos Archipelago, Vitória, Rio, Paratí, Paranaguá, and Curitiba as well as Montevideo, Uruguay, and Buenos Aires, Argentina.

To learn how to plan, choose, and book a cruise-ship voyage, check out Cruise How-To's on www.fodors.com and consult *Fodor's FYI: Plan & Enjoy Your Cruise* (available in bookstores everywhere).

➤ CRUISE LINES: **Abercrombie & Kent** (☎ 800/323–7308). **Amazon Tours and Cruises** (☎ 800/423–2791). **Clipper Cruise Line** (☎ 800/325–0010). **Celebrity Cruises** (☎ 800/437–4111). **Crystal Cruises** (☎ 800/446–6620). **Cunard** (☎ 800/5–CUNARD). **Fred. Olsen Cruises** (☎ 800/661 1119). **Holland America Line** (☎ 800/426–0327). **Lindblad Expeditions** (☎ 800/397–3348). **Orient Lines** (☎ 800/333–7300). **Radisson Seven Seas Cruises** (☎ 800/285–1835). **Royal Olympic Cruises** (☎ 800/872–6400). **Seabourne Cruise Lines** (☎ 800/929–9595). **Silversea Cruises** (☎ 800/722–9955).

CUSTOMS & DUTIES

When shopping, **keep receipts** for all purchases. Upon reentering the country, **be ready to show customs officials what you've bought.** If you feel a duty is incorrect or object to the way your clearance was handled, note the inspector's badge number and ask to see a supervisor. If the problem isn't resolved, write to the appropriate authorities, beginning with the port director at your point of entry.

IN BRAZIL

Formerly strict import controls have been substantially liberalized as part of the Brazilian government's efforts to open up the nation's economy. In addition to personal items, you're now permitted to bring in, duty-free, up to R$1,085 ($500) worth of gifts purchased abroad, including up to 2 liters of liquor. If you plan to bring in plants, you may do so only with documentation authenticated by the consular service.

IN AUSTRALIA

Australian residents who are 18 or older may bring home $A400 worth of souvenirs and gifts (including jewelry), 250 cigarettes or 250 grams of tobacco, and 1,125 ml of alcohol (including wine, beer, and spirits). Residents under 18 may bring back $A200 worth of goods. Prohibited items include meat products. Seeds, plants, and fruits need to be declared upon arrival.

➤ INFORMATION: **Australian Customs Service** (Regional Director, ✉ Box 8, Sydney, NSW 2001, Australia, ☎ 02/9213–2000, FAX 02/9213–4000, WEB www.customs.gov.au).

IN CANADA

Canadian residents who have been out of Canada for at least seven days may bring home C$500 worth of goods duty-free. If you've been away fewer than seven days but more than 48 hours, the duty-free allowance drops to C$200; if your trip lasts 24–48 hours, the allowance is C$50. You may not pool allowances with family members. Goods claimed under the C$500 exemption may follow you by mail; those claimed under the lesser exemptions must accompany you. Alcohol and tobacco products may be included in the seven-day and 48-hour exemptions but not in the 24-hour exemption. If you meet the age requirements of the province or territory through which you reenter Canada, you may bring in, duty-free, 1.14 liters (40 imperial ounces) of wine or liquor *or* 24 12-ounce cans or bottles of beer or ale. If you are 16 or older you may bring in, duty-free, 200 cigarettes and 50 cigars. Check ahead of time with Revenue Canada or the Department of Agriculture for policies regarding meat products, seeds, plants, and fruits.

You may send an unlimited number of gifts worth up to C$60 each duty-free to Canada. Label the package UNSOLICITED GIFT—VALUE UNDER $60. Alcohol and tobacco are excluded.

➤ INFORMATION: **Revenue Canada** (✉ 2265 St. Laurent Blvd. S, Ottawa, Ontario K1G 4K3, Canada, ☎ 613/993–0534; 800/461–9999 in Canada, FAX 613/991–4126, WEB www.ccra-adrc.gc.ca).

IN NEW ZEALAND

Homeward-bound residents 17 or older may bring back $700 worth of souvenirs and gifts. Your duty-free allowance also includes 4.5 liters of wine or beer; one 1,125-ml bottle of spirits; and either 200 cigarettes, 250 grams of tobacco, 50 cigars, or a combination of the three up to 250 grams. Prohibited items include meat products, seeds, plants, and fruits.

➤ INFORMATION: **New Zealand Customs** (Custom House, ✉ 50 Anzac Ave., Box 29, Auckland, New Zealand, ☎ 09/300–5399, FAX 09/359–6730), WEB www.customs.govt.nz.

IN THE U.K.

From countries outside the EU, including Brazil, you may bring home, duty-free, 200 cigarettes or 50 cigars; 1 liter of spirits or 2 liters of fortified or sparkling wine or liqueurs; 2 liters of still table wine; 60 ml of perfume; 250 ml of toilet water; plus £136 worth of other goods, including gifts and souvenirs. If returning from outside the EU, prohibited items include meat products, seeds, plants, and fruits.

➤ INFORMATION: **HM Customs and Excise** (✉ St. Christopher House, Southwark, London, SE1 OTE, U.K., ☎ 020/7928–3344, ☎ 020/7202–4227, WEB www.hmce.gov.uk).

IN THE U.S.

U.S. residents who have been out of the country for at least 48 hours (and who have not used the $400 allowance or any part of it in the past 30 days) may bring home $400 worth of foreign goods duty-free.

U.S. residents 21 and older may bring back 1 liter of alcohol duty-free. In addition, regardless of your age, you are allowed 200 cigarettes and 100 non-Cuban cigars. Antiques, which the U.S. Customs Service defines as objects more than 100 years old, enter duty-free, as do original works of art done entirely by hand, including paintings, drawings, and sculptures.

You may also mail or ship packages home duty-free: up to $200 worth of goods for personal use, with a limit of one parcel per addressee per day (except alcohol or tobacco products or perfume worth more than $5); label the package PERSONAL USE and attach a list of its contents and their retail value. Do not label the package UNSOLICITED GIFT or your duty-free exemption will drop to $100. Mailed items do not affect your duty-free allowance on your return.

➤ INFORMATION: **U.S. Customs Service** (✉ 1300 Pennsylvania Ave. NW, Washington, DC 20229, WEB www. customs.gov; inquiries ☎ 202/354–1000; complaints c/o ✉ 1300 Pennsylvania Ave. NW, Room 5.4D, Washington, DC 20229; registration of equipment c/o ✉ Resource Management, ☎ 202/927–0540).

DINING

Eating is a national passion, and portions are huge. In many restaurants, plates are prepared for two people; when you order, ask if one plate will suffice. The restaurants (all of which are indicated by an ✕) that we list are the cream of the crop in each price category. Properties indicated by an ✕☒ are lodging establishments whose restaurant warrants a special trip. Price categories are as follows:

CATEGORY	COST*
$$$$	over R$40
$$$	R$30–$40
$$	R$20–R$30
$	R$10–R$20
¢	under R$10

*per person for a dinner entrée

MEALS & SPECIALTIES

Between the extremes of sophistication and austere simplicity, each region has its own cuisine. You'll find exotic fish dishes in the Amazon, African-spiced dishes in Bahia, and well-seasoned bean mashes in the mining country of Minas Gerais. In major cities, the variety of eateries is staggering: restaurants of all sizes and categories, snack bars, and fast-food outlets line downtown streets and fight for space in shopping malls. In São Paulo, for example, Italian eateries—whose risottos rival those of Bologna—sit beside Pan-Asian restaurants, which, like the chicest spots in North America and Europe, serve everything from Thai *satay* to sushi to Vietnamese summer rolls. In addition, there's excellent Portuguese, Chinese, Japanese, Arab, Hungarian, and Spanish cuisine. Outside the cities you'll find primarily typical, low-cost Brazilian meals that consist simply of *feijão preto* (black beans) and *arroz* (rice) served with beef, chicken, or fish. Manioc, a root vegetable that's used in a variety of ways, and beef are adored everywhere. Note that Brazilians eat few vegetables, and these often must be ordered separately.

Many Brazilian dishes are adaptations of Portuguese specialties. Fish stews called *caldeiradas* and beef stews called *cozidos* (a wide variety of vegetables boiled with different cuts of beef and pork) are popular, as is *bacalhau*, salt cod cooked in sauce or grilled. *Salgados* (literally, "salteds") are appetizers or snacks served in sit-down restaurants as well as at stand-up *lanchonetes* (luncheonettes). Dried salted meats form the basis of many dishes from the interior and northeast of Brazil, and pork is used heavily in dishes from Minas Gerais. The national dish of Brazil is *feijoada* (a stew of black beans, sausage, pork, and beef), which is often served with arroz, shredded kale, orange slices, and manioc flour or meal—called *farofa* if it's coarsely ground, *farinha* if finely ground—that has been fried with onions, oil, and egg.

One of the most avid national passions is the *churrascaria*, where meats are roasted on spits over an open fire, usually *rodízio* style. Rodízio means "going around," and waiters circulate nonstop carrying skewers laden with charbroiled hunks of beef, pork, and chicken, which are sliced onto your plate with ritualistic ardor. For a set price you get all the meat and side dishes you can eat.

The mainstay of *comida mineira* (the cuisine of Minas) is *tutu*, a tasty mash of black beans, bacon, and manioc meal served with meat dishes. Another bracing favorite is *feijão tropeiro,* a combination of brown beans, bacon, and manioc meal. Among meat dishes, pork is the most common, in particular the famed *lingüiça* (Minas pork sausage) and *lombo* (pork tenderloin). The most typical chicken dish is *frango ao molho pardo,* broiled chicken served in a sauce made with its own blood. The region's very mild white cheese is known throughout Brazil simply as *queijo do Minas* (cheese from Minas).

Seafood is the thing in Bahia, in great variety and quantity, prepared either Bahian style or using more traditional Continental recipes. A happy mix of African and local ingredients has been passed down through the centuries, first from the hands and hearts of slave women and then from maids working in Bahian kitchens.

The basic raw materials are coconut milk, lemon, coriander, tomato, *dendê* (palm oil), onions, dried shrimp, salt, and hot chili peppers. The ubiquitous *moqueca*, which has all these ingredients plus the seafood catch of the day, is cooked quickly in a clay pot over a high flame. Other main dishes include *vatapá*, a fish purée made of bread, ginger, peanuts, cashews, and olive oil; *caruru*, okra mashed with ginger, dried shrimp, and palm oil; *ximxim de galinha*, chicken with peanuts and coconut; and *efo*, a bitter chicorylike vegetable cooked with dried shrimp. Most restaurants serve hot pepper sauce on the side, as well as farofa or farinha, which do a delicious job of soaking up sauces. (Note that palm oil is high in saturated fat and hard to digest; you can order these dishes without it. And most Bahian restaurants are happy to prepare simpler fish or shrimp dishes even if they're not on the menu.)

Brazilian *doces* (desserts), particularly those of Bahia, are very sweet, and many are descendants of the egg-based custards and puddings of Portugal and France. *Cocada* is shredded coconut caked with sugar; *quindim* is a small tart made from egg yolks and coconut; *doce de banana* (or any other fruit) is banana cooked in sugar; ambrosia is a lumpy milk-and-sugar pudding.

Coffee is served black and strong with sugar in demitasse cups and is called *cafezinho*. (Note that requests for *descafeinado* [decaf] will be met with a firm shake of the head "no," a blank stare, or outright amusement—it's just not a Brazilian thing.) Coffee is taken with milk—called *café com leite*—only at breakfast. Bottled mineral water is sold in two forms: with and without bubbles (*com gas* and *sem gas*, respectively).

MEALTIMES

You'll be hard-pressed to find breakfast outside a hotel restaurant. At lunch and dinner, portions are large. Often a single dish will easily feed two people; no one will be the least surprised if you order one entrée and two plates. In addition, some restaurants automatically bring a *couberto* (an appetizer course of such items as bread, cheese or pâté, olives, quail eggs, and the like). You'll be charged extra for this, and you're perfectly within your rights to send it back if you don't want it.

Mealtimes vary according to locale. In Rio and São Paulo, lunch and dinner are served later than in the United States. In restaurants, lunch usually starts around 1 and can last until 3. Dinner is always eaten after 8 and, in many cases, not until 10. In Minas Gerais, the northeast, and smaller towns in general, dinner and lunch are taken at roughly the same time as in the States.

PAYING

Credit cards are widely accepted at restaurants in the major cities. In the countryside, all but the smallest establishments generally accept credit cards as well.

RESERVATIONS & DRESS

Reservations are always a good idea: we mention them only when they're essential or not accepted. Book as far ahead as you can, and reconfirm as soon as you arrive. We mention dress only when men are required to wear a jacket or a jacket and tie.

WINE, BEER, & SPIRITS

The national drink is the *caipirinha*, made of crushed lime, sugar, and *pinga* or *cachaça* (sugarcane liquor). When whipped with crushed ice, fruit juices, and condensed milk, the pinga/cachaça becomes a *batida*. A *caipivodka*, or *caipiroska*, is the same cocktail with vodka instead of cachaça. Some bars make both drinks using a fruit other than lime, such as kiwi and *maracujá* (passion fruit). Brazil's best bottled beer is Cerpa, sold at most restaurants. In general, though, Brazilians prefer tap beer, called *chopp*, which is sold by all bars and some restaurants. Be sure to try the carbonated soft drink *guaraná*, made using the Amazonian fruit of the same name.

DISABILITIES & ACCESSIBILITY

Although international chain hotels in large cities have some suitable rooms and facilities and it's easy to hire private cars and drivers for excursions, Brazil isn't very well equipped to handle travelers with disabilities. There are few ramps and curb cuts, and it takes effort and planning to negotiate cobbled city streets, get around museums and other buildings, and explore the countryside.

City centers such as Rio de Janeiro are your best bets; indeed, some areas on the south side of Rio *do* have ramps and wide sidewalks with even surfaces. Legislation concerning people with disabilities has been approved but has yet to be enforced. There's no central clearinghouse for information on this topic, so the best local resource is the staff at your hotel.

RESERVATIONS

When discussing accessibility with an operator or reservations agent, **ask hard questions.** Are there any stairs, inside *or* out? Are there grab bars next to the toilet *and* in the shower/tub? How wide is the doorway to the room? To the bathroom? For the most extensive facilities meeting the latest legal specifications, **opt for newer accommodations.**

TRANSPORTATION

➤ COMPLAINTS: **Aviation Consumer Protection Division** (☞ Air Travel, *above*) for airline-related problems. **Civil Rights Office** (✉ U.S. Department of Transportation, Departmental Office of Civil Rights, S-30, 400 7th St. SW, Room 10215, Washington, DC 20590, ☎ 202/366–4648, FAX 202/366–9371, WEB www.dot.gov/ost/docr/index.htm) for problems with surface transportation. **Disability Rights Section** (✉ U.S. Department of Justice, Civil Rights Division, Box 66738, Washington, DC 20035-6738, ☎ 202/514–0301 or 800/514–0301; 202/514–0383 TTY; 800/514–0383 TTY, FAX 202/307–1198, WEB www.usdoj.gov/crt/ada/adahom1.htm) for general complaints.

TRAVEL AGENCIES

In the United States, the Americans with Disabilities Act requires that travel firms serve the needs of all travelers. Some agencies specialize in working with people with disabilities.

➤ TRAVELERS WITH MOBILITY PROBLEMS: **Access Adventures** (✉ 206 Chestnut Ridge Rd., Scottsville, NY 14624, ☎ 716/889–9096, dltravel@prodigy.net), run by a former physical-rehabilitation counselor. **CareVacations** (✉ 5-5110 50th Ave., Leduc, Alberta T9E 6V4, Canada, ☎ 780/986–6404 or 877/478–7827, FAX 780/986–8332, WEB www.carevacations.com), for group tours and cruise vacations. **Flying Wheels Travel** (✉ 143 W. Bridge St., Box 382, Owatonna, MN 55060, ☎ 507/451–5005 or 800/535–6790, FAX 507/451–1685, WEB www.flyingwheelstravel.com).

DISCOUNTS & DEALS

Be a smart shopper and **compare all your options** before making decisions. A plane ticket bought with a promotional coupon from travel clubs, coupon books, and direct-mail offers or on the Internet may not be cheaper than the least expensive fare from a discount ticket agency. And always keep in mind that what you get is just as important as what you save.

DISCOUNT RESERVATIONS

To save money, **look into discount reservations services** with toll-free numbers, which use their buying power to get a better price on hotels, airline tickets, even car rentals. When booking a room, always **call the hotel's local toll-free number** (if one is available) rather than the central reservations number—you'll often get a better price. Always ask about special packages or corporate rates.

When shopping for the best deal on hotels and car rentals, **look for guaranteed exchange rates,** which protect you against a falling dollar. With your rate locked in, you won't pay more, even if the price goes up in the local currency.

➤ AIRLINE TICKETS: ☎ **800/AIR–4LESS.**

➤ HOTEL ROOMS: **Players Express Vacations** (☎ 800/458–6161, WEB www.playersexpress.com). **Steigenberger Reservation Service** (☎ 800/223–5652, WEB www.srs-worldhotels.com).

Travel Interlink (☎ 800/888–5898, WEB www.travelinterlink.com). Turbotrip.com (☎ 800/473–7829, WEB www.turbotrip.com).

PACKAGE DEALS

Don't confuse packages and guided tours. When you buy a package, you travel on your own, just as though you had planned the trip yourself. Fly/drive packages, which combine airfare and car rental, are often a good deal. In cities, ask the local visitors' bureau about hotel packages that include tickets to major museum exhibits or other special events.

ECOTOURISM

Ecotourism is an ever more popular form of travel. Some ecotour operators are more trustworthy than others, however. Those recommended in this guide are good bets. You can also contact the Brazilian Institute of Ecotourism (Instituto Brasileiro de Ecoturismo, or IEB), a highly respected organization that's dedicated to preserving Brazil's natural resources while promoting tourism. Staffers there should have information about special-interest tours.

➤ INFORMATION: IEB (✉ Rua Minerva 156, Bairro Perdizes, São Paulo, ☎ 011/3672–7571).

ELECTRICITY

The current in Brazil isn't regulated: in São Paulo and Rio, it's 110 or 120 volts, 60 cycles alternating current (the same as in the United States and Canada); in Recife and Brasília it's 220 volts (the same as in Europe); and in Manaus and Salvador, it's 127 volts. **Bring a converter.**

Wall outlets take Continental-type plugs, with two round prongs. **Consider buying a universal adapter;** the the Swiss Army knife of adapters, a universal has several types of plugs in one handy unit. If your appliances are dual-voltage (as many laptops are), you'll need only an adapter. Don't use 110-volt outlets, marked FOR SHAVERS ONLY, for high-wattage appliances such as blow-dryers.

EMBASSIES & CONSULATES

➤ IN AUSTRALIA: Brazilian Embassy (✉ Box 1540, Canberra, ACT 2601, ☎ 616/273–2372).

➤ IN BRAZIL: American Embassy (✉ Lote 3, Unit 3500, Av. das Nações, 70403-900, Brasília, DF, ☎ 061/321–7272), Australian Embassy (✉ SES, Quadra 9 Conjunto 16, Casa 1, 70469-900, Brasília, DF, ☎ 061/248–5569), British Embassy (✉ SES, Av. das Nações, Quadra 801, Loto 8, Conjunto K, 70408-900, Brasília, DF, ☎ 061/225–2710), Canadian Embassy (✉ SES, Av. das Nações, Quadra 803, Lote 16, 70410-900, Brasília, DF, ☎ 061/321–2171), New Zealand Consulate-General (✉ Rua Paes de Araújo, 29-6 Andar, Conjunto 85, 04531-090, São Paulo, SP, ☎ 011/82–5532).

➤ IN CANADA: Brazilian Embassy (✉ 450 Wilbrod St., Ottawa, Ontario, K1N 6M8, ☎ 613/237–1090).

➤ IN THE U.K.: Brazilian Embassy (✉ 32 Green St., London, W1K 4AT, ☎ 020/7629–6909).

➤ IN THE U.S: Brazilian Embassy (✉ 3006 Massachusetts Ave. NW, Washington, DC 20008, ☎ 202/238–2700 or 202/238–2800 to cultural section).

ENGLISH-LANGUAGE MEDIA

Outside the programs on cable TV in large chain hotels, you'll be hard-pressed to find anything in English. In movie theaters, some British and American films are shown in English with Portuguese subtitles. In major cities, large newsstands and bookstores sell most American and a few British publications—albeit at prices much higher than you would pay at home. Some bookstores also carry English-language books.

ETIQUETTE & BEHAVIOR

Although Brazil is a predominately Catholic country, in many places there's an anything-goes outlook. As a rule, coastal areas (particularly Rio and parts of the northeast) are considerably less conservative than inland areas and those throughout the south. People dress nicely to enter churches, and hats are frowned upon during mass.

Whether they tend toward the conservative or the risqué, Brazilians are a very friendly lot. Don't be afraid to smile in the streets, ask for directions, or strike up a conversation with a local (be aware, however, that a Brazilian may give you false directions before admitting that he or she doesn't know where to point you). The slower pace of life in much of the country reflects an unwavering appreciation of family and friendship (as well as a respect for the heat); knowing this will help you understand why things may take a little longer to get done.

Throughout the country, use the thumbs-up gesture to indicate that something is OK. The gesture created by making a circle with your thumb and index finger and holding your other fingers up in the air has a very rude meaning.

GAY & LESBIAN TRAVEL

Brazil is South America's most popular destination for gay and lesbian travelers, and major cities such as Rio de Janeiro, São Paulo, and Salvador have numerous gay bars, organizations, and publications. Realize, however, that the acceptance of same-sex couples in the major cities may be limited to more touristy areas. Outside these destinations use discretion about public displays of affection.

The great Carnaval celebrations include many gay parades. At the end of the year, Mix Brasil International Festival of Sexual Diversity takes place in São Paulo, Rio de Janeiro and Porto Alegre.

➤ GAY- & LESBIAN-FRIENDLY TRAVEL AGENCIES: **Different Roads Travel** (✉ 8383 Wilshire Blvd., Suite 902, Beverly Hills, CA 90211, ☎ 323/651-5557 or 800/429-8747, FAX 323/651-3678, lgernert@tzell.com). **Kennedy Travel** (✉ 314 Jericho Turnpike, Floral Park, NY 11001, ☎ 516/352-4888 or 800/237-7433, FAX 516/354-8849, WEB www.kennedytravel.com). **Now Voyager** (✉ 4406 18th St., San Francisco, CA 94114, ☎ 415/626-1169 or 800/255-6951, FAX 415/626-8626, WEB www.nowvoyager.com). **Skylink Travel and Tour** (✉ 1006 Mendocino Ave., Santa Rosa, CA 95401, ☎ 707/546-9888 or 800/225-5759, FAX 707/546-9891, WEB www.skylinktravel.com), serving lesbian travelers.

HEALTH

DIVERS' ALERT

Don't fly within 24 hours of scuba diving. Neophyte divers should have a complete physical exam before undertaking a dive. If you have travel insurance that covers evacuations, **make sure your policy applies to scuba-related injuries,** as not all companies provide this coverage.

FOOD & DRINK

If you've just two weeks, you don't want to waste a minute stuck in your hotel room battling Montezuma's revenge, so **watch what you eat and drink**—on and off the beaten path. **Drink only bottled water** or water that has been boiled for at least 20 minutes. Stay away from ice, uncooked food, and unpasteurized milk and milk products. Peel or thoroughly wash fresh fruits and vegetables.

MEDICAL PLANS

No one plans to get sick while traveling, but it happens, so **consider signing up with a medical-assistance company.** Members get doctor referrals, emergency evacuation or repatriation, hot lines for medical consultation, cash for emergencies, and other assistance.

➤ MEDICAL-ASSISTANCE COMPANIES: **International SOS Assistance** (WEB www.internationalsos.com; ✉ 8 Neshaminy Interplex, Suite 207, Trevose, PA 19053, ☎ 215/245-4707 or 800/523-6586, FAX 215/244-9617; ✉ 12 Chemin Riantbosson, 1217 Meyrin 1, Geneva, Switzerland, ☎ 4122/785-6464, FAX 4122/785-6424; ✉ 331 N. Bridge Rd., 17-00, Odeon Towers, Singapore 188720, ☎ 65/338-7800, FAX 65/338-7611).

OVER-THE-COUNTER REMEDIES

Mild cases of diarrhea may respond to Imodium (known generically as loperamide) or Pepto-Bismol (not as strong), both of which can be purchased over the counter. Drink plenty of purified water or *chá* (tea)—*camomila* (chamomile) is a good folk remedy. In severe cases, rehydrate yourself with a salt–sugar solution: ½ teaspoon *sal* (salt) and 4 tablespoons *açúcar* (sugar) per quart of *agua* (water). The word for aspirin is *aspirinha*; Tylenol is pronounced *tee-luh-nawl*.

PESTS & OTHER HAZARDS

Bichos de pé, parasites found in areas where pigs, chickens, and dogs run free, embed themselves in humans' feet. To avoid these parasites, never walk barefoot in areas where animals are loose.

Sunshine, limes, and skin don't mix well. The oil in lime-skin juice, if left on human skin and exposed to the sun, will burn and scar. If you're using lime and will be exposed to a lot of sun, be sure to wash well with soap and water. Should spots appear on skin areas that have been exposed, pharmacies will know which creams work best to heal the burns. (Note that affected areas shouldn't be exposed to the sun for three months following the burn.)

Heatstroke and heat prostration are common though easily preventable maladies. The symptoms for either can vary but always start with headaches, nausea, and dizziness. If ignored, these symptoms can worsen until you require medical attention. In hot weather be sure to rehydrate regularly, wear loose, lightweight clothing, and avoid overexerting yourself.

Aside from the obvious safe-sex precautions, keep in mind that Brazil's blood supply isn't subject to the same intense screening as it is in North America, western Europe, Australia, or New Zealand. If you need a transfusion and circumstances permit it, ask that the blood be screened. Insulin-dependent diabetics or those who require injections should pack enough of the appropriate supplies—syringes, needles, disinfectants—to last the trip. In addition, you might want to resist the temptation to get a new tattoo or body piercing while you're in Brazil.

SHOTS & MEDICATIONS

All travelers should have up-to-date tetanus boosters, and a hepatitis A inoculation can prevent one of the most common intestinal infections. If you're heading to tropical regions, you should get yellow fever shots, particularly if you're traveling over-land from a country where yellow fever has been prevalent, such as Peru or Bolivia. Children must have current inoculations against measles, mumps, rubella, and polio.

According to the Centers for Disease Control (CDC) there's a limited risk of contracting cholera, typhoid, malaria, hepatitis B, dengue, and chagas. Although a few of these can be contracted anywhere in the country, most cases occur in jungle areas. If you plan to visit remote regions or stay for more than six weeks, **check with the CDC's International Travelers' Hot Line.**

In areas with malaria and dengue, which are both carried by mosquitoes, take mosquito nets, wear clothing that covers the body, apply repellent containing DEET, and use a spray against flying insects in living and sleeping areas.

The hot line recommends chloroquine (analen) as an antimalarial agent. (Note that in parts of northern Brazil, a particularly aggressive strain of malaria has become resistant to chloroquine and may be treated with mefloquine (also known by its trade name Lariam), an expensive alternative that can also have some rather unpleasant side effects—from headaches, nausea, and dizziness to psychosis, convulsions, and hallucinations.)

Dengue has become an increasing problem in the Amazon and Pantanal regions. Unlike malaria, it's primarily a concern in urban areas and is spread by mosquitoes that are more active during the day than at night. No vaccine exists against dengue.

➤ HEALTH WARNINGS: **National Centers for Disease Control and Prevention** (CDC; National Center for Infectious Diseases, Division of Quarantine, Traveler's Health Section, ✉ 1600 Clifton Rd. NE, M/S E-03, Atlanta, GA 30333, ☎ 888/232–3228 or 800/311–3435, FAX 888/232–3299, WEB www.cdc.gov).

HOLIDAYS

Major national holidays include: New Year's Day (Jan. 1); Epiphany (Jan. 6); Carnaval, the week preceding Ash Wednesday (which falls on Feb. 13 in 2002 and Mar. 5 in 2003); Good

Friday (Mar. 29, 2002; Apr. 18, 2003); Easter (Mar. 31, 2002; Apr. 20, 2003); Tiradentes Day (Apr. 21); Labor Day (May 1); Corpus Christi (May 30, 2002; June 9, 2003); Independence Day (Sept. 7); Our Lady of Aparecida Day (Oct. 12); All Souls' Day (Nov. 1); Declaration of the Republic Day (Nov. 15); Christmas (Dec. 25).

INSURANCE

The most useful travel-insurance plan is a comprehensive policy that includes coverage for trip cancellation and interruption, default, trip delay, and medical expenses (with a waiver for pre-existing conditions).

Without insurance you will lose all or most of your money if you cancel your trip, regardless of the reason. Default insurance covers you if your tour operator, airline, or cruise line goes out of business. Trip-delay covers expenses that arise because of bad weather or mechanical delays. Study the fine print when comparing policies.

If you're traveling internationally, a key component of travel insurance is coverage for medical bills incurred if you get sick on the road. Such expenses are not generally covered by Medicare or private policies. U.K. residents can buy a travel-insurance policy valid for most vacations taken during the year in which it's purchased (but check pre-existing-condition coverage). British and Australian citizens need extra medical coverage when traveling overseas.

Always **buy travel policies directly from the insurance company**; if you buy them from a cruise line, airline, or tour operator that goes out of business you probably will not be covered for the agency or operator's default, a major risk. Before making any purchase, **review your existing health and home-owner's policies** to find what they cover away from home.

➤ TRAVEL INSURERS: In the U.S.: **Access America** (✉ 6600 W. Broad St., Richmond, VA 23230, ☎ 804/285–3300 or 800/284–8300, FAX 804/673–1586, WEB www.previewtravel.com). **Travel Guard International** (✉ 1145 Clark St., Stevens Point, WI 54481, ☎ 715/345–0505 or 800/826–1300, FAX 800/955–8785, WEB www.travelguard.com).

➤ INSURANCE INFORMATION: In the U.K.: **Association of British Insurers** (✉ 51–55 Gresham St., London EC2V 7HQ, U.K., ☎ 020/7600–3333, FAX 020/7696–8999, WEB www.abi.org.uk). In Canada: **Voyager Insurance** (✉ 44 Peel Center Dr., Brampton, Ontario L6T 4M8, Canada, ☎ 905/791–8700, 800/668–4342 in Canada). In Australia: **Insurance Council of Australia** (✉ Level 3, 56 Pitt St., Sydney NSW 2000, ☎ 03/9614–1077, FAX 03/9614–7924). In New Zealand: **Insurance Council of New Zealand** (✉ Level 7, 111–115 Customhouse Quay, Box 474, Wellington, New Zealand, ☎ 04/472–5230, FAX 04/473–3011, WEB www.icnz.org.nz).

LANGUAGE

The language in Brazil is Portuguese, not Spanish, and Brazilians will appreciate it if you know the difference. The two languages are distinct, but common origins mean that many words are similar, and fluent speakers of Spanish will be able to make themselves understood. English is spoken among educated Brazilians and, in general, by at least some of the staff at hotels, tour operators, and travel agencies. Store clerks and waiters may have a smattering of English; taxi and bus drivers won't. As in many places throughout the world, you're more likely to find English-speaking locals in major cities than in small towns or the countryside. (Note that in the northeast you may even have difficulty in the cities.)

LODGING

When you consider your lodgings in Brazil, add these three terms to your vocabulary: *pousada* (inn), *fazenda* (farm), and "flat" or "block" hotel (apartment-hotel). Flat hotels are popular with Brazilians, particularly in cities and with families and groups. Some have amenities such as pools, but for most folks, the biggest draw is affordability: with kitchen facilities and room for a group, flat hotels offer more for the money.

In the hinterlands, it's good to **look at any room before accepting it;** expense is no guarantee of charm or cleanliness, and accommodations can vary dramatically within one hotel. Also, **be sure to check the shower:** some hotels have electric-powered shower-heads rather than central water heaters. In theory, you can adjust both the water's heat and its pressure. In practice, if you want hot water you have to turn the water pressure down; if you want pressure, expect a brisk rinse. Careful! Don't adjust the power when you're under the water—you can get a little shock.

If you ask for a double room, you'll get a room for two people, but you're not guaranteed a double mattress. If you'd like to avoid twin beds, **ask for a cama de casal** ("couple's bed"; no wedding ring seems to be required).

The lodgings (all indicated with a 🏨) that we list are the cream of the crop in each price category. We always list the facilities that are available—but we don't specify whether they cost extra: when pricing accommodations, always ask what's included. All hotels listed have private bath unless otherwise noted. Properties indicated by ✕🏨 are lodging establishments whose restaurant warrants a special trip.

Assume that hotels operate on the European Plan (**EP,** with no meals) unless we specify that they're all-inclusive (including all meals and most activities) or use the Breakfast Plan (**BP,** with a full breakfast daily), Continental Plan (**CP,** with a Continental breakfast daily), Full American Plan (**FAP,** with all meals), or Modified American Plan (**MAP,** with breakfast and dinner daily). Price categories are as follows:

CATEGORY	COST*
$$$$	over R$400
$$$	R$300–R$400
$$	R$200–R$300
$	R$100–R$200
¢	under R$100

for a double room in high season, excluding taxes

APARTMENT & VILLA RENTALS

If you want a home base that's roomy enough for a family and comes with cooking facilities, **consider a furnished rental.** These can save you money, especially if you're traveling with a group. Home-exchange directories sometimes list rentals as well as exchanges.

➤ INTERNATIONAL AGENTS: **Hide-aways International** (✉ 767 Islington St., Portsmouth, NH 03801, ☎ 603/430–4433 or 800/843–4433, FAX 603/430–4444, WEB www.hideaways.com; membership $129). **Villas International** (✉ 950 Northgate Dr., Suite 206, San Rafael, CA 94903, ☎ 415/499–9490 or 800/221–2260, FAX 415/499–9491, WEB www.villasintl.com).

CAMPING

There are campgrounds all over the country, and some are well situated in areas such as the beach resort of Búzios in Rio de Janeiro State and the beautiful mesa of Chapada dos Guimarães in Mato Grosso State. Those with basic facilities (running water and electricity) cost as little as R$11 ($5) a day per person. Some campgrounds also have picnic areas, kitchen and laundry facilities, recycling bins, playgrounds, soccer fields, and courts for volleyball and/or basketball.

Although it isn't illegal to camp outside campgrounds, you should inquire with locals for additional information and permission. Note that most conservation areas have restricted access, and some natural preserves forbid camping altogether.

HOSTELS

No matter what your age, you can **save on lodging costs by staying at hostels.** There are about 100 hostels scattered across Brazil, all of them affiliated with Hostelling International (HI). Many Brazilian hostels' names are preceded by the letters *AJ* (Albergues de Juventude). The Federação Brasileira dos Albergues de Juventude (FBJA; Brazilian Federation of Youth Hostels) is based in Rio.

Membership in any HI national hostel association, open to travelers of all ages, allows you to stay in HI-affiliated hostels at member rates; one-year membership is about $25 for adults (C$26.75 in Canada, £9.30 in the U.K., $30 in Australia, and $30 in New Zealand); hostels run about $10–$25 per night. Members have priority if the hostel is full; they're also eligible for discounts around the world, even on rail and bus travel in some countries.

➤ ORGANIZATIONS: **Federação Brasileira dos Albergues de Juventude** (✉ Rua da Assembleia 10, Sala 1211, Centro, Rio De Janeiro, RJ 20011, ☎ 021/2531–2234 or 021/2531–1302). **Hostelling International—American Youth Hostels** (✉ 733 15th St. NW, Suite 840, Washington, DC 20005, ☎ 202/783–6161, FAX 202/783–6171, WEB www.hiayh.org). **Hostelling International—Canada** (✉ 400–205 Catherine St., Ottawa, Ontario K2P 1C3, Canada, ☎ 613/237–7884; 800/663–5777 in Canada, FAX 613/237–7868, WEB www.hostellingintl.ca). **Youth Hostel Association of England and Wales** (✉ Trevelyan House, 8 St. Stephen's Hill, St. Albans, Hertfordshire AL1 2DY, U.K., ☎ 0870/8708808, FAX 01727/844126, WEB www.yha.org.uk). **Youth Hostel Association Australia** (✉ 10 Mallett St., Camperdown, NSW 2050, Australia, ☎ 02/9565–1699, FAX 02/9565–1325, WEB www.yha.com.au). **Youth Hostels Association of New Zealand** (✉ Box 436, Christchurch, New Zealand, ☎ 03/379–9970, FAX 03/365–4476, WEB www.yha.org.nz).

HOTELS

Hotels listed with EMBRATUR, Brazil's national tourist board, are rated using stars. Note, however, that the number of stars awarded appears to be based strictly on the number of amenities, without taking into account intangibles such as service and atmosphere.

Carnaval (Carnival), the year's principal festival, occurs during the four days preceding Ash Wednesday. For top hotels in Rio, Salvador, and Recife—the three leading Carnaval cities—you must make reservations a year in advance. Hotel rates rise 20% on average for Carnaval. Not as well known outside Brazil but equally impressive is Rio's New Year's Eve celebration. More than a million people gather along Copacabana Beach for a massive fireworks display and to honor the sea goddess Iemanjá. To ensure a room, book at least six months in advance.

Hotels accept credit cards for payment, but first ask if there's a discount for cash. Try to bargain hard for a cash-on-the-barrel discount, then pay in local currency.

➤ TOLL-FREE NUMBERS: **Best Western** (☎ 800/528–1234, WEB www.bestwestern.com). **Choice** (☎ 800/221–2222, WEB www.hotelchoice.com). **Clarion** (☎ 800/252–7466, WEB www.clarionhotel.com). **Comfort** (☎ 800/228–5150, WEB www.comfortinn.com). **Forte** (☎ 800/225–5843, WEB www.forte-hotels.com). **Hilton** (☎ 800/445–8667, WEB www.hilton.com). **Holiday Inn** (☎ 800/465–4329, WEB www.basshotels.com). **Inter-Continental** (☎ 800/327–0200, WEB www.interconti.com). **Le Meridien** (☎ 800/543–4300, WEB www.lemeridien-hotels.com). **Sheraton** (☎ 800/325–3535, WEB www.starwoodhotels.com).

MAIL & SHIPPING

Post offices are called *correios,* and branches are marked by the name and a logo that looks something like two interlocked fingers; most are open weekdays 8–5 and Saturday until noon. Mailboxes are small yellow boxes marked CORREIOS that sit atop metal pedestals on street corners. Airmail from Brazil takes at least 10 or more days to reach the United States, possibly longer to Canada and the United Kingdom, definitely longer to Australia and New Zealand.

OVERNIGHT SERVICES

Brazil has both national and international express mail service, the price of which varies according to the weight of the package and the destination. International express mail companies operating out of Brazil include Federal Express and DHL.

POSTAL RATES

An airmail letter from Brazil to the United States and most parts of Europe, including the United Kingdom, costs about R$2.16 ($1). Aerograms and postcards cost the same.

RECEIVING MAIL

Mail can be addressed to "poste restante" and sent to any major post office. The address must include the code for that particular branch. American Express will hold mail for its cardholders.

MONEY MATTERS

Prices throughout this guide are given for adults. Substantially reduced fees are almost always available for children, students, and senior citizens. For information on taxes, *see* Taxes, *below.*

Top hotels in Rio and São Paulo go for more than R$430 ($200) a night, and meals can—but do not have to—cost as much. Outside Brazil's two largest cities and Brasília, prices for food and lodging tend to drop considerably. Self-service salad bars where you pay by weight (per kilo, about 2.2 pounds) are inexpensive alternatives everywhere, though be sure to choose carefully among them. Taxis can be pricey. City buses, subways, and long-distance buses are all inexpensive; plane fares aren't.

ATMS

Nearly all the nation's major banks have automated teller machines. MasterCard and Cirrus are rarely accepted (some airport Banco Itaú ATMs are linked to Cirrus); Visa and Plus cards are. American Express card holders can make withdrawals at most Bradesco ATMs marked 24 HORAS. To be on the safe side, carry a variety of cards. Note also that if your PIN is more than four digits long and/or uses letters instead of numbers, it might not work; talk to your bank. Finally, for your card to function on some ATMs, you may need to hit a screen command (perhaps, *estrangeiro*) if you are a foreign client.

➤ ATM LOCATIONS: **MasterCard Cirrus** (☎ 800/424–7787). **Visa Plus** (☎ 800/843–7587).

CREDIT CARDS

In Brazil's largest cities and leading tourist centers, restaurants, hotels, and shops accept major international credit cards. Off the beaten track, you may have more difficulty using them. Many gas stations in rural Brazil don't take credit cards.

For costly items use your credit card whenever possible—you'll come out ahead, whether the exchange rate at which your purchase is calculated is the one in effect the day the vendor's bank abroad processes the charge or the one prevailing on the day the charge company's service center processes it at home.

Throughout this guide, the following abbreviations are used: **AE**, American Express; **DC**, Diners Club; **MC**, MasterCard; and **V**, Visa.

CURRENCY

Brazil's unit of currency is the real (R$; plural: *reais,* though it's sometimes seen as *reals*). One real has 100 centavos (cents). There are notes worth 1, 5, 10, 50, and 100 reais, together with coins worth 1, 5, 10, 25, and 50 centavos, and 1 real, all of which feel and look similar.

CURRENCY EXCHANGE

At press time, the real was at 3.08 to the pound sterling, 2.15 to the U.S. dollar, 1.37 to the Canadian dollar, 1.07 to the Australia dollar, and 0.89 to the New Zealand dollar.

For the most favorable rates, **change money through banks.** Although ATM transaction fees may be higher abroad than at home, ATM rates are excellent because they are based on wholesale rates offered only by major banks. You won't do as well at *casas de câmbio* (exchange houses) in airports or rail and bus stations, in hotels, in restaurants, or in stores.

To avoid lines at airport exchange booths, **get local currency before you leave home.** (Don't wait until the last minute to do this as many banks—even the international ones—don't have reais on hand and must order them for you. This can take a couple days.) Outside larger cities, changing money in Brazil becomes more of a challenge. It's best when leaving a large city for a smaller town to travel with enough cash. For an average week in a Brazilian city, a good strategy is to convert $500 into reais. This provides sufficient cash for most expenses, such as taxis and small purchases and snacks.

➤ EXCHANGE SERVICES: **International Currency Express** (☎ 888/278–6628 for orders, WEB www.foreignmoney. com). **Thomas Cook Currency Services** (☎ 800/287–7362 for telephone orders and retail locations, WEB www. us.thomascook.com).

TRAVELER'S CHECKS

Do you need traveler's checks? It depends on where you're headed. If you're going to rural areas and small towns, go with cash; traveler's checks are best used in cities. Lost or stolen checks can usually be replaced within 24 hours. To ensure a speedy refund, buy your own traveler's checks— don't let someone else pay for them: irregularities like this can cause delays. The person who bought the checks should make the call to request a refund.

Traveler's checks can be exchanged at hotels, banks, casas de câmbio, travel agencies, and shops in malls or stores that cater to tourists. Many small tradesmen are at a total loss when faced with traveler's checks. Note, however, that the rate for traveler's checks is lower than that for cash, and hotels often change them at a rate that's lower than that available at banks or casas de câmbio.

PACKING

If you're doing business in Brazil, you'll need the same attire you would wear in U.S. and European cities: for men, suits and ties; for women, suits for day wear and cocktail dresses or the like for an evening out. For sightseeing, casual clothing and good walking shoes are appropriate; most restaurants don't require very formal attire. For beach vacations, you'll need lightweight sportswear, a bathing suit, a beach cover-up, a sun hat, and really good sunscreen.

Travel in rain-forest areas will require long-sleeve shirts, long pants, socks, sneakers, a hat, a light waterproof jacket, a bathing suit, and plenty of insect repellent. Other useful items include a screw-top water container that you can fill with bottled water, a money pouch, a travel flashlight and extra batteries, a Swiss Army knife with a bottle opener, a medical kit, binoculars, a pocket calculator, and lots of extra film. A sarong or a light cotton blanket makes a handy beach towel, picnic blanket, and cushion for hard seats, among other things.

In your carry-on luggage, **pack an extra pair of eyeglasses or contact lenses and enough of any medication** you take to last the entire trip. You may also ask your doctor to write a spare prescription using the drug's generic name since brand names may vary from country to country. In luggage to be checked, **never pack prescription drugs or valuables.** To avoid customs delays, carry medications in their original packaging. And don't forget to carry with you the addresses of offices that handle refunds of lost traveler's checks. Check *Fodor's How to Pack* (available in bookstores everywhere) for more tips.

CHECKING LUGGAGE

How many carry-on bags you can bring with you is up to the airline. Most allow two, but not always, so make sure that everything you carry aboard will fit under your seat or in the overhead bin, and get to the gate early. Note that if you have a seat at the back of the plane, you'll probably board first, while the overhead bins are still empty.

If you are flying internationally, note that baggage allowances may be determined not by piece but by weight— generally 88 pounds (40 kilograms) in first class, 66 pounds (30 kilograms) in business class, and 44 pounds (20 kilograms) in economy.

Airline liability for baggage is limited to $1,250 per person on flights within the United States. On international flights it amounts to $9.07 per pound or $20 per kilogram for checked baggage (roughly $640 per 70-pound bag) and $400 per passenger for unchecked baggage. You can buy additional coverage at check-in for about $10 per $1,000 of coverage, but it excludes a rather extensive list of items, shown on your airline ticket.

Before departure, **itemize your bags' contents** and their worth, and label the bags with your name, address, and phone number. (If you use your home address, cover it so potential thieves can't see it readily.) Inside each bag, **pack a copy of your itinerary.** At check-in, **make sure that each bag is correctly tagged** with the destination airport's three-letter code. If your bags arrive damaged or fail to arrive at all, file a written report with the airline before leaving the airport.

2 copies of passport

PASSPORTS & VISAS

When traveling internationally, **carry your passport** even if you don't need one (it's always the best form of I.D.) and **make two photocopies of the data page** (one for someone at home and another for you, carried separately from your passport). If you lose your passport, promptly call the nearest embassy or consulate and the local police.

ENTERING BRAZIL

To enter Brazil, all U.S. citizens, even infants, must have both a passport and a tourist visa (valid for five years). To obtain one, you must submit the following to the Brazilian embassy or to the nearest consulate: a passport that will be valid for six months past the date of first entry to Brazil; a passport-type photo; a photocopy of your round-trip ticket or a signed letter from a travel agency with confirmed round-trip bookings or proof of your ability to pay for your stay in Brazil; and cash, a money order, or a certified check for $45 (there's also a $10 handling fee if anyone other than the applicant submits the visa).

If you're a business traveler, you may need a business visa (valid for 90 days). It has all the same requirements as a tourist visa, but you'll also need a letter on company letterhead—addressed to the embassy or consulate and signed by an authorized representative (other than you)—stating the nature of your business in Brazil, itinerary, business contacts, dates of arrival and departure, and that the company assumes all financial and moral responsibility while you're in Brazil. The fee is $105 (plus the $10 fee if someone other than you submits the visa). In addition to the forms of payment detailed above, a company check is also acceptable.

Canadian nationals, Australians, and New Zealanders also need visas to enter the country. For Canadians, the fee is US$40; for New Zealanders, US$20; and for Australians, there's no charge. Citizens of the United Kingdom don't need a visa.

In the United States there are consulates in Atlanta, Boston, Chicago, Houston, Los Angeles, Miami, New York, San Francisco, and San Juan. To get the location of the Brazilian consulate to which you must apply, contact the Brazilian embassy. Note that some consulates don't allow you to apply for a visa by mail. If you don't live near a city with a consulate, consider hiring a concierge-type service to do your legwork. Many cities have these companies, which not only help with the paperwork for such things as visas and passports but also send someone to wait in line for you.

PASSPORT OFFICES

The best time to apply for a passport or to renew is in fall and winter. Before any trip, check your passport's expiration date, and, if necessary, renew it as soon as possible.

➤ AUSTRALIAN CITIZENS: **Australian Passport Office** (☎ 131–232, WEB www.dfat.gov.au/passports).

➤ CANADIAN CITIZENS: **Passport Office** (☎ 819/994–3500; 800/567–6868 in Canada, WEB www.dfait-maeci.gc.ca/passport).

➤ NEW ZEALAND CITIZENS: **New Zealand Passport Office** (☎ 04/494–0700, WEB www.passports.govt.nz).

➤ U.K. CITIZENS: **London Passport Office** (☎ 0870/521–0410, WEB www.ukpa.gov.uk) for fees and documentation requirements and to request an emergency passport.

➤ U.S. CITIZENS: **National Passport Information Center** (☎ 900/225–5674; calls are 35¢ per minute for automated service, $1.05 per minute for operator service; WEB www.travel.state.gov/npicinfo.html).

REST ROOMS

The word for "bathroom" is *banheiro*, though the term *sanitários* (toilets) is also used. *Homens* means "men" and *mulheres* means "women." Around major tourist attractions and along the main beaches in big cities, you'll find public rest rooms. In other areas you may have to rely on the kindness of local restaurant and shop owners. If a smile and polite request (*"Por favor, posso usar o banheiro?"*) doesn't work, become a customer—the purchase of a drink or a knickknack might just buy you a trip to the bathroom. Rest areas with relatively clean, well-equipped bathrooms are plentiful along major highways. Still, carry a pocket-size package of tissues in case there's no toilet paper. Bathroom attendants will *truly* appreciate a tip of a few spare centavos.

SAFETY

By day, the countryside is safe. Although there has been a real effort to crack down on tourist-related crime, particularly in Rio, petty street thievery is still prevalent in urban areas, especially in places around tourist hotels, restaurants, and discos. **Avoid flashing money around.** To safeguard your funds, **lock traveler's checks and cash in a hotel safe,** except for what you need to carry each day. Money (and important documents) that you do carry are best tucked into a money belt or carried in the inside pockets of your clothing. Wear the simplest of timepieces and **do not wear any jewelry you aren't willing to lose**— stories of thieves yanking chains or earrings off travelers aren't uncommon. **Keep cameras in a secure camera bag,** preferably one with a chain or wire embedded in the strap. Always **remain alert for pickpockets,** particularly in market areas, and **follow local advice about where it's safe to walk.**

Note that Brazilian law requires everyone to have official identification with them at all times. Carry a copy of your passport's data page and of the Brazilian visa stamp (leave the actual passport in the hotel safe).

LOCAL SCAMS

Most tourist-related crimes occur in busy public areas: beaches, sidewalks or plazas, bus stations (and on buses, too). In these settings, pickpockets, usually young children, work in groups. One or more will try to distract you while another grabs a wallet, bag, or camera. **Beware of children who suddenly thrust themselves in front of you** to ask for money or who offer to shine your shoes. Another member of the gang may strike from behind, grab whatever valuable is available, and disappear in the crowd. It's best not to protest if you're mugged. Those on the take are sometimes armed or will tell you that their backup is, and although

they're often quite young, they can be dangerous.

WOMEN IN BRAZIL

Although women are gradually assuming a more important role in the nation's job force, machismo is still a strong part of Brazilian culture. Stares and catcalls aren't uncommon. Although you should have no fear of traveling unaccompanied, you should still take a few precautions.

Ask your hotel staff to recommend a reliable cab company, and **call for a taxi instead of hailing one on the street,** especially at night. **Dress to avoid unwanted attention.** For example, always wear a cover-up when heading to or from the beach. **Avoid eye contact** with unsavory individuals. If such a person approaches you, discourage him by politely but firmly by saying, "*Por favor, me dê licença*" ("Excuse me, please") and then walk away with resolve.

SENIOR-CITIZEN TRAVEL

There's no reason why active, well-traveled senior citizens shouldn't visit Brazil, whether on an independent (but prebooked) vacation, an escorted tour, or an adventure vacation. The country is full of good hotels and competent ground operators who will meet your flights and organize your sightseeing. Before you leave home, however, determine what medical services your health insurance will cover outside the United States; note that Medicare doesn't provide for payment of hospital and medical services outside the United States. If you need additional travel insurance, buy it.

To qualify for age-related discounts, **mention your senior-citizen status up front** when booking hotel reservations (not when checking out) and before you're seated in restaurants (not when paying the bill). When renting a car, ask about promotional car-rental discounts, which can be cheaper than senior-citizen rates.

➤ EDUCATIONAL PROGRAMS: **Elderhostel** (✉ 11 Ave. de Lafayette, Boston, MA 02111-1746, ☎ 877/426–8056, FAX 877/426–2166, WEB www.elderhostel.org).

SHOPPING

Centers and malls—many based on the American model—abound, though well-to-do Brazilians prefer the personal attention they get in smaller shops. Price and quality vary dramatically; as a rule, you get what you pay for, though shops that cater to tourists invariably charge more. Prices in department stores are fixed, but in smaller shops and boutiques there might be some room for discussion, and some stores give discounts for cash. At outdoor fairs and markets, bargaining is a way of life. If you wish to haggle, the Portuguese phrase for "That's too expensive" is *Está muito caro.*

SIGHTSEEING GUIDES

If you're in Olinda and want to be shown around, the guides with official ID badges in the Praça do Carmo may be the way to go. Under any other circumstances, though, **don't hire sightseeing guides who approach you on the street.** Hire one through the museum or sight you're visiting (once you get inside), a tour operator, the tourist board, your hotel, or a reputable travel agency—and no one else.

STUDENTS IN BRAZIL

Although airfares to and within Brazil are high, you can **take buses to most destinations** for mere dollars, and you can usually find safe, comfortable (if sparse) accommodations for a fraction of what it might cost back home. Most Brazilian cities also have vibrant student populations. In stalwart university towns like Ouro Preto in Minas Gerais State, you may find inexpensive lodging at fraternity houses (*repúblicas*). Students are supposed to be given a 50% discount at movie theaters and concert halls, although some places don't observe this practice. Foreign visitors may also qualify for discounts at some sporting events. **Contact a travel agency for full details on discounts and how to qualify for them.**

➤ I.D.s & SERVICES: Council Travel (CIEE; ✉ 205 E. 42nd St., 15th floor, New York, NY 10017, ☎ 212/822–2700 or 888/268–6245, FAX 212/822–2699, WEB www.councilexchanges.org) for mail orders only, in the U.S. Travel Cuts (✉ 187 College St., Toronto, Ontario M5T 1P7, Canada, ☎ 416/979–2406 or 800/667–2887 in Canada, FAX 416/979–8167, WEB www.travelcuts.com).

TAXES

Sales tax is included in the prices shown on goods in stores. Hotel, meal, and car rental taxes are usually tacked on in addition to the costs shown on menus and brochures. At press time, hotel taxes were roughly 5%; meal taxes, 10%; car rental taxes, 12%.

Departure taxes on international flights from Brazil aren't always included in your ticket and can run as high as R$86 ($40); domestic flights may incur a R$22 ($10) tax. Although U.S. dollars are accepted in some airports, be prepared to **pay departure taxes in reais.**

TELEPHONES

Telephone numbers in Brazil don't always have the same number of digits. Public phones are everywhere and are called *orelhões* (big ears) because of their shape. To use them, buy a phone card, a *cartão de telefone,* at a *posto telefônico* (phone office), newsstand, or post office. Cards come with a varying number of units (each unit is usually worth a couple of minutes), which will determine the price. Buy a couple of cards if you don't think you'll have the chance again soon.

Even with a phone card, you may not be able to make long-distance calls from some pay phones—and the logic behind which ones will and which ones won't allow such calls varies from region to region, making it as baffling as it is Brazilian. First, do as the locals do: shrug your shoulders and smile. Second, do as the locals say: ask the staff at your hotel for insight.

Commercial establishments don't usually have public phones, although a bar or restaurant may allow you to use its private phone for a local call if you're a customer. Phone offices are found at airports, many bus stations, and in downtown neighborhoods of large cities.

COUNTRY & AREA CODES

To call Brazil from overseas, dial the country code, 55, and then the area code, omitting the first 0. The area code for Rio is 021, for São Paulo, 011. Other area codes are listed in the front of local phone directories and in chapter A to Z sections throughout this guide.

DIRECTORY & OPERATOR INFORMATION

For local directory assistance, dial 102. For directory assistance in another Brazilian city, dial the area code of that city plus 121.

LONG-DISTANCE CALLS

Long-distance calls within and international calls to and from Brazil are extremely expensive. Hotels also add a surcharge, increasing this cost even more. For operator-assisted international calls, dial 000111. For international information, dial 000333.

With the privatization of the Brazilian telecommunications network, everyone now has a choice of long-distance companies. Hence, to make direct-dial long-distance calls you must find out which companies serve the area you're calling from and then get their access codes—the staff at your hotel can help. (Note, however, that some hotels have already made the choice for you, so you may not need an access code when calling from the hotel itself.) For international calls, dial 00 + the long-distance company's access code + the country code + the area code and number. For long-distance calls within Brazil, dial 0 + the access code + the area code and number. AT&T, MCI, and Sprint operators are also accessible from Brazil; before you leave home, **get the local access codes** for your destinations.

LONG-DISTANCE SERVICES

AT&T, MCI, and Sprint access codes make calling long distance relatively convenient, but you may find the local access number blocked in many hotel rooms. First ask the hotel operator to connect you. If the hotel operator balks, ask for an international operator, or dial the international operator yourself. One way to improve your odds of getting connected to your long-distance carrier is to travel with more than one company's calling card (a hotel may block Sprint, for example, but not MCI). If all else fails, call from a pay phone.

TIME

Although Brazil technically covers several time zones, most Brazilian cities are three hours behind GMT (Greenwich mean time), which means that if it's 5 PM in London, it's 2 PM in Rio and noon in New York. Manaus is an hour behind Rio.

TIPPING

Note that wages can be paltry, so a little generosity can go a long way. At hotels, it can go even farther if you tip in U.S. dollars or pounds sterling (bills, not coins). At restaurants that add a 10% service charge onto the check, it's customary to give the waiter an additional 5% tip. If there's no service charge, leave 15%. In deluxe hotels, tip porters R$2 ($1) per bag, chambermaids R$2 ($1) per day, bellhops R$4–R$6 ($2–$3) for room and valet service. Tips for doormen and concierges vary, depending on the services provided. A good tip would be R$22 ($10) or higher, average R$11 ($5). For moderate and inexpensive hotels, tips tend to be minimal (salaries are so low that virtually anything is well received). If a taxi driver helps you with your luggage, a per-bag charge of about 75 centavos (35¢) is levied in addition to the fare. In general, tip taxi drivers 10% of the fare.

At the barber shop or beauty salon, a 10%–20% tip is expected. If a service station attendant does anything beyond filling up the gas tank, leave him a small tip of some spare change. Tipping in bars and cafés follows the rules of restaurants, although at outdoor bars Brazilians rarely leave a gratuity if they had only a soft drink or a beer. At airports and at train and bus stations, tip the last porter who puts your bags into the cab (R$1/50¢ a bag at airports, 50 centavos/25¢ a bag at bus and train stations). In large cities, you'll often be accosted on the street by children looking for handouts; 50 centavos (25¢) is an average "tip."

TOURS & PACKAGES

Because everything is prearranged on a prepackaged tour or independent vacation, you spend less time planning—and often get it all at a good price.

BOOKING WITH AN AGENT

Travel agents are excellent resources. But it's a good idea to collect brochures from several agencies as some agents' suggestions may be influenced by relationships with tour and package firms that reward them for volume sales. If you have a special interest, **find an agent with expertise in that area** the American Society of Travel Agents (ASTA; ☞ Travel Agencies, *below*) has a database of specialists worldwide.

Make sure your travel agent knows the accommodations and other services of the place they're recommending. Ask about the hotel's location, room size, beds, and whether it has a pool, room service, or programs for children, if you care about these. Has your agent been there in person or sent others whom you can contact?

Do some homework on your own, too: local tourism boards can provide information about lesser-known and small-niche operators, some of which may sell only direct.

BUYER BEWARE

Each year consumers are stranded or lose their money when tour operators—even large ones with excellent reputations—go out of business. So **check out the operator.** Ask several travel agents about its reputation, and try to **book with a company that has a consumer-protection program.** (Look for information in the company's brochure.) In the United States, members of the National Tour Association and the United States Tour Operators Association are required to set aside funds to cover your payments and travel arrangements in the event that the company defaults. It's also a good idea to choose a company that participates in the American Society of Travel Agents' Tour Operator Program (TOP); ASTA will act as mediator in any disputes between you and your tour operator.

Remember that the more your package or tour includes the better you can predict the ultimate cost of your vacation. Make sure you know exactly what is covered, and **beware of hidden costs.** Are taxes, tips, and transfers included? Entertainment and excursions? These can add up.

➤ TOUR-OPERATOR RECOMMENDATIONS: **American Society of Travel Agents** (☞ Travel Agencies, *below*). **National Tour Association** (NTA; ✉ 546 E. Main St., Lexington, KY 40508, ☎ 859/226–4444 or 800/682–8886, WEB www.ntaonline.com). **United States Tour Operators Association** (USTOA; ✉ 342 Madison Ave., Suite 1522, New York, NY 10173, ☎ 212/599–6599 or 800/468–7862, FAX 212/599–6744, WEB www.ustoa.com).

THEME TRIPS

Among companies that sell theme-trip tours to Brazil, the following are well known, have a proven reputation, and offer plenty of options.

➤ AMAZON JUNGLE LODGES: **Ecotour Expeditions** (✉ Box 128, Jamestown, RI 02835, ☎ 401/423–3377 or 800/688–1822, WEB www.naturetours.com). **Explorers Travel Group** (✉ 1 Main St., Suite 304, Eatontown, NJ 07724, ☎ 732/542–9006 or 800/631–5650, WEB www.explorerstravelgroup.com). **Naturequest** (✉ 30872 S. Coast Hwy., Box 185, Laguna Beach, CA 92651, ☎ 949/499–9561 or 800/869–0639, WEB www.naturequesttours.com). **Swallows and Amazons** (✉ Box 771, Eastham, MA 02642, ☎ 508/255–1886, WEB www.swallowsandamazonstours.com).

➤ AMAZON RIVER TRIPS: **Abercrombie & Kent** (✉ 1520 Kensington Rd., Suite 212, Oak Brook, IL 60523, ☎ 630/954–2944 or 800/323–7308, WEB www.abercrombiekent.com). **Amazon Tours & Cruises** (✉ 275 Fontainebleau Blvd., Suite 173, Miami, FL 33172, ☎ 305/227–2266 or 800/423–2791, WEB www.amazontours.net). **Brazil Nuts** (✉ 1854 Trade Center Way, Naples, FL 34109, ☎ 941/593–0266 or 800/553–9959, WEB www.brazilnuts.com). **Clipper Cruise Line** (✉ 7711 Bonhomme Ave, St. Louis, MO, 63105, ☎ 314/727–2929 or 800/325–0010, WEB www.clippercruise.com). **Ecotour Expeditions** (✉ Box 128, Jamestown, RI 02835, ☎ 401/423–3377 or 800/688–1822, WEB www.

naturetours.com). **Explorers Travel Group** (✉ 1 Main St., Suite 304, Eatontown, NJ 07724, ☎ 732/542–9006 or 800/631–5650, WEB www.explorerstravelgroup.com). **G.A.P. Adventures** (✉ 19 Duncan St., Suite 401, Toronto, Ontario, M5H 3H1, Canada, ☎ 416/260–0999 or 800/465–5600, WEB www.GAPadventures.com). **Southwind Adventures** (✉ Box 621057, Littleton, CO 80162, ☎ 303/972–0701 or 800/377–9463, WEB www.southwindadventures.com). **Swallows and Amazons** (✉ Box 771, Eastham, MA 02642, ☎ 508/255–1886, WEB www.swallowsandamazonstours.com). **Tours International** (✉ 12750 Briar Forest Dr., Suite 603, Houston, TX 77077, ☎ 281/293–0809 or 800/247–7965, WEB www.toursinternational.com). **Travcoa** (✉ 2350 S.E. Bristol St., Newport Beach, CA 92660, ☎ 949/476–2800; 800/992–2003; or 800/992–2004 in California, WEB www.travcoa.com).

➤ BIRD-WATCHING: **Field Guides** (✉ 9433 Bee Cave Rd., Bldg. 1, Suite 150, Austin, TX 78733, ☎ 512/262–7295 or 800/728–4953, WFB www.fieldguides.com). **Focus Tours** (✉ 103 Moya Rd., Santa Fe, NM 87505, ☎ 505/466–4688, WEB www.focustours.com). **Swallows and Amazons** (✉ Box 771, Eastham, MA 02642, ☎ 508/255–1886, WEB www.swallowsandamazonstours.com). **Victor Emanuel Nature Tours** (✉ Box 33008, Austin, TX 78764, ☎ 512/328–5221 or 800/328–8368, WEB www.ventbird.com).

➤ CANOEING: **Explorers Travel Group** (✉ 1 Main St., Suite 304, Eatontown, NJ 07724, ☎ 732/542–9006 or 800/631–5650, WEB www.explorerstravelgroup.com). **Swallows and Amazons** (✉ Box 771, Eastham, MA 02642, ☎ 508/255–1886, WEB www.swallowsandamazonstours.com).

➤ CULTURE: **Ecotour Expeditions** (✉ Box 128, Jamestown, RI 02835, ☎ 401/423–3377 or 800/688–1822, WEB www.naturetours.com). **Swallows and Amazons** (✉ Box 771, Eastham, MA 02642, ☎ 508/255–1886, WEB www.swallowsandamazonstours.com).

➤ FISHING: **Fishing International** (✉ Box 2132, Santa Rosa, CA 95405, ☎ 707/542–4242 or 800/950–4242,

WEB www.fishinginternational.com), **Quest Global Angling Adventures** (✉ 3595 Canton Hwy., Suite C11, Marietta, GA 30066, ☎ 770/971–8586 or 888/891–3474, WEB www.fishquest.com). **Rod & Reel Adventures** (✉ Box 1187, Eugene, OR 97440, ☎ 541/338–0367 or 800/356–6982, WEB www.rodreeladventures.com.

➤ NATURAL HISTORY: **Ecotour Expeditions** (✉ Box 128, Jamestown, RI 02835, ☎ 401/423–3377 or 800/688–1822, WEB www.naturetours.com). **Focus Tours** (✉ 103 Moya Rd., Santa Fe, NM 87505, ☎ 505/466–4688, WEB www.focustours.com). **Southwind Adventures** (✉ Box 621057, Littleton, CO 80162, ☎ 303/972–0701 or 800/377–9463, WEB www.southwindadventures.com). **Swallows and Amazons** (✉ Box 771, Eastham, MA 02642, ☎ 508/255–1886, WEB www.swallowsandamazonstours.com).

➤ PHOTOGRAPHY: **Focus Tours** (✉ 103 Moya Rd., Santa Fe, NM 87505, ☎ 505/466–4688, WEB www.focustours.com). **Joseph Van Os Photo Safaris** (✉ Box 655, Vashon Island, WA 98070, ☎ 206/463–5383, WEB www.photosafaris.com).

➤ SCIENTIFIC RESEARCH TRIPS: **Earthwatch** (✉ 3 Clocktower Pl., Suite 100, Maynard, MA 01754, ☎ 978/461–0081 or 800/776–0188, WEB www.earthwatch.org).

➤ TREKKING & HIKING: **Brazil Nuts** (✉ 1854 Trade Center Way, Naples, FL 34109, ☎ 941/593–0266 or 800/553–9959, WEB www.brazilnuts.com). **Eldertreks** (✉ 597 Markham St., Toronto, Ontario, M6G 2L7, Canada, ☎ 416/588–5000 or 800/741–7956, WEB www.eldertreks.com). **Explorers Travel Group** (✉ 1 Main St., Suite 304, Eatontown, NJ 07724, ☎ 732/542–9006 or 800/631–5650, WEB www.explorerstravelgroup.com). **Swallows and Amazons** (✉ Box 771, Eastham, MA 02642, ☎ 508/255–1886, WEB www.swallowsandamazonstours.com).

TRAIN TRAVEL

Brazil has an outdated and insufficient rail network, the smallest of any of the world's large nations. Although there are commuter rails to destinations around major cities, don't plan on taking passenger trains between major cities. There's one exception: the ride from Curitiba to Paranaguá—in the southern state of Paraná—offers spectacular vistas of ravines, mountains, and waterfalls from bridges and viaducts.

TRAVEL AGENCIES

A good travel agent puts your needs first. Look for an agency that has been in business at least five years, emphasizes customer service, and has someone on staff who specializes in your destination. In addition, **make sure the agency belongs to a professional trade organization.** The American Society of Travel Agents (ASTA)—the largest and most influential in the field with more than 26,000 members in some 170 countries—maintains and enforces a strict code of ethics and will step in to help mediate any agent-client disputes if necessary. ASTA (whose motto is "Without a travel agent, you're on your own") also maintains a Web site that includes a directory of agents. (If a travel agency is also acting as your tour operator, *see* Buyer Beware *in* Tours & Packages, *above*.)

➤ LOCAL AGENT REFERRALS: **American Society of Travel Agents** (ASTA; ☎ 800/965–2782 24-hr hot line, FAX 703/739–7642, WEB www.astanet. com) **Association of British Travel Agents** (✉ 68–71 Newman St., London W1T 3AH, U.K., ☎ 020/7637–2444, FAX 020/7637–0713, WEB www. abtanet.com). **Association of Canadian Travel Agents** (✉ 130 Albert St., Ste. 1705, Ottawa, Ontario K1P 5G4, Canada, ☎ 613/237–3657, FAX 613/237–7502, WEB www.acta.net). **Australian Federation of Travel Agents** (✉ Level 3, 309 Pitt St., Sydney NSW 2000, Australia, ☎ 02/9264–3299, FAX 02/9264–1085, WEB www.afta.com. au). **Travel Agents' Association of New Zealand** (✉ Box 1888, Wellington 10033, New Zealand, ☎ 04/499–0104, FAX 04/499–0827, WEB www. taanz.org.nz).

VISITOR INFORMATION

EMBRATUR, Brazil's national tourism organization, doesn't have offices overseas, though its Web site is helpful. For information in your home country, contact the Brazilian embassy or the closest consulate—some of which have Web sites and staff dedicated to promoting tourism. Cities and towns throughout Brazil have local tourist boards, and some state capitals also have state tourism offices.

➤ U.S. GOVERNMENT ADVISORIES: **U.S. Department of State** (✉ Overseas Citizens Services Office, Room 4811 N.S., 2201 C St. NW, Washington, DC 20520, ☎ 202/647–5225 for interactive hot line, WEB http://travel. state.gov/travel/html); enclose a self-addressed, stamped, business-size envelope.

WEB SITES

Do check out the World Wide Web when planning your trip. You'll find everything from weather forecasts to virtual tours of famous cities. Be sure to **visit Fodors.com** (www.fodors.com), a complete travel-planning site. You can research prices and book plane tickets, hotel rooms, rental cars, vacation packages, and more. In addition, you can post your pressing questions in the Travel Talk section and, in the site's Rants & Raves section, read comments about some of the restaurants and hotels in this book—and chime in yourself. Other planning tools include a currency converter and weather reports, and there are loads of links to travel resources.

Be prepared to really surf. For good information, you may have to **search by region, state, or city**—and hope that at least one of them has a comprehensive official site of its own. **Don't rule out foreign-language sites;** some have links to sites that present information in more than one language, including English. On Portuguese-language sites, watch for the name of the region, state, or city in which you have an interest. The search terms in Portuguese for "look," "find" and "get" are *olhar/achar, buscar,* and *pegar*; "next" and "last" (as in "next/last 10") are *próximo* and *último/anterior.* Keep an eye out for such words as: *turismo* (tourism), *turístico* (tourist-related), *hoteis* (hotels), *restaurantes* (restaurants), *governo* (government), *estado* (state), and *cidade* (city).

The following sites should get you started: www.embratur.gov.br (the official Brazilian tourist board site, with information in English provided by the Brazilian embassy in London), www.varig.com (Varig Airlines's site, with English information), www.brazilny.org (the official consular Web site in New York, with details about other consulates and the embassy as well as travel information and links to other sites), www.brazilinfocenter.org (a Washington, D.C.–based organization that promotes political and business issues, rather than tourism, but whose Web site has an incredible number of helpful links), www.vivabrazil.com (a site with background and travel info on Brazil's different regions as well as links that will help you arrange your trip).

WHEN TO GO

CLIMATE

Seasons below the equator are the reverse of the north—summer in Brazil runs from December to March and winter from June to September. The rainy season in Brazil occurs during the summer months, but this is rarely a nuisance. Showers can be torrential but usually last no more than an hour or two. The areas of the country with pronounced rainy seasons are the Amazon and the Pantanal. In these regions, the rainy season runs roughly from November to May and is marked by heavy, twice-daily downpours.

Prices in beach resorts are invariably higher during the high season (Brazilian summer). If you're looking for a bargain, stick to the off-season (May–June and August–October; July is school-break month). In Rio and at beach resorts along the coast, especially in the northeast, these months offer the added attraction of relief from the often oppressive summer heat, although in Rio the temperature can drop to uncomfortable levels for swimming in June through August.

Rio de Janeiro is on the tropic of Capricorn, and its climate is just that—tropical. Summers are hot and humid, with temperatures rising as high as 105°F (40°C), although the average ranges between 84°F and 95°F (29°C–35°C). In winter, temperatures stay in the 70s (20s C), occasionally dipping into the high 60s (15°C–20°C). The same pattern holds true for all of the Brazilian coastline north of Rio, although temperatures are slightly higher year-round in Salvador and the northeastern coastal cities. In the Amazon, where the equator crosses the country, temperatures in the high 80s to the 90s (30s C) are common all year. In the south, São Paulo, and parts of Minas Gerais, winter temperatures can fall to the low 40s (5°C–8°C). In the southern states of Santa Catarina and Rio Grande do Sul, snowfalls occur in winter, although they're seldom more than dustings.

➤ FORECASTS: **Weather Channel Connection** (☎ 900/932–8437), 95¢ per minute from a Touch-Tone phone.

FESTIVALS AND SEASONAL EVENTS

Note that country-wide events and celebrations related to Brazil's biggest festival, Carnaval, start in January and peak in the days preceding Lent, sometime in February or March. Manaus takes its Carnaval a step further by combining it with the traditions of *boi bumba* (dancing competitions) in a festival known as Carnaboi. Holy Week,

The following are the average daily maximum and minimum temperatures for Rio de Janeiro.

Jan.	84F	29C	May	77F	25C	Sept.	75F	24C
	69	21		66	19		66	19
Feb.	85F	29C	June	76F	24C	Oct.	77F	25C
	73	23		64	18		63	17
Mar.	83F	28C	July	75F	24C	Nov.	79F	26C
	72	22		64	18		68	20
Apr.	80F	27C	Aug.	76F	24C	Dec.	82F	28C
	69	21		64	18		71	22

The following are the average daily maximum and minimum temperatures for Salvador.

Jan.	87F	31C	May	80F	27C	Sept.	78F	26C
	76	24		70	21		69	21
Feb.	88F	31C	June	80F	27C	Oct.	80F	27C
	76	24		67	19		69	21
Mar.	87F	31C	July	78F	26C	Nov.	83F	28C
	77	25		66	19		72	22
Apr.	84F	29C	Aug.	80F	27C	Dec.	86F	30C
	73	23		67	19		77	25

in March or April, is marked by many events throughout the country, including Passion plays. Remember: the country's seasons are the reverse of those in the northern hemisphere.

➤ MAY: Many communities throughout Brazil celebrate the **Festa do Divino Espírito Santo,** with food donations for the poor, processionals, and folklore festivals. The central-west town of Pirenópolis observes the holiday with the *cavalhadas,* equestrian events that reenact battles between Christians and Moors.

➤ JUNE: The **Festas Juninas** celebrations last from mid-June to mid-July and honor St. John (June 24) and St. Peter (June 29). The festivals are noteworthy in Rio de Janeiro State and in several interior regions of the northeast. Typical foods are prepared especially for these occasions. Look for fresh corn and other salty and sweet-corn products (*pamonha, curau, canjica*) as well as sweets made with coconut or peanuts, such as cocada, *cuscuz, pé de moleque and paçoca.* Fireworks and barn dances are among the festival traditions.

In São Paulo, the annual **Carlton Dance Festival** starts in June and continues through July. During Brasília's **Festa dos Estados,** held the last weekend of June, each of the nation's 26 states gets a chance to showcase its traditions. Outside Salvador, the town of Cachoeira celebrates the **Feast of St. John** (June 23–24), which commemorates the harvest season. There are many special music and dance activities, and the children dress up in traditional garb. The **Parintins Folk Festival** (June 28–30) takes place 400 km (250 mi) downriver from Manaus and is the Amazon's largest folkloric festival. The chief event is the boi bumba

dancing competition between two groups—the Garantidos (who wear red) and the Caprichosos (who wear blue)—that have slightly different styles. Among the more than 40,000 spectators, all wearing the color of their favorite group, there's a mania not unlike that of a soccer match.

➤ JULY: The **Festival de Inverno,** in Campos do Jordão, São Paulo, is one of Brazil's most important classical musical events. Young musicians can learn from more experienced ones, and everyone can watch performances at the Auditório Cláudio Santoro. On Ilhabela, July sees the **Semana da Vela,** which brings sailors from throughout Brazil to the island for competitions. During Ouro Preto's weeklong **winter festival** in mid-July the town is overtaken by musical and theatrical performances. In the west the **Chapada dos Guimarães Festival de Inverno** takes place the last week of July. Young hippies flock here for the variety of bands that perform and because this town—as the uncontested geodesic center of South America— has some really good vibes.

During Fortaleza's **Regata de Jangadas,** held in late July, you can watch fishermen race their *jangada* boats between Praia do Meireles and Praia Mucuripe. **Fortal,** Fortaleza's lively out-of-season Carnaval, is held the last week of July. The **Animamundi International Animation Festival,** showcasing national and international animated films, takes place every year in Rio de Janeiro and São Paulo during two weeks in July. Workshops, lectures, and children's programs are also offered.

➤ AUG.: São Paulo's Museu da Imagem e do Som sponsors the **International Short Film Festival** in August. The month also sees São Paulo's annual, three-day **Free Jazz Festival.** During Ilhabela's August **Festival do Camarão,** restaurants get together to organize cooking contests and offer lectures.

Salvador's **Festin Bahia** is a three-day international music festival held every August or September featuring foreign and local performers; past participants have included Maxi Priest, Youssou N'Dour, China Head, Carlinhos Brown, Pepeu Gomes, and Olodum. Many of the events are free. In Cachoeira, west of Salvador, the Irmandade da Boa Morte (Sisterhood of the Good Death; once a slave women's secret society) holds a **half-Candomblé, half-Catholic festival** August 14–16 honoring the spirits of the dead. In Fortaleza, each August 15 the **Iemanjá Festival** honors the water goddess on Praia do Futuro. August 22–29 sees Fortaleza's **Semana do Folclore,** the city's folklore week.

➤ SEPT.: Ouro Preto's giant, weeklong **Julibeu do Senhor Ben Jesus do Matosinhos** religious festival is held in mid-September. One of Belém's two out-of-season Carnavals, **Paráfolia,** takes place at the end of September. The most interesting and eagerly awaited week on Ilha do Marajó (Amazon) comes in September when Soure hosts the annual **ExpoBúfalo.** The finest water buffalos in Brazil are brought here to compete in such categories as the prettiest and the best milk producer. The weeklong **Cairé Festival,** held in Alter do Chão (Amazon) the second week of September, features folkloric music and dance presentations.

➤ OCT.: Not only is October 12 the official day (celebrated all over the country and particularly in Aparecida in São Paulo State) of Brazil's patron saint, **Nossa Senhora da Aparecida,** but it's also **Children's Day.** São Paulo's international film festival, **Mostra Internacional de Cinema,** is held in October. The world-renowned biennial art exhibition (South America's largest), the **São Paulo Biennial,** is held from mid-October to mid-December in each even-numbered year in Ibirapuera Park.

Porto Alegre's monthlong **Feira do Livro** (Book Fair) is the largest and most famous event of its kind in Brazil. Blumenau's **Oktoberfest** lasts three weeks and emulates the original in Munich. The citizens of Recife repeat Carnaval in the weekend-long **Recifolia** festival; dates vary each year. On the second Sunday in October, thousands of worshipers flock to Belém for the **Círio de Nazaré** processional honoring the city's patron saint. There's also a procession on the river involving hundreds of boats bedecked in flowers.

➤ NOV.: In November, Ouro Preto's **Aleijadinho Week** honors the great 18th-century sculptor whose work adorns many of the city's churches. The second of Belém's out-of-season Carnavals, **Carnabelém,** takes place in mid-November.

➤ DEC.: Although December 8 is the actual date of the **Festa de Nossa Senhora da Conceição,** thousands of celebrants start to fill Santarém's streets during the last week of November. The weeklong celebration culminates with a procession through the city.

➤ JAN.: On **Ano Novo** (New Year's Eve), followers of Candomblé (a spiritualist cult) honor Iemanjá, goddess of the sea, with fireworks, songs, rituals, and offerings along Rio's beaches, particularly Copacabana. Salvador's four-day **Festival of the Good Lord Jesus of the Seafarers** starts on the first Sunday of the month. It features samba and capoeira performances, feasts of Bahian food, and a processional—with hundreds of small vessels—along the coast to Boa Viagem Beach.

➤ FEB.: In Salvador the **Festival of Iemanjá** is held on the second Sunday of February. Devotees of the Afro-Brazilian Candomblé cult begin singing the sea goddess's praises at the crack of dawn along the beaches.

➤ MARCH: The **Formula I Grand Prix** is held during March in São Paulo. In Salvador, March sees **PanPerc,** a percussion festival in which such music notables as Gilberto Gil and Caetano Veloso perform alongside percussion groups. In Macapá (Amazon), the most important local holiday is the **Festa de São José,** a weeklong celebration honoring the city's patron saint. The festivities, which consist mostly of traditional music and dance presentations, end on March 19.

➤ APRIL: April 21 is **Tiradentes Day,** a national holiday honoring the father of Brazil's 18th-century independence movement, the Inconfidência. On this date, Joaquim José da Silva Xavier, known as Tiradentes (Tooth Puller) because he was a dentist, was executed for treason by the Portuguese crown in Ouro Preto. The city celebrates over a four-day period (April 18–21) with many ceremonies.

PORTUGUESE VOCABULARY

Words and Phrases

English	Portuguese	Pronunciation
Basics		
Yes/no	Sim/Não	**see**ing/nown
Please	Por favor	pohr fah-**vohr**
May I?	Posso?	**poh**-sso
Thank you (very much)	(Muito) obrigado	(**moo**yn-too) o-bree **gah**-doh
You're welcome	De nada	day **nah**-dah
Excuse me	Com licença	con lee-**ssehn**-ssah
Pardon me/what did you say?	Desculpe/O que disse?	des-**kool**-peh/o.k. **dih**-say?
Could you tell me?	Poderia me dizer?	po-day-**ree**-ah mee dee-**zehrr**?
I'm sorry	Sinto muito	**seen**-too **moo**yn-too
Good morning!	Bom dia!	bohn **dee**-ah
Good afternoon!	Boa tarde!	**boh**-ah **tahr**-dee
Good evening!	Boa noite!	**boh**-ah **noh**ee-tee
Goodbye!	Adeus!/Até logo!	ah-**deh**oos/ah-**teh loh**-go
Mr./Mrs.	Senhor/Senhora	sen-**yor**/sen-**yohr**-ah
Miss	Senhorita	sen-yo-**ri**-tah
Pleased to meet you	Muito prazer	**moo**yn too prah-**zehr**
How are you?	Como vai?	**koh**-mo **vah**-ee
Very well, thank you	Muito bem, obrigado	**moo**yn-too **beh**-in o-bree-**gah**-doh
And you?	E o(a) Senhor(a)?	eh oh sen-**yor** (**yohr**-ah)
Hello (on the telephone)	Alô	ah-**low**

Numbers

1	um/uma	oom/**oom**-ah
2	dois	**doh**ees
3	três	**treh**ys
4	quatro	**kwa**-troh
5	cinco	**seen**-koh
6	seis	**seh**ys
7	sete	**seh**-tee
8	oito	**oh**ee-too
9	nove	**noh**-vee
10	dez	**deh**-ees
11	onze	**ohn**-zee
12	doze	**doh**-zee
13	treze	**treh**-zee

14	quatorze	kwa-**tohr**-zee
15	quinze	**keen**-zee
16	dezesseis	deh-zeh-**seh**ys
17	dezessete	deh-zeh-**seh**-tee
18	dezoito	deh-**zoh**ee-toh
19	dezenove	deh-zeh-**noh**-vee
20	vinte	**veen**-tee
21	vinte e um	**veen**-tee eh **oom**
30	trinta	**treen**-tah
32	trinta e dois	**treen**-ta eh **doh**ees
40	quarenta	kwa-**rehn**-ta
43	quarenta e três	kwa-**rehn**-ta e **treh**ys
50	cinquenta	seen-**kwehn**-tah
54	cinquenta e quatro	seen-**kwehn**-tah e **kwa**-troh
60	sessenta	seh-**sehn**-tah
65	sessenta e cinco	seh-**sehn**-tah e **seen**-ko
70	setenta	seh-**tehn**-tah
76	setenta e seis	sch-**tehn** ta e **seh**ys
80	oitenta	ohee-**tehn**-ta
87	oitenta e sete	ohee-**tehn**-ta e **seh**-tee
90	noventa	noh-**vehn**-ta
98	noventa e oito	noh-**vehn**-ta e **oh**ee-too
100	cem	**seh**-ing
101	cento e um	**sehn**-too e **oom**
200	duzentos	doo-**zehn**-tohss
500	quinhentos	key-**nyehn**-tohss
700	setecentos	seh-teh-**sehn**-tohss
900	novecentos	noh-veh-**sehn**-tohss
1,000	mil	meel
2,000	dois mil	**doh**ees meel
1,000,000	um milhão	oom mee-lee-**ahon**

Colors

black	preto	**preh**-toh
blue	azul	a-**zool**
brown	marrom	mah-**hohm**
green	verde	**vehr**-deh
pink	rosa	**roh**-zah
purple	roxo	**roh**-choh
orange	laranja	lah-**rahn**-jah
red	vermelho	vehr-**meh**-lyoh
white	branco	**brahn**-coh
yellow	amarelo	ah-mah-**reh**-loh

Days of the Week

Sunday	Domingo	doh-**meehn**-goh
Monday	Segunda-feira	seh-**goon**-dah **fey**-rah
Tuesday	Terça-feira	**tehr**-sah **fey**-rah
Wednesday	Quarta-feira	**kwahr**-tah **fey**-rah

Thursday	Quinta-feira	**keen**-tah **fey**-rah
Friday	Sexta-feira	**sehss**-tah **fey**-rah
Saturday	Sábado	**sah**-bah-doh

Months

January	Janeiro	jah-**ney**-roh
February	Fevereiro	feh-veh-**rey**-roh
March	Março	**mahr**-soh
April	Abril	ah-**breel**
May	Maio	**my**-oh
June	Junho	gy**oo**-nyoh
July	Julho	gy**oo**-lyoh
August	Agosto	ah-**ghost**-toh
September	Setembro	seh-**tehm**-broh
October	Outubro	owe-**too**-broh
November	Novembro	noh-**vehm**-broh
December	Dezembro	deh-**zehm**-broh

Useful Phrases

Do you speak English?	O Senhor fala inglês?	oh sen-**yor fah**-lah een-**glehs**?
I don't speak Portuguese.	Não falo português.	nown **fah**-loh pohr-too-**ghehs**
I don't understand (you)	Não lhe entendo	nown ly**eh** ehn-**tehn**-doh
I understand	Eu entendo	**eh**-oo ehn-**tehn**-doh
I don't know	Não sei	nown say
I am American/ British	Sou americano (americana)/ inglês/inglêsa	sow a-meh-ree-**cah**-noh (a-meh-ree-**cah**-nah/ een-**glehs** (een-**glah**-sa)
What's your name?	Como se chama?	**koh**-moh seh **shah**-mah
My name is . . .	Meu nome é . . .	mehw **noh**-meh eh
What time is it?	Que horas são?	keh **oh**-rahss **sa**-ohn
It is one, two, three . . . o'clock	É uma/São duas, três . . . hora/horas	eh **oom**-ah/**sa**-ohn **oo**mah, **doo**-ahss, **treh**ys **oh**-rah/**oh**-rahs
Yes, please/No, thank you	Sim por favor/ Não obrigado	seing pohr fah-**vohr**/ nown o-bree-**gah**-doh
How?	Como?	**koh**-moh
When?	Quando?	**kwahn**-doh
This/Next week	Esta/Próxima semana	**ehss**-tah/**proh**-see-mah seh-**mah**-nah
This/Next month	Este/Próximo mêz	**ehss**-teh/**proh**-see-moh mehz
This/Next year	Este/Próximo ano	**ehss**-teh/**proh**-see-moh **ah**-noh
Yesterday/today tomorrow	Ontem/hoje amanhã	**ohn**-tehn/**oh**-jeh/ ah-mah-**nyan**
This morning/ afternoon	Esta manhã/ tarde	**ehss**-tah mah-**nyan** / **tahr**-deh

Tonight	Hoje a noite	**oh**-jeh ah **noh**ee-tee
What?	O que?	oh **keh**
What is it?	O que é isso?	oh **keh** eh **ee**-soh
Why?	Por quê?	pohr-**keh**
Who?	Quem?	**keh**-in
Where is . . . ?	Onde é . . . ?	**ohn**-deh **eh**
the train station?	a estação de trem?	ah es-tah-**sah**-on deh train
the subway station?	a estação de metrô?	ah es-tah-**sah**-on deh meh-**tro**
the bus stop?	a parada do ônibus?	ah pah-**rah**-dah doh **oh**-nee-boos
the post office?	o correio?	oh coh-**hay**-yoh
the bank?	o banco?	oh **bahn**-koh
the hotel?	o hotel . . . ?	oh oh-**tell**
the cashier?	o caixa?	oh **kah**y-shah
the museum?	o museo . . . ?	oh moo-**zeh**-oh
the hospital?	o hospital?	oh ohss-pee-**tal**
the elevator?	o elevador?	oh eh-leh-vah-**dohr**
the bathroom?	o banheiro?	oh bahn-**yey**-roh
the beach?	a praia de . . . ?	ah **prah**y-yah deh
Here/there	Aqui/ali	ah-**kee**/ah-**lee**
Open/closed	Aberto/fechado	ah-**behr**-toh/feh-**shah**-doh
Left/right	Esquerda/ direita	ehs-**kehr**-dah/ dee-**ray**-tah
Straight ahead	Em frente	ehyn **frehn**-teh
Is it near/far?	É perto/ longe?	eh **pehr**-toh/**lohn**-jeh
I'd like to buy . . .	Gostaria de comprar . . .	gohs-tah-**ree**-ah deh cohm-**prahr** . . .
a bathing suit	um maiô	oom mahy-**owe**
a dictionary	um dicionário	oom dee-seeoh-**nah**-reeoh
a hat	um chapéu	oom shah-**peh**oo
a magazine	uma revista	**oo**mah heh-**vees**-tah
a map	um mapa	oom **mah**-pah
a postcard	cartão postal	kahr-**town** pohs-**tahl**
sunglasses	óculos escuros	**ah**-koo-loss ehs-**koo**-rohs
suntan lotion	um óleo de bronzear	oom **oh**-lyoh deh brohn-zeh-**ahr**
a ticket	um bilhete	oom bee-ly**eh**-teh
cigarettes	cigarros	see-**gah**-hose
envelopes	envelopes	eyn-veh-**loh**-pehs
matches	fósforos	**fohs**-foh-rohss
paper	papel	pah-**pehl**
sandals	sandália	sahn-**dah**-leeah
soap	sabonete	sah-bow-**neh**-teh
How much is it?	Quanto custa?	**kwahn**-too **koos**-tah
It's expensive/ cheap	Está caro/ barato	ehss-**tah kah**-roh / bah-**rah**-toh

A little/a lot	Um pouco/muito	oom **pohw**-koh/ **moo**yn-too
More/less	Mais/menos	**mah**-ees /**meh**-nohss
Enough/too much/too little	Suficiente/ demais/ muito pouco	soo-fee-see-**ehn**-teh/ deh-**mah**-ees/ **moo**yn-toh **pohw**-koh
Telephone	Telefone	teh-leh-**foh**-neh
Telegram	Telegrama	teh-leh-**grah**-mah
I am ill.	Estou doente.	ehss-**tow** doh-**ehn**-teh
Please call a doctor.	Por favor chame um médico.	pohr fah-**vohr shah**-meh oom **meh**-dee-koh
Help!	Socorro!	soh-**koh**-ho
Help me!	Me ajude!	mee ah-**jyew**-deh
Fire!	Incêndio!	een-**sehn**-deeoh
Caution!/Look out!/ Be careful!	Cuidado!	kooy-**dah**-doh

On the Road

Avenue	Avenida	ah-veh-**nee**-dah
Highway	Estrada	ehss-**trah**-dah
Port	Porto	**pohr**-toh
Service station	Posto de gasolina	**pohs**-toh deh gah-zoh-**lee**-nah
Street	Rua	**who**-ah
Toll	Pedagio	peh-**dah**-jyoh
Waterfront promenade	Beiramar/ orla	behy-rah-**mahrr**/ **ohr**-lah
Wharf	Cais	**kah**-ees

In Town

Block	Quarteirão	kwahr-tehy-**rah**-on
Cathedral	Catedral	kah-teh-**drahl**
Church/temple	Igreja	ee-**greh**-jyah
City hall	Prefeitura	preh-fehy-**too**-rah
Door/gate	Porta/portão	**pohr**-tah/porh-**tah**-on
Entrance/exit	Entrada/ saída	ehn-**trah**-dah/ sah-**ee**-dah
Market	Mercado/feira	mehr-**kah**-doh/ **fey**-rah
Neighborhood	Bairro	**buy**-ho
Rustic bar	Lanchonete	lahn-shoh-**neh**-teh
Shop	Loja	**loh**-jyah
Square	Praça	**prah**-ssah

Dining Out

A bottle of . . .	Uma garrafa de . . .	**oo**mah gah-**hah**-fah deh

A cup of . . .	Uma xícara de . . .	**oo**mah **shee**-kah-rah deh
A glass of . . .	Um copo de . . .	oom **koh**-poh deh
Ashtray	Um cinzeiro	oom seen-**zeh**y-roh
Bill/check	A conta	ah **kohn**-tah
Bread	Pão	**pah**-on
Breakfast	Café da manhã	kah-**feh** dah mah-**nyan**
Butter	A manteiga	ah mahn-**teh**y-gah
Cheers!	Saúde!	sah-**oo**-deh
Cocktail	Um aperitivo	oom ah-peh-ree-**tee**-voh
Dinner	O jantar	oh **jyahn**-tahr
Dish	Um prato	oom **prah**-toh
Enjoy!	Bom apetite!	bohm ah-peh-**tee**-teh
Fork	Um garfo	**gahr**-foh
Fruit	Fruta	**froo**-tah
Is the tip included?	A gorjeta esta incluída?	ah gohr-**jyeh**-tah ehss-**tah** een-clue-**ee**-dah
Juice	Um suco	oom **soo**-koh
Knife	Uma faca	**oo**mah **fah**-kah
Lunch	O almoço	oh ahl-**moh**-ssoh
Menu	Menu/ cardápio	me-**noo** / kahr-**dah**-peeoh
Mineral water	Água mineral	**ah**-gooah mee-neh-**rahl**
Napkin	Guardanapo	gooahr-dah-**nah**-poh
No smoking	Não fumante	nown foo-**mahn**-teh
Pepper	Pimenta	pee-**mehn**-tah
Please give me	Por favor me dê	pohr fah-**vohr** mee **deh**
Salt	Sal	sahl
Smoking	Fumante	foo-**mahn**-teh
Spoon	Uma colher	**oo**mah koh-ly**ehr**
Sugar	Açúcar	ah-**soo**-kahr
Waiter!	Garçon!	gahr-**sohn**
Water	Água	**ah**-gooah
Wine	Vinho	**vee**-nyoh

INDEX

NOTES

NOTES

NOTES

NOTES

FODOR'S BRAZIL

EDITORS: Carissa Bluestone; Lisa Dunford; Laura M. Kidder, senior editor

Editorial Contributors: Rob Aikins, Karla Brunet, Joyce Dalton, José Fonseca, Denise Garcia, Joan Gonzalez, Alan Ryan, Carlos Tornquist, Ana Lúcia do Vale

Editorial Production: Tom Holton

Maps: David Lindroth, Inc., Mapping Specialists Ltd., cartographers; Rebecca Baer and Bob Blake, map editors

Design: Fabrizio La Rocca, creative director; Guido Caroti, art director; Jolie Novak, senior picture editor; Melanie Marin, photo editor

Cover Design: Pentagram

Production/Manufacturing: Yexenia Markland

COPYRIGHT

Second Edition

ISBN 0-676-90191-3

ISSN 0163-0628

SPECIAL SALES

Fodor's Travel Publications are available at special discounts for bulk purchases for sales promotions or premiums. Special editions, including personalized covers, excerpts of existing guides, and corporate imprints, can be created in large quantities for special needs. For more information, contact your local bookseller or write to Special Markets, Fodor's Travel Publications, 280 Park Avenue, New York, NY 10017. Inquiries from Canada should be directed to your local Canadian bookseller or sent to Random House of Canada, Ltd., Marketing Department, 2775 Matheson Boulevard East, Mississauga, Ontario L4W 4P7. Inquiries from the United Kingdom should be sent to Fodor's Travel Publications, 20 Vauxhall Bridge Road, London SW1V 2SA, England.

PRINTED IN THE UNITED STATES OF AMERICA

10 9 8 7 6 5 4 3 2 1

IMPORTANT TIP

Although all prices, opening times, and other details in this book are based on information supplied to us at press time, changes occur all the time in the travel world, and Fodor's cannot accept responsibility for facts that become outdated or for inadvertent errors or omissions. So always confirm information when it matters, especially if you're making a detour to visit a specific place.

PHOTOGRAPHY

The Image Bank: Andrea Pistolesi, cover (zoo in Manaus, the Amazon)

Bahiatursa, 2 top left. Aristides Alves, 2 bottom center. Jota Freitas, 2 top right, 2 bottom right.

Contexto: Peter Feibert, 16B. Tom Rica, 26C. Américo Vermelho, 7D.

Copacabana Palace, 28C.

Corbis: 2 bottom left, 3 top left, 3 top right, 30J. AFP, 11B. Yann Arthus-Bertrand, 7C. Richard Bickel, 4–5. Barnabas Bosshart, 27F. Tom Brakefield, 24 center left. James Davis/Eye Ubiquitous, 19C. Owen Franken, 8 bottom, 27 bottom right. Dave G. Houser, 1. Danny Lehman, 24 bottom right. Stephanie Maze, 15B, 22 top. Inge Yspeert, 21 bottom. Jim Zuckerman, 6B, 26D.

Fundação Maria Luisa e Oscar Americano, 12E.

Bernard Grilly, 28A.

Blaine Harrington III, 9J.

Houserstock: Steve Cohen, 24A. Dave G. Houser, 7E, 11C, 32.

Gustavo Laceroa, 28E.

MS Tourismo, 28B.

Museu da Inconfidencia: Rômulo Fialdini, 3 bottom right, 16A.

Museu de Arte Naif do Brasil, 30I.

Donald Nausbaum, 21C, 23B, 23C.

PhotoDisc, 3 bottom left, 14A.

Reflexo: Alberto Alves, 20B. Bruno Alves, 13G. Luiz Braga, 27G. Jose Caldas, 17 bottom right. Rubens Chaves, 28F. Mario Friedlander, 19E. Felipe Goifman, 9H. Carlos Goldgrub, 10A, 11D, 12F, 15D, 17C, 18A, 19D, 30G, 30H. Christian Knepper, 18B. Zig Koch, 15C. Frédéric Mertens, 13H, 20A. Roberto Negraes, 22A. Lau Polinésio, 10 top. Nelson Toledo, 13I.

Refúgio Ecológico Caiman, 30K.

Riotur: 8G. Marluce Balbrino, 6A.

H. Stern, 8F, 17 bottom left.

Stone: Jacques Jangoux, 25B.

Travel Stock: Buddy Mays, 25 bottom, 26E.

Tropical Hotels Brasil, 28D.

The Viesti Collection: Jeffrey Dunn, 9I.

ABOUT OUR WRITERS

The more you know before you go, the better your trip will be. Brazil's most fascinating small museum (or its most reliable jeweler or most happening *churrascaria*) could be just around the corner from your hotel, but if you don't know it's there, it might as well be on the other side of the globe. That's where this book comes in. It's a great step toward making sure your next trip lives up to your expectations. As you plan, check out the Web as well. Guidebooks have been helping smart travelers find the special places for years; the Web is one more tool. Whatever reference you consult, be savvy about what you read, and always consider the source. Images and language can be massaged to make places appear better than they are. And one traveler's quaint is another's grimy.

Here at Fodor's, and at our on-line arm, Fodors.com, our focus is on providing you with information that's not only useful but accurate and on target. Every day Fodor's editors put enormous effort into getting things right, beginning with the search for the right contributors—people who have objective judgment, broad travel experience, and the writing ability to put their insights into words. There's no substitute for advice from a like-minded friend who has just come back from where you're going, but our writers, having seen all corners of Brazil, are the next best thing. They're the kind of people you'd poll for tips yourself if you knew them.

Rob Aikins makes his home in the beach community of Leucadia, California, where he writes about music, art, travel, and adventure sports for a variety of newspapers and magazines. He has previously worked on *Fodor's San Diego*.

São Paulo chapter writer **Karla Brunet** is a photographer and designer who studied art in San Francisco and who teaches digital photography in Brazil. Her major passion is travel, and she has done a great deal of it. Her most recent expedition took her to the Inca sites in Ecuador, Peru, and Bolivia.

Joyce Dalton, who contributed to Smart Travel Tips, has been traveling for more years than she cares to count. Her travel articles and photos appear in numerous trade and consumer publications. Joyce also has revised chapters for *Fodor's South America* and *Fodor's Eastern and Central Europe*.

Denise Garcia is a journalist and a producer of animated cartoons and has traveled to and lived in various places around the world. She put her talents to work on Smart Travel Tips from her home in Rio de Janeiro.

Joan Gonzalez, who updated the chapter on Brazil's northeastern cities, has updated the Bolivia, Ecuador, and Peru chapters of *Fodor's South America* and co-authored the first edition of *Fodor's Pocket Los Cabos*. She also writes for travel-industry publications.

Carlos Tornquist, who covered the south and Brasília and the west, is a soil scientist who is highly qualified to write about travel in his native turf. When he's not visiting farmers as a technical advisor, he's traveling. Carlos has seen much of the New World—from the U.S.–Canada border to the tip of Tierra del Fuego.

Compulsive traveler and Rio native **Ana Lúcia do Vale,** who updated the Rio de Janeiro and Minas Gerais chapters, has been a working journalist for several years. Her career has included producing and directing Brazilian television shows as well as work with a news agency and writing for the *carioca* newspaper *O Dia*.

Don't Forget to Write

Your experiences—positive and negative—matter to us. If we have missed or misstated something, we want to hear about it. We follow up on all suggestions. Contact the Brazil editor at editors@fodors.com or c/o Fodor's, 280 Park Avenue, New York, New York 10017. And have a fabulous trip!

Karen Cure
Editorial Director